NOLO *Products & Services*

"In Nolo you can trust." —THE NEW YORK TIMES

Books & Software

Nolo publishes hundreds of great books and software programs on the topics consumers and business owners want to know about. And every one of them is available in print or as a download at Nolo.com.

Plain-English Legal Dictionary

Free at Nolo.com. Stumped by jargon? Look it up in America's most up-to-date source for definitions of cutting edge legal terminology. Emphatically not your grandmother's law dictionary!

Legal Encyclopedia

Free at Nolo.com. Here are more than 1,200 free articles and answers to frequently asked questions about everyday consumer legal issues including wills, bankruptcy, small business formation, divorce, patents, employment and much more. As *The Washington Post* says, "Nobody does a better job than Nolo."

Online Legal Forms

Make a will or living trust, form an LLC or corporation or obtain a trademark or provisional patent at Nolo.com, all for a remarkably affordable price. In addition, our site provides hundreds of high-quality, low-cost downloadable legal forms including bills of sale, promissory notes, nondisclosure agreements and many more.

Lawyer Directory

Find an attorney at Nolo.com. Nolo's unique lawyer directory provides in-depth profiles of lawyers all over America. From fees and experience to legal philosophy, education and special expertise, you'll find all the information you need to pick a lawyer who's a good fit.

Nolo's Aim:
to make the law...

 **easy-to-understand**

 **affordable**

 **hassle free**

Keep Up to Date!

*Old law is often bad law. That's why Nolo.com has free updates for this and every Nolo book. And if you want to be notified when a revised edition of any Nolo title comes out, sign up for this free service at **nolo.com/ legalupdater**.*

"Nolo is always there in a jam."
—NEWSWEEK

11th edition

The Criminal Law Handbook

Know Your Rights, Survive the System

By Attorneys Paul Bergman & Sara J. Berman

ELEVENTH EDITION   AUGUST 2009

Editor   RICHARD STIM

Cover Design   JALEH DOANE

Proofreading   SUSAN CARLSON GREENE

Index   JULIE SHAWVAN

Printing   DELTA PRINTING SOLUTIONS, INC.

Bergman, Paul, 1943-
  The criminal law handbook : know your rights, survive the system / by Paul Bergman &
Sara J. Berman. -- 11th ed.
      p. cm.
  ISBN-13: 978-1-4133-1053-5 (pbk.)
  ISBN-10: 1-4133-1053-2 (pbk.)
  1. Criminal procedure--United States--Popular works. I. Berman-Barrett, Sara J., 1964-
II. Title.
  KF9619.85.B47 2009
  345.73'05--dc22

                        2009011881

International Standard Serial Number (ISSN): 1940-722X

Dedication

With love to Kevin, Hilary, and Vincent; and to Julia and Daniel.

Acknowledgments

Our thanks:

To attorneys Jake Warner and Steve Elias of Nolo for first envisioning a book about the criminal justice process.

To Janet Portman and Rich Stim for their hard work and dedication to the text.

To Dean Laurie Levenson, a former prosecutor and legal commentator; Michael Roman, an experienced criminal defense attorney; and Ron Schlesman, a longtime probation officer, each of whom was kind enough to read through the entire text; and law professors David Sklansky, Peter Arenella, and David Dolinko of the UCLA School of Law and Michael Graham of the Miami School of Law for their many insights, critiques, and immensely helpful suggestions.

To public defender and Concord law professor John Ciroli for his many insights into criminal defense practice.

To attorney Steve Harvey for his insightful comments about the nature of the U.S. criminal justice system.

To the many resourceful employees of Nolo who put their heart and energy into producing such warm and helpful books and making sure the public knows about them.

Much appreciation to Dr. LaVera Otoyo for sharing wisdom and stories gathered from her many years of service to America's juvenile justice system.

To the Martinez family, whose loving care enabled the long hours of research and writing.

To UCLA School of Law Professor Robert Goldstein for his help with the domestic violence and child abuse sections.

Table of Contents

Your Legal Companion

Introduction: A Walk-Through of the Case of *State v. Andrea Davidson*, a Fictional Robbery Prosecution

13 Defensespeak: Common Defenses to Criminal Charges

14 Discovery: Exchanging Information With the Prosecution

15 Investigating the Facts

16 Preliminary Hearings

17 Fundamental Trial Rights of the Defense

18 Basic Evidence Rules in Criminal Trials

19 Motions and Their Role in Criminal Cases

Index

Your Legal Companion

When can a police officer make an arrest? Is it a good idea to talk to the police? Who decides whether to charge someone with a crime, and what crime to charge? Is self-representation ever a good idea in criminal cases? Should defendants conceal their guilt from their attorneys? What factors might convince a judge to release a jailed person on low bail—or waive bail altogether? All of these questions can be perplexing, particularly if you're not familiar with the criminal justice system.

You may be asking these questions because you, a relative, or a friend have been arrested and charged with a crime. Or perhaps you've been the victim of one. Maybe you're a teacher, social worker, or counselor who needs clear answers to pressing questions so you can help others understand how the criminal justice system works. Or perhaps you're just glued in front of Court TV and you want to know a little more about the real-life courtroom drama onscreen.

This book is for all of you.

It is written in an easy to understand question-and-answer format to explain the criminal justice system, inside and outside the courtroom.

- If you are facing criminal charges, this book will help you know enough about what's going on to intelligently participate in important decisions that are likely to affect the outcome.
- If someone close to you faces criminal charges, you'll want to know what is happening and how you can be of help—for example, does it matter whether you are there in the courtroom when your friend or relative is arraigned?
- If you are a victim of a crime, you too will want to understand how the process works and where in the process you can expect to have an effect on how the case is prosecuted.

Whatever prompts your interest, the criminal justice system belongs to you. You have a right to know how it works. The information in this book tells you what you never learned in high school civics.

In summary, our goal in this book is to cultivate educated clients, educated relatives and friends of defendants, educated victims, and educated citizens.

Our book is in no way intended as a detailed guide to self-representation. While the information in the book will no doubt assist those defendants who choose self-representation, the authors assume that those facing criminal charges for which jail or prison is a possibility are represented by an attorney, either privately retained or appointed at government expense. The book is, however, designed to empower criminal defendants by helping them understand every phase of the criminal justice process and what types of defenses and strategies are available to them.

If you are charged with a crime and seek to represent yourself, understand that criminal laws and procedures can be so complex that even judges can get them wrong. In one California case, for example, Garcia (a prison inmate) was charged with carrying a concealed weapon in prison. Garcia represented himself, and he asked the judge to order the sheriff to bring a few other prisoners to court so that they could testify on his behalf at the trial. The judge refused Garcia's request, on the ground that Garcia first had to serve subpoenas on the prisoners and Garcia hadn't done that. As the judge told Garcia during the trial,

"That's your problem, Mr. Garcia, that's not the court's problem. We're not here to practice law or do your work for you … I will not give you suggestions. I will not give you advice. I have previously encouraged you to consult with counsel … you've declined that."

Despite this rather condescending lecture, the judge was wrong. Under California law, the judge could order the prisoners to be brought to Garcia's trial even if Garcia had not subpoenaed them (*People v. Garcia,* CA Ct. of Appeal 2008).

Throughout the book, we have included examples that illustrate specific questions, sample dialogues of court proceedings, and specific tips for the reader. Sample documents commonly used in the criminal justice process are located at the end of the chapter in which they are discussed. The examples are provided as illustrations only. They are not designed to predict exactly what will happen in a particular case.

This book describes the criminal justice system as it tends to operate throughout the country. But each state, as well as the federal government, has its own set of criminal laws and procedures. Thus, if you need to know the terms of a specific law, or the procedures your local court will follow, you will need to consult the rules for your jurisdiction. Chapter 27 explains how to find such rules and other important information in a law library and on the Internet.

You may need to consult more than one chapter to get answers to your question. For example, if you want to know when the police can search your home, you will find answers in Chapter 2, *Search and Seizure*, and Chapter 3, *Arrest: When It Happens, What It Means*.

We encourage readers to use the registration card at the back of the book to pose questions of general concern. We'll incorporate the answers to these questions in future editions.

Introduction:
A Walk-Through of the Case of *State v. Andrea Davidson*, a Fictional Robbery Prosecution

This walk-through is intended to quickly familiarize you with what may happen as a case wends its way through the criminal justice system. While no two cases follow the identical procedural path, the example provides an overview of the entire process and serves as a guide to where you'll find answers to the questions posed in the walk-through, as well as loads of additional important information.

1. **Andrea Davidson is walking along a public street when Officer Kevin Daniels walks up to her and says, "Excuse me, I'd like to ask you a few questions."**

   - Can the officer legally do this?
   - Does Officer Daniels have to possess reliable information connecting Andrea to criminal activity before he can question her?
   - Does Andrea have to answer the officer's questions? Is it a good idea for her to talk to the officer even if she doesn't have to?
   - If Andrea believes that she has done nothing wrong, does she have anything to lose by talking to the officer?

   See Chapter 1, *Talking to the Police.*

2. **For many folks who are stopped and questioned, lawfully or otherwise, contact with the criminal justice system ends after the police finish "on the street" questioning. But as an example in our walk-through, Andrea has a long road ahead of her. Before questioning Andrea, Officer Daniels proceeds to "frisk" her (pat down her outer clothing).**

   - What's the difference between a frisk and a search?
   - Can police officers search suspects as a matter of routine?
   - If, during the frisk, the officer feels what seems to be a suspicious object, can the officer remove it from Andrea's clothing?

   See Chapter 2, *Search and Seizure.*

3. **Officer Daniels removes a gun from Andrea's coat and arrests her for carrying a concealed weapon.**

   - What constitutes an arrest?
   - Do police always take an arrested suspect to jail?
   - Was the officer required to get a warrant before arresting Andrea?

   See Chapter 3, *Arrest: When It Happens, What It Means.*

4. Andrea is taken to jail by Officer Daniels.

- What will happen to Andrea when she's booked into jail?
- How soon will Andrea have a chance to bail out of jail?
- What's the difference between posting cash bail and buying a bail bond?

See Chapter 5, *Booking and Bail: Checking In and Out of Jail.*

5. Feeling very alone and scared, Andrea considers contacting a lawyer.

- Does Andrea have a right to an attorney? What if she can't afford to hire one?
- If Andrea wants to represent herself, does she have a right to do so? Is self-representation generally a good idea?
- How can Andrea find a lawyer if she's in jail?
- What's the difference between private lawyers and public defenders?
- If Andrea is represented by a lawyer, does the lawyer make all the decisions?
- If Andrea talks to the lawyer while she's in jail, is their conversation confidential?
- What does it mean for the government to have to provide Andrea with "due process of law"?

See Chapter 7, *Criminal Defense Lawyers,* Chapter 8, *Understanding the Attorney-Client Relationship in a Criminal Case*; and Chapter 17, *Fundamental Trial Rights of the Defense.*

Multiple Coverage of Some Subjects

As you read through the book, you may notice that the same topic may arise in more than one chapter. For example, we refer to "motions *in limine*" in Chapters 19 and 21. We do this to reduce cross-referencing and to help readers who want to read about a particular part of the criminal justice process before reading the book from beginning to end.

---

6. Suspecting that Andrea was the culprit who had robbed a convenience store a short time before her arrest, Officer Daniels and another police officer question Andrea about her whereabouts at the time of the robbery.

- What are the "*Miranda* rights" that police officers often read to suspects?
- If the police fail to warn Andrea of her *Miranda* rights, does the case have to be thrown out?
- If Andrea starts talking to the police before they can warn her about her *Miranda* rights, can what she says be used against her in court?

See Chapter 1, *Talking to the Police.*

7. Officer Daniels asks Andrea to participate in a lineup to determine whether the store owner who was robbed at gunpoint, Hilary Julia, is able to identify Andrea as the robber.

- What happens at a lineup?
- Does Andrea have to participate in the lineup?
- Instead of conducting a lineup, could the police have shown the store owner a picture of Andrea?
- If Andrea has a lawyer, does she have the right to have her lawyer attend the lineup?
- Can the police compel Andrea to speak during the lineup?

See Chapter 4, *Eyewitness Identification: Psychology and Procedures*, and Chapter 17, *Fundamental Trial Rights of the Defense*.

8. Andrea's answers to Officer Daniels's questions lead the officer to suspect that evidence linking Andrea to the robbery is inside her home (such as some of the loot and a cap that the robber wore during the robbery). Officer Daniels wants to get hold of this evidence.

- Does the officer need to obtain a search warrant before entering Andrea's home?
- If the officer legally enters Andrea's house looking for evidence connecting her to the robbery and finds illegal drugs, can the officer seize the drugs and charge Andrea with another crime?
- If the officer enters Andrea's house illegally, does the case against her have to be dismissed?

See Chapter 2, *Search and Seizure*.

9. Andrea is formally charged with armed robbery.

- Does Officer Daniels make the decision about whether to charge Andrea with a crime?
- How long does the government have to decide whether to charge Andrea with a crime?
- Does the prosecutor have to seek an indictment from a grand jury?
- What does the prosecution have to prove to convict Andrea of armed robbery?

See Chapter 6, *From Suspect to Defendant*, and Chapter 12, *Crimespeak: Understanding the Language of Criminal Laws*.

10. Andrea is taken to court and "arraigned" on the armed robbery charge.

- What will the courtroom be like?
- If Andrea doesn't have a lawyer yet, what should she do? Can she represent herself?
- What happens at an arraignment?
- Is the arraignment judge authorized to release Andrea from jail?

See Chapter 9, *A Walk Through Criminal Court*; and Chapter 10, *Arraignments*.

11. Andrea tells the arraignment judge that she wants a lawyer but can't afford to hire one, so the judge appoints a lawyer to represent her.

- Will the attorney ask Andrea to tell her side of the story?

- Can the attorney do anything to help Andrea if she tells the attorney that she committed the robbery?
- What kinds of legal challenges can a defense attorney make before a case goes to trial?
- Does the lawyer have to keep everything Andrea says confidential?
- What decisions about her case does Andrea have the right to make?

See Chapter 8, *Understanding the Attorney-Client Relationship in a Criminal Case*; Chapter 11, *Developing the Defense Strategy*; and Chapter 19, *Motions and Their Role in Criminal Cases*.

12. Andrea's lawyer talks to her about the possibility of entering into a plea bargain.

- What rights would Andrea give up by pleading guilty?
- Can her lawyer insist that Andrea enter into a plea bargain?
- What does Andrea have to gain by pleading guilty?
- What factors will influence any "deal" that Andrea is offered?
- What is the judge's role in the plea bargaining process?

See Chapter 10, *Arraignments*, and Chapter 20, *Plea Bargains: How Most Criminal Cases End*.

13. Andrea pleads not guilty at the arraignment, and decides that even though she has a lawyer she should try to find out more about the crime she's charged with.

- Andrea's lawyer tells her that robbery is a specific intent crime. What does "specific intent" mean, and how will the prosecutor try to prove it?
- What are the possible defenses that Andrea can raise at trial?
- If Andrea wants to do legal research in a library or on a computer, how can she find information relevant to her case?

See Chapter 11, *Developing the Defense Strategy*; Chapter 12, *Crimespeak: Understanding the Language of Criminal Laws*; Chapter 13, *Defensespeak: Common Defenses to Criminal Charges*; and Chapter 27, *Looking Up the Law*.

14. At the conclusion of Andrea's arraignment, the judge schedules a date for a preliminary hearing.

- What is the purpose of a preliminary hearing?
- Do Andrea and her lawyer have a right to be present at the preliminary hearing?
- How can a preliminary hearing benefit the defense?

See Chapter 16, *Preliminary Hearings*.

15. At the conclusion of Andrea's preliminary hearing, the judge finds there is probable cause to try her for robbery and sets her case for trial. Andrea's attorney tells her, "I'll continue gathering information in preparation for trial."

- Does the prosecutor ever have to turn information over to the defense?

- Does the defense ever have to turn over information to the prosecutor?
- Does the defense have a right to interview prosecution witnesses?
- What can Andrea do to help her attorney investigate the case?

See Chapter 14, *Discovery: Exchanging Information With the Prosecution*, and Chapter 15, *Investigating the Facts*.

16. Though most cases end with dismissals or guilty pleas before trial, Andrea's case does go to trial.

- Why does the prosecution get to present its evidence first?
- What is the hearsay rule?
- If Andrea testifies, can the prosecutor offer evidence of her previous illegal conduct?
- Is Andrea entitled to a jury trial?
- Can the prosecution force Andrea to testify?
- Does Andrea have to convince the judge or jury of her innocence?

See Chapter 17, *Fundamental Trial Rights of the Defense*; Chapter 18, *Basic Evidence Rules in Criminal Trials*; and Chapter 21, *The Trial Process*.

17. Andrea is found guilty of armed robbery and a date is set for sentencing.

- What happens at a sentencing hearing?
- How might Andrea be punished other than or in addition to going to jail?
- What factors are likely to affect Andrea's sentence?
- What can Andrea do to earn the lightest possible sentence?

- If, after she's been found guilty, Andrea uncovers for the first time an important witness who supports her alibi defense, what can she do?

See Chapter 19, *Motions and Their Role in Criminal Cases*, and Chapter 22, *Sentencing: How the Court Punishes Convicted Defendants*.

- Andrea believes that her conviction was a mistake and wants to appeal it.
- How do appellate court judges find out about what took place at Andrea's trial?
- Will appellate court judges consider Andrea's argument that the jury shouldn't have believed the prosecutor's witnesses?
- If the trial judge made an error of law, will the appellate court necessarily overturn Andrea's conviction?

See Chapter 23, *Appeals: Seeking Review by a Higher Court*.

18. The conviction is overturned because the judge mistakenly barred certain evidence from the trial. Andrea is retried and this time is found not guilty.

- Can the prosecutor appeal the not guilty verdict to a higher court?
- Can the prosecutor refile the armed robbery charge in the future if new evidence turns up?
- Can the prosecutor ask the judge to order a new trial on the ground that the jurors afterwards said that they thought that Andrea was guilty but that she didn't deserve punishment?

See Chapter 13, *Defensespeak: Common Defenses to Criminal Charges*; Chapter 17, *Fundamental Trial Rights of the Defense*; and Chapter 19, *Motions and Their Role in Criminal Cases.*

19. **Andrea's conviction and five-year prison sentence are upheld on appeal, so Andrea has to serve time in state prison.**

   • Can Andrea do anything to improve bad prison conditions?

   • If Andrea has a child, will she lose custody of her child?
   • Can Andrea vote while she is in prison or after she is released?
   • Can Andrea earn money while she is in prison?
   • Does Andrea have a chance to be released early on parole?

See Chapter 26, *Prisoners' Rules.*

Comparison of Federal and State Systems

The vast majority of criminal prosecutions take place in state courts. The list below highlights some of the key differences between state and federal criminal systems:

   • **Jurisdiction ("power" to decide cases).** A state has power over defendants who violate the laws of that state. The federal government has power over defendants who commit criminal acts on federal property (for example, an assault in a national park) or whose criminal acts cross state lines (for example, a kidnapper who transports a victim from Iowa to Missouri). The federal government also has jurisdiction over a group of federally-defined crimes such as offenses related to immigration fraud and U.S. customs violations. A state and the federal government can have "concurrent" power over a defendant when the same criminal activity violates both state and federal laws (for example, selling drugs or robbing banks). In those situations, state and federal prosecutors make case-by-case decisions as to whether a defendant will be prosecuted in state or federal court.

   • **Police Officers.** Typical state police officers are county sheriffs and city police officers. Typical federal police officers are agents of the FBI and DEA (Drug Enforcement Administration).

   • **Prosecutors.** Federal criminal prosecutions are handled by U.S. attorneys, who are appointed by and are ultimately responsible to the U.S. Attorney General. State prosecutors, many of whom are elected on a countywide basis, carry a variety of titles; common ones are district attorney, state's attorney, and city attorney.

Comparison of Federal and State Systems (continued)

- **Defense Attorneys.** Most criminal defendants qualify for government-paid defense attorneys. Government-paid attorneys are usually employed either by an office of the Federal Public Defender or a county's Public Defender office. (For information about the differences between government-paid and privately-retained defense attorneys, see Chapter 7.)

- **Trial Courts.** Most federal criminal prosecutions occur in United States District Courts. State courts carry such titles as "superior court," "municipal court," "police court," or "county court," depending on the state and the seriousness of criminal charges.

- **Judges.** Federal trial judges are known as District Court judges; they are appointed for life by the president, subject to confirmation by the U.S. Senate. State court judges are typically initially appointed by governors and then are subject to election every few years. State court trial judges carry such titles as Superior Court Judge, Municipal Court Judge, and (in New York) Supreme Court Judge. In both state and federal courts, magistrates may preside over pretrial hearings such as bail hearings, as well as less serious criminal trials.

- **All-Purpose vs. Specialized Judges.** Federal courts use the "all-purpose judge" system. This means that the same judge almost always presides over a case from beginning to end—that is, from a defendant's first court appearance to final acquittal or sentencing. Some states also follow the all-purpose judge model. In many states, however, judges are specialized. For example, one judge may determine bail (see Chapter 5), another judge may hear pretrial motions (see Chapter 19), and a third judge may preside over a trial (see Chapter 21).

Talking to the Police

The overbearing police interrogation designed to wrench a confession from a quivering suspect is an enduring dramatic image. Though the image is largely a relic of the past, police officers do question individuals in a variety of circumstances. For example, aside from seeking a confession, police officers may question an arrestee to uncover information about additional suspects, or officers may simply seek information from people they have no intention of arresting. This chapter examines common situations in which police officers are likely to ask questions, and describes the typical legal consequences both of talking and of remaining silent.

TIP
Prosecutors can be counted on to use your words against you. Even a seemingly innocuous or innocent explanation may appear to link you to a crime when your words are recounted by a police officer. Your statements to a police officer may return to haunt you throughout your entire case, from the charges, to the amount of bail, to the trial itself. People who have even a remote suspicion that they may be accused of a crime should *never* talk to police officers before first talking to a lawyer.

Section I: Police Questioning of People Who Haven't Been Taken Into Custody

This section deals with police attempts to question you in situations in which you have not yet been placed in custody.

These commonly include:
- on-the-street, in-your-face questioning
- car stops for traffic violations
- investigatory visits to homes or offices, and
- telephone conversations.

(See Section II for police questioning after you have been taken into custody.)

1. Can a police officer stop me on the street and question me even if I have done nothing wrong?

Yes. Even if an officer has no reason to suspect that you have done anything wrong, the officer can approach you to ask questions and ask to search you or objects in your possession (such as a briefcase). So long as the officer doesn't suggest that you are legally compelled to talk or agree to a search, the officer has done nothing wrong (*U.S. v. Drayton,* U.S. Sup. Ct. 2002). At the same time, a person is generally not required to answer a police officer's questions or allow a police officer to conduct a search.

2. Is it a crime to refuse a police officer's request for identification?

Possibly. Many states have "stop and identify" laws. Under these laws, if a police officer reasonably suspects that a person has engaged in criminal activity, the officer can detain the person and ask for identification. A person who refuses to provide identification commits the crime of resisting an officer's lawful order (*Hiibel v. Nevada,* U.S. Sup. Ct. 2004).

Also, laws typically require drivers who are stopped for speeding and similar infractions to provide identification when an officer requests it.

CASE EXAMPLE: Jones is standing outside his parked truck. Noticing that Jones fits the description of a man who took clothing from a nearby store about a half hour earlier, Officer Juarez asks Jones for identification and questions Jones about where he's been for the last half hour. Jones refuses to say anything to the officer.

Question: Has Jones committed any crimes by refusing to answer?

Answer: Since Officer Juarez reasonably suspected that Jones might have stolen the clothing, Jones's refusal to provide identification would violate a "stop and identify" law. However, Jones has a constitutional right under the Fifth Amendment to remain silent. Jones cannot be punished for refusing to answer the officer's other questions.

3. Can I walk away from a police officer who is questioning me?

Unless a police officer has "probable cause" to make an arrest (see Chapter 3, Question 4), or a "reasonable suspicion" to conduct a "stop and frisk" (see Chapter 2, Section VI), a person has the legal right to walk away from a police officer. However, at the time of the encounter, there is no real way to tell what information the officer is using

---

Do You Have to Report a Crime to the Police?

Generally, neither a crime victim nor a witness who sees a crime take place has a legal obligation to report the crime to the police. Though a crime is an offense to the public as a whole, reporting is usually a matter for people's individual consciences and circumstances. However, you should be aware of the following:

- Laws in many states do require some individuals to report particular types of crimes. For example, teachers, social workers, and medical professionals may have to report suspected child abuse.
- You may be guilty of a crime as an "accessory after the fact" if you take active steps to conceal either the crime or the perpetrator. For more information about this, see Chapter 12, Section III.
- A few states, including Ohio, Massachusetts, and Washington, have enacted laws that make it a crime to see a felony occur yet fail to report it. Few prosecutions have taken place under such laws.

For background information about mandatory reporting laws, see Eugene Volokh, "Duties to Rescue and the Anti-Cooperative Effects of Law," 88 *Georgetown Law Journal* 105 (1999).

as a basis for her actions. In fact, an officer may have information that gives her a valid legal basis to make an arrest or to conduct a stop and frisk, even if the individual is, in truth, innocent of any wrongdoing. If that is the case, an officer may forcibly detain an innocent individual who starts to leave the scene of an interview. Common sense and self-protection suggest that people who intend to walk away from a police officer make sure that the officer does not intend to arrest or detain them. A good question might be, "Officer, I'm in a hurry, and I'd prefer not to talk to you right now. You won't try to stop me from leaving, right?" If the officer replies that you are not free to leave, you should remain at the scene and leave the issue of whether the officer had a legal basis for detaining you for the courts to determine at a later time.

4. If I start to answer a police officer's questions, can I change my mind and stop the interview?

Yes. You can halt police questioning at any time merely by indicating your desire not to talk further.

5. A police officer told me that if I didn't answer his questions I'd be arrested for loitering. Is that legal?

In certain circumstances, it may be. Laws in many states define loitering as "wandering about from place to place without apparent business, such that the person poses a threat to public safety." Under these laws, if a police officer sees a person loitering,

the officer can demand identification and an explanation of the person's activities. If the person fails to comply, the officer can arrest the person for loitering. Therefore, the refusal to answer questions is only a problem if the officer has also observed the person to be loitering.

CASE EXAMPLE: Officer Icia Yu is dispatched to Upscale Meadows after a resident calls the police to complain that a woman has been walking back and forth along the streets for over an hour, with no apparent purpose. From a distance, the officer observes the woman for a few minutes, and sees her stopping occasionally to peer into residents' back yards. Believing that she may be planning a burglary, Officer Yu confronts the woman, asks for identification and asks her to explain what she is doing in the neighborhood. The woman refuses to respond.

Question: Can Officer Yu arrest her?

Answer: Under loitering laws in effect in many states, yes. Officer Yu had reasonable grounds to believe that the woman posed a danger to the community. Since she didn't identify herself or explain why she was in the neighborhood, the officer could arrest her. Had the woman responded to Officer Yu, the officer might not arrest her for loitering. However, she might be subject to arrest for a different offense, such as trespass (unlawful entry on someone else's property).

The Questionable Legality of Loitering Laws

Many people argue that police officers use loitering laws to clear neighborhoods of "undesirables." Some courts have held loitering laws to be unconstitutional on the grounds that they are enforced discriminatorily against poor persons and ethnic minorities and that they unduly restrict people's rights to travel on public streets. However, the safest place to challenge the validity of a loitering law is in the courts, not on the streets to a police officer's face.

6. An officer pulled me over for suspicion of drunk driving and questioned me about where I'd been and what I'd had to drink. Can I be arrested for refusing to answer these questions?

No. An officer has the right to conduct a field sobriety test of a suspected drunk driver. But the driver has the right to refuse to answer questions. In such a situation, the validity of an arrest would depend solely on the person's driving pattern and performance on the field sobriety tests. (See Chapter 24 for more on drunk driving and field sobriety tests.)

7. If I don't have to answer questions, does this mean I can sue a police officer for trying to question me?

No. Even in the complete absence of probable cause to arrest or suspicion to conduct a stop and frisk, police officers have the same right as anyone else to approach people and try to talk to them. Of course, if the person refuses to talk, the officer must stop.

CASE EXAMPLE 1: Officer Stan Doff knocks on the front door of Dee Fensive's home. When Dee answers the door, the officer says, "I'd like to ask you a few questions about a robbery that took place across the street a few minutes ago. Have you noticed any suspicious people hanging around the neighborhood lately?" Dee indicates that she does not want to talk and closes the door. Officer Doff then leaves.

Question: Has the officer violated Dee's rights?

Answer: No. The officer has a right to try to question Dee. When Dee indicated that she did not want to talk, the officer ended the interview. The officer's actions are legally proper.

CASE EXAMPLE 2: Martinez is arrested for assaulting Police Officer Haskell. Martinez is shot during the altercation, and very seriously injured. Therefore, Officer Haskell has Martinez taken to a hospital emergency room. A second police officer, Officer Chavez, questions Martinez while he is receiving medical treatment, and Martinez admits to Officer Chavez that before Officer Haskell shot him, he was trying to grab Officer Haskell's gun. Officer Chavez should have but failed to advise Martinez of his *Miranda* rights before questioning him. (See Question 13.)

However, Martinez is never charged with a crime and the statements he made to Officer Chavez are never offered against him in court.

Question: Can Martinez sue Officer Chavez for violating his civil rights and receive money damages?

Answer: No. Because Martinez's statements to Officer Chavez were never offered into evidence against Martinez in a criminal trial, Officer Chavez did not violate Martinez's constitutional rights. In other words, suspects cannot recover money from police officers simply because the officers' questioning violates *Miranda*. On the other hand, suspects' civil rights are violated and suspects can sue and receive money damages when police officers use "egregious" questioning methods, such as torture or other methods of brutality (*Chavez v. Martinez*, U.S. Sup. Ct. 2003).

8. Doesn't a police officer always have to read me my "*Miranda* rights" before questioning me?

No. A "*Miranda* warning" (see Section II) is required only if a suspect is in custody and the police intend to interrogate the suspect. In other words, both "custody" and "interrogation" have to occur for *Miranda* rights to kick in. One upshot is that a statement by a person who is not in custody, or a statement made voluntarily rather than in response to police interrogation, is admissible in evidence at trial even though no *Miranda* warning was given.

CASE EXAMPLE: Officer Dave Bouncer is investigating a barroom brawl. The bartender indicates that a patron named Bob Sawyer might be able to identify the instigator of the brawl. When Officer Bouncer interviews Bob, Bob makes statements implicating himself in the brawl. Officer Bouncer did not read Bob his *Miranda* rights.

Question: If Bob is charged with a crime concerning the brawl, will Bob's statements to Officer Bouncer be admissible as evidence?

Answer: Yes. At the time Officer Bouncer spoke to Bob, Bob was not in custody. Thus, *Miranda* warnings were not required as a condition of admissibility.

9. A police officer wants to question me about a crime I know I didn't commit. Can I harm my own interests by talking?

Quite possibly. It is often perfectly sensible and socially desirable for innocent people to cooperate in a police investigation. However, they should be aware of the risks. Here are several important questions to ask yourself before agreeing to a police interview:

a. Even if I haven't done anything wrong, how sure am I about the events that the police officer is asking me about?

Unfortunately, people who haven't done anything wrong are sometimes mistakenly accused of crimes. Equally unfortunately, these same innocent people may unwittingly add to the evidence against them if they talk to police officers before they are prepared to do so. Individuals who are unprepared to talk about certain events may become confused and answer incorrectly, especially when confronted by police officers. These individuals may then want to change what they've said to "set the record straight." But the police (or a judge or jury) may regard the change of story as itself suspicious and indicative of guilt. Thus, even individuals who want to cooperate with police officers ought to make sure that they have a clear recollection of the events about which the officers are asking. Individuals who are unsure of what to do should at least ask the officer to return at a later time.

Delay the Interview

People who are uncertain about whether to talk to a police officer needn't feel trapped into giving an immediate "yes" or "no." Being confronted by a police officer tends to make many people nervous and anxious, which renders them unable to give completely accurate answers. A good alternative is to delay the interview by saying something such as, "This is a bad time," or, "I didn't expect this so I'm a bit muddled now, please come back another time." Among other things, delay provides an opportunity to consult with a lawyer, and perhaps to have the lawyer present during the interview if the person ultimately decides to talk.

---

b. Might the police learn about any unrelated crimes I have committed as a result of the interview?

People may talk to police officers because they are confident that they can demonstrate that they are not involved in the crimes that the officers are investigating. However, they may unwittingly disclose information implicating themselves in other criminal activity.

> **CASE EXAMPLE:** While voluntarily answering a police officer's questions and denying any involvement in a burglary that took place on May 15, Sol Itary nervously mentions that he was using illegal drugs with someone else at another location.
>
> **Question:** If Itary is charged with possession of illegal drugs based on other evidence, can the prosecution offer Itary's statement to the officer into evidence?
>
> **Answer:** Yes. Itary voluntarily spoke to the officer, so the statement is admissible.

c. Will previous contacts I've had with the police possibly lead them to distort what I say?

People who think that they may be police targets (perhaps because of past criminal records) should be especially careful about voluntarily talking to a police officer. Police officers sometimes distort people's oral statements, either because the officers are lying or because they have heard only what they want to hear. By repeating in court only part of a person's statement or changing a few words around, a police officer may make an innocent remark seem incriminating.

> **CASE EXAMPLE:** A humorous example of police officer distortion occurred in the 1992 comedy film, *My Cousin Vinny*. In the film, a police officer questions a college student who has been arrested for killing a grocery store clerk. The stunned student, who at first thought that he had been arrested for shoplifting a can of tuna fish, repeats in a dazed, questioning voice, "I shot the clerk?" In court, however, the police officer makes it sound as if the student confessed to the murder by testifying that the student asserted, "I shot the clerk." In real life, of course, police distortion is no laughing matter.

Recording Statements Made to Police Officers

People who want to cooperate with police officers but fear that the police will distort their statements should insist that the police officers tape-record the conversation or prepare a written summary of it for the person to sign. The tape or summary minimizes a police officer's opportunity to distort at a later time. But there is a potential downside to having the statement recorded. Once the words are on tape, a defendant will have to live with them if the case goes to trial, rather than argue that the police got it wrong.

d. How knowledgeable am I about the law governing the events about which I'm being questioned?

People sometimes unwittingly provide evidence of their own guilt because they inaccurately believe that their behavior does not amount to criminal conduct. They may think they are explaining their innocence, while the police officers are using their explanation to amass evidence of a crime.

> **CASE EXAMPLE:** Moe gets into a fist fight with Curly, which results in a severe cut to Curly's head. A police officer contacts Moe, seeking his version of the fight. Thinking that he acted in self-defense, Moe fully describes his version of events. However, as the police officer interprets Moe's story, Moe used excessive force, and the officer arrests Moe for aggravated assault. Had Moe more clearly understood the law, he might not have talked to the police officer.

10. Can it ever help me to answer a police officer's questions?

Yes. Police officers may be as interested in clearing the innocent as in convicting the guilty. People can often clear their names as well as help the police find the real perpetrators by answering a few straightforward questions. For example, assume that Wally, a possible suspect, can demonstrate that "I was at dinner with Andre" at the moment a crime was committed. Wally both removes himself as a suspect and enables the police to concentrate their efforts elsewhere.

And legal rights aside, the truth on the street is that people often can make life easier for themselves by cooperating with police officers—so long as they don't have a good reason not to. "Contempt of cop" has resulted in the arrest and even physical injury of more than one innocent person. When innocent people who are pulled over or questioned by police officers stand on their rights too forcefully, events can sometimes get out of control rather quickly.

Lie Detector Tests

Police officers sometimes ask suspects to take lie detector tests to "clear their names." In general, suspects should refuse to take lie detector tests. Police sometimes use the tests as tools for obtaining confessions, falsely telling suspects that because they are flunking a test, they might as well confess. Moreover, lie detector tests are notoriously inaccurate. Innocent people often test guilty. Though lie detector test results are not usually admissible in court, even a false "guilty" result may prompt the police to make an arrest. (For more on lie detector tests, see Chapter 18, Question 36.)

---

11. A police officer wants to talk to me about a crime that I took part in. Is it ever a good idea to try to talk my way out of it?

Usually, no. The golden rule of defense is that suspects who think that they may be implicated in a crime should keep their mouths tightly shut. Suspects all too frequently unwittingly reveal information that later can be used as evidence of guilt. The right to not incriminate oneself, guaranteed by the Fifth Amendment to the U.S. Constitution, is especially powerful in this situation, and a suspect should politely decline to answer questions, at least until consulting with an attorney.

12. A police officer wants to ask me about a crime that a friend or relative of mine committed. What do I risk by providing false information?

A lot. When people lie to the police or otherwise intentionally assist a known criminal to avoid arrest, they may be charged as "accessories after the fact." They can also be charged with obstruction of justice. Obviously, the decision as to whether to furnish information leading to the arrest of a relative or close friend is a personal one. However, a person who chooses not to do so should simply decline to answer an officer's questions rather than lie. Rarely, if ever, would an individual who simply declines to give information to a police officer qualify as an accessory after the fact.

CASE EXAMPLE: Cain comes running into his brother Abel's house, and tells Abel that he, Cain, just robbed a market and that the police might be on his tail. A few minutes later, a police officer knocks on Abel's door and asks him if Cain is in the house. Abel responds,

"No, he left town permanently to go back east weeks ago."

Question: Is Abel subject to criminal prosecution?

Answer: Yes, Abel might be prosecuted as an accessory after the fact. By affirmatively misleading the police, he has aided Cain in avoiding arrest. To protect himself while not giving up his brother, Abel might have said, "I'm sorry, I can't talk to you about that." (Admittedly, the police might view such a response as a red flag that Cain is close at hand. Abel must rely on his own balancing of personal risk, private loyalty, and public duty.)

Section II: Police Questioning of Arrestees

This section deals with police attempts to question you in situations in which you are in custody. It explains the *Miranda* rule and when it does and does not apply.

13. What is a *"Miranda* warning"?

When police officers make an arrest, they commonly interrogate (question) the arrestee. Usually they are trying to strengthen the prosecution's case by getting the arrestee to provide some evidence of guilt. An interrogation may have other purposes as well, such as developing leads to additional suspects.

By answering police questions after arrest, a suspect gives up two rights granted by the U.S. Constitution:

- the Fifth Amendment right to remain silent, and
- the Sixth Amendment right to have a lawyer present during the questioning.

Although people are entitled to voluntarily give up these and other rights, the courts have long recognized that voluntariness depends on knowledge and free will, and that people questioned by the police while they are in custody frequently have neither.

To remedy this situation, the U.S. Supreme Court ruled in the case of *Miranda v. Arizona* (1966) that information obtained by police officers through the questioning of a suspect in police custody may be admitted as evidence at trial only if the questioning was preceded by certain cautions known collectively as a *"Miranda* warning." Accordingly, police officers usually begin their questioning of a person in custody by first making the following statements:

- You have the right to remain silent.
- If you do say anything, what you say can be used against you in a court of law.
- You have the right to consult with a lawyer and have that lawyer present during any questioning.
- If you cannot afford a lawyer, one will be appointed for you if you so desire.
- If you choose to talk to the police officer, you have the right to stop the interview at any time.

If a suspect is in police custody, it doesn't matter whether the interrogation takes place in a jail or at the scene of a crime, on a busy downtown street, or in the middle of an open field. Other than routine automobile stops and brief on-the-street detentions, once a police officer deprives a suspect of freedom of action in any way, the suspect is in police custody and *Miranda* is activated. (See Question 20 for more on when a person is in custody.)

The *Miranda* Case

Ernesto Miranda was arrested for kidnapping and raping a young woman in Arizona. Ten days after the rape took place, the victim picked Miranda out of a lineup and identified him as her attacker. The police took Miranda into an interrogation room and questioned him for two hours. Eventually, Miranda broke down and confessed in writing to committing the rape. The police did not physically abuse Miranda or trick him into confessing. At trial, the prosecution offered Miranda's confession into evidence, and he was convicted. On appeal, the U.S. Supreme Court overturned the conviction and granted Miranda a new trial. The Supreme Court decided that the confession should not have been admitted into evidence at Miranda's trial because the police had not advised Miranda of his right to remain silent and to consult with counsel. Miranda was convicted again after a second trial, even though the prosecution was not able to offer Miranda's confession into evidence.

CASE EXAMPLE: Kelly Rozmus is arrested for assault. At the police station, Officer Mayorkas seeks to question Rozmus about the events leading up to the assault.

Question: Does Rozmus have to answer the officer's questions?

Answer: No. Rozmus has a constitutional right to remain silent, and if Officer Mayorkas fails to warn Rozmus of the *Miranda* rights before questioning begins, then nothing Rozmus says is later admissible in evidence.

14. What happens if a suspect who is in custody isn't given a *Miranda* warning and answers a police officer's questions?

If a police officer questions a suspect without giving the suspect the *Miranda* warning, nothing the suspect says can be used against the suspect at trial. The purpose of this "exclusionary rule" is to deter the police from violating the *Miranda* rule, which the U.S. Supreme Court has ruled is required by the Constitution (*Dickerson v. U.S.*, U.S. Sup. Ct. 2000).

15. Can the government ever use statements against defendants if they were obtained in violation of *Miranda*?

Yes, assuming that the only reason that a defendant's statement is inadmissible is the police *Miranda* violation and not other police misconduct such as physical coercion.

If the defendant gives testimony at trial that conflicts with the statement made to the police, the prosecutor can offer the statement into evidence to impeach (attack) the defendant's credibility. (See *Kansas v. Ventris*, U.S. Sup. Ct. 2009.) Similarly, rules in many jurisdictions allow prosecutors to offer statements obtained in violation of *Miranda* against defendants in sentencing hearings (*U.S. v. Nichols*, 4th Cir., 2006). For example, assume that in an improperly-obtained statement, a defendant admits to the police that he was armed with a weapon when he committed a crime. The defendant's confession may not be admissible at trial to prove the defendant's guilt, but the prosecutor may offer it into evidence during sentencing to try to obtain a harsher sentence.

Also, the government may be able to use the "fruits" of statements taken in violation of *Miranda*. If police officers learn about evidence by taking a defendant's statement in violation of *Miranda*, that evidence might be admissible against the defendant. Here are some common examples:

- In dangerous situations, the "public safety" exception allows police officers to question suspects about weapons without giving a *Miranda* warning, and if the interrogation leads the police to a weapon, it can be used against the suspect at trial (*N.Y. v. Quarles*, U.S. Sup. Ct. 1984).
- Dangerous situation or not, any tangible evidence (such as a threatening note or the loot from a robbery) that the police learn about through questioning that violates *Miranda* can generally be used against a suspect in court (*U.S. v. Patane*, U.S. Sup. Ct. 2004).

- If a statement taken in violation of *Miranda* leads the police to another witness, that witness can testify against a suspect at trial (*Michigan v. Tucker*, U.S. Sup. Ct. 1974).
- The "inevitable discovery" doctrine means that if the police would have eventually found tangible evidence on their own, the evidence can be used against a suspect at trial even if the police find out about it during questioning that violates *Miranda*.

These interpretations of the *Miranda* rule give the police a real incentive to violate the *Miranda* rule. Moreover, they mean that suspects have to protect themselves. Suspects who think that what they say can't be used against them at trial because they weren't given *Miranda* warnings need to understand that the fruits of their improperly obtained statements may well be admissible in evidence.

CASE EXAMPLE 1: Mal Addy is arrested for assault with a deadly weapon. The police question Addy without giving him the *Miranda* warning. Addy confesses to the crime and tells the police where he hid the knife that he used in the attack. The police then locate the knife.

Question: What evidence can the prosecutor use against Addy at trial?

Answer: The prosecutor cannot offer Addy's confession into evidence at trial. However, the knife can be used at trial because the knife is a tangible object, not a statement.

CASE EXAMPLE 2: Same case. While the police question Addy without giving him a *Miranda* warning, he tells them that he has illegal drugs in the backpack that he is carrying when he is arrested.

Question: Can Addy be charged with possession of illegal drugs?

Answer: Yes, because the police would have inevitably found the drugs when they inventoried the contents of the backpack during the booking process.

16. Are there circumstances in which a statement by a suspect can't be used against that suspect even if a *Miranda* warning is given?

Yes, but only in unusual circumstances. If a police officer gives a suspect a *Miranda* warning and then physically coerces the suspect into talking (say, refusing a suspect's requests for medicine that the suspect has to take), the resulting statement cannot be used against the suspect.

A confession following the giving of a *Miranda* warning also cannot be used against a suspect if it's the result of a ploy known as "question first, warn later." Police using this technique question a suspect without giving a *Miranda* warning. If a suspect confesses, the police then give a *Miranda* warning and convince the suspect that having already confessed, the suspect should waive (give up) the right to remain silent and repeat the confession. Even though the second confession follows a *Miranda* warning, neither the first nor the second confession can be used against the suspect at trial (*Missouri v. Seibert,* U.S. Sup. Ct. 2004).

17. Am I entitled to have my case dismissed if the police questioned me without advising me of my *Miranda* rights?

No. One popular misconception about the criminal justice system is that a case has to be thrown out of court if the police fail to give the *Miranda* warning to people they arrest. What *Miranda* says is that the warning is necessary if the police interrogate a suspect in custody and want to offer something the suspect says into evidence at trial. This means that the failure to give the *Miranda* warning is utterly irrelevant to the case if:

- the suspect is not in custody (see Question 20)
- the police do not question the suspect, or
- the police do question the suspect, but the prosecution does not try to use the suspect's responses as evidence.

In essence, if the prosecution can win its case without using the illegally-obtained evidence, a *Miranda* violation will not cause dismissal of the case.

18. After I'm arrested, is it ever a good idea to talk to the police?

Not without talking to a lawyer first. Talking to the police is almost always hazardous to the health of a defense case, and defense attorneys almost universally advise their clients to remain silent until the attorney has assessed the charges and counseled the client about case strategy.

19. How do I assert my right to remain silent if I am being questioned by the police?

Suspects do not need to use any magic words to indicate that they want to remain silent. Indeed, they don't have to use any words at all. Arrestees may invoke their *Miranda* rights by saying things like the following:

- "I want to talk to an attorney."
- "I refuse to speak with you."
- "Please leave me alone."
- "I don't have anything to say."
- "I claim my *Miranda* rights."

If the police continue to question an arrestee who says anything like the above, the police have violated *Miranda*. As a result, nothing the arrestee says after that point is admissible in evidence.

20. If the police question me before arresting me, does the *Miranda* rule apply?

Not necessarily. *Miranda* applies only to "custodial" questioning. A person is not in custody unless a police officer has "deprived a [person] of his freedom of action in a significant way." Whether a suspect is in custody and therefore not free to leave is an objective issue that judges decide without taking into account a suspect's inexperience or psychological condition (*Yarborough v. Alvarado*, U.S. Sup. Ct. 2004).

When it decided the *Miranda* case, the Supreme Court said that its ruling did not apply to "general on-the-scene questioning as to facts surrounding a crime or other general questioning of citizens in the fact-finding process." Thus, unless a person is in custody, an officer can question the person without giving the *Miranda* warning, and whatever the person says is admissible in evidence.

CASE EXAMPLE: Officer Roy Altie responds to a call to investigate a purse-snatching incident. The officer learns from the victim that the culprit was a white male, about 5'10" tall, weighing about 175 pounds and wearing a light-colored sweatshirt. About ten minutes later, about a mile from where the purse-snatching took place, Officer Altie sees a man generally fitting the attacker's description walking alone. Officer Altie realizes that he lacks sufficient evidence to make an arrest, and approaches the man merely to question him about his activities and whereabouts during the preceding one-half hour.

Question: Does Officer Altie have to precede the questioning with the *Miranda* warning?

Answer: No. The victim's description was so general that it could apply to many men. Thus, Officer Altie lacked probable cause to make an arrest, and did not intend to make an arrest. Officer Altie was engaged in general on-the-scene questioning, and therefore did not have to give the *Miranda* warning.

Police Officers May Mischaracterize a Custodial Situation in Court

Police officers generally believe that suspects are more likely to speak with them voluntarily in the absence of a *Miranda* warning. Thus, police officers have an incentive not to give the warning. One way they may attempt to evade the *Miranda* rule is by delaying the arrest of a suspect until after they're through with the questioning. If an officer can convince a judge that the officer was engaged only in general questioning, and would have let the suspect walk away had the suspect chosen to do so, anything the suspect says to the officer can be used against the suspect at trial despite the lack of *Miranda* warnings.

21. Do the police have to give me a *Miranda* warning if I'm stopped for a traffic violation?

No, so long as the police officer simply asks a motorist for identification and limits discussion to the traffic offense for which the officer stopped the motorist. Routine traffic violations are infractions, not crimes. A motorist's statement to a police officer relating to events leading up to a ticket is therefore admissible even if the officer did not give the motorist the *Miranda* warning. However, a *Miranda* warning would be

required if an officer detains a motorist in order to question the motorist about crimes unrelated to the traffic stop.

CASE EXAMPLE: Officer Starsky stops Hutch for running a red light. After issuing a ticket, the officer orders Hutch from the car and questions him about a burglary that had taken place nearby. Officer Starsky does not give Hutch the *Miranda* warning.

Question: Is what Hutch says to the officer about his whereabouts at the time of the burglary admissible in evidence?

Answer: No. Hutch was ordered out of the car and thus was not free to leave. Because Hutch was in custody and Officer Starsky questioned him about a crime unrelated to the traffic offense without giving Hutch the *Miranda* warning, Hutch's statements are inadmissible in evidence.

22. Are statements that I make voluntarily before I'm questioned admissible in evidence?

In general, yes. *Miranda* applies only to statements that are the product of police questioning. If an arrestee volunteers information to a police officer, the information is admissible in evidence.

CASE EXAMPLE: After failing a series of sobriety tests, Ina Bryate is arrested for drunk driving. As the officer is taking her toward the police vehicle, Ina says, "I couldn't possibly be drunk. I only had a few beers at the sorority party." Before Ina said this, the officer had neither given her a *Miranda* warning nor questioned her.

Question: Is what Ina said admissible in evidence?

Answer: Yes. Ina volunteered the remark; the officer did not elicit it with a question. Thus, the fact that Ina had not been given a *Miranda* warning does not bar admission of her statement into evidence.

23. What does it mean to "waive" my *Miranda* rights?

Suspects waive (give up) their *Miranda* rights by talking to police officers after having been advised that they have the right not to. To avoid disputes in court about whether *Miranda* warnings were given and waived, police officers often ask suspects who indicate a willingness to talk to sign waiver forms acknowledging that they've received and understood their *Miranda* rights, and that they want to talk to the police anyway.

24. Once I've waived my *Miranda* rights, is it possible to change my mind and invoke my right to silence?

Yes. Suspects can invoke their right to silence at any time, even if they have begun talking to the police. Of course, statements made before invoking the right to silence are admissible, so deciding to remain silent after previously answering questions may be the equivalent of locking the barn

door after the horse has run away. To stop police questioning, a suspect merely has to say something like, "I don't want to say anything else," or, "I want to talk to a lawyer before we go any farther." If the police continue to question a suspect who invokes *Miranda*, nothing the suspect says after indicating a desire to halt the interview is admissible in evidence.

25. What effect has the *Miranda* rule had? Do most suspects invoke their right to remain silent and to be represented by an attorney during police questioning?

When *Miranda* was decided, police and prosecutors predicted a dire effect on their ability to secure convictions. (In a 1998 book about Miranda, Prof. Richard Leo estimates that at least 80% of suspects waive their *Miranda* rights and voluntarily talk to the police.) The following psychological factors that police regularly use to their advantage explain why suspects often make "voluntary" confessions that they later regret:

- Suspects who are in custody are psychologically vulnerable. Many suspects are intimidated by jail conditions, and talk in order to please the jailers who are suddenly in control of their lives.
- Police often lead a suspect to believe that a confession or cooperation in naming other suspects will result in leniency. Although courts generally consider this to be improper police conduct (see, for example, *United States v. Johnson*, 6th Cir., U.S. Court

How the Police Can Benefit From Delayed *Miranda* Warnings

Crafty police officers may intentionally delay giving *Miranda* warnings to suspects following an arrest for at least two reasons:

- If they don't question the suspect, police officers don't have to give *Miranda* warnings. In the absence of the warnings, some suspects will blurt out voluntary statements that the prosecution can then offer into evidence at trial. For example, instead of immediately interrogating a suspect, a police officer may reveal the evidence that the officer has thus far gathered from other sources. Figuring that there's nothing to be gained from silence, the suspect may indicate a willingness to confess. The officer can then advise the suspect of his *Miranda* rights, making the subsequent confession admissible in evidence against the defendant at trial (*U.S. v. Gonzalez-Lauzan*, 11th Cir. 2006).

- Even if a suspect remains silent, the prosecution can sometimes use that silence against the suspect at trial. Assume that a suspect who remained silent after arrest testifies in essence that, "I didn't do it." The prosecution may be able to attack the suspect's credibility (believability) by having the arresting officer testify to the suspect's silence following arrest. The prosecution's argument would be, "If the suspect really didn't do it, why didn't the suspect immediately say that to the arresting officer?" This tactic can only be used, however, if the defendant takes the stand.

of Appeals (2003)), the police will usually deny that they promised leniency, and the judge will usually believe them.

- Police use the "good cop–bad cop" routine. In this ploy, one police officer is aggressive and overbearing toward a suspect. A second officer is helpful and courteous. Suspects believe the second officer is on their side, and so they gratefully and voluntarily talk to the second officer.

- Many suspects talk voluntarily in the belief that only explicit confessions will be admissible in evidence. They are mistaken. Anything they say to the police, even if at the time it seems to be in their favor, is admissible in evidence.

- Police may make suspects feel that their situations are already hopeless. For example, police officers may tell a suspect he failed a lie detector test, that a codefendant confessed and incriminated the suspect, or that the police have a videotape of the suspect committing the crime. Even if the police have lied, the resulting confession is usually admissible in evidence.

- Taking advantage of a suspect's pangs of guilt, police officers may emphasize the harm that the suspect has caused to the victim, and stress that the suspect can begin to repay the victim by owning up to the misdeed. A resulting confession turns the suspect's feeling of moral guilt into legal guilt.

- Police sometimes emphasize that a confession will speed things up. Many suspects, especially first-time offenders, want to put a criminal charge behind them as soon as possible. To them, a confession represents the shortest line between two points.

- Police officers tell suspects, "We'll put what you say in our reports, so this is a chance to make sure that the district attorney hears your side of the story." Then in an effort to minimize their guilt, suspects often furnish evidence that eventually helps convict them.

- When two or more suspects commit a crime, police officers sometimes extract confessions by falsely telling some of the suspects that the police regard them as witnesses rather than culprits.

False Confessions and the "Central Park Jogger" Case

Confessions carry great weight with juries because most people believe the precept, "innocent people don't confess to serious crimes." However, the psychological factors mentioned in the response to Question 25 are so powerful that they can produce false confessions. Research carried out by The Innocence Project indicates that about 25% of suspects who were convicted and later proved innocent (usually based on DNA testing) had confessed their guilt. One of the most infamous examples of erroneous convictions based largely on false confessions occurred in the Central Park Jogger case. In 1989, a woman was raped and horribly beaten while jogging in New York's Central Park. Police officers extracted confessions from five teenage boys, and they were convicted and sentenced to prison even though their stories varied and DNA testing failed to link any of the boys to the attack. Thirteen years later, an individual named Reyes confessed that he alone had attacked the jogger. Reyes' confession provided details known only to the police, and DNA testing confirmed that Reyes was the source of the semen found at the crime scene. The innocent teenage boys' convictions were vacated. More information about the case and suggestions for reforms that might reduce the risk of false confessions generally can be found in an article by Prof. Richard Leo (and others) entitled *Bringing Reliability Back In: False Confessions and Legal Safeguards in the Twenty-First Century* in the Wisconsin Law Review of 2006.

Empty Promises

Police officers' promises of leniency are usually empty. Police officers may recommend a light sentence (then again, they may not even fulfill that part of the bargain), but at the end of the day it's prosecutors and judges who normally determine punishment on the basis of statutory requirements and political expediency.

CASE EXAMPLE 1: Dee Nyal is arrested and charged with burglary. At the police station, Dee waives her *Miranda* rights and voluntarily tells the police that she is innocent, because she was at the movies at the time the burglary took place. At trial, the prosecutor wants to offer Dee's statement to the police into evidence to show it was false, because the movie Dee said she watched was not playing the night of the burglary. Dee protests that what she said to the police shouldn't be admissible because she didn't make a confession; instead she said she wasn't guilty.

Question: Is Dee's statement to the police admissible in evidence?

Answer: Yes. Dee waived her *Miranda* rights, so the statement is admissible, regardless of whether she made the statement to help herself or to admit guilt.

CASE EXAMPLE 2: Len Scap is arrested for murder. The police give Len his *Miranda* warning, then tell him that he might as well confess because the police found Len's fingerprints at the crime scene and because they have an eyewitness who can easily identify him. Feeling all is lost, Len confesses to the murder. It turns out that the police lied to Len—they had neither his fingerprints nor an eyewitness.

Question: Is Len's confession admissible in evidence?

Answer: Very probably. Judges generally rule that confessions are voluntary even if they are obtained by the police through trickery. (See *Frazier v. Cupp*, U.S. Sup. Ct. 1969.)

26. **If my boss questions me about drug use or my landlord asks me about illegal activities in my apartment, can my responses be used as evidence against me if they didn't first give me a *Miranda* warning?**

Yes. *Miranda* only applies to questioning by the police or other governmental officials.

27. If the police plant informants in jails in violation of suspects' right to counsel, are statements that the suspects make to the informants admissible in evidence?

Yes, but only for impeachment. Planting an informant in jails violates the suspects' right to counsel. But if suspects testify at trial and contradict what they've said to an informant, prosecutors offer the contradictory statements into evidence. Allowing impeachment in these circumstances promotes the integrity of the trial process. (See *Kansas v. Ventris*, U.S. Sup. Ct. 2009.)

> **CASE EXAMPLE:** Ventris is in jail, charged with murder. Hoping to develop additional evidence against Ventris, the police place an undercover informant in his jail cell. The informant is prepared to testify that Ventris admitted committing the murder. At trial, however, Ventris testifies that his girlfriend committed the murder.
>
> **Question:** Can the prosecutor call the informant to testify to Ventris' admission that he was the murderer?
>
> **Answer:** Yes. Since Ventris' trial testimony contradicted his jailhouse statement to the informant, the prosecution can offer the statement into evidence to impeach Ventris' credibility.

Private Individuals May Sometimes Be Police Agents for Purposes of *Miranda*

Courts sometimes hold private individuals to the same *Miranda* standards as police officers if the individuals act in concert with the police. For example, assume that the police arrest Rose Ettastone for embezzlement from the bank that employs her. Hoping to find out how Rose carried out the scheme, the police ask the bank manager to come down to the jail and interview Rose. Rose tells the bank manager details of the scheme, which the prosecutor wants to offer into evidence. Because the manager was acting as a police agent, he would have had to advise Rose of her *Miranda* rights before interviewing her if the statements were to be admitted as evidence.

Recent years have seen an explosion of private security guards—according to one estimate, the United States now has three times as many private security guards as police officers. Because private security guards are not governmental employees, rules such as *Miranda* have not been applied to them. However, courts may soon be called upon to impose some of the same restrictions on private security guards as they do on police officers.

28. Besides *Miranda*, are there other restrictions placed on the police when they seek information from an arrested person?

Yes. Confessions that are deemed to be involuntary are not allowed as evidence. Under this rule, the police are not allowed to use brutality, physical threats, or other means of intimidation to coerce suspects into confessing. If the police obtain information by any of these illegal means, the information is not admissible, whether or not they read the suspect his *Miranda* warning. In addition, under the fruit of the poisonous tree rule, any evidence that the police obtain as the result of the coerced confession would be equally inadmissible.

> **CASE EXAMPLE 1:** Clark Kent is arrested for indecent exposure. After he is booked, the police read the *Miranda* rights to Clark. The police then proceed to question Clark over a 36-hour period, keeping him in solitary confinement when they are not questioning him and withholding almost all food and water. Clark finally agrees to talk to the police and confesses to the crime.
>
> **Question:** Are Clark's statements admissible in evidence?
>
> **Answer:** No. Clark did not freely and voluntarily waive his *Miranda* rights, because the interrogation methods were highly coercive.

> **CASE EXAMPLE 2:** Moe Money is charged with obtaining money by fraudulent means. Following the *Miranda* warning, Moe voluntarily agrees to talk to the police and denies any fraudulent conduct. The police then tell Moe that they will arrest his wife and bring her to the station for questioning. Moe tells the police that his wife is pregnant but very ill, and has been instructed by her doctor to remain in bed as much as possible to protect her health and that of the baby. The police tell Moe that's his problem, they're going to arrest his wife unless he confesses and "the health of your wife and your kid is up to you."
>
> **Question:** If Moe then confesses, is the confession admissible in evidence?
>
> **Answer:** No. Moe's confession was involuntary. This is especially true if the police lacked probable cause to arrest Moe's wife and threatened to arrest her only to coerce Moe into talking. (See *Rogers v. Richmond*, U.S. Sup. Ct. 1961.)

Cops Usually Win "Swearing Contests"

Defendants' claims that they were coerced into talking often turn into swearing contests, with the police contending that everything was honest and aboveboard. Defendants who are physically coerced by police into talking can support their claims with photos of marks and bruises. But actual police brutality is unusual, and defendants cannot usually offer independent evidence to support their claims of psychological coercion. Judges, believing that defendants have a greater motivation to lie than police officers, usually side with the police and conclude that no coercion took place.

29. How do intoxication or mental limitations affect the voluntariness of a confession?

Very little. Defendants often ask judges to rule that their confessions were involuntary on the grounds that at the time the defendants confessed they were drunk, were high on drugs, or had mental limitations. Unless the defendant was practically unconscious at the time of confessing, judges usually decide that confessions are voluntary—despite the existence of factors that strongly suggest an opposite conclusion. (See *United States v. Curtis,* 344 F.2d 1057 (2003).)

CASE EXAMPLE 1: Sarah Bellum is arrested for armed robbery, and confesses after receiving *Miranda* warnings. Defense evidence shows that Sarah is mentally retarded, with a mental age of nine. In addition, she suffers from attention deficit disorder and depression.

Question: Was her confession voluntary?

Answer: Probably. Judges usually rule that confessions by suspects with mental limitations are voluntary.

CASE EXAMPLE 2: Same case, except that this time Sarah's evidence is that at the time of her confession, the police had just awakened her from a deep sleep produced by her having ingested three tranquilizers a few hours earlier. The police testify that Sarah was fully awake and lucid.

Question: Was her confession voluntary?

Answer: Yes. While the drugs may have impaired Sarah's cognitive functions, she was not legally incapable of making a voluntary confession.

CASE EXAMPLE 3: Same case, except that this time Sarah's evidence is that she confessed to armed robbery while in an ambulance on the way to the hospital. At the time she confessed, she was in pain from injuries she suffered when she was captured, she was under the effects of tranquilizers she had ingested just prior to the robbery and she passed out a number of times during the interrogation.

Question: Was her confession voluntary?

Answer: Probably not. Sarah's physical condition was so impaired that she was legally incapable of confessing voluntarily.

Search and Seizure

The Fourth Amendment to the U.S. Constitution places limits on the power of the police to make arrests, search people and their property, and seize objects, documents, and contraband (such as illegal drugs or weapons). These limits are the bedrock of "search and seizure law."

Search and seizure law is constantly in flux and so complex that entire books are devoted to it. This chapter answers the most basic questions that people might have about search and seizure law, but if you have more specific questions about arrest (technically, a kind of seizure), see Chapter 3.

RESOURCE

Other resources go into search and seizure in more detail. Readers wanting additional information might want to consult *Marijuana Law*, by Richard Glen Boire (Ronin Publishing); *Search and Seizure*, by Wayne LaFave (West Publishing); or *Criminal Justice*, by James A. Inciardi (Harcourt Publishers). (See Chapter 27 for more on legal research and using a law library.)

Section I: The Constitutional Background

This section provides an overview of the limitations on searches and seizures provided by the Fourth Amendment to the U.S. Constitution.

1. What are the search and seizure provisions of the Fourth Amendment all about?

They are about privacy. Most people instinctively understand the concept of privacy. It is the freedom to decide which details of your life shall be revealed to the public and which shall be revealed only to those you care to share them with. To honor this freedom, the Fourth Amendment protects against "unreasonable" searches and seizures by state or federal law enforcement authorities. However, the Fourth Amendment does not protect against searches initiated by nongovernmental people, such as employers, landlords, and private security personnel, unless the search is made at the behest of a law enforcement authority.

The Text of the Fourth Amendment

The right of the people to be secure in their persons, houses, papers, and effects, against unreasonable searches and seizures, shall not be violated, and no Warrants shall issue, but upon probable cause, supported by Oath or affirmation, and particularly describing the place to be searched, and the persons or things to be seized.

Unfortunately for privacy itself, the Fourth Amendment does permit searches and seizures that are considered to be reasonable. In practice, this means that the police may override your privacy concerns and conduct a search of your home, barn, garage, car, boat, office, personal or business documents, bank account records, trash barrel, or wherever, if:

- the police have probable cause to believe they can find evidence that you committed a crime, and a judge issues a search warrant (see Section II), or
- the search is proper without a warrant because of the particular circumstances.

2. Are all searches subject to Fourth Amendment protection?

No. American judges have written thousands of opinions interpreting the Fourth Amendment and explaining what a "reasonable" search is. But before getting to that question, another question must be answered first. Did the search in question violate the defendant's privacy in the first place? Or more precisely, as framed by the U.S. Supreme Court, did the defendant have a "legitimate expectation of privacy" in the place or thing searched? (*Katz v. U.S.,* 1967). If not, then no search occurred for the purpose of Fourth Amendment protection. If, however, a defendant did have a reasonable expectation of privacy, then a search did occur, and the search must have been a reasonable one.

Courts use a two-part test (fashioned by the U.S. Supreme Court) to determine whether, at the time of the search, the defendant had a legitimate expectation of privacy in the place or things searched:

- Did the person subjectively (actually) expect some degree of privacy?
- Is the person's expectation objectively reasonable, that is, one that society is willing to recognize?

Only if the answer to both questions is "yes" will a court go on to ask the next, ultimate question: Was the search reasonable or unreasonable?

For example, a person who uses a public restroom expects not to be spied upon (the person has a subjective expectation of privacy) and most people—including judges and juries—would consider that expectation to be reasonable (there is an objective expectation of privacy as well). Therefore, the installation of a hidden video camera by the police in a public restroom will be considered a search and would be subject to the Fourth Amendment's requirement of reasonableness.

On the other hand, when the police find a weapon on the front seat of a car, it is not a search for Fourth Amendment purposes because it is very unlikely that the person would think that the front seat of the car is a private place (a subjective expectation of privacy is unlikely), and even if the person did, society is not willing to extend the protections of privacy to that particular location (no objective expectation of privacy).

3. How can an illegal search affect my criminal case?

In *Mapp v. Ohio* (1961), the Supreme Court established what has come to be known as the "exclusionary rule." This rule states that evidence seized in violation of the Fourth Amendment cannot be used as evidence against defendants in a criminal prosecution, state or federal. To this day, some commentators continue to criticize the *Mapp* case on the ground that it unfairly "lets the criminal go free because the constable has erred." In recent years, the U.S. Supreme Court has appeared to agree with these commentators by deciding that improperly seized evidence is admissible at trial when the police officers who carry out the searches act on information that they believe to be correct (see *Herring v. U.S.*, U.S. Sup. Ct. 2009). But supporters of *Mapp* argue that excluding illegally seized evidence is necessary to deter police from conducting illegal searches. According to this deterrence argument, the police won't conduct improper searches if the resulting evidence is barred from the trial.

> **CASE EXAMPLE:** Officer Joe Friday notices teenager Bunny Schwartz walking in a mall. Officer Friday demands to look into Bunny's purse. The officer finds three pairs of earrings with the price tags still attached. A mall jewelry store owner identifies the earrings as having been stolen minutes earlier, when Bunny was the only customer in the store. A judge rules that Officer Friday's search of Bunny's purse was improper.
>
> **Question:** How will this ruling affect the case against Bunny?

> **Answer:** The charges will have to be dropped. Because the search of Bunny's purse was illegal, the earrings are not admissible in evidence against her. The prosecution has no case without the earrings, so the case must be dismissed. Realizing that Bunny went free ought to deter Officer Friday from conducting illegal searches in the future, exactly what the exclusionary rule is supposed to accomplish.

4. If the police conduct an illegal search, does the case against me have to be dismissed?

No. A judge will exclude evidence that the police seized or learned about as the result of an illegal search. But if a prosecutor has enough other evidence to prove the defendant guilty, the case can continue.

> **CASE EXAMPLE:** Dick McCallous is charged with possession of stolen property—cleaning products stolen from a local janitorial supply business. Half of the missing janitorial products that McCallous is charged with possessing were discovered by the police at McCallous's home in the course of a warrantless search of the home by the police after they had properly arrested McCallous for possession of the other half. In response to a defense motion to exclude evidence, the judge rules that the police illegally seized the janitorial products from McCallous's home, but

that the other products were seized properly.

Question: How will these rulings affect the case against McCallous?

Answer: The prosecution can go forward, limited to possession of properly seized stolen janitorial products.

5. If a police officer finds contraband or evidence of crime in the course of a search, does that make the search valid even if it was initially illegal?

No. A well-established rule is that a search can't be justified by what it turns up. If a search is illegal to begin with, the products of that search, no matter how incriminating, are inadmissible in evidence.

6. Can illegally seized evidence be used in court for any purpose?

Yes. Cases decided after *Mapp* have established that the Fourth Amendment is not a complete bar to the use of illegally seized evidence. For example, a judge may consider illegally seized evidence when deciding on an appropriate sentence following conviction, and illegally seized evidence is admissible in civil cases and deportation cases. Also, in some circumstances a prosecutor can use improperly seized evidence to impeach (attack the credibility of) a witness who testifies during a court proceeding.

CASE EXAMPLE: Flo Kane is on trial for possessing illegal drugs. During a pretrial hearing, the trial judge had ruled that the police had illegally seized a gun from Flo's bedroom, and that the prosecutor could not admit the gun into evidence. While testifying, Flo states, "I've never owned a weapon of any kind."

Question: Following this testimony, could the prosecutor show Flo the illegally seized gun and ask her to admit that she owned it?

Answer: Yes. Once Flo denies ever owning a weapon, the prosecutor may use the illegally seized gun to attack the credibility of her testimony.

7. Do Fourth Amendment protections apply in every state?

Basically, yes. The Fourth Amendment provides rights for defendants that are binding on every state. In addition, many state constitutions contain language similar to that in the Fourth Amendment, and a state can validly interpret its own constitution to provide defendants with greater protection—but not less—than the Fourth Amendment requires.

8. If the police illegally seize evidence, can they use the illegally seized information to find other evidence to use against the defendant?

No, because of a legal rule colorfully known as the "fruit of the poisonous tree doctrine." This doctrine makes inadmissible any evidence that police officers seize or any information that police officers obtain as a direct result of an improper search. The tree is the evidence that the police illegally seize in the first place; the fruit is the second-generation product of the illegally seized evidence. Both tree and fruit are inadmissible at trial. The fruit of the poisonous tree doctrine removes what would otherwise be a big incentive for police officers to conduct illegal searches.

CASE EXAMPLE: Officer Wiley arrests Hy Lowe for selling phony telephone cards. A judge ruled that Officer Wiley had illegally entered Lowe's home and improperly seized a map showing the location where Lowe hid the phone cards. At trial, the prosecutor doesn't try to offer the map into evidence. The prosecutor does, however, seek to offer into evidence the phone cards that Officer Wiley located by using the map.

Question: Are the phone cards admissible in evidence?

Answer: No. Officer Wiley obtained the map through an illegal search. The phone cards are the fruit of that unlawful search, and therefore inadmissible in evidence.

9. Can I plead guilty but reserve the right to challenge a search and have my guilty plea set aside if the search is held to be illegal?

In most states, by pleading guilty, a defendant waives (gives up) any claim

that evidence was illegally seized. This rule can be a dilemma for defendants who unsuccessfully challenge the legality of a search at the trial court level, for these reasons:

- After a defendant's unsuccessful challenge to the admissibility of seized evidence, a guilty verdict may be an all-but-certain result at trial.
- To save the time and expense of a useless trial, the defendant may decide to plead guilty.
- By pleading guilty, however, the defendant loses the right to appeal the trial court's decision on the search and seizure issue.

Some states do allow defendants to plead guilty and then challenge the seizure of evidence on appeal. Self-represented defendants who plan to challenge the legality of a police officer's search on appeal must never plead guilty without knowing whether their jurisdiction permits such a procedure.

10. As a self-represented defendant, what are my chances of successfully challenging a search's legality?

Very small, except if the search is obviously illegal. The rules are not only complex, but also hard to find. The rules regulating the legitimacy of searches and seizures are not set out neatly in statutes or regulations. Rather, arguments that a search is illegal usually have to be pieced together from a number of appellate court decisions involving similar facts. Moreover, in many states, a special body of rules governs the procedures for challenging the legality of a search. For example, a defendant may have to challenge a search in a special proceeding before trial or lose the right to do so. (See Chapter 19, Section II.) For these reasons, when the outcome of a case turns on the legality of a search, self-represented defendants should almost always get a lawyer. (Self-represented defendants should at least have a "legal coach" available to spot possible search-and-seizure issues. (More on legal coaches in Chapter 7.))

Section II: Search Warrants

This section describes search warrants and explains when they are and are not necessary.

11. What is a search warrant?

A search warrant is an order signed by a judge that authorizes police officers to search for specific objects or materials at a definite location at a specified time. For example, a warrant may authorize the search of "the premises at 11359 Happy Glade Avenue between the hours of 8 a.m. to 6 p.m.," and direct the police to search for and seize "cash, betting slips, record books, and every other means used in connection with placing bets on horses." Police officers can take reasonable steps to protect themselves when conducting a search, such as handcuffing occupants while searching a house for weapons (*Mena v. City of Simi Valley,* U.S. Sup. Ct. 2005).

12. How do police officers obtain search warrants?

Police officers obtain warrants by providing a judge or magistrate with information that the officers have gathered. Usually, the police provide the information in the form of written statements under oath, called affidavits, which report either their own observations or those of private citizens or police undercover informants. In many areas, a judicial officer is available 24 hours a day to issue warrants. If the magistrate believes that an affidavit establishes "probable cause" to conduct a search, she will issue a warrant. The suspect, who may be connected with the place to be searched, is not present when the warrant issues and therefore cannot contest the issue of probable cause before the magistrate signs the warrant. However, the suspect can later challenge the validity of the warrant with a pretrial motion. (See Chapter 19.) A sample affidavit for search warrant and a sample search warrant are in the back of this chapter.

Police officers can obtain *anticipatory* search warrants, meaning that if the police can show probable cause, they can obtain a warrant before contraband arrives at the location to be searched (*U.S. v. Grubbs*, U.S. Sup. Ct. 2006). For example, if the police demonstrate to a magistrate that illegal drugs are about to be shipped to a suspect's home, they can get a warrant that allows the police to search the home once the drugs are delivered.

13. How much information do police officers need to establish that probable cause for a search warrant exists?

The Fourth Amendment doesn't define probable cause. Its meaning remains fuzzy. What is clear is that after 200 years of court interpretations, the affidavits submitted by police officers to judges have to identify objectively suspicious activities rather than simply recite the officer's subjective beliefs. The affidavits also have to establish more than a suspicion that criminal activity is afoot, but do not have to show proof beyond a reasonable doubt.

The information in the affidavit need not be in a form that would make it admissible at trial. (For example, a judge or magistrate may consider hearsay that seems reliable.) However, the circumstances set forth in an affidavit as a whole should demonstrate the reliability of the information (*Illinois v. Gates,* U.S. Sup. Ct. 1983). In general, when deciding whether to issue a search warrant, a judicial officer will likely consider information in an affidavit reliable if it comes from any of these sources:

- a confidential police informant whose past reliability has been established or who has firsthand knowledge of illegal goings-on
- an informant who implicates herself as well as the suspect
- an informant whose information appears to be correct after at least partial verification by the police
- a victim of a crime related to the search

- a witness to the crime related to the search, or
- another police officer.

CASE EXAMPLE 1: Hoping to obtain a warrant to search Olive Martini's backyard, a police officer submits an affidavit to a magistrate. The affidavit states that "the undersigned is informed that Olive operates an illegal still in her backyard."

Question: Should the magistrate issue a search warrant?

Answer: No. The affidavit is too vague, and does not identify the source of the information so that the magistrate can properly judge its reliability. Probable cause therefore does not exist.

CASE EXAMPLE 2: Same case. The affidavit states that "I am a social acquaintance of Olive Martini. On three occasions in the past two weeks, I have attended parties at Martini's house. On each occasion, I have personally observed Martini serving alcohol from a still in Martini's backyard. I have personally tasted the drink and know it to be alcoholic with an impertinent aftertaste. I had no connection to the police when I attended these parties."

Question: Should the magistrate issue a warrant authorizing the police to search Martini's backyard?

Answer: Yes. The affidavit provides detailed, firsthand information from an ordinary witness (without police connections) that indicates criminal activity. The affidavit is reliable enough to establish probable cause for issuance of a warrant.

"No Entry While We Obtain a Warrant"

It may take an hour or two (or longer) for police officers to obtain a warrant. To prevent suspects from destroying evidence inside homes while the police are waiting for a judge to issue a warrant, the police may station themselves outside homes and prevent suspects from entering them (*Illinois v. McArthur*, U.S. Sup. Ct. 2001).

---

14. What if a police officer makes a search under a warrant that shouldn't have been issued in the first place?

In most situations the search will be valid. In *U.S. v. Leon* (1984), the U.S. Supreme Court ruled that if the police conduct a search in good-faith reliance on the warrant, the search is valid and the evidence admissible even if the warrant was in fact invalid through no fault of the police. The Court's reasoning is that:

- it makes no sense to condemn the results of a search when police officers have done everything reasonable to comply with Fourth Amendment requirements, and
- the purpose of the rule excluding the results of an invalid search as

evidence is to curb the police, not a judge, and that if a judge makes a mistake, this should not, therefore, be grounds to exclude evidence.

For example, assume that a judge decides that an affidavit submitted by a police officer establishes probable cause for the issuance of a warrant. Even if a reviewing court later disagrees and decides that the warrant shouldn't have been issued in the first place, the officer's search in good-faith reliance on the validity of the warrant will be considered valid, and whatever the search turns up will be admissible in evidence. If, however, the warrant is issued on the basis of statements in the affidavit that the police knew to be untrue or that were made recklessly without proper regard for their truth, the evidence from a search based on the warrant may later be excluded upon the proper motion being made by the defendant.

CASE EXAMPLE 1: Officer Furlong searches a residence for evidence of illegal bookmaking pursuant to a search warrant. The officer obtained the warrant by submitting to a magistrate an affidavit containing statements known by the officer to be false.

Question: Is the search valid because it was conducted pursuant to a warrant?

Answer: No. By submitting a false affidavit, Officer Furlong did not act "in good faith." The search was thus improper, and whatever it turned up is inadmissible in evidence.

CASE EXAMPLE 2: Officer Cal Ebrate stops a motorist for a traffic violation. A computer check of the driver's license reveals the existence of an arrest warrant for the driver. Officer Ebrate places the driver under arrest, searches the car, and finds illegal drugs. It later turns out that the computer record was wrong, and that an arrest warrant did not in fact exist.

Question: Are the illegal drugs admissible in evidence against the driver?

Answer: Yes. The officer acted in good-faith reliance on the computer record. The seizure was therefore valid even though the record was wrong (*Arizona v. Evans*, U.S. Sup. Ct. 1995; see also, *Herring v. U.S.*, U.S. Sup. Ct. 2009).

15. **If the police have a warrant to search my backyard for marijuana plants, can they legally search the inside of my house as well?**

No. The police can only search the place described in a warrant, and usually can only seize whatever property the warrant describes. The police cannot search a house if the warrant specifies the backyard, nor can they search for weapons if the warrant specifies marijuana plants. However, this does not mean that police officers can only seize items listed in the warrant. Should police officers come across contraband or evidence of a crime that is not listed in the warrant in the course of searching for stuff that is listed, they can lawfully seize the unlisted items.

"Well, Look What We Have Here"

The rule that police officers can seize items not listed in a search warrant in the course of searching for the stuff that is listed creates obvious disincentives for police to list all the items they hope to find. For example, perhaps a police officer suspects that a defendant carries a weapon, but can't establish probable cause to search for it. No problem. The officer can obtain a search warrant for other items, and then seize a weapon if the officer comes upon it in the course of the search. The defendant's only hope of invalidating the seizure of the weapon would be to convince a judge that the officer did not just happen to come across the weapon, but in fact searched for it.

For example, assume that a search warrant authorizes police to search for shotguns. Carrying out the search, a police officer finds cocaine inside a small box in the defendant's sock drawer. The defendant is arrested and charged with possession of cocaine. The judge might rule that the drugs are inadmissible in evidence and dismiss the charges, because the police officer searched a container that could not possibly conceal a shotgun.

16. **The police had a warrant to search a friend I was visiting and they searched me as well. Is this legal?**

No. Normally, the police can only search the person named in a warrant. Without probable cause, a police officer cannot search other persons who happen to be present at the scene of a search. However, if an officer has reason to suspect that an onlooker is also engaged in criminal activity, the officer might be able to "frisk" the onlooker for weapons. (See Section VI, below.)

17. If a police officer knocks on my door and asks to enter my dwelling, what should I do?

You should ask to see a search (or arrest) warrant. The officer may have no right to enter your home without a warrant. If the officer displays a warrant, allow the officer to enter. While the officer is inside your dwelling, observe the officer's activities and if possible make notes about them. The notes can help you testify fully and accurately in the event that you later want to challenge the officer's actions in court.

If the police officer does not have a warrant, you may decide to allow the officer to enter your dwelling anyway. You will then have "consented" to the entry and you will probably have no right to challenge the search later in court. (See Section III, below.)

Alternatively, if the officer does not have a warrant, you can tell the officer that you refuse entry into your dwelling. You may do so loudly enough for others to hear, so that they may testify to your refusal in court if necessary. The officer may insist on entering anyway, and if so you should not try to interfere. Here are a few reasons why:

- It is much safer to challenge a police officer's actions in court than in your home. Also, you do not want to risk being charged with interfering with a police officer.
- Perhaps a valid warrant has been issued, even though the officer does not have it. If so, the officer probably has the right to enter your dwelling (*United States v. Hector*, 9th Cir. 2007).
- The officer may have a legal right to enter your dwelling without a warrant. As you'll read later in this chapter, police officers often have the right to conduct searches and make arrests without a warrant.

If an officer does insist on entering your dwelling despite your refusal and the absence of a warrant, it is even more important that you observe and make a record of the officer's activities that you can refer to should you challenge the officer's actions in court.

"Knock and Notice" Laws

Generally, police officers executing a search warrant on a residence must knock on the door, announce their presence, and give someone inside a chance to open the door. The rule protects individuals' safety, privacy, and dignity. The Fourth Amendment has been interpreted to require the knock and notice procedure (*Wilson v. Arkansas*, U.S. Sup. Ct. 1995), and federal law also requires it (18 U.S.C. § 1309).

Police officers don't have to follow the knock and notice procedure if they reasonably fear that it will result in violence or destruction of evidence, or if the procedure seems futile under the circumstances (*Richards v. Wisconsin*, U.S. Sup. Ct. 1997). Moreover, after knocking and announcing their presence, police officers need only delay entry for a reasonable time, which can be only a few seconds depending on the circumstances (*U.S. v. Banks*, U.S. Sup. Ct. 2003). Finally, the "exclusionary rule" does not apply to violations of the knock and notice rule (*Hudson v. Michigan*, U.S. Sup. Ct. 2006). That means that evidence is admissible at trial even if police officers violate the knock and notice rule when carrying out an otherwise valid search.

Section III: Consent Searches

This section discusses when a warrantless search may be legally justified because the person in control of the property is said to have agreed to it.

18. If I agree to a search, is the search legal even if a police officer doesn't have a warrant or probable cause to search?

Yes. If a defendant freely and voluntarily agrees to a search, the search is valid and whatever the officers find is admissible in evidence.

For example, assume that Officer Mayer knocks on the door of Caryn-Sue's house. Officer Mayer suspects that Caryn-Sue is part of a group of suspects who are making pirated DVDs, but the officer lacks probable cause to search her house or arrest her. When Caryn-Sue answers the door, the following conversation takes place:

Officer: Good afternoon. I'm Officer Mayer. Is your name Caryn-Sue?

Caryn-Sue: Yes, it is. What can I do for you, officer?

Officer: I'm investigating the production of pirated DVDs, and I'd like to talk to you.

Caryn-Sue: Well, I'm not sure I can help you. I'm not under arrest or anything, am I?

Officer: No, but you may have information that can help the investigation. Do you mind if I come in and look around?

Caryn-Sue: I'm in the middle of a couple of things. Could you come back later?

Officer: If that's necessary. But it won't take long.

Caryn-Sue: We might as well get it over with if you can hurry. Look around all you want, there's nothing here of interest to you.

Officer Mayer enters Caryn-Sue's house, and in a corner of her living room closet notices hundreds of blank DVDs. The officer arrests Caryn-Sue for producing pirated DVDs, and seizes the blank DVDs.

Under these circumstances, a judge would undoubtedly rule that the officer legally seized the blank DVDs. Though the officer had neither a warrant nor probable cause to search Caryn-Sue's house, Officer Mayer's search was valid because Caryn-Sue agreed to let the officer search her house. The fact that the officer was politely insistent on entering the house does not overcome the fact that Caryn-Sue consented to the entry before it was made.

19. Does a police officer have to warn me that I have a right to refuse to consent to a search?

No. No equivalent to *Miranda* warnings (see Chapter 1, Section II) exists in the search and seizure area. Police officers do not have to warn people that they have a right to refuse consent to a search (*Ohio v. Robinette*, U.S. Sup. Ct. 1996).

CASE EXAMPLE 1: Jaime Costello is sitting on a park bench. Officer Abbot approaches Costello and asks to look through his backpack. Costello replies, "Sure, go ahead, I guess I can't stop you." The officer finds illegal drugs in Costello's backpack, and arrests him.

Question: Are the drugs admissible in evidence?

Answer: Yes. The search was valid, since Costello gave his consent. Officer Abbot had no duty to clear up Costello's misconception that he had no choice but to consent.

CASE EXAMPLE 2: Officer Nemir boards a public bus as part of a routine drug and weapons search and asks George, "Mind if I check you?" George agrees, and a pat down suggests hard objects similar to drug packages. George is arrested, and a further search reveals that George had taped cocaine in both thigh areas.

Question: Is the cocaine admissible in evidence?

Answer: Yes, the search was valid because George gave his consent. The Fourth Amendment does not require that police officers advise individuals of their right not to cooperate and to refuse consent to searches (*U.S. v. Drayton*, U.S. Sup. Ct. 2002).

20. If a police officer tricks or coerces me into consenting to a search, does my consent make the search legal?

No. To constitute a valid consent to search, the consent must be given "freely and voluntarily." If a police officer wrangles a consent through trickery or coercion, the consent does not validate the search. Often, a defendant challenges a search on the grounds that consent was not voluntary, only to have a police officer testify to a conflicting version of events that establishes a valid consent. In these conflict situations, judges tend to believe police officers unless defendants can support their claims through the testimony of other witnesses.

CASE EXAMPLE 1: In the example above, assume that before Caryn-Sue consents to Officer Mayer's entry into her home, Officer Mayer falsely tells her, "It will do you no good to refuse entry to me. I've got a warrant, so I'm prepared to come in whether or not you consent." Caryn-Sue replies, "If you've got a warrant, I might as well let you in. Look around all you want."

Question: Has Caryn-Sue validly consented to the search?

Answer: No. Her consent is not voluntary. It is the result of the officer's false claim of having a warrant. However, it may be Caryn-Sue's word against the officer's as to whether the officer tricked her into consenting.

CASE EXAMPLE 2: Undercover cop Jones, posing as an employee of the gas company, asks Casey to allow him into Casey's home to check for an alleged gas leak. Casey agrees. Jones enters and sees drugs and drug paraphernalia in the kitchen.

Question: Is the police search of Casey's home valid under the Fourth Amendment?

Answer: No, consent that is obtained by fraud is not considered voluntary, and Jones's lying and saying he was a gas company employee would be fraud.

CASE EXAMPLE 3: Same case, but this time Jones has been posing as a parent in Casey's son's school and has made friends with Casey independent of his undercover mission. Casey invites his "friend" Jones in to play cards. Once inside the home, undercover agent Jones unexpectedly sees illegal drugs. He seizes the drugs and arrests Casey.

Question: Was the police entry into Casey's home valid under the Fourth Amendment?

Answer: Yes. Casey was not tricked or coerced in any way to let Jones in. He just didn't know who his friend really was. The Constitution does not prevent the consequences of having what the courts call a "false friend."

21. If I agree to open my door to talk to a police officer and the officer enters without my permission and searches, is the search valid?

No. Merely opening the door to a police officer does not constitute consent to entry and search. Thus, whatever such a search turns up would be inadmissible in evidence. Of course, if contraband or evidence of a crime is in "plain view" from the doorway, the officer may seize it. (See Section IV, below.)

22. Can I consent to a police search of my living room but not my bedroom?

Technically, yes. Where only limited consent is given, that limitation is supposed to be honored. But if in the course of making their limited search the police see evidence of illegal activity elsewhere, they may properly search and seize it. Also, once in a home, the police are very skilled at obtaining consent from the homeowner to expand the scope of the search.

> **CASE EXAMPLE 1:** Officer Zack asks permission to search Mike's residence for marijuana plants. Mike agrees. Officer Zack proceeds with the search and goes into Mike's desk and reviews some of the documents he finds there.
>
> **Question:** Is the search valid under the Fourth Amendment?
>
> **Answer:** No. Searching the documents was illegal because Mike only agreed to the limited search for marijuana plants, and there were obviously no such plants in the desk or the words Officer Zack was reading.

> **CASE EXAMPLE 2:** Officer Zack asks, and Mike agrees, to allow a search of Mike's home for narcotics. In the course of the search, the officer finds a closet containing an illegal weapon, which the officer seizes.
>
> **Question:** Is the search valid under the Fourth Amendment?

> **Answer:** Yes. The weapon was readily seen in a place where narcotics might be found.

23. Is a search valid if the reason I consent to it was because I felt intimidated by the presence of the police officer?

Yes. Many people are intimidated by police officers, and may even perceive a request to search as a command. However, so long as an officer does not engage in threatening behavior, judges will not set aside otherwise genuine consents.

> **EXTREME CASE EXAMPLE:** The owner of a massage parlor agrees to allow police officers to search her business premises. At the time the owner consents, she has been handcuffed, is in the presence of seven male police officers, the officers had already physically subdued and pointed a gun at an employee, the officers had threatened to tear up the premises, and the owner was of foreign descent and unfamiliar with the American criminal process.
>
> **Question:** Is her consent valid?
>
> **Answer:** Yes, at least this was the result in *State v. Kyong Cha Kim,* 779 P.2d 512 (1989). Despite the outcome of this case, it is possible that another judge in another jurisdiction might find this type of police conduct so coercive or threatening as to make the consent involuntary.

24. If I share my residence with the person who consents to a police officer search (for example, a spouse or a roommate) and the search turns up evidence that incriminates me, can the evidence be used against me?

No, so long as you are personally present when the police ask for permission to search and you refuse to consent. Even if the person you share the residence with has agreed to the search, your refusal means that evidence cannot be used against you (*Georgia v. Randolph*, U.S. Sup. Ct. 2006). (Of course, if the police have probable cause, they might obtain a search warrant and conduct a search after you refuse to give permission.)

If your spouse, roommate, or cotenant agrees to a search in your absence, and the search turns up evidence that incriminates you, the evidence might well be admissible in evidence against you at trial. An adult in rightful possession of a house or apartment usually has legal authority to consent to a search of the entire premises. But if there are two or more separate tenants in one dwelling, courts often rule that one tenant has no power to consent to a search of the areas exclusively controlled by the other tenants (for instance, their separate bedrooms).

A tricky twist is that the consent will be considered valid if the police reasonably believe that the consenting person has the authority to consent even if it turns out they don't. (See the example below.)

CASE EXAMPLE: Bob's ex-wife Jan knows where Bob hides his cocaine. She calls the police and tells them about the cocaine. She directs them to Bob's house. When they get there, she opens the door with a key (she never returned it to Bob). She puts her purse on the entry hall table, opens the hall closet, and puts on a sweater that appears to be hers. She then leads the police to the place where Bob stores his cocaine. As far as the police know, Jan lives in the apartment and has full authority to consent to the search.

Question: Even though Jan and the police enter the apartment without Bob's permission, did the search violate Bob's Fourth Amendment rights?

Answer: No. Although the police mistakenly thought that Jan had the authority to consent to the search, the mistake would be considered a reasonable one because every fact surrounding the search (including Jan's having a key and knowing her way around the apartment) pointed to that authority.

25. While I'm out, the landlord of the apartment building where I live gives a police officer permission to search my apartment. Does the landlord's consent make the search legal?

No. The landlord is not considered to be in possession of an apartment leased to a tenant, and therefore lacks authority to consent to a search of leased premises. The same is true for hotel operators.

26. Can the police search my hotel room without a warrant?

The general rule is, no. Again, however, an exception (such as consent or an emergency) may exist that would justify a warrantless hotel room search.

27. If my employer consents to a police search of my workspace, are the results of the search admissible in evidence?

Probably. An employer can validly consent to a search of company premises. An employer's consent extends to employees' work areas, such as desks and machinery. However, police officers might need a warrant to search a clearly private area, such as an employee's clothes locker.

28. Can my child let the police search our home while I am at work?

This would primarily depend on the child's age. The younger the child, the less authority he would have to consent to a search. The California courts, for example, require a child to be at least 12 to consent, and even then the child must appear to be "in charge" of the house at that time.

Section IV: The Plain View Doctrine

This section is about warrantless searches and seizures that are considered valid because the police officer initially spotted contraband or evidence that was in the officer's plain view.

29. I agreed to talk to a police officer in my house. The officer saw some drugs on a kitchen counter, seized them, and arrested me. Is this legal?

Yes. Police officers do not need a warrant to seize contraband or evidence that is in plain view if the officer is where he has a right to be. An officer's seizure of an object in plain view does not violate the Fourth Amendment because the officer technically (and legally) has not conducted a search.

CASE EXAMPLE 1: During daylight hours, Officer Mendoza stops a car for having an expired license plate. When Officer Mendoza approaches the driver, the officer sees a packet of what appears to be illegal drugs on the front seat of the car. The officer seizes the packet and arrests the driver.

Question: Was the seizure of the drugs legal?

Answer: Yes. The drugs were in plain view. Though the officer had no probable cause to search the car at the moment the officer pulled the car over, seeing the illegal drugs on the front seat gave the officer a valid basis for seizing them.

CASE EXAMPLE 2: Same case, except that the traffic stop occurs at night and Officer Mendoza sees the packet of drugs on the front seat only after shining a flashlight into the interior of the car.

Question: Is the officer's seizure of the packet still legal?

Answer: Yes. As long as police officers are standing where they have a right to be, objects that they see with the aid of a flashlight are in plain view.

CASE EXAMPLE 3: Officer Tanaka pulls a car over for running a red light. When the driver rolls down the window, Officer Tanaka detects a strong odor of marijuana emanating from inside the car. The officer orders the driver out of the car and conducts a search. Underneath the driver's seat, the officer finds a pouch filled with marijuana.

Question: Did the officer legally find the marijuana?

Answer: Yes. Smelling the marijuana gave Officer Tanaka probable cause to believe that the car contained illegal drugs (under what has come to be called the "plain smell" doctrine). The officer could therefore conduct an immediate search, without having to obtain a search warrant first.

30. If a police officer illegally enters a house and observes evidence in plain view, can the officer seize the evidence?

No. A police officer can seize objects in plain view only if the officer has a legal right to be in the place from which the objects can be seen or smelled. If an officer has no legal right to be where she is when the evidence or contraband is spotted, the plain view doctrine doesn't apply.

CASE EXAMPLE: Two police officers in a helicopter fly over the backyard of a home as they are returning from the scene of a highway collision. Aided by binoculars, one of the officers sees a large number of marijuana plants growing in a greenhouse in the backyard. The officers report what they have seen, a search warrant is obtained, and the occupant of the house is arrested and charged with growing illegal drugs for sale.

Question: Was the officers' aerial search of the backyard legal?

Answer: Yes. The police officers had a right to be in public airspace, and the occupant had no reasonable expectation of privacy for what could be seen from public airspace. (Maybe this is an example of "plane view.") The outcome might be different if the police officer had spotted the plants from a space station by using advanced technology spying equipment. The homeowner might reasonably expect that the backyard would not be subjected to that type of surveillance.

"Dropsy" Cases

Dropsy cases are a familiar setting in which police officers are often accused of misleading courts about how they got hold of illegal drugs. In dropsy cases, police officers find drugs or other incriminating evidence through searches that might not withstand judicial scrutiny. To eliminate the Fourth Amendment problem, the officers testify that the defendants dropped the contraband on the ground just before they were arrested. Voilà, the contraband was in plain view. Over the years, an amazing number of defendants have developed dropsy problems!

Section V: Warrantless Searches That Are Incident to Arrest

This section deals with warrantless searches that are considered valid because they were made in the course of making a valid arrest.

31. Can an officer legally search me after arresting me?

Yes. Police officers do not need a warrant to make a search "incident to an arrest." After an arrest, police officers have the right to protect themselves by searching for weapons and to protect the legal case against the suspect by searching for evidence that the suspect might try to destroy. Assuming that the officer has probable cause to make the arrest in the first place, a search of the person and the person's surroundings following the arrest is valid, and any evidence uncovered is admissible at trial.

If probable cause exists, the Fourth Amendment allows police officers to arrest and search suspects for committing minor offenses that usually result in citations rather than arrests. (See *Virginia v. Moore*, U.S. Sup. Ct. 2009.)

> **CASE EXAMPLE:** Police Officer Leigh Werlinich issues Miller a traffic ticket for driving with a broken taillight. After noticing that Miller's driver's license was suspended, Werlinich arrests Miller even though the law authorized Werlinich only to cite and release Miller. Werlinich searches Miller incident to the arrest, finds illegal drugs in Miller's purse, and also arrests Miller for possession of illegal drugs.
>
> **Question:** Under the Fourth Amendment, did Werlinich have the right to arrest and search Miller?
>
> **Answer:** Yes. Since Werlinich had probable cause to make an arrest, the search is constitutional even though Werlinich was only supposed to issue a citation to Miller.

32. If I'm arrested on the street or in a shopping mall, can the arresting officer search my dwelling or car?

No. To justify a search as incident to an arrest, a spatial relationship must exist between the arrest and the search. The general rule is that after arrest the police may search a defendant and the area within a defendant's immediate control (*Chimel v. California,* U.S. Sup. Ct. 1969). For example, an arresting officer may search not only a suspect's clothes, but also a suspect's wallet or purse. If an arrest takes place in a kitchen, the arresting officer can probably search the kitchen, but not the rest of the house. If an arrest takes place outside a house, the arresting officer cannot search the house at all. To conduct a search broader in scope than a defendant and the area within the defendant's immediate control, an officer would have to obtain a warrant.

CASE EXAMPLE: Officer Montoya arrests Sarah Adams for driving under the influence of illegal drugs. Before taking Sarah to jail, Officer Montoya takes Sarah's key and enters her apartment. Inside, Officer Montoya finds a number of computers that turn out—after a check of their serial numbers—to have been stolen. Officer Montoya seizes the computers as evidence and adds possession of stolen property to the charges against Sarah.

Question: Are the computers admissible in evidence?

Answer: No. The officer should have obtained a search warrant before entering Sarah's apartment. Since Officer Montoya had no right to be inside the house in the first place, it doesn't matter that the computers were in plain view once the officer was inside.

Don't Go Back in the House

When the police arrest suspects outside their residences and have no basis for making a protective sweep, officers may try to expand the scope of a permissible search by offering to let suspects go inside to get a change of clothes or feed a pet before taking the suspect to jail. While accompanying the suspect inside the residence, officers can seize whatever may be in plain view (for instance, drugs). Thus, suspects may wisely refuse an invitation by the arresting officers to let the suspect enter the residence, and instead rely on their friends if they need clothes or pet care.

---

33. If I'm arrested in my car, or shortly after leaving it, do the police need a warrant to search the interior of the car?

No. If the police arrest a suspect in or around a car, they don't need a warrant to search its interior (*Thornton v. U.S.,* U.S. Sup. Ct. 2004). They probably would need a warrant to search the trunk, however.

34. If I'm arrested outside my place of residence, can the police go inside to look for accomplices?

Sometimes. Police officers can make protective sweeps following an arrest (*Maryland v. Buie,* U.S. Sup. Ct. 1990). When making a protective sweep, police officers can walk through a residence and make a cursory visual inspection of places where an accomplice might be hiding. For example, police officers could look under beds and inside closets. To justify making a protective sweep, police officers must have a reasonable belief that a dangerous accomplice might be hiding inside a residence. If a sweep is lawful, the police can legally seize contraband or evidence of crime that is in plain view.

CASE EXAMPLE: Police officers have warrants to arrest Fox and Mulder for armed bank robbery. Fox and Mulder live together in a house. Officers Spock and Kirk stake out the house and arrest Fox coming up the driveway. With Fox in custody, Spock goes into the house to conduct a protective sweep. Spock goes into a bedroom, lifts up a mattress and seizes a gun hidden between the mattress and the box spring. Witnesses later identify the gun as the one used in the bank robbery.

Question: Did Officer Spock lawfully seize the gun?

Answer: No. Because (1) Fox and Mulder live together, (2) Fox was arrested outside the house, and (3) they were suspected of committing a violent crime together, Spock probably had the right to make a protective sweep to look for Mulder. However, Spock had no right to lift up the mattress, because nothing suggested that Mulder might be hiding under it. After making sure that Mulder wasn't in the house, the officers should have secured the house and gotten a search warrant.

35. If the police properly arrest me in my home, can they also search the home?

They can to a certain extent. They may search the person arrested and the area within that person's immediate control. Immediate control is interpreted broadly to include any place a suspect may lunge to obtain a weapon. If the alleged crime is particularly violent, or if the police have reason to believe other armed suspects may be in the residence, the police may do a protective sweep to search in any place such accomplices may be hiding. Also, while they are making a lawful arrest or protective sweep, the police may typically search and seize anything apparently related to criminal activity that is in plain view.

36. Do guests in a home have the same privacy rights as the homeowner or tenant?

The answer depends on why the guests are there. If they are there for purely social reasons or to spend the night, they are probably protected against unreasonable searches and seizures to the same extent as the homeowner or tenant. However, if the guests are there for a brief commercial transaction or illegal purpose and are not staying overnight, then they do not have the same privacy rights as social overnight guests and thus may not be able to successfully challenge a police search that took place in their host's home (*Minnesota v. Carter*, U.S. Sup. Ct. 1998).

CASE EXAMPLE: Mark hosts a weekly poker game at his apartment. One night the game included his neighbor Bobby. After a neighbor complained about a strange smell coming from Mark's apartment, the police arrived and, though they didn't have a warrant, searched the premises. On a cabinet in the bathroom, they found a baggie of illegal drugs belonging to Bobby. Bobby is arrested and charged with possession of illegal drugs.

Question: Can Bobby exclude the drugs from evidence because the police searched Mark's apartment improperly?

Answer: No. As a temporary guest, Bobby has no privacy right in Mark's apartment.

37. Is a search following an illegal arrest valid?

No. If an officer lacks probable cause to make an arrest, the invalid arrest cannot validate a search. Any evidence found during a search following an improper arrest is inadmissible in evidence.

38. If an officer searches me after a valid arrest and finds evidence for an entirely different crime, is the evidence admissible?

Yes. An officer can seize whatever evidence a proper search incident to an arrest turns up. So long as the search is valid, it doesn't matter if a seized object has nothing to do with the crime for which the defendant was arrested.

Section VI: "Stop and Frisk" Searches

This section describes when a police officer may conduct a limited search of a person for the purpose of assuring the officer's safety.

39. What is the "stop and frisk" rule?

Using a procedure known as stop and frisk, authorized by *Terry v. Ohio*, U.S. Sup. Ct. 1968, a police officer need only have a reasonable suspicion of criminal behavior to detain and question a person (the "stop"). For self-protection, the officer can at the same time carry out a limited pat-down search for weapons (the "frisk"). This rule applies whether you are on foot or in your car. A "reasonable suspicion" requires more than a hunch or a mere distrust; the officer must have reasonable grounds, based on all of the circumstances, to suspect that the person is involved in criminal activity.

CASE EXAMPLE 1: Officer Crosby sees Stills and Nash talking normally on a street corner. Having a hunch that a drug transaction may be underway, the officer detains and frisks the pair. The officer finds a gun in Nash's pocket, and arrests him.

Question: Was the gun validly seized?

Answer: No. Officer Crosby had no right to detain Stills and Nash in the first place. A "hunch" doesn't authorize detention; an officer must have "articulable facts supporting a reasonable suspicion" (*U.S. v. Hensley,* U.S. Sup. Ct. 1985). Since the initial detention was improper, the frisk incident to that detention was improper, and the fruits of the frisk are inadmissible.

CASE EXAMPLE 2: Officer Jacks sees Jill hiding under the steps of an apartment building. As the officer approaches, Jill runs away. Officer Jacks captures Jill and pats her down for weapons. The officer removes a hard object that turns out to be a plastic envelope containing burglar's tools.

Question: Can Officer Jacks legally seize the tools?

Answer: Yes. Officer Jacks had reasonable grounds for suspecting that Jill was engaged in criminal activity. The officer had the right to detain and pat down Jill, and remove an object that might have been a weapon.

CASE EXAMPLE 3: Officer Ross spots Wade's minivan on a little-used road sometimes frequented by drug smugglers. Wade is driving at a time when border patrol officers commonly change shifts. Officer Ross knows that drug smugglers often use minivans, runs a check on the vehicle, and finds that it is registered to an address in a block notorious for drug smuggling. Officer Ross stops Wade, asks to search the van, and Wade consents. A subsequent search of the minivan reveals 130 pounds of marijuana.

Question: Can Officer Ross seize the marijuana?

Answer: Yes. Based on all of the circumstances, Officer Ross had a reasonable suspicion that Wade was engaged in illegal behavior and had the right to detain him. Since the stop was legal and the resulting search was consensual, the marijuana is admissible as evidence (*U.S. v. Arvizu*, U.S. Sup. Ct. 2002).

40. What's the difference between a search and a frisk?

A search is more extensive. An officer conducting a full search can probe extensively for any type of contraband or evidence. A frisk allows officers only to conduct a cursory pat-down and to seize weapons, such as guns and knives or objects that the officer can tell from a plain feel are contraband (*Minnesota v. Dickerson,* U.S. Sup. Ct. 1993).

CASE EXAMPLE 1: Officer Mace pulls over a driver who resembles a person wanted for bank robbery. Officer Mace asks the driver to get out of the car, then frisks the driver. The officer feels a soft packet in the driver's back pocket. With the packet still in the driver's pocket, the officer pokes a finger through the packaging into the packet, rubs powder from the packet onto the finger, removes the finger and decides from the powder's appearance and smell that it is an illegal drug. The officer removes the packet and arrests the driver for possession of illegal drugs.

Question: Are the contents of the packet admissible in evidence?

Answer: No. The officer had reasonable grounds for detaining the driver, but lacked probable cause to arrest the driver and conduct a full search. Therefore, all the officer could do was frisk the driver and seize either a weapon or contraband in plain feel. Since the soft packet could not reasonably have been mistaken for a weapon, and the officer had to manipulate the packet before deciding that it contained illegal drugs, the officer had no right to remove it from the driver's pocket.

CASE EXAMPLE 2: Same case, except that Officer Mace testifies that, "When I frisked the driver, I felt a packet of little pebbles that felt like rock cocaine, so I seized it."

Question: Is the rock cocaine admissible in evidence?

Answer: Yes. The officer could tell from plain feel that the packet contained illegal drugs, so the seizure is valid. (Note: Police officers are generally very "up" on the law of search and seizure, and know how to testify so that seizures stand up in court.)

41. Does the stop and frisk rule give police officers the right to regularly detain and hassle me, maybe because of my ethnicity?

No. No matter what a person's appearance, the type of neighborhood or time of day, an officer can detain a person only if the officer can point to objective facts showing a reasonable basis that the particular person is engaged in suspicious behavior. Undoubtedly, however, some police officers illegally use stop and frisk to harass "undesirables," confident that they can later articulate enough circumstances to justify the detention. Again, for their own personal safety, people who believe that they are unfair targets of police harassment should put their claims before a judge rather than act belligerently on the street.

42. Seeing a police officer walking in my direction, I tossed away a packet of illegal drugs. Can the officer pick it up and use it as evidence against me?

Yes. The officer neither detained the defendant nor conducted a search. The officer had the right to pick up whatever the defendant tossed away and make an arrest when the object turned out to be illegal drugs.

Section VII: Searches of Cars and Occupants

Based on the mobility of cars and the potential risks of traffic stops both for police officers and citizens, judges are reluctant to second-guess officers' decisions to pull drivers over and search cars' occupants.

43. What are the basic "dos and don'ts" for police officers who pull drivers over for traffic violations?

Police officers who detain motorists for traffic violations typically issue tickets and allow them to proceed. However, if they have probable cause to believe that motorists have committed a traffic offense, police officers may arrest and search motorists (*Virginia v. Moore*, U.S. Sup. Ct. 2009). Even if they plan only to issue a ticket, police officers can order drivers and any passengers to get out of a car. If police officers "reasonably believe" that drivers or passengers might be carrying weapons, they can conduct a short "frisk" (pat down the car's occupants) (*Maryland v. Wilson*, U.S. Sup. Ct. 1998). A traffic stop generally continues until police officers tell drivers that they are free to leave. Before telling drivers that a stop has ended, police officers can briefly question drivers and occupants about matters unrelated to the purpose of the stop (*Arizona v. Johnson*, U.S. Sup. Ct. 2009).

On the other hand, police officers cannot use traffic stops as a pretext to launch extensive investigations. Unless the police have probable cause to believe that a car or its trunk contains weapons or contraband, the police cannot search a car that has been pulled over for a traffic violation. Similarly, unless police officers have probable cause to believe that a driver or passenger has committed a serious crime; the officers cannot use the stop as a pretext to interrogate a car's occupants about other possible crimes.

CASE EXAMPLE 1: Officer Colombo pulls a car over for making an illegal left turn. Inside the car are four teenagers. The officer has no reason to believe that criminal activity has taken place. Nevertheless, Officer Colombo orders the driver and passengers out of the car. As one of the passengers gets out of the car, a packet of cocaine falls out of his shirt pocket. Officer Colombo arrests that teenager for possession of illegal drugs.

Question: Is the arrest valid?

Answer: Yes. Officer Colombo had the right to order the car's occupants out of the car. Seeing the packet of cocaine in plain view gave the officer the right to arrest the passenger.

CASE EXAMPLE 2: Officer Colombo pulls a car over for making an illegal left turn. Inside the car are four teenagers. The officer has no reason to believe that any of the occupants are armed or involved in criminal activity. Nevertheless, Officer Colombo orders the driver and passengers out of the car and frisks them. In the course of one of the frisks, the officer feels what he believes to be a weapon in the jacket pocket of one of the teenagers. The officer reaches in, pulls out a packet of cocaine and arrests the teenager for possession of illegal drugs.

When Can Police Use Checkpoints?

In recent years, police forces in many communities have set up roadblocks—also called checkpoints—at which police officers stop and inspect all drivers and vehicles passing along a road. Because the police typically lack probable cause to believe that any particular driver who is stopped has broken a law, checkpoints potentially violate the Fourth Amendment.

For a checkpoint to be valid the police must follow the same procedures with respect to all motorists on a route; they cannot discriminatorily target any particular driver. Even if the police do follow the same procedures for all drivers, a roadblock may still be illegal if its purpose is not closely tied to highway safety and instead is directed only at general crime control. A few of the recent U.S. Supreme Court cases illustrate this distinction:

- "Sobriety" checkpoints are valid. The goal of improving highway safety, combined with checkpoints' minimal intrusiveness, means that police officers can stop drivers at checkpoints and detain those suspected of driving under the influence. (*Michigan State Police v. Sitz*, U.S. Sup. Ct. 1990.)

- "Illegal immigrant" checkpoints in areas near border crossings are also valid. (*U.S. v. Martinez-Fuerte*, U.S. Sup. Ct. 1976.)

- "Narcotics checkpoints" set up for detecting the presence of illegal drugs are not valid. The goal of apprehending people carrying drugs—while socially beneficial—is not sufficiently tied to roadway safety to overcome the Fourth Amendment prohibition of unreasonable searches and seizures. (*Indianapolis v. Edmond*, U.S. Sup. Ct. 2000.)

- "Investigatory checkpoints" are often lawful. If the police set up a roadblock in order to gather evidence to help solve a crime, they can temporarily stop and question motorists in the same area and around the same time of day that the crime occurred. The police can also lawfully arrest a driver for drunk driving if the driver enters an investigatory checkpoint while under the influence of alcohol. (*Illinois v. Lidster*, U.S. Sup. Ct. 2004.)

Question: Was the arrest valid?

Answer: No. Officer Colombo had the right to order the car's occupants out of the car, but had no basis to conduct a frisk. Since a frisk can't be justified by what it turns up, the arrest based on the illegal frisk is itself illegal. (See Section VI.)

CASE EXAMPLE 3: Officer Colombo pulls a car over for making an illegal left turn. Inside the car are four teenagers. The officer had received a police radio call indicating that four youths had robbed a liquor store and escaped in a car resembling the one pulled over. Therefore, Officer Colombo orders the driver and passengers out of the car and frisks them. In the course of one of the frisks, the officer feels what he believes to be a weapon in the jacket pocket of one of the teenagers. The officer reaches in, pulls out a packet of cocaine and arrests the teenager for possession of illegal drugs. It turns out that none of the car's occupants were connected to the liquor store robbery.

Question: Was the arrest valid?

Answer: Yes. The radio call gave Officer Colombo reason to suspect that the car's occupants had been involved in the robbery. Thus, the officer had a right to frisk the occupants. The officer could then seize the drugs discovered during the frisk, and arrest their owner. (See Section VI for more on frisks.)

44. Can police officers pull a car over for a traffic violation when their true motive is to find evidence of criminal activity?

Yes. Judges generally ignore police officers' subjective motivation when evaluating the legality of their conduct. If a police officer has a valid basis for detaining a motorist (even a nit-picky one like a broken rear taillight), the stop is valid no matter what the officer's subjective purposes might be (*Whren v. U.S.*, U.S. Sup. Ct. 1996; *Arkansas v. Sullivan*, U.S. Sup. Ct. 2001).

CASE EXAMPLE: Officer Colombo sees an old, battered car being driven at night by an unkempt driver in a wealthy section of town, and suspects that the driver might be planning to commit a crime. The officer notices a minor traffic infraction—the light over the car's rear license plate isn't illuminated. The officer uses that as an excuse to pull the car over, and sees illegal drugs on the passenger seat. Officer Colombo then arrests the driver for possession of illegal drugs.

Question: Was the arrest valid?

Answer: Yes. Whatever his motivations, the minor infraction gave Officer Colombo the right to stop the vehicle. Seeing the drugs in plain view gave the officer the right to make the arrest.

"Driving While Black"

Many dark-skinned drivers are convinced that the police stop them for that reason alone. In other words, they are pulled over solely because they are "driving while Black." The police uniformly deny that this occurs, but some do admit to acting on the basis of criminal profiles that often include racial or ethnic factors. For instance, cars driven by people who appear to be of Hispanic descent arguably are more likely to be stopped near the Mexico–U.S. border— because of suspicion of illegal immigration activity—than are cars driven by folks with other characteristics. Similarly, cars driven by African Americans may be more susceptible to a stop in neighborhoods populated by rich Caucasian people than those driven by people with Caucasian characteristics, especially if the hour is late and the car is an expensive model.

As long as the police have a legitimate reason to stop the vehicle (such as a minor traffic violation), then the stop doesn't violate the Fourth Amendment, even if the real reason for the stop is the person's race or ethnic background (*Whren v. U.S.*, U.S. Sup. Ct. 1996). However, the *Whren* case also suggests that this sort of police behavior may violate the Fourteenth Amendment's guarantee of equal protection of the law to all U.S. citizens.

The issue of racial profiling remains controversial, especially in the wake of the September 11, 2001 terrorist attacks. For more on this issue, see www.aclu.org/profiling.

45. Does a traffic stop constitute a seizure of a car's passengers as well as of its driver?

Yes. When police officers pull cars over, neither the drivers nor the passengers generally believe that they are free to simply walk off. Therefore, for purposes of the Fourth Amendment, police officers who carry out traffic stops "seize" all of a car's occupants (*Brendlin v. California*, U.S. Sup. Ct. 2007). One upshot is that drivers and passengers alike can challenge the legality of a stop and any ensuing searches and arrests. The consequence is that police officers have the same power over passengers as over drivers. For example, officers may run the criminal histories of all of a car's occupants.

46. If the police have probable cause to search a car, do they have to obtain a warrant first?

No. Cars are not like houses. If the police have probable cause to search a car, they can do so. They do not need a warrant, even if they have adequate time to obtain one (*Maryland v. Dyson*, U.S. Sup. Ct. 1999). The basic reason for this exception to the warrant rule is that cars can easily be moved and the court believes that people don't have the same expectation of privacy in their vehicles as they do in their homes. (See Section II for more on the search warrant requirement.)

CASE EXAMPLE: Officer Ness receives information from a reliable informant that Jones has just purchased a large shipment of illegal weapons. The informant tells the officer that the weapons are in Jones's car, and gives the officer a full description of the car and the location to which Jones is taking the weapons. With this information, Officer Ness has probable cause to obtain a search warrant. However, instead of obtaining a warrant, Officer Ness goes directly to the location, searches Jones's car and finds the weapons, and places Jones under arrest.

Question: Was the arrest valid?

Answer: Yes. Officer Ness had probable cause to believe that contraband was present in the car and was therefore entitled to search it without first obtaining a warrant. (See Section II for more on the search warrant requirement.)

47. If the police have probable cause to search a car, can they also search objects belonging to passengers?

Yes. Once they have probable cause to search a car, the police don't have to worry about whether the objects they are searching belong to the driver or to any passengers. The officers have the right to search any object that might be capable of concealing whatever object the police are searching for (*Wyoming v. Houghton*, U.S. Sup. Ct. 1999). If the search turns up incriminating evidence (such as drugs or loot from a crime), the police can arrest the driver and the passengers (*Maryland v. Pringle*, U.S. Sup. Ct. 2003).

CASE EXAMPLE 1: Officer Colombo pulls a car over for making an illegal left turn. Inside the car are four teenagers. The officer notices a hypodermic syringe and traces of drugs in the driver's shirt pocket. The officer orders all the passengers out of the car, frisks them, and begins to search the car looking for drugs. The officer picks up a purse from the back seat, which one of the occupants identifies as hers. Officer Colombo opens the purse, finds drugs inside and places the purse's owner under arrest.

Question: Was the arrest valid?

Answer: Yes. Since Officer Colombo had the right to search the car, the officer also had the right to search objects belonging to any passengers, assuming that the object could reasonably contain drugs.

CASE EXAMPLE 2: Officer Colombo pulls a car over for making an illegal left turn. Inside the car are four teenagers. The officer notices an illegal automatic weapon sticking out under the front passenger seat. Officer Colombo orders all the passengers out of the car, frisks them and begins to search the car looking for other evidence of weapons. The officer picks up a wallet from the back seat, which one of the occupants identifies as his. Officer Colombo carefully searches the wallet and finds drugs inside. He places the wallet's owner under arrest.

Question: Was the arrest valid?

Answer: Probably not. Because Officer Colombo had the right to search the car, the officer also had the right to search property belonging to any passengers if the property could reasonably contain the objects the police are searching for, in this case weapons. Since no weapon could be concealed in the wallet, the search of the wallet was arguably illegal and the arrest based on it invalid.

48. Can a police officer who stops a motorist for a traffic violation have a police dog sniff around the car for illegal substances such as drugs?

Yes. Even if a police officer has no reason to believe that a car contains an illegal substance, the officer can use a trained "sniffer dog" to check for illegal substances. Any illegal substances that the officer finds with the dog's help can be used against the motorist at trial (*Illinois v. Caballes*, U.S. Sup. Ct. 2005).

Safe and Sane Stopping Procedures

Should a police officer pull your car over, these few tips can help keep you safe and help you get on your way as soon as possible:

- When you become aware that a police officer has signaled you to pull over, slow down and pull off the road (usually to the right) when it is safe to do so. Use your turn signal to indicate your intent to the officer.
- Turn off the engine, turn on the interior light (if it is dark out), and then keep your hands on the steering wheel. This should lessen officers' fears for their own safety. (Remember they know nothing about you, and you know nothing about any descriptions they've been given about cars and occupants involved in recent crimes.)
- Avoid actions that suggest that you are hiding something. For example, if an officer sees you lean forward, the officer may think that you have hidden an object under the front seat. This may be enough for the officer to order you out of the car, pat you down and search under the front seat.
- Stay in the car unless the officer asks you to get out.
- Obey the officer's instructions. Until the officer tells you that you can drive off, the officer is in charge of the situation.
- Answer the officer's questions, but don't volunteer information or "mouth off." Save any arguments for the courtroom.
- Tell any passengers to follow these same rules.
- Remember that many police cars have equipment that visually records traffic stops.
- If you have reason to doubt that the person who pulled you over is a police officer, ask to talk to a supervisor or say that you will follow the police officer to the police station.

49. Are the rules for car searches different near the U.S. borders?

Yes. Because the government has a unique interest in policing its borders at and around border crossings, police officers can search cars and their occupants even if they have no reason to be suspicious. The right to search in the absence of suspicion even extends to a vehicle's gas tank (*U.S. v. Flores-Montano*, U.S. Sup. Ct. 2004).

Section VIII: Warrantless Searches or Entries Under Emergency (Exigent) Circumstances

This section is about the right of the police to make a warrantless search when the time it takes to get a warrant would jeopardize public safety or lead to the loss of important evidence.

50. What are some examples of emergency situations that eliminate the need for search warrants?

Here are some situations in which most judges would uphold a warrantless search or entry into a residence:

- An officer checks an injured motorist for possible injuries following a collision and finds illegal drugs.
- Following a street drug arrest, an officer runs into the house after the suspect shouts into the house, "Eddie, quick, flush our stash down the toilet." The officer arrests Eddie and seizes the stash.

- A police officer in hot pursuit of a fleeing armed robbery suspect continues the chase into the suspect's house, where the officer arrests and searches the suspect.
- A police officer on routine patrol hears shouts and screams coming from a residence, rushes in and arrests a suspect for spousal abuse.
- A police officer responding to a "loud party" complaint observes underage drinking and fighting going on inside the residence where the party is taking place (*Brigham City v. Stuart*, U.S. Sup. Ct. 2006).

In these types of emergency situations, an officer's duty to protect people and preserve evidence outweighs the warrant requirement.

51. Can a judge decide after the fact that a claimed emergency did not justify a warrantless search?

Yes. If a judge decides that an officer had time to obtain a search warrant without risking injury to people or the loss of evidence, the judge should refuse to allow into evidence whatever was seized in the course of the warrantless search. Judges always have the final word on whether police officers should have obtained warrants.

CASE EXAMPLE 1: Responding to a call from a neighbor, Officer Jules finds a three-year-old wandering around an apartment building without adult supervision. The neighbor, Jim Roman, tells the officer that the child lives alone with her mother, that the mother left about two hours earlier, and that the child has been outside alone ever since. Officer Jules knocks on the mother's door a number of times. Getting no response, he breaks in and looks through the apartment. There he finds stolen food stamps in the bedroom.

Question: Are the food stamps admissible in evidence against the mother?

Answer: Probably not. Officer Jules was not faced with an emergency situation. The child was safely in custody, and the officer had no reason to suspect that the mother or anyone else was inside the apartment. Officer Jules should have gone to a judge to try to establish probable cause for the issuance of a search warrant.

CASE EXAMPLE 2: Officer McNab arrests Ruby, who is alone in her apartment, for stealing jewelry. Officer McNab immediately searches Ruby's apartment and finds a number of pieces of stolen jewelry in a shoebox in a corner of Ruby's basement.

Question: Should a judge admit the pieces of jewelry into evidence?

Answer: No. Exigent circumstances do not justify the warrantless search. Officer McNab had time to obtain a search warrant, because no one else was in the apartment who might have destroyed the evidence. If necessary, a police officer could secure the apart-

ment until a warrant was issued. (Nor could the search be justified as incident to an arrest, since Officer McNab's search went beyond Ruby's immediate surroundings. See Section V.)

Section IX: Miscellaneous Warrantless Searches

This section explains some of the other situations in which the police are authorized to conduct a warrantless search.

52. Can police secretly listen in on telephone conversations without a search warrant?

No. People reasonably expect their telephone conversations to be private, whether made from home or a public telephone booth. Police need a search warrant before recording or listening in on telephone conversations (*Katz v. U.S.,* U.S. Sup. Ct. 1967). Federal laws enacted in 1996 extend the general privacy in telephone conversations to electronic devices like cell phones and email (18 U.S.C. § 2510).

Under the Patriot Act as reenacted in 2006, the National Security Administration claims the power to listen in on private conversations that may involve domestic terrorism. Any phone call placed to or received from a non-U.S. exchange is currently subject to a warrantless search. How widespread the domestic surveillance —and the legality of such surveillance—is a subject of furious debate.

53. Do the police need a warrant to search my trash?

No. People do not have a reasonable expectation of privacy in garbage that they leave out for collection (*California v. Greenwood*, U.S. Sup. Ct. 1988).

CASE EXAMPLE: Fausto prunes his marijuana plants, placing the dead leaves and stems in a kitchen garbage bag, which he later puts in a garbage can outside his home for collection on trash day. Without Fausto's knowledge, the local police have asked the trash collector to deliver Fausto's trash directly to them rather than mixing it with other trash. The police search the trash, find the leaves and stems, and seize them as evidence. Fausto is charged with marijuana cultivation, a felony.

Question: Did the police procedures in this case violate Fausto's rights under the Fourth Amendment?

Answer: No. Trash put out for collection is not within the Fourth Amendment's zone of protection. Because the trash is freely accessible to others (such as scavengers, snoops, and the police) the owner has no reasonable expectation of privacy in it.

54. Is my backyard as subject to Fourth Amendment protection as the inside of my house?

Yes. However, as a practical matter, a person's privacy in his backyard is harder to protect than that inside the home. For instance, there is no privacy in the yard if members of the public can see into it from where they have a right to be.

CASE EXAMPLE: Officer Alex pulls into an alley behind Joshua's house, stops his car and climbs on the car roof to see over a high fence into Joshua's back yard. He spots a number of stacked boxes in an open shed. He shines his flashlight on the boxes and observes that they appear to contain electronic components. Officer Alex is aware of a recent burglary in which similar components were stolen. Officer Alex obtains a search warrant and returns to Joshua's house for a closer look. The components in the boxes match the description of the stolen ones, and Joshua is charged with the crime of receiving stolen property.

Question: Did Officer Alex violate Joshua's Fourth Amendment rights by standing on his car to peer into Joshua's backyard and shining his flashlight on the boxes?

Answer: No. Officer Alex was in a public place where he had a right to be. Even climbing onto the car and using his flashlight was fine since anyone driving in a high truck in the daytime could have made the same observations.

55. I live in a house with large acreage in a rural area. Are the fields around my house private?

No. As long as the police are in a place they have a right to be, they can use virtually any type of surveillance device to observe the property. However, they can't trespass onto your property to obtain a better view. Furthermore, the police cannot use specialized heat-scanning devices to obtain evidence of criminal activity inside a home (*Kyllo v. U.S.*, U.S. Sup. Ct. 2001).

56. Can public school officials search students without a warrant?

Public school students have fewer Fourth Amendment protections than adults. School officials do not need probable cause or search warrants; they can search students and their possessions as long as they have a reasonable basis for conducting a search and as long as the search is appropriate based on the age of the student and what's being sought. For example, if a school official has a reasonable belief that a student has a weapon, drugs, or other illegal substances, the official may pat down the student's clothes or request that the student empty pockets or any personal belongings such as backpacks.

CASE EXAMPLE: A junior high school student tells the school's vice principal that someone in a group of five to six children had brought a gun to school. The vice principal searches the clothes and backpacks of all the students in the group. The vice principal finds a gun and calls the police.

Question: Is the gun admissible in evidence?

Answer: Yes. The student's initial report gave the vice principal a reasonable basis to conduct the search.

57. Can public school officials require drug testing for students participating in extracurricular activities?

Yes, public school officials have the power to conduct drug tests on any student who is engaged in extracurricular school activities, even if the officials have no reason to think that a student is using drugs (*Board of Education v. Earls*, U.S. Sup. Ct. 2002).

CASE EXAMPLE: The Fidelity School District requires all middle school students participating in extracurricular activity to consent to urinalysis testing for drugs. Jack refuses and is prohibited from working on the yearbook.

Question: Can the school require that Jack take a drug test in order to work on the yearbook?

Answer: Yes, the Supreme Court has determined that drug testing of high school and middle school students participating in extracurricular activity —even nonathletic activity—is a reasonable means of preventing drug use among schoolchildren and does not violate the Fourth Amendment.

58. Can the government agency to which I've applied for a job force me to take a drug test before hiring me?

Possibly. The U.S. Supreme Court has upheld drug tests for prospective federal government employees (*National Treasury Employees' Union v. Von Raab,* U.S. Sup. Ct. 1989). The court has likewise upheld drug testing of current employees, even in the absence of a reasonable basis to suspect that an employee might be using drugs. Legality of drug testing in the employment context depends in part on the type of work carried out by a government agency. The more an agency's work involves public safety or sensitive government policies, the more likely a court is to uphold drug testing.

59. Can a government medical facility perform drug tests on pregnant women for police purposes?

No. If a medical professional comes across evidence of a pregnant woman's illegal drug use by means of testing done for valid medical purposes, it would probably not violate the Fourth Amendment to turn that evidence of illegal drug use over to the police. But a medical facility and the police cannot constitutionally join together to set up a drug testing program for the purpose of catching pregnant women who are illegally using drugs. (*Ferguson v. Charleston,* U.S. Sup. Ct. 2001.) However, testing a pregnant woman for the purpose of finding evidence of illegal drug use

is valid if she gives informed consent to such testing, or if medical personnel have probable cause to believe that she was using illegal drugs.

60. Can police officers secretly peek into public restrooms?

No. People have a reasonable expectation of privacy in public restrooms.

61. Can police officers use high-tech devices to search for evidence of criminal activity within a residence?

No, without a warrant, police cannot use high-tech "sense-enhancing" technology that is not in general use to collect information regarding the interior of a home or to monitor a person's conduct within her home.

CASE EXAMPLE: The police suspect that Wheeler is illegally growing marijuana inside his home. Knowing that indoor marijuana growers often rely on lamps that emit unusually high levels of heat, the police scan the outside of Wheeler's home with a thermal imager, a high-tech device that scans for heat. The scan indicates that portions of Wheeler's walls and roof are unusually hot. The police use this information to obtain a search warrant to search Wheeler's home and find marijuana being grown inside.

Question: Did the use of the thermal imager constitute an illegal "search" of Wheeler's home?

Answer: Yes. Wheeler had a reasonable expectation of privacy in his home. By intruding into Wheeler's privacy by means of a high-technology device not in general use, the police conducted an illegal search. If the police did not have probable cause to obtain a search warrant in the absence of the information gained by using the thermal imager, the search was illegal and the evidence inadmissible (*Kyllo v. U.S.*, U.S. Sup. Ct. 2001).

62. Can shops legally use closed-circuit cameras in dressing rooms?

Yes. Shops and other private enterprises are not government agencies and therefore not subject to the Fourth Amendment.

Searches Performed by Private Security Guards

Private security personnel currently outnumber police officers in the United States by 3 to 1. As a result, whether you're shopping in a supermarket or a pharmacy, working in an office building, or visiting a friend in a housing project, you may be more likely to be confronted by a security guard than by a police officer. At the present time, the Fourth Amendment does not apply to searches carried out by nongovernmental employees such as private security guards. For example, assume that a shopping mall security guard acting on a pure hunch (that is, lacking probable cause) searches a teenager's backpack. Inside the backpack the guard finds a baggie containing an illegal drug. The guard can detain the teenager, call the police, and turn the drug over to a police officer. The drug is admissible in evidence, because the search was conducted by a private security guard. As private security guards increasingly exercise traditional police functions, courts may one day apply Fourth Amendment guidelines to their conduct.

---

63. I'm on probation in connection with an earlier criminal charge. Does that give a police officer a right to search me without a warrant?

Probably. Probation normally comes with strings attached. A common string requires probationers to submit to searches by peace officers, whether or not they have a warrant. This condition of probation allows police or probation officers to conduct warrantless searches of probationers based on "reasonable suspicion" (not "probable cause") that the probationers are in possession of contraband such as drugs or of other evidence of criminal activity (*U.S. v. Knights,* U.S. Sup. Ct. 2001).

CASE EXAMPLE: Mark was convicted of a drug offense and placed on probation subject to a condition that he submit to searches of himself, his house, his vehicle, and any of his other possessions at any time by any law enforcement officer, without the need for a warrant. While Mark is on probation, a police officer observes Mark carrying objects that closely resemble some items that were recently reported stolen from a nearby home. The officer later searches Mark's home, finds other stolen objects, and places Mark under arrest.

Question: Was the search of Mark's home valid?

Answer: Yes. The police officer reasonably suspected that Mark might be in possession of stolen goods. Since Mark is on probation and subject to a condition that he submit to searches, the officer does not need probable cause to justify the search.

64. Can government officers search passengers in airports, subways, and other mass transit locales even if they have no reason to suspect them of criminal activity?

Yes. Because of concerns about terrorism and other forms of mass violence, so-called warrantless "special needs" or "administrative" searches are valid so long as they are reasonably limited in scope. For example:

- Airport screening searches are valid because they help to protect airline passengers from terrorism and they are minimally intrusive (*U.S. v. Hartwell,* 3d Cir. 2006).
- New York subway rules authorizing random searches of subway passengers are valid because they allow officers to search only for explosives, and riders are advised when they enter a subway station that they are subject to search and are subject to arrest if they enter a station and refuse a search request (*MacWade v. Kelly,* 2d Cir. 2006).
- Searches of passengers' bags and vehicles on the Lake Champlain ferry (between Vermont and New York) are valid even though a rural ferry may be a less likely target of an attack than an urban subway system (*Cassidy v. Chertoff,* 2d Cir. 2006).

Sample Affidavit for Search Warrant

United States District Court

FOR THE

Eastern District of Missouri

UNITED STATES OF AMERICA	Docket No. _____A_____
	Case No. _____11246_____
vs.	
John Doe	AFFIDAVIT FOR
	SEARCH WARRANT

BEFORE Michael J. Thumb, Federal Courthouse, St. Louis, Missouri
Name of Judge or Federal Magistrate   *Address of Judge or Federal Magistrate*

The undersigned being duly sworn deposes and says:

That he has reason to believe that (on the person of) Occupants, and (on the premises known as) 935 Bay Street, St. Louis, Missouri, described as a two story, residential dwelling, white in color and of wood frame construction ....

in the Eastern   District of Missouri

there is now being concealed certain property, namely   *here describe property*

Counterfeit bank notes, money orders, and securities, and plates, stones, and other paraphernalia used in counterfeiting and forgery,

which are   *here give alleged grounds for search and seizure*

in violation of 18 U.S. Code § 471–474

And that the facts tending to establish the foregoing grounds for issuance of a Search Warrant are as follows: (1) Pursuant to my employment with the Federal Bureau of Investigation, I received information from a reliable informant that a group of persons were conducting an illegal counterfeiting operation out of a house at 935 Bay Street, St. Louis, Missouri. (2) Acting on this information, agents of the FBI placed the house at 935 Bay Street under around-the-clock surveillance. During the course of this surveillance officers observed a number of facts tending to establish the existence of an illegal counterfeiting operation. These include: observation of torn and defective counterfeit notes discarded in the trash in the alley behind the house at 935 Bay Street, and pick-up and delivery of parcels at irregular hours of the night by persons known to the FBI as having records for distribution of counterfeit money.

Mary M. Dunton, Special Agent
Signature of Affiant

Federal Bureau of Investigation
Official Title, if any.

Sworn to before me, and subscribed in my presence   December 3rd, 20xx

Michael J. Thumb
Judge or Federal Magistrate

Sample Search Warrant

United States District Court
FOR THE
Eastern District of Missouri
_____

UNITED STATES OF AMERICA   Docket No. _____ A _____

                                         Case No. _____ 11246 _____

vs.

John Doe   SEARCH WARRANT

To Any sheriff, constable, marshall, police officer, or investigative officer of the United States of America.

Affidavit(s) having been made before me by
Special Agent, Mary M. Dunton

that he has been reason to believe that { on the person of
on the premises known as }

on the occupants of, and

on the premises known as 935 Bay Street, St. Louis, Missouri
described as a two story, residential dwelling, white in color and of wood frame construction ....

in the Eastern   District of Missouri

there is now being concealed certain property, namely

Counterfeit bank notes, money orders, and securities, and plates, stones, and other paraphernalia used in counterfeiting and forgery,

and as I am satisfied that there is probable cause to believe that the property so described is being concealed on the person or premises above described and that the foregoing grounds for application for issuance of the search warrant exist.

You are hereby commanded to search within a period of __10__ (not to exceed 10 days) the person or place named for the property specified, serving this warrant

and making the search { ~~in the daytime (6:00 a.m. to 10:00 p.m.)~~
at anytime in the day or night [1] } and if the

property be found there to seize it, leaving a copy of this warrant and a receipt for the property taken, and prepare a written inventory of the property seized and promply return this warrant and bring the property before me as required by law.

Dated this 3rd day of December, 20xx

Michael J. Thumb
_____
Judge or Federal Magistrate

[1] The Federal Rules of Criminal Procedure provide: "The warrant shall be served in the daytime, unless the issuing authority, by appropriate provision in the warrant, and for reasonable cause shown, authorizes its execution at times other than daytime." (Rule 41(C))

Arrest: When It Happens, What It Means

An arrest occurs when police officers take a suspect into custody. An arrest is complete the moment the suspect is no longer free to walk away from the arresting police officer, a moment that often comes well before the suspect actually arrives at a jail. (See Question 1, below.)

The U.S. Constitution's Fourth Amendment authorizes arrests only if the police have probable cause to believe that a crime was committed and that the suspect did it. (See Question 4.) This probable cause requirement restrains the power of the police to deprive people of liberty. It prevents the random roundup of "undesirables" that sometimes occurs in other countries.

Legislatures and courts have picked up where the Fourth Amendment leaves off, developing rules setting forth how, when, and why people can be arrested. This chapter answers commonly asked questions about the most important arrest procedures.

Arresting Material Witnesses

A "material witness" is an individual who is not a suspect but who can provide important evidence implicating a suspect in a crime. If the police can convince a judge that a material witness will likely flee the jurisdiction before a case can come to trial, the judge can authorize the police to arrest the witness and keep the witness in jail until the case concludes.

Common Consequences of Arrest

In addition to depriving a person of liberty, an arrest often triggers a variety of other events. Some of these are:

- The arrested person will have an official record of arrest, which may have to be reported to employers and licensing agencies, such as a State Board of Dentistry.
- Arrested people who are taken to jail commonly try to secure quick release by posting bail or convincing a judge to order "own recognizance" release. (See Chapter 5.)
- The arresting police officer will usually issue *Miranda* warnings before questioning the arrestee. (See Chapter 1, Section II.)
- The arrestee—and sometimes the arrestee's car or home, depending on where the arrest occurs—may be searched. (See Chapter 2.)
- Any contraband or evidence of a crime will be seized for later use in court. (See Chapter 2.)
- An arrested person who remains in jail after the arrest will be taken before a judge as quickly as practicable for a hearing typically called an "arraignment" or "initial appearance." (See Chapter 10.)

Readers seeking to understand the full panoply of events that typically are associated with an arrest should consult these other chapters as well as this one.

Section I: General Arrest Principles

This section describes the basic legal principles governing arrests in most circumstances, including what an arrest consists of and what laws authorize arrests to be made.

1. When exactly is a person under arrest?

An arrest occurs when a police officer takes a person into custody. However, arrest is not synonymous with being taken to jail. The following common situations suggest the scope of arrest:

- A driver is stopped for a routine traffic violation. The driver technically is under arrest because the driver is not free to leave until the officer has written a ticket (or if it's the driver's lucky day, only issued a warning). But the arrest is temporary. Assuming the officer has no basis to suspect that the driver is engaged in criminal activity other than the traffic violation, the officer must release the driver so long as the driver produces identification and signs a promise to appear in court (assuming a ticket was written). Traffic stop arrests do not become part of a person's arrest record, and do not count as arrests for the purpose of the question: "Have you ever been arrested?"

- A shopper in a mall is stopped by a police officer who says, "I'd like to know whether you saw the robbery that took place a few minutes ago in the jewelry store." No arrest has taken place. People questioned by police officers are not under arrest unless the officers indicate that they are not free to leave. (But for reasons of personal safety, the shopper should not simply walk away from the officer without the officer's permission.) Even if the officer refuses permission, thereby placing the shopper under arrest, this arrest, like the traffic stop arrest, doesn't count as an arrest if the shopper is allowed to leave after the questioning and is not charged with a crime.

- A police officer yells, "Hold it right there, you're under arrest!" to a suspect who assaulted another individual on the street. The suspect flees. The suspect has not been arrested, because the suspect has neither been taken into custody nor voluntarily submitted to the police officer's authority.

- A police officer yells, "Hold it right there, you're under arrest!" to two suspects who assaulted an individual on the street. As the officer handcuffs Suspect 1, the officer tells Suspect 2, "Stay right there and don't move." Suspect 2 does not move. By submitting to the police officer's authority, Suspect 2 has been arrested though the suspect has not physically been taken into custody.

- A store security guard who has arrested an individual for shoplifting turns the suspect over to a police officer. The police officer issues a citation instructing the suspect to appear in court on a charge of petty theft. The suspect has been arrested, but does not have to go to jail.

Would the answer be different in the last example if the suspected shoplifter were a juvenile? No—an arrest of the juvenile would have taken place. (However, in many states juveniles can eventually expunge (delete) an arrest from their record.)

2. Can I be charged with a crime without being arrested?

Yes. An alternative procedure—called "citation"—exists in most states. In lieu of arresting people for traffic offenses (like speeding) and minor misdemeanors (such as shoplifting), officers can issue citations. A citation is a notice to appear in court. By signing the citation, a person promises to appear in court on or before the date specified in the notice in exchange for remaining at liberty.

Need for Citation Procedures in Urban Areas

The jails in many urban areas are overcrowded. In some cases, jails are subject to court orders limiting the number of inmates they can hold. Because of this, many police departments instruct their officers to issue citations to suspects who in the past would have been arrested. One unfortunate by-product of this is that some suspects who might benefit from going to jail and "cooling off" remain free, and thus may pose a danger to themselves and to the persons who called the police.

3. Does the Constitution limit the power of the police to make arrests?

Yes. As mentioned above, to be lawful, all arrests must comply with the Fourth Amendment to the U.S. Constitution. That amendment protects people against "unreasonable searches and seizures," and provides that warrants can issue only on a showing of probable cause. Arrests are covered by this Fourth Amendment provision because they are a type of seizure (of the body).

As interpreted by the courts, the Fourth Amendment requires police officers to obtain arrest warrants *only* when they enter a suspect's dwelling to make an arrest (*Payton v. New York,* U.S. Sup. Ct. 1980). However, the police do not need an arrest warrant in emergency situations such as when they pursue a fleeing suspect into the dwelling.

4. What exactly does "probable cause" mean?

The Fourth Amendment makes probable cause the key term in the arrest process. The police need probable cause to make an arrest, whether they are asking a judge to issue an arrest warrant or justifying an arrest after it has been made. Some principles of probable cause are well-settled:

- To establish probable cause, police officers must be able to point to objective factual circumstances that lead them to believe that a suspect committed a crime. A police officer can't establish probable cause by saying something like, "I just had a hunch that the defendant was a burglar."

- Judges, not police officers, have the last word on whether probable cause exists. A police officer may be sincere in believing that enough factual information to constitute probable cause exists. But if a judge examines that same information and disagrees, then probable cause does not exist (or did not exist if the question is being decided after the arrest occurred).
- Probable cause to arrest may have existed at the time of the arrest, even if the police later turn out to be wrong. Put differently, an arrest is valid so long as it is based on probable cause, even if the arrested person is innocent. In this situation, probable cause protects the police against a civil suit for false arrest if the charges are later dismissed or the defendant is acquitted at trial.

These principles leave open the most important issue concerning probable cause: How much information do police officers need to convince a judge to issue an arrest warrant or to justify a warrantless arrest? In general, probable cause requires more than a mere suspicion that a suspect committed a crime, but not so much information that it proves a suspect guilty beyond a reasonable doubt.

Because it is an abstraction, a firm definition of probable cause is impossible.

The Fourth Amendment doesn't provide a definition, so it's up to judges to interpret the meaning of probable cause on a case-by-case basis, taking into account:

- what the judge thinks the amendment's drafters meant by the term probable cause
- previous judges' interpretations in similar fact situations, and
- the judge's views about police rights vs. criminals' rights.

Judges help to define the meaning of probable cause each time they issue a warrant or decide a case in which the issue arises.

CASE EXAMPLE 1: Officer Furman arrives at Simpson's Jewelry store moments after it's been robbed. Officer Furman sees broken glass inside the jewelry store. A man claiming to be Simpson, the owner, tells the officer that a man approximately 6'5" tall and weighing over 300 pounds held up the store at gunpoint and escaped with rings and watches in a small brown paper bag. A few minutes later, less than a mile away from the jewelry store, Officer Furman pulls a car over for speeding. The driver matches the description of the robber, and on the seat next to the driver is a small brown paper bag and a couple of watches with the price tags intact.

Question: Does Officer Furman have probable cause to arrest the driver?

Answer: Yes. The driver matches the unusual physical description of the robber, and has the property that

Simpson said was missing. Though the officer did not see the actual robbery, the officer has probable cause to arrest the driver.

CASE EXAMPLE 2: Same case. Assume that the person claiming to be Simpson, the jewelry store owner, was actually the robber's accomplice. The accomplice gave Officer Furman a phony description, and then fled after the officer drove off. The driver pulled over by the officer for speeding later is able to prove that he is the lawful owner of the watches that the officer saw on the seat.

Question: Under these circumstances, was the arrest proper?

Answer: Yes. Officer Furman had no reason to doubt the word of the person claiming to be Simpson, and the broken glass corroborated "Simpson's" statement that a robbery had occurred. Thus, the officer had probable cause to make the arrest, even though the information turned out to be incorrect.

CASE EXAMPLE 3: Officer Seesit pulls over a car and its three occupants for speeding. The officer searches the car with the driver's consent and finds baggies of cocaine stashed behind an armrest in the back seat. All three occupants of the car say that they didn't know that the cocaine was in the car.

Question: Does the officer have probable cause to arrest the three people in the car?

Answer: Yes. In the absence of evidence demonstrating that the cocaine belonged to a specific occupant, the officer could reasonably conclude that all of them knew about and possessed the cocaine (*Maryland v. Pringle,* U.S. Sup. Ct. 2003).

Probationers and Parolees

The probable cause requirement for arrest does not generally apply to people who are on probation or parole. As a condition of being placed on probation or parole, they typically have to agree to submit to arrest without probable cause.

Pursuant to these agreements, a police officer needs only "reasonable suspicion" (not "probable cause," a harder condition for an officer to satisfy) that a probationer is involved in criminal activity to justify a search (*U.S. v. Knights,* U.S. Sup. Ct. 2001). And a police officer can search a parolee even if the officer has no basis to suspect that the parlee is engaged in criminal activity (*Samson v. California,* U.S. Sup. Ct. 2006).

5. What happens if the police arrest me and it turns out that they lacked probable cause?

A judge will not issue an arrest warrant if it appears to the judge that probable cause for the arrest is lacking. However, police officers are authorized to make warrantless arrests without getting a judge's permission, unless they arrest the suspect at his home. Many times these arrests hold up. Other times, though, a judge may later decide that the police lacked probable cause to make the arrest and order the charges dismissed and the suspect released.

Probable Cause Formed After the Arrest

A judge's decision that the police lacked probable cause at the time of the arrest does not always mean that the defendant is in the clear. By the time a judge makes that decision, the police may have gathered enough additional information to have probable cause. If so, a defendant might be released, only to be immediately and properly rearrested based on the additional information.

Apart from the possibility that the suspect will be released from custody, a judge's determination that the police lacked probable cause to make an arrest may result in any of the following:

- **Exclusion of evidence.** Any evidence seized by the police in connection with an illegal arrest cannot be used as evidence in court.
- **Civil tort action.** An improperly arrested person may be able to sue the arresting officer (and the city or other government entity that

employed the officer) for damages in a civil case. In practice, civil tort actions against police officers for improper arrest tend to succeed only when a rogue cop physically abuses a suspect in the course of an improper arrest.

 CAUTION
People under arrest cannot use force to resist an improper arrest. Most courts have ruled that arrestees have no right to use force to resist an arrest, even if the arresting police officer clearly lacks probable cause. An improperly arrested person who resists arrest may be charged with resisting arrest or battery on a police officer. To protect arrestees and police officers alike, judges and legislators want issues of probable cause to be fought out in court after the fact, not on the streets.

Section II: Arrest Warrants

This section describes arrest warrants—what they are, when they are necessary for an arrest, and how one is obtained.

6. What exactly is contained in an arrest warrant?

An arrest warrant is an official document, signed by a judge (or magistrate), authorizing a police officer to arrest the person or persons named in the warrant. Warrants typically identify the crime for which an arrest has been authorized, and may restrict the manner in which an arrest may be made. For example, a warrant may state that a suspect can be arrested "only between the hours of 6 a.m. and 6 p.m." Finally, some warrants also specify the bail that a defendant must post to regain freedom following arrest. If the warrant is for a previous failure of the suspect to appear in court—called a bench warrant— it will probably specify that the arrested person may not be released on bail at all (sometimes termed a "no-bail warrant").

7. The police officer who arrested me didn't have an arrest warrant. Does that mean that my arrest was improper?

Not necessarily. So long as a police officer has probable cause to believe that a crime was committed and that the arrestee committed it, a warrantless arrest usually is valid. For further discussion of warrantless arrests, see Section III, below. In general, police officers need to obtain arrest warrants only when they intend to enter a suspect's dwelling in a nonemergency situation to make an arrest.

8. How do the police obtain an arrest warrant?

To obtain a warrant, a police officer typically submits a written affidavit to a judge or magistrate. The affidavit, given under oath, must recite sufficient factual information to establish probable cause that a crime was committed and that the person named in the warrant committed it. A description

so broad that it could apply to hundreds of people or more will not suffice. For instance, a judge will not issue a warrant to arrest "Rich Johnson" based on an affidavit that "a liquor store was held up by a bald potbellied man of medium height, and Rich Johnson matches that description." That description doesn't establish probable cause to believe that Rich Johnson robbed the liquor store, because the vague description would apply to numerous people. On the other hand, probable cause to arrest Rich Johnson probably would be adequate if the affidavit included the factual information that "the liquor store clerk and three witnesses identified a photo of Rich Johnson as depicting the individual who held up the liquor store."

If the Arrest Warrant Contains Incorrect Information

Sometimes arrest warrants contain factual mistakes. The suspect's name may be misspelled or the wrong crime may be specified. Ideally, the police should show the warrant to the suspect. And, if the suspect is able to prove that the officer has the wrong person, then the officer should not proceed. As a practical matter, the police sometimes don't show the warrant to the suspect for a variety of reasons real or imagined, and any mistakes as to identity are sorted out later. As for clerical errors, these alone won't invalidate the warrant.

Section III: Warrantless Arrests

This section deals with situations where the police may arrest a suspect without an arrest warrant.

9. What is a warrantless arrest?

As the name implies, a warrantless arrest is simply an arrest without a warrant. When police officers make a warrantless arrest, a judge does not have a chance to determine ahead of time whether the police have probable cause to make the arrest. Nevertheless, the Fourth Amendment probable cause requirement remains the same. For a suspect to remain in custody following an arrest, the police must speedily satisfy a judge or magistrate that they had probable cause to make the arrest (*Gerstein v. Pugh,* U.S. Sup. Ct. 1975).

10. When can a police officer legally make a warrantless arrest?

Assuming that they have probable cause to make an arrest, police officers can legally make warrantless arrests in these two circumstances:

- When the crime is committed in the officer's presence. For example, a police officer, on routine patrol, sees a driver strike a pedestrian and drive off without stopping (the crime of "hit and run"). The police officer can pursue the driver and place him in custody.
- When the officer has probable cause to believe that the suspect committed

a felony, whether or not the deed was done in the officer's presence. (See Chapter 6 for more on how crimes are classified.)

CASE EXAMPLE 1: While on routine patrol, Officer Martin comes upon Fred Rowan, an individual possessing—and apparently under the influence of— cocaine. Rowan tells Officer Martin that he had bought the cocaine moments earlier from a man around the corner wearing a dark business suit and white loafers. Peering around the corner, Officer Martin sees a suspect matching that description standing on the street.

Question: Does Officer Martin have probable cause to place the suspect described by Rowan in custody?

Answer: Yes. The officer did not personally see the suspect sell the cocaine to Rowan. But selling drugs is a felony everywhere, and Rowan's appearance and information gives the officer probable cause to believe that the suspect had committed that crime.

CASE EXAMPLE 2: Officer Winter is told by Mr. Summer, a security guard in an electronics store, that Summer personally saw a red-haired teenage girl wearing a leather jacket bearing the logo "Cafe Rock Hard" and tennis shoes take a $75 Panasonic Portable CD player from the store without paying for it. A few hours later, Officer Winter sees a red-haired girl dressed as Summer described sitting in a park listening to a Panasonic Portable CD player.

Question: Can Officer Winter place the girl in custody?

Answer: No. Even if the girl is guilty, the information given to Officer Winter indicates that, at most, the girl committed a misdemeanor commonly called shoplifting. Since Officer Winter did not personally see the act, he would need to submit an affidavit and obtain an arrest warrant before placing the girl in custody. The officer can, however, issue the girl a citation ordering her to appear in court to answer to a misdemeanor shoplifting charge. However, if the CD player had been worth more than several hundred dollars, Officer Winter could make the arrest on probable cause because the theft would be a felony rather than a misdemeanor.

The bottom line: Warrantless arrests are generally okay if probable cause exists, except if a police officer arrests a suspect for a misdemeanor not committed in the officer's presence.

11. Can the police make a warrantless arrest for an offense that is punishable only by a small fine?

Yes. If a police officer has probable cause to believe that an offense has been committed, the officer can make an arrest even if the crime is a very minor one that is punishable only by a small fine (*Atwater v. Lago Vista,* U.S. Sup. Ct. 2001). As a practical matter, police officers rarely make arrests in these situations. However, in the Supreme Court's opinion, a rule making the validity of an arrest depend on the seriousness of an offense would be too difficult for police officers to follow because they would have to know the punishment for every criminal offense.

> **CASE EXAMPLE:** Officer Buckle spots Whip Lash driving without a seat belt. In the state where the offense occurs, driving without a seat belt is an offense that can be punished only with a small fine. Whip cannot be punished with jail time even if he is found guilty of the offense.
>
> **Question:** Can Officer Buckle arrest Whip and take him to jail?
>
> **Answer:** Yes. Because Officer Buckle has probable cause to believe that Whip committed an offense, the officer can arrest him even though the offense is a minor one that doesn't carry jail time.

12. Can the police make a warrantless entry into my home to arrest me?

Police officers generally need to obtain arrest warrants before arresting suspects in their dwellings (*Payton v. New York,* U.S. Sup. Ct. 1980). If necessary, another officer can be posted outside a home to prevent a suspect's escape during the time it takes to obtain the warrant.

However, warrantless in-home arrests are valid under certain circumstances if "exigent circumstances" exist that make it impracticable for the police to obtain a warrant. Examples of exigent circumstances are:

- A police officer who is in hot pursuit of a fleeing suspect who runs into a house or apartment will not generally be required to break off the chase and obtain a warrant.

CASE EXAMPLE: Officer Hernandez arrests Frick for taking part in a string of burglaries. After Frick is taken into custody, he confesses and names Frack as the other person who took part in the burglaries. Frick also tells Officer Hernandez where Frack lives. Officer Hernandez immediately goes to Frack's house, demands admittance, and arrests Frack.

Question: Is Frack's arrest proper?

Answer: No. Officer Hernandez should first have gotten a warrant for Frack's arrest. Officer Hernandez was not in hot pursuit of Frack, and no other emergency circumstances justify the officer's going into Frack's home without a warrant.

- A police officer who believes that someone in the home is in danger and gains entry for that reason may then arrest the owner without a warrant.

- A police officer who is let into the home by someone answering the door may make the arrest without a warrant.

Section IV: Use of Force When Making Arrests

This section deals with what force the police are permitted to use when making an arrest.

13. Do the police have to knock before entering my home to arrest me?

It depends. In the typical case where the police are entering a home to arrest a suspect pursuant to a warrant, the police are supposed to follow what are sometimes called "knock and notice" rules that vary from state to state. But, the police usually need not announce their presence in advance if:

- they are in hot pursuit of a fleeing suspect
- they believe that someone is being harmed in the house
- they have reasonable grounds to suspect that announcing their presence might put them in danger, or
- they have reasonable grounds to suspect that announcing their presence would allow a suspect to escape or destroy evidence.

The Fourth Amendment has been interpreted to require the knock and notice procedure (*Wilson v. Arkansas*, U.S. Sup. Ct. 1995). However, violations of the rule do not require judges to exclude evidence or dismiss criminal charges (*Hudson v. Michigan*, U.S. Sup. Ct. 2006).

14. How much force can police officers use when making arrests?

Police officers are generally allowed to use reasonable force to take a person into custody. For example, if a suspect's only resistance consists of a momentary attempt to run away or a token push, a police officer would not be justified in beating the suspect senseless. Officers who use unnecessary force may be criminally prosecuted, and may also have to pay civil damages to the injured suspect.

Courts decide whether an officer's use of force was unreasonable on a case-by-case basis, taking into account the severity of the crime, whether the suspect posed a threat, and whether the suspect was resisting or attempting to flee (*Graham v. Connor*, U.S. Sup. Ct. 1989).

In a perfect world, suspects informed that they were under arrest would meekly submit to a police officer's authority. But then again, a perfect world would contain neither suspects nor police officers. In this world, suspects sometimes try to flee or to fight off arrest. In such situations, police officers can use force (and sometimes even deadly force) to make an arrest.

The amount of force that police officers can use when making an arrest is a subject of much concern and controversy. Police officers often seek discretion to use as much force as they—at the time of the arrest—think necessary, to protect both society and their personal safety. But citizens' groups, especially those made up of ethnic or racial minorities, often oppose any extension of police officers' authority to use force, on the ground that the police are too likely to use force discriminatorily against disfavored minorities.

CASE EXAMPLE: Officer Smitts and his partner observe Delany punch somebody outside a bar and then run away. The officers give chase. When they catch up, Delany struggles and strikes at the officers in an effort to escape. While Officer Smitts applies a chokehold, the partner manages to handcuff Delany and manacle his legs. However, Officer Smitts continues to apply the chokehold for another minute, until Delany passes out.

Question: Did Officer Smitts use excessive force?

Answer: Yes. Once Delany was shackled, there was no further need for the chokehold. However, Officer Smitts would probably be able to convince a judge or jury that his continued use of the chokehold was reasonable under the circumstances.

Should Police Officers Fire Into Moving Vehicles?

A car driven in a police officer's direction can be a deadly weapon. An officer may shoot at it in self-defense. Or an officer may fire into a moving vehicle to prevent a suspect from escaping. Either situation creates serious hazards for passersby. Moreover, in the "heat of battle" an officer may overreact. In one case that drew national attention to the issue in 2005, Los Angeles police officers pursued a stolen vehicle that crashed and then backed up towards them. The officers shot and killed the driver, a 13-year-old boy. To try to prevent unwarranted shootings, many police departments are in the process of developing policies to guide police officers' decisions about when they should fire into moving vehicles. One common guideline advises officers to get out of the way of a moving vehicle when they can safely do so. Another recommendation is that police officers not fire into vehicles unless the people inside have weapons that create a serious risk of harm to the officers or others. While policies such as these may be helpful, they cannot eliminate the risk of shootings that in retrospect were unjustified; speeding cars tend to force officers into immediate and emotional decisions.

15. Can the police legally use deadly force to make an arrest?

Sometimes. A police officer may use deadly force to capture a suspect only if a suspect threatens an officer with a weapon or an officer has probable cause to believe that the suspect has committed a violent felony (*Tennessee v. Garner*, U.S. Sup. Ct. 1985). The police can also use deadly force to protect the life of a third person. But police officers cannot routinely use deadly force whenever they seek to arrest a suspect for committing a felony. The police should allow some felony suspects to escape rather than kill them.

> **CASE EXAMPLE:** Officer Fish sees a suspect take a camera from an outdoor sales stall and run off without paying for it. The officer calls for the suspect to stop, but the suspect continues to run away.
>
> **Question:** What force may the officer use to arrest the suspect?
>
> **Answer:** Officer Fish has personally observed the suspect commit a misdemeanor, and therefore has probable cause to make an arrest. But the officer cannot shoot the suspect or use other serious force. If the suspect refuses to halt and the officer cannot chase down the suspect, the officer would have to try to make an arrest at a later time.

Always Consider the Police Officer's Perspective

The probable cause rule allows police officers to act based on the information available to them, even if it later turns out that the information is wrong. Thus, a person stopped by police officers who thinks herself innocent of any wrongdoing should act cautiously, because the officers may have information causing them to think that the person is dangerous.

For example, assume that a young man with red hair driving a late model convertible is pulled over by a police officer. The driver, confident that he's done nothing wrong, is indignant and belligerent. He gets out of the car and shakes his fists at the officer. But unknown to the driver, the police officer has information that five minutes earlier, a young red-headed man robbed a nearby convenience store at gunpoint and escaped in a late model convertible. The officer may interpret the young man's belligerence as a threat, and use force. The officer would probably have the right to do so, even though it later turns out that the young man is innocent and has no weapon.

The moral: People should keep their hands in view at all times so that the police don't think they are hiding any weapons. And they should act courteously toward police officers, because they don't know what the officers know. (When police officers are investigated for shooting unarmed suspects, they can often credibly claim that they thought the suspect was armed and reaching for a weapon.)

16. Can police officers use deadly force to terminate high-speed car chases?

Yes. Motorists who drive off at high speed instead of stopping in response to a police officer's blinking lights and siren often place the lives of other drivers and pedestrians at risk. To prevent harm to innocent bystanders, police officers have the right to use deadly force to put an end to the car chase and arrest fleeing motorists. (See *Scott v. Harris*, U.S. Sup. Ct. 2007.)

17. The officer who arrested me placed me in a chokehold even though I wasn't putting up a struggle. Was I entitled to defend myself without being guilty of a crime?

Technically, yes. If police officers use excessive force in the course of an arrest, arrestees are entitled to use self-defense to protect themselves. It doesn't matter whether an officer has probable cause to make the arrest in the first place. The use of more force than is necessary to make an arrest is improper. However, an arrestee should use self-defense only when absolutely necessary to prevent severe injury or death. Judges and jurors are likely to blame any escalation in violence on the person being arrested, so self-defense should always be considered a last-ditch option.

Section V: Citizens' Arrests

This section covers when a non-law-enforcement officer can make an arrest without being held liable for false imprisonment.

18. Is it legal for an ordinary citizen to make an arrest?

All states authorize private citizens to make arrests. For example, a car owner may arrest a teenager trying to break into her car, or a store security guard may arrest a shoplifter.

"Here Comes the Posse!"

The posse is a familiar staple in most westerns. Yet, reminiscent of the Wild West, in emergency situations law enforcement officers can still conscript private citizens into serving on posses to capture suspects. Though the laws are rarely enforced, a citizen who refuses an officer's order to join a posse can technically be guilty of a misdemeanor.

19. What kind of legal trouble can I get myself into if I make a citizen's arrest?

In order to encourage citizens to leave arrests to the professionals, laws in almost all states afford less protection to private citizens who make mistakes during the arrest process than they do to police officers.

Most states authorize private citizens to make arrests if:

- they personally observe the commission of a crime
- the person arrested has actually committed a felony, even if not in the private citizen's presence, or
- a felony has in fact been committed, and the private citizen has probable

cause to believe that the arrested person committed it.

Compare these rules to those that apply to police officers. So long as they act on probable cause, police officers are not civilly liable for mistakenly arresting an innocent person. But if a private citizen makes an arrest for a felony not committed in the citizen's presence, the citizen had better not mistakenly arrest an innocent person. If a private citizen is mistaken—that is, if it turns out that the arrested person did not commit a felony, or that nobody committed a felony, or that the private citizen had no reasonable basis to believe that the arrested person committed a felony—then the private citizen may be civilly liable to the arrested person for false imprisonment.

CASE EXAMPLE 1: While eating lunch in the park, Ella Mentry overhears two people talking about a plan to rob Haro's Jewelry Store. As the two people walk away, Ella realizes that one of the speakers is her next-door neighbor. About an hour later, Ella sees a crowd and two police officers gathered in front of Haro's Jewelry Store. Ella immediately rushes to the neighbor's house and places the neighbor under arrest for robbery. It turns out, however, that Haro's was not robbed; the police and crowd had gathered for a diamond-cutting demonstration.

Question: Is Ella civilly liable to her neighbor for false imprisonment?

Answer: Yes. Since no robbery took place, Ella may have to pay damages to her neighbor. As a private citizen, Ella is not protected by probable cause.

CASE EXAMPLE 2: Same case. Assume that after overhearing her neighbor talking about a plan to rob Haro's, Ella tells Officer Chang what she heard. About an hour later, Officer Chang sees a large crowd gathered in front of Haro's and sees the person who turns out to be Ella's next-door neighbor running away from the store. Officer Chang runs after and arrests the neighbor. Again, it turns out that Haro's was not robbed.

Question: Is Officer Chang civilly liable to the neighbor for false imprisonment?

Answer: No. Officer Chang had probable cause to believe that a robbery occurred. Though Officer Chang was wrong, probable cause protects the officer against a suit for false imprisonment.

CAUTION

Private citizens are at great legal risk if they try to use deadly force to make an arrest. Courts are especially hostile toward private citizens who use deadly force to make arrests. Courts are rightly fearful that any encouragement of private citizens' use of deadly force will lead to armed vigilantes roaming the streets and lessening public safety. Thus, a private citizen's use of deadly force while making a citizen's arrest is not justified unless the citizen's belief that the use of deadly force was necessary to protect the citizen or others from extreme

harm or death was accurate. Private citizens who are mistaken may be both sued civilly and prosecuted criminally.

20. Are there any other factors I should consider before making a citizen's arrest?

Legal problems aside, the biggest peril to keep in mind is the danger of confronting criminals. Police officers are highly trained and have excellent physical skills, yet even they are sometimes injured or killed when making arrests. Unless they are certain of their physical security, private citizens should turn their information over to the police rather than personally make arrests. And if they do make an arrest, private citizens must call the police and turn the suspect over as soon as possible.

CASE EXAMPLE: Officer Wachit, a store security guard, arrests a suspected shoplifter. In response to Wachit's request, a police officer takes the suspect into custody.

Question: Since the police officer did not personally witness the theft, does the officer's arrest of the shoplifter violate the rule forbidding police officers to make warrantless arrests for misdemeanors that are not committed in the officers' presence?

Answer: No. The person making the arrest is Wachit, the security guard. Wachit will fill out an arrest report (see sample at the end of this chapter), and the officer will take the suspect into custody as Wachit's representative.

Arrest Powers of Private Security Guards

The private security industry has grown to such an extent in recent years in the United States that security guards now outnumber police officers by a ratio of about 3 to 1. Most security guards have only the same legal rights as ordinary citizens when it comes to the power to make arrests. In some areas, however, local governments have given security guards a few police powers, including issuing traffic tickets and making arrests for nonviolent misdemeanors such as trespassing (entering someone else's property without permission). If the public continues to perceive that police departments lack adequate staffing, the blurring of the line between police officers and private security personnel may continue.

Just because the Constitution doesn't apply to private security guards, however, does not mean citizens have no legal rights if security guards' actions are inappropriate. For example, if a private security guard wrongfully detains, harasses, or physically injures a suspect, the injured person may have sufficient grounds to sue the security guard for a number of different torts (civil wrongs), including false imprisonment and battery.

Additionally, especially if the security guard works for a company that receives government funding, the injured citizen may have a civil rights violation claim under 42 U.S.C. § 1983. But remember: It is nearly always wiser to bring grievances to court after the fact than to physically stand up for your rights when the person you're standing up to is armed.

Sample Arrest Report

REPORT OF ARRESTING OFFICER

ARRESTEE'S LAST NAME   **FIRST**   **MIDDLE**
Daniels   Julian   M.

ARRESTEE'S ADDRESS:
252 Longside Lane, City, State

BOOKING NO.	**LOC. BKD.**	**DR. LICE. NO.**	**STATE**
12195	9990	DL9966033	

SEX	**HAIR**	**EYES**	**HEIGHT**	**WEIGHT**	**AGE**
M	BR	BR	57	140	21

DATE ARRESTED	**TIME ARR.**	**TIME BKD.**
121	2300	2351

CHARGE:	**BAIL:**
DUI, Section 23152 (A)(VC)	$500

LOCATION OF ARREST:
Seascape Village Drive and Oak Avenue, Pleasantville.

WITNESS/PASSENGER/VICTIM: ADDRESS & PHONE
Neighbor, Jake Ihara, head crash, phoned police: 111 Oak Street.
Ph: 222-3333.

ADMONITION OF RIGHTS:
1. You have the right to remain silent.
2. Anything you say can and will be used against you in a court of law.
3. You have the right to talk with an attorney and to have an attorney present before and during questioning.
4. If you cannot afford an attorney, one will be appointed for you free of charge, if you desire.

The above statement was read to the arrested by: Watt Charles

DETAILS OF ARREST:
Approached suspect Daniels, who was standing in front of his car. Suspect had red, watery eyes & suspect's car had hit tree. Suspect passed FTS, but BAC measured at Main County station 1/2 hour after arrest was .09. Suspect booked.

BOOKING INVENTORY:
Brown leather wallet, containing identification, photos and $25. 4-door white Corolla (license _____) impounded.

SIGNATURE OF ARRESTING OFFICER: *Watt Charles*
                                        Officer W. Charles

Eyewitness Identification: Psychology and Procedures

The popular media have made most people familiar with common tools of forensic science, such as finger-print analysis, DNA analysis, and ballistics.

Yet in approximately 80,000 criminal cases per year, the prosecution's main evidence consists of eyewitness identification. And in over half the cases in which it turns out that innocent people were wrongly convicted and are set free, sometimes after serving many years in prison, the culprit is that eyewitnesses were mistaken. For better or worse, then, eyewitness identification often determines case outcomes.

In response to the frequent importance of eyewitness identification, evidence rules allow eyewitnesses not only to identify suspects at trial, but also to testify to pre-trial identifications. The evidence of multiple identifications tends to strengthen a prosecutor's case. A second response, which acknowledges the problem of mistaken identifications, allows defendants to educate jurors about factors tending to undercut the accuracy of eyewitness identifications. With so much riding on the accuracy of eyewitness identification rather than forensic science, the principles and policies that this chapter discusses are critical to our system of justice.

Section I: An Overview of Eyewitness Identification Procedures

When eyewitnesses to a crime are available, the police typically want to find out as soon as possible whether they can identify the culprit. This section briefly describes the common identification procedures that eyewitnesses and suspects may encounter, and how those procedures can affect eyewitnesses' trial testimony.

1. What are the common pretrial identification procedures?

The three most common identification procedures, which the chapter later examines in more detail, are the following:

- **Lineups.** A lineup typically consists of five to six people. Usually one is the suspect, while the others may be police officers or other "decoys" who somewhat resemble the suspect or fit the description that the eyewitnesses gave to the police. Generally the police hold a lineup after they've made an arrest, and they want to know whether the eyewitnesses can identify the suspect ("make a positive identification").

- **Showups.** A showup is a "one on one" identification procedure. That is, an eyewitness views a single suspect, perhaps at a police station or sometimes at the crime scene. Again, the police generally conduct a showup after they've identified and arrested a possibly guilty suspect.

- **Photo identifications.** This procedure calls for eyewitnesses to view photo-graphs, typically head shots (called "mug shots") in a police department's files. The police may resort to photo identifications when they don't have enough information to make an arrest, and an eyewitness's positive identification of a suspect's photo is what allows the police to make an arrest.

In addition to identifying suspects, each of these procedures can also help to clear a suspect. For example, if an eyewitness fails to make a positive identification at a lineup, the police may release a suspect.

2. At trial, can eyewitnesses testify to pretrial identifications?

Yes. Typically, eyewitnesses testify to their opportunities to view suspects during the crime itself, and then pick out the defendant in the courtroom as the perpetrator. In addition, evidence rules in all states allow eyewitnesses to bolster their in-court identifications by testifying to their pretrial identifications. For example, an eyewitness may testify as follows:

Question: And what happened when you came to the police station the day after the robbery?

Answer: Officer Smith sat me at a computer and asked me to look through photos and to tell him if I recognized anyone.

Question: And did you recognize anyone?

Answer: Yes, as soon as I saw the photo of the defendant. I must have looked at 50 or 60 photos by that time, but when I came to the defendant's photo I stopped looking and immediately told the officer that this was the robber.

Of course, the defense can bring out an eyewitness's failure to make a positive identification when the eyewitness had an opportunity to do so. For example, a portion of a defense attorney's cross-examination of an eyewitness may go as follows:

Question: You've testified today that the defendant is the person who robbed the bank, right?

Answer: Yes.

Question: But you attended a lineup less than two weeks after the robbery, right?

Answer: That's true.

Question: And the defendant was in that lineup, wasn't he?

Answer: He was.

Question: Yet at that time you told the police that you didn't recognize anyone in the lineup as the robber, didn't you?

Answer: That's correct, but …

Question: Thank you. You've answered my question.

3. Are there safeguards against unduly suggestive pretrial identification procedures?

Yes. While the risks of mistaken identifications can probably never be overcome entirely, various safeguards lessen the chance that suggestive pretrial identification procedures will promote mistakes. Among the common safeguards are these:

- Police officers are trained not to suggest, directly or indirectly, who they want an eyewitness to identify. For example, eyewitnesses viewing a lineup should only be asked if they recognize anyone, and should not be told whether the suspect is in the lineup.

- Lineups are photographed, and records are kept as to which photos were shown to eyewitnesses. Thus, if the defendant was displayed in an unfair way that could lead an eyewitness to pick the defendant out of a group, the defense will have an opportunity to point that out. For instance, if an eyewitness described the perpetrator as "tall," and the defendant was noticeably taller than anyone else in a lineup, the defense may convince a judge that the lineup was unfair.

- The police keep eyewitnesses apart from each other during pretrial identification procedures. This eliminates the risk that at a lineup, one eyewitness will identify "the third person from the left" as the culprit simply because this witness was standing next to another eyewitness who made that same identification.

- If a judge concludes that a pretrial identification procedure was unfair, an eyewitness cannot testify at trial to having identified the defendant before trial. In an extreme case, a judge may decide that a pretrial identification was botched so badly that an eyewitness won't even be allowed to make an identification at trial.

CASE EXAMPLE: Shortly after receiving a report of a convenience store robbery, the police arrest a suspect who generally matches the clerk's description. Bringing the suspect to the store, the police tell the clerk, "This guy matches the description you gave. He's got a record a mile long, and his alibi doesn't hold water. Just tell us we've got the right guy, we'll haul him right off to jail and you won't have problems from him again." The clerk then says, "Good work. He's got to be the one who robbed me." The suspect is then charged with robbing the store.

Question: How is this showup likely to affect the clerk's trial testimony?

Answer: In this extreme example, the police virtually told the clerk to identify the suspect. The judge should rule that the clerk can't testify to the out-of-court identification. Moreover, the risk is so great that the unfair procedure tainted the clerk's memory that the clerk shouldn't even be allowed to identify the suspect at trial.

Find the Defendant

Inside the courtroom, witnesses ordinarily have no trouble figuring out who to identify: It's the person sitting next to the defense attorney. Arranging for a truer test of an eyewitness' credibility, famed defense lawyer Johnnie Cochran, Jr. on at least one occasion got a judge to allow the defendant to be seated among the spectators. A decoy sat next to Cochran at counsel table. When the eyewitness was asked to "look around the courtroom and tell us if you see the perpetrator," the arrangement forced the eyewitness to carefully consider before answering. Much earlier in the 20th century, legendary Los Angeles lawyer Earl Rogers did the same thing, actually having the defendant switch places with a courtroom spectator while Rogers cross-examined the eyewitness. Rogers stood so as to block the witness's view of the switch.

Section II: The Psychology of Eyewitness Identification

Cognitive psychologists have conducted literally thousands of experiments examining factors that might affect the accuracy of eyewitness identifications. This section summarizes some of what they've learned about eyewitness identification and discusses the type of testimony that eyewitness identification experts typically give at trial.

 RESOURCE
The literature on eyewitness identification is vast. Good places to start are the books by Elizabeth Loftus, *Eyewitness Identification* (Harvard University Press, 1996), and Edward Geiselman, *Eyewitness Expert Testimony* (Eagle Publishers, 1995). Both of these authors have conducted extensive research and testified as expert witnesses in hundreds of cases.

4. Is there reason to be skeptical of a crime victim who points to the defendant in court and says "I'm absolutely sure that's the robber, I'll never forget that face"?

Yes. Even the most convincing-sounding identifications can be mistaken because human memory does not act like a machine, accurately recording, storing, and retrieving images on demand. Like all of us, eyewitnesses construct and interpret what they see while events are ongoing. The process continues while images are stored in eyewitnesses' memories, and when they're called upon to "retrieve" the image when a police officer asks, "Do you recognize this person?" As one expert puts it, "Some memories are elaborations created by witnesses over time based on their own rationalizations for what must have happened and suggestions from others." (Geiselman, *Eyewitness Expert Testimony,* pp. 74-75, Eagle Publishers, 1995.)

5. What factors tend to cause eyewitnesses to identify the wrong person?

Some of the factors associated with mistaken identifications are matters of common sense and everyday experience. For example, all of us recognize the difficulty of making an accurate identification based on a "quick glance" as opposed to a "long look." Similarly, one does not have to be a cognitive scientist to know that lighting, distance, and an eyewitness's physical condition (for example, just awakened) can also cause an eyewitness to identify the wrong person. Below are some of the less obvious factors that have led eyewitnesses to make mistakes:

- **Stress.** While many people tend to believe that "stress sharpens the senses," research consistently shows that people who are under stress when they observe an event are more likely to misidentify a culprit.
- **Presence of a weapon.** Eyewitnesses confronted by a weapon are apt to focus on the weapon and not on the person holding it.
- **Confidence level.** Eyewitnesses who express great confidence in their identifications are no more accurate than those who admit to uncertainty. Confident eyewitnesses sometimes have higher error rates.
- **Cross-racial identification.** Eyewitnesses are less accurate when the person they are asked to identify is of a different race. This factor affects members of all racial groups.

- **Pressure to choose.** Eyewitnesses are more likely to make mistakes when they feel under pressure to make an identification, despite an admonishment that they don't have to make a choice.
- **Postevent influence.** Eyewitnesses are more likely to make mistakes when they rehash events with other observers. In these situations, witnesses may alter their memories so that they can be in agreement with others.
- **Transference.** Eyewitnesses may make a mistaken identification based on having seen the person they identify on a different occasion.
- **Multiple perpetrators.** Identification accuracy decreases as the number of people involved in an event increases.
- **Absence of an "employment boost."** Eyewitnesses who regularly interact with the public (store cashiers, bank tellers) are no better at making identifications than other people.

6. How do judges and jurors find out about factors that may lead to mistaken identifications?

Many cognitive psychologists not only do research experiments, but also qualify as expert witnesses and testify at trial. Based on the factors surrounding the commission of a crime, they can testify to how those factors might have affected eyewitness's ability to make an accurate identification.

Defendants who can't afford to hire a cognitive psychologist as an expert may ask a judge to appoint an expert at government expense. However, few court systems have enough money to allow judges to appoint eyewitness identification experts in every case in which their testimony is relevant. A less expensive option is for a judge to give a jury instruction that summarizes factors that might affect eyewitness' accuracy.

7. When they testify at trial, do eyewitness identification experts give an opinion about whether the identifications in that case are accurate?

No. Qualified experts can "educate the jury" by talking generally about factors that studies have shown tend to lead to inaccurate identifications. But experts have no way of assessing whether a particular eyewitness is accurate.

> **CASE EXAMPLE:** Sal Mander, a Caucasian male, is on trial for robbing Delores, a black female. After Delores identifies Sal as her attacker, Mander's eyewitness identification expert testifies about factors that existed at the time of the robbery that might cast doubt on Delores's ability to observe and recall accurately.
>
> **Question:** Can the expert testify that "In my opinion, there's less than a 50% chance that Delores's identification is accurate"?
>
> **Answer:** No. Eyewitness identification experts can talk about factors that in

experiments have been associated with mistaken identifications, but experts themselves admit that they cannot assess the accuracy of any particular identification.

Section III: Lineups

This section describes issues related to lineups, one of the most frequently used pretrial identification procedures.

8. Are live lineups more likely than showups and photo identifications to produce accuracy?

Generally, the answer seems to be "no." In experimental studies, assuming that eyewitnesses have a chance to view the actual perpetrator, their ability to make an accurate identification is no greater when they see the perpetrator in a lineup as opposed to another type of pretrial identification procedure.

Blind and Sequential Lineups

Erroneous eyewitness identifications are the leading cause of improper convictions. Blind and sequential lineups are two procedures that might reduce the risk of erroneous identifications.

In blind lineups, the police investigator conducting a lineup does not know which of the people in the lineup is thought to be the suspect. A lineup is "double-blind" if the investigator tells eyewitnesses that the investigator does not know whether the suspect is in the lineup. These procedures reduce the risk that an investigator will provide subconscious hints as to a suspect's identity.

With sequential lineups, eyewitnesses view individuals one at a time instead of in groups of five or six. Eyewitnesses must "pass" on one possible suspect before seeing another one. Sequential lineups may reduce the risk that an uncertain eyewitness will simply pick out the person in a group who most closely resembles the actual culprit.

9. In addition to witnesses and those in the lineup, who else may be present?

Police officers and often a prosecutor attend lineups. A defense attorney may be present as well, because a suspect who has been formally charged with a crime has a right to be represented by a lawyer at a lineup. (*Kirby v. Illinois,* U.S. Sup. Ct. 1972.) In large cities, public defender offices may have an attorney available to attend a lineup

24/7. The defense lawyer may also bring an investigator, a paralegal, a law clerk, or other observer to act as a witness in a later court hearing in case the lineup procedures are unfair to the defendant. To avoid having to provide a suspect with counsel, the police may try to convince a suspect to participate voluntarily in a lineup before charges are filed.

10. Can suspects be required to participate in a lineup?

Yes. The police can force arrested persons to participate in a lineup. Judges do not consider this a violation of the Fifth Amendment privilege against self-incrimination because in a lineup, suspects do not provide "testimony." (*U. S. v. Wade,* U.S. Sup. Ct. 1967.)

As a condition of granting bail or "release O.R." (see Chapter 5), a judge may require a suspect to participate in a lineup. However, being released from jail may reduce a suspect's chance of having to participate in a lineup because making the arrangements entails extra work for the police.

Unless they have a court order, the police cannot compel suspects who have not been arrested to participate in a lineup. The police may ask such suspects for voluntary participation, arguing that "this is our chance to clear you." While that may be true, even people who are confident of their innocence should think carefully and perhaps talk to a lawyer before agreeing to participate in a lineup voluntarily since witnesses can make mistakes. On the other hand, the police may regard refusal as evidence of guilt and investigate the suspect's activities more aggressively.

Types of Nontestimonial Evidence

Lineups are not the only nontestimonial activities in which arrested persons might have to participate. The police can compel arrestees to be photographed and to provide fingerprints and samples of their blood, hair, voice, handwriting, and other physical characteristics. (*Schmerber v. California*, U.S. Sup. Ct. 1967.) Arrestees can demand that qualified medical professionals perform invasive tests, and can also ask that their attorneys be present. Indigent persons who cannot afford to hire an attorney should ask the court to appoint one before testing takes place. An attorney's presence can help ensure that a test is done fairly and compassionately. For example, a police officer is unlikely to engage in improper coaching when a defense lawyer is looking on.

11. Can suspects demand that the police conduct a lineup?

Laws in many states give suspects the right to demand a lineup. Suspects and their attorneys should think carefully before demanding a lineup. The advantage of participating in a lineup is that if eyewitnesses are unable to make a positive identification, the police may drop their investigation of a suspect. Yet suspects risk a positive identification that strengthens the case against them.

12. During a lineup, do suspects see or have contact with eyewitnesses?

No. One-way mirrors or bright lights typically make it impossible for suspects to see witnesses. Even if contact is possible, suspects should not try to talk to witnesses. Even a plaintive "Tell them I'm innocent" may lead a witness to look extra hard at a suspect and identify the suspect as the perpetrator. The police may also construe a suspect's attempt to talk to a witness as intimidation and charge the suspect with a separate crime!

13. Can the police dictate what participants wear and say during a lineup?

Yes. Dressing the lineup participants as the culprit was dressed, and having them speak words that the culprit used, can increase the likelihood that an eyewitness's identification (or failure to identify) is accurate. Of course, for the lineup to be fair, conditions must be the same for all lineup participants.

CASE EXAMPLE: Ann Ekdote is arrested for burglarizing a home. Wilma, the next-door neighbor, tells the police that the burglar was a woman who wore large sunglasses, carried a big shopping bag, and yelled "It's all mine" while running out of the house. The police arrest Ann and ask Wilma to view her in a lineup.

Question: Can the police dress Ann in large sunglasses and have her carry a big shopping bag if the items match Wilma's description?

Answer: Yes, assuming all the lineup participants are displayed to the eye-witnesses in the same way.

Question: Can the police require each lineup participant to yell, "It's all mine"?

Answer: Yes. Refusal would not be a wise choice for Ann to make. Since the other participants will do as the police request, Ann is likely to draw more attention to herself by refusing to repeat the words (or whispering them). Moreover, the prosecution can use Ann's refusal as further evidence of her guilt at trial.

14. What happens after a lineup is over?

A positive identification makes it likely that a suspect will be formally charged with a crime (if charges have not already been filed). And the prosecution can bolster its case for plea bargaining purposes or at trial by showing that the eyewitness identified the defendant at a lineup.

An eyewitness's inability to make an ID doesn't necessarily mean that a suspect will be freed. The prosecutor may conduct additional lineups for other eyewitnesses, or may decide to move the case ahead based on forensic evidence such as fingerprints and DNA analysis.

15. What features might incline a judge to rule that a lineup was unfair?

Judges are likely to decide that lineups are unfair or impermissibly suggestive in the following types of circumstances:

- The suspect is the only person in the lineup who closely resembles the eye-witnesses' description of the perpetrator.
- The police drop not-so-subtle hints as to who the eyewitnesses should identify by handcuffing the suspect while the decoys' hands are free.
- The police allow eyewitnesses to confer with each other before or during the lineup.
- The police instruct an eyewitness along the lines of "Pay particular attention to number 3."

Events occurring before a lineup starts can also render it unfair. For example, assume that while the eyewitnesses are waiting outside the room where the lineup will take place, the police "accidentally" walk the handcuffed suspect past the eyewitnesses. Such a ploy would imper-missibly indicate who the officers think is guilty.

Whether mistakes such as these are purposeful or accidental, they taint the resulting identifications. When such mistakes occur, eyewitnesses should not be allowed to repeat their lineup identifications at trial. If a judge determines that a lineup was so impermissibly suggestive that it must have influenced eyewitnesses' recollections of the events themselves, eyewitnesses should not be permitted to identify defendants at trial either.

16. How can a defense lawyer's presence safeguard a suspect's rights at a lineup?

A defense lawyer's presence is likely to deter impermissibly suggestive police behavior. In addition, a defense lawyer may:

- **Object to unfair elements and suggest fairer ones.** For example, a lawyer who notices eyewitnesses starting to confer with each other might ask the police officers to separate them.
- **Make a record of unfair aspects for use in a later court challenge to the lineup identifications.** For example, the lawyer may take a photo of the eyewitnesses conferring with each other, or note that the angle of the lighting in the lineup room made the defendant in particular look sinister.
- **Observe the eyewitnesses' demeanor and attitudes.** The lawyer might get insights into how convincing the eyewitnesses might be at trial, and how confident they are in their own identifications. (Eyewitnesses who are uncertain at the time of a lineup sometimes retract their identifications before trial.)
- **Observe conversations that the eyewitnesses have with the police or a prosecutor.** Ostensibly, the attorney's task is to ensure that the eyewitnesses aren't improperly coached. But the attorney can also be alert to anything that witnesses say that might detract from the believability of their identifications. For example, an eyewitness may tell a police officer, "I'm as nervous now as during the holdup. It's really hard for

me to pay attention." That's the kind of statement that an attorney can mention to a prosecutor during plea bargaining discussions, because it indicates that the witness's identification may be mistaken. And if the case goes to trial, the defense attorney can cross-examine the witness as follows:

> **Question:** You were as nervous at the lineup as during the holdup, correct?
>
> **Answer:** I guess so, yes.
>
> **Question:** And that nervousness made it hard for you to pay attention to what was happening, right?
>
> **Answer:** I wouldn't say that.
>
> **Question:** Well, at the lineup, didn't you tell Officer Meachem that you were so nervous that it was hard for you to pay attention?
>
> **Answer:** Yes, I suppose I did say that.

- **Interview the eyewitnesses.** While defense attorneys are typically observers rather than active participants, they may have an opportunity to question the eyewitnesses. While victims and witnesses have no obligation to agree to an interview, the presence of police officers sometimes makes them comfortable talking to a defense attorney (especially if they hope that they can convince the lawyer that the suspect should plead guilty so they don't have to come back to court). If so, the attorney may gain helpful information about their ability to observe the culprit and how well the suspect corresponds to the descriptions given to the police.

17. I haven't been arrested, I don't want to pay for a lawyer, and the police ask me to "waive counsel" and participate in a lineup so they can "clear me." What should I do?

Innocent people may reasonably decide to participate voluntarily in a lineup without being represented by a lawyer, so long as they recognize the risk that eyewitnesses will mistakenly identify them. After all, the alternatives may be even more unpalatable, because police may continue to investigate their activities or resort to photo identifications. Reading through this chapter will help those who participate voluntarily to be aware and take note of factors making a lineup unfair.

CASE EXAMPLE: Warren Tees is an ex-felon who resembles the description of the man who held up a liquor store. The police lack probable cause to arrest Warren. However, they are suspicious of him because of his past record and they ask him to take part in a lineup. Warren knows that he did not hold up the liquor store, he does not have a right to appointed counsel, and he cannot afford to hire an attorney.

Question: Should Warren agree to participate in the lineup?

Answer: Warren has to decide for himself whether the risk that an unfair procedure will cause him to be mistakenly identified justifies the expense of a lawyer. If Warren refuses, the police may regard that as suspicious and keep investigating his whereabouts at the time of the robbery. Moreover, if Warren doesn't agree to a lineup the police can instead show the eyewitnesses a mug shot of Warren, which may create an even greater danger of mistaken identification.

Question: If Warren is mistakenly identified and arrested, might the judge be inclined to rule that the lineup was unfair because Warren wasn't represented by an attorney?

Answer: No. Since Warren voluntarily decided to go ahead without a lawyer, a judge will disregard that fact when considering the lineup's fairness.

18. How can suspects who don't have an attorney present protect their rights during a lineup?

Suspects who have already been charged with a crime have a right to have counsel present at a lineup, and should tell the police that they want a lawyer present, orally, and in writing if possible, before the lineup gets underway. Suspects should not sign a "Waiver of Attorney," which allows the police to conduct a lineup without having an attorney present. If the police refuse to wait for an attorney and go ahead with a lineup, the suspect should participate in it and later file a motion to suppress any resulting identification.

If no attorney is present, suspects can help protect their right to a fair lineup by paying attention to the lineup procedures and writing down as soon after the lineup as possible any elements that seemed unfair. For example, a suspect should make note of an unusually small number of participants. If a lineup consists of only three or four participants, for example, a judge may later decide that the prosecution can't offer evidence of an identification at trial. Likewise, suspects should be alert to ways in which they either looked or were dressed differently from the other participants, as well as to any conversations they overhear between the police and eyewitnesses.

Any notes that suspects make of their lineup observations should be marked "Privileged—For My Attorney Only" and not shown to anyone except a lawyer.

Section IV: Showups

Showups bring suspects and witnesses or victims together in face-to-face meetings.

19. What's the difference between a lineup and a showup?

With a showup, a witness or victim is confronted with only one person rather than with a group of people. Whereas lineups almost always take place in police stations, showups may take place in a police station or in the field, perhaps at the crime scene. The latter is especially likely when the police capture a possible suspect shortly after a crime has occurred.

20. Are showup identifications less reliable than those following lineups?

Research experiments have not demonstrated differences in reliability. Showups often take place soon after a crime, meaning that memory is less of a problem and witnesses are less likely to be influenced by others. On the other hand, witnesses may still be under great stress when the police return soon after a crime with a possible suspect in tow, and they may feel under pressure to make an identification regardless of what the police say.

21. Do suspects have a right to have an attorney present at showups?

Since showups almost always take place before charges are filed, suspects have no right to have an attorney present.

22. Might suspects have to participate in both a showup and a lineup?

Yes. The police might use a showup to avoid locking up a suspect whom eyewitnesses can't identify. If an identification is made and the suspect is charged with a crime, the police then might arrange for a lineup. The lineup can substantiate the showup identification, and determine if additional witnesses can also identify the suspect as the perpetrator.

Section V: Photo Identifications

Police may seek identifications by having victims and witnesses look at photographs rather than people.

23. What happens during photo identifications?

Typically, the police ask victims and witnesses to come to the police station and to try to identify a suspect by looking at photographs. The witnesses may look through large books of photos, or smaller groupings of six photos that police commonly call "six packs." The photos are almost always mug shots, so witnesses are aware that the people they are looking at have criminal records.

Tricking Suspects Into Confessing

Police officers sometimes tell suspects that they might as well confess, because witnesses have already identified them from a photo as the perpetrator. Even if no identification has taken place, a resulting confession will normally be admissible in evidence because police are allowed to use this type of trickery. See Chapter 1.

---

24. Why do the police use photo identifications?

The police use photo identifications when they lack probable cause to make an arrest. Since the process is nonintrusive, the police can display photos to eyewitnesses whether or not they have any information tying people to a crime. Thus, photo identifications are in essence a search for a suspect.

25. Do suspects have a right to have an attorney present at a photo identification?

No. (*U.S. v. Ash,* U.S. Sup. Ct. 1973.) Photo identifications invariably take place before charges are filed, and even suspects have no right to be present.

26. If neither suspects nor attorneys are present, how can the fairness of photo identifications be challenged?

The police are supposed to keep records of what photographs are shown to eyewitnesses, and the order in which they are shown. The defense can see the photos themselves prior to trial. Thus, if a photo display is unfair (for example, the defendant was the only person in a six pack who was fully facing the camera or was the only person whose picture was in color), the defense can seek to suppress the identification.

The photo identification process is informal, and no transcripts of conversations between police officers and eyewitnesses are made. To the extent that the police unfairly guide eyewitnesses to identify a suspect, the defense can find this out only by asking the participants what was said and relying on them to answer completely and accurately.

Section VI: Motions to Suppress Identifications

A motion to suppress an identification is a common defense method of seeking a judge's ruling that a pretrial identification is inadmissible in evidence because the process was unfair. More information about motions (including samples) is provided in Chapter 19.

27. By what standard do judges decide whether a pretrial identification procedure was unfair?

The general rule is that a pretrial identification is admissible in evidence unless the procedure was "so unnecessarily suggestive of the defendant's guilt that it created a substantial likelihood of misidentification." (*Neil v. Biggers,* U.S. Sup. Ct. 1972.) This standard makes it difficult for defendants to knock out prior identifications. As a result, juries are likely to hear evidence of pretrial identifications. Defendants typically bring up the same factors they raised in an unsuccessful attempt to get a judge to suppress an identification when arguing to jurors that an identification is unworthy of belief.

28. Do judges apply the same standard to all the pretrial identification procedures?

No. The burden is even higher for defendants seeking to suppress a showup identification. A showup identification is admissible in evidence unless there is a "very substantial likelihood of irreparable misidentification." (*Simmons v. U.S.,* U.S.

Sup. Ct. 1968.) The factors that judges look at when determining the validity of a showup include:

- How carefully did an eyewitness observe a suspect during the crime itself?
- How closely does the suspect match the description that the eyewitness gave the police?
- How confident was the eyewitness that the suspect was the perpetrator? (The eyewitness identification research described above casts doubt on the legitimacy of this factor.)
- How much time elapsed between the crime and the showup?

29. What options does a judge have when ruling on a motion to suppress an identification?

Judges' rulings on motions to suppress identifications typically consist of one of the following:

- When eyewitnesses identify suspects prior to trial more than once, a judge may limit how many identifications the witnesses can refer to at trial even if all the procedures were fair. For example, if an eyewitness identifies a suspect at a showup and later in a lineup, the judge may rule that the witness may testify to only one of the identifications (in addition to the in-court identification during trial, of course). This option means that prosecutors can't automatically "pile on" identification testimony.

Sample Waiver of Rights

WAIVER OF RIGHTS
LOS ANGELES MUNICIPAL COURT

DIVISION _____   CASE # _____   DATE _____

_____   _____   _____
Defendant's Name – print   Attorney's Name   Judge

DEFENDANT: PUT YOUR INITIALS IN EACH SET OF BRACKETS IF YOU HAVE READ AND UNDERSTAND THE STATEMENTS WHICH APPEAR BEFORE IT.

1. CHARGES. I understand that I am charged with the offenses of _____ and   [   ]
                                                                                   [if applicable]

    further a prior conviction of _____ on _____ .
                                              [if applicable]   [if applicable]

2. PENALTY. I understand that the maximum penalty for the offense(s) charged is _____   [   ]
    and the consequences are _____ .
                                                      [if applicable]

3A. WAIVER OF ATTORNEY. I understand that I have the right to be represented or assisted by an attorney   [   ]
    at all stages of this case and that if I cannot afford an attorney, one will be appointed at no cost to me.
    I understand that by proceeding without an attorney and representing myself instead, that there may be
    certain defenses of which I may be unaware and fail to assert which an attorney could use to acquit me. I
    understand that it is almost always unwise to proceed without an attorney, that I will not be shown any special
    favors by this court or the experienced prosecutor and that if I make a mistake in these proceedings, I cannot
    later claim that I made a mistake in deciding to represent myself. I give up my right to an attorney.

                                                              OR

3B. DISCUSSION WITH ATTORNEY. I have discussed my case with my attorney. We discussed the rights I am   [   ]
    giving up by my plea, the elements of the offense(s), possible legal and factual defenses available and the
    possible consequences of my plea.

4. JURY TRIAL. I understand that I have the right to a speedy and public <u>trial by jury</u>. I give up this right.   [   ]

5. COURT TRIAL. I understand that if the prosecution agrees. I may have a <u>court trial</u> instead of a jury. I give   [   ]
    up this right.

6. CONFRONTATION. I understand that I have the right to <u>confront and cross-examine</u> the witnesses against   [   ]
    me at trial. I give up this right.

7. SELF-INCRIMINATION. I understand that I have the constitutional right not to incriminate me and that   [   ]
    <u>I may remain silent</u>, and that by pleading guilty or no contest I am incriminating myself. I give up this right.

8. RIGHT TO SUBPOENA AND PRODUCE EVIDENCE. I understand that <u>I have the right to testify</u> in my own
    behalf and to use the power of the court to subpoena witnesses and produce other evidence for me at the
    trial. I give up this right.

9. PLEA OF NO CONTEST. I understand that a plea of "no contest" <u>is the same as a "guilty" plea</u>.   [   ]

10. PROBATION. I understand that the court may place me on probation instead of imposing a sentence; that   [   ]
    if I accept probation with its terms and conditions, the maximum sentence can be imposed if I am later
    found to have disobeyed any terms or conditions of probation.

11. CITIZENSHIP. I understand that if I am not now a United States citizen, a guilty or no contest pleas to the   [   ]
    charge(s) can result in my deportation or denial of immigration or naturalization.

12. There have been no promises or threats made to me to cause me to plead. I am aware of and understand   [   ]
    what I am charged with, the elements of the offenses, the defenses available to me and consequences of
    my plea. I have initialed the above paragraphs. I signed below to show my understanding of same and my
    waiver of rights.

13. I now plead _____ to the charge(s).   [   ]

14. I understand that the above rights apply with equal force to any priors alleged. I expressly and explicitly give   [   ]
    up each and every one of the above rights and admit to the following priors:

    _____
    _____

15. I stipulate to a commissioner for sentencing.   [   ]

    DATE: _____   SIGNED: _____
                                                      SEE REVERSE

CRIM. M-41 (10/94)

- A judge may rule that an eyewitness may not testify to a pretrial identification because it was conducted unfairly. For example, a judge may rule that a witness cannot testify to identifying a suspect at a showup because a police officer told the witness that "We're confident that this is the right guy."

- A judge may rule that an unfair identification procedure so tainted an eyewitness's memory that the witness cannot testify to the pretrial identification and also cannot identify the defendant at trial. If such a ruling eliminates the prosecution's only evidence of a perpetrator's identity, the ruling requires that charges be dismissed. Most police officers know and obey the rules, however, so such extreme rulings are rare.

Booking and Bail:
Checking In and Out of Jail

M any suspects are taken to jail upon arrest. Usually their first priority is to get out. Other than the old movie method of ordering a cake with a file in it, the usual method of leaving jail after arrest is posting bail. This chapter concentrates on the bail system and its alternative to Monopoly's "Get Out of Jail Free" card, "Own Recognizance Release" (also known as "Release O.R.").

Section I: The Booking Process

This section is about the procedures used by a jail booking officer to identify arrested persons and prepare them for incarceration.

1. What's likely to happen when I arrive at the jail after arrest?

As fans of crime dramas know, defendants taken to jail are normally booked shortly after arrival. Few booking officers were trained behind the reception desk of a luxury hotel. However, just as hotel registration cards provide information about hotel guests, so too do booking records provide information about the people detained in jail.

Since booking creates an official arrest record, individuals who are arrested who can post bail immediately often can't be released until after the booking process. Even suspects who are given citations in lieu of being taken to jail often must go through a booking process within a few days of their arrest.

Why Some Suspects Are Taken to Jail While Others Remain Free

While many suspects are taken to jail upon arrest, others receive citations to appear in court and are allowed to remain free in the interim. The factors that influence a police officer's decision about taking an arrestee to jail include:

- **The seriousness of the crime.** Suspects arrested for petty misdemeanors (such as shoplifting) are less likely to be jailed than those charged with felonies or crimes of violence.
- **The suspect's mental and physical condition.** Police officers often jail suspects who cause a disturbance during the arrest process. Likewise, suspects who are a danger to themselves or others (such as a suspect who is under the influence of drugs or alcohol) are likely to be jailed upon arrest.
- **Jail conditions.** Many jails are overcrowded, forcing police to cite and release suspects who might otherwise be taken to jail.
- **Police department policies.** Police officers often have discretion to decide whether to jail a suspect, and each police department sets its own policies.

2. What usually happens during the booking process?

The booking process is highly impersonal, and typically includes the following steps:

Step 1: Recording the suspect's name and the crime for which the suspect was arrested. In olden days, this information became part of a handwritten police blotter; now virtually all booking records are computerized.

Step 2: Taking a "mug shot," perhaps the only photo guaranteed to be less flattering than the one on the suspect's driver's license.

Use of Mug Shots

Mug shots have a variety of possible uses. For instance, a mug shot can help to determine which of two people with the same name was arrested. A mug shot can also help to establish a suspect's physical condition at the time of arrest. The suspect's physical condition at arrest can be relevant to a claim of police use of unlawful force or to whether the suspect had been in an altercation before being arrested.

Step 3: Taking the suspect's clothing and personal property (such as a wallet, purse, or keys) into police custody. At a suspect's request, some booking officers allow the suspect to hold on to small personal items like a wristwatch. Any articles taken from the suspect must be returned upon release from jail, unless they constitute contraband or evidence of a crime.

CASE EXAMPLE: Sticky Fingers is arrested for stealing a calculator. The police seize the calculator at the scene of the arrest. During the booking process, the police find in Fingers's backpack a packet of illegal drugs and a stolen camera.

Question: Will any of these items be returned to Fingers upon his release?

Answer: No. The calculator and the camera are evidence of the crime of shoplifting. The drugs are illegal contraband; the police can take them regardless of whether drug charges are filed against Fingers.

Arrested Suspects Should Get Receipts for Personal Items

During booking, suspects should request a receipt for all personal items taken by a booking officer. The receipt should describe the unique characteristics of any items of special value (for instance, "one Swiss Army knife, autographed by the Swiss Army"). Insisting on a written receipt is one way suspects can ensure that the police ultimately return all confiscated personal property and clothing.

Step 4: Taking fingerprints. Fingerprints are a standard part of a booking record, and are also normally entered into a nationwide database maintained by the FBI and accessible by most local, state, and federal police agencies. Comparing fingerprints left at the scene of a crime to those already in the database helps police officers identify perpetrators of crimes.

Step 5: Conducting a full body search. Police officers routinely make cursory pat-down inspections at the time of arrest. Far more intrusive (and to many people deeply humiliating) is the strip search that is often part of the booking process. To prevent weapons and drugs from entering a jail, booking officers frequently require arrestees to remove all their clothing and submit to a full body search.

Step 6: Checking for warrants. The booking officer checks to see if an arrestee has any other charges pending, ranging from unpaid parking tickets to murder charges in other states. Suspects with warrants pending are normally not released on bail.

Step 7: Health screening. To protect the health and safety of jail officials and other inmates, the booking process may include X-rays (to detect tuberculosis) and blood tests (to detect sexually transmitted diseases such as gonorrhea and AIDS).

CAUTION
Additional criminal charges can result from items found during the booking process. While searching the suspect's clothing, backpacks, and body cavities, police officers sometimes find drugs or stolen merchandise. Any such items can become the basis for additional criminal charges.

3. How long does booking take?

At its slowest, the booking process may take hours to complete. Its length depends on how many of the standard booking procedures are conducted, the number of arrestees being booked at the same time, and the number of police officers involved in the booking process.

4. Am I entitled to legal representation during the booking process?

No, although defendants in criminal cases have a constitutional right to legal representation at every critical stage of the proceeding. (See Chapter 7.) Courts regard booking as a routine administrative procedure, not a critical stage in a criminal proceeding.

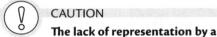

CAUTION
The lack of representation by a lawyer during booking can damage the defense case. For many suspects, the booking process is impersonal, long, and humiliating, which leaves them extremely vulnerable. With no attorney to provide comfort and advice, people being booked are prone to start talking to the police officers who suddenly hold sway over them. These voluntary statements can be used as evidence in court. Therefore, regardless of the psychological pressures of booking, suspects are well advised to say nothing about their case until they've spoken to an attorney.

Free Phone Calls

Laws in many states allow suspects to make one or more free local calls as soon as booking is completed. See, for example, Cal. Penal Code § 851.5. Suspects typically call attorneys, bail bond sellers, or friends and relatives, in an effort to bail out or at least talk to a friendly person. However, suspects need to be very careful about what they say over the phone, because police officers and other people may overhear their conversations or even monitor the calls.

CASE EXAMPLE: Cliff Hangar is arrested and taken to jail. He refuses to participate in the booking process, demanding that the police let him phone for a lawyer.

Question: Do the police have to allow Cliff to call a lawyer?

Answer: No. Cliff has no right to an attorney or even to phone for an attorney until the completion of the booking process. Until then, Cliff should just answer the booking officer's questions, and should not talk about his case.

Section II: Arranging for Bail

This section is about bail—what it is and how to arrange for it.

5. What is bail?

Bail is cash or its equivalent (such as a bail bond) that a court accepts in exchange for allowing a defendant to remain at liberty until the conclusion of the case. Bail creates a financial incentive for defendants to make all required court appearances. Should a defendant fail to appear in court, the bail is forfeited (that is, the court keeps the cash or collects on the bond) and the judge issues an arrest warrant. Bail jumping (not returning to court when required) is itself a crime.

6. What will courts and jails accept as bail?

Bail can be provided in any of the following ways:

- By cash or check for the full amount of the bail. For instance, if the police or a court set bail at $1,000, a defendant may post (pay) this full amount.
- By purchasing a bond from a bail bond seller, who typically charges a nonrefundable premium of about 10% of the amount of bail. For example, if the police or a court set bail at $1,000, a defendant can usually purchase a bail bond for $100. The bail bond seller has to forfeit the full bail amount to the court should a defendant who purchased a bail bond fail to appear in court.

Collateral for a Bail Bond

Often, bail bond sellers ask for collateral in addition to the cost of the bail bond. This means that the bond seller must be given a financial interest in enough real property (such as a house) or personal property (such as a car) to cover the bond seller's loss should the arrested person jump bail, leaving the bond seller liable for the full amount of bail. Collateral adds to the cost of a bail bond by tying up the collateralized property until the case concludes. This means, for example, a person is not free to sell property while it serves as collateral. Moreover, bond sellers often refuse to do business with an arrested person who lacks the ability to post collateral.

- By depositing with the court property worth at least the full amount of the bail in some courts. For example, if the police or court set bail at $1,000, and a suspect owns a fancy watch worth at least that amount, the defendant may be able to use the watch to post bail.

7. Am I better off buying a bail bond or posting the full cash amount?

For defendants who make all scheduled court appearances, posting full cash bail is cheaper than buying a bail bond. At the conclusion of the case, the defendant who posts full cash bail gets the money back (sometimes less a small administrative fee). Cash bail is refunded regardless of whether a defendant is convicted after a trial, pleads guilty before trial, or gets the charges dismissed. But defendants who buy a bail bond are out the purchase price regardless of the outcome of a case. The cost of a bail bond is a bail bond seller's nonrefundable fee. Moreover, a bail bond may be valid only for a limited time—perhaps a year. If a case drags on past that time, the defendant may have to pay a second fee.

Court-Financed Bail

Some states offer a hybrid between posting full cash bail and buying a bail bond from a private bail bond seller. Under the hybrid system, a qualifying arrested person pays a fee of 10% of the full cash bail directly to the court; collateral may also be required. Unlike when a bail bond is purchased from a private seller, the 10% fee (less an administrative charge) is eventually returned if the arrested person makes all required court appearances. Of course, if a defendant fails to appear at a required hearing, the defendant is liable for the full cash bail amount, as well as being subject to rearrest and a new criminal charge of bail jumping.

CASE EXAMPLE: Cala Mari is arrested for drunk driving and taken to jail. Bail is set at $1,000. Cala posts this amount and makes all required court appearances. She eventually pleads guilty to reckless driving.

Question: At the end of the case, what happens to the bail money?

Answer: All (or almost all) of the bail money will be returned to Cala. By contrast, had Cala paid $100 for a bail bond, the bail bond seller would not return that money to her.

8. Do I need to hire a lawyer to arrange for a bail bond?

No. Arrested persons can arrange for bail themselves. They can either post cash bail personally, or phone a bail bond seller and arrange for a bond directly with the bond seller.

9. Can relatives or friends pay my bail?

Yes. Relatives or friends can come to a jail or court and post cash bail for an arrested person, or purchase a bond from a bail bond seller.

10. How much bail will I have to pay? Who decides?

Judges ordinarily set bail at a suspect's first court appearance after an arrest, which may be either a bail hearing or an arraignment. Judges normally adhere to standard practices—for example, setting bail in the amount of $500 for nonviolent petty misdemeanors. However, judges can raise or lower the standard bail, or waive bail altogether and grant Release O.R., according

Is It Wise for Relatives and Friends to Post Bail?

A true test of a relative's or friend's trust in a person is when that person calls from jail and wants the relative or friend to post bail. A relative or friend who posts full cash bail for an arrested person may lose it all if the arrested person jumps bail. And if the friend or relative purchased a bail bond and the arrested person jumps bail, the bond seller can sue them to collect the full amount of the bond.

Even if the arrested person makes all required appearances, the person who buys a bail bond is out the bond seller's fee, and may have property tied up as collateral. Finally, people who post bail for a suspect may have to appear in court and answer questions under oath as to where they got the money used to post the bail. Thus, before agreeing to post bail for an arrested person, friends or relatives have to consider their own financial needs, the risk of the arrested person jumping bail, and the likelihood that the arrested person will repay any out-of-pocket costs (such as the bond seller's fee).

to the circumstances of an individual case. (See Section III for more on Release O.R.)

In addition to the seriousness of the charged crime, the amount of bail usually depends on factors such as a defendant's past criminal record, whether a defendant is employed, and whether a defendant has close ties to relatives and the community.

Judges may legally deny bail altogether in some circumstances. For example, if another jurisdiction has placed a warrant (hold) on a defendant, a judge is likely to keep the defendant in custody at least long enough for the other jurisdiction to pursue its charge. And bail may be denied to a defendant who is likely to flee the jurisdiction before the case concludes.

In many areas of the country, defendants can post bail with the police even before they are brought to court for a bail hearing or an arraignment. Many jails have posted bail schedules, which specify bail amounts for common crimes. An arrested defendant can obtain release immediately after booking by paying the amount of bail set forth in the jailhouse bail schedule.

> **CASE EXAMPLE:** Peter is arrested and charged with managing a large prostitution ring. He is a naturalized American citizen born in Spain, and his family still lives in Barcelona. While searching Peter after his arrest, the police found that he was carrying a passport and $5,000 in cash.
>
> **Question:** Is the judge likely to release Peter on bail?

Answer: No. Peter's family background and the fact that he was carrying a passport and a large amount of cash suggest that Peter may flee to Spain if he is released on bail. Unless Peter can explain why he was carrying his passport and an unusually large amount of cash, and can also demonstrate strong ties to the local community, a judge is likely to deny his request for bail.

Duty Judges

As an alternative or in addition to jailhouse bail schedules, some areas have duty judges. A duty judge is available to fix bail over the phone, without the necessity for a formal court hearing. Like a jailhouse bail schedule, the availability of a duty judge is an option for arrested persons who are anxious to bail out of jail before going to court.

11. What are the typical rates in a bail schedule?

Bail schedules can vary considerably according to locality, type of crime, and residency. Below are portions of recent bail schedules from Sacramento County, California, and Brevard County, Florida. The schedules demonstrate what law enforcement personnel consider to be the relatively serious and less serious offenses, and provide a rough idea of how much bail might be required for some common crimes in your area.

As a general rule, bail for offenses classified as felonies is five to ten times the bail required for misdemeanors. (See Chapter 6 for more on the differences between felonies and misdemeanors.) Also, the more serious and dangerous the crime, the higher the amount of bail is likely to be. As a general rule, a jailhouse bail schedule is inflexible. The police will not accept bail other than as set forth in a schedule; suspects wanting to pay less must go before a judge.

> **CASE EXAMPLE:** Rand Omly is arrested and jailed for possession of cocaine. Using a bail schedule such as the one above, the police refuse to release Omly unless he can post bail in the amount of $10,000. Omly argues that his bail should be lower because he has never previously been arrested, and he has a family and a job.
>
> **Question:** Will the police consider reducing the amount of Omly's bail?
>
> **Answer:** Probably not. A bail schedule applies equally to all suspects, regardless of their individual circumstances. Omly will have to wait to go before a judge and argue his special circumstances.

Sacramento County, California, Bail Schedule—Selected Offenses	
Offense	**Bail**
Bribery of a Judge or Juror	$30,000
Murder	No bail
Vehicular Manslaughter	$30,000
Vehicular Manslaughter (While Intoxicated)	$50,000
Rape	$50,000
Kidnapping	$50,000
Robbery	$25,000
Robbery (of Residence)	$50,000
Assault With a Deadly Weapon	$10,000
Child Abuse	$10,000
Spousal Abuse	$25,000
Bookmaking	$3,000
Arson (Causing Injury)	$30,000
Resisting Arrest (Causing Injury)	$10,000
Burglary	$20,000
Smuggling Weapon Into Jail	$50,000
Hit-and-Run (Personal Injury)	$15,000
Car Theft	$10,000
Drunk Driving (Personal Injury)	$25,000
Possession of Cocaine for Sale (up to ½ oz.)	$10,000
Possession of Cocaine for Sale (½ oz. to 2 oz.)	$50,000
Possession of Cocaine for Sale (2 oz. to 1 lb.)	$75,000
Possession of Cocaine for Sale (1 lb. to 3 lbs.)	$150,000
Possession of Marijuana for Sale (under 2 lb.)	$5,000

Brevard County, Florida, Bail Schedule—Selected Offenses				
	Residency			
Offense	Local	Florida	Out-of State	Out-of Country
Capital Felony	No Bail	No Bail	No Bail	No Bail
Life Felony	No Bail	No Bail	No Bail	No Bail
First Degree Felony Punishable by Life	No Bail	No Bail	No Bail	No Bail
Attempt/Solicitation/Conspiracy to Commit First or Second Degree Murder	No Bail	No Bail	No Bail	No Bail
Third Degree Murder	$15,000	$20,000	$25,000	$35,000
Manslaughter	$15,000	$20,000	$25,000	$35,000
Vehicular Homicide	$15,000	$20,000	$25,000	$35,000
Hit-and-Run Involving Death or Personal Injury	$5,000	$8,000	$10,000	$15,000
Armed Robbery or Burglary	No Bail	No Bail	No Bail	No Bail
Burglary With an Assault or Battery	No Bail	No Bail	No Bail	No Bail
Carjacking	No Bail	No Bail	No Bail	No Bail
Kidnapping	No Bail	No Bail	No Bail	No Bail
Drug Trafficking and Conspiracy to Traffic in Drugs	No Bail	No Bail	No Bail	No Bail
Domestic Violence	No Bail	No Bail	No Bail	No Bail
Burglary of an Occupied Dwelling	$10,000	$15,000	$25,000	$30,000
All Other Non-Armed Burglaries	$5,000	$8,000	$10,000	$15,000
Sexual Offenses—First or Second Degree Felony	$35,000	$40,000	$50,000	$60,000
DUI Involving Personal Injury	$5,000	$8,000	$10,000	$15,000
DUI Manslaughter	$15,000	$20,000	$25,000	$35,000
Non-Specifically Enumerated Felonies				
First Degree Felony (Violent)	$8,000	$10,000	$15,000	$25,000
First Degree Felony (Nonviolent)	$4,500	$6,000	$8,000	$15,000
Second Degree Felony (Violent)	$5,000	$8,000	$10,000	$15,000
Second Degree Felony (Nonviolent)	$2,000	$3,000	$4,500	$8,000

Why Police Often Charge the Most Serious Crime Possible

Unfortunately for many suspects who want to bail out of jail quickly, the police tend to report the most serious criminal charge that can possibly be supported by the facts at their disposal. For instance, whenever possible the police may treat possession of a small amount of marijuana (a misdemeanor in most states) as an arrest for possession of marijuana with intent to sell (a felony in all states). Even though such a charge will almost certainly be reduced to a misdemeanor later in the case, it is a felony for the purposes of the bail schedule, and bail will be set accordingly.

12. Are there times when a person under arrest is better off waiting for a judge to set bail than using the posted bail schedule?

Yes. Bail schedules treat all arrested persons alike. But an arrested person with no previous arrests and strong ties to the community (for example, a job and family) may convince the judge to set much lower bail than the bail schedule provides—or even to grant own recognizance release. (See Section III.) In this situation, by remaining in jail a day or two before appearing in court, an arrested person might save considerable money. For example, if the bail schedule fixes bail at $10,000, a bond will cost $1,000

in a nonrefundable fee. If a day later the judge fixes bail at $1,000, the bond would then cost only $100. This means that by waiting for the judge to act, the defendant (or the defendant's family or friends) would save $900.

Of course, each individual suspect, and the suspect's family and friends, will have to weigh the opportunity to save money by asking the judge to lower the bail against the hardship of remaining in jail one hour longer than is absolutely necessary.

13. How soon after my arrest will I be able to ask a judge to lower my bail or release me O.R.?

Most jurisdictions require that an arrested person be taken "without unnecessary delay before the nearest available ... magistrate." (For instance, see Federal Rule of Criminal Procedure 5.) This first court appearance will be either a bail hearing or an arraignment, or both. In no event should more than 48 hours elapse between the time of booking and the time the suspect is brought to court—not counting weekends and holidays. This weekends and holidays exception unfortunately means that a suspect arrested on a Friday afternoon may not see a judge until Tuesday, or even Wednesday, if Monday is a holiday. On the other hand, a suspect arrested in the morning may sometimes be able to see a judge that afternoon if the prosecutor's office is quick with its paperwork. (See Chapter 6.)

14. Can I represent myself when seeking a lower bail or release O.R.?

Yes, but suspects typically benefit from legal representation at a bail hearing. Experienced attorneys know the factors that particular judges find important when considering a request for low bail or O.R. release. In addition, attorneys normally discuss cases with prosecutors before the bail hearing, and sometimes can assure the judge that the charges are not as serious as they look on paper. Finally, a simple reality is that judges often take attorneys' arguments more seriously than those of self-represented defendants.

15. I'm representing myself at my bail hearing. What can I say that might convince the judge to lower my bail or release me O.R.?

Just like lawyers, self-represented defendants seeking lower or no bail should try to convince the judge of these facts:

- The defendant doesn't pose a physical danger to the community. Obviously, this argument is mostly available to defendants charged with nonviolent crimes.
- The defendant has no previous criminal record, or has a minimal past record and made all required appearances.
- The defendant has strong ties to the community, such as a family and employment. (Judges are often impressed when family members and an employer personally appear to support a defendant at a bail hearing.)

16. What can I do if the judge rules against me on bail?

If you haven't already, hire a lawyer. Judges can always reconsider bail, and may lower bail when they receive information—from an attorney—that they were previously unaware of.

17. Are there limits on how much bail a judge can require?

Yes and no. The Eighth Amendment to the United States Constitution (which is binding on all states) requires that the amount of bail not be excessive. What this means is that bail should not be a way to raise money for the state, or to punish a person for being suspected of committing a crime. Nor can the police use bail to keep a suspect in jail simply to give themselves more time to gather evidence. Because a suspect is innocent until proven guilty, the amount of bail should be no more than reasonably necessary to keep the suspect from fleeing the jurisdiction before the case is over.

Despite these policies, many judges set unaffordably high bail in some types of cases to keep suspected offenders in jail pending trial. Judges can lose elections when defendants they've released on bail commit new crimes, but rarely take political heat for keeping a suspect behind bars. High bail is particularly likely when a defendant poses a danger to the community or has committed an offense against a child. A judge may also set higher bail if a defendant is likely to flee the jurisdiction before trial, or if the defendant has a prior criminal record. Although some legal commentators argue that preventive detention—keeping a defendant in jail out of fear that the defendant is dangerous—violates the Eighth Amendment, the U.S. Supreme Court upheld the practice in *U.S. v. Salerno,* U.S. Sup. Ct. 1987.

Because of terrorism concerns, foreign nationals may face special obstacles in the bail-setting process. Arrested foreign nationals may need to contact a lawyer with experience in both criminal law and immigration issues, and may also want to contact their country's consulate.

> **CASE EXAMPLE 1:** Rex Kars is charged with felony hit-and-run driving. At a bail setting hearing, the judge sets bail at $5,000. Kars argues that the bail is excessive, as he cannot afford to post that amount in cash nor does he have sufficient collateral to purchase a bail bond.
>
> **Question:** Is this argument likely to convince the judge to lower the bail?
>
> **Answer:** No. While a judge can consider Kars's personal history and financial ability when setting bail, the fact that Kars cannot afford to pay the bail that is set does not make it excessive.

> **CASE EXAMPLE 2:** Holly Woode is arrested for stealing two blouses from a clothing store (petty theft). During a bail hearing, the judge tells Holly, "In my opinion, once a petty thief always a petty thief. If I let you out on bail, you'll probably just go on stealing." With that, the judge denies bail to Holly. (Alternatively, the judge sets bail so high that Holly clearly has no way of paying it.)
>
> **Question:** Is the judge's action proper?
>
> **Answer:** No, the judge's decision is arbitrary and excessive. The crime that Holly is accused of committing is not one of violence, so preventive detention is unnecessary. Moreover, the judge's comments are based only on the judge's predisposition, not on information about Holly. Holly can file a petition for habeas corpus asking another judge to set reasonable bail. (See Chapter 23.)

18. Once the judge sets bail, can it be changed?

Yes. Judges have the power to change the amount of bail if new information emerges.

> **CASE EXAMPLE 1:** Phil Errup, an unemployed electrician, is charged with assault and battery. A judge initially sets bail in the amount of $10,000, commenting that Phil's lack of employment makes him a risk to flee. Phil cannot afford the bail, so he remains in jail. A week later, an

electrical contractor agrees to hire Phil to work on a job, and to continue to employ Phil at least until the charges are finally resolved.

Question: Might this information affect Phil's bail status?

Answer: Yes. Since the judge who originally set bail was influenced in part by Phil's unemployment, the job is a changed circumstance which might incline the judge (or a different judge) to lower the bail, since having a job makes Phil less likely to jump bail. Phil can file a Motion for Reconsideration of Bail, and ask the electrical contractor either to attend the court hearing or send a letter to the court verifying the job offer.

CASE EXAMPLE 2: Jenna Furr is charged with possession of cocaine. A judge initially sets bail in the amount of $1,000. Jenna posts bail and is released from jail. A week later, the district attorney receives new information that six months earlier, Jenna had been charged with possession of illegal drugs in another state, and had fled the state before the case was over.

Question: Might this information affect Jenna's bail status?

Answer: Yes. Upon the district attorney's request, the judge might schedule a new bail hearing, order Jenna to attend, and increase her bail or revoke it altogether.

19. Can my release on bail be accompanied by restrictions on my behavior?

Yes. Judges have the power to place restrictions on defendants as a condition of releasing them on bail. For example, depending on the offense charged, a defendant may have to agree to:

- abstain from alcohol, drugs, or weapons
- avoid contact with a victim or witnesses
- report regularly to a law enforcement officer
- undergo a medical or psychological counseling program
- maintain or seek employment
- maintain or seek an educational program, and
- remain in the custody of a designated relative or other person.

20. What happens if I violate a condition of bail?

Judges can revoke the bail of a suspect who violates a condition of bail. For example, if a suspect who is ordered to enroll in a counseling program fails to do so, the judge can revoke the suspect's bail and issue a warrant for the suspect's arrest. Or, if the judge does not consider the violation to be overly serious, the judge may simply raise the amount of bail (or require bail from a suspect previously released O.R.).

21. What happens if I'm out on bail and I don't show up in court?

This is a big no-no. Defendants who fail to appear at a scheduled court appearance may suffer both financial and criminal penalties. That is, a violator will forfeit the amount of bail and also, in most states, can be charged with a separate crime. Perhaps most seriously, if the person is ever arrested and detained again in the future—once the current case is resolved—the bail in that future case probably will be impossibly high, because the judge in the future case will consider the person a bail risk.

> **CASE EXAMPLE:** Della Ware is free on $1,000 bail after posting the full cash amount with the court. The judge orders Della to attend a pretrial settlement conference. However, Della fails to attend and does not explain her absence to her lawyer.
>
> **Question:** What is the likely result?
>
> **Answer:** Della will forfeit the entire $1,000 to the court. Della may also find herself charged with the crime of bail jumping, in addition to the crime she was charged with in the first place. A warrant will go out for her arrest, and when she's picked up neither the police nor a judge or magistrate are likely to offer her a second chance to post bail.

What if defendants such as Della fail to make a required court appearance after purchasing a bail bond for $100? Since the bail bond seller probably required her to post collateral, the bond seller may sell her car or fancy watch or whatever property she used as collateral. In addition, if the collateral is insufficient, the bond seller can hire a bounty hunter to find and arrest Della, and bring her back to the court's jurisdiction so that the bond seller no longer has to pay the full amount of the bail to the court—or gets the money back if it has already been paid. So by skipping bail, Della has two groups after her—the police and the bail bond seller/bounty hunter. All in all, once Della bails out, she had better make all her required court appearances.

22. The police have a strong case against me and I'm probably going to do some jail time anyway. Why bother bailing out?

If a person is convicted of a crime and given a jail sentence, the sentence will be reduced by the number of days that the person was detained in jail prior to conviction. (This is called "time served.") Thus, a suspect who expects to receive a jail sentence may consider saving the cost of a bail bond and in effect begin serving the sentence prior to conviction.

From an economic standpoint, forgoing bail in such a situation may make sense. But in practice it's usually to a suspect's benefit to seek pretrial release. One obvious reason is that the suspect may be wrong about receiving a jail sentence upon conviction. Many jails are overcrowded, and suspects who in the past might have been incarcerated are now allowed to remain free even if they are convicted.

A second reason to bail out is that jail conditions are normally worse for inmates awaiting sentencing than they are for inmates who have already been sentenced. For example, people serving jail sentences have access to exercise facilities and the jail's law library, and may be given work opportunities and other privileges. Prior to sentencing, none of these things may be true.

Third, defendants who are released prior to trial run no danger of making statements to jailers or even other inmates that can be used against them if their cases ultimately go to trial.

Fourth, prosecutors usually move cases along more slowly when defendants are not in custody. As a result, witnesses can disappear and cases can get stale, so that bailed-out defendants often wind up with better deals. As defense attorneys like to say, "Justice delayed is justice."

Finally, suspects who bail out have a chance to undertake constructive activities that may lead a prosecutor or a judge to dismiss or at least reduce the charges against them or lessen their punishment. For example, assume that Harold is charged with shoplifting. Harold bails out of jail quickly, makes restitution (pays back) to the store whose merchandise he attempted to steal, and begins a counseling program offered through a community mental health center. Weeks later, when Harold and his attorney meet with the prosecutor to see if the case can be settled without going to trial, Harold has a letter from the store

owner forgiving him and a letter from the head of the counseling program praising Harold's efforts. The prosecutor may be impressed enough with Harold's self-help efforts to place Harold on informal probation and dismiss the shoplifting charge after six months if Harold completes (or remains in) the counseling program and has no further arrests during that period.

Section III: Own Recognizance Release (Release O.R.)

This section is about getting out of jail without having to pay for bail.

23. What does it mean to be released on my own recognizance?

Simply put, O.R. release is no-cost bail. Defendants released on their own recognizance need only sign a written promise to appear as required. No amount of bail has to be paid, either to the court or to a bail bond seller. However, all other aspects of bail remain the same. That is, a judge can place conditions on a defendant released O.R. (such as to check in regularly with a probation officer and to abstain from the use of drugs or alcohol), and order the arrest of a defendant who fails to show up in court when required.

24. How will a judge decide if I'm eligible for O.R. release?

Judges have nearly absolute discretion when it comes to deciding whether to require bail or release a suspect O.R. Generally, the same factors that might incline a judge to set low bail may persuade a judge to grant release O.R. Thus, factors favoring O.R. release include a suspect's good past record, longtime residence in a community, support of family members, and employment.

25. I'm representing myself at a bail hearing; can I ask for release O.R.?

Yes. In fact, a suspect should request release O.R. if there is any reasonable chance that the judge will grant the request. Then, if the judge denies the O.R. request, the suspect can seek low bail as an alternative.

26. What is an O.R. officer?

Many communities rely on O.R. officers to help judges decide whether to release suspects O.R. (in some areas, O.R. officers are called pretrial officers). When a suspect requests release O.R., a judge may ask an O.R. officer to do a quick check of a suspect's general background, past criminal record, and ties to the community. The O.R. officer will then make a nonbinding recommendation to the judge. If possible, a suspect should ask an employer, religious leader, and others who can speak positively of the suspect to contact an O.R. officer to support the O.R. request.

Release Order and Bond Form

Many courts use a checklist that covers all possible options available to the judge when deciding the status of a defendant pending trial. A sample form used by the federal court in the Central District of California is included on the facing page.

Sample Release Order and Bond Form

UNITED STATES DISTRICT COURT FOR THE CENTRAL DISTRICT OF CALIFORNIA

| UNITED STATES OF AMERICA. | CASE NUMBER | |
| Plaintiff. | COMPLAINT | INDICTMENT/INFORMATION |

V.

Defendant/Material Witness

VERIFICATION OF BAIL:
BAIL FIXED BY COURT FOR DEFENDANT/WITNESS:

IN CASE NO. _____
IN THE AMOUNT OF $ _____

CLERK, U.S. DISTRICT COURT

BY: _____
Deputy Clerk

Violation of Title _____ Section _____

TYPE OF BOND
☐ PERSONAL RECOGNIZANCE (Signature only - no dollar amount)
☐ UNSECURED APPEARANCE BOND IN AMOUNT OF $ _____
☐ APPEARANCE BOND IN THE AMOUNT $ _____
☐ WITH CASE DEPOSIT (amount or %) _____
  ☐ WITH AFFIDAVIT OF SURETY (No Justification) (Form CR-4)
  ☐ WITH JUSTIFICATION AFFIDAVIT OF SURETY (Form CR-3)
  ☐ AND WITH DEEDING OF PROPERTY OR ☐
☐ COLLATERAL BOND IN THE AMOUNT OF $ _____
  (Cash or Negotiable Securities)
☐ CORPORATE SURETY BOND IN AMOUNT OF $ _____
  (Corporate Surety Bond requires separate form)

PRE-CONDITIONS TO RELEASE

☐ You are to surrender to the Clerk of Court all passports issued to you and not apply for the issuance of a passport during the pendency of this case.
☐ Bail is subject to Nebbia Hearing.

ADDITIONAL CONDITIONS OF RELEASE

☐ Travel is restricted to _____
☐ You are to reside with _____
☐ Pretrial Services supervision   [   ] Intensive
☐ You are not to use illegal drugs and are to cooperate with Pretrial Services in a drug treatment and testing program.
☐ You are to participate in a residential drug/alcohol treatment program as approved by Pretrial Services.
☐ Other conditions: _____

GENERAL CONDITIONS OF RELEASE

I will appear in person in accordance with any and all directions and orders relating to my appearance in the above entitled matter as may be given or issued by the Court or any judicial officer thereof, in that Court or before any Magistrate Judge thereof, or in any other United States District Court to which I may be removed or to which the case may be transferred.

I understand the next ordered appearance is at _____ _____ p.m.
                                                  (Place)   (Date/Time)

I will abide by any judgment entered in this matter by surrendering myself to serve any sentence imposed and will obey any order or direction in connection with such judgment as the Court may prescribe.

I will not leave the State of California except upon order of this Court, and I will immediately inform the Court, the United States Attorney and my counsel in writing of any change in my residence address or telephone number so that I may be reached at all times.

I will not commit a Federal, State, or local crime during the period of release.

I will not intimidate any witness, juror or officer of the court, or obstruct the criminal investigation in this case in violation of Title 18 USC Section 1503 and 1510. Additionally, I will not tamper with, harass or retaliate against any alleged witness, victim or informant in this case in violation of Title 18 USC Section 1512 and 1513.

ACKNOWLEDGEMENT OF DEFENDANT/MATERIAL WITNESS

AS CONDITION OF MY RELEASE ON THIS BOND, PURSUANT TO TITLE 18 OF THE UNITED STATES CODE. I HAVE READ OR HAVE HAD INTERPRETED TO ME AND UNDERSTAND THE GENERAL CONDITIONS OF RELEASE. THE PRE-CONDITIONS AND ADDITIONAL CONDITIONS OF RELEASE AS CHECKED ABOVE AND AGREE TO COMPLY WITH ALL CONDITIONS OF RELEASE IMPOSED ON ME AND TO BE BOUND BY THE PROVISIONS OF LOCAL CRIMINAL RULES 5.2, 5.4 AND 5.5

FURTHERMORE, IT IS AGREED & UNDERSTOOD THAT THIS IS A CONTINUING BOND (INCLUDING ANY PROCEEDINGS ON APPEAL OR REVIEW) WHICH SHALL CONTINUE IN FULL FORCE & EFFECT UNTIL SUCH TIME AS DULY EXONERATED.

I UNDERSTAND THAT VIOLATION OF ANY OF THE GENERAL AND/OR ADDITIONAL CONDITIONS OF RELEASE AS GIVEN ON THE FACE OF THIS BOND MAY RESULT IN A REVOCATION OF RELEASE, AN ORDER OF DETENTION AND A NEW PROSECUTION FOR AN ADDITIONAL OFFENSE WHICH COULD RESULT IN A TERM OF IMPRISONMENT AND/OR FINE.

I FURTHER UNDERSTAND THAT IF I FAIL TO OBEY AND PERFORM ANY OF THE GENERAL AND/OR ADDITIONAL CONDITIONS OF RELEASE AS GIVEN ON THE FACE OF THE BOND, THIS BOND MAY BE FORFEITED TO THE UNITED STATES OF AMERICA. IF SAID FORFEITURE IS NOT SET ASIDE, JUDGMENT MAY BE SUMMARILY ENTERED IN THIS COURT AGAINST MYSELF AND EACH SURETY, JOINTLY AND SEVERALLY, FOR THE BOND AMOUNT, TOGETHER WITH INTEREST AND COSTS, AND EXECUTION OF THE JUDGMENT MAY BE ISSUED OR PAYMENT SECURED AS PROVIDED BY THE FEDERAL RULES OF CRIMINAL PROCEDURE AND OTHER LAWS OF THE UNITED STATES AND ANY CASH, REAL OR PERSONAL PROPERTY OR THE COLLATERAL PREVIOUSLY POSTED IN CONNECTION WITH THIS BOND MAY BE FORFEITED.

DATE: _____   _____   (   ) _____
                               Defendant/Material Witness' Signature   Telephone Number

Address (please print)   City, State and Zip Code

☐ Check if Interpreter is used: I have interpreted into the _____ language all of the above conditions of release and have been told by the defendant that he or she understands all the conditions of release.

          Date: _____   _____
                                          Interpreter's signature

APPROVED: _____   DATE: _____
          UNITED STATES MAGISTRATE JUDGE

IF CASH DEPOSITED: RECEIPT # _____   FOR $ _____
          (This bond may require surety agreements and affidavits pursuant to Local Criminal Rules 5.2 or 5.3)

From Suspect to Defendant

To be "charged" with a crime means to be formally accused of that crime. Police officers usually start the charging process with an arrest or citation. (See Chapter 3.) They then send copies of their reports to a prosecutor's office staffed by government lawyers whose job it is to initiate and prosecute criminal cases. The prosecutor is supposed to either:

- make an independent decision as to what charges should be filed, or
- enlist the help of citizens serving as grand jurors in deciding what charges to file.

Section I: Crime and Criminal Cases

This section covers some basics about crime, including what makes a crime a crime, the difference between civil and criminal cases, and the general categories of crime. In Chapter 12 we go into more detail about the language used in common criminal laws.

1. What are the hallmarks of a criminal case?

There are two different types of court cases—criminal and civil. A criminal case takes place when the government seeks to punish an individual for an act that has been classified as a crime by Congress or a state legislature. A civil case, on the other hand, usually has to do with a dispute over the rights and duties that individuals and organizations legally owe to each other. Among the important differences between criminal and civil cases are these:

- In a criminal case a prosecutor, not the victim, institutes and controls the case. The prosecutor may file criminal charges even if the victim doesn't approve, or he may refuse to file criminal charges despite the victim's desire that criminal charges be filed. This method of initiating the case contrasts with civil cases, where the injured party is the one who starts the ball rolling—although if you view the prosecutor as a stand-in for the community injured by a crime, then there's not much difference.

- People convicted of crimes may pay a fine or be incarcerated or both. People held liable in civil cases may have to pay money damages or give up property, but do not go to jail or prison. (We don't have debtors' prisons for those who can't pay a civil judgment.)

- In criminal cases, government-paid lawyers represent defendants who want but can't afford an attorney. Parties in civil cases, on the other hand, usually have to represent themselves or pay for their own lawyers.

- In criminal cases, the prosecutor has to prove a defendant's guilt beyond a reasonable doubt. In a civil case, the plaintiff only has to show by a preponderance of the evidence that the defendant is liable for damages.

- Defendants in criminal cases almost always are entitled to a jury trial. A party to a civil action is entitled to a jury trial in some types of cases, but not in others.

 CAUTION
The same conduct may violate both criminal and civil laws. A defendant whose actions violate both criminal and civil rules may be criminally prosecuted by the state and civilly sued by a victim for monetary damages. For instance, in 1995 O. J. Simpson was prosecuted for murder and found not guilty. In an entirely separate case, Simpson was also sued civilly for wrongful death by the victims' families. At the close of the civil case in 1997, Simpson was found "liable" (the civil equivalent to guilty, meaning responsible for) for the victims' deaths and ordered to pay millions of dollars in damages.

2. What are felonies, misdemeanors, and infractions (petty offenses), and how do these terms relate to the seriousness of a criminal charge?

Like boxes of soap powder, criminal laws come in an array of shapes and sizes. To determine the seriousness of a charge, find out whether it's a felony, misdemeanor, or infraction:

- Felonies are the most serious kinds of crimes. Generally, a crime is considered a felony when it is punishable by more than a year in a state prison (also called a penitentiary). Examples of felonies are murder, rape, burglary, and the sale of illegal drugs.

What Makes a Crime a Crime?

In the United States, an act is a crime because Congress or a state or local legislative body has defined it as such. But why are some acts defined as crimes while others aren't? While whole books have been written on this subject, here are a few straightforward reasons why crimes are crimes:

- Many acts that we consider crimes today were considered crimes under English law when we became a country. In large part we adopted that law as our own.
- Many crimes have their origin in moral precepts that originally were enforced by churches and taken over by the secular state.
- Acts carried out with an antisocial or malicious intent usually are considered worthy of punishment.
- Acts that may have been acceptable at one time (such as physical punishment of a child, drinking while driving, or sexual harassment) are redefined as crimes when societal groups convince lawmakers to criminalize such acts.

At bottom, what is and is not a crime is, to an extent, arbitrary and a reflection of who has the power to decide. But with some notable exceptions—for example, drug laws—most common crimes have been considered crimes for centuries, and most people agree that they should be.

When the Judge or Prosecutor Has Authority to Classify an Offense as Either a Felony or a Misdemeanor

Prosecutors and judges sometimes are authorized by a criminal statute to treat the behavior defined in the statute as a crime as either a felony or a misdemeanor. Such crimes are often referred to as "wobblers." For example, under a wobbler statute that allows assault to be charged as a felony or a misdemeanor, the prosecutor usually will decide which charge to bring on the basis of the severity of the injury to the victim and the nature of the defendant's intent and past criminal record. Similarly, after hearing evidence of a crime charged as a felony under such a statute, a judge may decide to reduce the charge to a misdemeanor.

- Misdemeanors are less serious crimes, and are typically punishable by up to a year in county jail. Common misdemeanors include shoplifting, drunk driving, assault, and possession of an unregistered firearm. Often, an offense that is a misdemeanor the first time a person commits it becomes a felony the second time around.
- Infractions are still less serious violations, like those involving traffic laws, that typically subject a person to nothing more than a monetary fine. Defendants charged with infractions usually have no right to

a jury trial or to a court-appointed lawyer.
- Municipal laws, also called ordinances, are enacted by and effective only in a particular city or county. For example, a city ordinance may forbid overnight parking or prohibit smoking in elevators. Violators of municipal laws are typically fined.

Section II: To Charge or Not to Charge, That Is the Question

This section is about how charges come to be filed and some of the considerations that go into deciding on particular charges.

3. Do charges have to be dismissed if there is undue delay between the time that a crime is committed and the time that criminal proceedings begin?

Yes. Every state has laws known as "statutes of limitation" that establish time limits for starting criminal proceedings. Statutes of limitation generally start to "run" on the date that crimes are committed, and if an applicable time limit expires before criminal proceedings begin, charges have to be dismissed.

The time limits that statutes of limitation establish vary from one state to another and according to the seriousness of a crime. In general, the more serious a crime, the more time a state has to begin criminal proceedings. By way of example only, here are some time limits set forth in the current version of Section 1.06 of the "Model Penal

Code," which are similar to those of many states:

- murder charges: no time limit
- serious felony charges: six years
- misdemeanor charges: two years, and
- petty misdemeanors and infractions: six months.

States cannot retroactively change rules to allow prosecution of crimes that are already barred by an existing statute of limitations. For example, assume that Will sexually molests a teenager named Joe. Joe doesn't report what happened for many years, and by the time he tells the police about the molestation, the statute of limitations has expired. The legislature cannot enact a new law that would allow the state more time to prosecute Will. (*Stogner v. California,* U.S. Sup. Ct. 2003.)

CASE EXAMPLE 1: Larry breaks into a neighbor's house and steals an Italian lamp that he has always wanted for his own apartment. The neighbor reports the burglary to the police. However, the police misplace the report and as a result don't begin investigating the crime until many months later. By the time the police arrest Larry and the prosecutor is ready to begin criminal proceedings, the state's three-year statute of limitations on burglary has expired.

Question: How does the expiration of the statute of limitations affect Larry's case?

Answer: Larry cannot be prosecuted for burglary. If the prosecutor were

to begin criminal proceedings, Larry would be entitled to have the case dismissed.

CASE EXAMPLE 2: Same case. Assume that after committing the burglary, Larry moves to another state for three years. A few months after he returns, the police arrest him for burglary.

Question: Will the state's three-year statute of limitations prevent the prosecution of Larry for burglary?

Answer: No. Time counts for statute of limitations purposes only during the time that the person who commits a crime remains in the state where the crime was committed and has a fixed place of residence or work. Thus, the statute of limitations was not running during the three years that Larry was in a different state.

Note: Statutes of limitation which establish time limits for starting criminal proceedings are distinguished from the Sixth Amendment right to a speedy trial, which applies to the length of time between the beginning of criminal proceedings and cases going to trial. For information on the right to a speedy trial, see Chapter 17.

4. Who decides what criminal charges to file?

Generally, this is a job for the prosecutor's office. Arrest and prosecution functions are separated primarily to protect citizens against the arbitrary exercise of police power. Police officers usually make arrests based only on whether they have good reason (probable cause) to believe a crime has been committed. Prosecutors can take a broader perspective. They have what is called "prosecutorial discretion." Prosecutors can look at all the circumstances of a case, including the suspect's past criminal record. Prosecutors can file charges on all crimes for which the police arrested a suspect, can file charges that are more or less severe than the charges leveled by the police, or can decide not to file any charges at all. (*U.S. v. Batchelder,* U.S. Sup. Ct. 1979.)

Victims' Right to Consult on Charges

Laws in a few jurisdictions provide a limited right for victims to consult with prosecutors about the charging decision. For example, Arizona Statute 13-4408 requires prosecutors to notify victims if the prosecutors intend not to file charges, and to give victims a chance to consult with them before the decision not to file becomes final. Ultimately, however, the final charging decision rests with the prosecutor.

5. After I'm arrested, how long will I have to wait to find out whether the prosecutor will charge me with a crime

For suspects who are in custody, speedy trial laws typically require prosecutors to file charges, if at all, within 72 hours

of arrest. Some jurisdictions require prosecutors to charge a suspect even sooner. For example, California requires that charges be filed within 48 hours. (Cal. Penal Code § 825.) However, prosecutors' initial charging decisions are subject to change. For example, a prosecutor's final decision on charges may not be determined until after a preliminary hearing (see Chapter 16), which may take place more than a month after arrest.

6. How do prosecutors decide what crimes to charge?

Typically, prosecutors base their initial charging decisions on the documents sent to them by the arresting police officers (usually called police or arrest reports). Arrest reports summarize the events leading up to arrests and provide numerous other details, such as dates, time, location, weather conditions, and witnesses' names and addresses. (See the sample arrest report at the end of Chapter 3.)

7. How do prosecutors obtain arrest reports?

Police officers and prosecutors work closely together. The police complete an arrest report soon after they make an arrest and then quickly forward the report to a prosecutor assigned to do case intake. The intake prosecutor decides whether to formally file charges (or to submit the evidence to a grand jury) and what charges to file.

Use of Arrest Reports in Criminal Cases

Arrest reports are almost always one-sided. They recite only what the police claim took place, and may include only witness statements that support the police theory. While they are generally not admissible as evidence in a trial, arrest reports can have a major impact in criminal cases. Not only do arrest reports often determine what charges prosecutors file, but they also may play a key role in how much bail is required, the outcome of preliminary hearings (where hearsay evidence is often admissible), the willingness of the prosecutor to plea bargain, and trial tactics (for instance, the police report can be used to discredit testimony of the police officer who prepared the report).

8. Does a prosecutor ever conduct an independent investigation before deciding what charges to file?

In some parts of the country, prosecutors may personally talk to police officers, victims, and witnesses before filing charges. (Prosecutors do not normally talk to the suspect, especially if the suspect is already represented by counsel.) In most places, however, and in big cities especially, the charging process is usually too harried to allow independent investigations. For instance, a single intake prosecutor may process 200–300 cases a day. Thus, prosecutors usually make charging decisions based on little more than a cursory review of the police report and a defendant's criminal history. If laboratory testing was done (such as in under-the-influence cases), prosecutors may also check the results of those tests before filing charges.

9. Does this mean that the prosecutor just rubber-stamps the arresting officer's assessment of the suspect's probable guilt?

Not always, but many times yes. Though prosecutors technically have powerful discretion in their charging decisions, political realities are such that they often don't use it. Instead, if the police say charges should be brought, prosecutors charge. For a number of reasons, many prosecutors view their role as house counsel for the local police department. One reason is that prosecutors would be out of business without police. A second is that every time a prosecutor decides not to file charges, the prosecutor is implicitly, if not directly, snubbing the arresting officer. The prosecutor is saying to the officer in effect, "You didn't have enough evidence to make this arrest," or "You didn't follow correct procedures"—at least, that's what the officer often hears. Rather than have to play this role with the police, a prosecutor may go along with the officer's assessment and let the court and the defense worry about preventing any resulting injustice.

Prosecutors May Also File Charges to Satisfy Important Political Constituencies

Most prosecutors are elected officials. Many of them view their position as a stepping-stone to higher office. Their charging decisions are often, therefore, affected by public opinion or important support groups. For example, a prosecutor may file charges on every shoplifting case, no matter how weak, to curry favor with local store owners who want to get the word out that shoplifters will be prosecuted. For similar reasons, a prosecutor may pursue otherwise weak prostitution charges to avoid alienating powerful civic groups. Deputy or assistant prosecutors may feel that appearing tough will help their careers—either within the prosecutor's office or later if they want to become judges. Experienced defense attorneys understand that prosecutors must sometimes be seen as taking a strong stand publicly, even though they may be willing to respond to weaknesses in individual cases at a later stage of the process.

10. Does the typical process for deciding what charges to file mean that some bad cases get brought?

Yes. When prosecutors don't meticulously screen cases, some defendants end up charged with crimes even though the evidence is insufficient to prove them guilty. Other defendants face technically accurate charges supported by admissible evidence, but the charges stem from circumstances for which many of us would probably not impose punishment. Prosecutors may also file charges to discourage arrested persons from filing civil false arrest suits against the police.

CASE EXAMPLE 1: Officer Bremer arrested Marla Michaels for drunk driving as she left a fraternity house party. The arrest was questionable—Marla's blood alcohol reading was under the legal limit. The officer's police report indicates that Marla said, "I had a few drinks," but does not indicate whether the officer gave her the *Miranda* warning (that is, telling Marla she has the right to remain silent; see Chapter 1).

Question: Is an intake prosecutor likely to file charges against Marla under these facts?

Answer: Yes. The intake prosecutor probably won't take the time to find out first whether the officer gave the *Miranda* warning to Marla, even though that might affect whether the prosecution could offer Marla's statement into evidence. The intake prosecutor might also want to support the police officer by following through with the charge even if the intake prosecutor personally feels that the case shouldn't be brought. Finally, while recognizing that the charge might be weak, the intake prosecutor may reason that Marla will probably agree to plead guilty to a lesser charge and that at least some punishment will serve as a lesson to the local college students.

How Victims Can Affect a Prosecutor's Charging Decision

Prosecutors often consider a victim's views when deciding whether to file a criminal charge or how serious a charge to file. This is especially true when organized constituencies of crime victims exist. Organized groups often pressure prosecutors to go hard on certain types of crimes, on pain of campaigning against the prosecutor at the next election. For example, groups of spousal assault victims have formed in many communities. A prosecutor deciding whether to file a spousal assault charge or whether to file it as a misdemeanor or a felony is likely to consider the reactions both of the group and of the individual victim.

CASE EXAMPLE 2: Officer Krupke arrests Bernardo Gutierrez, a Puerto Rican male, for interfering with a police officer's duties. Krupke claims that Bernardo physically tried to prevent Krupke from making an arrest. Bernardo claims that he did nothing wrong, and simply tried to tell Krupke that he was arresting an innocent person. The prosecutors know that Krupke has a bad attitude towards racial and ethnic minorities.

Question: Is the intake prosecutor likely to file charges?

Answer: Yes. The intake prosecutor may fear that to drop charges would be to invite Bernardo to file a suit for false arrest against the police. Also, the prosecutor's office would not be able to work with Krupke in the future if they didn't follow through on his arrests. However, the intake prosecutor might also alert the police department to a problem officer and ask for a review of Krupke's performance.

Prosecutors May Extort Agreements Not to Sue

Defendants who have been wrongfully arrested can seek money damages by bringing civil suits for false arrest against the arresting officer, and sometimes the city or county employing the officer. So, even if a prosecutor realizes that a bust was a bad one, the prosecutor might file criminal charges anyway to head off a civil suit and then drop the criminal charges—but only if the defendant agrees not to sue for false arrest. Some judges would consider the prosecutor's motive to be improper. But other judges would hold the defendant to the agreement, and throw out a false arrest civil suit by a defendant who had previously agreed not to sue. Clearly, an accused person considering suing for false arrest must speak with an attorney before agreeing to forgo a civil suit in exchange for a dismissal of charges.

11. **With all the pressure on prosecutors to file charges, why do they sometimes decide not to prosecute?**

Intake prosecutors may decline to file charges for a number of reasons. Among the most common are:

a. The offense is trivial or low priority

Prosecutor offices may view certain types of crimes as insignificant or not worth pursuing. For example, a prosecutor may decline to prosecute all cases involving possession of very small quantities of marijuana. Or the prosecutor may decide not to pursue charges against a group of protesters arrested at a local political rally.

b. The police officer failed to observe the suspect's rights

If through obvious police error the prosecution lacks enough admissible evidence to make a criminal charge stick, the chances are the charge won't be brought in the first place.

> **CASE EXAMPLE:** Police officer Zena Phobic received a tip that Fanny Pack was growing marijuana in her backyard. That night, Officer Phobic drove to Fanny's house, hopped the fence, broke down the door to search the inside of the covered greenhouse and found marijuana plants. Officer Phobic immediately went into the house and arrested Fanny.
>
> **Question:** Is there any reason why an intake prosecutor might not charge Fanny with possession of marijuana?

Answer: Yes. The intake prosecutor might decide that Phobic violated Fanny's rights by not obtaining a search warrant before searching the greenhouse. (More on search warrants in Chapter 2.) If the prosecution couldn't introduce the marijuana as evidence against Fanny, there would be no way for it to win the case. For that reason, the prosecutor might decide not to file charges.

c. The victim asks that no charges be brought

Charging decisions are for prosecutors, not victims. However, if victims ask prosecutors not to bring charges and make it perfectly clear that they will not cooperate, prosecutors often won't file charges. In past years, this type of situation was common in family disputes. In the heat of an argument, battering, or other abuse, one spouse (often a wife or girlfriend) would call the police, leading to the arrest of another spouse (a husband or boyfriend). For personal reasons (whether fear of retaliation or hopes of making up), the complainant (the person who called the police) would then refuse to cooperate and charges would not be filed. In recent years, the law enforcement community has begun to take domestic abuse allegations more seriously, and many prosecutors now bring and prosecute domestic abuse charges even when the victim doesn't want to pursue the case. A famous example of this was the trial of Warren Moon (a well-known football player) on domestic abuse charges. The D.A. went ahead even though the alleged victim testified in favor of her husband. (The jury found Moon not guilty.)

Mediating Minor Nonviolent Criminal Cases

In some locations, minor criminal complaints are diverted out of the court system before prosecutors file charges. The alleged offender and complainant both are brought together to discuss their problem, sometimes with a facilitator or mediator, to come up with some sort of solution. Ask your defense attorney or public defender if mediating is available in your jurisdiction.

Civil Compromise

Defense lawyers often try to prevent the filing of criminal charges by arranging for a civil compromise. Much like mediated agreements, with a civil compromise a defendant agrees to reimburse a victim for damages. In return, the victim asks a prosecutor not to file charges. This option gives wealthier arrestees a ticket out of the criminal justice system that poorer arrestees may not have.

---

d. The prosecutor views the suspect as a good person

Occasionally, a prosecutor will decide that a basically good person made a stupid mistake that shouldn't result in a consequence as severe as a criminal charge. In such a situation, the prosecutor will refuse to prosecute, either in the interests of justice or because it would be a waste of resources (time and money) to charge such a person with a crime, even where the initial arrest was valid.

> **CASE EXAMPLE:** Lib Erty, a teenager, stood with a group of five girlfriends at a store cosmetics counter. A security guard saw two of the girls take some lipsticks and leave without paying for them. The guard detained all the girls and called the police. A police officer arrested them, including Lib, for shoplifting. After reviewing the case, the intake prosecutor believes that Lib did not take anything herself and was not aware that the other girls planned to steal the items. The prosecutor also learns that Lib has no prior criminal record, and that her chances for a college scholarship might be jeopardized if she is convicted of a crime. Under all the circumstances, the prosecutor decides that it would not be in the interests of justice to prosecute Lib. However, the store manager and police officer want the prosecutor to prosecute all the girls to send the teenage community a strong message that shoplifting will not be tolerated.

Question: Does the prosecutor have to bring charges against Lib?

Answer: No. Prosecutors can consider the views of citizens and police, but the ultimate decision of whom to formally charge with crimes is the prosecutor's alone to make.

e. The prosecutor wants one defendant

Commonly, a prosecutor will drop charges against one suspect in exchange for that suspect's testimony against another suspect.

12. Can a prosecutor file charges and then change her mind and dismiss them?

Yes. Prosecutors have the power to "nolle prosequi" (withdraw) charges any time before a verdict is entered. In most jurisdictions, however, prosecutors need a judge's permission to "nolle pros" a case. (See Federal Rule of Criminal Procedures 48(a).) Especially in cases of great notoriety, judges may refuse to grant permission.

13. If I have a criminal record, will that affect a prosecutor's charging decision?

Yes. Even if they conduct no other investigation, intake prosecutors almost always check to see if an accused has a criminal record (called a rap sheet or priors). A suspect's past criminal record, even for a different crime, makes it more likely that charges will be filed, and may affect the severity of those charges. For example, a shoplifting charge against

a defendant with a prior shoplifting conviction may be filed as a felony instead of a misdemeanor (where the laws support that type of escalation). Similarly, a charge of drunk driving with a prior always carries a more severe penalty than a first charge of drunk driving. (See Chapter 24 for more on drunk driving penalties.)

Section III: The Mechanics of Charging

This section is about how charges are actually brought against a criminal defendant.

14. Is the charging process always the same?

No. Prosecutors may follow one of two procedures, depending largely on local policies and the seriousness of a crime:

- If a crime is a misdemeanor, a prosecutor files an accusatory pleading directly in court. This pleading may be called a criminal complaint, an information, or a petition.
- If a crime is a felony, charges may be brought either in the form of an accusatory pleading (as with misdemeanors) or by an indictment handed down by a grand jury. About half the states (mostly eastern states) require prosecutors to use grand juries in felony cases. Other states allow prosecutors to choose which procedure to use. The Fifth Amendment to the U.S. Constitution requires the federal government to use grand juries in all felony cases.

15. How much will I be able to find out about the prosecution's case by reading the criminal complaint or information?

Very little. The initial charging document is little more than a formality. It doesn't divulge specifics about the prosecution's case, but simply identifies the defendant and the crime or crimes with which a defendant is charged. An intake prosecutor simply inserts this information into a preprinted form. (See the sample criminal complaint at the end of this chapter.)

16. Will the complaint or information indicate whether the prosecutor is using my past criminal record as a basis for a more severe charge?

Generally, yes. When prosecutors use prior convictions to increase the severity of a charge, those prior convictions usually are alleged in the accusatory pleading. (An Allegations of Prior Convictions section is included in the sample criminal complaint at the end of this chapter.)

Defendants Should Carefully Review Allegations of Prior Convictions

Prosecutors sometimes make mistakes in listing prior convictions, and such mistakes can be terribly costly to defendants. Defendants therefore must review the priors and consult with counsel about possible avenues to strike (convince a judge not to consider) some or all prior convictions.

---

17. Can I be charged with more than one crime for committing the same act?

Yes. A complaint may describe what seems like a single criminal act as separate criminal charges. For example, a shoplifter who steals five lipsticks in one incident may face a separate charge for each. Similarly, a defendant arrested for drunk driving may be charged with two separate "per se" crimes: violating the per se statute that prohibits driving with a blood alcohol level over the legal limit, and violating a separate statute that prohibits driving under the influence of drugs or alcohol. (More on these statutes in Chapter 24.)

Although defendants may be convicted of separate charges for the same act, they usually can't be punished separately for each charge. As a general rule, the government may not punish a defendant more than once for the same conduct. What constitutes the exact same conduct can be a tricky question, one best left to experienced defense lawyers.

> **CASE EXAMPLE 1:** Shamon Yu is charged with kidnapping and rape. Yu allegedly grabbed his victim, drove her to a secluded spot ten miles away, and raped her.
>
> **Question:** Upon conviction, can Yu be given one sentence for the kidnapping and a separate sentence for the rape?
>
> **Answer:** Yes. Though everything that Yu did might seem a single criminal act, he committed two separate crimes and could be punished for each separately.

CASE EXAMPLE 2: Bea Sotted is arrested for drunk driving. Bea faces two charges: violating a per se rule (driving with a blood alcohol level over the state's legal limit, regardless of whether driving is affected), and driving under the influence.

Question: If convicted of both crimes, can the judge hand down two separate sentences?

Answer: No. Bea committed only a single criminal act, and she should be given only a single penalty.

18. **Is it true that intake prosecutors commonly charge suspects with the most serious offense that the facts will reasonably support, and with as many offenses as possible?**

Yes. Defense attorneys often term this practice "overcharging." By filing as many charges as possible, the prosecution improves its chances of conviction should the evidence to support any particular charge not pan out. The prosecution may also overcharge as a bargaining chip to be used during plea bargaining: They can agree to drop one or more charges or reduce the seriousness of a charge in exchange for a guilty plea from the defendant. Finally, intake prosecutors like to err on the side of completeness, because it's easier for them to drop a charge from an existing complaint than to prepare a new complaint with additional charges.

CASE EXAMPLE 1: John George was arrested for robbing Paul Starr. John was arrested at Paul's home, after Paul tripped a silent alarm which summoned the police. John was charged with robbery (taking property from Paul by force or fear), burglary (breaking and entering into Paul's home), larceny (taking property from Paul), and carrying a concealed weapon—all from the same event, the one robbery.

Question: Why would the prosecutor charge John with four different crimes based on one incident?

Answer: Quite likely because the prosecutor hopes to avoid trial by scaring John into a quick plea bargain. John may be so fearful of receiving four separate sentences that he willingly pleads guilty to one or two of the crimes.

CASE EXAMPLE 2: Charles "Chuckles" Lorettian was caught by the police spray painting his signature ("laughs") inside an abandoned warehouse. Chuckles was charged with malicious mischief (a misdemeanor) for the graffiti and with burglary (a felony) for breaking and entering into a building for the purpose of stealing property. Chuckles is a young member of a tagging crew (group that does graffiti for fun) with no prior convictions.

Question: Is Chuckles likely to be convicted of burglary? If not, why would the prosecutor include a burglary charge?

Answer: A burglary conviction is unlikely if Charles is young and the warehouse was abandoned and empty. But by including the felony charge, the prosecutor may induce Charles to plead guilty to the misdemeanor.

The Politics of Overcharging

Many critics argue that both defense lawyers and prosecutors are involved in a cynical game of overcharging. If prosecutors file high, then defense lawyers can appear to be getting defendants a deal by convincing prosecutors to lower the charges. Said one prosecutor, "... we get what we want. The defendant thinks his attorney is great. The attorney gets his money." (Prosecutor cited in *Plea Bargaining: Critical Issues and Common Practices*, by William F. McDonald, (U.S. DOJ, National Institute of Justice, 1983, at 20).)

Section IV: Grand Juries

This section is about grand juries—what they are, the role they play in the charging process, and how they work.

19. What are grand juries?

Grand juries are similar to regular trial juries (technically called "petit juries") in that they are made up of randomly selected individuals who listen to evidence. However, crucial differences exist:

- Petit juries decide whether defendants are guilty. Grand juries decide whether to indict suspects (charge them with crimes).
- Grand juries meet in secret proceedings. Petit juries serve during public trials.
- Petit jurors usually serve for a short period, as little as ten days unless they serve on a longer trial. Grand jurors serve for longer periods that typically coincide with a term of court, often six to 18 months.
- Grand juries have 15–23 people, 16–23 in federal courts. (See Federal Rule of Criminal Procedure 6(a).) By contrast, a petit jury usually consists of between six and 12 people.
- Petit juries generally have to be unanimous to convict a defendant. Grand juries need not be unanimous to indict. In the federal system, for example, an indictment may be returned if 12 or more jurors agree to indict. (Federal Rule of Criminal Procedure 6(f).)

20. What happens in a grand jury indictment proceeding?

A prosecutor presents a bill (the charges) to the grand jury and introduces evidence—usually the minimum necessary, in the prosecutor's opinion, to secure an indictment. The proceedings are secret and are held without the suspect or his lawyer present. Indicted suspects can sometimes later obtain transcripts of grand jury proceedings, a big reason why prosecutors like to keep the evidence to the minimum. The prosecutor may call a suspect or other witnesses to testify. (Any witnesses who think that they might be a target of investigation have a right not to answer questions.) If the grand jury decides to indict, it returns what is called a "true bill." If not, the grand jury returns a "no-bill." However, charges may eventually be filed by the prosecutor even after a grand jury returns a no-bill. Prosecutors can return to the same grand jury with more evidence, present the same evidence to a second grand jury, or (in jurisdictions that give prosecutors a choice) bypass the grand jury altogether and file a criminal complaint.

21. Do grand juries usually indict?

Yes. The grand jury does not make its decision on the basis of an adversary proceeding. Rather, grand jurors see and hear only what prosecutors put before them. (Prosecutors technically have an obligation to present "exculpatory" evidence—evidence that suggests that a defendant might not be guilty—though there is not much other than the prosecutor's conscience to enforce this rule.)

In part because there's no one on the "other side" to contest the prosecutor's evidence, grand juries almost always return an indictment as requested by the prosecutor. According to a U.S. Department of Justice study on plea bargaining, "Grand juries are notorious for being "rubberstamps" for the prosecutor for

virtually all routine criminal matters." (*Plea Bargaining: Critical Issues and Common Practices*, by William F. McDonald, (U.S. DOJ, National Institute of Justice, 1983).)

22. Why might a prosecutor want to ask a grand jury to indict me rather than simply file a criminal complaint or information in court?

Where they have a choice, prosecutors often prefer grand juries because grand jury proceedings are secret. When prosecutors file an information, they usually are required to convince a judge in a public preliminary hearing that they have enough evidence to secure a conviction. (See Chapter 16.) Also, during a preliminary hearing, the defendant can see and cross-examine prosecution witnesses.

23. If I'm called to testify before the grand jury, what does that mean?

Prosecutors typically subpoena witnesses to appear before a grand jury either because:

- a prosecutor believes that a witness has information about a crime committed by a third party, and wants to elicit the information to secure an indictment against the third party, or
- a prosecutor regards a witness as a target, a person suspected of crime, and wants to develop evidence against the target.

Individuals called before a grand jury as witnesses do not have to be warned that they are or may become targets. *Miranda-*

type warnings are not required, and unless they are specifically given immunity, any testimony witnesses provide to a grand jury may be used against them in a later prosecution.

24. How can I find out whether I'm a target of a grand jury proceeding?

Defense lawyers can often confer with the prosecutor to find out whether a client is the target of a grand jury investigation. If so, the defense lawyer may try to work out a deal in which the target agrees to testify before the grand jury in exchange for immunity from prosecution.

25. Can I have my lawyer at my side when testifying before the grand jury?

No. Lawyers are not permitted to accompany clients into the grand jury room. Grand jury proceedings are closed, and witnesses are not entitled to be represented by counsel during the proceedings. Lawyers may, however, remain in a nearby hallway, and witnesses may leave the room to consult with their lawyers as needed. Lawyers sometimes advise their clients to leave the room and talk to them before answering every question. For example, a witness might repeatedly say, "I respectfully request permission to leave the room to consult with my lawyer before I answer that question."

26. Do I have to answer the prosecutor's questions in a grand jury proceeding?

Under the Fifth Amendment to the U.S. Constitution, witnesses do not have to answer questions if, in the witness's opinion, the answers might tend to incriminate the witness (provide evidence of criminal activity). To claim the privilege, a witness should simply say, "I respectfully decline to answer based on my state and federal privileges against self-incrimination." The prosecutor can negate the Fifth Amendment by granting the witness immunity from prosecution. Prosecutors often develop evidence against the big fish in a criminal scheme by granting immunity to the little fish. Without the immunity, the little fish could refuse to testify.

 RESOURCE
For more information on grand juries, see *Representation of Witnesses Before Federal Grand Juries—A Manual for Attorneys,* National Lawyers Guild (West Group, 4th ed., 1999).

Section V: Diversion

This section explains "diversion"—a process in which a person doesn't have to answer to criminal charges if she cooperates in a type of informal probation.

27. Do prosecutors have any choices other than charging me with a crime or dropping charges?

Yes. Cases can be diverted out of the criminal justice system. Defendants whose cases are diverted typically have to participate in a treatment or rehabilitation program. Since criminal charges are normally dropped when a defendant successfully completes a diversion program, diversion allows defendants to escape the stigma of a criminal conviction.

28. Does my chance of getting into a diversion program depend on the charge against me?

Yes, though eligibility rules vary from one locality to another. Diversion programs are most often available to defendants charged with misdemeanors and nonviolent felonies involving drugs or alcohol. In some jurisdictions, diversion may be available to defendants charged with domestic violence, child abuse or neglect, traffic-related offenses, or even writing bad checks.

29. Apart from the charge, what else might affect my eligibility for diversion?

Diversion eligibility often depends on two factors:

- A defendant's past criminal record. For example, in drug cases, a locality may offer diversion only to defendants with no prior drug convictions. Again, however, eligibility rules vary, and another locality may extend diversion to previously convicted defendants who have successfully completed probation or parole.
- A recommendation from a probation officer that a defendant is a fit candidate for diversion—that is, that a defendant is likely to benefit from and succeed at a treatment program.

30. Do I have to arrange for diversion at any specific time?

No. Typically, diversion is available any time before trial.

31. How do I arrange for diversion?

Prosecutors sometimes voluntarily offer diversion to defendants who are clearly eligible under a community's guidelines. Defense counsel may also suggest diversion to prosecutors, sometimes even before formal charges are filed. Finally, defense counsel may wait until a defendant's first court appearance and ask the judge to order an evaluation for diversion.

A defendant who is referred for diversion in any of these ways then meets with a probation officer, who conducts an investigation and prepares a report as to the defendant's suitability for diversion. The report may specify the type of program that is most suitable for the defendant. Judges normally follow a probation officer's recommendation.

32. Can I appeal a judge's decision to refuse diversion?

Defendants who are denied diversion and ultimately convicted can appeal a judge's refusal to admit them to a diversion program. However, these appeals rarely succeed.

33. What happens if a judge diverts my case?

Diverted defendants have to enter and complete a specified diversion program. Diversion programs range from periodic counseling to live-in treatment programs.

34. If I am diverted, will I have to pay for the diversion program?

Probably. Defendants often have to pay a fee both to the court and to the treatment center. The cost of the diversion program can sometimes be more than a fine. However, the defendant hopefully benefits from the treatment and from avoiding a criminal record. (See Question 35, below.)

35. What is the effect of diversion?

In most states, charges are dropped when defendants successfully complete a diversion program. Thus, diverted defendants avoid a conviction. However, diversion usually does not expunge arrest records; the record of arrest remains.

Those who do not complete the assigned program or meet conditions set by the treatment center, and those who are arrested on other charges during their treatment, will likely have the diversion revoked and the original charges reinstated. Sometimes, the judge will conduct a hearing before deciding whether to revoke diversion.

36. How is it that my friend who got sentenced to attend a drug treatment program still has a record?

Convicted defendants may have to attend drug and alcohol treatment programs as part of their sentence. But that is different from diversion. Defendants who plead or are found guilty have criminal records; no treatment program takes that away. But, where defendants are diverted, the criminal prosecution is actually suspended. They won't have a record of conviction if they successfully complete the program.

Sample Criminal Complaint

IN THE MUNICIPAL COURT OF LOS ANGELES JUDICIAL DISTRICT
COUNTY OF LOS ANGELES, STATE OF CALIFORNIA

THE PEOPLE OF THE STATE OF CALIFORNIA,)	MISDEMEANOR COMPLAINT
)	
OR 11/2 mc 5555555)	
Plaintiff,)	CASE NO.
vs.)	
)	EDWARD M. KRINGLE, Clerk
)	Court Administrator
)	By _____
)	Deputy Clerk
)	
V23333A)	Issued by
V23333B)	JOHN K. BUGLE, City Attorney
)	
Defendant(s).)	By B. ZAPPA
)	Deputy City Attorney

Comes now the undersigned and states that he is informed and believes, and upon such information and belief declares: That on or about MARCH 13, 2008 at and in the City of Los Angeles, in the County of Los Angeles, State of California, a misdemeanor, to wit, violation of the first paragraph of Subsection (a) of Section 23152 of the California Vehicle Code was committed by the above-named defendant(s) (whose true name(s) to affiant is (are) unknown), who at the time and place last aforesaid, did willfully and unlawfully drive a vehicle while being under the influence of alcoholic beverage and a drug and under the combined influence of an alcoholic beverage and a drug.

ALLEGATIONS OF PRIOR CONVICTIONS

Affiant further alleges that the defendant was convicted of having violated the following section(s) of the California Vehicle Code, said violation(s) and conviction(s) having occurred on or about the following date(s):

Code Section	Violation Date	Conviction Date	Docket No.	Court No.
NONE KNOWN				

COUNT II

For a further, separate and second cause of action being a different offense, belonging to the same class of crimes and offenses set forth in Count I hereof, affiant further alleges that on or about MARCH 13, 2008 at and in the City of Los Angeles, in the County of Los Angeles, State of California, a misdemeanor, to wit:
violation of Subdivision (b) of Section 23152 of the California Vehicle code was committed by the above-named defendant(s) (whose true name(s) to affiant is (are) unknown), who at the time and place last aforesaid, did willfully and unlawfully drive a vehicle with 0.08 percent or more, by weight, of alcohol in his or her blood.

Sample Criminal Complaint (continued)

The allegations of prior convictions listed in Count I of this complaint are hereby incorporated by reference as allegations of prior convictions for the purposes of this Count of the complaint.

All of which is contrary to the law and against the peace and dignity of the People of the State of California. Declarant and complainant therefore prays that a warrant may be issued for the arrest of said defendant(s) and that he may be dealt with according to law.

Attached hereto and incorporated by reference as though fully set forth are written states and reports, consisting of pages, which constitute the basis upon which I make the within allegations.

A declaration in Support of the Issuance of Such Warrant is Submitted.

Executed at Los Angeles, California, on March 19, 2008.

I declare under penalty of perjury that the foregoing is true and correct.

_____
Declarant and Complainant

INFORMAL DISCOVERY NOTICE

TO THE ABOVE-NAMED DEFENDANT(S) AND/OR ATTORNEY(S) FOR DEFENDANT(S):

Plaintiff, the People of the State of California, hereby requests discovery/disclosure from the defendant(s) and his or her attorney(s) in this case pursuant to Penal Code Sections 1054.3 and 1054.5.

YOU ARE HEREBY NOTIFIED that if complete disclosure is not made within 15 days of this request, plaintiff will seek—on or before the next court date, or as soon as practicable thereafter—a court order enforcing the provisions of Penal Code Section 1054.5, subdivisions (b) and (c). This is an ongoing request for any of the listed items which become known to the defendant(s) and his or her attorney(s) after the date of compliance.

The written statements and reports attached hereto constitute discoverable materials designated in Penal Code Section 1054.1 Any additional material discoverable pursuant to Penal Code Section 1054.1 that becomes known to plaintiff will be provided to the defense.

If prior to or during trial, as a result of this request plaintiff obtains additional evidence or material subject to disclosure under a previous defense request or court order pursuant to Penal Code Section 1054.1, plaintiff will disclose the existence of that evidence or material within a reasonable time.

DISCOVERY MATERIALS SHOULD BE DELIVERED TO A DEPUTY CITY ATTORNEY IN MASTER CALENDAR COURT ON THE FIRST TRIAL DATE.

Criminal Defense Lawyers

O ne of the most immediate concerns for people charged with crimes is how to secure legal representation. This chapter answers typical questions that defendants have when setting out to either hire their own attorney or have an attorney appointed for them at government expense. The chapter also addresses the issue of self-representation.

Section I: Do I Need a Lawyer?

This section explains why it's almost always better to be represented by a lawyer in a criminal case.

1. Are all criminal defendants represented by lawyers?

Not all are, but most criminal defendants choose to be represented by a lawyer, especially when jail or a prison sentence is a possible result. This is because it is very difficult for a person to competently handle his or her own criminal case. (See Question 3, below.) While there are no firm statistics on how many people choose to represent themselves in criminal cases, estimates range well below 1%.

2. Lawyers are expensive; how do people afford them?

Paradoxically, the biggest reason that most defendants are represented by lawyers in criminal cases is that most defendants can't afford to hire their own private defense attorney. When defendants are considered to be legally indigent—as most are—the court is constitutionally required to provide them with legal representation at government expense if jail or prison is a possible outcome of the case.

Indigent Defendants Are Not Always Entitled to Free Legal Representation

Indigent defendants are entitled to free legal representation only if there is an actual risk of a jail or prison sentence (*Alabama v. Shelton*, U.S. Sup. Ct. 2002). For example, indigent defendants charged with minor traffic offenses are not entitled to free legal services. And if a judge agrees at the start of a defendant's case not to impose a jail or prison sentence, no lawyer need be appointed. However, most judges prefer to appoint a lawyer rather than promise no jail time in advance.

---

3. If I'm not poor enough for a court-appointed attorney, how important is it that I hire my own?

Even with the high costs of legal representation, a nonindigent defendant faced with the possibility of going to jail or prison should almost always hire an attorney. The truth is, no matter what the person's intelligence or educational background, the criminal justice system makes it virtually impossible to do a competent job of representing oneself. Each criminal case is unique, and only a specialist who is experienced in assessing the particulars of a case—and in dealing with the many variables present in every criminal case—can provide the type of representation that every criminal defendant needs to receive if justice is to be done.

Criminal defense lawyers do much more than simply question witnesses in court. For example, defense lawyers:

- Negotiate "deals" with prosecutors, often arranging for reduced charges and lesser sentencing. By contrast, prosecutors may be uncooperative with self-represented defendants.
- Formulate sentencing programs tailored to a client's specific needs, often helping defendants avoid future brushes with the criminal justice system.
- Help defendants cope with the feelings of fear, embarrassment, reduced self-esteem, and anxiety that criminal charges tend to produce in many people.
- Provide defendants with a reality check—a knowledgeable, objective perspective on their situation and what is likely to happen should their cases go to trial. This perspective is vital for defendants trying to decide whether to accept a prosecutor's offered plea bargain. (See Chapter 20 for more on plea bargains.)
- Are familiar with important legal rules that people representing themselves would find almost impossible to locate on their own—because many criminal law rules are hidden

---

Examples of Hidden Costs of Pleading Guilty

Pleading guilty can have negative consequences far beyond the penalties imposed by law for that particular offense. Here are two examples.

EXAMPLE 1: Although the actual sentence for a first-time drunk driving charge may be a $500 fine and loss of a driver's license for six months, a future drunk driving conviction may require a mandatory jail sentence. Even more dramatically, people who earlier have pled guilty to certain violent offenses are at risk of greatly harsher sentences under many states' "three strikes" legislation if they are in the future convicted of any felony, even a nonviolent one.

EXAMPLE 2: Pleading guilty to a crime in which the person's property was used in the commission of the crime may result in that property being taken in a civil forfeiture proceeding. For instance, assume that Charlie pleads guilty to selling marijuana out of his Rolls-Royce automobile. In addition to being fined and/or jailed, Charlie may later find that the government has decided to take his automobile. Civil forfeiture proceedings following criminal convictions do not violate the constitutional rule against double jeopardy (*U.S. v. Ursery*, U.S. Sup. Ct. 1996).

The Gulf Between the Law on Paper and in Practice

Self-representation is made more difficult by the typical gulf between paper and practice in criminal cases. In books you can find laws that define crimes, fix punishments for their violation, and mandate courtroom procedures. Take the time and trouble to read these books, defendants might think, and they'll understand the system. Alas, the practice of criminal law can't be understood by reading books alone. To experienced criminal defense attorneys, the criminal law appears much the same as a droplet of water appears to a biologist under a microscope—a teeming world with life forms and molecules interacting unpredictably.

For example, prosecutorial discretion—the power of prosecutors to decide whether to file criminal charges, and what charges to file—determines much of what actually happens in the criminal courts. Which prosecutor has the power to make decisions, and when those decisions are made, can greatly affect the outcome of a case. An act that looks on paper to constitute one specific crime can be recast as a variety of other crimes, some more and others less serious. What in a statute book appears to be a fixed sentence for a particular crime can be negotiated into a variety of alternatives. In other words, the world of criminal law is vast, hidden, and shifting, and defendants enter it alone at their peril. At the very least, most self-represented defendants should arrange for a lawyer to be a legal coach and consult with their coaches as needed. (See Question 36.)

away in court interpretations of federal and state constitutions. For example, understanding what may constitute an unreasonable search and seizure often requires familiarity with a vast array of state and federal appellate court opinions.

- Are familiar with local court customs and procedures that are nowhere written down. For example, a defense lawyer may know which prosecutor has the real authority to settle a case, and what kinds of arguments are likely to appeal to that prosecutor.
- Understand the possible hidden costs of pleading guilty that a self-represented person might never think about.
- Spend time on a case that a defendant cannot afford to spend. Defendants who can afford to hire a lawyer usually have jobs, and therefore lack the time (and energy) to devote to such time-consuming activities as gathering and examining documents, doing legal research, and talking to witnesses.
- Gather information from prosecution witnesses. Witnesses often fear people accused of crimes and there-fore refuse to speak to people representing themselves. Witnesses

are more likely to talk to defense attorneys or their investigators.

• Hire and manage investigators. Investigators may be able to believably impeach (contradict) prosecution witnesses who embellish their stories at trial. By contrast, it is far less effective for a defendant to testify that "the prosecution witness told me something different before trial."

Section II: Court-Appointed Attorneys

This section is about attorneys appointed by the court to represent defendants who can't afford to hire their own. The section explains who these attorneys are, who is entitled to receive their services, and the type of services you are entitled to expect from them.

4. How do I qualify for free legal services?

Normally, a defendant who wants a lawyer at government expense must:

• ask the court to appoint the lawyer, and

• provide details under oath (in a financial eligibility questionnaire or in oral responses to questions posed by the judge) about his or her income and resources.

Unfortunately, it is impossible to say with certainty who will qualify for a court-appointed lawyer. Each state (or even county) makes its own rules as to who qualifies as indigent for the purpose of

getting a free lawyer. For example, one state defines indigent as a "person who is unable to pay for the services of an attorney, including the costs of investigation, without substantial hardship to the person or the person's family" (Florida Rule of Criminal Procedure 3.111). Another state with a similar statute provides that, when defining "hardship," a judge can consider "such factors as income, property owned, outstanding obligations, number and ages of any dependents, and other sources of family income" (Comment to Arizona Rule of Criminal Procedure 6.4).

The seriousness of a charge is also likely to affect a judge's decision as to whether a defendant is eligible for a free lawyer. For example, a judge may decide that a wage-earner charged with shoplifting has sufficient income and property to hire a private defense attorney, since the cost of such representation is likely to be relatively low. But the judge may decide that the same wage-earner is indigent and qualifies for a court-appointed lawyer if the wage-earner is charged with a complex and serious case of criminal fraud.

5. If I make just a little too much money to be considered indigent, can I obtain a court-appointed lawyer at a reduced fee?

Most states provide for partial indigency. This means that a judge may allow a defendant who exceeds the indigency guidelines but who cannot afford the full cost of a private lawyer to receive the services of a court-appointed attorney.

(See New Hampshire Statute 604-A:2-d; Florida Rule of Criminal Procedure 3.111.) At the conclusion of the case, the judge will require the defendant to reimburse the state or county for a portion of the costs of representation. Typically, the reimbursement rate will be much lower than the standard hourly fees charged by the private defense attorneys in that community.

6. Some of my close relatives are pretty well-heeled. Will a judge consider that when deciding if I'm eligible for free legal services?

No. Defendants are not legally required to ask relatives for money to hire an attorney. With rare exceptions, judges determine indigency only according to the income and property of the defendant. Adult defendants who are otherwise indigent remain eligible for court-appointed lawyers even if they have parents and other relatives who could afford to hire a private attorney.

7. Will anyone check up on the information I provide in my application for a free lawyer?

Perhaps. To protect the limited funds available for court-appointed lawyers, judges sometimes order audits on the accuracy of defendants' financial eligibility questionnaires. because these documents must be filled out under oath, defendants who make materially false claims can be prosecuted for perjury. However, such prosecutions are extremely rare. More likely, the consequence will be that the court will revoke the appointment of the lawyer and require the defendant to reimburse the appointed lawyer for services already rendered.

8. Where I live, the court-appointed attorney is called a public defender. What exactly is a public defender?

Most criminal defendants are legally indigent and can't afford to pay for an attorney. On the other hand, the state can't legally prosecute indigents unless it provides them with an attorney. To satisfy this requirement, many states have set up offices called public defender offices. Typically, each local office has a chief public defender (who may be either elected or appointed), and a number of assistant public defenders ("P.D.s"). P.D.s are fully licensed lawyers whose sole job is to represent indigent defendants in criminal cases. Because they typically appear in the same courts on a daily basis, P.D.s can gain a lot of experience in a short period of time.

The P.D. is in some respects a part of the same criminal justice community that includes the judge, prosecutor, police, and court personnel. As a result, defendants sometimes fear that a P.D. will pull punches in order to stay friendly with judges and prosecutors. However, most private attorneys also have regular contacts with judges and prosecutors and are rarely accused of being in league with them. Thus, this is an unfair criticism of P.D.s. All defense attorneys, whether private or government-paid, can maintain cordial relationships with judges and prosecutors while vigorously representing their clients' interests.

Some P.D. offices assign the same P.D. to a defendant's case from beginning to end. In other P.D. offices, the P.D.s are specialized. One P.D. may handle arraignments, another settlement conferences, another trials, and so forth. Under this method, a single defendant may be represented by a number of P.D.s as a case moves from beginning to end. This second approach can sometimes result in a particular defendant getting lost in the cracks, depending primarily on the level of communication between the different P.D.s as the case moves from one phase to the next.

9. Some areas offer indigents panel attorneys instead of public defenders. Is there any difference between these two systems?

Yes. Panel attorneys are private attorneys who agree to devote part or all of their practice to representing indigent defendants at government expense. Panel attorneys handle most of the criminal cases in states that have not set up public defender offices. When the judge has to appoint an attorney for a defendant, the judge appoints the panel attorney whose turn it is to be in the judge's courtroom. Usually, the same panel attorney continues to represent a defendant until the case concludes.

Availability of Free Legal Assistance by Nonprofit Groups

Indigent persons can sometimes get free legal assistance in civil cases from various civil rights organizations. For example, an indigent person who wants to sue a city for stopping her from handing out political leaflets might seek help from the ACLU. However, such free legal assistance is rarely available to criminal defendants. In part because a system of government-appointed attorneys is already in place, few civil rights organizations represent indigent criminal defendants. However, defendants should not entirely discount the possibility. For instance, a woman charged with assault who claims that she was defending herself after years of physical abuse might seek legal help from an organization such as NOW (National Organization for Women).

---

10. My friend and I were charged with committing a crime together. My friend got a public defender while I got a panel attorney. Why?

Even jurisdictions with public defender offices usually maintain panels of private counsel whom judges appoint to represent those indigent defendants the P.D. is not able to represent, because of what is called a conflict of interest.

A P.D. would not be allowed to represent a defendant because of a conflict of interest in the following situations:

- Where two defendants are charged with jointly committing a crime. Even if both are indigent, the public defender's office cannot represent both because each defendant may try to point the finger at the other as being more to blame.
- Where the victim is a former public defender client. In this situation the P.D. would have two conflicting duties: (1) to vigorously represent the current client's interests, and (2) to not disclose any information learned from the previous client in confidence. To fulfill the duty of vigorous representation in the current case, the P.D. would have to use any information known about the victim that might put the victim's testimony in doubt. Yet this could easily violate the duty owed by the P.D. to the previous client (the victim in the present case) to not use that information. Note: In this case, public defender offices sometimes avoid conflict of interest problems by following a "don't peek" policy. Under this policy, a P.D. stays on a case by promising not to look in the P.D. files to dig up nasty but confidential information against a former client. Judges have an economic incentive to accept such promises: It's almost always cheaper to appoint a second P.D. than a private panel attorney.

11. Can I choose which lawyer the judge appoints to represent me?

Generally, no. In communities served by public defender offices, a judge simply appoints the public defender's office to represent indigent defendants. The individual P.D. who actually provides the representation is normally the P.D. who happens to be assigned to the courtroom in which a defendant's case is heard. Similarly, panel attorneys are appointed according to which panel attorney is available for assignment in the courtroom in which a defendant's case is heard.

12. Do court-appointed attorneys provide competent legal representation?

Despite the increasingly severe fiscal constraints on their offices, public defenders usually provide representation that is at least as competent as that provided by private defense attorneys. This was demonstrated by a 1992 study conducted by the National Center for State Courts entitled, "Indigent Defenders Get the Job Done and Done Well." The study concluded that P.D.s and private counsel achieve approximately equal results. For example, in the nine counties surveyed in the study, 76% of public defender clients were convicted, compared to 74% of private counsel clients.

Additionally, public defender jobs tend to be so competitive that P.D. offices can select highly qualified attorneys. True, many P.D.s stay for a few years, gain intensive experience, and then leave for the supposedly greener pastures of private practice. However, most public defender offices offer excellent training programs, so that even recently arrived P.D.s can rapidly build expertise.

Panel Attorneys Are Good, Too

In the past, many private defense counsels shunned panel work. As a result, panel attorneys were often like bookends: either novice lawyers with no other source of clients, or older lawyers for whom panel work was a way to ease into retirement. However, private defense attorneys now tend to look at panel work as a plum assignment that can supplement their private practices. They are sure to get paid, and because they appear in court regularly they can quickly build their reputations. Hence, judges in many areas can be quite picky, and panel attorneys are often experienced and highly competent.

Despite these good points, there is much that is wrong with many appointed-counsel programs:

- **Too much work, not enough money.** Regardless of the competence of individual court-appointed attorneys, they are often asked to perform too much work for not enough money. This is especially true of public defender programs. Local politicians don't win many votes by expanding the budget for court-appointed lawyers to keep up with

the growth in criminal prosecutions. For example, courts in Louisiana and Minnesota have ruled that the system of free legal defense services is so badly underfunded that it is unconstitutional. And in a California case, *Williams v. Superior Court,* 53 Cal. Rptr. 2d 832 (1996), the court noted that a deputy public defender was representing 21 defendants whose cases were beyond the time limit to take them to trial—yet was eligible for additional assignments.

Caseload Guidelines Are Often Incompatible With Quality Representation

Even nationally approved caseload guidelines sound staggering. Under those guidelines, one attorney may handle 150 felonies in addition to 400 misdemeanors, 200 juvenile cases, or 25 appeals in a year. Even assuming compliance with these guidelines, indigent defendants may languish in jail for a week or more before they see an attorney. And high caseloads often force court-appointed lawyers to give short shrift to individual cases and pressure defendants to plead guilty. For example, even in an older study of convicted felons, the author wrote, "Most [of the defendants] spent 5 to 10 minutes with their P.D., and the P.D.'s first words were, 'I can get you _____ if you plead guilty'" (*American Criminal Justice: The Defendant's Perspective,* by Jonathan Caspar (Prentice Hall, 1972)).

- **Don't rock the boat.** Court-appointed lawyers often appear in the same courtrooms day in and day out, and therefore know their way around the courthouse better than other criminal defense attorneys in the area. This can be a boon for one defendant but bad news for another. For example, the court-appointed attorney may use that familiarity so as to achieve the best result possible for one client, yet resist rocking the boat in another case to maintain friendly relationships with the judges and prosecutors he or she has to work with every day. The danger is perhaps most acute with panel attorneys. Panel attorneys owe their jobs to the judges who appoint them, and some panel attorneys may fear that to take a position that offends a judge is to bite the hand that feeds them.

CASE EXAMPLE: Hedda Drynk is charged with drunk driving and is represented by Joe Riley, a court-appointed panel attorney. Hedda's case has been assigned to Judge Hawk for trial. Hedda has a previous conviction for reckless driving, and Riley knows that Judge Hawk is especially stern on second-time offenders. Riley could automatically have the case assigned to another judge by filing an affidavit asserting that Judge Hawk cannot give his client a fair shake.

Question: Why might Riley fail to file the affidavit?

Answer: Riley might fear that Judge Hawk will take revenge if he finds out that Riley has challenged his fairness. When Riley's current panel term expires, Riley may find that he has been replaced by another lawyer. Judge Hawk could not properly remove Riley from the panel for exercising a proper procedure. However, Riley would have difficulty proving that this is the reason he was removed, and Riley might prefer not to rock the boat.

13. Should I get a second opinion on any advice my court-appointed lawyer gives me?

Defendants who think their court-appointed attorneys are not representing them adequately out of a fear of rocking the boat or any other reason should consider:

- **Checking the court-appointed lawyer's advice with a private defense attorney.** Even an indigent defendant may be able to pay for a short second opinion consultation with a private defense attorney. Or, a defendant may have friends who can check with an attorney who has represented them.
- **Talking to other defendants facing similar charges to find out if their attorneys have provided different advice.** Note, though, that because each case is unique, advice for different defendants—even those charged with the same crime—may be valid, yet vary greatly. Also remember that the conversation will not be confidential and can be disclosed to the prosecution.

14. If I'm unhappy with my court-appointed lawyer, can I get a replacement?

Defendants sometimes ask judges to fire their appointed counsel (P.D. or panel attorney) and appoint a new one. Often, the stated reason is something like, "My attorney and I don't see eye to eye about case strategy," or, "My attorney won't talk to me." However, judges rarely grant such requests, believing that most of them arise from frustration with the system rather than from the reason actually stated by the defendant. Most indigent defendants must therefore either accept whatever lawyer the judge appoints, or represent themselves if they are qualified to do so. The right to counsel of choice does not extend to defendants who require appointed attorneys (*U.S. v. Gonzales-Lopez*, U.S. Sup. Ct. 2006). However, if a defendant is able to offer concrete proof that communications with a court-appointed lawyer have completely broken down, the defendant may be able to successfully pursue a Motion for Substitution of Attorney.

A Court-Appointed Attorney May Voluntarily Agree to a Substitution

Instead of asking a judge to order a change of a court-appointed attorney, a defendant may have better luck asking the attorney to agree to the change. Rather than continue to represent a defendant with whom communications have broken down, court-appointed attorneys tend to honor such a request, and judges tend to go along.

Section III: Private Defense Attorneys

This section is about private attorneys— who they are, how to find them, and what they charge.

15. What kinds of attorneys offer private criminal defense services?

Defendants who want to be represented by an attorney, and who can secure a qualified private attorney on their own, have a Sixth Amendment right to be represented by the attorney of their choice (*U.S. v. Gonzales-Lopez*, U.S. Sup. Ct. 2006).

Private criminal defense lawyers tend to practice either on their own or in small partnerships, and in a specific geographical setting. By contrast, attorneys who handle civil cases tend to congregate in large corporate law firms with branch offices in many cities.

While personality differences between civil and criminal attorneys may account for some of the variance, the biggest factor is the differing nature of the work:

- Big-firm civil attorneys tend to represent companies who do business all over the country or the world. Criminal defense lawyers represent individuals whose problems are usually quite local.
- Companies represented by big-firm civil lawyers have a continual need for legal advice and representation. Individual criminal defendants tend to be one-shot players with nonrecurring or sporadic legal needs.

- The typical private defense attorney has had several years of experience working for the government before going into private practice, either as a prosecutor (often, a district attorney or city attorney) or as a public defender.

CASE EXAMPLE: Carson O'Genic is charged with hit-and-run driving, a felony. Carson wants to hire her own attorney, and a friend strongly recommends an attorney named Brette Simon. Carson is impressed with Brette, but is worried when Brette mentions that she spent seven years as a prosecutor with the district attorney's office. Carson's concern is that Brette is prosecution-oriented and may not do everything she can for Carson.

Question: Should Carson look elsewhere for a lawyer?

Answer: Not necessarily. Brette's previous prosecutorial experience alone should not cause Carson to hire a different attorney. Many excellent criminal defense attorneys have previous prosecutorial experience. If anything, Brette's years as a prosecutor are likely to benefit Carson. Brette is apt to be familiar with the district attorney's policies and practices, and may know just who to talk to in an effort to resolve the matter in Carson's favor.

16. How can I find a private lawyer if I'm in jail because I couldn't bail out?

While they are in jail, defendants have to overcome two obstacles to hire a lawyer:

- **Paying the lawyer's fee.** Criminal defense lawyers often want the bulk of their money up front, meaning, "You want to talk to me, you pay me first." Since jailed defendants usually have no money, they have to find family members or friends who will put up the money.
- **Finding a satisfactory lawyer.** If an arrested suspect has previously been satisfactorily represented by a criminal defense lawyer, that is usually the lawyer whom the suspect should call.

But how should other arrested suspects proceed? Probably the most fruitful approach is to get a referral from one or more of the following sources:

- **Civil practitioners.** Defendants who know an attorney in civil practice can ask that attorney to recommend a criminal defense lawyer. (Some civil practitioners, of course, are also competent to represent clients in criminal matters, at least for the limited purpose of arranging for release from jail following an arrest.)
- **Family members or friends,** who may either know of a criminal defense lawyer or who, not being in custody, have the time to pursue additional reference sources, such

as family clergy, doctors, or other professionals.

- **Bail bond sellers,** who are usually in regular contact with private defense lawyers.

If none of these resources pan out, and only as a last resort, defendants sometimes may consider referrals from other jailed suspects who are satisfied with their lawyers.

Bail Out of Jail, Then Shop for a Lawyer

It may be difficult to find and hire a competent lawyer while in jail. The atmosphere is usually psychologically oppressive, a defendant can't comparison-shop, and the police and other defendants are notoriously poor judges of lawyers' competence. Defendants who can quickly bail out of jail on their own are often better off doing so, and then hiring a lawyer.

---

17. How should I go about finding a lawyer if I'm not in custody?

Many defendants facing criminal charges are not in custody at the time they seek to hire an attorney. Either the police issue them a citation and a court date and never take them to jail, or they bail out of jail on their own, without first hiring an attorney.

Like defendants who are in custody, defendants who are not in jail can seek referrals from civil lawyers, friends and relatives, and bail bond sellers. However,

nonjailed defendants have additional options. The additional sources include:

- **A local bar association's lawyer referral panel.** Attorneys are usually recommended according to their experience and the type and seriousness of a criminal charge.
- **Martindale-Hubbell.** Martindale-Hubbell publications identify lawyers according to their specialties in specific geographic areas, and even rate the lawyers for competency. Defendants can either try to find attorneys by looking in Martindale-Hubbell, or check references on attorneys who have been recommended to them. All law libraries have Martindale-Hubbell books; many general public libraries have them as well. Defendants who have access to the Internet will also find Martindale-Hubbell online. (See Chapter 27.)
- **Courthouse visits.** Defendants can visit a local courthouse and sit through a few criminal hearings. If a particular lawyer impresses a defendant, the defendant can ask for that lawyer's card (after the hearing has concluded) and then call for an appointment.

18. How do I know if a particular lawyer is right for me?

No matter what the source of a lawyer referral, defendants should always personally interview a lawyer before hiring one. Noncustodial defendants should consider "comparison shopping" by speaking with at least two lawyers before hiring one. A private defense attorney often consults with a potential client at no charge, and a personal interview increases the likelihood that the defendant will be satisfied with the attorney's services.

A personal interview is desirable because a successful attorney-client relationship depends on more than just an attorney's background and legal skills. A good relationship is a true partnership, with both partners actively involved in decision making. (See Chapter 8.) Because there's no guarantee that a lawyer who works well with one client will work equally well with another, even a strong recommendation from a trusted friend is not a substitute for a personal consultation.

More than simply hiring a known criminal law defense attorney, a defendant should try to hire an attorney whose experience is in the courthouse where the defendant's case is pending. Though the same laws may be in effect throughout a state, procedures vary from one courthouse to another. For example, the D.A. in one county may have a no-plea-bargaining policy with respect to a certain offense, while the D.A. in a neighboring county may have no such policy. Defendants should prefer attorneys experienced in local procedures and personnel.

A defendant should also try to find an attorney who has represented defendants charged with the same or very similar offenses. Modern criminal law is so complex that many lawyers specialize in particular types of offenses. For example, one may specialize in drunk driving, another in drug offenses, and another in white-collar crimes (generally referring to nonviolent, money-related crimes such as tax fraud or embezzlement).

It is perfectly appropriate for a defendant to inquire during the initial consultation about the attorney's experience. A defendant should not hire a lawyer who refuses to specifically discuss her experience or who gives vague, unrevealing answers. For example, assume that Zach Michaels is charged with driving under the influence of alcohol (drunk driving). Zach might ask the lawyer he's thinking of retaining such questions as:

- "Have you represented people who have been charged with drunk driving before?"
- "What percentage of your practice involves representing people charged with drunk driving?"
- "Are you certified as a specialist in drunk driving cases?" (Some states allow attorneys to qualify as specialists in specific areas of practice; others do not.)
- "What percentage of your practice involves appearing in the courts that my case will be assigned to?"

Because most private lawyers have years of criminal law experience either as a prosecutor or as a P.D. before going into private practice, defendants should not have to sacrifice quality to find attorneys who have local experience with their types of cases.

A defendant's lawyer speaks for the defendant. No matter how highly recommended a lawyer may be, it is also important that the lawyer be someone with whom the defendant is personally comfortable. The best attorney-client relationships are those in which clients are full partners in the decision-making process, and defendants should try to hire lawyers who see them as partners, not as case files.

Thus, defendants should ask themselves questions such as these when considering whether to hire a particular lawyer:

- "Does the attorney seem to be someone I can work with and talk openly to?"
- "Does the attorney explain things in a way that I can understand?"
- "Does the lawyer show personal concern and reflect a genuine desire to want to help?"
- "Do the lawyer's concerns extend to my overall personal situation, as opposed to being narrowly limited to the crime with which I'm charged?"
- "Does the lawyer appear to have characteristics that make it likely she will engender trust in prosecutors, judges, and, if necessary, jurors?"

19. Should I expect a lawyer to guarantee a good result?

No. Toasters come with guarantees, attorneys don't. Defendants should be wary of lawyers who guarantee satisfactory outcomes. Too much of what may happen is beyond a defense lawyer's control for a hard guarantee to make sense. A lawyer who guarantees an outcome may simply be trying a hard-sell tactic to induce the defendant to hire him. On the other hand, it may make perfect sense for a lawyer to express strong confidence about the outcome, as long as he doesn't express this confidence in absolute terms.

20. I'm happy with the lawyer I hired, but she's part of a law firm. Can I reasonably insist that only the lawyer I select work on my case?

Defendants generally assume that the lawyer they hire will personally attend to all aspects of their cases, from legal research to trial. Lawyers (especially those who are members of a law firm), however, often delegate work to others. For example, a lawyer may hire a law student (often called a law clerk) to do legal research, ask an associate lawyer in her firm to appear with the client at a pretrial conference with the D.A., and ask a paralegal to meet with and prepare the client for trial. These are common lawyer practices, and are one way that lawyers can hold down legal fees. (Clients who pay by the hour ordinarily pay less for an hour of a paralegal's time than for an attorney's time.) However, these practices are appropriate only if the client knows about them in advance and agrees. Therefore, before retaining a lawyer a defendant should take the following steps:

- Find out whether the lawyer is currently involved in any unusually complex cases. If the lawyer is in the middle of a month-long jury trial, the lawyer is more likely to assign work to an associate.
- Ask whether the lawyer's practice is to assign work to an associate.
- Check the written retainer agreement that the lawyer asks you to sign. (See Question 25, below.) If it provides for work done by people other than the lawyer, consider specifying what duties the lawyer can't delegate to others. (For instance, "Unless otherwise agreed to in advance, Lawyer will be personally present at all court appearances.")

21. What's a private criminal defense lawyer likely to cost?

More than most people feel comfortable paying. However, as is so often the case in legal matters, a definitive answer to this question is impossible. Attorneys set their own fees, which vary according to such factors as:

- **The probable complexity of the case.** Most attorneys charge more for felonies than for misdemeanors, since felonies carry greater penalties, are likely to involve more court appearances, etc.
- **The attorney's experience.** Generally, less experienced attorneys set lower fees than their more experienced colleagues.

- **Geography.** Just as gasoline and butter cost more in some parts of the country than others, so do attorneys.

Because of factors such as these, standard legal fees do not exist. According to a survey of readers reported in *Consumer Reports,* the median legal fee charged by lawyers in criminal cases was $1,500. (Median means that the fees were over the amount in as many cases as they were under the amount.) Because many of these cases only involve a consultation or a single court appearance, most defendants can expect to pay much more for full representation. For example, a defendant charged with a misdemeanor that goes to trial should not be surprised by a legal fee in the neighborhood of $2,000–$3,000; an attorney may want an advance of around $2,500, and $1,000 per day of trial in a felony case. Moreover, most attorneys want all or a substantial portion of their fees paid up front (in advance).

22. How do criminal defense lawyers decide what to charge?

Criminal defense lawyers usually charge either by the hour or by the case. Increasingly, the latter type of billing arrangement is more common in criminal cases.

a. Hourly billing

Defendants who are billed by the hour pay for the actual time their lawyers devote to their cases—say, $150 per hour. They may also pay for expenses a lawyer incurs in the course of the representation, such as copying fees, subpoena fees, and so on.

From the defendant's standpoint there are advantages and disadvantages to hourly billing. The most important advantage is that defendants who pay by the hour benefit if a case concludes quickly. However, if the case becomes unexpectedly complicated, it can get very costly. Moreover, hourly fees give attorneys a financial incentive to devote more time to a case than it may warrant or the defendant is prepared to pay. Also, most criminal defense attorneys set a minimum retainer fee that they keep even if a case is resolved with one phone call. (See Question 23, below.)

Fortunately, experienced defense attorneys usually can anticipate how many hours they are likely to spend on a case, and a defendant should not agree to an hourly charge without getting the attorney's good-faith estimate of how much time the case is likely to take.

b. Case billing

Lawyers who charge by the case represent defendants for a fixed fee. For example, a lawyer may set a fee of $1,500 for a defendant charged with drunk driving. The fee would not change according to the number of hours the lawyer devotes to the case.

As with hourly billing, the case billing approach has its advantages and disadvantages. The primary advantage is certainty. Defendants know going in what their cost will be, and the attorney bears the risk of unforeseen complications. However, a defendant may feel ripped off if the case settles very quickly. (In some quick settlement circumstances, attorneys will refund a portion of their fee.) Also, the fee may cover only the pretrial phase of the case; the attorney may require an additional substantial fee to actually try the case. As with other types of information, the defendant should clarify this point before hiring the attorney. (See Question 25, below.)

Beware Super-Low Hourly Rates

With legal fees so high, most defendants understandably want to pay as little as possible for effective representation. However, a low hourly rate can be misleading. An experienced attorney with a high hourly rate may be able to resolve a case more speedily and satisfactorily than a novice with a much lower hourly rate, and therefore be less expensive in the long run.

Hourly Fee With a Cap

A defendant may also agree to pay an hourly fee but only up to an agreed-upon fixed sum. After that amount, the lawyer finishes the representation at no extra cost to a defendant. This approach combines the advantages of both of the fee arrangements discussed above while minimizing the disadvantages.

23. What is a retainer fee?

Whether they bill by the hour or by the case, defense lawyers typically want defendants to pay a retainer fee up front— that is, before the attorney begins working on the case. For example, a lawyer who bills at the rate of $100 an hour may want clients to pay up front for 20 hours of the lawyer's time, or $2,000. The lawyer will send the client regular statements showing how much time she has put into the case, what was done, and how much of the retainer has thus far been used. If the balance in a defendant's account approaches zero, the lawyer will probably ask the defendant for an additional payment (unless the lawyer is working for a set fee). The lawyer will refund to the defendant whatever portion of the retainer remains at the end of the case.

24. I've heard of contingency fees, where an attorney gets paid only if the attorney wins the case. Can I arrange for a contingency fee in a criminal case?

No. Contingency fees are common in some types of civil cases, particularly personal injury cases. Lawyers who work on a contingency basis take their fees from money their clients recover as damages; if the clients collect nothing, the lawyers get nothing. However, in criminal cases contingency fees are considered unethical and are not permitted (Rule 1.5(d) of the ABA Model Rules of Professional Conduct). One reason why the no-contingency-fee rule makes sense is that defendants in criminal cases don't recover money damages if they win, so there's no pot of money from which an attorney can collect fees.

25. How do I find out what services I'll be getting for my fees?

Defendants should carefully examine the terms of the attorney-client agreement they are asked to sign. Until recently, this would have been difficult, because many attorney-client arrangements were oral and based on handshakes. Today, after reaching agreement with a defendant about fees, a lawyer will almost certainly ask the defendant to sign a written retainer agreement or fee agreement. The agreement is a written contract, fully enforceable in court, that specifies the attorney's fee and the services that the lawyer will perform for that fee. (See the sample retainer agreement at the end of this chapter.)

Knowing the amount of an attorney's fee is one thing; knowing what services it covers is quite another. Many defendants who are fully aware of what their attorneys will charge are surprised when their attorneys inform them that services that the defendants thought were included in the fee are extra.

For example, the reality is that most cases are settled before trial. Because of this, a fee agreement may include an attorney's services only up until the time of trial. A defendant who wants to go to trial may therefore get a jolt when the attorney says, "My additional fee to take the case to trial will be $$$." Other extras that may come as a surprise to a defendant include:

- the cost of a private investigator
- the fees of an expert witness
- the costs of copying documents and subpoenaing witnesses, and
- the attorney's fees to handle an appeal from a conviction.

There are no standard agreements, and just because one attorney performed a set of legal services for one all-inclusive fee does not mean that another attorney will do likewise. The key is for defendants to read retainer agreements carefully and ask their attorneys to explain possible extras.

26. Can I change lawyers if I'm unhappy with the one I hired?

Yes. Defendants who hire their own attorneys have the right to discharge them without court approval. A defendant does not need to show good cause or even justify the discharge to the lawyer. (Most attorney-client agreements explicitly advise clients that they have the right to discharge their attorneys.) After discharging a lawyer, defendants can hire another or, if qualified, represent themselves. Of course, the decision to change lawyers can be costly. In addition to paying the new lawyer, the defendant will have to pay the original lawyer whatever portion of the fee the original lawyer has earned.

When Changing Lawyers Might Unfairly Prejudice the Prosecution's Case

A defendant's right to change lawyers must be weighed against the prosecutor's right to keep the case moving on schedule. Assume, for example, that a defendant seeks to change attorneys on the eve of trial. The new attorney is likely to agree to represent the defendant only if the trial is delayed so that the new attorney can prepare. The prosecutor may oppose delay, perhaps for the reason that the prosecution witnesses will not be available to testify at a later date. In these circumstances, the judge may deny the defendant's request to delay the trial. This would mean—realistically—that the defendant will have to stay with the original attorney rather than bring in an unprepared new attorney.

---

27. What can I do if I think my lawyer overcharged me?

In many states, bar associations (that is, organized groups of lawyers) can protect defendants against fee gouging. Many lawyer-client fee agreements provide for arbitration in case of a dispute between attorney and client over fees. Often, a state's bar association selects the arbitrator. Many arbitrators are very sensitive to fee gouging, and will often reduce the fee of an attorney whose charges are out of line with others in the same geographical area.

Negotiating a Reduced or Alternative Fee

Many attorneys will settle with clients who are unable to pay their full fees—especially when the alternative is a hearing before a bar association arbitrator. Before filing a claim with the state bar, a defendant should seek a friendly resolution with the lawyer. The lawyer may well agree to extend payments or reduce the fee. An attorney might even accept an "in-kind" payment in lieu of part of the fee—say, a painting from an artistic defendant, or a piece of handmade furniture from a carpenter. Be creative!

28. Do I have to hire a lawyer selected by my relatives or friends to get me out of jail?

No. Defendants who are in jail commonly ask relatives or friends to contact a lawyer for help in securing a speedy release. But a defendant doesn't have to hire that lawyer. If the attorney wants to be paid for arranging for bail, the attorney will have to look to the relative or friend who contacted the lawyer.

29. How can I be sure that I have my attorney's undivided loyalty?

Attorneys have a duty of loyalty to their clients and should not take on a defendant's case if representing the defendant would cause a conflict with other cases handled by that lawyer, or the lawyer's own personal or business interests. (See Rule 1.7, ABA Model Rules of Professional Conduct.)

Here are the types of questions that defendants can ask to make sure that they have a lawyer's loyalty:

- "Even though my mom (or uncle, etc.) is paying your fees, am I the one with whom you will discuss all important case strategies, including plea bargains?" No matter who is paying a lawyer's fee (even if it's the government paying the fee), a lawyer's duty is to the client and not to the fee-payer. For example, a lawyer cannot disclose a defendant's confidential communications to whomever is paying the defendant's fee. And it's up to the defendant, not the fee-payer, to decide whether the defendant will plead guilty.
- "I'm charged with embezzling money from the city department where I worked, and I think I'm being made a scapegoat for political reasons. Do you represent any local agencies or politicians that will prevent you from showing who's really responsible for the money that disappeared?" Defense attorneys often try to show that others are responsible for the crimes with which their clients are charged, and defendants do not want to be represented by lawyers whose hands may be tied.
- "If I decide that I want to go to trial, will you support that decision?" Sometimes attorneys take cases expecting them to settle and have

no real desire to go to trial. As a result, a lawyer's advice may reflect the lawyer's agenda rather than the client's.

CASE EXAMPLE: Attorney Frieda Mann represents Jowanna Bashin, who is charged with the unauthorized practice of law. Jowanna insists that she's not guilty and wants to go to trial. However, in an effort to get more court referrals, Mann is trying to establish a reputation in the local courts as a lawyer who can settle cases before trial. Therefore, Mann repeatedly urges Jowanna to plead guilty in exchange for a very small penalty and no jail time.

Question: Has Mann violated her duty of loyalty to Jowanna?

Answer: Yes. Mann's primary motive is to develop her law practice rather than to represent her client. Jowanna should ask Mann to return all or most of the money she has already paid her, and hire a different lawyer. If Mann fails to return Jowanna's money, Jowanna should file a complaint with her state or local bar association.

> ## Public Defenders and the Duty of Loyalty
>
> No less than private attorneys, public defenders owe a duty of loyalty to their clients. However, many P.D.s have far more cases than they can reasonably handle. As a result, P.D.s may resemble sausage makers—they try to stuff all their clients into the same mold. For example, many P.D.s routinely recommend that their clients accept standard deals, regardless of the clients' individual circumstances. The reason is that P.D.s may perceive of their duty of loyalty as owed to their clientele as a whole, and to spend a large block of time on any single client's case would mean neglecting too many other clients. Nevertheless, P.D.s do give some cases more priority than others, and defendants should seek to ensure that their cases receive individualized attention. (See Section II for more on public defenders.)

Section IV: Self-Representation

This section is about self-representation in a criminal case—why some people self-represent, and some tips on how to decide whether it's feasible in your situation.

CAUTION
Few defendants are capable of representing themselves competently. (See Section I, above.)

A Famous Case of Self-Representation

Occasionally, high-profile defendants choose self-representation—though generally without much success. One of the most famous cases of self-representation involved Colin Ferguson, the so-called "Long Island Railroad Killer." Ferguson was tried in 1995 for gunning down six commuters on the Long Island Railroad. Though he faced life in prison without possibility of parole, Ferguson insisted on representing himself at trial. There was a huge public outcry against allowing him to do so, especially from people who thought that it would be cruel to allow Ferguson to personally question survivors of the attack. Nevertheless, the judge ruled that Ferguson was legally capable of waiving his right to an attorney and participating in the trial, and allowed him to represent himself. The jury convicted him on all counts after a short deliberation.

30. If the criminal justice system is so complex, why do some defendants choose to represent themselves?

Statistically, few defendants represent themselves in criminal cases. Those who do, do so for a variety of reasons:

- Some defendants who have the financial ability to hire lawyers don't do so because they think that the likely punishment is not severe enough to warrant the expense.
- Some defendants believe (often mistakenly) that their court-appointed or even hired attorneys in previous cases were ineffective, and figure they can do just as well by representing themselves.
- Some defendants believe that lawyers are part of an overall oppressive system and try to make a political statement by representing themselves.
- Some defendants want to take responsibility for their own destiny.
- Some defendants who are in jail pending trial can gain privileges through self-representation, such as access to the jail's law library. Also, not bound by lawyers' ethical codes, self-represented defendants can delay proceedings and sometimes wreak havoc on an already overloaded system by repeatedly filing motions.

When Self-Representation Probably Isn't a Good Idea

Defendants seriously considering representing themselves should probably pay for or accept free legal representation when it's available when one or more of the following factors exists:

- Conviction is likely to result in a prison sentence.
- The case is likely to go to trial.
- A defendant has a prior criminal record.
- The defendant is in custody and as a result may not have access to a law library.
- A defendant is anxious and feels overwhelmed about being charged with a crime.

31. Does a judge have to let me represent myself?

No. Defendants cannot represent themselves unless a judge determines that they are competent to do so. No less than a defendant, the community as a whole has an interest in achieving justice. A trial in which an incompetent defendant self-represents does not constitute a fair trial.

The case that established that defendants have a right to represent themselves was *Faretta v. California*, U.S. Sup. Ct. 1975. The *Faretta* case said that a judge must allow self-representation if a defendant is competent to understand and participate in the court proceedings.

To determine competence, the judge often weighs factors such as:

- the defendant's age
- the defendant's level of education
- the defendant's familiarity with English, and
- the seriousness of the crime with which the defendant is charged.

No single factor determines the result, and a defendant doesn't need the legal skills of a professional lawyer to qualify for self-representation. As long as a defendant is competent, knowingly gives up the right to an attorney, and understands court proceedings, the defendant is entitled to represent herself. However, a judge has the power to decide that a defendant is mentally competent to stand trial, yet not competent enough to represent himself (*Indiana v. Edwards*, U.S. Sup. Ct. 2008).

CASE EXAMPLE 1: Ella Mental is charged with burglary. Ella has only an elementary school education, and she has been in and out of mental institutions for much of her life. Ella tells the judge that she wants to represent herself in the burglary case. The judge allows Ella to do so, on the ground that Ella has been convicted of various crimes three times in the past and is thus familiar enough with criminal law to represent herself. Ella goes to trial, and her questions to prosecution witnesses are garbled and for the most part ruled improper by the judge. Ella is convicted.

Question: Was the judge's decision to allow Ella to represent herself proper?

Answer: No. The mere fact that Ella has three prior convictions does not demonstrate that she is capable of knowingly giving up her right to an attorney and representing herself. In view of her limited education, her history of mental problems, and her inability to participate meaningfully in the trial, the judge should have ignored Ella's wishes and appointed a lawyer to represent her.

CASE EXAMPLE 2: Lexi Khan is charged with assault and battery, and wants to represent herself. Lexi speaks English, but has trouble understanding some words. She also has trouble reading a lawbook that the judge asks her to read. In the arraignment court, Lexi refused to enter a plea, and repeatedly said that the whole system is biased and that she wanted nothing to do with it. Over Lexi's objection, the judge appoints an attorney to represent her.

Question: Did the judge act properly?

Answer: Yes. Taking all the circumstances into account, the judge properly exercised discretion when denying Lexi's request for self-representation. In view of Lexi's language difficulties and refusal to participate in the arraignment proceedings, Lexi is not capable of participating in the trial in a meaningful way.

CASE EXAMPLE 3: Dane Gerous is charged with aggravated sexual assault, and asks to represent himself. The judge's questioning reveals that Dane did not finish high school, and that he has no previous legal experience. However, Dane accurately summarizes the charge that he is facing. Also, when the judge reads a statute to Dane, he is able to explain what it means in his own words.

Question: Should the judge allow Dane to represent himself?

Answer: Yes. The charge is serious, and the judge may believe that Dane should have a lawyer. However, Dane has demonstrated sufficient ability to understand and participate in the proceedings, and is entitled to represent himself.

32. Can I be represented by a nonattorney relative or friend?

No. Only licensed attorneys can represent defendants in court. For example, one spouse who is not a lawyer can't represent another, and a nonlawyer parent can't represent a child. No matter how much a defendant trusts and respects a relative or friend, defendants must choose between self-representation and representation by an attorney.

33. If I give a power of attorney to a nonattorney relative or friend, can that relative or friend represent me?

The answer is still no. A "power of attorney" is a document that can enable a relative or friend to handle a defendant's property (such as a house or a bank account) as an "attorney in fact." A power of attorney can even designate one person to make health care decisions for another. But a power of attorney cannot convey the power to represent a defendant in a criminal case. State and federal statutes give lawyers a monopoly on this activity. This is true even though one of the powers often set out in a power of attorney document allows the attorney in fact to prosecute and defend actions in court (which has been interpreted to mean *hire* an attorney to do the court work).

34. Can I start out representing myself, and then hire an attorney if I get in over my head?

Yes. Just as defendants can generally substitute one attorney for another, defendants representing themselves can substitute an attorney for themselves. Many defendants choose to represent themselves in the hope of working out a speedy resolution with a prosecutor, and then hire an attorney if a speedy resolution is not possible.

35. How should I go about deciding whether to represent myself?

As a general rule, the less severe the charged crime, the more sensible is self-representation. Defendants charged with minor traffic offenses should rarely hire an attorney; defendants charged with serious misdemeanors and felonies should rarely be without one.

The most difficult decisions involve less-serious misdemeanors such as drunk driving, possession of small amounts of drugs, shoplifting, and the like. Hiring an attorney in these situations may make sense because jail time and a fine are possibilities, and convictions may carry hidden costs (for example, more severe punishment for a second conviction). On the other hand, first-time offenders are not usually sentenced to jail, and judges and prosecutors often offer standard deals to all defendants for these types of offenses, whether or not they are represented by counsel.

Therefore, the most critical piece of information that defendants should try to learn before deciding whether to hire an attorney is what the likely—rather than possible—punishment would be upon conviction. Often the likely punishment for an offense is far less than the maximum possible punishment set out in the law.

> **CASE EXAMPLE 1:** A law states that the offense of shooting a deer out of season is punishable by a $1,000 fine and six months imprisonment. However, the

How Do I Find Out What a Likely Sentence Is?

It can be hard for a defendant like Jay (in the preceding example) to find out what sentence a judge is likely to hand out in a given case. This information can't be found in statutes or court rules. Rather, information about a judge's sentencing proclivities is part of the hidden law that lawyers learn from being in the trenches. Defendants who want to know what the punishment is likely to be upon conviction might take the following steps:

- Pay a private defense attorney for an hour of consultation. An experienced defense attorney can often make accurate predictions as to likely punishment, and may well advise the defendant to plead guilty without hiring an attorney.
- Call your local public defender's office. Public defenders often have an

"attorney of the day" or "duty attorney" assigned to answer questions. While you may not get advice specific to your case, the attorney will probably tell you what the standard sentence is.

- At the first court appearance, ask the prosecutor, "If I plead guilty (or "nolo contendere"—in which you do not admit guilt, but do not contest the facts) today, what kind of sentence am I likely to get?" While the judge rather than the prosecutor will impose the sentence, the case may be routine enough that the prosecutor's estimate will be pretty close to the mark. But be careful on this one. The prosecutor is not normally the person you want to get your advice from.

actual punishment routinely meted out for a first offense may be a $50 fine and an administrative suspension of the offender's hunting permit. Comparing the likely sentence to the costs of an attorney, the defendant may choose self-representation.

CASE EXAMPLE 2: Jay Walker is charged with drunk driving. According to the statute, upon conviction Jay may lose his license for up to a year, be sent to county jail for up to six months, and fined $2,000. Jay learns that the judge

does not send first offenders like Jay (whose blood alcohol reading was just barely over the limit) to jail. Instead, the judge routinely imposes a fine of $400 and sends offenders to driving school. Balancing the likely consequences of a conviction in this judge's court against the cost of an attorney (and the substantial possibility that a conviction will result anyway), Jay decides to plead guilty without hiring an attorney.

36. Can I represent myself and pay a lawyer to advise me as I go?

Yes. Defendants considering self-representation might seek out an attorney willing to serve as a legal coach. The idea of a legal coach is to combine an attorney's knowledge with the defendant's time. Since a defendant pays only for the periodic use of the attorney's time, the cost of a legal coach can be far less than turning a case over to a private attorney.

Some examples of how legal coaches can help are:

- A legal coach can advise a defendant to make a pretrial motion and even draft the motion; the defendant can go to court and argue the motion.
- A legal coach can advise a defendant what documents to look for and where they might be found; the defendant can conduct the actual document search.
- A legal coach can advise a defendant on a variety of strategies, such as whether to accept a prosecutor's plea offer.
- If a defendant wants an attorney to handle a trial at the last minute, the legal coach who's been working with the defendant can probably step in and take over without unnecessary delay.

Not All Attorneys Are Willing to Serve as Legal Coaches

Some attorneys are worried about their liability if they give wrong advice based on incomplete information; others do not want to be involved with a case unless they are in control of it. Therefore, it may make sense for a defendant thinking about self-representation to line up a legal coach before making the final decision to self-represent. As a general rule, the greater the effort you have made to understand your case and learn some basics of criminal law, the more likely it is that an attorney will agree to serve as your law coach. Reading this book is a good start.

Sample Retainer Agreement

NOTICE: FEES IN THIS CONTRACT ARE NEGOTIABLE;
ATTORNEY FEES ARE NOT SET BY LAW

1. **IDENTIFICATION OF PARTIES.** This agreement, executed in duplicate with each party receiving an executed original, is made between _[name of attorney]_ , hereafter referred to as "Attorney," and _[name of client]_ , hereafter referred to as "Client.

    This agreement is required by Business and Professional Code section 6148 and is intended to fulfill the requirements of that section.

[Option 1: One fee for case through sentencing]

2. **LEGAL SAVING TO BE PROVIDED.** The legal services to be provided by Attorney to Client are as follows: Representation in Case No. _[number]_ , _[court, e.g., San Bernardino County Superior Court]_ , now set for arraignment on _[date]_, through disposition, whether by trial, sentencing, or otherwise. No promises or representations have been made, express or implied, regarding the results in this case.

3. **LEGAL SERVICES SPECIFICALLY EXCLUDED.** Legal services that are not to be provided by Attorney under this agreement specifically include, but are not limited to, the following: _[List services excluded, e.g., representation following a mistrial or granting of a motion for a new trial, appellate work, work on any petition for an extraordinary writ, and representation on any other case (including cases related to this case, such as any later probation or parole revocation).]_

    If client wishes Attorney to provide any legal services not included under this agreement, a separate written agreement between Attorney and Client will be required.

4. **ATTORNEY FEES.** Client will pay to Attorney the fixed sum of _[dollar amount]_ for attorney fees for the legal services to be provided under this agreement, payment in full on or before _[date]_ . This payment is nonrefundable even if Client pleads guilty or the case is dismissed.

[Option 2: Fee Structure for Case Up to Trial]

2. **LEGAL SERVICES TO BE PROVIDED.** The legal services to be provided by attorney to client are as follows: making court appearances concerning client's release from custody, plea negotiations, and setting a trial date; preparation of case for trial; and work on plea

Sample Retainer Agreement (continued)

negotiations, including discussions with prosecution. No promises or representations have been made, express or implied, regarding the results in this case.

3.   LEGAL SERVICES SPECIFICALLY EXCLUDED. This contract does not cover payment for attorney services for the following:

Appeals to [*the superior court appellate department/the court of appeal/the California Supreme Court/any federal court*] .

Writs or similar proceedings to any court.

Representation in any administrative hearing, even if related to this case.

Representation in any [*probation/parole*] violation arising out of any case, even if the revocation is triggered by this case.

 [*Representation at the preliminary hearing in this case.*]

Representation at the trial in this case.

Representation at evidentiary hearings in this case.

Representation at the sentencing hearing in this case.

Representation at a retrial in this case.

Representation if this case is dismissed and then recharged.

As the case progresses, Attorney will notify Client of any proceeds not covered by this contract that require a new contract and the payment of additional fees.

4.   ATTORNEY FEES. Client will pay to Attorney the sum of [*dollar amount*] for attorney fees for the legal services to be provided under this agreement, payable in full on or before [*date*] . This payment is nonrefundable even if Client pleads guilty or the case is dismissed on the first day Attorney makes a court appearance.

[Continue]

5.   RESPONSIBILITIES OF ATTORNEY AND CLIENT. Attorney will perform the legal services called for under this agreement, keep Client informed of progress and developments, and respond promptly to Client's inquiries. Client will be truthful and cooperative with Attorney; keep Attorney reasonably informed of developments and of Client's address, telephone number, and whereabouts; and timely make any payments required by this agreement.

Sample Retainer Agreement (continued)

6. COSTS. Client will pay all "costs" in connection with Attorney's representation of Client under this agreement. Costs are separate from attorney fees. Costs include, but are not limited to, expert fees and expenses, investigation costs, long-distance telephone charges, messenger service fees, photocopying expenses, and process server fees. Costs will be advanced by Attorney and then billed to Client, unless the costs can be met out of client deposits that are intended to cover costs.

7. DEPOSIT. Client will pay to Attorney an initial deposit of _[dollar amount]_ to be received by Attorney on or before _[date]_ , and to be applied against costs incurred by Client. This amount will be deposited by Attorney in an interest-bearing trust account. Client authorizes Attorney to withdraw the principal from the trust account to pay costs as they are incurred by client. Any interest earned will be paid, as required by law, to the State Bar of California to fund legal services for indigent persons. If, at the termination of services under this agreement, the total amount incurred by Client for costs is less than the amount of the initial deposit, the difference will be refunded to Client.

   Attorney will notify Client whenever the full amount of any deposit has been applied to costs incurred by Client. Within 15 days after each notification is mailed, client will pay to Attorney an additional deposit in the same amount, and to be applied in the same manner, as the initial one. Deposit of such additional amounts and payment of any interest earned will be made in the same manner as for the initial deposit. Client authorizes Attorney to withdraw the principal from the trust account to pay costs as they are incurred by Client. If, at the terminations of services under this agreement, the total amount incurred by Client for costs is less than the total amount of all deposits, the difference will be refunded to Client.

8. STATEMENTS AND FACTS. Attorney will send client a monthly statement indicating costs incurred and their basis, any amounts applied from deposits, and any current balance owed. If no costs are incurred for a particular month or if they are minimal, the statement will be held and combined with that for the following month unless a statement is requested by Client. Any balance will be paid in full within 30 days after the statement is mailed.

9. ERRORS AND OMISSIONS INSURANCE COVERAGE. Attorney maintains errors and omissions insurance coverage that would apply to the services to be rendered under this agreement. The policy limits of the coverage are _[dollar amount]_ per occurrence up to a maximum of _[dollar amount]_ per policy term.

   This statement is required by Business and Professions Code section 6148.

Sample Retainer Agreement (continued)

10. EFFECTIVE DATE OF AGREEMENT. The effective date of this agreement will be the date when, having been executed by Client, one copy of the agreement is received by Attorney and Attorney receives the payment required by Paragraph 5 of this agreement and the initial deposit required by Paragraph 7, provided that the copy, payment, and deposit are received on or before __[date]__ , or Attorney accepts late receipt.

The foregoing is agreed to by:

Date:_____   [Signature of client]_____

[Typed name]_____
Client

Date:_____   [Signature of attorney]_____

[Typed name]_____
Attorney

Understanding the Attorney-Client Relationship in a Criminal Case

Most defendants are represented by criminal defense lawyers. (See Chapter 7.) This chapter focuses on the attorney-client relationship, and examines the legal and ethical obligations that lawyers owe to their clients. Defendants need to understand these obligations to work effectively with the lawyers who represent them.

RESOURCE

For a more detailed description of the ethical and legal obligations of lawyers to their clients, consult a professional responsibility treatise such as *Professional Responsibility of the Criminal Lawyer,* by John Wesley Hall, Jr., usually available in academic and large public law libraries.

How Effective Lawyer-Client Relationships Benefit Society

Regardless of its impact on the outcome of a particular case, an effective lawyer-client relationship often produces important long-range social benefits. Defendants who feel that they got "the shaft" from their own lawyers may lose respect for the entire criminal justice system and as a result be at risk of future antisocial behavior. By contrast, defendants whose own efforts contribute to an effective attorney-client relationship are more likely to feel empowered by the system and may thus be less likely to break the law in the future.

Section I: Confidentiality

This section is about the duty of a lawyer to not disclose any information imparted to the lawyer in confidence by a client.

CAUTION

Write the words "Privileged and Confidential" on any written information you send to your lawyer, whether by letter, email, or other means. This shows that you intend what you say to remain private.

1. Can my lawyer repeat what I say to anyone without my permission?

No, with one important exception (discussed below). The most basic principle underlying the lawyer-client relationship is that lawyer-client communications are privileged, or confidential. This means that lawyers can't reveal clients' oral or written statements (nor lawyers' own statements to clients) to anyone, including prosecutors, employers, friends, or family members, without their clients' consent. It matters not whether defendants confess their guilt or insist on their innocence—attorney-client communications are confidential. Both court-appointed lawyers and private defense attorneys are equally bound to maintain their clients' confidences.

> **CASE EXAMPLE 1:** Heidi Hemp is charged with possession of illegal drugs. At the request of Heidi's mother, attorney Joe Lawless talks with Heidi in jail and offers to represent her. Heidi

decides not to hire Lawless, and instead retains Bill Mucho as her lawyer after she bails out. At trial, the prosecutor calls Lawless as a witness and asks him to reveal what Heidi told him in their jail conversation.

Question: Can Lawless testify?

Answer: No. Lawless was talking to Heidi in his capacity as an attorney, and their conversation is confidential even though Heidi decided to hire a different attorney.

CASE EXAMPLE 2: Same case. Heidi tells her lawyer that the drugs belonged to her, and that she bought them for the first time at a time when loss of her job put her under great stress. Heidi authorizes her lawyer to reveal this information to the D.A., hoping to achieve a favorable plea bargain. However, the D.A. refuses to reduce the charges and the case goes to trial. Cross-examining Heidi, the D.A. asks, "Isn't it true that you admitted to your lawyer that the drugs were yours?"

Question: Is this a proper question?

Answer: No. Heidi authorized her lawyer to reveal her confidential statement to the D.A. But a statement made for the purpose of plea bargaining is also confidential, so the D.A. cannot ask about it in trial.

CASE EXAMPLE 3: Same case. Soon after her arrest, Heidi speaks to her mother in jail. Heidi's case goes to trial, and the prosecutor calls Heidi's mother as a witness and asks her to reveal what Heidi told her.

Question: Must her mother testify?

Answer: Yes. Most states do not regard conversations between parents and their children as privileged. Thus, Heidi's mother would have to answer questions under oath about what Heidi said to her.

> CAUTION
>
> **Clients' statements to lawyers concerning an intention to commit a crime or a fraud in the future are usually not confidential.** Judges can compel lawyers to testify to such statements. (For more on the future crimes exception to the lawyer-client confidentiality rule, see Question 7, below.)

2. I discussed my case with my attorney in a restaurant, loud enough for other diners to overhear me. Can they testify to what I said?

Yes. Lawyer-client communications are confidential only if they are made in a context where it would be reasonable to expect that they would remain confidential (*Katz v. U.S.*, U.S. Sup. Ct. 1967). A defendant who talks to a lawyer in such a loud voice that others overhear what is said has no reasonable expectation of privacy and thus waives (gives up) the privilege.

Similarly, people who talk about their cases on cell phones in public places risk losing confidentiality.

3. Are conversations I have with my attorney while I'm in jail considered confidential?

Jailhouse conversations between defendants and their attorneys are considered confidential as long as the discussion takes place in a private portion of the jail and the attorney and defendant do not speak so loudly that jailers or other inmates can overhear what is said. Also, defendants must be very careful not to allow jailers or other prisoners to overhear what they say on the telephone. These people sometimes eavesdrop, in person or on the telephone, and then claim that they were able to overhear incriminating information because the defendant spoke in a loud voice. (Inmates often try to curry favor with prosecutors through such tactics.) If a judge believes them, the privilege is lost and a jailer or other prisoner can testify to a defendant's remarks.

CAUTION

If a jailer warns a prisoner that phone calls are or may be monitored, then phone conversations between prisoners and their lawyers may not be privileged. If a jailer monitors a phone call and overhears a prisoner make a damaging admission to the prisoner's lawyer, then the jailer can probably testify to the defendant's statement in court.

4. I'd like my mom (best friend, etc.) to be present when I talk to my attorney. Does that mean that our conversation won't be considered confidential?

Quite possibly. Defendants who bring strangers (people who are not part of the attorney-client relationship) into a meeting risk losing the right to claim as confidential what is said during the meeting. This means that the D.A. might be able to ask the stranger or even the defendant about what was said during the conference. However, the lawyer can maintain the privilege by convincing a judge that it was necessary to include the stranger in the conversation.

> **CASE EXAMPLE:** Geri Attrix is charged with filing fraudulent income tax returns. Geri brings her son, who helped her prepare the returns in question, to the meeting with her lawyer.
>
> **Question:** Is Geri's conversation with her lawyer confidential?
>
> **Answer:** Yes. Since Geri's son helped her prepare the tax returns, the son's input is necessary for the lawyer to gain a full understanding of the case.

5. If I repeat what I told my lawyer to someone else, is my conversation with the lawyer still considered confidential?

No. Blabbermouth defendants waive (give up) the confidentiality of lawyer-client communications if they disclose those statements to someone else (other than a spouse, because a separate privilege exists for spousal communications). Defendants have no reasonable expectation of privacy in conversations they reveal to others.

CASE EXAMPLE: Benny Dikshun is charged with possession of stolen merchandise. The day after discussing the case with his lawyer, Benny discusses it with a neighbor.

Question: Does talking about the case with a neighbor mean that Benny's statements to his lawyer are no longer confidential?

Answer: No. So long as Benny does not say something to his neighbor like, "Here's what I told my lawyer yesterday …," the attorney-client communications remain confidential. Of course, Benny's conversation with the neighbor is not confidential, and the persecutor can properly ask the neighbor to testify about what Benny told him.

6. Can I have my lawyer confidentially hold on to stuff that I don't want the police to know about?

Usually no. A defendant may want his or her lawyer to hold on to an incriminating tangible object, such as a knife that was used in a stabbing, or documents showing income that the defendant failed to report to the IRS. Because what they say to their lawyers is supposed to be confidential, many defendants assume that they can keep the police from seizing objects by turning them over to their attorneys. However, if an

object is an instrumentality of a crime (the means used to commit a crime, such as a knife used in a stabbing), a lawyer has to turn it over to the police. Defendants can't conceal instrumentalities of crime by giving them to their attorneys.

CASE EXAMPLE 1: Sly Sims comes rushing into the office of an attorney, Sue Menow, and hands her a knife. Sly tells Sue, "This is the blade that I stuck Gibson with. Keep it safe so the cops don't find it." Sly is eventually arrested and charged with stabbing Gibson.

Question: Does Sue have to turn the knife over to the police?

Answer: Yes. Sue cannot conceal the instrumentality of a crime. However, what Sly told her is confidential, so Sue would have to turn over the knife anonymously. Sue could not reveal how she acquired the knife or her conversation with Sly.

CASE EXAMPLE 2: Same case. Assume that instead of handing Sue a knife, Sly Sims phones her and says, "I tossed the knife into the bushes behind the bowling alley on 8th Avenue." Sue goes to the location, looks at the knife, but leaves it exactly where it is.

Question: Does Sue have to tell the police where to find the knife?

Answer: No. Because Sue did not move the knife, she did not interfere with the ability of the police to find the knife on their own. And she does not have to reveal what Sly Sims told her, because that is confidential.

CASE EXAMPLE 3: Same case. Again, Sue gets a phone call from Sly Sims telling her of the location of a knife used in a stabbing. Sue goes to the location and removes the knife so that she can have it tested.

Question: What are Sue's obligations with respect to the knife?

Answer: Because Sue removed physical evidence from its original location, she has an obligation to turn it over to the police. She probably also has to reveal exactly where she found it (see *Alhambra Police Officers Ass'n v. City of Alhambra Police Dep't.,* 7 Cal. Rptr. 3d 432 (2003)), but doesn't have to say how she found out where it was.

CASE EXAMPLE 4: Same case. After stabbing Gibson, Sly Sims comes into Sue's office and hands her a letter written by Gibson threatening Sly with disclosure of a past indiscretion and demanding money. Sly asks Sue to keep the letter to prevent the police from finding out that he had a motive to stab Gibson.

Question: Must Sue turn the letter over to the police?

Answer: Probably not. The letter is not a crime instrumentality: it was not a means by which Sly committed the crime. Thus Sue can treat the letter as confidential.

7. I told my lawyer about my plan to commit a crime in the future. Does my lawyer have a duty to keep my statement confidential?

No. The confidentiality of attorney-client communications usually does not extend to statements pertaining to future frauds or crimes. The government can compel a defense lawyer to testify to a client's statement pertaining to a future crime. In emergency or life-threatening situations, a lawyer might have to reveal such a statement to the police even before a crime is committed.

CASE EXAMPLE: (Based on the John Grisham book and film, *A Time to Kill*): Two defendants are arrested for brutally raping Carl Lee's daughter. Carl Lee tells Jake, a lawyer and friend, of his plan to kill his daughter's attackers, and asks Jake to represent him after he's arrested.

Question: What steps should Jake take next?

Answer: Jake should first urge Carl Lee not to take the law into his own hands. But if Carl Lee insists that he will take personal revenge against the defendants, Jake should report the threat to the police so that they can prevent harm both to Carl Lee and to the attackers. In many states, Jake's failure to report Carl Lee's threat would be an ethical violation that could lead to Jake's suspension or disbarment.

8. Is the fact that the defendant has met with an attorney considered to be confidential?

No. Attorney-client confidentiality mainly extends to communications, so details such as the following are normally not considered confidential:

- the dates and times of attorney-client meetings
- the identities of people who were present during such meetings, and
- the amount of the attorney's fee, and who paid it.

Prosecutors do not routinely seek such information. Its relevance is often limited to conspiracy cases, when a prosecutor wants the information to show that a number of people were part of the same conspiracy. When the information is relevant, attorneys usually must disclose it upon request.

Section II: Client-Centered Decision Making

This section is about who makes what decisions in the course of a criminal case.

9. Should I expect my lawyer to involve me in important decisions?

Yes. Lawyers' ethical responsibilities require that they involve clients in decision making. For example, Rule 1.4 of the ABA Model Rules of Professional Conduct states that, "A lawyer shall explain a matter to the extent necessary to permit the client to make informed decisions regarding the

representation." Moreover, Standard 4-5.2 of the ABA Standards for Criminal Justice lists a number of decisions that "are to be made by the accused after full consultation with counsel." (See Question 10, below.)

Don't be fooled by movie and TV defense attorneys who often say things to clients like, "Do it my way or else." As lawyers' ethical codes recognize, cases belong to defendants, not to their attorneys. It is always the client, not the attorney, who pays a fine or serves the time. Thus, defendants have the right to have input into important case decisions.

On the other hand, lawyers are not "mouthpieces." They are not required to fulfill all of their clients' demands, especially where doing so conflicts with ethical rules or the lawyers' own professionalism.

10. How do I know which decisions are important ones?

Standard 4-5.2 of the ABA Standards for Criminal Justice identifies decisions that are for defendants to make after consultation with their attorneys. They include:

- what plea to enter (usually, guilty or not guilty)
- whether to accept a plea bargain
- whether to waive (give up) a jury trial
- whether to personally testify at trial, and
- whether to appeal.

Decisions about these matters are entrusted to clients not only because the matters are important, but also because lawyers normally have time to consult with their clients before the decisions are made. "Consultation" is a key term. Before making any decision, defendants should insist on meeting with their attorneys to review their options and the likely consequences of each.

11. Are there other decisions that I should think about making?

Because each case is unique, no bright dividing line separates important decisions that are for defendants to make from other decisions that lawyers can be expected to make. Generally, a decision is important if it is likely to have a substantial legal or nonlegal impact on a client.

Two lawyers handling the same case may sometimes reasonably disagree about whether to leave a particular decision to the defendant. In the final analysis, defendants who want to make as many potentially important decisions as possible should do the following:

- repeatedly tell their attorneys that they want to participate in the decision making whenever feasible
- include in their lawyers' fee agreements (see Chapter 7) a clause allocating decision-making to the defendant whenever feasible
- insist that their lawyers counsel them with respect to their alternatives, and the likely consequences of each, and
- match deeds to words by making decisions expeditiously as the opportunities arise.

12. If it's my case, why can't I make all the decisions?

It simply isn't feasible for defendants to make all the decisions regarding their cases. Some decisions, such as how to question potential jurors, involve attorneys' professional craft and, because of the extemporaneous nature of that procedure, are largely beyond the control of defendants. Similarly, in the heat of trial, attorneys often can't turn over to their clients decisions about what questions to ask or objections to make.

Nevertheless, Standard 4-5.2 does identify some trial-related decisions that defense attorneys should make only after consultation with clients, provided that time permits. These decisions include:

- what witnesses to call
- whether and how to cross-examine prosecution witnesses
- what jurors to accept or strike
- what trial motions to make, and
- what evidence to introduce.

Many attorneys think these decisions should be entirely in their hands. Thus, clients who want a voice in as many decisions as possible should discuss their wishes with their attorneys at the outset of the case.

> **CASE EXAMPLE:** (Based again on *A Time to Kill*) Carl Lee is charged with murder for shooting and killing two men who brutally raped his daughter. In the course of the shooting, Carl Lee also accidentally wounded a policeman, causing the policeman to lose a leg.

During cross-examination of the policeman, Carl Lee wants his lawyer, Jake, to ask the policeman whether Carl Lee should be punished for killing the rapists. Jake does not want to ask the question, fearing that the policeman will want to see Carl Lee punished for causing him to lose a leg. When Carl Lee finally convinces Jake to ask the question, the policeman dramatically supports Carl Lee's actions.

Question: Did Jake have to comply with Carl Lee's wishes and ask the question?

Answer: Probably not. In the heat of trial, lawyers normally have the tactical authority to decide what questions to ask. Besides, the witness's opinion about the legitimacy of Carl Lee's actions is irrelevant.

13. My lawyer is urging me to accept a plea bargain; I want to go to trial. Who gets to make the decision?

When lawyers and defendants can't agree about an issue as fundamental as whether to go to trial, it's normally the defendant's desire that prevails. Assuming that a defendant's decision is neither unethical nor illegal ("My decision is that you should bump off the prosecution witness"), the lawyer is the defendant's agent and must either carry out the defendant's decision or convince the judge to let him withdraw from the case. But defendants should not obstinately refuse their attorneys' advice. Defendants should ask questions to make sure that they understand the advice and

why the lawyers think it's in their best interests.

CASE EXAMPLE: Randy Even is charged with aggravated assault, and has insisted to his lawyer that he struck the alleged victim in self-defense. One day, Randy's lawyer phones him to say that he's worked out a good deal with the prosecutor: If Randy pleads guilty (or *nolo contendere*) to simple assault, the prosecutor will recommend that Randy be given a sentence of time served (the jail time he already served while waiting to make bail), and a small fine. However, Randy still believes that he is not guilty and is not sure that he wants to settle the case.

Question: What can Randy do?

Answer: Randy can tell his lawyer to tell the D.A. that there is still no deal. Despite what the lawyer said, the lawyer has no power to make a deal without Randy's personal approval. However, Randy can expect a letter from the lawyer outlining the deal and stating that Randy has decided to reject it in spite of the lawyer's recommendation that he accept it.

14. I want to propose a plea bargain. Does my lawyer have to present it to the prosecutor? And does my attorney have to tell me about the prosecutor's counter-proposal?

Like the decision about whether to go to trial, decisions about whether to offer or accept plea bargains are for defendants to make. To enforce this right, defense attorneys are ethically required to:

- relay their client's offer to plead to the prosecutor, and
- relay the prosecutor's offer to accept a particular plea to their client.

It doesn't matter that the defense attorney believes the defendant's offer won't be accepted, or that the prosecutor's offer is unacceptable.

The Ethical Rule Governing Disclosure of Plea Bargain Offers

Comment to Rule 1.4, ABA Model Rules of Professional Conduct, states: "A lawyer who receives ... a proffered plea bargain in a criminal case should promptly inform the client of its substance unless prior discussions with the client have left it clear that the proposal will be unacceptable."

---

15. What information do I need to decide intelligently whether to plead guilty or make other important decisions?

Before making an important decision in the case, the defendant is entitled to know what alternatives are reasonably available, and so far as can be predicted, the likely consequences of each. For example, assume that the defendant is charged with assault with a deadly weapon. The defense attorney tells the defendant, "The D.A. is willing to accept a guilty plea to simple assault and recommend a sentence of six months in county jail and a fine of $500. The decision is yours—what do you want to do?"

The defendant's response should be something like, "Let's see what my options are, and try to figure out the likely consequences of each one." Here, the defendant and the attorney should readily identify at least three possible options:

- plead guilty now
- plead guilty later, or
- refuse to plead guilty and go to trial.

Before making a decision, the defendant and attorney should discuss the likely consequences of each option. For example, the defendant may ask questions such as:

- "Is there a chance that I'll get a better deal if I wait until closer to the trial to plead guilty?"
- "What sentence am I likely to receive if I go to trial and I'm convicted of assault with a deadly weapon?"
- "I'm trying to get a job. Do you think a conviction for assault with a deadly weapon will look worse than one for plain assault?"

Defendants should not count on having perfect information about the likely consequences of each option. For instance, a defense attorney may have to respond to Question 2 by saying, "It's really hard to predict what sentence you'll receive if you're convicted of assault with a deadly weapon. The judge to whom we've been assigned is very unpredictable, and a lot will depend on the recommendation in the probation report that will be prepared after you enter your plea." (See Chapter 22 for more on probation reports.)

Nevertheless, only if the attorney reviews in as much detail as feasible the likely consequences of all available options can defendants be assured of making the most responsible decisions possible.

Defendants as a Source of Options and Consequences

Attorneys are not always the drivers and defendants always the passengers in an effective attorney-client relationship. Defendants should not hesitate to bring up options and consequences on their own. In fact, when it comes to nonlegal consequences (such as the impact of a conviction on a defendant's job or family), defendants often can make more accurate predictions than attorneys. For example, assume that a stockbroker charged with making unauthorized trades has to decide whether to plead guilty to a lesser charge. The defendant may be better able than the lawyer to predict the effect of a conviction of a lesser offense on the defendant's license.

To make sure that they carefully consider their options and consequences before making a decision, defendants should write them down. Make a heading for each option, and underneath note the likely consequences of that option.

CASE EXAMPLE: Penny Seagram is charged with drunk driving. At the time of her arraignment, Penny's lawyer tells her, "The D.A. will drop the charge to reckless driving. You'll pay a fine of $400, won't have any jail time, you'll give up your driver's license for three months, and will be on probation for a year. I think it's a pretty good deal, but it's up to you. Should we take the deal?"

Question: What should Penny do?

Answer: Penny should insist on a more thorough discussion with her lawyer before making a decision. Almost certainly, Penny's lawyer can postpone the arraignment for a week, at which time the same deal will be available. In the meantime, Penny can discuss her options and alternatives with her lawyer.

16. Can my attorney properly offer an opinion as to what I should do, even if it's my decision to make?

Yes. Attorneys have a professional obligation to offer "candid advice" (Rule 2.1, ABA Model Rules of Professional Conduct). Attorneys should offer their best professional judgment, not simply tell defendants what they want to hear.

CASE EXAMPLE: Carrie Oka is charged with drunk driving. The prosecutor has offered Carrie a chance to plead guilty to a lesser charge of reckless driving. Carrie wants to go to trial, mentioning various reasons why she is confident that a jury will disbelieve the police officer's testimony about how Carrie was driving. Carrie's lawyer is sympathetic to some of her arguments, but believes on balance that a judge or jury will believe the police officer, and that the prosecutor's offer is a good one and Carrie should take it.

Question: Once Carrie has indicated her desire to refuse the prosecutor's offer, can her lawyer still advise her to accept it?

Answer: Yes. Defendants all too often see their cases through rose-colored glasses. Carrie's lawyer has an obligation to provide dispassionate advice, but in the end should follow her wishes.

17. My lawyer threatened to withdraw from the case if I did not follow her advice. Can she do that?

Occasionally, lawyers and defendants have such strongly opposing views that the lawyer cannot effectively carry out the defendant's desired strategy. In such a situation, the attorney may seek to withdraw as the defendant's counsel, or the defendant may seek to have the attorney replaced with another. Whether this will be permitted in either case depends on whether the prosecutor will be prejudiced or the proceedings will be unnecessarily delayed or disrupted. (See Chapter 7.)

CASE EXAMPLE: Denise Baylout is charged with burglary, and is represented by a public defender. Unfortunately, Denise and her attorney do not always agree on the best strategy, and Denise thinks that her attorney is cold and aloof and not committed to her defense. Denise asks the judge to appoint a different public defender.

Question: Is the judge likely to do so?

Answer: A change of counsel in this context is very unlikely. Defendants who hire private counsel can replace them at will, so long as doing so doesn't unduly delay proceedings. But defendants who are represented at government expense get whomever the judge appoints or a public defender's office assigns. Unless attorney-client communications have broken down to such an extent that Denise cannot get a fair trial, the judge will probably refuse to appoint a new attorney.

18. I hired a private lawyer to represent me, but cannot continue paying him. Can the lawyer withdraw from the case over my objection?

Possibly, subject to approval by the judge. Professional rules in many states allow a lawyer to withdraw from the case if the client fails to pay the lawyer's fees, or if continuing to represent the client causes financial hardship to the lawyer. However, before a judge permits a lawyer to withdraw from a case, the lawyer usually has to give sufficient advance warning to give the client time to hire a new attorney. And a judge might not permit the attorney to withdraw at all under these circumstances:

- the attorney seeks to withdraw on the eve of trial
- the attorney has put in so much work on a case that the client would be prejudiced by having to start all over with another lawyer, or
- the client has already paid substantial legal fees to a lawyer and is financially unable to pay additional fees.

Section III: Lawyer-Client Communication

This section covers the ethical rules that govern the degree to which lawyers must keep their clients informed about the progress of the case.

19. Does my lawyer have to keep me informed about my case?

Yes. Defendants frequently grouse to friends after a case is over, "My lawyer didn't tell me what was going on." To prevent this from happening, defendants should insist that their lawyers adhere to their ethical obligation to inform them about the progress of cases.

Rule Requiring Lawyers to Communicate With Clients

ABA Standard for Criminal Justice 4-3.8 states: "Defense counsel should keep the client informed of the developments in the case and the progress of preparing the defense and should promptly comply with reasonable requests for information." (See also Rule 1.4, ABA Model Rules of Professional Conduct.)

As defined by ethical rules, a lawyer's duty to keep clients informed has two primary components:

- to advise the defendant of case developments (such as a prosecutor's offered plea bargain or locating an important defense witness), and
- to respond reasonably promptly to a defendant's request for information.

20. My lawyer thinks that I am being kept reasonably informed about my case. I disagree. What's going on?

Without labeling either party to the relationship "wrong," lawyers and clients usually have different perspectives on the lawyer's duty to inform the defendant of case developments.

CASE EXAMPLE: Anita Consult's arraignment has just concluded; she and her attorney Sol Vent are supposed to return to court in a month. As they are leaving the courthouse, attorney Vent tells defendant Anita, "I'm going to set up a meeting with the D.A. in the next few days to try to work things out; I'll let you know what happens." As it turns out, Vent and the D.A. can't get together for three weeks. Vent does not bother to tell this to Anita. Anita is upset with Vent. Having heard nothing, Anita worries that the case may have been settled without her knowledge, or that the D.A. refused to meet with Vent.

Question: Did Vent violate the ethical rule requiring an attorney to keep his client informed?

Answer: Probably not, since no developments took place. However, since Vent indicated that he would be speaking to the D.A. in the next several days, he certainly would have been wise, from a customer service standpoint, to have informed Anita about the delay.

21. What can I do to make sure my lawyer communicates with me?

The duty to keep clients informed rests on attorneys, not clients. But on the theory that if the attorney screws up it's the client who usually suffers, here are a few steps that defendants can take to try to secure effective communication with their lawyers:

- Establish, in advance, clear understandings about case updates. If an attorney's practice is to initiate contact only when a development occurs, the attorney should indicate that to the client at the outset of the representation. If a client wants (and can pay for) regular updates

regardless of whether developments have taken place, that too can be spelled out in advance—even included in a written retainer agreement. (See Chapter 7 for more on retainer agreements.)
- A defendant who phones his or her attorney with a request for information can indicate a willingness to speak with the lawyer's associate, secretary, or paralegal. The lawyer may be too tied up on other cases to return the call personally, but may have time to pass along information through an assistant. And because some lawyers have poor communication skills, the information coming from an assistant may be superior to what would have come from the lawyer.

Section IV: Representing Guilty Defendants

This section is about how lawyers handle the sometimes onerous task of representing a defendant the lawyer knows is guilty of the crime.

22. Can my lawyer represent me if she knows I'm guilty?

Yes. Defense attorneys are ethically bound to zealously represent all clients, the guilty as well as the innocent. (See Canon 7, ABA Model Code of Professional Responsibility.) Perhaps no one has ever put the duty so eloquently as Henry VIII's soon-to-be-

beheaded ex-Chancellor Sir Thomas More, who, before going to the scaffold, insisted, "I'd give the Devil benefit of law, for mine own safety's sake." A vigorous defense is necessary to protect the innocent and to ensure that judges and citizens and not the police have the ultimate power to decide who is guilty of a crime.

Another way of looking at this is that the defense lawyer almost never really knows whether the defendant is guilty of the crime he or she has been charged with. Just because the defendant says he did it doesn't make it so. The defendant may be lying to take the rap for someone he wants to protect, or may be guilty, but guilty of a different and lesser crime than the one being prosecuted by the district attorney. For these reasons, among others, many defense lawyers never ask their clients if they committed the crime. Instead, the lawyer uses the facts to put on the best defense possible and leaves the question of guilt to the judge or jury.

23. If my lawyer knows I'm guilty, can my lawyer argue at trial that I should be found not guilty?

Yes. The key is the difference between factual guilt (what the defendant did) and legal guilt (what a prosecutor can prove). A good criminal defense lawyer asks not, "What did my client do?" but rather, "What can the government prove?" No matter what the defendant has done, he is not legally guilty until a prosecutor offers enough evidence to persuade a judge or jury to convict. However, the defense lawyer may not lie to the judge or jury by specifically stating that the defendant did not do something the lawyer knows the defendant did do. Rather, the lawyer's trial tactics and arguments focus on the government's failure to prove all the elements of the crime.

CASE EXAMPLE: Sam Anella is charged with shoplifting. Sam admits to his lawyer that he took the watch, as charged. Sam's lawyer realizes that the store's hidden camera videotape is fuzzy and practically useless as prosecution evidence. In addition, Sam's lawyer learns that the store's security guard was at the end of a long overtime shift and had been drinking alcohol.

Question: Can Sam's lawyer argue for Sam's acquittal?

Answer: Yes. Before trial, Sam's lawyer can argue to the D.A. that the D.A.'s case is too weak to prosecute. At trial, Sam's lawyer can argue to a judge or jury to acquit Sam. No matter what Sam has done, Sam is not legally guilty unless the prosecutor can prove it beyond a reasonable doubt. But note that Sam's lawyer cannot ethically state in his argument that Sam "didn't do it," only that the D.A. didn't prove that Sam did do it. While the line between ethical and unethical behavior may seem like—indeed, is—a fine one, it is a line that criminal defense lawyers walk every day they are on the job.

How to Become an Unpopular Defense Lawyer

Criminal defense attorneys may vigorously defend guilty clients, but as a couple of examples make clear, they risk committing professional suicide by doing so. Way back in 1840, Charles Phillips, one of the finest British barristers of his era, defended Benjamin Courvoisier against a charge that Courvoisier brutally murdered his employer, wealthy man-about-town Lord Russell. Courvoisier privately confessed to Phillips that he was guilty. Nevertheless, Phillips's aggressive cross examinations suggested that the police officers were liars and that other members of Lord Russell's staff might have killed him. Courvoisier was convicted and executed. But when it became generally known that Phillips had known that his client was guilty, Phillips became a pariah to the profession and the public.

Moving forward to 2002, San Diego lawyer Steven Feldman got the "Phillips treatment" when he represented David Westerfield, who was charged with molesting and murdering seven-year-old Danielle van Dam. Feldman knew privately that Westerfield was guilty. Nevertheless, at trial Feldman aggressively attacked Danielle's parents. He offered evidence that they frequently invited strangers into their home for sex orgies, and suggested that one of the strangers could have been the killer. Westerfield was convicted and sentenced to death. Yet like Phillips, Feldman was viciously attacked in the media. TV commentators and members of the public called for his disbarment.

Although Phillips and Feldman gave their clients the best defense possible, their experiences suggest that defense lawyers risk their reputations and perhaps their careers when they go all-out for obviously guilty clients.

Section V: Competent Clients

This section is about how a defendant can help his attorney present the most effective defense possible.

24. What is a competent client?

Competent clients share in the responsibility for an effective attorney-client relationship. Competent clients needn't possess an attorney's knowledge and skills. Instead, competent clients:

- understand and hold attorneys to the ethical duties outlined in this chapter
- participate in making important case decisions, and
- follow through on their attorneys' advice, for example by making and showing up to appointments with counselors. In the event of conviction, such activities lend support to an argument that a defendant has already begun rehabilitation.

Just as educated patients elicit better information from their doctors, so do competent clients tend to receive improved legal services.

25. Can I learn any important client skills by attending court sessions unrelated to my case?

Sure. Courtrooms are public places, and defendants can learn a lot simply by taking an hour or two to watch a court in session. The defendant can examine the demeanor and dress of other defendants, and identify what impresses him or her and what seems off-putting. The defendant can then mirror effective behavior during his or her own court appearance.

26. Should I consider doing my own legal research about issues that arise in my case?

Competent clients need not play amateur lawyer or second-guess every bit of legal advice their lawyer gives. But a defendant should understand the charges against her and the basic procedures followed by the local criminal courts. The procedures described in this book are a good starting point, and the defendant can supplement what she learns in one court by checking for local variations in other courts. The defendant should also read the statutes she allegedly has violated, and make sure she understands how the courts have interpreted those statutes. (See Chapter 12 for more on interpreting criminal statutes and Chapter 27 for how to do legal research.)

A Walk Through Criminal Court

ontrary to the popular notion of courthouses as solemn places— much like churches where people are quiet, well-dressed, and respectful— state courts devoted to criminal cases tend more often to resemble train stations: crowded, confusing, and noisy. The "action" seems to be (and is) happening in the courtroom and in the halls outside; the people seem (and are) tense and scared.

The reality is that the last place most people want to be is criminal court, except perhaps the lawyers and court staff who work there. For anyone else who must go, however, the best way to cope is to first learn what's what, who's who, and the basic rules of the game.

Section I: The Courthouse

This section is about finding your way around the courthouse—that is, the general layout and organization of the building where criminal courts tend to be located.

1. How do I find where I'm supposed to be in the courthouse?

Courthouses, like most public office buildings, usually have guards or directories at the main entrance. Either can direct defendants, witnesses, or anyone else who wants to attend court to "Department J," "Judge Paul's courtroom," or any other location. People who do not know the name or number of the court they need should go to the courthouse clerk's office for help in finding the appropriate courtroom. If both civil and criminal matters are handled in the courthouse, there often will be separate courthouse clerk's offices for the criminal and civil courts.

Finding the Right Courthouse

Obviously, before visitors can find the right courtroom, they need to be in the right courthouse. Criminal courts are often located in the same building as civil (noncriminal) courts, but, especially in large urban areas, they may be in a different building. Anyone asked or told to appear in a criminal court should be sure to get the correct address and building number. Visitors who want to observe criminal proceedings should phone the clerk's office of any nearby court and ask where criminal cases are heard.

---

2. What happens in the courthouse clerk's office?

The courthouse clerk's office is the courthouse's central nervous system. Here, documents relating to all the cases in a courthouse are filed and stored. The courthouse clerk's office may also issue subpoenas (orders to appear in court), collect fines, and manage other administrative details. Courthouse clerks also work with clerks assigned to individual courtrooms (called "courtroom clerks" in this book to distinguish them from those who work in the courthouse clerk's office). (More on courtroom clerks in Section III, below.)

3. Do courthouses have the facilities I need to do legal research?

Many courthouses have law libraries that are open to the public. Attorneys and some criminal defendants, especially those who represent themselves, find courthouse law libraries convenient when they need quick answers to questions that have been raised in the course of a court hearing or trial.

4. I'd like to go to court and observe the judge who I've learned will be in charge of my case. Will the judge always be in the same courtroom?

Most judges conduct open-court hearings in the same courtroom every day, though some are assigned different courtrooms on different days. Visitors should check with the courthouse clerk's office if they are unsure where a particular judge is holding court on a particular day. If there is a line at the courthouse clerk's office, visitors might look on the walls and doors, where clerks often post daily lists of all the cases to be heard in each courtroom. Those lists typically also include the names of the judges.

5. I've wandered down the halls of the courthouse and seen lots of other office-like rooms. They don't look like courtrooms. What are they?

Courthouses also may provide business offices for:

- court personnel—from judges to secretaries
- court-related officials, including prosecutors and public defenders

- law enforcement, such as the marshal's office, and
- local legal newspapers.

Courthouses in which criminal matters are handled also have jails. Visitors won't usually see them, though, because they are typically located behind courtrooms, in basements, or on a separate floor. These jails (sometimes called "holding cells," "pens," or "bullpens") provide a temporary place to keep in-custody defendants while they wait for their cases to be heard. Most often, they are for day use only.

Section II: The Courtroom

This section offers a general orientation of the courtroom.

Where's Justice?

Because so much activity relating to criminal cases goes on outside the court-room—and reflecting a loss of confidence in the courts that was prevalent among certain segments of the community at the time—a saying cropped up in the 1960s that "In the halls of justice, the only justice is in the halls."

6. My neighbor has asked me to go with her to her arraignment for a criminal charge. Where will I sit?

Most courtrooms have a spectator area in the back, often separated by a "bar" or partition from the rest of the courtroom. Members of the public, including those who come to court to support a family member or friend, sit in this area.

7. Where do I wait before my case is called?

Defendants who are free on bail usually sit in the spectator area of the courtroom until their cases are called by the courtroom clerk, bailiff, or judge. In-custody defendants wait in holding cells and are escorted into the courtroom by a bailiff.

8. Will I sit or stand when the judge considers my case?

Defendants should sit or stand as directed by their attorneys (if they have counsel) or by the judge, courtroom clerk, or bailiff. The custom is different in different proceedings and different courtrooms. For example, during arraignment (see Chapter 10), defendants typically stand, facing the judge. However, at trial or a hearing on a motion they may sit at counsel table in the area at the front of the courtroom. (See diagram.)

9. Where will the lawyers be?

Again, it depends on the proceeding. In pretrial hearings, lawyers may stand right in front of the judge. In trials, however, lawyers usually sit or stand at counsel table, the prosecutor usually on the side closest to the jury box.

Most defense lawyers stand when addressing the judge or questioning witnesses. Self-represented defendants should do the same.

10. Who sits in the rows of seats near the judge?

Jurors sit in those seats, called the "jury box," during jury trials. (See diagram.) The jury box may remain empty during nonjury proceedings (or when a jury is deliberating), or the judge may use it to seat in-custody defendants during arraignments and motions.

11. Judges sit at the front of the courtroom, I know. But what is the thing they sit on?

The "bench." The judge's bench is the raised wooden desk or podium at the front of the courtroom where the judge sits. Attorneys and defendants alike should not go near the bench unless they ask for and receive the judge's permission "to approach the bench." This forbidden territory includes the "well," the space between counsel table and the bench, where the courtroom clerk and the court reporter may sit.

12. Does the judge have a separate office, or does everything happen in the courtroom itself?

Typically, judges have private offices called "chambers" located in a room adjacent to or behind the courtroom. A judge and the attorneys may have a conference in chambers during a trial or other proceeding, especially if they want to go "off the record" and have a quiet place to confer. Also, some judges prefer to hold plea bargaining negotiations in chambers.

Attorneys (or self-represented defendants) may request that in-chambers conferences be put "on the record" if they become uncomfortable with what is being said. This means the conference will be recorded word for word by a court reporter and preserved as part of the case for possible later review. (See Chapter 23, on appeals.)

13. Who is the person sitting on the other side of the judge (not the witness)?

Courtroom clerks, often present during court proceedings, may sit in the well, as mentioned above, or on the side of the judge's bench opposite the witness box.

Section III: The Courtroom Players

This section describes the major players in a typical criminal case.

14. What do judges really do?

The judge, the man or woman seated at the bench wearing a black gown (called a "robe"), typically does some or all of the following:

- conducts hearings and makes rulings concerning pretrial business such as preliminary hearings and motions (more on preliminary hearings in Chapter 16 and on motions in Chapter 19)
- determines how cases will be tried, subject to established legal rules of evidence and procedure
- makes legal rulings during trial, such as whether to admit or exclude particular evidence (more on criminal trials in Chapter 21)

- decides on the guilt or innocence of the defendant when the defendant has opted for a nonjury trial ("bench trial")
- instructs the jury on the law they must follow to decide the defendant's guilt or innocence, when there is a jury, and
- sentences convicted defendants following a guilty verdict or negotiated plea of guilty. (More on sentencing in Chapter 22.)

15. Do all judges do all of those things?

Not necessarily. Though many do, other judges only perform some of these functions. For example, some judges—especially in large metropolitan areas—are assigned to hear only pretrial motions, conduct only misdemeanor trials, or handle only preliminary hearings in felony cases.

16. Are there other words that mean the same thing as "judge"?

"Court," "Bench," "Magistrate," and "Commissioner" are sometimes used interchangeably with the word "Judge." For example, a trial before a judge alone without a jury may be called a "bench trial."

Sometimes a judicial title suggests a particular function. For example, the term "Justice" usually refers to a judge in the highest appeals court in a state or in the United States Supreme Court.

Commissioners and magistrates are typically lawyers appointed by the judges in a court system (for example, U.S.

The Difference Between Trial and Appellate Courts

In both state and federal courts, there are trial courts (lower courts, where cases are first heard) and higher or appellate courts, which review decisions of the trial courts. To appeal a case means to petition an appellate court to overturn or modify the decision of the lower or trial court. Usually, a defendant can appeal a case only if the judge in the trial court made a mistake about the law that affected the outcome of the case. Appellate courts normally won't reconsider the evidence and try to second-guess the verdict. (See Chapter 23 for more on appeals.)

In the federal court system, the courts, in order from lowest to highest, are district courts, circuit courts of appeal, and the United States Supreme Court (the highest of the federal courts). While most criminal actions (such as theft, drunk driving, and murder) are processed in state courts, an increasing number of crimes are being handled in the federal courts—those occurring on federal property and crimes involving more than one state (such as interstate drug trafficking).

In the state systems, the names of criminal courts vary greatly from state to state. In some states, the lowest-level criminal courts (often hearing bail motions and arraignments) may be called magistrate courts, police courts, or traffic courts. The next level courts may be called municipal courts, superior courts, or county courts, and the highest court the State Supreme Court. Check a public or law library to find out more about the court structure in your state.

magistrates are appointed by federal district court judges) to act as judges. The judges may delegate full judicial authority to magistrates and commissioners or limit them to certain types of cases or certain functions within cases. For example, a magistrate might have authority to set bail, conduct arraignments, and issue search and arrest warrants, but not to conduct trials.

17. What do courtroom clerks do?

Courtroom clerks are court officials who work for particular judges. Courtroom clerks have many duties. Typically, they:

- Verify that the parties are present in court. If a defendant fails to come to court when required, the courtroom clerk may assist the judge in preparing a bench warrant for that defendant's arrest.
- Prepare and maintain the court calendar (sometimes called the "docket"), which lists the dates and times for trials and other matters.
- Prepare court orders for the judge to sign, such as an order granting a motion to exclude evidence.

- Keep custody of exhibits entered as evidence in a case and administer oaths to witnesses, jurors, and interpreters.
- Obtain for the judge's reference and keep custody of case files maintained and stored in the Courthouse Clerk's Office.
- Assist the judge during a hearing or trial by marking and handling documents and other exhibits.

What Are Case Files?

A case file consists of the legal papers (indictments, bail orders, and other documents) having to do with the case, which have been "filed," that is, delivered to the court's custody to be stored as permanent public records.

18. I've seen another person walk in and out of the courtroom, sometimes sitting with the courtroom clerk. Who is that?

It may be a law clerk. Some judges hire lawyers or law students as law clerks to research legal issues and assist with legal questions that arise prior to and sometimes even during trials. Law clerks may also help draft the written documents (often referred to as findings and conclusions) that judges sometimes produce to explain their rulings.

19. Who is the person in uniform? Is that a real cop?

There may be police officers in the spectator section of the courtroom, waiting to testify. But there will also usually be a uniformed, armed peace officer who is a court official: the bailiff. (Bailiffs may also be deputy sheriffs.) The bailiff's job is to maintain order and decorum in the courtroom. This includes a wide range of duties, from removing disruptive spectators to telling attorneys where to stand when they address the judge. The bailiff also brings defendants from holding cells into court, and escorts juries to and from the jury room and jury box.

20. Do criminal courts come with court reporters?

Usually yes, although some types of proceedings, such as sentencing, may routinely be conducted without a court reporter unless the defense or prosecution requests one. Also, some courts now use tape recorders instead of court reporters. Court reporters:

- Record every word that is said during the proceeding. At trial, upon request of the judge, the reporter will read back testimony of a witness or a statement of counsel, and
- Prepare transcripts (written booklets containing what was said at a particular court session), for a fee, upon the request of a party or the judge.

21. Do courts provide interpreters for non-English speakers?

Yes, at all critical stages of a case. Thus, judges will appoint interpreters to translate for defendants (and often victims as well) who have substantial difficulty speaking and understanding English. The law that applies in federal court is commonly called the Court Interpreters Act, 28 U.S.C. § 1827. States with such laws include Virginia (Va. Code Ann. § 19.2), Florida (Fla. Stat. Ann. §§ 90.606 and 90.6063), California (Constitution, Art 1, § 14), and New York (Crim. Proc. Law § 260.20). Under the Americans with Disabilities Act, hearing-impaired individuals may also obtain sign language interpreters.

Even if they have some ability to speak and understand English, defendants may need the help of an interpreter to understand fully what is happening in court. At the same time, their need for an interpreter may not be fully apparent to judges and even their own lawyers. Thus, defendants who need an interpreter may have to tell their own lawyers or the judge that they want an interpreter.

Defendants who have interpreters should communicate through them at all times. For example, even if Jim thinks that he understands a question without waiting for it to be translated and can answer it in English, Jim should listen to the translation before answering and should answer in his primary language.

The presence of an interpreter in no way interferes with the confidentiality of attorney-client communications.

> **CASE EXAMPLE:** Su has been charged with shoplifting for trying to steal an expensive dress. Su's first language is Mandarin and her knowledge of English is quite limited. Therefore, Su walked out of the store with the dress in the mistaken belief that the dress store clerk had agreed to let her borrow it before buying it so she could get an estimate of alterations. Su is not really sure why she was arrested when she walked out of the store, and has not been able to understand fully what the police officers have said to her.
>
> **Question 1:** Su has hired a lawyer, but should she also ask for an interpreter?
>
> **Answer:** Yes. Even if Su's lawyer speaks Mandarin fluently, the lawyer cannot participate in courtroom proceedings while simultaneously translating for Su. Su should ask the judge to appoint an interpreter. (If Su knows someone who can interpret for her, she can ask the judge to appoint that person.)
>
> **Question 2:** Su wants to give her lawyer information that she does not want the prosecutor, the judge, or anyone else to know about. If Su talks to her lawyer through an interpreter, does the interpreter have to keep the information confidential?

Answer: Yes. The interpreter has the same obligation of confidentiality that Su's lawyer does.

22. Who are the jurors, and what do they do?

Jurors are randomly drawn from the court's geographical area—typically from voter and motor vehicle registration lists—to evaluate evidence during trials and render verdicts. Jurors decide, according to the evidence, whether the defendant is guilty beyond a reasonable doubt of the charged crime. Jurors are not supposed to decide legal questions, such as what evidence is admissible. And jurors usually do not decide what sentence the defendant should receive in case of a conviction, except in capital punishment cases.

It is increasingly common for judges to involve jurors in the questioning of witnesses. Before excusing witnesses, many judges invite jurors to submit written questions. After reviewing the jurors' proposed questions with attorneys from both sides, the judge decides which questions (if any) to ask.

Most Cases Don't Involve Juries

Juries are not formed unless and until a case goes to trial. Since at least 90% of criminal cases end in plea bargains (never getting to trial), and many trials are handled by judges alone, most criminal cases go from start to finish without the involvement of a jury.

23. Who are the parties in a criminal case?

In criminal cases, the parties are the state or federal government bringing the charges (also known as the "People" or the prosecution), and the defendant(s), the person or people accused of the charged crimes.

24. What will I be called if I represent myself?

A self-represented defendant typically is referred to as a *pro se* (pronounced pro say) defendant, from the Latin meaning "[f]or oneself," or a *pro per* defendant (or just a *pro per*), from the Latin term "*in propria persona*," defined as "[f]or one's own person." (*Black's Law Dictionary*, 8th ed., West Publishing Co.) Several self-represented defendants may simply be called *pro pers* (pronounced pro purz). Since these Latin labels originate from the legal profession, some members of the legal self-help movement prefer the term "self-represented."

25. Who are the lawyers who work in a criminal court?

Lawyers (also called attorneys, counsel, or counselors) are legal representatives of either the defendant (defense counsel) or the government (prosecutors—sometimes called district attorneys, state's attorneys, or city attorneys). They must be licensed to practice law. Defendants may not have a nonlawyer friend or family member represent them.

In court, lawyers present evidence and arguments, make objections to evidence presented by the opposing party, and handle all aspects of a case for the party they represent. They also perform many out-of-court functions, such as interviewing witnesses, surveying the crime scene, arranging for scientific tests, conducting legal research, drafting motions, counseling defendants about their options, and negotiating settlements or plea bargains (sometimes in the presence of the judge). (See Chapter 7 for more on defense counsel.)

26. Will my lawyer speak for me?

In court, most of the time, lawyers speak for their clients. However, defendants may speak for themselves in a few instances, for example when they enter a plea, if they testify, if they address the judge during sentencing, or, obviously, if they are representing themselves. Represented defendants are advised to, and usually do, prepare with their lawyers any time they are going to address the judge directly.

Outside of court, lawyers also speak for their clients. Under lawyers' professional rules, clients must communicate with represented opposing parties through their lawyers—not directly. So prosecutors, for instance, contact the lawyers of represented defendants to discuss cases.

(!) CAUTION

Keep your mouth shut! With some minor exceptions (such as giving your name and address if arrested), if you are accused of a crime, you do not have to (and should not) speak to anyone about the matter except your lawyer unless your lawyer is present and agrees to your speaking.

27. Who else might be in court who would have an interest in my case?

Included among the people in the court-room who might have an interest in a particular case are:

- The police officers who arrested the accused or those officers investigating the crime. They may be in court to testify about some aspect of the arrest or investigation, or just remain present to let the prosecution know they are interested in the outcome of the case.

- Victims. For many years regarded as peripheral, victims now play a greater role in the criminal justice process. Frequently they attend every court session to observe. Sometimes victims assist in identifying suspects. And victims may speak to the judge during sentencing about the crime's impact on their lives and the type of sentence they think is appropriate.

- Personnel from both governmental and nonprofit victim/witness assistance programs, who counsel and may accompany a victim or witness to court.

- Probation officers, who may be assigned to investigate the defendant's background and prepare a report to help the judge decide on a sentence. (For more on sentencing, see Chapter 22.)

- Family and friends lending moral support to the defendant or victim.
- Reporters for newspapers and radio and television stations.
- Courthouse groupies. Even total strangers may come to the courtroom, since most court proceedings are open to the public.

Section IV: Courtroom Behavior

This section is about how defendants ought to behave when they appear in court.

28. Am I the only one who feels unnerved by my court appearances?

Most defendants are, understandably, nervous and insecure in the courtroom. Not only might it be their first time in court—an intimidating arena even to trained professionals—but they usually face serious consequences. Family and friends trying to help a loved one cope with criminal charges are also likely to be confused and overwhelmed if not outright disgusted with the experience.

The best way to cope is to prepare, and learn about what is likely to happen, and what, if anything, can be done to positively affect the outcome. The more prepared one is, the less unpleasant, hopefully, the experience will be.

29. How should I dress to go to court?

Attorneys almost always advise their clients on how to dress for court appearances. If not, defendants should dress as if they were

going for a job interview for a professional job. This means suits for men, suits or dresses for women. Most courts have dress codes, too: no hats (except for religious purposes), shorts, tank tops, or bare feet. In general, it is better to overdress than to underdress. If nothing else, the jury and judge may perceive the defendant's effort to look nice as respect for the system. Jurors and judges are human, and a well-dressed defendant may get the benefit of the doubt over someone who has come to court dressed sloppily.

The same is true for family and friends of the defendant. Seeing appropriately dressed family and friends out in numbers to support the defendant may have a conscious or subconscious impact on the jury, judge, or prosecutor (for the purposes of plea bargaining).

30. How nice should I be to the courtroom personnel?

The short answer is, "Very nice." Defendants should go out of their way to be courteous to everyone, especially to official court personnel and prosecutors. Judges, clerks, prosecutors, and even defense lawyers are so used to dealing with defendants who are rude or who simply don't care, that if the defendant and his or her family are polite, they will stand out—and quite likely make a favorable impression. Even such simple things as saying "please" and "thank you" and showing up on time may make the difference between a two-minute, nameless consultation in the hallway before a guilty plea, and having meaningful representation and a fair shot in the courtroom.

The long answer is more complex, but still the same. The system, in many ways, is biased against the accused. Clearly, it's not supposed to be that way, since one of the most important legal principles in this country holds that people are presumed to be innocent until they are proven guilty beyond a reasonable doubt. But many people just don't buy it anymore. Or, they do in theory, but in practice they don't trust (or consciously or unconsciously fear and dislike) anyone even accused of a crime. One reminder of this is the number of times defense lawyers are asked, "How Can You Defend Those People?" (the title of one public defender's memoirs and a comment the authors have personally heard asked of defense lawyers time and time again).

The authors certainly hope that on a large scale, this attitude will change. But in the meantime, accused persons are forewarned that in practice they may well face a presumption of guilt rather than the presumption of innocence to which they technically have the right. Hopefully, the simple suggestions above and many more throughout this book will help people accused of crime cope with what is often a deck stacked against them.

31. How should I address the judge?

There are certain times when represented defendants must talk directly to the judge —for example, when a plea is entered, or during sentencing, when defendants may speak on their own behalf. The most important thing for a defendant to remember in these situations is to be polite, and, where appropriate, to show remorse. (More on this in Chapter 22, on sentencing.)

In addition, it is critical to follow certain basic rules and customs:

- Stand when addressing the judge. Those unable to stand for medical reasons should mention that to the judge at the outset so that their remaining seated is not interpreted as a sign of disrespect.
- Call the judge "Your Honor"—not "Judge," not "Sir," and especially not "Ma'am." In court, by long-running tradition, "Your Honor" is the neutral, respectful term used by all. It is a term judges expect and one they like to hear.
- Speak slowly and clearly, directly into the microphone if one is provided. If not, stand tall and project so that the judge, attorneys, and court reporter can hear easily.
- Represented defendants should only speak when asked to, and, if possible, only after their attorney has had an opportunity to counsel them on what to say. They should also be careful to wait until counsel and the judge finish before speaking. Talking over another courtroom participant is discourteous, and court reporters can only take down the words of one person at a time.

32. I understand that I'm not supposed to discuss my case after I'm arrested, but is there anything wrong with talking once we're in court?

Inside a courtroom, defendants should not discuss their cases with witnesses, reporters, family members, or anyone else.

Defendants should take special care not to say anything, even to their own lawyers, in a public place such as a bathroom or elevator, where they may be overheard. (For more on attorney-client communications, see Chapter 8.)

Arraignments

An arraignment is the usually brief hearing that commonly starts the courtroom phase of a criminal prosecution. The typical arraignment consists of some or all of the following:

- The suspect—now called the defendant—is provided with a written accusation prepared by the prosecutor's office.
- The defendant is allowed to apply for court-appointed counsel.
- The defendant responds to the written charges—usually orally and almost always with a not-guilty plea.
- The judge sets a tentative schedule for such later courtroom activities as a pretrial conference, a preliminary hearing (see Chapter 16), a hearing on pretrial motions (see Chapter 19), and the trial itself (see Chapter 21).
- The judge decides unresolved bail issues (bail may be set, raised, or lowered, or the defendant may be released O.R.; see Chapter 5).

Section I: Timing of Arraignments

This section is about when arraignments are held in the typical criminal case.

1. When does an arraignment take place?

Arraignments are usually held within 48 hours of a suspect's arrest (excluding weekends and holidays) if the suspect is in jail. If the suspect has bailed out or was issued a citation, the arraignment typically occurs several weeks later. The exact timing of arraignments varies from one locality to another. For example, Arizona Rule of Criminal Procedure 14.1 requires that an arraignment be held within ten days after charges are filed; California law does not specify a time requirement.

All states must adhere to the U.S. Supreme Court's ruling that an arraignment should take place "as quickly as possible" after arrest (*Mallory v. U.S.*, U.S. Sup. Ct. 1957).

Dog Years and Court Days

Like dog years, court days often don't correspond to the normal calendar. Court holidays can expand the typical "arraignment within 48 hours of arrest" period for jailed suspects. If a suspect is arrested Friday evening, and Monday is a court holiday, the arraignment may not take place until Wednesday. Saturday, Sunday, and Monday typically are not considered court days that count toward the 48 hours.

---

2. Why are speedy arraignments required under the U.S. Constitution?

The requirement that a suspect be arraigned shortly after arrest is intended to protect the suspect. A quick arraignment before a judge means that police must have evidence of a crime in hand before making the arrest. Otherwise, the police could arrest the suspect on a whim and force the suspect to languish in jail while the police rummage around for evidence of crime.

The Tactical Advantages of Delay

In most cases, delays help defendants. Prosecution witnesses may forget what they saw and heard, prosecutors lose evidence, and cases simply lose momentum. The older a case, the easier it typically is to negotiate a plea bargain favorable to the defense. Also, delays provide a defendant the opportunity to undertake counseling, get a job, or otherwise establish a course of behavior that will favorably impress the judge at a later sentencing (if one occurs).

As with all general rules, there are exceptions. In 1995, in the famous O.J. Simpson criminal trial, the defense pushed for the earliest possible trial date. The defense strategy substantially reduced the prosecution's ability to prepare an extraordinarily complex case.

3. I posted stationhouse bail and was released from jail shortly after I was arrested. Will that delay my arraignment?

Probably. By bailing out, a suspect can count on the arraignment being delayed for at least two weeks. The delay is rarely of legal consequence, because speedy arraignments are intended primarily to benefit jailed suspects. However, in an unusual case, a bailed-out suspect might still ask the judge to dismiss charges because of a delayed arraignment. To be successful, the suspect would have to demonstrate that the delay was extraordinary, that it was not the fault of the suspect, and that the delay ruined the suspect's opportunity to present an effective defense (perhaps because it allowed a crucial defense witness to flee the country).

4. How does an arraignment compare to a trial?

Life inside an arraignment courtroom tends to be far more hectic than at trial. The court's calendar (the cases a judge will hear on a given day) is likely to be crowded, and the judge often has to move quickly from one case to the next. The courtroom will be buzzing with prosecutors, defense attorneys, and defendants, all of whom are waiting for the judge to call their cases. Sometimes, a judge will interrupt one case to make a ruling or take a plea on another. No juries are present at arraignment.

In addition to the hectic atmosphere of an arraignment courtroom, judges, clerks, prosecutors, and even defense counsel often sound as if they are speaking in a strange code. They routinely refer to courtroom procedures by statute numbers or the names of the cases that mandated the procedures. For example, an attorney might tell the defendant, "We're going to have a *McDonald* conference with the D.A.," or "We'll schedule a 605 motion." The latter remark doesn't mean that the motion will be heard on an interstate highway. The attorney may simply be referring to a hearing to review a lab analysis of alleged drugs. Defendants confused by unfamiliar jargon should always ask for a translation.

Where Defendants Sit During Arraignments

During arraignment, defendants who were unable to make bail (known as "custodies") will be brought into the courtroom by a sheriff from holding cells located behind the courtroom, and often will be seated in the jury box if the courtroom has one. If there is no place to put them, they will be ushered in one at a time. Defendants who were given a citation or who were released on bail or O.R. enter the courtroom through the public doors and sit in the audience until their cases are called.

CASE EXAMPLE 1: Al Dente appears at an arraignment on drunk driving charges. After Al enters a not guilty plea, the judge asks, "Do you want me to set this for a 605 conference?" Al does not understand what this means, but is fearful of displaying his ignorance in open court.

Question: What should Al do?

Answer: Al should ask the judge to explain what a "605 conference" is. The opinions of court personnel and others as to Al's legal knowledge are much less important than Al making an intelligent decision about his case. If Al is excessively image-conscious, he can ask to "approach the bench." If the judge agrees, Al can go up to the judge and ask his question out of earshot of other people in the courtroom.

CASE EXAMPLE 2: Same case. Assume the same facts as above, except that Al is represented by a lawyer. When the judge asks whether the lawyer wants a "605 conference," Al's lawyer says, "Yes." Al does not know what a 605 conference is.

Question: Since Al is represented by a lawyer, does it matter whether or not he knows what a 605 conference is?

Answer: Yes. Cases belong to defendants, not to their lawyers, and defendants can't participate in making important decisions if they don't understand what's going on in their cases. Even though Al may prefer to save face in front of his attorney rather than show ignorance, Al should interrupt and ask his lawyer to explain the purpose of a 605 conference before answering.

5. What happens during a typical arraignment?

The primary purpose of an arraignment is to give the defendant written notice of the charged crime or crimes and to take the defendant's plea. In addition, the judge may do any of the following.

a. Appoint counsel

The judge will appoint an attorney to represent an indigent defendant if jail time is a possible outcome. (See Chapter 7.) Defendants who are ineligible for court-appointed counsel and who need additional time to hire an attorney can ask the judge to "continue" (delay) the arraignment for a week or so.

b. Hear a bail motion

Whether or not they earlier had a bail hearing, defendants can ask the arraignment judge to review their bail status (for example, reduce the bail, or convert bail to O.R. release). (See Chapter 5.) Similarly, if bail has previously been posted, the prosecutor may ask the court to raise the amount of the bail if it appears necessary to assure the defendant's appearance or protect the public.

c. Set a date to hear pretrial motions

Defendants and their attorneys often raise issues at arraignment that the judge may wish to consider at a future time when both sides have had an opportunity to fully prepare their arguments. For example, the defendant may file a motion claiming that the case has been filed in the wrong court, or that the activity in which the defendant was engaged doesn't constitute a crime. (See Chapter 19.)

d. Set dates for upcoming hearings not involving motions

Depending on a state's procedures and whether the charge involves a felony or a misdemeanor, the judge may schedule a number of upcoming hearings before other judges. For example, in one case an arraignment judge may schedule a preliminary hearing (see Chapter 16), in another the judge may schedule a plea bargaining settlement discussion. (See Chapter 20 for more on plea bargaining.)

One Arraignment and Out

An arraignment can be the first and last court appearance for a defendant who pleads guilty (or *nolo contendere*, which is the same as "no contest"). In simple cases, the arraignment judge may accept a guilty plea and sentence the defendant immediately according to an agreement worked out by the defendant and the prosecutor. In more complex cases, or cases where significant jail time is a possibility, the judge may accept the plea but set a future date for sentencing.

Criminal defense attorneys routinely discourage their clients from pleading guilty at the arraignment. However, there are instances when a guilty plea may get the best result for the defendant. For example:

- The defendant is arrested far from home and doesn't want to return for future court proceedings.
- The defendant can't afford to take time off from work to fight the case.
- The defendant can't afford an attorney, doesn't qualify for a court-appointed attorney, and isn't inclined to self-represent.
- Delay may bring harmful evidence to light that leads the prosecutor to insist on a harsher punishment.

6. My arraignment has been scheduled. I'm not eligible for a court-appointed attorney. I haven't hired an attorney yet, and I'm not sure I want to. What should I do?

Defendants who are uncertain about whether to represent themselves at arraignment (or for the duration of the case) may buy additional time to make a decision by asking for a continuance (postponement). Judges routinely grant continuances of at least a week to give the defendant a chance to hire an attorney. In return, the defendant may have to "waive time," meaning he or she gives up the right to be arraigned within statutory time limits. The continuance does not obligate the defendant to hire an attorney. The defendant can appear at the next scheduled date for the arraignment and self-represent.

To obtain a continuance, the defendant usually must appear in court on the date set for arraignment and ask the judge for more time to find an attorney. However, some courts allow defendants to arrange continuances by phone. A defendant who wants a continuance and finds it inconvenient to appear in court on the date set for arraignment should phone the arraignment court clerk ahead of time to find out if an informal continuance is possible.

7. I'm represented by a lawyer, but I need to be at work on the day set for my arraignment. Can my lawyer appear without me?

Many states excuse defendants from having to appear at their arraignments if their attorneys are present. However, even these states are likely to impose some limitations. For example, many states excuse defendants from personally attending arraignments only if the defendants are charged with misdemeanors; defendants charged with felonies have to appear in court, with or without an attorney. (For examples of such rules, see Kentucky Rule of Criminal Procedure 8.28(1); Arizona Rule of Criminal Procedure 14.2; Florida Rule of Criminal Procedure 3.180; California Penal Code § 977(a).)

Most judges won't allow the defendant's lawyer to plead guilty or enter a no-contest plea for the defendant (with some exceptions for defendants who live outside the court's jurisdiction). This is because constitutional considerations require the judge to question the defendant face to face before accepting a plea that might result in a criminal conviction. The judge needs to determine for the record that:

- a factual basis for the plea exists (that is, the defendant admits to facts that justify conviction of the crime charged)
- the defendant is pleading guilty voluntarily (that is, the plea is not the result of illegal threats or promises)
- the defendant is aware of all the rights he or she is giving up by pleading guilty or no contest (such as the right to a jury trial, the right to cross-examine adverse witnesses, and the right against self-incrimination), and
- the defendant understands the charges and recognizes the potential

consequences of the guilty or no-contest plea.

8. Any prosecutor who took the time to analyze my case would realize my arrest was due to a misunderstanding. Is there any way I can get my case thrown out before my arraignment?

Yes. But unfortunately, this possibility generally exists only for defendants who hire private attorneys prior to arraignment. Defendants who are represented by court-appointed counsel (see Chapter 7) often do not even have counsel appointed until the time of arraignment. And a self-represented defendant should not risk additional legal difficulties by discussing the case with a prosecutor before arraignment—assuming that a prosecutor would agree to meet with the defendant in the first place.

Defendants who hire private counsel before arraignment have a chance to derail the case for several reasons. First, in most parts of the country, intake prosecutors (not the police) are supposed to analyze cases to make sure that there is evidence of guilt and that prosecution is in the interests of justice. Frequently, however, the caseload is so heavy that reviews are cursory, and weak cases sometimes slip into the pipeline. (See Chapter 6.) If an attorney who is well known to the courtroom prosecutor can convince that prosecutor of the weaknesses in the case, the case may get dismissed.

Second, prior to arraignment, no one in the prosecutor's office has invested a lot of time or money in the case, and there is no need to justify the effort with at least some kind of conviction.

Third, intake prosecutors normally work in offices tucked away from the courtroom spotlight. Courtroom prosecutors, however, who arraign and try cases, have to take heat from judges if they show up in court with weak cases.

Finally, especially in urban areas, courtroom dockets are crowded. By quickly disposing of weak cases, prosecutors can devote the little time they have to the most serious cases.

For all these reasons, if defense counsel can point out weaknesses that the intake prosecutor did not consider, or convince the prosecutor that further proceedings would not be in the interests of justice, a prearraignment meeting between the defendant's attorney and the prosecutor may result in the case being derailed before arraignment.

> **CASE EXAMPLE:** Redd Emption was arrested for carrying a concealed weapon. Rushing to make an airplane, Redd forgot that the gun that he was supposed to leave at his parent's house was still in his backpack. He was arrested when the airport metal detector revealed the gun. Redd has no prior arrests, and the only reason that he had the gun in the first place is that a series of robberies had taken place in his apartment house, and his father had loaned him the gun for protection. Redd is out on bail and is scheduled for arraignment in a week. Thinking that

his arrest is a misunderstanding, Redd is uncertain about whether to hire an attorney.

Question: Might an attorney be helpful in derailing Redd's case before it reaches arraignment?

Answer: Yes. Unlike Redd personally, Redd's attorney may be able to contact the arraignment prosecutor to seek a mutually-agreeable outcome. Redd's attorney can point out information that the intake prosecutor may not have been aware of—Redd didn't own the gun; he had borrowed it for protection, and inadvertently had it in his backpack. Though Redd is technically guilty as charged, these factors may convince the prosecutor that prosecution of Redd is not in the interests of justice. As a result, the prosecutor may agree to dismiss the case or offer Redd diversion (that is, agree to temporarily not file the charges and end the case permanently if Redd stays out of trouble for a period of time).

9. My case was dismissed at arraignment. Does the double jeopardy rule against being tried twice for the same crime protect me from being arrested again on the same charges?

No. As long as the statute of limitations (period of time within which a case can be filed following a crime) has not run out, the police can rearrest defendants whose cases have been dismissed at arraignment.

Defendants are not considered to be "in jeopardy" for purposes of the double jeopardy rule until the trial actually begins. Dismissal followed by rearrest can be expensive—a defendant may have to obtain a second bail bond and pay a second fee.

10. I'm in jail. How do I get to my arraignment?

Jailed suspects get free rides to arraignments, courtesy of the local sheriff. Upon arriving at the courthouse, jailed suspects are put into "holding cells" or "pens" located near the courtroom. Then they are called into court singly or as a group, depending on local practice. They usually remain in jail attire for the arraignment, since no jury is present.

11. What happens if I'm going to be late for my arraignment or get sick and can't make it at all?

Defendants who cannot for any reason appear in court as scheduled must phone either their attorneys (if they are already represented) or the courtroom clerk (if they are not) as soon as possible. As long as the defendant notifies the clerk in advance and has a valid reason to be late or absent, most judges will put the case on hold until the defendant arrives, or even reschedule it for a later day. But if the defendant fails to contact the court and is absent from the courtroom when the judge calls the defendant's case, the judge may immediately revoke bail and issue a warrant for the defendant's arrest.

12. I want the judge to appoint an attorney for me. How will this happen?

Defendants who think they may financially qualify for a court-appointed attorney (see Chapter 7) should ask the judge for one when their case is called. Usually, an attorney is present in the arraignment courtroom to represent indigent defendants who want legal help. It's only necessary for you to say something like, "Your Honor, I want to talk to a lawyer before I do anything." At that point, the judge will put the case aside until after the defendant has spoken to the lawyer.

13. How soon will my case be handled?

Arraignment judges typically call cases in the following order:

- cases in which defendants are represented by private counsel
- noncustody defendants who are representing themselves, and
- defendants who are represented by the public defenders or other court-appointed counsel, or defendants who are in custody.

This order awards first preference to private attorney cases and lowest priority to public defender cases, perhaps on the grounds that public defender clients are not paying for their attorneys' time and public defenders often have to spend the whole day in court anyway.

14. A lawyer told me that if I plead guilty or no contest at my arraignment, I'll be waiving my constitutional rights. What does this mean?

Defendants who are charged with crimes have a variety of constitutional rights—most fundamentally the right to trial by jury, the right to present their own witnesses, and the right to confront and cross-examine prosecution witnesses. By pleading guilty or *nolo contendere* (no contest), a type of guilty plea, defendants give up these rights. Especially if the judge plans to sentence the defendant to jail, the judge usually will insist that the defendant give up these rights "on the record" in open court. This explicit waiver insulates the conviction that results from the plea from being declared invalid at a later time.

Attacking Prior Convictions

Most states have laws that punish a defendant progressively more severely for repeat offenses. The most extreme example of this tendency are laws mandating a life sentence for anyone convicted of a third felony (the so-called three strikes laws). When faced with this type of statute, the defense will obviously benefit if it can invalidate an earlier conviction (called "striking a prior"). A frequent way to attack a prior conviction based on an earlier guilty plea has been to show that the plea was not knowingly or intelligently made and that the defendant therefore gave up constitutional rights out of ignorance.

15. A close relative is due in court for arraignment. Would my presence be of any value?

Though arraignments tend to be quite brief, defendants often derive psychological support from the presence of relatives as well as close friends and employers. Their very presence can produce tangible benefits if the defendant is seeking lower bail or release O.R. Seeing that defendants retain the support of others notwithstanding their arrest may incline the judge to exercise discretion in a defendant's favor, where possible.

16. Is it possible to have two arraignments in the same case?

Yes, in felony cases, in states that operate a two-tiered system of trial courts. One arraignment takes place in the lower tier, and a second arraignment in the higher tier court if the lower tier court decides in a preliminary hearing that the case should proceed as a felony.

Section II: Self-Representation at Arraignment

This section is about the pros and cons of self-representation at the arraignment.

17. Is it advisable for me to represent myself at my arraignment?

Many defendants are capable of representing themselves at an arraignment. They can plead not guilty and even ask the judge to reduce bail. (See Chapter 5 for more on bail.) During the interval between the arraignment and the next court appearance (rarely less than two weeks and often longer), the defendant can decide whether to hire a lawyer for postarraignment proceedings.

Nevertheless, going it alone at arraignment is not a good idea for most defendants. For example, if a technical defect exists in the prosecution's case, the defendant may have the right to raise the defect only prior to entering a plea. Also, a particular prosecutor's office may have a policy of offering the best deals to defendants who plead guilty (or no contest) at their arraignments. Defendants who intend at some point to plead guilty but who are unaware of such a policy may suffer a harsher punishment by putting off the guilty plea until after the arraignment. Finally, arraignment judges are more likely to lower bail when defendants have legal representation. Thus, most defendants considering self-representation should postpone the arraignment by asking the judge for a continuance, and then consult with a criminal defense lawyer before deciding to self-represent.

18. I'm out on bail. What should I do when I arrive in court for the arraignment?

Defendants first need to make sure they are in the correct courtroom, and then check in with the clerk or bailiff. (See Chapter 9.)

19. Can I ask for priority as a self-represented defendant?

Normally, arraignment judges give priority to private attorney cases. This means that the judge tends to handle all "private attorney matters" before hearing other cases. Self-represented defendants who have a special reason why their cases should be taken out of order can request priority. To make a priority request, the defendant should notify the courtroom clerk or bailiff at the time of checking in of the need for priority. If the request is valid, the clerk or bailiff will inform the judge, who should call the case along with the private attorney cases.

20. What happens when my case is called?

Subject to local variation, most arraignments tend to unfold as follows: When the judge calls the defendant's case, the bailiff normally directs the defendant where to stand. The judge reads the charge; at that time a defendant who has not already gotten them usually receives a written copy of the complaint (the charge) and the written report prepared by the arresting officer (the arrest report). The judge then asks the defendant if she has an attorney or wants the court to appoint one. Upon learning that the defendant wants to self-represent, the judge then asks the defendant to enter a plea. As mentioned, defendants usually plead not guilty at arraignment. However, a self-represented defendant alternatively may:

- ask for a continuance of a week or two
- in unusual circumstances, make a motion to dismiss the case, or
- plead guilty (or no contest).

Assuming that the defendant enters a plea, the judge typically schedules the next court appearance. After a not guilty plea, the next appearance may be for a pretrial conference, a preliminary examination, or a trial date, depending on local procedures and whether the case involves a felony or a misdemeanor. In the event of a guilty plea, the judge may pronounce sentence immediately, or schedule a later "sentencing hearing," which occurs after a probation officer investigates a defendant's background and submits a report. (See Chapter 22.)

The Effect of a No Contest (*Nolo Contendere*) Plea

For criminal law purposes, no contest and guilty pleas have an identical effect. In jurisdictions that allow no contest pleas (and not all do), the effect of such a plea is limited to civil cases. This is because no contest pleas are sometimes inadmissible as evidence in civil cases. This can make it possible for a criminal defendant who might later face a lawsuit by the victim for civil damages to plea bargain a criminal case without giving a potential adversary ammunition to use against the defendant in a civil case.

If the arraignment is combined with a bail hearing, which is typical, the judge will set bail at some point in the course of the arraignment. If the defendant's bail status has already been determined, the judge normally concludes the arraignment by continuing that same status. (See Question 21, below.)

21. I bailed out of jail prior to arraignment and will represent myself at arraignment. Can the bail issue arise again?

Yes. Judges often conclude arraignments by continuing defendants on the same bail status they had prior to arraignment. However, the arraignment judge has the power to reset bail, either lower or higher. Bailed-out defendants can ask the arraignment judge to release them O.R. or lower the bail in order to free up cash and collateral for other purposes (including hiring an attorney). Unfortunately, even if the judge lowers the bail or grants the defendant O.R., the bail premium already paid to the bail bond seller cannot be recaptured.

It is also possible that the prosecutor will seek higher bail (for instance, because the defendant has a criminal record). If the arraignment judge does increase a bailed-out defendant's bail, the defendant can be returned to custody until the higher bail is met. Self-representing defendants who have any reason to fear an increase in bail should come to the arraignment prepared to pay the additional cost. For example, a defendant might ask a bail bond seller to come to court and immediately post bond for the higher amount.

22. I'm in jail; does this affect my right to self-representation?

No. The procedures are the same. Of course, defendants who are in custody at the time of arraignment are likely to ask a judge to set bail (if this has not already occurred at an earlier bail hearing) or to lower the bail previously set. A defendant's bail status is always subject to review, and defendants should never hesitate to inform judges of changed circumstances (for example, a job offer) that might lead the judge to reduce bail.

Developing the Defense Strategy

This chapter examines the crucial process by which defendants and their lawyers often jointly formulate a defense strategy. A defense strategy typically emerges as a defense attorney finds out about the prosecution's evidence and a defendant's version of events. The process of developing a defense strategy is fluid, and it varies from one case to another. For example, the attorney's tentative theory of defense will influence the topics the attorney asks about. The defendant's answers to those questions may in turn affect the attorney's defense strategy.

This does not mean that defendants and their attorneys collaborate to make up false stories. For various reasons explained in this chapter, defendants usually benefit from telling their attorneys the truth as the defendants perceive it. However, multiple versions of truth can coexist in the defense of criminal charges. For instance, assume that a woman is charged with murdering her boyfriend. The "truth" may consist of the woman's acting in self-defense, or it may consist of the boyfriend's physical and verbal abuse of the woman in the months preceding the killing, or it may consist of both. A defense strategy is a product of a defendant and defense attorney fitting together the version of the truth that is most likely to produce a satisfactory defense outcome (a verdict of not guilty, a verdict of guilty of a lesser charge, or an acceptable plea bargain).

Overcoming a Failure to Communicate

The process by which attorneys work with a defendant to develop the defendant's version of events, and the impact of the defendant's version on the overall defense strategy, usually can be seen and understood only during confidential attorney-client meetings. Few books for nonlawyers address this process, and few nonlawyers understand it. Hopefully, the information in this chapter will make it easier for defendants to work harmoniously with their attorneys to develop an accurate and effective defense account of events.

Section I: Overview

This section provides an introduction to the ways defendants recount their version of events when meeting with their attorney.

1. Is a version of events something that I or my attorney make up?

No. The term "version" is not a pejorative implying falsity. A version of events is simply the defendant's account of the events leading up to the defendant's arrest. However, a version of events is not like a diamond, lying intact in the ground waiting to be found. Instead, defendants and their attorneys usually piece the defendant's version together—over the course of one or more interviews—on the basis of the defendant's recollections and objectively verifiable facts, and informed by the lawyer's knowledge of the laws and defenses that apply to the type of behavior in question. The result of this cooperation between the defendant and the attorney is hopefully a full and accurate defense story that is consistent with the truth and can withstand any challenge that the prosecution may mount.

2. Isn't a lawyer who helps me develop my version of events in effect asking me to lie?

No. The fact that a story may be told in a variety of ways does not prevent each version from being accurate. By way of analogy, consider two maps of the United States, one in which the states are depicted according to geographical boundaries, the other in which the states are depicted according to density of population. The maps will look different, yet both will be accurate. It's up to an attorney and a defendant to develop together the most legally helpful, accurate version of events relevant to the case. The result will hopefully have such characteristics as:

- Consistency with objectively verifiable evidence. For example, if the police found the defendant's fingerprints at the scene of a crime, hopefully the defendant's version accounts for the presence of the fingerprints. ("Defendant was at the apartment the day before the burglary.")

- The potential to gain the sympathy of a judge or jury. For example, the defendant's version may demonstrate that he or she tried to withdraw from the criminal activity in question and prevent it from happening.

- Explaining why events took place as the defendant claims. For example, if the defendant claims to have been out of town on the date of the crime, the defendant's version explains why the defendant was out of town.

As may be apparent, the account of events a defendant might tell spontaneously could omit these and other elements that are both accurate and helpful. This is why defendants and their attorneys have to work together to develop a version of events that will best benefit the defense.

3. What kinds of versions of events do defendants tell their attorneys?

While no two defendants will ever come up with a factually identical version of events, a defendant's account almost always falls into one of three broad categories:

- **"Confession" story.** Defendants who tell their lawyers confession stories admit that they did what the prosecution claims: "Yes, I did break into the house through a window and steal the computer."

- **"Complete denial" story.** Defendants who tell their lawyers complete denial stories assert that the prosecution's claims are totally false. An "alibi" is a familiar type of complete denial story: "I was out of town with a friend when the burglary they say I committed took place. I have no idea what they're talking about."

- **"Admit and explain" story.** This story falls between the "confession" and "complete denial" stories. Defendants who tell "admit and explain" stories agree that part of the prosecution's claims are accurate, but assert legally critical differences: "I did go into the house and take the computer, but I went in through the front door with a key after the person who lived there gave me permission to borrow the computer."

4. How will my version of events affect the defense strategy?

The ultimate defense strategy grows out of, but is not the same as, a defendant's version of events, regardless of which of the three broad categories above it falls into. When formulating a defense strategy, an attorney also considers such factors as the reliability of defense and prosecution witnesses, community attitudes toward crime and the police, and a defendant's moral culpability. A defense attorney uses these factors to develop a "theory of the case" that is consistent with provable facts and explains events in a way that favors the defense.

For example, assume that a defendant is charged with burglary. The prosecution's evidence consists of the defendant's confession to the police shortly after the defendant's arrest, and an eyewitness who "is pretty sure that the defendant was among the burglars." The defendant has told his attorney that a couple of the defendant's friends planned and carried out the burglary, that he had never been in trouble but stupidly went along with them so as to look good in their eyes, and that the police didn't tell him that he had a right to remain silent or have an attorney present during questioning.

This is in essence a "confession" story. Nevertheless, the defendant and the defense attorney may adopt a defense theory that "overzealous police officers tried to paper over weak eyewitness identification evidence by improperly extracting a confession from a naive suspect." This theory is consistent with the defendant's version of events, and it describes events in a way that favors the defense.

Pursuing this strategy, the defense attorney might file a pretrial motion seeking to bar the prosecution from offering the confession into evidence because the police failed to comply with *Miranda* procedures. (See Chapter 1.) In addition, the defense attorney might develop arguments that the eyewitness identification evidence is too weak to prove guilt beyond a reasonable doubt. The goal of this strategy may be either to achieve a not guilty verdict at trial, or to weaken the prosecutor's case enough to persuade the prosecutor to agree to the defense's desired plea bargain. Even if the defendant is convicted, the defense attorney may rely on the defendant's lack of a prior criminal record, and the fact that he was a dupe who passively participated in a crime orchestrated by others, to argue for minimum punishment.

5. So long as I tell the truth, why not tell my version of events to the police after I'm arrested?

Even assuming that they want to tell the truth, almost all suspects should talk to a defense attorney before talking to the police. In part, this is because the police may accidentally or purposefully distort the suspect's statement at trial. (See Chapter 1 for more on talking to the police.) Moreover, many suspects are too nervous and unaware of the law to tell the police an accurate story that will also benefit their defense. Remember that there are many ways to accurately recount a series of events (see Question 2, above); suspects are almost always better off talking to an attorney before talking to the police.

6. Can the prosecution find out about my version of events before trial?

Since the defense version of events is developed in the course of confidential attorney-client conversations (see Chapter 8), it can remain confidential until the defendant discloses it or the attorney discloses it with the defendant's permission. However, in most states, the prosecutor has the right to know before trial if the story involves an alibi or insanity defense. (See Chapter 14 for more on what information the defense must share with the

prosecution.) Also, the defense may have to provide the prosecution with the identities of defense witnesses and any written statements they've made. By reading the statements or interviewing the witnesses, the prosecutor may be able to glean many aspects of the defendant's story.

Although the details of the defendant's version of events need not be disclosed, except as noted, the general contours of the story tend to be imparted to the prosecution early in the case, when the possibility of a plea bargain is first discussed. Just how much of a defense story should be disclosed prior to trial to facilitate a possible plea bargain (or in some jurisdictions, a court-engineered settlement) will depend on such factors as:

- how likely it is that disclosure will result in a settlement favorable to the defendant
- whether the defense will gain from keeping the story under wraps as long as possible, and
- how obvious the story is, or how much of the story is already known to the prosecution.

7. I'm representing myself. Any tips as to how I can develop my version of events?

The following guidelines can help self-represented defendants develop accurate and credible stories that are consistent with a sound overall case strategy:

- Self-represented defendants should not talk to the police, at least not until after they've had an opportunity to think through and develop their stories. Just as defense attorneys often suggest, thinking through events chronologically and visiting the scene of important events are effective story-development techniques.

- Self-represented defendants should write out their stories in a format that allows them to add to and delete information from the stories as they continue to think through all that happened. Whether the writing consists of pen on paper or a computer disk, it should be labeled "confidential attorney work product" (because the defendant is acting as his or her own attorney) and kept in a safe and secure place.

- Self-represented defendants should be sure they understand exactly what they are charged with, and the meaning of those charges in everyday language, before finalizing their story. (See Chapter 27 for tips on reading and understanding criminal statutes.)

- Self-represented defendants should look at the police report and written witness statements to find out what the witnesses have to say. The stories of prosecution witnesses can often help the defendant remember important details and understand what topics to cover in the defendant's own story.

Section II: How the Defendant's Version of Events May Limit Defense Strategies

This section discusses the important intersection between the defendant's version of events and the ethical rules under which criminal defense attorneys operate.

8. Can I tell my attorney one version and testify to a different one?

No. An important ethical rule governing attorneys is that they cannot knowingly encourage or help a witness to give perjured testimony (testimony that the attorney knows to be false). (See Rule 3.3, ABA Model Rules of Professional Conduct.) If a defendant has told an attorney one version of events, the defendant cannot change the version for trial just because a different story would be stronger. This means that defendants have to be careful when giving their version to their lawyers, because a defendant may have to live with that version should the case go to trial (or get another lawyer if he or she is in a position to do so). (See Question 10, below, for more on when a defendant's version may be modified.)

> **CASE EXAMPLE:** Rusty Nails is charged with assault and battery. Rusty has repeatedly insisted to his attorney that it's a case of mistaken identity, and that he was nowhere near the bar where the attack took place. In the course of

investigation, Rusty's lawyer talks to two witnesses who say that they saw the fight and that Rusty acted in self-defense.

Question: Can Rusty testify to self-defense at trial?

Answer: No. Unless Rusty can satisfactorily explain the sudden change of story (for instance, "I was nervous," or, "I lied at first because I was afraid you wouldn't believe the truth"), Rusty's lawyer may conclude that Rusty's self-defense testimony constitutes perjury. If Rusty plans to stick to the self-defense story on the stand, Rusty's lawyer might be unable to call Rusty as a witness.

Ethical Rules and Self-Represented Defendants

Self-represented defendants are not subject to the ethical rules constraining attorneys. Therefore, a self-represented defendant who testifies untruthfully is not subject to the discipline that attorneys might face if they assisted in such behavior. Nevertheless, an untruthful self-represented defendant runs the risk of a perjury charge, as well as being given a harsher sentence. If a conviction results and the judge concludes that the defendant lied, he may choose to unofficially punish the defendant by imposing a stiffer sentence than might otherwise have been the case. (See Chapter 22 for more on sentencing.)

9. If my lawyer knows I'm guilty, can he or she call friends of mine to testify to a version of events that indicates I'm innocent?

No. It doesn't matter whether the person who will give false testimony is a defendant or a defense witness. In either event, ethical rules forbid attorneys from calling witnesses who they know will perjure themselves.

> **CASE EXAMPLE:** In the Rusty Nails example above, assume that Nails cannot testify to self-defense in his own behalf.
>
> **Question:** Could the defense attorney call the two witnesses to testify that Nails acted in self-defense?
>
> **Answer:** No. If Nails would be committing perjury by testifying to self-defense, then so would his witnesses. The ethical constraint on the attorney is the same.

10. Does this mean I can never change the version of events I first tell my lawyer?

Of course not. Defendants are not forever locked in to the first versions of events they tell their lawyers. Defendants can and often do change what they initially tell their attorneys. For example, a defendant might recall additional information, or realize after talking to others or seeing photos that the first version was inaccurate. A defense attorney's first commitment is to the client, and the attorney will not conclude that a defendant's modified version of events is perjured unless the circumstances leave the attorney no other choice. As long as the attorney is subjectively satisfied that helping the client formulate a different version is not a breach of professional ethics, the attorney can present the defendant's modified version at trial.

CASE EXAMPLE: Rusty Nails remains charged with assault and battery. As before, Rusty's initial version is that it's a case of mistaken identity, and that he was nowhere near the bar where the attack took place. Sometime later, Rusty tells his lawyer that the truth is that he acted in self-defense. Rusty explains that he did not initially admit to participating in the fight because he had promised his girlfriend not to go near the bar where the fight took place. Rusty has decided to tell the truth now and patch up things with the girlfriend later.

Question: Can Rusty testify to self-defense at trial?

Answer: Yes. Rusty's explanation for the changed story is plausible enough for almost any defense attorney. Even if the defense attorney subjectively distrusts Rusty's new version, the attorney has a sufficient basis to help Rusty tell it while avoiding an ethics violation.

Subjective Interpretations of Ethical Rules

It would be misleading to suggest that all criminal defense attorneys subscribe to the same view of their ethical obligations regarding perjured testimony. In fact, some believe that any limitation on their right to present testimony interferes with a defendant's right to an effective defense. Most defense attorneys agree that it's wrong to present perjured testimony, but are likely to vary when it comes to making a subjective judgment as to whether proposed testimony is perjured.

As a practical matter, attorneys who decide to elicit perjured testimony in violation of their ethical responsibilities are rarely caught. Usually, the only witness to the unethical deed is the defendant, who has little incentive to rat on an attorney whose strategy, while unethical, was effective. About the only time that abuses come to light is when defendants who are unhappy with the outcomes of their cases complain about their attorneys. Even then, proving that an attorney broke ethical rules is difficult. To many judges and prosecutors, convicted defendants who complain about their lawyers come across as people just looking to blame someone else for their troubles.

11. Is it my lawyer's role to coach me as part of developing the defense story?

Defense lawyers have a duty to help defendants formulate the strongest defense story possible. To that end, lawyers can and do coach defendants in a variety of ways. For instance, attorneys can:

- use interviewing techniques that stimulate memory, such as asking defendants to relate events chronologically
- conduct interviews at the scene of important events, or
- ask defendants to write down in their own words their versions of important events. (To maintain the confidentiality of what they've written, defendants should write "Confidential Document—For My Attorney Only" at the top of the first page, and if possible hand whatever they've written directly to their attorneys.)

In addition, attorneys can coach defendants by fully explaining the charges against them, and by imparting as much as is known of the prosecution's story, before starting to question them about a version of events. Defendants need such information if they are to tell an accurate version that does not leave out information potentially helpful to the defense.

For example, assume that Rhoda is charged with the crime of "receiving stolen goods." Before seeking to elicit Rhoda's version, Rhoda's lawyer may ethically tell her something along these lines:

"Rhoda, you're charged with receiving stolen property. What that means in plain English is that you personally are not charged with stealing anything; the claim is that you obtained property even though you knew for a fact that someone else had stolen it. Now, I'd like to find out from you as much as you can tell me about what happened. But first let me tell you that the police report and a brief talk I had with the D.A. indicate that they claim you are a middleperson in a ring that deals in stolen watches. A couple of guys named Bernie and Chuck supposedly steal watches from warehouses and drop some of the cartons off in your garage, and you later distribute them to jewelry stores around town. They've got the names of some of the stores you supposedly deal with. Unless you have any questions, why don't you tell me what you know about all this?"

CASE EXAMPLE 1: As before, Rusty Nails is charged with assault and battery growing out of a barroom brawl. When Nails meets with his attorney, the attorney tells him, "They've got you charged with assault and battery, but I've talked to a couple of people and I think we can make a good case for self-defense. Now, I'm going to tell you exactly what to say, and if you want me to represent you, you better do as I tell you."

Question: Is the defense attorney's approach legitimate?

Answer: No. The attorney has violated ethical rules by making up a story for the client to tell, and the attorney would be subject to discipline if the client revealed what happened. A defendant confronted by such an approach should look elsewhere for another attorney as soon as possible. An attorney who will so cavalierly violate one ethical rule is likely to violate others, including the one mandating loyalty to the client's case.

CASE EXAMPLE 2: Same case. Before asking Nails to give his version of events, Nails's lawyer says, "Before talking to you, I asked my investigator to stop by the cafe and talk to a couple of the employees. They remember that the guy you hit took a swing at you first, so it looks like we might have a good case for self-defense. But before I know if this will fly, I'll need to know from you what happened."

Question: Is the defense attorney's approach legitimate?

Answer: Though some defense attorneys might dissent, most would probably agree that the defense attorney has acted unethically by telegraphing the story that the attorney expects the client to tell. The attorney should stick to telling Nails what he's charged with and summarizing what he knows of the prosecution's evidence, and then carefully elicit Nails's story.

More About How Defense Attorneys Help Develop the Defense Story

A dramatic example of an attorney struggling with the ethics of how much information to give a defendant before asking for the defendant's version is the lecture scene in the classic courtroom film, "Anatomy of a Murder." In the film, a defendant is charged with murder. The defendant admits the shooting, but claims that it was the result of an "irresistible impulse" caused by his wife's telling him that the deceased had raped and beaten her. After some urging by his old mentor, the defense attorney delivers to the defendant a short lecture on the possible defenses to murder, explains which don't apply, and then asks the defendant to consider the remaining defense when telling his story of why he shot the deceased. Attorneys disagree as to whether the lawyer in the film overstepped ethical bounds.

---

12. If I've told one story to the police and testify to a different one at trial, can the prosecutor use the difference between the two stories against me?

Yes. When a defendant's story at trial varies in some way from the story she told to the police, prosecutors typically call a police officer as a witness to testify to the differences. The prosecutor can then argue to the judge or jury that the changes in story mean that the defendant is unworthy of belief. This is another reason that defendants should always talk to their attorneys before talking to the police.

Section III: When Attorneys Ignore a Defendant's Version of Events

This section is about miscommunication and misunderstanding between attorneys and defendants regarding the defendant's version of events.

13. Has my attorney acted incompetently by visiting me in jail soon after my arrest but not asking me to give my side of the story?

Probably not. Experienced defense attorneys know that many defendants who have just been arrested and jailed are not in a psychological condition to relate accurate stories. The attorney may also be concerned that guards or other prisoners may try to eavesdrop. Instead, the attorney may cover only what are likely to be a defendant's more pressing needs. For example, during an initial jailhouse interview an attorney may do no more than:

- reassure the defendant that the attorney's sole obligation is to the defendant, and that the attorney will do everything possible to secure a satisfactory outcome
- explain the charges and bail proce-dures, and advise the defendant that the immediate priority is to seek the defendant's release on bail, or on his or her own recognizance (O.R.)

- ask if the attorney can help take care of any of the defendant's personal matters until the client bails out of jail, such as canceling a business meeting or phoning relatives, and
- advise the defendant to say nothing to the police or any other person before the next meeting.

Initial Interviews by Court-Appointed Lawyers

Because of large caseloads, court-appointed lawyers often ask defendants about their version of events during an initial meeting immediately prior to arraignment. Their goal is to identify and dispose of "guilties" as quickly as possible (often through quick plea bargains) in order to devote the bulk of their time to cases that may go to trial.

14. Might my attorney reasonably handle my case without ever asking for my version of events?

Paradoxically, despite the frequent impor-tance of defense stories, some experienced and successful criminal defense attorneys make it a practice never to ask for the defendant's version unless there is a good reason to know it. Since it is up to the prosecution to prove a defendant guilty beyond a reasonable doubt, these defense attorneys prefer to focus their efforts on contesting the prosecution's case rather than on proving the truth of the defendant's story. For these attorneys, the danger of having ethical blockades put in the way of an effective defense outweighs the benefits of knowing the defendant's version.

> **CASE EXAMPLE:** Return to the case of Rusty Nails, who is charged with assault and battery. The defense attorney never asks for Nails's story. Two employees of the cafe where the fight took place tell the attorney that the so-called victim threw the first punch, and that Nails hit back in self-defense. The employees admit to the attorney that they do not like the victim, and the attorney suspects that they may not be telling the truth.
>
> **Question:** Can the attorney call the employees as witnesses at trial?
>
> **Answer:** Yes. The employees' story does not conflict with anything that Nails said, since the defense attorney never asked for Nails's version of events. And defense attorneys can call witnesses whom they only suspect may not be telling the truth, because credibility is for the judge or jury to decide, not the defense attorney.

15. If my attorney doesn't ask for my version of events, can I still help prove that some of the prosecution witnesses are mistaken?

Yes. Even if the defense attorney does not develop the defendant's affirmative story, the attorney may enlist the defendant's help in disproving the prosecutor's case. For example, a defense attorney may go line by line through a police report or the statement of a prosecution witness with a defendant and ask, "Can we disprove that?" By seeking out only information that casts doubt on the prosecution's case, the defense attorney can involve the defendant in the defense effort without asking for the defendant's complete story.

16. If my attorney doesn't seem interested in my side of the story, should I volunteer to tell it anyway?

No. An attorney's disinterest in a defendant's account of events is usually a strategic decision not to find out information that might hamstring an effective defense.

Section IV: The Importance of Honesty in Developing a Defense Strategy

This section is about why it's usually better for a defendant to trust the attorney and be truthful when responding to the attorney's questions.

17. The truth is that I did what the prosecution claims. If I say that to my attorney, can the attorney still represent me effectively?

Yes. The duty of defense attorneys to zealously represent their clients extends to the guilty as well as the innocent. Thus, even if they know that a client is guilty, defense attorneys can cross-examine prosecution witnesses and argue that the prosecution has failed to prove guilt beyond a reasonable doubt. This is because the defense has the right, in our justice system, to raise every possible doubt about the prosecution's case, no matter whether the defendant committed a crime or not. Guilt or innocence is for a judge or jury to determine, not the defense attorney.

18. If my story shows that I'm guilty, can that ever help my attorney?

Yes. Morality and strategic defense planning often mandate the same result: Defendants can usually best help their cases by telling their attorneys the truth—as the defendants perceive it. By concealing information, defendants may prevent their attorneys from mounting the most effective possible response to the prosecution's evidence. Ironically, innocent defendants who conceal information because they believe it makes them look guilty often end up doing more harm to their cases than good.

> **CASE EXAMPLE 1:** Cal Amity, a former police officer, is charged with murdering his fiancée after she refused to move with him to another state. The prosecution claims that, on the morning that he resigned as a police officer, Amity took a gun with him when he went to meet his fiancée at the café where she worked. He then shot his fiancée when she refused to leave with him. Amity insists to his lawyer that he shot his fiancée by accident after she

pulled a gun on him; he didn't take a gun with him when he went to talk to his fiancée. At trial, however, the prosecution surprises the defense by calling two police officers who testify that they saw Amity leaving the station after he resigned with a gun tucked in his waistband. Amity later admits to his lawyer that he had the gun on him all along.

Question: Has Amity's concealing information from his attorney hurt his case?

Answer: Yes. Had Amity's attorney known that Amity was carrying the gun, the attorney might well have been able to show that Amity was carrying the gun for a different reason than because he intended to kill his fiancée. For example, perhaps Amity carried it out of force of habit: Police officers routinely carry guns when off duty, so Amity continued this habit even though he had just resigned. But by concealing evidence, even if the shooting was in fact accidental, Amity makes it difficult for his attorney to effectively respond to the prosecution's evidence.

> **CASE EXAMPLE 2:** Will Hurt is charged with assault and battery on Ken Tusion. Hurt tells his attorney that Tusion attacked him, and that he hit Tusion in self-defense. Hurt also denies any previous problems between him and Tusion. At trial, the prosecution offers evidence that a few days before the

fight, Hurt got angry with Tusion for trying to date Hurt's girlfriend.

Question: Should Hurt have mentioned the earlier incident to his attorney?

Answer: Yes. Again, Hurt may well have struck Tusion in self-defense. But by failing to disclose the earlier incident to his attorney, Hurt allows the prosecution to surprise the attorney at trial. Had Hurt told the truth, the attorney might have been able to negate the importance of the earlier incident.

How It's Possible to Be Guilty and Still Come Out Ahead

Another reason to tell attorneys the truth is that the truth may reveal the defendant to be guilty, but only of a less serious offense. For example, a defendant's truthful story may reveal that a defendant charged with assault with a deadly weapon is at most guilty of simple assault, a much less serious crime. If the defendant lies and insists on complete innocence, the defense attorney may be unable to arrive at a realistic plea bargain. And if the case goes to trial, the defense attorney may not be able to ask the jury to convict on the lesser offense rather than the greater offense, because the facts suggesting such a result were not disclosed by the defendant to his attorney.

Though truth usually is the soundest strategy for a defendant, common sense suggests that defendants may sometimes gain by concealing the truth from their attorneys. Some attorneys may expend less effort on behalf of defendants who are guilty. And unlike defendants who privately admit guilt to their lawyer, defendants who tell false stories of innocence can testify at trial, and they can enable their attorneys to call witnesses who corroborate the defendants' stories.

The ultimate decision is up to the defendant. If the defendant believes herself guilty, should she admit guilt to the lawyer? If the defendant believes herself innocent, should she conceal harmful evidence from the lawyer? Defendants have to decide for themselves. They should understand, however, that they are much more likely to do their defense more harm than good by concealing the truth.

CASE EXAMPLE: Cal Purnia is charged with shoplifting. Unwilling to admit guilt to his lawyer, Cal makes up a phony story. Cal tells his lawyer that he came into the store with the watch that he is charged with stealing, and gives the lawyer what looks like a receipt for its purchase, dated about a month before the theft. Cal's lawyer shows the receipt to the D.A., and asks the D.A. to dismiss the charges. The D.A. refuses, and shows Cal's lawyer film from a hidden camera clearly showing

Cal stealing the watch. Because of Cal's phony story, the D.A. refuses to plea bargain and takes the case to trial. Cal is convicted and given a substantial fine.

Question: Could Cal's attorney have achieved a better outcome had Cal told the truth?

Answer: Yes. Had Cal told his lawyer the truth, the lawyer could have helped Cal enroll in a counseling program. That might have led the D.A. to reduce the charges and place Cal on probation. By lying, Cal prevented his lawyer from providing effective representation.

Crimespeak: Understanding the Language of Criminal Laws

This chapter will help you interpret criminal laws. Criminal laws are often hard to understand for several reasons:

- They may include unfamiliar concepts, such as the term "malice aforethought" in many murder statutes.
- Familiar concepts, such as "maliciously," are often what lawyers call terms of art. That is, they can take on special meanings when used in criminal laws.
- The legal definition of a crime is often different from its popular meaning. For example, if Yolanda comes home to find that her house was broken into, she's likely to yell, "I've been robbed!" No, she hasn't. Yolanda's house may have been burgled, but technically Yolanda wasn't robbed.
- Laws may vary from one state to another. For example, talking on a mobile phone while driving is illegal in some states but permissible in other states.
- Verdicts often depend on how judges and jurors subjectively interpret vague, abstract rules regarding defendants' mental states. For example, a killing may not be a crime at all or it may be first-degree murder, depending on how a jury evaluates the defendant's pre-killing thought processes. (The controversial "Nanny case" of 1997–1998 illustrated some of the subtle mental state distinctions in the murder laws. See Section IV, below.)

As a result, though "ignorance of the law is no excuse," people are often justifiably uncertain about the meaning of many criminal rules.

To help you understand criminal laws, this chapter begins by explaining the concept of "*mens rea*" ("the guilty mind"). *Mens rea* is the premise upon which our society thinks it is fair and just to punish wrongdoers. The chapter then explains the legal language you're likely to find in commonly charged crimes. The chapter should enable you to understand:

- the meaning of the legal language in common criminal statutes
- how to distinguish similar offenses such as murder and manslaughter from each other, and
- how to work backward from a statute's legal language to the type of evidence that a prosecutor is likely to offer to prove a violation of the statute.

Once you have read this chapter, you can find out in more detail what your state's laws provide by either visiting your local library or searching for them on the Internet. See Chapter 27 for more on legal research.

Section I: *Mens Rea*

This section discusses the meaning of *mens rea*, a concept that provides the foundation for labeling people as guilty and punishing them.

1. What does *mens rea* mean?

Mens rea is Latin for "guilty mind." The *mens rea* concept expresses a belief that people should be punished (fined or imprisoned) only when they have acted with an intent or purpose that makes them morally blameworthy.

2. Will I find the term *mens rea* in criminal laws?

No. *Mens rea* is never identified as a distinct element of a crime. Instead, moral blame is almost always the underlying justification for the enactment of a criminal law. In the legal system's eyes, people who intentionally engage in the behavior prohibited by a law have *mens rea*; they are morally blameworthy. For example, a murder law may prohibit "the intentional and unlawful killing of one human being by another human being." Under this law, one who intentionally and unlawfully kills another person had the mental state, or *mens rea* at the time of the killing to make them morally blameworthy for that death.

3. Can a criminal law be valid even if it doesn't require *mens rea*?

Yes, though such laws are relatively few in number. Laws that don't require *mens rea*—that is, laws that punish people despite their state of mind—are called "strict liability laws." The usual justification for a strict liability law is that the social benefits of stringent enforcement outweigh the harm of punishing a person who may be morally blameless. Examples of strict liability laws include:

- Statutory rape laws, which, in some states, make it illegal to have sexual intercourse with a minor, even if the defendant honestly and reasonably believed that the sexual partner was old enough to consent legally to sexual intercourse. (For more on statutory rape, see Section V, below.)
- Sale of alcohol to minors laws which, in many states, punish store clerks who sell alcohol to minors even if the clerks reasonably believe that the minors are old enough to buy liquor.

Strict liability laws like these punish defendants who make honest mistakes and therefore may be morally innocent. Because the legal consequences of innocent mistakes can be so great in certain circumstances, people who find themselves in situations governed by strict liability rules need to take special precautions before acting.

4. Do people who commit an illegal act by mistake have *mens rea*?

Not necessarily. In most cases, moral blame attaches when a person intentionally engages in conduct that is illegal. The corollary of this principle is that people who *unintentionally* engage in illegal conduct may be morally innocent. People can unintentionally break the law when they make a mistake of fact. A person who breaks the law because he honestly misperceives reality lacks *mens rea* and should not be charged with or convicted of a crime. (Mistake of fact is often irrelevant to guilt under strict liability laws, since they are not based on *mens rea*. See Question 3, above.)

CASE EXAMPLE 1: John owes Barbara $100. At a party, John tells Barbara that the money he owes her is in a desk drawer and that she should take it. Assuming that it adds up to $100, Barbara puts the wad of money that she finds in the desk drawer in her purse and leaves the party. The next day, John realizes that the $200 he had in his desk drawer is missing.

Question: Is Barbara guilty of stealing $100?

Answer: Not if a judge or jury believes that Barbara honestly thought that she was only taking $100. Barbara's honest mistake indicates that she did not have a guilty mind. Since theft is a *mens rea* crime, not a strict liability crime, Barbara is not guilty.

CASE EXAMPLE 2: Jane borrows a raincoat from Jean. Unbeknownst to Jane, one of the pockets contains a packet of illegal drugs. A police officer standing in a mall sees Jane take off the raincoat and the packet of drugs fall out of the pocket. The officer then arrests Jane.

Question: Is Jane guilty of possession of illegal drugs?

Answer: No. Jane lacked *mens rea* because she didn't know that the drugs were in the borrowed raincoat.

Mistake of Law vs. Mistake of Fact

Make no mistake, mistake of fact can negate *mens rea*, but "mistake of law"—that is, not knowing the law—usually cannot. People who intentionally commit illegal acts are almost always guilty, even if they honestly don't realize that what they are doing is illegal. For example, if Jo sells cocaine in the honest but mistaken belief that it is sugar, Jo may lack *mens rea*. However, if Jo sells cocaine in the honest but mistaken belief that it is legal to do so, Jo is considered morally blameworthy. Perhaps the best explanation for the difference is that if a mistake of law allowed people to escape punishment, the legal system would be encouraging people to remain ignorant of legal rules.

5. Can careless behavior amount to *mens rea*?

In some situations, yes. Ordinary carelessness is not a crime. For example, negligent drivers are not usually criminally prosecuted, though they may have to pay civil damages to those harmed by their negligence.

However, more-than-ordinary carelessness can demonstrate *mens rea*. Common terms for morally blameworthy carelessness are "recklessness" and "criminal negligence." Unfortunately, no clear line separates noncriminal negligence from recklessness and criminal negligence. In general, carelessness can amount to a crime when a person recklessly disregards a substantial and unjustifiable risk. Indefinite language like that cannot always rationally draw a line between ordinary and criminal carelessness. Police officers and prosecutors have to make the initial decisions about whether to charge a careless person with a crime. At that point, it's up to judges and juries to evaluate a person's conduct according to community standards and decide whether the carelessness is serious enough to demonstrate a morally blameworthy mental state (*mens rea*).

CASE EXAMPLE 1: Eddie gets a slingshot for his 25th birthday. He is so excited that he runs into the street, picks up a small rock, and, without aiming, shoots the rock as far as he can. The rock hits and severely injures Marsha as she crosses the street about 40 yards away. The street tends to be a busy one, and Eddie has lived on the street for 15 years.

Question: Does Eddie's conduct demonstrate *mens rea*?

Answer: Yes. Eddie may not have intended to injure Marsha. However, he acted recklessly. He knew from experience that people were likely to be out walking on his street, and nevertheless fired off an object capable of causing severe physical injury. Eddie is morally blameworthy for his conduct.

CASE EXAMPLE 2: Bobbie gets a slingshot for her 25th birthday. She is

so excited that she runs to an open field near her house, picks up a small rock, and without aiming shoots the rock as far as she can. The rock hits and severely injures Michael as he walks across the field about 40 yards away. The field is surrounded by a fence displaying a number of "No Trespassing" signs, and the incident took place at midnight.

Question: Does Bobbie's conduct demonstrate *mens rea*?

Answer: No. Under the circumstances, Bobbie could reasonably believe that the field would be deserted and that no one would be hurt by the rock. Even if her conduct is unreasonable, it is not so reckless that it demonstrates *mens rea*.

CASE EXAMPLE 3: Good friends Smith and Wesson go deer hunting. When they stop for lunch, Smith has a couple of beers. An hour later, Smith shoots in the direction of moving branches, thinking he's shooting at a deer. He hits Wesson instead, killing him.

Question: Does Smith's carelessness amount to criminal negligence?

Answer: Probably. Smith should know that drinking alcohol is especially dangerous when he is carrying a loaded weapon. Also, Smith should have known that his hunting companion was likely to be in the vicinity. Smith's reckless disregard of a substantial and unjustifiable risk demonstrates *mens rea*.

6. Can a young child have *mens rea*?

It depends on the age of the child and the state in which a crime is committed. Laws in all states exempt some young children from criminal responsibility. These laws assume that very young children do not have the capacity for *mens rea*. However, the *mens rea* age limit varies from state to state. Some states exempt only children under the age of seven. Other states have a presumption that even older children (perhaps up to age 14) lack *mens rea*, but leave room for judges to determine that a particular youthful offender did have *mens rea*.

Children who are legally old enough to have *mens rea* may be guilty of crimes, but be eligible to be treated as juveniles rather than as adults. For more information about juvenile offenders, see Chapter 25.

Section II: The Meaning of Frequently Used Legal Language

This section explains the legal language that is often found in criminal law statutes.

7. What does the term "knowing" or "knowingly" mean?

Many laws punish only violators who knowingly engage in illegal conduct. The "knowingly" requirement indicates that a crime involves *mens rea*, and prevents people who make innocent mistakes from being convicted of crimes. What a person has to know to be guilty of a crime depends on the behavior that a law makes illegal. For example:

- A drug law makes it illegal for a person to knowingly import an illegal drug (often referred to as a controlled substance) into the United States. To convict a defendant of this crime, the prosecution would have to prove that he knew that what he brought into the United States was an illegal drug.

- Another drug law makes it illegal to furnish drug paraphernalia with knowledge that it will be used to cultivate or ingest an illegal drug. To convict a defendant of this crime, the prosecution would have to prove that a defendant who sold or supplied drug paraphernalia knew the improper purposes to which the paraphernalia would be put.

- A perjury law makes it illegal for a person to testify to any material matter which she knows to be false. To prove perjury, the prosecution would have to prove that the defendant knew at the time she testified that her testimony was false.

- A school safety law makes it illegal for a person to knowingly possess a firearm in a school zone. To prove a violation of this law, the prosecution would have to prove both that the defendant knew that he was carrying a gun and that he was in a school zone.

CASE EXAMPLE: Donald, an Oregon resident, vacations in Canada. As Donald is about to leave Canada, his friend Brandi gives him a satchel.

Brandi tells Donald that the satchel contains wedding presents for Brandi's friend who lives in Oregon, and that the friend will collect the satchel from Donald in a few days. After he crosses the border, a police officer finds the satchel in Donald's car. The officer opens it and finds that it contains packages of cocaine. Donald is charged with knowingly importing illegal drugs.

Question: Did Donald knowingly import drugs into the United States?

Answer: No, if a judge or jury accepts Donald's story. If Donald did not know that the satchel contained illegal drugs, he did not knowingly import them and therefore lacked *mens rea*. Of course, Donald might reasonably expect judges and jurors to have a skeptical attitude toward his somewhat fishy story.

8. How can the government possibly prove what a defendant knew?

A defendant might confess to a police officer, or admit knowledge in a phone call or a letter. However, in most cases the government has to offer circumstantial evidence of a defendant's knowledge. That is, the government offers evidence of circumstances surrounding the defendant's actions and asks the judge or jury to infer the defendant's knowledge from those circumstances. For example, in Donald's case above, the government might offer the following circumstantial evidence to show that Donald knew that the satchel contained illegal drugs:

- Brandi (or others) had on an earlier occasion asked Donald to carry presents across the border in a satchel; on this earlier occasion, Donald found out that the satchel contained illegal drugs.
- Donald had tried to conceal the satchel in his car.
- The satchel was too heavy (or too light) to account for the presents that Brandi told Donald it contained.
- The satchel emitted a strong odor of drugs.
- Donald is a drug user.
- Donald was aware that Brandi's friend was a drug user.

9. What are "specific intent" crimes?

Specific intent laws require the government to do more than show that a defendant acted knowingly. Specific intent laws require the government to prove that a defendant had a particular purpose in mind when engaging in illegal conduct. Each specific intent law identifies the particular purpose that the government has to prove. For example:

- Many theft laws require the government to prove that a defendant took property with the intent to permanently deprive a person of the property. To convict a defendant of theft, the government has to prove that a thief's plan was to forever part a victim from his property. For example, a culprit who drives off in another's car without permission and returns it a few hours later might be convicted only of joyriding. However, the same culprit who drives off in another's car without permission and takes it across the country probably demonstrates a specific intent to permanently deprive the owner of the car and would be guilty of the more serious crime of car theft. (For more information about theft laws, see Section VIII, below.)

- Insurance fraud laws often require proof that a defendant destroyed insured property with the intent to defraud the insurer. To convict a defendant of insurance fraud, a prosecutor has to prove that a defendant's purpose in destroying insured property was to collect money from the property's insurer. For instance, a prosecutor might offer evidence that the owner of a decaying factory hired an arsonist to set fire to it and then filed an insurance claim.

- A serious drug crime involves possession of drugs with the intent to sell them. To prove this crime, a prosecutor would have to prove that the defendant intended to sell the drugs found in the defendant's possession rather than keep them for his own use. For example, the prosecutor might offer evidence that the drugs found in the defendant's apartment were bundled into separate packages, that the defendant also owned a set of scales commonly used by drug pushers to weigh drugs, and

that customers were frequently seen going in and out of the apartment.

CASE EXAMPLE 1: Veecee Arr is charged with stealing a video recorder. The prosecutor offers evidence that Arr took a video recorder from an electronics shop without paying for it and tried to pawn it the next day.

Question: Is this evidence adequate to prove Arr's specific intent to steal the video recorder?

Answer: Yes. Arr's efforts to pawn the video recorder the day after taking it is strong circumstantial evidence that Arr planned to permanently deprive the electronics shop of possession of the video recorder.

CASE EXAMPLE 2: Hank O'Hare is charged with kidnapping with intent to commit rape. The victim testifies that as she was walking home one evening, O'Hare jumped out from behind some bushes, grabbed her, and pushed her into his car. Inside his car, O'Hare covered the victim's mouth and secured her hands with adhesive tape. O'Hare drove around for 15 minutes before the victim managed to free her hands and escape from the car.

Question: Is O'Hare guilty as charged?

Answer: No. O'Hare is clearly guilty of the lesser (but still very serious) crime of kidnapping. However, the circumstantial evidence is probably not strong enough to prove that O'Hare kidnapped the victim for the purpose of committing a rape.

Question: What additional evidence might the government introduce to demonstrate that O'Hare intended to commit rape?

Answer: Any one of the following items of evidence would be legally sufficient to prove that O'Hare kidnapped the victim with the intent of committing rape: (1) statements by O'Hare to the victim (or to O'Hare's cronies) indicating his sexual intent; (2) O'Hare's sexual touching of the victim before she managed to escape; or (3) evidence that O'Hare had previously used the same "m.o." (methods) to kidnap and rape other young women on previous occasions.

10. A statute makes it illegal to maliciously deface a building. What does the term "maliciously" mean?

In everyday usage people often use the term malicious to mean spiteful or wicked. In most criminal statutes, however, "malicious is simply synonymous with intentionally" and knowingly. (Section IV, below, discusses the term "malice afore-thought" in murder statutes.) As a result, the term "maliciously" usually adds nothing to the general *mens rea* requirement.

CASE EXAMPLE: Red Brown is charged with spray painting graffiti on Wood Siding's house. The statute under which Red is charged requires that the prosecution prove that Red acted maliciously.

Question: Does Red have a valid defense if he admits to spraying the house with graffiti, and testifies that he was playing a birthday joke on Wood and didn't act out of spite or nastiness?

Answer: No. The prosecution has to prove only that Red intentionally sprayed paint on Wood's house. The fact that Red may have done it as a joke is irrelevant.

11. How does the term "willfully" affect the meaning of a statute?

As with maliciously, the term "willfully" usually adds nothing to the general *mens rea* requirement. In most statutes, to commit an illegal act willfully is simply to commit it intentionally. For example, consider these statutes:

- "It is unlawful to willfully disturb another person by loud and unreasonable noise."
- "Anyone who willfully encourages another to commit suicide is guilty of a felony."

Each of these statutes merely requires the government to show that a person intentionally committed the act made illegal by the statute.

CASE EXAMPLE: Raye Dio deliberately cranks up the volume on her stereo at 3 a.m. The volume is so high that it wakes up a number of other tenants, who call the police.

Question: Has Raye willfully disturbed others by making loud and unreasonable noise?

Answer: Yes. Raye acted willfully because she knew that she was playing her stereo at a high volume.

Question: What if Raye deliberately turned up the volume only because she is hard of hearing?

Answer: A serious hearing problem may prevent Raye from realizing that what seems like a normal volume to her is in reality unreasonably loud. If so, Raye did not knowingly create unreasonable noise and so did not behave willfully. However, if Raye persists in playing her stereo loudly even after the neighbors have advised her that the volume is unreasonably loud, Raye may be guilty of disturbing the peace notwithstanding her hearing problem. She has acted willfully, especially because reasonable alternatives (such as headphones) are available.

Less commonly, the term "willfully" in a statute has been interpreted to require the government to prove not only that a person acted intentionally, but also that the person intended to break the law. (This is an unusual instance in which ignorance of the law actually IS an excuse!) For example, in one case, a federal law made it illegal to willfully bring in to the country more than $10,000 in cash without declaring it to customs officials. The U.S. Supreme Court decided that to convict a person of violating this law, the government had to prove that the person knew the law's requirements (*Ratzlaf v. U.S.*, U.S. Sup. Ct. 1994). This more exacting interpretation of "willfully" preserves the *mens rea* foundation of criminal law where, as in the cash-declaring law, many people might be morally innocent yet break the law.

12. How does the term "feloniously" affect the meaning of a statute?

The term "felonious" is sometimes included in a law when prohibited conduct can in some circumstances be legal. Its presence is a reminder that a law applies only to a prohibited form of conduct. For example, consider this law:

"Anyone who feloniously takes the property of another is guilty of theft."

Taking another's property is often perfectly legal. For example, one sister may give another sister general permission to wear her sweaters. And shoppers certainly commit no crime when they take an item off a shelf when deciding whether to buy it. The statute makes only felonious taking illegal— that is, taking property without permission and with the intent to permanently deprive another of the property.

13. What does the term "motive" mean?

Motive refers to the reason why a person committed an illegal act. For example, a person's need to raise money quickly to pay off a bookie may be the motive for a robbery; revenge for a personal affront may be the motive for a physical attack.

Prosecutors often offer motive evidence as circumstantial evidence that a defendant acted intentionally or knowingly. The reason is that, like most people, judges and jurors believe in cause and effect. They are more likely to believe that a defendant had *mens rea* if they know that the defendant had a motive to commit an illegal act.

14. Does the government have to prove motive?

No. While prosecutors frequently do offer motive evidence, they are not required to do so. By the same token, defendants may offer evidence showing that they had no motive to commit a crime, and then argue that the lack of a motive demonstrates reasonable doubt of guilt.

> **CASE EXAMPLE:** Lucretia Borgia is charged with murdering her husband, Sid. The government offers evidence that Lucretia had begun secretly dating another man in the months before Sid died. Lucretia offers evidence that under the terms of Sid's father's will, Lucretia would inherit $1 million, but only if Sid was alive when the father died. Sid's father was still alive at the time of Sid's death.
>
> **Question:** What impact might the motive evidence have on the outcome of the case?
>
> **Answer:** The government's evidence suggests that Lucretia had an emotional motive to knock off Sid; Lucretia's evidence suggests that she had a

financial motive not to. It's up to the judge or jury to weigh the conflicting motive evidence together with all the other evidence in the case and arrive at a verdict.

Crimes and the Constitution

While the U.S. Congress and state legislatures have broad powers to define crimes, courts have the ultimate power to decide whether a criminal statute is constitutional. For example, the U.S. Supreme Court decided that a District of Columbia law banning the possession of handguns was invalid because it violated the Second Amendment (*District of Columbia v. Heller*, 2008). The federal government still has wide powers to control weapons. For example, it can ban specific types of weapons, it can ban weapons in particular places (such as around airports and schools), and it can prevent certain people (such as ex-felons and people who have been convicted of crimes involving domestic violence) from owning weapons. Moreover, since the Second Amendment is a restriction on the power of the federal government, state gun control laws may be unaffected by it (*Maloney v. Cuomo*, 2d Cir. Court of Appeals, 2009).

Section III: Derivative Criminal Responsibility

This section looks at situations in which a person might not commit the primary criminal act yet still be guilty of a crime.

15. Who is an accomplice?

An accomplice is one who intentionally helps another to commit a crime. Even if an accomplice does not participate in carrying out the crime, in the eyes of the law the accomplice's precrime assistance makes an accomplice just as guilty as the person who does carry out the crime. For example, assume that Lars Senny breaks into a warehouse and steals property belonging to the warehouse owner. Hal Perr would be Lars's accomplice and just as guilty as Lars if Hal took any of the following steps to help Lars commit the theft:

- Hal works in the warehouse, and drugged the warehouse night watchman before leaving work on the day of the theft
- Hal cut the wires to the burglar alarm (or cut a hole in the fence) so that Lars could enter the warehouse without being detected
- Hal has a blueprint of the warehouse, and he met with Lars a week before the theft to review warehouse layouts and exit routes

- Hal rented a U-Haul truck and left it parked outside the warehouse on the night of the robbery, or
- Hal agreed to babysit for Lars's infant child so that Lars could break into the warehouse.

The Accomplices in the Oklahoma City Bombing Tragedy

In 1995, a bomb exploded in front of the federal building in Oklahoma City; 168 people were killed and more than 500 were injured. A jury convicted Timothy McVeigh of first degree murder for carrying out the bombing; McVeigh was sentenced to death. McVeigh was executed in 2001. A separate jury convicted Terry Nichols of conspiracy for helping McVeigh plan the bombing and gather bomb components. However, the jury acquitted Nichols of murder because of its uncertainty over whether Nichols realized that McVeigh planned to carry out the bombing at a time when the federal building was open for business. Nichols was sentenced to life in prison in June 1998. Michael Fortier, another accomplice, was sentenced to 12 years in prison in May 1998 after pleading guilty to four charges, including failure to warn authorities of the bomb plot and transporting stolen weapons. In part, Fortier's lighter sentence was due to his cooperation with the government; he provided crucial testimony that helped convict McVeigh and Nichols.

Barbara Graham: The Executed Accomplice

In 1953, Barbara Graham was convicted in California of helping three others murder and rob a widow. Graham's role consisted mainly of helping her cohorts gain entry into the widow's home. Graham was sentenced to death, though she may not have participated in the actual killing. She was executed in 1955 after two last-minute stays of executions were lifted, becoming one of four women ever executed in California. The case was dramatized in the 1958 film *I Want To Live!,* for which Susan Hayward won the Academy Award for Best Actress.

16. Does an accomplice need *mens rea* to be guilty of a crime?

Yes. To prove that a defendant is an accomplice, the government must prove that the defendant intentionally aided in the commission of a crime. This means that the defendant must realize that the principal is going to commit a crime and that the accomplice intends to help the crime come off.

CASE EXAMPLE 1: Jill Lester manages a warehouse. Jill takes Lars Senny on a tour of the warehouse after Lars informs the warehouse owner that he is interested in purchasing it. The night of the tour, Lars uses the information he gained from Jill to successfully enter the warehouse and steal property.

Question: Did Jill act as Lars's accomplice in the warehouse theft?

Answer: No. Jill did not intentionally help Lars commit the theft. Thus, Jill lacked *mens rea* and did not commit a crime.

CASE EXAMPLE 2: Les Sorr rents a room in Sorr's apartment house to Les See. See tells Sorr, "I'm glad the apartment is available. The mayor is coming by in a motorcade in a couple of weeks, and I plan to shoot him." Sorr replies, "I hope you don't do that." See does in fact shoot the mayor from a window of his apartment.

Question: Is Sorr guilty as See's accomplice in the shooting of the mayor?

Answer: Probably not. Many courts would conclude that Sorr is not guilty, because Sorr intended only to rent the apartment, not to help See shoot the mayor.

Question: What if, after See mentioned his plan to shoot the mayor, Sorr had replied, "In that case, the apartment is an extra fifty bucks per month"?

Answer: Probably all judges would conclude that Sorr is guilty as an accomplice, because Sorr has financially benefited from See's criminal act.

Accomplices, Accessories, Aiders and Abettors, and Principals

To distinguish the criminal culpability of one crime helper from another, the common law has developed specialized terms for the various ways in which one could be a party to the crime. For instance, a principal in the first degree is the person who actually carries out a crime. A principal in the second degree (an aider and abettor) is a helper who is present at a crime scene but in a passive role, such as acting as a lookout. An accessory before the fact is a helper who is not present at the crime scene.

While some state laws retain the common law terminology, few states make any distinction between the criminal liability of crime perpetrators and their accomplices. All can be punished equally, whether they actually perpetrate a crime or only help bring it about.

17. Who is an accessory after the fact?

An accessory after the fact is someone who, knowing that a felon has finished committing a crime (and generally the crime has to be a felony), helps the felon avoid arrest or trial. Perhaps because by the time an accessory after the fact becomes involved a crime has already occurred, in most states accessories after the fact face far smaller punishment than accomplices or principals.

CASE EXAMPLE 1: Abbe Citron is driving past the Last National Bank when she sees her husband Alan run out of the bank carrying a bag of cash and being chased by a security guard. Alan jumps into Abbe's car and asks her to drive him to a secret hideaway. She does so.

Question: Is Abbe guilty of a crime, and if so, what crime?

Answer: Abbe is an accomplice, just as guilty as Alan of the bank robbery because she helped Alan to escape. Abbe does not qualify for the lesser crime of being an accessory after the fact because Alan had not yet finished committing the crime of bank robbery when Abbe assisted him. A crime is not finished until the criminal has reached a place of temporary or permanent safety.

CASE EXAMPLE 2: As in the previous example, Alan has robbed the Last National Bank. Alan runs home, tells Abbe what he did and hides in the basement. A short time later, when the police come looking for Alan, Abbe tells them that she has not seen Alan and does not know where he is.

Question: Is Abbe guilty of a crime, and if so, what crime?

Answer: Abbe is guilty of being an accessory after the fact to bank robbery. Abbe is not an accomplice because Alan had finished committing the crime before Abbe tried to help him evade capture.

CASE EXAMPLE 3: Tippycanoe and Tyler meet at a movie theater. Once inside, Tippycanoe shows Tyler a bag of candy and snack food, tells Tyler that he stole it from a shop and offers some to Tyler. Between them, Tippycanoe and Tyler finish the whole bag.

Question: Is Tyler guilty of being an accessory after the fact?

Answer: No. Tyler helped Tippycanoe to conceal the crime by eating some of the stolen food. However, Tippycanoe's crime was petty theft, which is almost certainly a misdemeanor and not a felony. As mentioned in the text above, in most states, an accessory after the fact is guilty of a crime only if the underlying crime is a felony.

The Law's Suspicious Attitude Toward Accomplice Testimony

Judges have historically had a suspicious attitude toward accomplice testimony because of accomplices' obvious motive to minimize their own responsibility (and punishment) by shifting most of the blame to somebody else. As a safeguard, most states have a rule that a defendant cannot be convicted merely upon the testimony of an accomplice. If a prosecution witness qualifies as an accomplice, the prosecution has to corroborate the witness's testimony with independent evidence linking the defendant to a crime.

18. Who are conspirators?

Conspirators are two or more people who agree to commit a crime. (The distinction between accomplices and conspirators is that the former are helpers, while each conspirator is a principal.) Conspiracy is a controversial crime, in part because conspirators can be guilty even if the crime that they agree to commit never occurs. As a result, conspirators can be punished for their illegal plans rather than for what they actually do. But as some protection against convicting people purely for their private thoughts, in most states conspirators are not guilty of the crime of conspiracy unless at least one of them commits an overt act. An "overt act" is an activity which in some way moves a conspiracy into motion.

CASE EXAMPLE 1: Bonnie and Clyde agree to rob the Last National Bank. The night before the planned robbery, Bonnie brags about the plan to a friend, who notifies the police. Bonnie and Clyde are arrested early the next morning, before they can carry out their plan.

Question: Are Bonnie and Clyde conspirators?

Answer: No. They formed a mental plan but took no overt act towards its completion. Therefore they are not conspirators.

CASE EXAMPLE 2: Same case. Before bragging about her plan to the friend, Bonnie had called the Last National

Bank to ask what time it would open the next morning.

Question: Are Bonnie and Clyde conspirators?

Answer: Yes. Bonnie's phone call, though not itself a crime, is an overt act that helped put the conspiracy into motion. Bonnie and Clyde can be convicted of conspiracy even though the robbery never occurred.

Overt Acts Can Be Trivial

States that require prosecutors to prove overt acts in conspiracy cases add little to their burden. Almost any objectively provable act, even one that standing alone is entirely innocent, can be sufficient to prove a conspiracy. Writing a letter, making a phone call, attending a lawful meeting, and hiring a lawyer are examples of overt acts that have satisfied conspiracy statutes.

19. How does the government prove that a conspiracy exists?

Few conspiracies are reduced to writing. Usually, as when trying to prove intent or knowledge, a prosecutor relies on circumstantial evidence. Just as a person might infer the existence of a fire from smoke, prosecutors ask judges and juries to infer from conspirators' behavior the illegal agreement that gave rise to that behavior.

CASE EXAMPLE: Laurel and Hardy drive through the streets of a city. They pass three piano stores. Each time, Laurel stops the car, Hardy gets out with a hammer, walks into the piano store and smashes a piano to bits.

Question: Could a judge or jury infer from this behavior that Laurel and Hardy are conspirators?

Answer: Yes. Laurel and Hardy's behavior suggests that they are carrying out a plan to which they agreed earlier.

20. Can conspirators receive double punishment?

Yes. Conspiracy is itself a crime. As a result, conspirators can be convicted both of conspiracy and of the crime which they carry out in furtherance of the conspiracy. For instance, assume that Bonnie and Clyde conspire to rob a bank, then actually rob it. Bonnie and Clyde can be convicted and separately punished for conspiracy and for bank robbery.

21. Can a conspirator be convicted of crimes committed by co-conspirators regardless of whether the conspirator agreed to those crimes in advance?

Yes. Another broad feature of conspiracy law in most states is that each conspirator is legally responsible for crimes committed by any other conspirators—so long as those crimes fall within the scope of the conspiracy. Because the precise goal of a conspiracy is rarely written down, a conspirator's criminal liability can easily be much more than the conspirator anticipated. A conspirator may intend to take part only in a single crime, yet be responsible for additional crimes committed by co-conspirators who intended for the conspiracy to perpetrate a number of crimes.

> **CASE EXAMPLE 1:** Bonnie and Clyde agree to rob the Last National Bank. Bonnie waits in the getaway car while Clyde holds up the bank. To prevent being captured, Clyde shoots and severely wounds a bank security guard.
>
> **Question:** Can Bonnie be charged both with bank robbery and with shooting the security guard?
>
> **Answer:** Yes. As explained earlier, a successful getaway is an inherent part of a crime scheme. Since shooting the security guard furthers the purpose of Bonnie and Clyde's conspiracy, Bonnie and Clyde are equally responsible for the shooting.

> **CASE EXAMPLE 2:** Bonnie and Clyde carry out a plan to rob the Last National Bank. The same evening, they divide up the money and go their separate ways. The next morning, Bonnie robs the Next to Last National Bank.
>
> **Question:** Is Clyde legally responsible for the Next to Last National Bank robbery?
>
> **Answer:** Probably not. On this information, Bonnie and Clyde were conspirators only for the limited purpose of robbing the Last National Bank. That

plan was carried out—the money had already been divided and the conspirators had gone their separate ways. The robbery that Bonnie carried out the next morning was therefore not in furtherance of the original plan, and Clyde is not legally responsible for it.

> **CASE EXAMPLE 3:** Bonnie, Clyde, Barker, and Dillinger get together and plan to each rob a bank on the same day and later divide up the total proceeds equally. Dillinger later recruits Capone, who helps Dillinger rob a bank.
>
> **Question:** Could each robber, including Capone, be convicted of the robberies committed by the other robbers?
>
> **Answer:** Yes. The conspiracy encompassed all the bank robberies, so each conspirator is legally responsible for each of them. Even though Capone may only have agreed to help Dillinger, Capone is bound by the conspiracy's wider scope.

Section IV: Murder and Manslaughter

This section explains the important but often subtle distinctions between murder and manslaughter, and between different degrees of those crimes. Often, the language of both murder and manslaughter can reasonably be applied to a defendant's conduct. A judge's or jury's verdict may be less dependent on the abstract language of the rules than on a judgment about just how morally blameworthy a defendant is.

22. Is homicide the same thing as murder?

No. A homicide is any killing of a human being by another human being. Many homicides are legal, such as a justifiable killing of a suspect by the police and a killing done in self-defense.

23. What is the definition of murder?

Murder is an intentional killing that is:
- unlawful (in other words, the killing isn't legally justified), and
- committed with "malice aforethought."

Malice aforethought doesn't mean that a killer has to have acted out of spite or hate. Malice aforethought exists if a killer intends to kill a person. In addition, in most states malice aforethought isn't limited to intentional killings. Malice aforethought can also exist if:
- a killer intentionally inflicts very serious bodily harm that causes a victim's death, or
- a killer's behavior, which demonstrates extreme reckless disregard for the value of human life, results in a victim's death.

Under this scheme, intent to do serious bodily harm and extreme reckless disregard become legal equivalents to intent to kill. To be consistent, from here on we'll refer to murders as intentional killings.

24. If a victim is dead in any event, why distinguish between first degree and second degree murder?

Even within the universe of those who kill unlawfully and with malice aforethought, the law regards some killers as more dangerous and morally blameworthy than others; this group can be convicted of first degree murder. Unlawful and intentional killings that don't constitute first degree murder are second degree murder.

The rules vary somewhat from state to state as to what circumstances make an intentional killing first degree murder. The following circumstances are common:
- The killing is deliberate and premeditated. In other words, the killer plans the crime ahead of time. For example, premeditation exists if a wife goes to the store, buys a lethal dose of rat poison, and puts it in her husband's tea.
- The killing occurs during the course of a dangerous felony. This is often known as the felony murder rule. A felon can be guilty of murder whenever a death occurs in the course of a dangerous felony, even if the felon is not the killer. For example, assume that A and B commit an armed bank robbery. As they attempt to flee with the loot, a police officer shoots and kills A. B could be convicted of first degree murder because a death occurred in the course of a dangerous felony—even though the killer was a police officer and the dead person was B's co-conspirator.
- The killer uses an explosive device such as a bomb.

25. Is the punishment for first degree murder usually more severe than for second degree murder?

Yes. Many states have mandatory minimum sentences for murder, and the mandatory minimum for first degree murder is almost always higher than for second degree. Defendants convicted of first degree murder can also be eligible for a state's ultimate penalty. Currently, in 37 states and under some federal laws, the ultimate penalty is death. In others, it is life in prison without the possibility of parole (LWOP). Defendants convicted of second degree murder are often sentenced to a term of years rather than to life in prison, and are almost always eligible for parole.

26. What is the difference between murder and manslaughter?

Manslaughter (in some states called third degree murder) is an unlawful killing that does not involve malice aforethought. The absence of malice aforethought means that manslaughter involves less moral blame than either first or second degree murder. Thus, while manslaughter is a serious crime, the punishment for manslaughter is generally less than for murder.

27. Do degrees of manslaughter exist, as they do for murder?

Yes, though the two types of manslaughter are usually referred to as voluntary and involuntary manslaughter.

Voluntary manslaughter is often called "the heat of passion" crime. Voluntary manslaughter arises when a person is suddenly provoked (in circumstances which are likely to provoke many reasonable people) and kills in the heat of passion aroused by the provocation. That the killing is not considered murder is a concession to human weakness. Killers who act in the heat of passion may kill intentionally, but the emotional context prevents them from having the ability to fully control their behavior. As a result, the heat of passion reduces their moral blameworthiness.

The common example of voluntary manslaughter involves a husband who comes home unexpectedly to find his wife committing adultery. If the husband is provoked into such a heat of passion that he kills the paramour right then and there, a judge or jury might very well consider the killing to be voluntary manslaughter.

A killing can be involuntary manslaughter when a person's reckless disregard of a substantial risk results in another's death. Because involuntary manslaughter involves carelessness and not purposeful killing, it is a less serious crime than murder or voluntary manslaughter.

The subtleties between the degrees of murder and manslaughter reach their peak with involuntary manslaughter. Suppose that Rosencrantz is driving a car and runs over and kills Guildenstern. Rosencrantz might be:

- Not guilty of a crime at all. If Guildenstern's family sues Rosencrantz in a civil case, Rosencrantz might have to pay damages to Guildenstern's heirs if Rosencrantz was negligent—that is,

The "Nanny" Case: Murder or Manslaughter?

The subtle distinctions between murder and manslaughter were at the heart of 1997–1998's controversial and internationally-televised nanny trial in Massachusetts. A 19-year-old British au pair babysitter was charged with second degree murder for killing an infant that had been left in her care. The prosecution claimed that she shook the baby so violently that he died. In crimespeak, the prosecution claimed that the babysitter's behavior demonstrated extreme reckless disregard for human life. The defense claimed that the baby died as the result of an unforeseeable reaction to normal shaking, so she committed no crime.

Under Massachusetts law, the defense could have asked the judge to instruct the jury about involuntary manslaughter, which would have allowed the jury to conclude that the babysitter was criminally negligent for shaking the baby too hard. However, the defense asked the judge not to instruct on involuntary manslaughter, gambling that the jury would acquit rather than convict the babysitter of murder. (Other states don't allow the defense to play tactical games like this one, and require the judge to instruct on every verdict reasonably warranted by the evidence.)

The defense lost the gamble—the jury convicted the babysitter of second degree murder, which carried a mandatory minimum sentence of 15 years in prison. A few weeks later, the defense asked the judge either to acquit the babysitter or reduce the verdict to involuntary manslaughter. The judge did the latter, sentenced the babysitter to time served, and freed her from prison immediately. The Massachusetts Supreme Court upheld the judge's decision in June 1998.

if Rosencrantz failed to use ordinary care.

- Convicted of involuntary manslaughter if Rosencrantz recklessly disregarded a substantial risk, meaning that Rosencrantz was more than ordinarily negligent. For example, a judge or jury might convict Rosencrantz of involuntary manslaughter if Rosencrantz killed Guildenstern while driving under the influence of alcohol.
- Convicted of second degree murder if Rosencrantz's behavior demonstrated such an extreme reckless disregard for human life that a judge or jury decides that Rosencrantz's behavior demonstrates malice aforethought. For example, if Rosencrantz not only kills Guildenstern as a result of drunk driving, but does so with a stolen car after his license had been taken away for previous drunk driving convictions, a judge or jury might convict Rosencrantz of second degree murder.

CASE EXAMPLE 1: Fast Boyle is walking along a busy street. Clay bumps into Boyle and continues walking without saying "Sorry." Angered by Clay's rudeness, Boyle immediately pulls out a gun and kills Clay.

Question: What crime should Boyle be convicted of?

Answer: Second degree murder, because Boyle killed Clay intentionally. A judge or jury is unlikely to conclude that the killing was premeditated, which would elevate the shooting to first degree murder. On the other hand, this was not a heat of passion killing that might reduce the conviction to voluntary manslaughter. While Boyle might personally have been provoked into killing Clay, the circumstances were not so extreme that many ordinary and reasonable people would have been provoked to kill.

Question: What crime should Boyle be convicted of if instead of shooting Clay, Boyle had pulled out a knife and thrown it at Clay, meaning just to hurt him and teach him a lesson? However, the knife punctured Clay's liver and he bled to death.

Answer: Boyle should again be convicted of second degree murder. Boyle may not have intended to kill Clay. Nevertheless, Boyle intended to inflict a very serious bodily injury on Clay, and that injury caused Clay's death. In most states, malice aforethought would be implied from Boyle's intent to do serious harm.

CASE EXAMPLE 2: Standing next to each other in a bookstore a few feet away from the top of a flight of stairs, Marks and Spencer argue over the proper interpretation of free will in Hobbes's philosophy. The argument becomes increasingly animated, and culminates when Spencer points a finger at Marks and Marks pushes Spencer backwards. The push is hard enough to cause Spencer to fall backwards and down the stairs. Spencer dies from the resulting injuries.

Question: What crime should Marks be convicted of?

Answer: Marks would probably be guilty of involuntary manslaughter. It was criminally negligent of Marks to shove a person standing near the top of a stairway. But circumstances don't suggest that Marks's behavior was so reckless as to demonstrate extreme indifference to human life, which would have elevated the crime to second degree murder.

CASE EXAMPLE 3: Lew Manion comes home to find that his wife Lee has been badly beaten and sexually abused. Manion takes Lee to the hospital. On the way, Lee tells Manion that her attacker was Barnett, the owner of a tavern that she and Manion occasionally visit. After driving Lee home from the hospital about four hours later, Manion goes to a gunshop and buys a gun. Manion then goes to the tavern and shoots and kills Barnett.

Question: What crime should Manion be convicted of?

Answer: Manion could be convicted of first degree murder, because his purchase of the gun suggests that the shooting was intentional and premeditated. Voluntary manslaughter is a somewhat less likely alternative. Most judges and jurors are likely to think that enough time elapsed between the time Manion found out about Lee's injuries and the time he shot Barnett for any heat of passion to have cooled. Manion should have left his gun at home and reported the crime to the police.

Section V: Sexual Violence

This section describes common crimes that involve sexual violence.

Part 1: Rape

28. What is rape?

Rape is unlawful (nonconsensual) sexual intercourse, often consisting of unwanted intercourse accomplished by means of force or fear. For purposes of rape laws, sexual intercourse occurs at the moment of sexual penetration, however slight.

The most typical form of rape is forcible rape, in which a rapist uses violence or threats of violence to coerce a victim into sexual intercourse. In most states, however, rape can also occur in a number of other ways. For example, rape generally also consists of sexual intercourse occurring under these conditions:

- the rapist prevents a victim from resisting by plying the victim with alcohol or drugs
- the rapist poses as a public official and threatens to arrest or deport the victim unless the victim agrees to sexual intercourse, or
- the rapist knows that the victim has a disorder or disability that prevents the victim from legally consenting to sexual intercourse.

CASE EXAMPLE 1: Amanda goes out to dinner with her boss Fred. After dinner Fred suggests that "we go back to my office and enjoy ourselves." Amanda has heard that Fred has been violent in the past. Fearing both that Fred may hurt her and that her career may suffer if she doesn't go along, Amanda agrees to go back to the office and engages in sexual intercourse with Fred.

Question: Is Fred guilty of raping Amanda?

Answer: No. Fred neither used force nor threatened harm to Amanda. Her subjective fear based on what she has heard about Fred doesn't invalidate her consent. Of course, Amanda may have a valid civil claim against Fred and the company for workplace sexual harassment.

CASE EXAMPLE 2: Belinda is sleeping when Stan breaks into her apartment, pulls out a knife, and threatens to use it unless Belinda agrees to sexual intercourse. Belinda pleads with Stan to leave, but he refuses and begins to strike her. Eventually Belinda hands Stan a condom and says, "At least use protection." Stan uses the condom while having sexual intercourse with Belinda.

Question: Is Stan guilty of rape?

Answer: Yes. The sexual intercourse was forcible, not consensual. Belinda's request that Stan use a condom is not evidence of consent, but rather an effort to suffer as little future harm as possible.

Dramatic Changes in Rape Evidence Rules

Until the mid-1970s, evidence rules tended to discourage rape victims from reporting the crime. Since then, largely as the result of political pressure from women's rights groups and their allies, two dramatic shifts in rape evidence laws favorable to rape victims have taken place. First, rape shield laws often prevent defendants from inquiring into rape victims' sexual histories. (See Federal Rule of Evidence 412; see also Chapter 18.) Second, in most states, the general rule forbidding inquiry into defendants' past crimes has been abandoned in sexual offense cases. (See Chapter 18.) When a defendant is charged with rape or another sexual offense, the prosecution can offer evidence of the defendant's past sexual offenses. (See Federal Rule of Evidence 413.)

29. Can a husband be guilty of raping his wife?

In most states, yes. If sexual intercourse is nonconsensual within the meaning of the rape laws, the fact that the parties are married is irrelevant. Of course, the fact that the alleged rapist is her husband may make it more difficult for a wife to convince the police or a judge or jury that rape rather than consensual intercourse took place.

30. Can a woman be guilty of rape?

Yes, though such cases are rare. In a few instances, females have been convicted of rape when they have been the accomplices of males and have lured a victim to a place where a rapist awaits.

31. Do degrees of rape exist?

In many states, yes. First degree rape may consist of rape accompanied by severe physical injuries. First degree rape carries a harsher punishment than second degree rape, which may involve no physical injuries beyond the rape itself.

32. What is the difference between "stranger rape" and "date rape"?

"Stranger rape" occurs when a rape victim is attacked by a previously unknown person. For example, an assailant who violently drags a passerby into a secluded spot and rapes her commits a stranger rape. Date rape occurs when the rapist and the rape victim have an existing social relationship and the rapist strikes in the course of that relationship. For example, a date rapist may prevent a woman from refusing to have sexual intercourse by drugging her drink while they are out on a date. Date rape is far more common than stranger rape. While both are equally illegal, the ambiguities that are inherent in many social situations make date rape a far more difficult crime to prove than stranger rape.

33. What is statutory rape?

Statutory rape consists of sexual intercourse with a minor, defined in most states as someone who is under age 18 at the time intercourse takes place. The minor's outward consent to intercourse is irrelevant. Statutory rape laws are strict liability laws that make a minor legally incapable of consenting to sexual intercourse. The (perhaps outmoded) assumption behind statutory rape laws is that someone under the age of 18 does not have the mature mental capacity to voluntarily consent to intercourse.

34. Can a minor be guilty of statutory rape of another minor?

Yes. If two 16-year-olds engage in sexual intercourse, in many states each could be prosecuted for statutory rape. In other states, only males can be prosecuted for statutory rape. Of course, such cases are rarely prosecuted. Even when they are, laws in many states make concessions to the frequency of sexual intercourse among minors in modern society. So long as one minor is not more than three years older than the other minor, statutory rape is often a misdemeanor rather than a felony.

Part 2: Domestic Violence

35. What is domestic violence?

Domestic violence is a catch-all term for violence that occurs between people who have a social relationship. They may be married, living together, or even just dating. They may be heterosexual, lesbian, or gay. While anyone can become a domestic violence perpetrator or victim, serious injuries resulting from domestic violence typically result from males attacking females. Though murder and rape can be forms of domestic violence, most often domestic violence consists of lesser forms of physical abuse such as hitting. Stalking can also be a form of domestic violence.

36. Is there a crime called "domestic violence"?

Many states define domestic violence as a distinct crime. As a result, a suspect who strikes a "significant other" may be charged with domestic violence instead of or in addition to other crimes such as assault and battery. Recognizing that domestic abusers take advantage of their victims' trust and confidence, convictions for domestic violence often result in harsher punishment compared to similar crimes committed against strangers.

37. Is it true that most acts of domestic violence go unreported?

Yes. Women, who are usually the victims of domestic violence, are often reluctant to report the abuse. Abused women may hope that the abuse was an isolated act that will not be repeated. Or they may be fearful that reporting the violence will only goad their attackers into further violence. If a woman and her children are dependent on their abuser's income, she may fear that reporting the violence will result in loss of financial support. Understandable though such reactions may be, they combine to produce estimates that most crimes of domestic violence go unreported.

38. What is the other half of the "double whammy" that confronts police and prosecutors in domestic violence cases?

Even when victims of domestic violence report attacks to the police, prosecutors often are unable to convict abusers because so many victims refuse to testify against their attackers at trial. As defendants have a constitutional right to confront and cross-examine their accusers (see Chapter 17), prosecutors cannot offer domestic violence victims' statements to the police into evidence in lieu of the victims' testimony. As a result, charges often have to be dismissed (*Davis v. Washington*, U.S. Sup. Ct. 2006).

The combination of failing to report and refusing to cooperate with prosecutors makes domestic violence one of the hardest crimes to prosecute successfully. Thus, many abusers remain free to continue their pattern of abuse.

39. Are there special evidence rules that help prosecutors convict perpetrators of domestic violence?

Some states (including California; see Cal. Evid. Code Sec. 1109) have special rules for domestic violence cases that allow prosecutors to offer evidence that defendants charged with domestic violence have committed other acts of domestic violence. These rules are an exception to the general rule that prosecutors can't offer evidence of defendants' past crimes. (See Chapter 18.)

Also, an abuser may attack or threaten a victim for the purpose of frightening the victim into refusing to testify at trial for earlier acts of abuse. If this happens, an abuser waives (gives up) the right to confront and cross-examine the victim at trial and police officers may testify to the victim's pretrial description of what happened (*Giles v. California*, U.S. Sup. Ct. 2008).

40. Apart from prosecuting abusers, what other help is available to domestic violence victims?

Domestic violence victims may call 911; statements made to 911 operators may be admissible in court to prove that a domestic abuser is guilty (*Davis v. Washington*, U.S. Sup. Ct. 2006). Many localities also have domestic violence hotlines. People who have reason to fear becoming victims of domestic violence should always know how to contact a domestic violence hotline. People who have been subjected to domestic violence may also go to court and secure a protective order. An abuser who violates the terms of a protective order (for example, by showing up at a victim's home or place of work) may be arrested and charged with a crime. Finally, a federal gun control law (18 U.S.C. 922(g)(9)) makes it a crime for people who have been convicted of crimes involving domestic violence to own guns. (For a discussion of the law, see *United States v. Hayes*, U.S. Sup. Ct. 2009.)

Part 3: Sexual Violence Involving Children

41. Is child sexual abuse a pervasive problem?

Common estimates are that as many as a third of females and a fifth of males in the U.S. experience sexual violence or at least sexualized touching before the age of 18. However, the practice of many researchers to lump together abuse of young children with consensual sexual conduct of older teenagers makes the prevalence of sexual abuse of young children uncertain. Despite the popular image of the pedophile as a "stranger with candy" who lures victims into a secluded area, most sexual abusers know their victims. Most sexual abusers are male.

42. What constitutes a crime of child sexual abuse?

Since children are legally incapable of consenting to sexual activity, virtually any form of sexual activity involving a child is likely to constitute sexual abuse. The distinct crimes that constitute child sexual abuse are of two general types, sexual assault and sexual exploitation.

Some types of violent child sexual abuse (such as rape and oral copulation) are the same as adult crimes. But all states also have special laws criminalizing less violent types of sexual abuse of children. Examples of such laws include various forms of sexual molestation, such as fondling and touching a child's private parts for purposes of sexual gratification, indecent exposure (exposing one's genitals to a child), luring a child into a secluded area for sexual purposes, and displaying pornography or exposing a child to other sexual behavior.

Sexual exploitation includes possessing or distributing pictures of minors engaged in obscene acts, coercing minors into engaging in prostitution and pressuring children into engaging in sexual conduct.

43. Is child sexual abuse an underreported crime?

Yes. Young children especially may not realize that an adult's conduct constitutes sexual abuse. Also, children are often fearful of telling an adult that they have been molested. One reason is that the molester is often a family member or trusted friend; another is that molesters often try to silence their victims with threats. Children also may be too embarrassed or ashamed to report that they have been abused.

44. Do laws exist that are directed specifically at child sexual abuse?

Many laws are directed specifically at child sexual abuse cases. For example, many professionals, such as teachers and physicians, have a legal obligation to report suspected child sexual abuse. During child abuse prosecutions, judges may appoint a lawyer called a "guardian ad litem" to represent the interests of the minors. Also, prosecutors can offer evidence that a defendant charged with child sexual abuse has committed other similar acts of abuse, regardless of whether the defendant was convicted of or even charged with committing the other abusive acts.

Defendants convicted of sexual abuse of minors are often punished more harshly than defendants who sexually abuse other adults. If they are proved to represent a continuing threat to children's safety, sexual abusers may be kept in prison for longer than their original sentences. Sexual abusers may also have to register with the police once they are released from prison, and may be restricted as to where they can live. For example, the "Adam Walsh Child Protection and Safety Act of 2006" (42 U.S.C. § 16901) establishes national registration requirements; failure to register is a felony

45. Is it a crime to possess or distribute child pornography?

Yes. Laws prohibit the possession or distribution of pictures showing children engaged in sexually explicit activity.

The laws cover printed and electronic pornography, and transmission from one person to another is illegal regardless of whether the sender charges a fee or sends it for free.

Possession of *virtual* child pornography, where the images are generated by computers—for example, computer-generated animations—is not itself illegal. (*Ashcroft v. Free Speech Coalition*, U.S. Sup. Ct. 2002.) However, a law making it illegal to knowingly offer to distribute child pornography (whether the children depicted are real or virtual) is constitutional. (*United States v. Williams*, U.S. Sup. Ct. 2008.)

Section VI: Burglary

The two previous sections focused on crimes of violence. This section explains burglary laws, which primarily protect property.

46. What is burglary?

Burglary laws protect buildings. A burglary occurs when a culprit:
- breaks into and
- enters
- a building
- without consent, and
- with the intent to commit a felony or to steal property, even if the theft itself would only be a misdemeanor.

Burglary is thus a specific intent crime. (See Question 9, above.) What distinguishes the felony of burglary from less serious misdemeanors such as trespassing is that with burglary the prosecution has to prove that a defendant intended to commit a felony or a theft inside a building at the very moment that the defendant entered it.

CASE EXAMPLE: Phil O'Nee is charged with burglary. The prosecution claims that Phil, wanting a birthday present for his girlfriend, went into a drugstore and took a bottle of perfume from the cosmetics area. Phil admits taking the perfume, and asks the judge to convict him only of petty theft, a misdemeanor.

Question: Might the judge convict Phil of burglary?

Answer: Yes—if the prosecution proves that Phil intended to steal the perfume at the moment he entered the drugstore. One way the prosecution might prove Phil's intent to steal is to show that Phil told a friend ahead of time that Phil planned to steal the perfume. Another way the prosecution might prove Phil's intent to steal is to show that Phil went into the drugstore carrying a large sack in which he could conceal the perfume bottle.

47. Does burglary require a forcible breaking and entry?

No. Years ago burglary laws were more rigid, and they required the government to prove that a defendant forced open a door, a window, or some other part of a building to gain entry. Now, going into a building without consent through an open window or an unlocked door constitutes a

---

In Burglary Laws, Buildings Are Not Just Residences

In early common law days, the burglary laws applied only to homes—and then only if the burglary occurred at night. Burglary laws now extend to almost all kinds of structures, even portable ones like cars, boats, and mobile homes. Shops, barns, stables, and outhouses are some of the other structures covered by modern burglary laws.

Any Felony Will Often Do for Burglary

The term "burglary" probably connotes a masked crook with a sack breaking into a residence and stealing personal property. In reality, the crime of burglary is broader than that. Entry into a building with the specific intent to commit any type of felony crime often satisfies burglary laws. For instance, a suspect may enter a building with the intent to burn it down or molest a child. Both are sufficient for burglary. This is why chronic petty thieves often end up with burglary convictions. By following their usual m.o. (*modus operandi*, or method of committing the crime), they make it easy for prosecutors to prove that they entered a shop with the intent to steal.

break and entry for purposes of almost all burglary statutes. Even a partial entry can constitute a burglary. For example, assume that the police arrest a suspect just as the suspect reaches her arm through an open window. If the other requirements are met, one arm in is sufficient entry to constitute a burglary.

48. Do degrees of burglary exist?

Yes. The danger of physical injury is greatest when a burglar enters an inhabited building, so in many states this constitutes first degree burglary. Under some statutes, entry at night rather than in the daytime also constitutes a first degree burglary, regardless of whether a building is inhabited.

49. Is it a burglary if a person enters a building intending to commit a crime, but is arrested or scared off before the crime can take place?

Yes. With burglary, the key moment is the burglar's entrance into a building. If at that moment the burglar intends to commit a felony or steal property inside the building, a burglary has taken place even if no other crime actually takes place. On the other hand, it may constitute some other crime, but not burglary, if a culprit first decides to commit a crime only after entering a building.

> **CASE EXAMPLE 1:** Klaus Santo enters the home of his ex-wife Wilma by climbing down the inside of a chimney. Santo has previously threatened to harm his wife, and he has a tire iron protruding from his back pocket. Wilma hears Santo coming, runs to a neighbor's house, and calls the police. The police arrest Santo as he tries to run away through the back door.
>
> **Question:** Has Santo committed a burglary?
>
> **Answer:** Yes. Santo entered Wilma's house without consent. The prior threats and the tire iron in his back pocket are circumstantial evidence showing that at the moment Santo entered her house, he intended to attack Wilma with a deadly weapon.

> **CASE EXAMPLE 2:** Same case, except assume that Santo offers evidence at trial that at the time he came down Wilma's chimney he'd been drinking heavily for three days and was too drunk to understand what he was doing.
>
> **Question:** Might Santo's evidence constitute a defense to the burglary charge?
>
> **Answer:** In some states, Santo's evidence would constitute a partial defense. To be convicted of burglary, Santo must have had a specific intent to commit a felony. Some states would allow Santo to claim that he was so intoxicated that he was unable to form the required specific intent. The defense would be a partial one because Santo could still be convicted of the lesser crime of breaking into Wilma's home. (For more on the intoxication defense, see Chapter 13, Section VI.)

CASE EXAMPLE 3: Same case, except assume that Santo and Wilma are high school classmates on the eve of graduation. As a prank, Santo climbs down a chimney in Wilma's house, toilet papers the inside of Wilma's house, and leaves by the front door.

Question: Has Santo committed a burglary?

Answer: No. Santo's actions show that he did not enter Wilma's house with the intent to commit a felony or steal property. Nevertheless, Santo could be charged with less serious crimes such as trespassing or, if he did some damage, malicious mischief.

50. A house is broken into. No one can identify who broke into the house, but the police find a suspect in possession of items taken from the house. Can the suspect be convicted of burglary?

Yes. Even in the absence of an eyewitness identification, it is possible that the prosecution could offer enough circumstantial evidence to prove that it was the suspect who broke into the house. As a fall-back, the prosecutor might convict the suspect of possession of stolen property. (See Question 48, below.)

CASE EXAMPLE: Goldie Locks returns to her apartment one afternoon to find that her front door has been forced open. A number of items are missing, including Goldie's favorite chair that had been left to her by her great-aunt.

Three weeks later, the police arrest Bear Withus on drug charges. Inside Bear's house, the police find Goldie's chair. In response to police questions, Bear claims that the chair had been given to him years earlier by a friend whose name he cannot remember.

Question: Is this information sufficient to prove that Bear burgled Goldie's apartment?

Answer: Yes. The circumstantial evidence (including Bear's false story to the police as to how and when he acquired the chair) suggests that it was Bear who entered Goldie's apartment without permission and committed a theft once he was inside.

Section VII: Robbery

This section looks at robbery laws.

51. What is robbery?

Robbery is a crime both of theft and violence. It consists of using means of force or fear to take personal property directly and permanently from another person. A classic though sadly all-too-common example of robbery involves the holdup of a convenience store. A robber pulls a gun (thus using means of force or fear, even if it's unloaded or a toy gun) and demands money from the clerk. Purse-snatching can also constitute robbery if the victim is confronted by the robber.

CASE EXAMPLE: Opper Tunist comes upon a person lying on the pavement, apparently passed out from the effects of alcohol. Seeing no one else around, Opper removes the wallet from the sleeper's pocket and runs away.

Question: Has Opper committed a robbery?

Answer: No, since Opper didn't use means of force or fear. Opper did, however, commit the crime of theft (taking the sleeper's property without permission).

52. Is robbery a specific intent crime?

Yes. Robbery is a type of theft crime, and as is often true with theft crimes, the government has to prove that a robber took property with the intent to forever deprive the victim of the stolen property.

53. How can the government prove that a thief intended to permanently deprive a victim of stolen property?

A prosecutor typically relies on circum-stantial evidence to prove intent, just as is true with statutes requiring proof of knowledge and other state of mind elements that can't be directly proven. In other words, a prosecutor asks a judge or jury to use common sense to infer a thief's intent from the circumstances under which property was stolen.

CASE EXAMPLE: Cal Lechter accosts Cora Spondent outside a baseball card show, believing that Cora had just bought the "Puddinhead Jones" card that Lechter wants for his collection. Lechter points a gun at Cora and says, "Give me the cards you just bought." Cora complies. Lechter flips through the cards, then asks, "Where's the Puddinhead Jones card?" Cora replies, "I don't know what you're talking about. I don't have it." Lechter then throws the cards to the ground in disgust and runs off.

Question: Lechter did not actually take any of Cora's cards. Nevertheless, could Lechter be convicted of robbery?

Answer: Yes. Lechter took property (Cora's cards) by means of force or fear, and the circumstances suggest that at the time Lechter took the cards, Lechter intended to permanently deprive Cora of the Puddinhead Jones card had Cora bought it.

54. Do degrees of robbery exist?

Yes. In some states, first degree robbery consists of a robbery committed inside a residence, or against certain classes of people, such as taxicab drivers or passengers. Other robberies are second degree robberies.

Section VIII: Theft

Theft laws protect people's personal property. This section outlines some of the common forms of theft.

55. What is theft?

Theft (or larceny) is an umbrella term that applies to various methods of stealing another's personal property with the specific intent (see Section II, above) to permanently deprive the other of possession. (Theft laws generally don't apply to land, since land can't be carried off. Of course, other laws protect landowners who are swindled out of their property.) In addition to the standard form of theft, simply carrying off someone else's property, two other common forms of theft are:

- embezzlement, in which an employee or other personal representative diverts money or property intended for the employer or principal to the employee's or personal representative's personal use, and
- fraud (or false pretenses), which typically occurs when a thief tricks a victim into voluntarily handing over money or property.

CASE EXAMPLE 1: Joy Rider sees a new Lexus parked on a residential street. The doors are unlocked and the keys are in the ignition. Never having driven a Lexus, Joy impulsively gets behind the wheel. Joy drives around for about ten minutes and leaves the car a block away from where she found it.

Question: Is Joy guilty of car theft?

Answer: Probably not. To convict Joy of theft, a prosecutor would have to prove that Joy took the car with the specific intent of permanently depriving the car's owner of possession. Since Joy returned the car near to where she found it a short time after taking it, she probably had no such intent. Most states have enacted a less serious crime of joyriding (or operating a vehicle without the owner's consent) to cover these types of situations.

Question: What if Joy drives the car until it runs out of gas, and abandons it on the road a few miles away from where she took it?

Answer: Joy would probably still be convicted of joyriding rather than car theft. The circumstances do not clearly indicate that Joy intended to permanently deprive the Lexus owner of possession.

CASE EXAMPLE 2: N. V. Uss is furious to learn that his ex-girlfriend has become engaged to another man. One day, Uss sees his ex-girlfriend sitting at a table in a restaurant, showing her engagement ring to a companion. Uss rushes up to the table, grabs the ring, runs outside and throws the ring into a sewer pipe. The ring is never found.

Question: Is Uss guilty of theft of the ring?

Answer: Yes. The fact that Uss did not keep the ring for himself is irrelevant. The gist of theft is permanently depriving a victim of the property that was stolen. Since Uss's actions suggest that Uss intended his ex-girlfriend to do without the ring permanently, Uss is guilty of theft.

CASE EXAMPLE 3: Em Bezzler works behind the counter at an ice cream shop. Over a period of weeks, Em pocketed part of the money that customers gave her. Em hid her activities from the shop owner by failing to ring up some ice cream sales. Finally, the shop owner catches on, fires Em, and starts to call the police. Em immediately offers to return all the money that she took, with interest.

Question: If Em fully pays back the shop owner, is Em still guilty of embezzlement?

Answer: Yes. Returning stolen property may count in a defendant's favor at the time of sentencing, but it is no defense to a theft or embezzlement charge. Em is guilty of theft because the circumstances suggest that she intended to permanently deprive the shop owner of the money at the time she took it.

56. What is the difference between grand theft and petty theft?

Grand theft is the equivalent of first degree theft. Theft can be grand theft, and therefore more serious, for a variety of reasons. Laws in many states deem a theft to be grand theft when:

- The property taken is worth more than a minimum amount, perhaps $200–$400 depending on the state.
- Property is taken directly from a person, but by means other than force or fear. (If force or fear were used, the crime would be robbery. See Section VII, above.) An example would be picking the pocket of an unsuspecting victim.
- Particular types of property are taken. For example, the theft of cars and some types of animals is often grand theft regardless of their actual market value.

A theft that does not qualify as a grand theft is petty, or second degree, theft.

 CAUTION

"Petty with a prior" can be grand theft. A prior conviction for petty theft can elevate a second charge of petty theft from a misdemeanor to felony grand theft. If the prosecution intends to use the prior conviction as the basis for a more serious charge, the complaint or information must refer to the prior conviction. A prosecutor might also elevate a petty theft charge to a felony by charging the culprit with burglary, alleging that the culprit entered a shop with the intent to steal merchandise. (See Section VI, above.)

57. Is it theft for one who finds lost property to keep it?

Keeping lost property can qualify as theft if the finder could reasonably return the property to its owner. For example, if Sue is bicycling along a deserted lane and sees a $100 bill floating on a puddle next to the curb, Sue would not be guilty of theft if she kept it. However, it's different if as she's bicycling, Sue sees Charles drop a $100 bill as Charles is getting out of the car. Charles is unaware that he has dropped the money and begins to walk away. If Sue rides over, picks up the $100 bill and keeps it, Sue has committed theft. Since Sue knows that the money belongs to Charles, and she has a reasonable opportunity to return it to him, Sue commits theft by not attempting to return the money to Charles. From a legal standpoint, Sue's keeping the money when she could easily return it to its rightful owner is what is known as a "constructive" taking.

58. Is it theft to steal property from a thief who has previously stolen it?

Yes. Theft is illegal even if the person from whom property is stolen had no right to the property in the first place. This rule is necessary to prevent successive thieves from taking the same property with no fear of punishment.

59. Is it theft to steal contraband such as illegal drugs or weapons?

Yes. Stealing contraband from one who has no right to have it is illegal. Again, the rationale is to deter the act of theft, no matter what the character of the stolen property.

60. Is it illegal to buy or keep stolen property?

Yes. This crime is popularly known as receiving stolen goods. To convict a defendant of receiving stolen goods, the government has to prove that property in the defendant's possession was stolen, and that the defendant acquired the property knowing that it was stolen. As is typical when a statute requires proof of knowledge and other state of mind elements, the government usually has to rely on circumstantial evidence to try to prove a defendant's knowledge that property had been stolen. Usually, the government's case relies on evidence that would have alerted any reasonable person that the items were "hot."

CASE EXAMPLE 1: Hu Gnu is an avid collector of rock-and-roll memorabilia, and he subscribes to a number of computer websites devoted to such items. A few days after a theft of rock-and-roll items from a museum is widely reported on TV and in newspapers in Hu's hometown, Hu receives an email message offering to sell a collection of Beatles memorabilia at a very low price. The seller claims that a quick sale is necessary because the seller has suffered a number of business losses. In fact, the Beatles items were stolen from the museum. Hu buys the Beatles items.

Question: Is the evidence sufficient for Hu to be convicted of receiving stolen property?

Answer: Yes. Circumstantial evidence suggests that Hu knew that he was buying "hot" merchandise. Hu is an experienced collector, the prices were very low, and the offer came on the heels of a widely reported museum theft.

CASE EXAMPLE 2: Luke Away owns Pawn City and is in the business of lending money in exchange for taking possession of personal property. Rose Anfell is known to Luke as a drug user who often sleeps in the doorways of Pawn City and other shops. One day Rose brings two diamond rings into Pawn City, tells Luke that they were left to her by a distant relative and asks to pawn them. Luke gives Rose $2,000 in exchange for the rings. Two days later, the police examine the rings and identify them as two of the rings stolen from a jewelry store the day before Rose brought the rings into Pawn City. The police arrest Luke on a charge of receiving stolen property.

Question: Could Luke be convicted of receiving stolen property?

Answer: Yes. Laws in many states obligate professional dealers in secondhand goods to investigate suspicious deals. Here, a woman known to Luke to be homeless and a drug user suddenly turns up in possession of two diamond rings and a fishy story about how she got them. Even though Luke did not actually know that the rings were stolen, and may not even have known about the jewelry store theft, the circumstances strongly suggested the possibility that the rings were stolen. As a pawnshop owner who failed to investigate how Rose got the rings, Luke is likely to be convicted of receiving stolen property.

Section IX: Hate Crimes

Hate crime laws punish violators who commit crimes against persons who belong to distinct social groups that legislators think deserve and need special protection.

61. Do hate crime laws make it a crime to hate?

No. Hatred may be lamentable, but it is not against the law to have a mental attitude of hate towards specific individuals or social groups. Moreover, in many circumstances, the First Amendment to the U.S. Constitution prevents punishment for expressing hatred toward specific individuals or social groups.

62. What is a hate crime?

While hate crime laws may vary from one state to another, in general a hate crime occurs when an illegal act is committed because of a victim's race, color, religion, ancestry, national origin, disability, gender, or sexual orientation. (We'll call this hate crime intent or hate crime purpose in this section so as not to have to repeatedly refer to each possible illegal purpose.) This does not mean that every crime committed against a victim who belongs to one of the groups identified by a hate crime law is a hate crime. A hate crime occurs when an illegal act is committed *because* a victim belongs to one of the groups identified in a hate crime law.

> **CASE EXAMPLE 1:** While an accomplice asks Jesse for directions, Fingers Malloy removes the wallet from Jesse's rear pocket and tries to run away. However, Fingers is captured less than a block away. Jesse immigrated to this country from Samoa about three years earlier.
>
> **Question:** Could Fingers be convicted of a hate crime under a law that provides that a hate crime is one that is committed because of a victim's national origin?
>
> **Answer:** No, because no evidence suggests that Fingers committed the crime because Jesse is from Samoa. Fingers may be guilty of theft, but he did not commit a hate crime.
>
> **CASE EXAMPLE 2:** Same case as above, except that the prosecution offers evidence that Fingers intentionally singled out Jesse as a victim because Jesse came to this country from Samoa.
>
> **Question:** Could Fingers be convicted of a hate crime under a law that

provides that a hate crime is one that is committed because of a victim's national origin?

> **Answer:** Yes, because Fingers committed the crime because Jesse is from Samoa.

63. What is the purpose of hate crime laws?

Hate crime laws seek to protect people who belong to groups that have frequently been the target of illegal acts. Hate crime laws also send a message that targeting these victims because of their status (for example, as gays or women or Muslims) is antithetical to maintaining a free and pluralistic society.

64. What are the two forms of hate crime laws?

One form of hate crime law defines a type of illegal conduct that is punishable in and of itself. For example, interfering with a person's civil rights with a hate crime intent may itself be a crime, regardless of whether the perpetrator violates any other criminal laws. Thus, just as the crime of murder is distinct from that of theft, so may a hate crime be a separately defined crime.

A second form of hate crime law increases the punishment of those who commit other crimes with a hate crime purpose. For example, a crime that is ordinarily a misdemeanor may become a felony if a perpetrator commits it with a hate crime intent. Similarly, a felony that is ordinarily punishable by up to five years in state prison may become punishable by up to eight years in state prison if a perpetrator commits it with a hate crime intent.

Hate crime laws have been challenged by defendants on the ground that they violate their free speech rights, but thus far courts have generally upheld and enforced them. (For an example, see *Wisconsin v. Mitchell*, U.S. Sup. Ct. 1993.)

CASE EXAMPLE: The prosecution proves that Damian, a Caucasian ex-convict, fired several shots through the window of a home near Damian's home that is owned by an African American family. Damian fired the shots into the home because the family was African American and Damian wanted to intimidate the owners into selling their home and moving out of the neighborhood.

Question: What crimes might Damian have committed and how might he be punished?

Answer: Damian may be convicted of committing a hate crime, because he attempted to interfere with an African American's right to own a home and did so because the family was African American. Damian might also be convicted of the separate crimes of assault with a deadly weapon and being an ex-convict in possession of a firearm, and his sentence for committing these crimes may be increased because he committed them with a hate crime intent. (Even if Damian were convicted of three separate crimes, he would probably not have to serve separate sentences for each crime because he committed only a single illegal act. Another way to say this is that he would serve all the sentences concurrently.)

65. Who decides whether a defendant had a hate crime intent?

At trial, a defendant may be convicted of committing a hate crime only if the prosecutor proves beyond a reasonable doubt that an illegal act was committed with a hate crime intent. It is up to the jury and not the judge to decide whether the defendant acted with a hate crime purpose. (*Apprendi v. New Jersey*, U.S. Sup. Ct. 2000.)

Proving that a defendant acted with a hate crime purpose can be difficult. A prosecutor normally must find and offer evidence that the reason that a defendant committed an illegal act was the victim's belonging to a group identified in a hate crime law. The evidence might consist of a statement made by a defendant. For example, to show that an act is a hate crime because it was committed against a gay man, a prosecutor may offer evidence that a defendant told a friend something like, "I plan to attack the next person I see who is homosexual." Or, the prosecutor may offer evidence that a defendant committed a series of illegal acts against different victims, each of whom were members of an ethnic minority group identified in a hate crime law.

Section X: The Patriot Act

The "Patriot Act" is the shorthand label for a lengthy and complex package of federal antiterrorism and general crime control laws that President Bush signed into law less than two months after the September 11, 2001 terrorist attacks on the World Trade Center and the Pentagon. The legislation's formal name is almost as complicated as its provisions; it's titled the "Uniting and Strengthening America by Providing Appropriate Tools Required to Intercept and Obstruct Terrorism Act" (Public Law 107-56, 115 Statutes § 272, 2001).

The Patriot Act was reenacted in 2006. Some sections of the original law were deleted or amended. The new law also added new provisions, such as the one creating a new Assistant Attorney General for National Security, whose office consolidates diverse national security and intelligence operations. Some provisions of the new law, including the authority for roving wiretaps, expire in 2009 unless they are reenacted.

66. What new federal crimes resulted from enactment of the Patriot Act?

The Patriot Act creates several new federal crimes, including:

- **Committing domestic terrorism.** It is now a federal crime to commit dangerous and illegal acts on U.S. soil with the intent to intimidate or coerce the government or a civilian population.

CASE EXAMPLE: Winters, who is vehemently anti-Muslim, rams a truck through the doors and walls of a mosque during religious services.

Question: Has Winters committed an act of domestic terrorism?

Answer: Yes, Winters committed domestic terrorism by carrying out a dangerous and intimidating act with the intent to coerce members of a religious group.

- **Possessing biological or chemical weapons.** It is a federal crime to possess substances that can be used for biological or chemical weapons for nonpeaceful purposes.

CASE EXAMPLE: Johnson stores anthrax powder in his basement. He intends to put the powder into food at the cafeteria where he works.

Question: Has Johnson committed a federal crime?

Answer: Yes, because Johnson possesses a chemical weapon and intends to use it for harm, he has violated the Patriot Act.

- **Committing cyberterrorism.** Cyberterrorism, which consists of hacking into government computer systems or breaking into and damaging any Internet-connected computer, is punishable by up to 20 years in prison.

CASE EXAMPLE: Kevin programs several computers to create denial-of-service attacks on CNN, Yahoo!, E*Trade, and other major websites.

Question: Has Kevin violated the Patriot Act?

Answer: Yes, federal agents can prosecute Kevin for breaking into and damaging the companies' Internet-connected computers.

- **Giving financial assistance to or recruiting members for terrorist organizations.** The State Department has the authority to identify groups as terrorist organizations. Giving financial assistance to or recruiting members for terrorist organizations is illegal. Members of such groups are barred from entering the United States, and group members already in the country can be deported regardless of whether they have engaged in wrongdoing.

CASE EXAMPLE: Following the October 12, 2002 bombing of a nightclub in Bali that killed at least 180 people, the State Department declared that Jemaah Islamiyah was an Indonesian-based terrorist organization that may have been involved in the bombing. Alannis learns of the status of the organization but continues to provide free space on her computer server to Jemaah Islamiyah, allowing the organization to maintain its website.

Question: Can the federal government prosecute Alannis?

Answer: Yes. By providing free services, Alannis is giving financial assistance to a terrorist group and can be prosecuted under the Patriot Act.

67. How did the Patriot Act expand the powers of federal agents?

The Patriot Act provides the federal government with a broad array of procedural tools to counter terrorism and investigate illegal activity, including:

- **Immigrant detention.** Immigrants may be held up to seven days for suspicion of involvement in terrorism and deported for engaging in violent acts or for soliciting funds or members on behalf of terrorist organizations.
- **Sneak and peek searches.** Federal agents with search warrants can conduct "sneak and peek" searches of people's homes or offices whenever they have reasonable grounds to believe that advance notification would have an adverse result. For example, a federal agent can use the procedure if he reasonably believes that notifying the person at the outset of a drug search would allow that person to have the drugs destroyed. This exception to the usual rule—that people are entitled to be shown search warrants before searches are carried out—is not limited to terrorism investigations.

- **Roving wiretaps.** Federal agents can obtain court orders for "roving wiretaps" on people suspected of engaging in terrorist activities, allowing them to secretly monitor (listen in on) suspects' telephone conversations on any telephone they may use. Under this provision, for example, agents can monitor phone calls that a suspect makes or receives while he is in a hotel, in his home, or on a cell phone.

- **Cyber sleuthing.** Federal agents can obtain court orders authorizing them to gather information about the computer usage of suspected terrorists whenever the information is relevant to an ongoing criminal investigation. Under this provision, an agent can obtain a court order to use computer tracking technology to find out what Internet sites have been visited by a suspect and the names of the persons and organizations that the suspect communicated with via email. (However, government agents would need additional authority to access the *contents* of email communications.)

In addition, the Patriot Act creates a special "Intelligence Court" to enforce many of the powers it grants to federal agents.

Does the Patriot Act Violate the Constitution?

Despite the 2006 reenactment of an amended version of the Patriot Act, debate over the constitutionality of many of its key provisions continues. Opponents argue that the expanded search and seizure powers violate the right to privacy, and that the definition of "domestic terrorism" is so vague that it might allow the federal government to arrest demonstrators exercising their First Amendment rights to express disagreement with government policies. Another argument is that the new rules curtailing immigrants' activities violate the right to due process of law.

Supporters of the Patriot Act argue that it gives the federal government the power it needs to counter terrorism, and that neither federal agents nor judges will allow it to be used to interfere with legitimate activities.

Whether the Patriot Act can be an important tool in the fight against terrorism without encroaching on privacy rights and legitimate activities will depend on how broadly federal agents construe their authority and how judges interpret its provisions when federal agents' actions are challenged in court.

Section XI: White Collar Crimes

The term "white collar crime" usually refers to a type of complex crime in which a criminal uses business paraphernalia such as computers and financial statements instead of weapons. Offenders are often bankers, businesspeople, doctors, lawyers, and other professionals—hence the term "white collar"—however, white collar criminals may occupy any social position. Many modern computer-related white collar crimes are even committed by juveniles.

68. What are some examples of white collar crimes?

Common white collar crimes include the following:

- **Securities fraud.** Example: Megafoods Inc. induces people to overpay for shares of its stock by concealing information that it has been losing money.
- **Insider trading.** Example: Megafoods' corporate officers find out that the government is going to file a huge lawsuit against the company the next day, and they sell their shares of stock in Megafoods immediately, before the general public can find out about the lawsuit and drive the value of the shares way down.
- **Credit card fraud.** Example: Jim runs up thousands of dollars in credit card charges, knowing that he cannot pay them back.
- **Bankruptcy fraud.** Example: Barbara runs up huge debts with the intention of declaring bankruptcy so that she will not have to pay back her creditors.

- **Telemarketing fraud.** Example: Bob phones people and solicits charitable donations, even though Bob keeps most of the money he collects for himself.
- **Embezzlement.** Example: Sally, an accountant working for Megafoods, underreports the money that the company has earned and puts the difference in her private bank account.
- **Money laundering.** Example: A husband and wife finance their bakery business with the money they earn by selling illegal drugs.
- **Home repair fraud.** Example: A repairman convinces a senior citizen that the roof of her house is about to collapse, takes a large down payment for materials, then is never seen again.

Based on information that white collar criminals often carry out their schemes by sending out unsolicited electronic mail messages (a type of email popularly called "spam"), Congress enacted a new law in 2003—the "Controlling Assault of Non-Solicited Pornography and Marketing Act"—that severely punishes offenders who use spam to commit crimes such as fraud, identity theft, and child pornography.

> **CASE EXAMPLE 1:** Daniel filed for bankruptcy, but did not list all of his assets on the forms he filed with the court.
>
> **Question:** Did Daniel commit a crime?
>
> **Answer:** Probably. Concealing assets in bankruptcy proceedings with the intent

to defraud creditors is a crime. On the other hand, if Daniel honestly forgot about an asset or did not know he owned it, then his actions may not be criminal.

CASE EXAMPLE 2: Laurie wanted to look really spiffy for an upcoming dinner party. Laurie took her friend Taimie's credit card without her permission, went to the mall, and used it to pay for a brand new outfit.

Question: Did Laurie commit a crime?

Answer: Yes. Unauthorized use of another's credit card constitutes theft.

The Martha Stewart "Insider Trading" Case

Martha Stewart (famous for her TV shows and magazines devoted to decorating and food) was convicted of crimes related to insider trading in March 2004. Stewart had sold all of her stock in a company called ImClone Systems the day before ImClone publicly announced that it was virtually worthless. Stewart denied to government agents that she sold her stock based on a tip from ImClone's president. The government offered plenty of evidence that she had been tipped off in advance to ImClone's problems, and a jury convicted Stewart of obstruction of justice. ImClone's president had earlier pleaded guilty to insider trading and had been sentenced to prison.

69. Can I be convicted of a crime if I don't pay income taxes?

Yes. Failure to file an income tax return when required or failing to report income is a crime if done with the intent to avoid paying taxes. The Internal Revenue Service estimates that at least 17% of all taxpayers cheat on their taxes and most of that dishonesty is accomplished by deliberately underreporting income. Only a fraction of these people are ever convicted of tax crimes, however (as low as 0.0022% in a recent year). In addition to or instead of criminal penalties, taxpayers who are caught cheating may face civil penalties of up to 20% of their tax bill for making mistakes on their tax returns and up to 75% of their tax bill for tax fraud.

70. Is white collar crime often more difficult to detect and prove than violent "street crimes"?

Yes. White collar crime often takes place noiselessly in private offices rather than out in public. The offenders are often educated and sophisticated, and they try to conceal their crimes in secret computer files, complex financial reports, offshore bank accounts, and the like. Thus, the "cop on the beat" is unlikely to uncover evidence of white collar crime. Instead, the detection of white collar crime is often the domain of state and federal agencies that employ private (and often undercover) investigators, lawyers, accountants, and professionals. Also, the government hopes that "whistle-blowers" will come forward to report their own organizations' misdeeds. (See "Encouraging and Protecting 'Whistle-Blowers,'" below.)

71. Can a corporation be guilty of committing a white collar crime?

Yes. A corporation as well as its employees can be guilty of a crime. Of course, a corporation cannot be put in prison. However, corporations can be ordered to pay fines and provide restitution (payments to crime victims).

72. Do white collar criminals "get off easy" compared to people who commit other types of crime?

A general perception exists that the punishment that white collar criminals tend to receive does not adequately reflect the harms they cause and the public trust they abuse. However, the accuracy of this perception is debatable. First, many white collar criminals have received jail time in recent years, including Bernard Ebbers, former CEO of WorldCom (who was sentenced to 25 years), Martha Stewart, Timothy and John Rigas of Adelphia, Enron's Andrew Fastow, and Frank Quattrone of Credit Suisse First Boston. Second, a seemingly light prison sentence may reflect an offender's willingness to make restitution to fraud victims. Because complex white collar schemes can be difficult for the government to prove in court, a light sentence may also reflect an offender's

willingness to provide information that enables the government to arrest others and to prove its case in court.

Encouraging and Protecting "Whistle-Blowers"

Whistle-blowers are employees who report wrongdoing by the private businesses or government agencies for which they work. Whistle-blowers have often taken the risk that their willingness to report on their colleagues' misdeeds will cause them to lose their jobs and be blacklisted for future jobs. However, they perform a valuable function, because as insiders they are privy to information that the government could not otherwise find out about.

A federal law known as the False Claims Act, like similar laws in many states, encourages whistle-blowing by providing that whistle-blowers may be entitled to a portion of the money that white collar criminals are ordered to pay to the government. False claims acts also protect whistle-blowers from being fired for reporting illegal or fraudulent activities.

CASE EXAMPLE: Don, a medical doctor, runs a busy clinic where he sees lots of patients. In order to see Medicare patients while earning what he considers to be an acceptable income, Don occasionally instructs his office manager, Mary, to bill Medicare for more expensive tests than those he has actually performed; for services at his hourly rate even when patients were seen only by Nancy, his office nurse; and for reviewing X-rays that were already reviewed by a radiologist. Unbeknownst to Don, Mary falsified information when applying for Don's office to become a qualified Medicare provider. Nancy found out that the office overbills Medicare for services, but likes her job so decides to play along and keep her mouth shut.

Question: Have Don, Mary, or Nancy committed any crimes?

Answer: Yes. Don and Mary both committed numerous acts of Medicare fraud and are subject to a fine and/or imprisonment. Don could also lose his license to practice medicine. Nancy did not commit a crime by failing to report Don's and Mary's misdeeds.

If Nancy does report Don and Mary to the government and they have to pay fines under a false claims act, Nancy may be entitled to a portion of the money. Moreover, Don and Mary could be ordered not to retaliate by harassing Nancy.

On the other hand, however, if Nancy lies about what she knows to a Medicare or other government investigator, she might be guilty of the crimes of obstruction of justice or lying

to federal authorities. (See 18 U.S.C. § 1001, Material Misrepresentation to the Federal Government.) Nancy might then be fined and might also lose her nursing license.

RESOURCE

For more information on false claims acts. If you are an employee who suspects that others in your company are violating the law, contact your state's department of justice and ask about the existence of a false claims act. The following references may also help:

Taxpayers Against Fraud/The False Claims Act Legal Center (www.taf.org), 1220 19th Street NW, Suite 501, Washington, DC 20036.

False Claims Act: Whistleblower Litigation, by James B. Helmer, Jr., (Michie) and

Civil False Claims and Qui Tam Actions, by John T. Boese (Aspen Publishers).

73. Are white collar crimes more likely than crimes of violence to lead to civil lawsuits?

Yes. Perpetrators of white collar crimes are more likely than violent criminals to have substantial assets. Thus, victims of white collar crimes may have a good chance of collecting on the judgments they obtain in civil lawsuits. By contrast, violent criminals are often "judgment proof." They have so few assets that a civil judgment obtained by a crime victim is likely to be worthless.

74. How can targets of government investigations into fraud claims protect themselves?

Anyone who thinks of themselves as the target of a white collar crime investigation should hire a lawyer with experience in these types of cases. White collar crime investigations can be lengthy and complex. An investigation may involve requests for business and personal records that government officials are not entitled to without obtaining a court order. In addition, white collar offenses may lead to the government filing either civil or criminal charges, so nonlawyers usually need the help of experienced lawyers to know where they stand. Finally, government prosecutors may offer various forms of immunity in exchange for information, and nonlawyers usually need help to understand how to protect their interests during immunity negotiations.

Concealment Often Results in Harsher Penalties

Individuals and companies suspected of committing white collar crimes have sometimes responded by trying to conceal information. For example, they may destroy records that they think are harmful or instruct employees to lie to government investigators. Frequently, such conduct only "compounds the crime" in various ways:

- To a government investigator or a judge or jury, evidence of concealment is seen as a sign of wrongdoing.
- Hiding information from government investigators may itself constitute a crime. Thus, even if the government couldn't prove that a white collar crime had taken place, it may win by proving the concealment of evidence.
- Hiding information often dramatically increases the penalty for engaging in white collar crime. Judges may show mercy towards those who admit to wrongdoings and make efforts to make up for the harms they've caused. However, those who do everything they can to conceal their misdeeds are likely to face harsh criminal and civil penalties. They are also likely to suffer in the "court of public opinion." For example, Arthur Anderson was once one of the biggest accounting firms in the world. Faced with charges that it helped a company, Enron, produce false business statements, many of Arthur Anderson's managers ordered the destruction of records. The destruction came to light, and Arthur Anderson lost so much credibility with the public that it dissolved virtually overnight.

"Pigeon Drop" Schemes

One form of fraud familiar to many in law enforcement is the pigeon drop scheme. In one variation, a con artist convinces a dupe that the con artist has won a lot of money on a bet. To collect the winnings, the con artist needs to prove that he could have paid up if he had lost the bet. Alas, the con artist has no money. However, the con artist offers to split the winnings with the dupe if the dupe will simply give the con artist cash temporarily so the con artist can show that he could have paid if he'd lost the bet. The dupe hands over the cash and never sees the con artist again.

75. How can consumers avoid becoming fraud victims?

Most people try to protect themselves from becoming victims of violent crime. For example, they lock the doors of their houses and cars and avoid walking alone at night in unfamiliar neighborhoods. Consumers should exercise that same level of vigilance to avoid becoming victims of white collar crime. The steps that people can take include:

- Realize that a get-rich-quick investment program that sounds "too good to be true" probably is.
- A consumer who is pressured into making a decision by being told that it's "now or never" should choose "never."

- Don't be fooled into trusting seemingly friendly, honest-sounding people if you don't know them. Don't make decisions before you've checked their backgrounds and references.
- Don't give solicitors your credit card or Social Security number.
- If you are suspicious, end the dialogue quickly. Then report what happened to your state's attorney general's or district attorney's office; these offices have consumer fraud divisions. You may also report suspected fraud to the FBI.

Many community organizations, such as the Better Business Bureau and the AARP, publish booklets on how consumers can avoid becoming fraud victims. Moreover, using keywords like "consumer fraud" will enable Internet users to pull up numerous websites with information on how they can protect themselves against specific types of fraudulent schemes. Among the websites are the Department of Justice's Office for Victims of Crime (OVC) (www.ojp.usdoj.gov/ovc/help/wc.htm) and the Directory of Crime Victims Service (http://ovc.ncjrs.org/findvictimservices).

Also, the National Consumer League's Fraud Center (www.fraud.org) has information on telemarketing, internet fraud, fraud scams against the elderly, and more.

76. What is "identity theft"?

Identity theft consists of stealing another person's identifying information—for example, a Social Security number, credit card number, or bank account number—

and using the information to take money or make purchases. Identity theft can not only cause direct financial losses, but it may force victims to spend weeks trying to re-establish credit and their good names. Unless corrected, identity theft can hamper a victim's ability to obtain employment, college loans, or buy a car or home. Examples of identity theft include:

- Electronically accessing a victim's computer (perhaps with the aid of "spyware") and then using passwords to access online bank accounts.
- Sifting through trash (sometimes called "dumpster diving") and finding account numbers on credit card receipts or bank statements.
- Making phone calls or sending emails to convince people to reveal their Social Security numbers or other data.
- Obtaining personal financial data via a phony email or website made to resemble a legitimate business (known as "phishing").

Identity theft can be a crime of unbelievable cruelty. In one scam, families of soldiers serving overseas were contacted by callers who falsely said that they represented the Red Cross and that they needed the family member's personal identifying information in order to get money to their loved one immediately. Many people were victimized and the Red Cross responded by publicly announcing that it never asks for personal identifying information by phone.

77. What can I do if I suspect that someone has stolen my identity?

First, make sure that a theft has taken place. Review bank and credit card statements and look for unauthorized transactions. Obtain credit reports to see if they show unauthorized loans.

If someone is using your identity, contact your local police department at once. Close accounts that you believe have been compromised. Immediately call one of the three major credit reporting agencies (TransUnion, Experian, or Equifax) and ask that a fraud alert be placed on all your accounts. With a fraud alert in place, anyone trying to obtain credit using your identity will be refused or questioned extensively to verify that the person is really you.

You yourself may have difficulty obtaining credit while you have a fraud alert in place.

> **CASE EXAMPLE:** Bridgette received a letter from the college that she had attended notifying her that thieves may have gained electronic access to her personal data. Bridgette immediately phoned Experian and requested a fraud alert. All three of the leading credit reporting agencies placed a 90 day fraud alert on her account—at no charge to Bridgette. Two months later, having forgotten about the fraud alert, Bridgette set out to open a new bank account. Later that day, a person claiming to be a bank employee phoned Bridgette and asked for

personal information. Bridgette politely refused to give the person any information at that time, but took down the caller's phone number. She then phoned her local bank branch and —after confirming that the call was genuine—Bridgette returned the call. Once the bank employee was satisfied with Bridgette's proffer of information about her identity, Bridgette's new bank account was opened. Sometimes, unlike in Bridgette's case, victims of identity theft are refused credit until a fraud alert has expired or until identity can be established by more substantial proof.

78. How can I avoid becoming a victim of identity theft?

Be familiar with the basic tools of online safety. Use virus protection, firewalls, and other basic safety methods. Change passwords often, don't share them with people, and choose unusual passwords. OnGuard Online (www.onguardonline.gov) is a government site offering information on computer safety.

Shred bills and statements before you throw them away, and keep others in safe, locked places. Do not give out personal information in response to unsolicited phone calls or emails. If you receive a request for identifying information or money and want to verify its legitimacy, a good place to start may be with your local Better Business Bureau. You can also get a free copy of your credit report annually by contacting Annual Credit Report Request Service (www.annualcreditreport.com).

CASE EXAMPLE: Michele, while paying bills, realized that she had not received her monthly bill from the alarm security company.

Question: Should Michele ignore this and be happy that she has one less bill to pay?

Answer: No. The absence of a bill was a red flag indicating that someone had tampered with Michele's identify. Michele phoned the company and found out that someone had changed the mailing address on her account. She followed up by contacting the Postal Inspection Service and determined that someone had falsely completed a change of address form. Because she acted promptly, Michele was able to correct the problem and was able to get her mail promptly re-routed back to her.

CASE EXAMPLE 2: Kathi received yet another of those unsolicited "You are preapproved" notices for a new credit card, and she promptly threw it in the trash.

Question: What should Kathi have done before tossing away the unsolicited notice?

Answer: She should have shredded the application so that an identity thief could not complete the application in Kathi's name.

79. As a business owner, can I do anything to prevent my customers' identities from being stolen?

Yes. You can lock cabinets in which written records are stored, and you can encrypt electronic data. For other suggestions, consult a booklet on privacy protection published by the Federal Trade Commission (FTC). It's available in downloadable form at www.ftc.gov/bcp/edu/pubs/business/privacy/bus69.pdf.

If you'd like more information, several government agencies have websites on identity theft including:

- Federal Trade Commission (FTC) (www.ftc.gov/idtheft)
- U.S. Department of Justice (USDOJ) (www.usdoj.gov/criminal/fraud/websites/idtheft.html), and
- Social Security Administration (SSA) (www.ssa.gov/pubs/idtheft.htm).

As noted in the section on general fraud information above, many non-government organizations also have helpful information on identity theft prevention and what to do if you are a victim, including the National Consumer League's Fraud Center (www.fraud.org), Better Business Bureaus (www.bbb.org), the AARP (www.aarp.org), CALPIRG (www.calprig.org/issues/identity-theft-prevention), and the Center for Democracy and Technology (www.cdt.org).

Defensespeak: Common Defenses to Criminal Charges

D efendants have a constitutional right to present evidence that might create a reasonable doubt about their guilt. This does not mean that judges have to admit any evidence a defendant might want to offer. For example, judges can exclude defense evidence because it constitutes inadmissible hearsay, because it is speculative, because it is unduly misleading, or because it violates rules of evidence. However, a state cannot arbitrarily take away a defendant's right to present a defense.

While a myriad of crimes exist, only a limited number of defenses are available. This chapter examines the most common defenses.

"Due Process" Defenses

In addition to the types of defenses described in this chapter, on rare occasions a court may decide that the Due Process clause in the Fourteenth Amendment to the U.S. Constitution prevents the government from making certain conduct a crime. For example, the government cannot make it a crime for two adults of the same sex (or opposite sexes, for that matter) to engage in private, intimate sexual conduct. (*Lawrence v. Texas*, U.S. Sup. Ct. 2003.)

Section I: Prosecutor's Failure to Prove Guilt

This section is about the defense most frequently used in criminal trials—the inability of the prosecution to prove guilt beyond a reasonable doubt.

1. What is the most common defense argument?

Undoubtedly, the most common defense argument is that the prosecution has failed to prove the defendant guilty. Because of the constitutional principles that a defendant is presumed innocent and that the prosecution has to prove guilt beyond a reasonable doubt, this is often the strongest argument the defendant can make. (See Chapter 17, Section II, for more on the prosecution's burden of proof.)

2. Can I ask a judge or jury to find me not guilty if I don't testify or call witnesses?

The defendant can sit silently through the entire trial and present no witnesses, but still argue that the prosecution case is simply too weak to prove guilt beyond a reasonable doubt—even assuming everything the prosecution witnesses said was accurate. More likely, even if the defense presents no case of its own, it will try to strengthen the not guilty argument by cross-examining prosecution witnesses and poking as many holes in their stories as possible. Taken together, the defense argument goes, the holes create a reasonable doubt as to the defendant's guilt. At the same time, the absence of a defense case denies the prosecution a target to poke holes at in return, as the prosecution generally is not permitted to comment on the fact that defendant chose to not testify, or failed to put on an affirmative case. (See Chapter 17, Section III, for more on the right to remain silent.)

"Will They Think I'm Guilty If I Don't Testify?"

Defendants have a constitutional right not to testify, and judges and jurors are legally prohibited from taking a defendant's silence as an indication of guilt. However, a risk exists that some jurors may disregard this rule, if only subconsciously. For further discussion, refer to Chapter 17, Section III, where the defendant's right to remain silent is explored in more detail.

CASE EXAMPLE: Noah Counting is charged with a nighttime burglary. The only evidence of his guilt is an eyewitness who thought she recognized Noah running out of the burglarized house about the time of the crime. Cross-examining this witness, Noah's attorney gets her to admit that she really couldn't be absolutely sure it was Noah. After the prosecution rests, the defense must decide whether to put on its case. It can present a witness to testify that Noah and the witness were playing cards at the time of the burglary. However, the prosecution can attack the defense witness's credibility on several grounds. Also, the defense witness is easily rattled when asked questions.

Question: Should the defense put this witness on the stand?

Answer: Probably not. The prosecution eyewitness's testimony is so weak that it is unlikely to persuade a judge or jury of Noah's guilt. By presenting its own shaky witness, the defense would risk making the prosecution's case look stronger.

Motion to Dismiss

A useful defense strategy is to make a motion to dismiss at the close of a shaky prosecution case. If the judge grants the motion, the case is over without the defendant having to choose whether to present evidence and create the risk of inadvertently strengthening the prosecutor's case. (For more on motions to dismiss, see Chapter 21.)

3. What are some of the ways the defense can poke holes in the testimony of prosecution witnesses?

Cross-examining prosecution witnesses and bringing out weaknesses in their testimony requires skill and preparation. The aim is to undermine the credibility (believability) of the witness. The more the defense undercuts the government witnesses, the more likely it is that the judge or jury will form a reasonable doubt as to the defendant's guilt and be willing to acquit her. The issues that the defense typically uses when attempting to cast doubt on prosecution witness testimony are these:

a. Bias

A prosecution witness is biased against the defendant, and therefore is lying or grossly exaggerating.

> **EXAMPLE:** "You're making this up to get back at the defendant for firing you from your job, aren't you?"

b. No opportunity to accurately observe

A prosecution witness's observations are mistaken because (1) the lighting was bad; (2) the witness was under the influence of drugs or alcohol; (3) the witness was too far away; etc.

> **EXAMPLE:** "You only got a side view of the robber from across the street, correct?" "And you'd drunk three beers in the hour before you saw the robbery, right?"

c. Faulty police methods

Evidence from police laboratories is unreliable because machines were not properly maintained, technicians were not properly trained, evidence was not carefully collected or stored, etc.

> **EXAMPLE:** "You personally have no idea whether the breathalyzer machine was operating properly, right?" "Lots of spectators were wandering in and out of the house while you were gathering evidence, weren't they?"

d. A prosecution witness cuts a deal

A prosecution witness lies to curry favor with the prosecution to get a good deal on criminal charges the witness is facing.

> **EXAMPLE:** "You're hoping to stay out of jail by testifying against the defendant, right?"

e. Implausible story

A prosecution witness's story is not believable (flies in the face of common experience).

> **EXAMPLE:** "Your reason for being out on the street at 3 a.m. is that you suddenly remembered you had to return a library book?"

Of course, it is not always possible for the defense to find weaknesses in a prosecution witness's testimony. And the presence of a weakness or two does not automatically mean that the judge or jury will disbelieve the prosecution witness. However, confining the defense case to attacking the credibility of prosecution witnesses on cross-examination, and then arguing reasonable doubt, is a frequent defense strategy.

4. Can I use the not guilty defense argument if I take the stand to testify or call witnesses?

Yes. Even when defendants testify or call witnesses, they typically still rely on the argument that the prosecution has failed to prove guilt beyond a reasonable doubt. It's important for defendants to realize that even when they present evidence, they usually are not legally obligated to convince the judge or jury that the defense story is accurate. The burden of proving guilt rests at all times on the prosecutor. As defense attorneys frequently remind judges and jurors, "It's not up to us to convince you that the defendant is innocent. The defendant is presumed innocent, and the burden remains on the prosecution to convince you beyond a reasonable doubt of guilt."

Keep the Jury's Attention Focused on the Prosecution's Weak Case

Sometimes, defense attorneys decide not to call witnesses for fear that jurors will erroneously think that by doing so the defense assumes the burden of proving the defense case accurate. The benefits of not presenting a defense case—hopefully impressing on jurors the fact that the entire burden of proof is on the prosecution—may outweigh the risk that jurors will think that the failure to call defense witnesses is evidence of guilt.

5. Can a defendant try to create a reasonable doubt by introducing evidence that someone else committed the charged crime?

Yes. A defendant can offer evidence that someone else committed a charged crime. However, in order to prevent defendants from "blowing smoke" by throwing blame at numerous possible suspects, evidence of "third-party guilt" is admissible only if the trial judge believes that the defendant's evidence is sufficient to raise a reasonable doubt about the defendant's guilt. Before they can offer evidence of third-party guilt, defendants generally have to produce evidence linking the third party to the crime. Rumors that the third party committed the charged crime, or even evidence that a third party had a motive to commit the crime, is not enough to create a reasonable doubt about the defendant's guilt.

Criminal defendants have a constitutional right to present a defense. Therefore, a judge cannot forbid a defendant from offering evidence of third-party guilt simply because the judge believes that the prosecutor has presented an exceptionally strong case (*Holmes v. South Carolina*, U.S. Sup. Ct. 2006).

CASE EXAMPLE 1: Watson is charged with armed robbery of an elderly lady. At trial, the victim identifies Watson as the attacker, and the prosecutor offers DNA evidence connecting Watson to the crime. Watson claims that Moriarty committed the robbery, and seeks to offer evidence that a couple of years ago, Moriarty had claimed that the robbery victim failed to pay off a debt she owed him. At that time, Moriarty swore that, "I'll get even with her if it's the last thing I do."

Question: Is Watson's evidence sufficient to raise a reasonable doubt about his guilt?

Answer: No. The judge would not allow Watson to offer the evidence about Moriarty. Watson's evidence shows that Moriarty had a motive to rob the victim, but does not otherwise connect Moriarty to the crime.

CASE EXAMPLE 2: In the same case, in addition to offering the evidence above, Watson also wants to offer evidence from an eyewitness that Moriarty ran out of the victim's house carrying a gun around the time the robbery was committed.

Question: Is Watson's evidence sufficient to raise a reasonable doubt about his guilt?

Answer: Watson's evidence not only shows that Moriarty had a motive to commit the crime, but also it ties Moriarty directly to the crime scene. The evidence is admissible because it is sufficient to raise a reasonable doubt about Watson's guilt.

Scotch Verdicts

Juries in Scottish criminal trials have a choice of three verdicts: guilty (or "proven"), not proven, and not guilty. While the latter two verdicts both result in acquittal, the not proven verdict implies that while a defendant may be guilty, the prosecution failed to offer sufficient proof. A not guilty verdict allows Scottish jurors to signal their belief that a defendant is factually innocent. By contrast, U.S. jurors have no way to declare its belief that a defendant is innocent. In the United States, every "not guilty" verdict leaves open the possibility that the jury believed that a defendant may be guilty but that the prosecution failed to offer sufficient proof. (If you'll pardon a bad pun, Scottish juries do not have the right to find a defendant "not kilty," meaning that the defendant failed to come to court in traditional Scottish male garb.)

Section II: "Partial" Defenses

This section is about defenses that may not entirely acquit the defendant but that do work to defeat the most serious charges in the case.

6. If I go to trial, are a conviction or an acquittal of the crime I'm charged with my only options?

Not necessarily. Defendants often go to trial expecting to be convicted of something, and aim for a conviction of a less serious crime than the crime they're charged with. Conviction of lesser crimes (also known as lesser included offenses) is often a possibility because for most crimes, the prosecution has to prove a number of discrete elements. (See Chapter 24.) These elements are like building blocks. And if the defendant can create a reasonable doubt about a necessary block in the more serious offense, the defendant may be found guilty only of a lesser crime that requires proof of fewer blocks. When defendants can reasonably argue for lesser charges, they will offer "partial defenses," concentrating their attack on the prosecution's lack of proof for a block or element, the absence of which converts a serious charge into a lesser crime. For example:

- A defendant charged with the felony of assault with a deadly weapon may argue that the object used in the fight was not a dangerous weapon, and therefore that the evidence at most supports a conviction for simple assault, a misdemeanor.
- A defendant charged with the felony of possession of drugs for sale may argue that the defendant possessed

The Common Partial Defense of Lack of Intent

In many serious crimes, the prosecution has to prove not only what a defendant did, but also that the defendant acted with a certain mental state known as intent. For example, assume that the prosecution proves that Smith fired a gun and hit Wesson in the shoulder. Depending on what the prosecution can prove about Smith's intent in firing the gun:

- Smith may be completely innocent (Smith fired the gun completely by accident)
- Smith may be guilty of a minor misdemeanor (Smith fired the gun on purpose but had no way of anticipating that Wesson was around)
- Smith may be guilty of assault with intent to commit great bodily injury, a serious felony (Smith was trying to wound but not kill Wesson), or

- Smith may be guilty of attempted murder (Smith was actually trying to kill Wesson).

Because intent can be so critical to the outcome of a case, defendants often offer partial defenses designed to show that they didn't have the intent required for the more serious offenses. In one recent case, for example, a mother was charged with murder when she allegedly failed to secure her infant child in a car seat and then lost control of her car, resulting in the child's death. To prove the mother guilty of murder, the prosecution had to prove that the mother acted with a recklessness amounting to intent to kill. The jury concluded that the mother did not have that intent and convicted her only of a misdemeanor.

only a small quantity of drugs, and that therefore the evidence at most supports a conviction of possession of drugs for personal use, a misdemeanor.

- A defendant charged with the felony of car theft may argue that the evidence does not establish that the defendant intended to steal the car but rather supports a conviction for the lesser crime of borrowing the car without permission—that is, joyriding.

- A defendant charged with assault with intent to commit murder may offer evidence that she has a mental impairment which makes her incapable of forming the intent to kill, and that therefore the evidence supports at most a conviction for the lesser crime of assault with a deadly weapon.

7. In a jury trial, how and when do the jurors find out about the possibility of convicting the defendant for lesser crimes than those charged?

The defense has two ways of informing jurors about the possibility of convicting the defendant of lesser crimes. One is through argument. At the close of the evidence, the defense argues that, at most, the prosecution's evidence supports conviction for a lesser crime. Second, the defense asks the trial judge to include a lesser crime instruction with the rest of the jury instructions. (See Chapter 21, Section XII, for more on jury instructions.) If the judge agrees that the evidence could support conviction of a lesser crime, the judge may give an instruction along these lines:

> "Jurors, Mr. Hatfield (the defendant) is charged with assault with a deadly weapon. To convict Mr. Hatfield of this crime, you must be convinced beyond a reasonable doubt that Mr. Hatfield struck Mr. McCoy with an object that is inherently dangerous to human life. If you are not convinced beyond a reasonable doubt that the object was inherently dangerous to life, then Mr. Hatfield can be guilty at most of the lesser crime of simple assault."

8. Can I argue both that I am not guilty of any crime and that if I am guilty, I am guilty only of a lesser crime?

Legally, yes. For example, the defendant can argue, "I hit McCoy in self-defense, and therefore I'm not guilty of anything, but even if you decide that I didn't act in self-defense, you should decide that the object I used, a small stick, was not inherently dangerous to human life. Therefore I cannot be guilty of anything more than simple assault."

This kind of in-the-alternative argument can be hard for jurors to follow. Jurors may also be put off by the defendant's morally ambiguous argument that "I didn't do it, but if I did, it wasn't as bad as they say." Self-represented defendants should consult their legal coach before deciding to make such an argument. (See Chapter 7, Section IV, for more on legal coaches.) Experienced defense attorneys often stick with what they consider the stronger argument rather than risk alienating or confusing the jury.

CASE EXAMPLE: Harley Quinn is charged with armed robbery.

Question: Can Quinn sensibly argue both that someone else committed the robbery (that is, that he has an alibi), and that even if Quinn was the robber, he didn't use a weapon and therefore should be convicted of a lesser crime?

Answer: Yes. Quinn can argue that the prosecution's evidence is too weak to prove beyond a reasonable doubt that the robber had a weapon. Quinn can also argue that he was not the robber, because he was out of town at the time it took place. The alibi defense is logically possible so long as Quinn doesn't claim any firsthand knowledge of the robbery.

9. Does the judge always have to instruct jurors about possible lesser crimes?

No. A judge will not give a lesser crime instruction unless the evidence supports the possibility that a defendant is guilty of a lesser crime. If a judge refuses to instruct on a lesser crime, then the defendant cannot argue it to a jury.

CASE EXAMPLE: Dr. Crippin is charged with murdering her husband by drowning him in a bathtub. Dr. Crippin does not deny that her husband was intentionally murdered, but claims to

have been out of town at the time the murder was committed.

Question: Based on this defense, should the judge instruct the jury that it may convict Dr. Crippin of the lesser crime of manslaughter?

Answer: No. The defense story gives the jury only two choices: either Dr. Crippin committed the murder, or she didn't. No evidence exists to support conviction of a lesser crime, so the judge will not tell the jurors about it.

10. Is it always in my interest as a defendant for the judge to instruct the jury about a lesser crime?

No. Defendants are sometimes better off not having jurors consider the possibility of convicting them of a lesser crime. For example, assume that jurors are uncertain whether a defendant is guilty of a serious charge, and have the option of convicting the defendant of a lesser crime. After wrangling with the issue for several hours or days, jurors may compromise by convicting the defendant of the lesser crime. If these same jurors had to choose between convicting the defendant of the serious crime or acquitting the defendant, they might well choose to acquit. In this situation, the defendant could be worse off if the jurors had the option of a lesser charge. Therefore, whether or not to ask the judge to give a lesser crime instruction requires careful thought. Self-represented defendants should not ask a judge to give a lesser crime instruction without first consulting their legal coach. (See Chapter 7, Section IV.)

11. Can the judge give a lesser crime instruction over an objection by the defense?

Yes. Judges sometimes instruct jurors about lesser crimes on their own, regardless of the defendant's wishes. The reason is that appellate courts sometimes rebuke trial judges for not giving lesser crime instructions—even when defendants request the trial judge not to give the instructions.

12. Can I base a partial defense on something other than a lesser offense?

Yes. Sometimes the seriousness of a charge depends on the defendant's past criminal record. If the defendant can invalidate a past conviction, the defendant may be subject only to a lesser charge, or to a lesser punishment. Self-represented defendants with past criminal records should review their records and the charge to determine if the seriousness of the current charge is based in part on a past conviction. If it is, they should consider arguing that the prior conviction is inadmissible in evidence (perhaps because it is too old, or because the record is erroneous).

Section III: Self-Defense

This section is about when a person accused of a violent crime can legitimately claim that the violence was necessary for self-defense. A legitimate self-defense claim legally justifies an acquittal.

13. In what kinds of cases can I argue self-defense?

Self-defense is a possible defense when the defendant is charged with a violent crime. Typical violent crimes include:

- battery (striking someone against his or her will)
- assault with a deadly weapon
- assault with intent to commit serious bodily injury
- manslaughter, and
- first or second degree murder.

14. Do I have to admit that I struck the so-called victim in order to use a self-defense argument?

Yes. Inherent in the concept of self-defense is that the defendant did strike the alleged victim. The defense asserts that the striking was legally justified because the "victim" who was struck was in actuality the attacker, and was necessary to prevent the defendant from being physically harmed. Thus, the basic issue in many self-defense cases boils down to, "Who started it?" An important secondary issue is whether the defendant's violence was a proportionate and necessary response. (See Question 15.)

15. Can I claim self-defense if I hit someone before they hit me?

Yes. If a reasonable person would think that physical harm is in the immediate offing, the defendant can use force to prevent the attack. People do not have to wait until they are actually struck to act in self-defense.

CASE EXAMPLE 1: Attila and Genghis begin arguing after their cars collide. The argument gets heated, and Attila suddenly lifts his arm and forms his hand into a fist. Thinking that Attila is about to hit him, Genghis quickly knocks Attila to the ground and twists Attila's arm behind Attila's back. A police officer arrives.

Question: Should the officer arrest Genghis for battery on Attila?

Answer: No. Under the circumstances, a reasonable person would think that Attila was about to hit Genghis. People don't have to wait to be hit before protecting themselves. Thus, Genghis acted in self-defense and is not guilty of a crime. In fact, the officer could arrest Attila for assaulting Genghis (making Genghis fear that he was about to be hit).

CASE EXAMPLE 2: Popeye sees Bluto walking down the street. They've had a few scuffles in the past. Though Bluto is paying no attention to Popeye, Popeye has a hunch that Bluto may trip him walking by. To prevent this, Popeye socks Bluto.

Question: Does Popeye have a valid self-defense claim?

Answer: No. The circumstances would not suggest to a reasonable person that Bluto was about to attack Popeye.

16. How much force can I use in self-defense?

A defendant can use reasonable force in self-defense. How much force is reasonable depends on the circumstances of each situation—particularly the amount of force a supposed victim is using against the defendant. A defendant who acts in self-defense, but who uses more force than is necessary for self-protection, is still guilty of a crime (anything from simple assault to murder, depending on how disproportionate the force is).

CASE EXAMPLE: David is charged with striking Goliath with a beer bottle. David claims that he and Goliath got into a verbal argument at a lodge meeting, that Goliath gave David a light push and that David then picked up the beer bottle and smashed it over Goliath's head.

Question: If the jury believes David, should it find that David acted in self-defense?

Answer: No. A person acting in self-defense can only use as much force as is reasonable to prevent harm. A light push that causes no injury does not justify a beating with a glass bottle.

The Menendez Case—A Famous Case of Imperfect Self-Defense

Some states allow a partial defense known as "imperfect self-defense." This defense reduces the charges of defendants who use force because they honestly (but mistakenly) believe that they are under attack.

In a highly publicized California case, the Menendez brothers were charged with murder for brutally killing their wealthy parents, and they relied on imperfect self-defense at trial. The brothers claimed that they killed their parents because the father had been so abusive in the past that they honestly (though incorrectly) believed that their father was planning to kill them. Had the jury accepted the brothers' imperfect self-defense, it would have reduced the crime to manslaughter. The first trial ended in a hung jury. The Menendez brothers were convicted of murder after a second trial and sentenced to life in prison.

Using Self-Defense to Expand the Scope of Admissible Evidence

Self-defense can make some evidence admissible that would not be admissible in the absence of the defense. For example, witnesses cannot ordinarily testify to rumors. But a defendant who claims self-defense can testify to any information that led the defendant to reasonably believe that the use of force was necessary. If one factor in that belief was a rumor as to the violent tendencies of the victim, the defendant can probably testify to the rumor.

17. If I argue self-defense, do I have to convince the judge or jury that I was justified in my action?

No. A defendant who offers self-defense evidence does not have to convince the judge or jury that he or she *was justified* in using force. The burden remains on the prosecution to prove beyond a reasonable doubt that the defendant's use of force *was not justified*. However, to raise the defense in the first place, the defendant has to produce some evidence that supports his self-defense theory.

18. If I claim that the supposed victim of my assault attacked me first, will I be allowed to offer evidence showing that the attacker had been violent in the past?

Yes. Defendants can support a self-defense claim with evidence that a supposed victim was prone to violence. Of course, it's open to the prosecution to produce evidence that the supposed victim was not prone to violence. Some states (such as California) go beyond this, and also allow the prosecution to offer evidence of the defendant's past history of violence. In these states, defendants have to think carefully before offering evidence of a supposed victim's violent past.

Battered Wife Syndrome

Traditionally, self-defense arises when defendants protect themselves against contemporaneous attacks. In a modern variation, women have argued that they acted in self-defense when they have struck or even killed their male spouses or partners—even though their partners or spouses were not then attacking them. (For example, a woman might strike her partner or spouse while he is sleeping.)

Many states now extend self-defense to these situations. These states authorize judges and juries to find that women have acted in self-defense when their male partners' or spouses' history of physical, sexual, and/or mental abuse has reasonably put the women in fear of serious harm or death in the near future. Many states also allow women to support their self-defense claims with testimony from psychological experts who testify to the characteristics of battered wife syndrome.

Section IV: Alibi

This section is about when and how a defendant can produce evidence to show that he or she wasn't on the scene when the crime occurred.

19. Can I offer evidence that I was somewhere else when a crime took place?

Yes. This is the classic alibi defense. An alibi consists of evidence that a defendant was somewhere other than the scene of the crime at the time it was committed. For example, assume that Freddie is accused of committing a burglary on Elm Street at midnight on Friday, September 13. Freddie's alibi defense might consist of testimony that at the time of the burglary, Freddie was watching *Casablanca* at the Maple Street Cinema.

20. Doesn't the word "alibi" imply that I'm lying?

Alibi is a perfectly respectable legal defense. Yet to some people the term connotes a phony defense. Defense attorneys usually are careful to remind jurors that alibi is simply a legal term referring to evidence that a defendant was elsewhere at the time a crime was committed, and that it in no way suggests falsity.

21. Can I offer alibi evidence if I choose not to testify?

Yes. The defense can call whomever it wants as witnesses. For example, a defendant who claims to have been at the movies with Ellen DeGeneres at the time a crime was committed can call Ellen as a witness to testify to the alibi.

22. Do I have to convince a judge or jury to accept my alibi?

No. As is true for self-defense, defendants who rely on alibis do have to offer evidence to support their claims, but do not have to convince the judge or jury that they were elsewhere at the time the crime was committed. The burden is still squarely on the prosecution to prove beyond a reasonable doubt that the defendant who offers the alibi is nevertheless guilty. (Remember, however, that some jurors may erroneously think that the defendant takes on an affirmative burden simply by putting on a defense case; see Question 2.)

23. Do I have to notify the prosecution before trial that I will present alibi evidence?

Yes, in many jurisdictions. Federal courts and many states require defendants to advise prosecutors prior to trial of the defendants' intention to rely on an alibi defense, and to supply the names and telephone numbers of their alibi witnesses. (See Federal Rule of Criminal Procedure 12.1.) The notice provisions allow prosecutors to ask the police to check out an alibi before trial and try to disprove it. For example, if at trial Freddie will claim to have been watching *Casablanca* at the Maple Street Cinema at the time the crime was committed, in many states Freddie will have to advise the prosecutor of his intention to offer that evidence. The pretrial notice gives the police time to investigate, and perhaps counter the defense with

evidence that *Treasure of the Sierra Madre* was the Maple Street Cinema's feature film that evening.

Supporting an Alibi Defense

Because some jurors may be suspicious of an alibi defense, alibi claims should be supported with as much independent evidence as possible. For example, a defendant who claims to have been in another town when a crime was committed might offer evidence such as:

- the testimony of a stranger who saw the defendant in the other town
- a receipt for the purchase of gasoline or another item, or
- evidence that the defendant had a preexisting appointment to be in the other town.

Section V: Insanity

This section is about when and how a defendant can claim insanity as a defense to a criminal charge.

24. Why do we allow a guilty defendant to be found not guilty by reason of insanity?

The insanity defense is based on the principle that punishment for serious crime is justified only if defendants were capable of controlling their moral behavior and could appreciate the wrongfulness of their behavior at the time the crime was committed. Insane people (people suffering from a mental disease) are not moral actors, the reasoning goes, and so should not be criminally punished for acts committed because of the insanity.

The Insanity Defense Remains Controversial

Though the insanity defense was recognized in England as early as 1505, it remains controversial. Many people point out that a person killed by an insane person is just as dead as one killed by someone who is sane, and argue that people should be punished for the harms they cause regardless of their mental functioning. Opponents of the insanity defense also doubt the competence of psychiatrists, judges, and jurors to determine after the fact whether someone suffered from a mental disease at the time the crime was committed, and the connection, if any, between mental disease and the commission of crime. Perhaps due to popular dissatisfaction with the insanity defense, few defendants actually rely on it. And of the defendants who do, very few are actually found not guilty by reason of insanity.

25. What is the most widely used definition of insanity?

The most popular definition is the "*M'Naghten* rule," established in England in the 1840s. Under the *M'Naghten* rule, defendants are not guilty by reason of insanity if at the time of a crime they were afflicted with a mental disease which caused them not to know what they were physically doing (lack of cognitive capacity), or if they did know, that what they were doing was wrong (lack of moral capacity).

States have the power to adopt their own insanity definitions. (See *Clark v. Arizona*, U.S. Sup. Ct. 2006.) Arizona, for example, recognizes only the "lack of moral capacity" aspect of *M'Naghten*. In other words, defendants are sane under Arizona law if they understand that their actions are wrong.

CASE EXAMPLE: Bentley and Craig are charged with murder after Craig kills a police officer who interrupts Bentley's and Craig's attempt to rob a warehouse. Bentley's evidence shows that Bentley is mentally impaired; a head injury that Bentley suffered as a young child has left him with the mental ability of an eight-year-old. Also, Bentley didn't think that Craig should try to steal, but went along with Craig so that Craig would be his friend.

Question: If the jury believes Bentley's evidence, should it find Bentley not guilty by reason of insanity?

Answer: No. To be considered insane in most states, a person has to be unable to distinguish right from wrong. Because Bentley knew that it was wrong to steal from the warehouse, the jury should conclude that he was sane. However, Bentley could have a partial defense. The jury could also conclude that Bentley's mental impairment rendered him incapable of forming an intent to kill, so that Bentley should be found guilty only of manslaughter. (See Question 6.)

26. Do courts use other definitions of insanity (besides the *M'Naghten* rule)?

Yes. Courts within the same state may use different definitions of insanity. A defendant who is not insane under one definition may be insane under another. For example, another common definition of insanity accepted in some states is known as "irresistible impulse." (This defense was the focus of the famous courtroom movie *Anatomy of a Murder.*) Defendants who acted because of an irresistible impulse knew that their actions were wrong, and thus would be considered sane under the *M'Naghten* rule. However, they may still be considered insane under the irresistible impulse rule if at the time of the crime they were afflicted with a mental disease that rendered them unable to control actions that they knew were wrong.

27. If I'm found not guilty by reason of insanity, will I be set free?

Probably not. Defendants found not guilty by reason of insanity usually are confined to mental institutions, and not released until a court determines that whatever insanity they experienced at the time of the crime is no longer present. Because judges do not want repeat performances from insane defendants, a defendant found not guilty by reason of insanity can easily spend more time in a mental institution than the defendant would spend in prison had the defendant been convicted of the crime.

28. Can defendants be found both guilty and insane?

Yes. Many states follow a "guilt first" procedure. In these states, a defendant's sanity is not determined until after a defendant has been found guilty of a crime. Then, if a defendant is found to have been insane when a crime was committed, the defendant is placed in a mental hospital. When (and if) the defendant's sanity is restored, the defendant goes to prison to serve any remaining time on the sentence.

29. Do I need a psychiatrist to testify that I was insane?

In almost all cases involving insanity, yes. When a defendant enters a plea of not guilty by reason of insanity, a psychiatric expert examines the defendant on behalf of the defense. The psychiatrist's investigation will normally include the circumstances of the crime, the defendant's past history, and one or more personal interviews of the defendant. The prosecutor can, and usually will, request that the defendant be examined by a government psychiatrist. It is not unusual in this kind of case to see the two learned experts emphatically disagree on just about everything (which causes some to question whether psychiatry is an exact enough science to be used as expert testimony in the first place).

30. I'm indigent—how can I afford to hire a psychiatrist?

Judges appoint psychiatrists at government expense to assist indigent defendants who cannot afford to hire psychiatrists.

Friends and Relatives as Defense Witnesses

Jurors tend to be suspicious of defense medical experts who pronounce a defendant insane based on a conversation or two and a review of records. The strongest evidence of insanity is often provided by friends and relatives who have known the defendant long enough to form a reliable opinion that the defendant is mentally ill. Most jurisdictions allow nonexpert witnesses to give an opinion regarding the sanity of a person with whom the witness is well acquainted.

---

31. Do I have to convince the judge or jury that I was insane?

Probably. In most states and in federal court, defendants do have the burden of convincing a judge or jury of their insanity. Normally, the defendant's burden is to prove insanity only by a preponderance of the evidence, the lower burden of proof commonly used in civil cases. However, some jurisdictions make things even harder for defendants by requiring them to prove insanity by clear and convincing evidence, a burden of proof somewhere in between the lower preponderance and a reasonable doubt standards.

The Partial Defense of Diminished Capacity

Diminished capacity is a partial defense akin to insanity. Where it is allowed, diminished capacity can reduce the criminal responsibility of defendants whose acts are the result of mental defects that fall short of the legal definitions of insanity. Diminished capacity played a central role in an important California trial in the early 1980s, when a jury accepted a diminished capacity defense and convicted Dan White of manslaughter for killing San Francisco Mayor George Moscone and Harvey Milk, an openly gay county supervisor, in San Francisco. White relied on the so-called "Twinkie defense," claiming that eating food high in sugar content had left him temporarily unable to control his actions. The verdict so aroused the public's anger that California outlawed the diminished capacity defense (Cal. Penal Code § 28-b); many other states have done likewise.

---

32. Do I have to notify the prosecution before trial that I will present an insanity defense?

Yes. As with the alibi defense, pretrial rules in many jurisdictions require defendants to advise prosecutors prior to trial that they will rely on an insanity defense at trial. (See Federal Rule of Criminal Procedure 12.2.)

Competence to Stand Trial

Whether or not a defendant pleads insanity as a defense to criminal charges, an issue can arise as to a defendant's sanity at the time of trial. A defendant cannot be put on trial if she suffers from a mental disease that prevents her from understanding the proceedings and assisting in the preparation of the defense. If a defendant claims incompetence to stand trial, a judge will hold a hearing and take evidence concerning the defendant's current competence. At this hearing, the defendant has the burden of proving incompetence to stand trial by a preponderance of the evidence (*Cooper v. Oklahoma*, U.S. Sup. Ct. 1996). If the judge decides that the defendant is mentally incompetent, the defendant will probably be placed in a mental institution until competency is reestablished. In what the U.S. Supreme Court has said are likely to be "rare" circumstances, prison officials can legally force prisoners to take medications that would make them competent to stand trial (*Sell v. United States*, U.S. Sup. Ct. 2003). Once a prisoner regains competence, with or without the help of medication, the trial will take place.

Defendants can be mentally competent to stand trial, yet not sufficiently mentally competent to represent themselves (*Indiana v. Edwards*, U.S. Supreme Court 2008).

One good but extreme example of how competency to stand trial works involved the alleged mob boss Vincent "The Chin" Gigante, who was indicted for a variety of crimes including murder, mail fraud, and extortion. Gigante claimed that he was incompetent to stand trial, based in part on evidence that for years his life consisted only of wandering around the block where he lived in pajamas and a bathrobe. In 1996, a federal judge ruled that Gigante had engaged in an elaborate deception for over 20 years and ordered him to stand trial. Gigante reportedly told other mobsters that "pretending to be crazy just wasn't worth it."

Prosecutors often respond by demanding that a defendant be examined by a government psychiatrist before trial.

Section VI: Intoxication (Under the Influence of Drugs or Alcohol)

Defendants do not have a constitutional right to offer an intoxication defense (*Montana v. Egelhoff*, U.S. Sup. Ct. 1996). This section explains why the voluntary ingestion of alcohol or drugs does not usually excuse a defendant from resulting criminal behaviors.

33. Can I use the fact that I committed a crime because I got high on drugs or alcohol as a defense?

No. Defendants know (or should know) that alcohol and drugs affect their ability to control their behavior. Therefore, voluntary intoxication is rarely a complete defense to a criminal charge. (It may be a partial defense; see Question 34, below.) Defendants who voluntarily consume alcohol or drugs, and because of that engage in criminal conduct, may be just as subject to punishment as defendants who commit crimes while stone cold sober.

> **CASE EXAMPLE:** Frank Lee is charged with attempted rape of Kay Dence. Lee claims that he had been drinking heavily at a party on the night of the attempted rape, and that his mental functioning was so impaired by the effects of alcohol that he lost control and attacked Dence.
>
> **Question:** If believed by a judge or juror, would Lee have a valid defense to the charge?
>
> **Answer:** No. Lee cannot escape punishment by claiming that his actions were the result of intoxication.

34. If I commit a crime because I get high on drugs or alcohol, might that qualify me for a partial defense?

In some states, voluntary intoxication can serve as a partial defense to crimes requiring a prosecutor to prove that a defendant acted with a specific intent. The intoxication does not entirely excuse the defendant's crime. But if intoxication produced mental impairment that rendered a defendant unable to form the required specific intent, the defendant can be convicted of a lesser crime. (Like insanity, this defense must usually be supported with medical or psychiatric testimony.)

> **CASE EXAMPLE:** Buck Shot is charged with assault with intent to commit murder. The prosecution claims that Buck shot at Vic Timm with the intention of killing Timm, but missed. Buck admits firing the shot, but claims that he had no intention of killing Timm. Buck claims that about an hour before the shooting he'd ingested an illegal drug that so impaired his mind that he was incapable of forming an intent to kill Timm.
>
> **Question:** Might Buck have a partial defense to the charge?
>
> **Answer:** In some jurisdictions, yes. The prosecution has charged Buck with a crime that requires the prosecutor to prove that Buck had a specific intent to kill Timm. If, because of drug consumption, Buck was incapable of forming an intent to kill, then Buck should be found guilty of a lesser crime, such as assault.

Intoxication Defense Rules Vary

Rules governing the intoxication defense vary greatly from state to state. For example:

- **Hawaii.** Voluntary intoxication can serve as a defense to any crime requiring specific intent (Haw. Rev. Stat. § 702-230(1)). California law is similar (Cal. Penal Code § 22(b)).
- **Virginia.** Voluntary intoxication is a defense only in murder cases (*Griggs v. Commonwealth*, 220 Va. 46, 1979).
- **South Carolina.** Voluntary intoxication is not a defense to any criminal charge (*State v. Vaughn*, 268 S.C. 119, 1977).

Because the rules vary greatly and can change quickly, self-represented defendants who hope to rely on a voluntary intoxication defense must discuss the matter thoroughly with their legal coaches. (See Chapter 7, Section IV, for more on legal coaches.)

---

35. Can I go free if I commit a crime because I involuntarily consumed drugs or alcohol?

Yes. Defendants sometimes through no fault of their own consume drugs or alcohol and lose the ability to control their behavior. If a judge or jury agrees that a defendant consumed drugs or alcohol involuntarily, and because of the resulting mental impairment committed a crime, the defendant should be found not guilty.

Section VII: Entrapment

This section explains the circumstances when a defendant may properly claim that the only reason he or she committed a crime was because the police led him or her into it.

36. Am I guilty of a crime if a government agent talks me into committing it?

No. The government cannot induce a defendant to commit a crime and then punish the defendant for committing it. However, if a judge or jury believes that a defendant was predisposed to commit the crime anyway, the defendant is guilty even if a government agent suggested the crime and helped the defendant to commit it. Entrapment defenses are therefore pretty difficult for defendants with prior convictions.

> **CASE EXAMPLE 1:** Solely on the basis of a statement made by a confidential informant, a police officer suspects that Hy Poe is a drug dealer. Wearing a concealed recorder, the officer tries to buy illegal drugs from Hy. Hy refuses to sell any drugs, and claims to know nothing about drugs. The officer repeatedly pleads with Hy to sell drugs, indicating that the officer needs the drugs to treat a medical condition. Hy says that he thinks he knows someone who can procure drugs, and arranges to meet the officer an hour later. Hy returns in an hour, offers to sell the drugs to the officer, and is immediately arrested.

Question: Would a jury be justified in convicting Hy of selling illegal drugs?

Answer: Probably not. A judge or jury would be justified in concluding that the officer entrapped Hy by inducing Hy to commit a crime that Hy would not otherwise have committed.

CASE EXAMPLE 2: Same case. When the officer approaches Hy to buy illegal drugs, Hy replies, "This isn't a good place—we could be under surveillance from cops." The officer convinces Hy to conclude the drug deal in a secluded alley. The officer then arrests Hy.

Question: Is Hy guilty of selling illegal drugs?

Answer: Yes. The officer talked Hy into selling the drugs, but Hy was evidently predisposed to the sale under the right circumstances. A judge or jury would be justified in convicting Hy.

37. Do I have to convince a judge or jury that I was entrapped?

Yes. Defendants who claim that they were entrapped into committing illegal acts normally have the burden of convincing a judge or jury (by a preponderance of the evidence) that they were induced to commit crimes they were not predisposed to commit.

Section VIII: Jury Nullification

This section explains that juries are not supposed to ignore the judge's instructions but do so on occasion when they feel that justice requires it.

38. Does a jury have the power to find me not guilty no matter what the evidence against me?

Yes. Jurors, not prosecutors, judges, or police officers, have the ultimate power to decide whether a defendant is guilty. As the conscience of the community, jurors can acquit a defendant even if they think the defendant really did it. When jurors nullify a law by acquitting a defendant who has obviously broken it, judges and prosecutors can do nothing about it. A jury's not guilty verdict is final.

CASE EXAMPLE: Mother Hubbard is charged with child abuse for using a switch on her ten-year-old child, leaving welts on the child's arms and legs. Mother Hubbard testified that she used the switch only after trying many nonphysical punishments and seeing her child still on the verge of getting into gangs and drugs. The jury acquits Mother Hubbard. Jurors tell the judge that while they believed that Mother Hubbard used excessive force on her child, under all the circumstances it would be unjust to convict her of a crime.

Question: Will the jury's verdict stand?

Answer: Yes. As the community's ultimate conscience, the jurors have the power to decide that Mother Hubbard is not guilty. Their not guilty verdict is final.

Judges and Nullification

Judges have the same power to nullify a law with a not guilty verdict. However, defendants who hope for a nullification outcome normally choose jury trials in the belief that jurors will be more sympathetic and feel less bound by the law.

---

39. Can the defense argue nullification to the jury as a defense?

No. The defense cannot explicitly ask jurors to nullify the law. For example, a judge would quickly silence a defendant who said, "Jurors, I was only trying to protect my community against a poisonous waste dump. You should find me not guilty even if you think I did break the law." In fact, judges do not instruct jurors about their nullification power. Jurors who might consider a nullification verdict have to realize on their own that they have the power.

40. What are the two most common situations in which a jury might nullify a law?

Jurors might consider a nullification if:

- The jurors believe a law to be politically unjust. For example, during Vietnam War protests in the 1970s, some jurors refused to convict war protestors who were charged with criminal trespass because they thought that a law banning nonviolent protests was unjust. In more recent times, jury nullification has occurred when defendants who nonviolently protest nuclear testing or toxic waste dumps are charged with crimes.
- The jurors believe that a valid law is being unjustly applied. For example, in the film *A Time to Kill*, jurors acquitted an African American father of murder after the father killed the two men who had brutally raped his daughter. The jurors did not consider the murder law itself unjust. Instead, the jurors thought that it was not fair to apply that law to the father's conduct.

41. Should I turn down a good plea bargain and hope for jury nullification?

No. Defendants who rely on jury nullification are usually disappointed. Jurors almost always limit their deliberations to whether a defendant committed the charged crime. Political overtones and feelings of sympathy or hostility notwithstanding, jurors rarely acquit a defendant they think is guilty as charged.

Evidence That May Lead to Nullification

While defendants cannot offer a nullification defense, they can sometimes present a case in a way that leads jurors to consider nullification on their own. Cases that result in nullification often have these characteristics:

- The defendant acted out of strong moral convictions shared by jurors. For example, a defendant acted out of a desire to close a toxic waste dump, and jurors believe the goal to be legitimate.
- Evidence portrays a defendant in a sympathetic light. For example, jurors may sympathize with a defendant who broke the law trying to close a toxic

waste dump only after making a number of legal efforts. (Note: Any sympathy evidence must be relevant to a valid defense. Judges don't admit evidence simply because it may arouse sympathy for a defendant.)

- Evidence arouses jurors' hostility to the government. For example, jurors may be hostile to police officers who were too aggressive when arresting a person engaged in a peaceful but illegal protest.
- The defendant is not charged with a crime of violence.

Discovery: Exchanging Information With the Prosecution

iscovery is the process through which defendants find out from the prosecution as much as they can about the prosecution's case. For example, through standard discovery techniques, the defendant can:

- get copies of the arresting officers' reports and statements made by prosecution witnesses, and
- examine evidence that the prosecution proposes to introduce at trial.

Traditionally, the prosecutor was not entitled to information held by the defendant. But in recent years discovery has become more of a two-way street. Just as defendants can discover information from prosecutors, so too can prosecutors examine certain evidence in the hands of defendants. See Section IV on reciprocal discovery.

Section I: Modern Discovery Policy

This section is about the general role that discovery plays in the criminal justice process.

1. Prosecutors in films and TV dramas always seem to have surprise evidence up their sleeves. Does that happen in real life?

It's very unlikely. Until recent years, prosecutors could guard evidence from defendants with the same fervor that toddlers protect toy trucks and dolls from their siblings. Defendants could not force unwilling prosecutors to hand over witness statements or even reveal the names of

their witnesses. Now the view is that the outcome of cases will be fairer if defendants know ahead of time what to expect at trial.

Surprise evidence may produce fine drama, but it leads to poor justice. Unlike prosecutors, defendants can't call on the services of police agencies to help them respond to evidence they find out about for the first time at trial. Thus, every jurisdiction has discovery rules obliging prosecutors to disclose evidence to defendants prior to trial.

2. Are discovery rules really intended to help the defense at trial?

The rule compelling prosecutors to pass along information to defendants is not intended purely to assure a fair outcome at trial. The rulemakers tend to believe that most defendants are guilty of something. Therefore, they think, if a defendant finds out before trial how strong a case the prosecution has, the defendant will be more likely to plead guilty and save the government the time and expense of taking the case to trial. Discovery may be an important part of why about 90% of criminal cases settle before trial.

3. Does discovery mean that the prosecution has to reveal its case strategy?

No. Discovery rules generally distinguish between raw information (names of witnesses, police reports, drug or alcohol test results) and attorney theories and strategies. The latter is called "attorney work product." Prosecutors don't have to turn over their work product to defendants. Each side has to prepare its own case for trial, and can protect its intellectual labors against a lazy adversary.

> **CASE EXAMPLE:** Vy Tummin is charged with assault and battery on a police officer. Vy claims that she reacted in self-defense to the police officer's use of illegal force. The prosecutor plans to show a videotape of the incident to the jury. The prosecutor also has prepared a file memorandum as a self-reminder about what portions of the tape to emphasize during the trial and why those portions are especially significant. Vy demands to see the videotape and all trial preparation memoranda written by the prosecutor.
>
> **Question:** Does the prosecutor have to turn all these documents over to the defense?
>
> **Answer:** Not all of them. Discovery rules allow Vy to see the videotape. But the prosecutor will not have to turn over the memorandum. The memorandum is the prosecutor's work product, because it's the prosecutor's strategic analysis of the significance of evidence.

4. Is there a particular period of time prior to trial when the defense is supposed to engage in discovery?

No. Various aspects of discovery can unfold over the entire pretrial period. For example, defendants may receive a copy of the arrest report at their first court appearance, but may not receive a prosecution expert's written analysis of blood evidence until shortly before trial.

Section II: Discovery of Helpful Information

This section is about the prosecutor's duty to turn over to the defense any information the prosecution has that might help to establish the defendant's innocence.

5. Does the prosecutor have to turn over information that helps my case?

Yes. Prosecutors have to provide defendants with any "exculpatory" information known to the prosecutor tending to prove that the defendant is not guilty of a crime (*Brady v. Maryland*, U.S. Sup. Ct. 1963). If the prosecutor fails to turn over exculpatory information and the defendant is convicted, an appellate court can overturn the conviction if the defendant appeals and the information that the prosecutor failed to disclose was important.

However, prosecutors are totally immune from personal liability if they improperly fail to turn over exculpatory information to the defense (*Van de Kamp v. Goldstein*, U.S. Sup. Ct. 2009). This means that defendants who may have been convicted and imprisoned due to a prosecutor's failure to disclose exculpatory information can't sue the prosecutor for monetary damages.

> **CASE EXAMPLE:** Maso Menos is charged with burglary. Two witnesses who saw Menos in a lineup identified him as the burglar. However, a third witness

present at the same lineup stated that Menos was not the burglar. The prosecutor does not think that the third witness is telling the truth.

Question: Does the prosecutor have to tell Menos about the third witness?

Answer: Yes. It's not up to the prosecutor to decide who's telling the truth. Information about the third witness is potentially helpful to Menos, and the prosecutor therefore has to disclose it.

6. How helpful to my case does information have to be before a prosecutor has to turn it over?

Information doesn't have to be so powerful that it proves the defendant conclusively innocent to qualify as exculpatory information. So long as information might contribute to doubt about the defendant's guilt in the mind of a reasonable judge or juror, the information must be revealed to the defendant. Examples of exculpatory information that prosecutors have to turn over to defendants include:

- a prosecutor's promise of leniency to a witness in exchange for the witness's testimony, and
- a prosecution witness's previous conviction of a crime that a defendant could offer into evidence to attack the witness's credibility.

However, if a defendant pleads guilty, the prosecution doesn't have to turn over the past records of government informants (*United States v. Ruiz*, U.S. Sup. Ct. 2002).

CASE EXAMPLE 1: Jane Austere is on trial for robbery of a small market; Jane's defense is mistaken identity. The prosecution's primary witness is Al Cohol, who identifies Jane as the robber. Jane is convicted. Jane then learns that the prosecutor knew prior to trial but failed to tell Jane that Cohol had undergone years of treatment for alcohol addiction. Jane asks the judge to set aside the conviction and order a new trial, based on the prosecution's failure to turn over this information. The prosecutor asks the judge to deny Jane's request, because she never specifically asked for information concerning Cohol's background.

Question: What should the judge do?

Answer: The judge should order a new trial. The information is important, because Cohol's years of alcohol abuse might cast doubt on his ability to identify Jane. Prosecutors have to disclose important exculpatory information even if the defendant fails to ask for it. This makes sense: How can defendants ask for information if they don't know it exists?

CASE EXAMPLE 2: Same case. In pretrial discussions with Cohol, the prosecutor learns that Cohol is a member of a white supremacist organization who uses derogatory epithets for members of minority groups. The prosecutor is personally repulsed by Cohol's activities and use of epithets, but does not reveal this information to Jane's lawyer.

After her conviction, Jane learns about Cohol's background and use of racial and ethnic slurs. Jane asks the judge to set aside the conviction and order a new trial based on the prosecution's failure to reveal this information to the defense prior to trial.

Question: Will the judge grant Jane's motion?

Answer: It's unlikely. In order to overturn Jane's conviction, the judge would have to decide that the information about Cohol was legally relevant and that it would tend to create a reasonable doubt in the mind of a rational juror. At least in the absence of evidence that Jane was a member of a group targeted by Cohol's white supremacist organization and that Cohol was an active member of the group, the judge is unlikely to rule that the prosecution had a duty to turn the information over to the defense.

7. Does the prosecution have to search for information that might help my case?

No. Prosecutors have to turn over exculpatory information that they know of. However, prosecutors don't have to search for information that might help a defendant, or even report every rumor that comes to the attention of the police.

8. If I don't know that helpful information exists, how can I find out whether a prosecutor is hiding it from me?

Though they have an ethical duty to achieve justice, not just to get convictions, prosecutors in an excess of zeal may fail to voluntarily reveal exculpatory information to the defense. Defendants should always be alert to the possibility that exculpatory information exists. They may learn of it in one of the following ways:

- by finding a reference to helpful information in a document that the prosecutor has had to turn over for other reasons
- by asking witnesses and police officers who are willing to talk before trial whether they know of any information that might support the defense version of events, or
- by interviewing witnesses after the trial results in a conviction. At this time, prosecution witnesses may be less guarded in their comments and may reveal exculpatory information that they made available to the prosecution prior to trial. The defendant would then have to go back to the trial judge to try to overturn the conviction based on the prosecution's failure to disclose that information.

9. Can I search police and prosecution files to see if they contain helpful information?

Defense attorneys often file pretrial motions (see Chapter 19) asking the judge to force the prosecutor to give the defense access to police and prosecution files and records for the purpose of discovering information that might help the defense. Prosecutors typically refuse to grant access on the ground that the defense has no right to rummage around in prosecution files hoping to find helpful information.

Generally, the only time that a judge will force the police and prosecution to open up their files is when the defense can demonstrate in advance that the files are likely to contain information that is critical to the defendant's case. Judges will not allow a defendant to go on a "fishing expedition."

Section III: Discovery of Harmful Information

This section is about how the defense obtains information from the prosecution prior to trial that the prosecution will be using against the defendant at the trial.

10. How can knowing about the prosecutor's evidence before trial help my case?

Knowing before trial what evidence the prosecutor plans to offer at the trial allows the defense to look for information that will undermine it. Discovery of prosecution evidence is vital for a defense attorney seeking to poke enough holes in the evidence to raise a reasonable doubt in the minds of a judge or a jury. On the other hand, a defendant who realizes that the prosecution's evidence is strong might accept a plea bargain that results in a lighter punishment than a guilty verdict following

a trial would produce. Thus, a defense attorney may have to file a discovery motion early in a case if the prosecutor doesn't turn over information without being asked for it, unless the law provides for automatic disclosure—as in the case of exculpatory evidence.

Local Discovery Variations

Despite the overall trend toward liberal discovery, discovery rules vary greatly from one jurisdiction to another. For example, in federal courts, defendants are not entitled to see pretrial statements of government witnesses until after the witnesses have testified (18 U.S.C. § 3500—the "Jencks Act"). Criminal defense attorneys usually are familiar with local discovery rules, and self-represented defendants should consult a legal coach to find out to what kind of information they can have access (and what kind of information they must turn over to prosecutors if reciprocal discovery laws apply). (See Section IV, below.)

---

11. What specific types of information does the prosecution have to turn over to me?

Section 1054.1 of the California Penal Code provides a typical example of pretrial disclosure requirements imposed on prosecutors. This law specifies that the prosecutor must disclose to the defense (normally at least 30 days before trial) the following information:

- **The names and addresses of all persons the prosecutor intends to call as witnesses at trial.**

When Lawyers Need Permission to Reveal Information to Their Clients

Recognizing the danger that may confront victims and witnesses were their addresses and phone numbers made available to certain defendants, many jurisdictions forbid defense attorneys from revealing this information to their clients without specific court authorization.

- **Any "real evidence" that the police have seized as part of their investigation.** For instance, if a defendant is charged with assault with a deadly weapon, and the police seized the beer bottle with which the defendant supposedly hit the victim, the prosecutor must allow the defense to examine the beer bottle.
- **Written statements prepared by the police that contain information relevant to the case,** such as police summaries of oral statements taken from witnesses or victims.
- **Written statements of any witnesses that the prosecutor intends to call at trial.** For example, if the police interviewed and made a written record of a statement by an eyewitness to a robbery, and the prosecutor expects to call the eyewitness at trial, the prosecutor must give the defense a copy of the statement. Defendants are also commonly entitled to see copies of statements they themselves have given to police officers.
- **Expert witness reports that a prosecutor intends to offer at trial.** For instance, assume that the police took a urine specimen from a defendant charged with drunk driving. A police laboratory technician analyzed the specimen and prepared a report stating that the percentage of alcohol in the defendant's blood was 0.11%. If the prosecutor plans to offer this report into evidence, the prosecutor must first reveal it to the defense.

12. Can I obtain a copy of my "rap sheet" (record of arrests and convictions)?

Yes. Defendants are entitled to discovery of their own rap sheets. Defense attorneys examine these carefully, because rap sheets often contain wrong information. For example, a conviction on a defendant's rap sheet may belong to another person with a similar name, or a conviction that shows up as a felony may have been only a misdemeanor, or charges long ago dismissed may show up as still pending. Correcting wrong information on a rap sheet may enable the defense to:

- deprive prosecutors of evidence with which to attack the credibility of a defendant who chooses to testify at trial, or
- obtain a more favorable plea offer from the prosecutor than would be possible in light of the uncorrected rap sheet.

Should the Defense Correct a Favorable but Erroneous Rap Sheet?

If a defendant notices that a rap sheet fails to mention an arrest or a conviction, should the defense bring the oversight to a prosecutor's attention? Generally, the answer is "no." It's not up to defendants to do the government's work. In rare instances, perhaps if a defendant is certain that a prosecutor is bound to learn of the mistake before the case concludes, the defendant might earn brownie points toward a favorable plea bargain by pointing out the mistake.

---

13. Can I find out about grand jury testimony?

In many states, yes. Defendants are often entitled to all pretrial statements of prosecution witnesses, whether given informally to police officers or formally under oath before a grand jury. (See Chapter 6, Section IV.) A grand jury transcript will reveal prosecution witnesses' trial testimony, and provide the defense with a basis for discrediting any witnesses who testify differently at trial than they did before the grand jury.

14. Will the prosecutor turn over to the defense a copy of the reports prepared by the police who investigated my case?

Yes. Police reports (sometimes called arresting officers' reports) typically detail the events leading up to a defendant's arrest. They may include the police officer's own observations, summaries of witness statements, and descriptions of seized evidence. The defense usually receives copies of police reports at the time of arraignment. (See Chapter 10.)

15. Will the prosecution turn over to the defense information about a search and seizure made in the case?

Yes. The defense receives copies of arrest and search warrants, and accompanying affidavits (statements of fact in support of the application for a warrant, given under oath). If the affidavits show that the police did not demonstrate probable cause for the issuance of a warrant, or lied about an important fact, the defense may file a motion challenging the legality of an arrest or the seizure of evidence.

Challenging Improper Arrests

Unless the police seized evidence in the course of an unlawful arrest, challenging the validity of an arrest warrant is often an act of futility. Even if the arrest was improper at the time, the prosecution has usually had sufficient time to gather additional evidence and secure another arrest warrant. However, a successful challenge to an arrest warrant can pay off if the police seized evidence when they made the arrest. Even if the police rearrest the defendant pursuant to a valid warrant, the prosecution may be unable to use the improperly seized evidence in court. (See Chapter 2 for more on search and seizure and the fruit of the poisonous tree doctrine.)

Section IV: Reciprocal Discovery

This section explains what information the defense must turn over to the prosecution.

16. Can the judge order the defense to disclose any evidence to the prosecutor?

Yes. Defendants have argued that forcing them to turn over evidence to the prosecutor violates their Fifth Amendment right to silence and their privilege against self-incrimination. However, judges have upheld so-called reciprocal discovery laws, which compel defendants to disclose some information to prosecutors before trial.

17. What information might the defense have to turn over to the prosecutor?

Again, each jurisdiction has its own reciprocal discovery rules, so self-represented defendants need to consult a legal coach for help in figuring out their discovery obligations. The following are examples of reciprocal discovery laws:

- **Federal courts.** Upon demand by a prosecutor, the defense must give written notice of intent to offer an alibi defense (assuming they plan to) and reveal the names and addresses of the alibi witnesses. If the defendant refuses to comply with the prosecutor's demand, then the defendant cannot offer the alibi defense or call the witnesses at trial (Federal Rule of Criminal Procedure 12.1). The U.S. Supreme Court upheld the legality of Florida's version of this rule in *Williams v. Florida* (U.S. Sup. Ct. 1970).
- **California.** Defendants must disclose to prosecutors (a) the names and addresses of all people other than themselves that they plan to call as witnesses; (b) any relevant written or recorded statements made by any of these witnesses; (c) any experts' reports upon which defendants intend to rely at trial; and (d) any real evidence (tangible objects) that defendants intend to offer into evidence (Cal. Penal Code § 1054).
- **Vermont.** Upon request by prosecutors, defendants must submit to reasonable physical or medical inspections of their bodies; permit the taking of hair and blood samples; and, if sanity is in issue, submit to psychiatric examinations (Vermont Rule of Criminal Procedure 16.1(a)(1)).

In the future, Congress and state legislatures are likely to impose further disclosure obligations on defendants. While defense attorneys are likely to object to their constitutionality, courts will probably uphold reasonable rules that correspond to discovery burdens imposed on prosecutors.

Investigating the Facts

I n addition to using established court discovery procedures to obtain the prosecution's evidence (see Chapter 14), defendants often gather evidence of their own in preparation for trial. Defense investigation methods can be as informal as talking to potential witnesses on the telephone, or as formal as a deposition under oath. Defendants who are not in custody can undertake some investigative tasks themselves, even if they are represented by a lawyer (private or government paid).

Section I: Interviewing Prosecution Witnesses

This section explains why it's important to interview the witnesses who will be testifying for the prosecution, and some common techniques for doing so.

1. Why would the defense want to interview prosecution witnesses?

The defense can gain three significant benefits through personally interviewing prosecution witnesses:

- The defense can gauge the witness's demeanor and credibility.
- Knowing what prosecution witnesses will say allows the defense time to think about how to poke holes in their testimony and to counter their testimony with defense evidence.
- If the prosecution witness's testimony at trial differs significantly from what he told the defense before trial, the defense may be able to undermine

his credibility by showing that his story changes from one telling to the next.

2. Why interview prosecution witnesses if the prosecution already is under a duty to turn witnesses' statements over to the defense?

Defendants cannot be certain the prosecution will play by the rules. Moreover, if a witness has only spoken orally to the police or prosecutor, there may be no evidence of that statement for the defense to obtain. Finally, witness statements prepared by the prosecution may not be an accurate guide to the testimony the witness will give at trial. This is because witness statements often are terse summaries, prepared by a police investigator for witnesses to sign, and don't fully portray what the witness has to say.

3. Is it completely legal for the defense to interview prosecution witnesses before trial?

Yes. Prosecutors do not own their witnesses, and they cannot prevent witnesses and crime victims from talking to the defense. It's up to individual witnesses, including victims, to decide whether to talk to the defense before trial.

4. Can I expect prosecution witnesses to voluntarily talk to someone from the defense team?

Prosecution witnesses do not normally voluntarily submit to defense interviews. Most prosecution witnesses are either the alleged crime victims, or people who are closely identified with the prosecution (like police officers), and therefore have no wish to help the defense. However, rules in most jurisdictions forbid prosecutors from explicitly instructing witnesses not to talk to the defense.

Defendants Should Not Personally Interview Crime Victims

Whatever the defendant's intent, an alleged victim may interpret any personal contact from the defendant as a threat. If the victim reports the "threat" to the police, the defendant might wind up having bail revoked and facing an additional criminal charge. Therefore, unless an attorney arranges for the contact in advance, the defendant should never personally contact a victim.

"I Can't Tell You What to Do, But ..."

Prosecutors sometimes subtly evade the rule forbidding them to instruct witnesses not to talk to the defense by simply advising witnesses of the law. Prosecutors can say something like, "I'm not telling you what to do, but I can tell you that the law doesn't require you to talk with the defense if you don't want to." Prosecutors realize that this word to the wise is enough in most cases to discourage prosecution witnesses from cooperating with defense interview requests.

5. If voluntary cooperation is unlikely, how should the defense go about interviewing prosecution witnesses?

The defense has two ways of increasing its chances of obtaining prosecution witness interviews before trial. However, both can be costly, and one is an option only in a few states. One possibility is for the defense to hire a private investigator. Private investigators specialize in finding and interviewing reluctant witnesses. The fact that many private investigators are former police officers enhances their chances of success. Private investigators can be costly, however, often charging about $75–$100 an hour (plus expenses) for their services. Thus, a defendant who hires a private attorney may not want to bear the added expense of an investigator.

Public defender offices, which serve indigent defendants in many parts of the country, sometimes employ investigators as part of their staffs. Demands on these investigators usually are very heavy, and it's up to the lawyers in the office, not an individual defendant, to decide which cases the investigators work on.

In some jurisdictions, a second way to interview a prosecution witness is to serve the witness with a subpoena (a court order) compelling the witness to attend and answer questions at a deposition (an out-of-court session at which the witness can be questioned under oath). Depositions are common in civil cases, but far less frequent in criminal cases. Florida is one state that permits the defense to subpoena witnesses for depositions without limitation (Florida Rule of Criminal Procedure 3.220(d)(1)). California takes a begrudging middle approach toward depositions. California allows the defense to depose only friendly witnesses, and only if the defense convinces a judge that the witness is unlikely to be available for trial, either because the witness is ill or because the witness is about to leave the state (Cal. Penal Code § 1336). Most jurisdictions simply don't allow depositions in criminal cases.

During a deposition, the witness is questioned under oath in front of a court reporter, who records the testimony and transcribes it into a booklet. Depositions can be expensive. A defendant represented by a private attorney would have to pay for the attorney's time to take the deposition, and for a court reporter to take down and transcribe the testimony.

6. Should I personally interview prosecution witnesses and save the cost of an investigator?

No. By personally interviewing prosecution witnesses, the defendant takes a risk that a witness will view the personal contact as threatening and report it to the police. Moreover, the defense can't do much about a sudden change in story at trial when it's the defendant who personally conducted the interview. To prove that the prosecution witness's story has changed, the defendant would have to testify. And even then, it would only be the defendant's word against that of the witness.

CASE EXAMPLE 1: Ruth Lessly is charged with trespass, but denies that she was among a group of youths who broke into a boarded-up house. Ruth personally contacts Bess, who lives next to the boarded-up house and who witnessed the break-in. Bess tells Ruth that Bess doesn't remember Ruth as one of the youths who broke into the house. At trial, however, Bess testifies that she is certain that Ruth trespassed.

Question: What can happen as a result of Ruth contacting Bess?

Answer: Bess might well report Ruth to the police, claiming that Ruth tried to threaten her into giving favorable testimony. Even if Bess doesn't do this, Ruth hasn't done much to help her case. Ruth can testify and say that Bess changed her story, at the cost of giving up her right to remain silent. Even if Ruth testifies to Bess's earlier statement, Bess is likely to deny making it. A judge or jury might choose to believe Bess rather than Ruth.

CASE EXAMPLE 2: Same case. Assume that a private investigator, rather than Ruth personally, interviews Bess before trial. When the investigator shows Bess a picture of Ruth, Bess tells the investigator that she doesn't remember Ruth as one of the youths who broke into the house. At trial, Bess identifies Ruth as one of the trespassers.

Question: Is the defense in a better position than in case example 1?

Answer: Yes. By using an investigator, Ruth can't be accused of trying to intimidate Bess. Furthermore, the defense can call the investigator as a witness to testify to Bess's earlier remark. A judge or jury might well regard the investigator as more believable than Ruth. Also, Ruth can stand on her right to remain silent while still attacking Bess's credibility through the investigator's testimony.

Section II: Finding and Interviewing Defense Witnesses

This section is about how the defense goes about finding appropriate witnesses to rebut the prosecution case and present facts favorable to the defense.

7. As the defendant, what can I personally do to help locate witnesses favorable to my defense?

Ideally, a defendant should note the presence of any bystanders at the scene of an alleged crime or the defendant's arrest, and try to remember such details as their gender, physical appearance, manner of dress, and the like—anything that might later help the defense locate and interview them.

The defendant can also revisit scenes of important events, and should visit these scenes at the same time of day that the actual events took place. That way, defendants are more likely to locate regular passersby who were on the scene earlier.

The defendant can also contact friends, employers, and other people who might testify to the defendant's good character. Such evidence is often admissible at trial, and in a close case may tip the scales in the defendant's favor. And even if the defendant is ultimately convicted at trial, these people can be invaluable in convincing the judge to be lenient when sentencing the defendant.

8. Should I personally interview someone who might give helpful testimony?

Defendants who are represented by attorneys should let their attorneys conduct interviews of potential witnesses. Attorneys are more likely to know which topics to probe. Sometimes, assuming the defense attorney agrees, it can be helpful for the defendant to accompany the attorney on an interview of a personal friend who wants to help the defendant. However, defendants should not be present at other interviews, because witnesses may regard the defendant's presence as intimidation, and report to the police that the defendant made a threat.

Section III: Other Investigation Tasks and Their Costs

This section is about other investigation options available to the defense and describes what they accomplish and what they cost.

9. Besides interviewing witnesses, what other investigation activities might the defense engage in?

The defense might:

- bring in a scientific expert to review the work of police laboratory technicians and, if necessary, testify
- hire a private investigator to locate and interview defense witnesses, or
- in states that allow them, take depositions of friendly or neutral witnesses to preserve their testimony should they move away or change their stories.

Whether to incur the costs associated with such additional investigative tasks is a judgment for each defendant to make. The defendant should try to determine what the costs are likely to be, what the chances are that the investigation will help the case, and the costs of conviction that might occur in the absence of such investigation. For example, a defendant may decide not to spend $1,000 for a private investigator if the fine upon conviction is likely to be no more than that. However, if the likely fine is $25,000 or there is a likelihood of substantial imprisonment, then the $1,000 may seem cheap, assuming the defendant can pay it.

10. What can I do as the defendant to help the investigation and hold costs down?

Defendants who are not in custody can (in cooperation with their attorneys) use a few self-help techniques to help their attorneys investigate the case. Some of these tasks include:

- Taking photographs. The defendant can photograph the scenes of important events. These photographs can become defense exhibits at trial. Or, the photos may raise issues that poke holes in the testimony of prosecution witnesses.
- Gathering receipts, records, and other documents from such places as government offices and private employers, if they will be helpful to the defense.
- Contacting counseling and community service agencies to find programs in which the defendant can enroll to learn how to control behaviors related to the crime. (Participation in such programs can be very persuasive when negotiating a plea or arguing for a lenient sentence.)

Studies suggest that, as a general rule, defendants who take an active role in their own defense do more than save money. They tend to achieve better outcomes than those who leave representation entirely in the hands of their attorneys.

11. What techniques are available to the defense to pry needed documents loose from government agencies or private businesses?

Defendants who need to obtain documents from uncooperative people or offices can serve them with a *subpoena duces tecum.* This rather forbidding term refers to a court order requiring the person or organization to whom it is directed to deliver the documents, records, or objects designated in the subpoena to court. (See Federal Rule of Criminal Procedure 17.) The order is easy to get; in some courthouses *subpoenas duces tecum* are prestamped and a defense attorney need only fill in the blanks. (A sample *subpoena duces tecum*, labeled "Subpoena (Criminal or Juvenile)," is at the back of Chapter 21.)

Use an "Early Return Date" on Subpoenas

It's often to a defendant's advantage to look through subpoenaed documents before the actual date of trial. To make this possible, the defense attorney can put an early return date on a subpoena—that is, have the documents due in court before the actual date of trial. Then the attorney can go to the courthouse and, with the judge's permission, examine the documents before trial.

---

12. Do subpoenas always work to produce the requested evidence?

No. A person whose books or records are subpoenaed can ask a judge to "quash" (nullify) the subpoena. The usual ground for such a request is that the subpoena is so broad that compliance is impossible or too costly. Judges often respond by asking the defendant to tailor the subpoena to specific records, and to describe the information the defendant expects the records to contain. Judges may even throw the subpoena out in its entirety if it appears the defendant is on a "fishing expedition."

Preliminary Hearings

The term "preliminary hearing" (sometimes called probable cause hearing, preliminary examination, PX, or prelim) refers to a hearing in which a judge decides whether there is probable cause to make the defendant stand trial for the crime with which she is charged. This does not mean the judge decides whether or not the defendant is guilty, but only whether the prosecution is able to present enough evidence to justify a belief that a crime occurred and that the defendant committed it. If the judge decides that the prosecution has such evidence, then the defendant is "bound over," meaning that the court will retain jurisdiction over the defendant until the case is either taken to trial or settled.

The Judge Can Reduce the Charges

If the judge does not find there is sufficient evidence to hold the defendant to answer at a trial for the charged crime, but that there is enough evidence of a lesser crime, the judge may hold the defendant to answer—after the preliminary hearing—for that lesser crime.

In essence, the preliminary hearing provides an independent judicial review of the prosecutor's decision to prosecute. But because the preliminary hearing requires the prosecution to produce enough evidence to convince the judge that the case should proceed to trial, it provides the defense with an excellent opportunity to find out more about the prosecution's case.

Section I: What Preliminary Hearings Are and When They Are Held

This section provides an overview of the function the preliminary hearing plays in the criminal justice process.

1. Will I have a preliminary hearing in my case?

Maybe or maybe not. First, preliminary hearings are only held in cases in which the defendant pleads not guilty at the arraignment or initial appearance. But even then, whether a preliminary hearing will be held depends upon the laws of each state. In some states, preliminary hearings are held in every criminal case. In other states they are held only if the defense requests them. In still other states they are only held in felony cases.

In many states the prosecutor may eliminate the need for a preliminary hearing altogether by convening a grand jury and obtaining an indictment. (See Question 14, below.) And for strategic reasons, defendants may decide to waive (give up) their right to the preliminary hearing altogether, and proceed directly to trial. (See Section III, below.)

2. If I do have a preliminary hearing in my case, when will it be held?

The preliminary hearing typically takes place soon after charges are officially filed against the defendant. For instance, under the Federal Speedy Trial Act, a preliminary hearing must normally be held within 30 days of the time the defendant is arrested. (See 18 U.S.C. § 3161.) Many states have similar time frames.

As it happens, defendants can and often do "waive time"—that is, give up their right to a speedy trial—which allows the preliminary hearing to be delayed to a time convenient for all the major players in the case. As noted in other parts of this book, delays usually benefit the defense, which is why it's very common for defendants—on the advice of their attorneys—to agree to waive time.

3. Are preliminary hearings open to the public?

Preliminary hearings usually are conducted in open court where the public, the defendant and defendant's family, any victims, the media, and any other interested people may all be present. In rare cases, however, the judge may decide to close the courtroom, for example in the case of a sex crime where the victim is a child.

4. What takes place in a preliminary hearing?

In some ways, preliminary hearings are previews of what the trial will be like, if the case gets that far (most don't). The prosecutor starts the hearing by putting witnesses on the stand to testify about what they saw or heard, and by introducing one or more pieces of physical evidence.

Typically, the prosecution doesn't present its whole case, but only enough evidence to convince the judge that there is probable cause to hold the defendant for trial.

The defense has the right to—and most often will—cross-examine prosecution witnesses both to find out more about their observations and to test their demeanor. This helps the defense prepare to cross-examine these witnesses later if the case goes to trial.

After the prosecution is finished with its presentation, the defense has the right to put on its own case, but is not required to do so—and often doesn't, for tactical reasons discussed in Section III.

5. In what important ways are preliminary hearings different from trials?

Though they are similar in some ways, preliminary hearings differ from trials in many important respects:

- Preliminary hearings are much shorter than trials. A typical prelim may take from a half hour to two hours, and some prelims only last a few minutes.
- Preliminary hearings are conducted in front of a judge alone—no jury.
- The burden of proof, while still on the prosecution, is much lower during a preliminary hearing than it is during trial. At trial, the prosecution has the burden of proving each element of the charged offense(s) beyond a reasonable doubt. But at the prelim, the prosecution only

has to show probable cause that the accused committed the crime; the prosecution, thus, only has to offer minimal evidence of each element of the crime.

- The goals differ. The goal of trial is to hear and test evidence to determine if the prosecution can prove beyond a reasonable doubt that the accused person(s) actually committed a particular crime or crimes. The goal of a preliminary hearing is to screen—to weed out weak cases and so protect defendants from unfounded prosecutions.

6. What procedural rules apply during preliminary hearings?

Many of the same procedural rules that govern trials apply in preliminary hearings. For example, ordinary witnesses (non-experts) may testify only to what they have perceived; they may not give opinions. And the defense and prosecution may object to evidence and testimony offered by the other side. (See Chapter 18 for more on rules of evidence and objections during trial.)

However, one important difference between preliminary hearings and trials is that frequently hearsay evidence is admissible in prelims.

7. What are the possible outcomes of a preliminary hearing?

A preliminary hearing usually has one of three outcomes:

- Most often, the defendant is held to answer at a trial (some say "bound over" for trial) on the original charge.
- Sometimes, when the charge is a felony, the judge may reduce the charge to a misdemeanor or a less serious felony.
- A small percentage of cases are dismissed by the judge (though the prosecution may refile them).

8. I've heard that the prosecution usually wins at the preliminary hearing. Why is that?

The prosecution usually wins at the preliminary hearing for a number of reasons:

- The burden of proof is fairly low. The prosecution does not have to demonstrate a great deal in order to show probable cause that the defendant committed the crime. As long as the evidence offered by the prosecution is enough to logically justify a guilty verdict if the judge or jury believes it, the judge will let the prosecution take the case to trial.
- Judges tend to defer to the prosecution at this stage, since the defendant is not actually being tried.
- The prosecution usually can use evidence during the preliminary hearing (such as hearsay evidence, discussed more in Chapter 18) that would not be allowed during a trial.
- The defense typically does not put up a strenuous fight at this stage,

most often because of strategic considerations. (See Section III, below.) Without putting on much or sometimes any evidence at all, it is difficult to rebut (or challenge) the prosecution's evidence enough to make a judge rule against the prosecution at this preliminary stage of the proceedings.

9. Assuming the judge does find probable cause to hold me for trial, what happens next?

The judge signs an order so stating (sometimes the judge writes directly on the criminal complaint). Then, the prosecutor files a separate document called an "information." The information serves the same purpose as a grand jury's indictment, to officially charge the defendant.

Defendants who are free on bail normally remain free following the prelim, but are required to appear in court at the next scheduled hearing. In-custody defendants stay in jail awaiting their next court appearance, although they can renew their request for bail at the prelim. Bail is always reviewable, and a judge might grant bail if the actual facts (as presented at the prelim) are not as bad as the police report made them sound. (More on bail in Chapter 5.)

At this point, depending on the jurisdiction and the seriousness of the crime:

- The defendant may be arraigned a second time before a higher level court in states that have two tiers of courts
- The parties may proceed directly to plea negotiations or trial in the court that conducted the preliminary hearing, or
- A judge may set a later date for either a pretrial conference, trial, or both.

10. Is a preliminary hearing ever a substitute for trial?

Yes. Prosecutors and defense attorneys sometimes agree to "submit on the record." When this happens, a judge (not a jury) determines the defendant's guilt or innocence based on the judge's review of the preliminary hearing transcript. A prosecutor might agree to submit on the record when the case is weak but the prosecutor's office doesn't want to dismiss charges outright. If the judge then dismisses the case, the prosecutor can deflect criticism from angry victims or police officers to the judge.

More often, a case submitted on the record favors the prosecution rather than the defense and in essence is a slow plea of guilty. In such cases, the defense knows that a guilty verdict is all but certain, but by submitting on the record, the defense can move the case more quickly to an appellate court, or simply offer an out to a defendant whose case is hopeless but who doesn't want to plead guilty or *nolo contendere.* (Defense attorneys can submit on the record only when the defendant agrees to waive trial.)

CHAPTER 16 | PRELIMINARY HEARINGS | 353

11. Other than the decision as to whether probable cause exists to hold me for trial, will anything else happen during the preliminary hearing?

Before or after the preliminary hearing, while the parties are still in court, the judge may handle other matters, such as hearing motions made by either party. (Motions, which are requests for court orders, are discussed in Chapter 19.)

12. Who will present the evidence against me at the preliminary hearing?

Most often, one of the attorneys who works for the local prosecutor's office presents the evidence. However, in some states and for certain offenses (such as less serious misdemeanors), instead of involving prosecutors at this early stage, police present evidence of the charges to the judge during the preliminary hearing, and prosecutors come on board only if the judge decides that probable cause does in fact exist to hold the defendant for trial.

13. The prosecutor at my preliminary hearing was not the same prosecutor who handled my arraignment. Why is that?

In some prosecutors' offices, the same prosecutor files the charges, handles the arraignment and preliminary hearing, and is responsible for all aspects of a particular defendant's case. In other offices, the routine practice is to assign a prosecutor to handle one particular phase of the criminal process in many different cases. For example, one assistant D.A. might do only felony preliminary hearings, while another will handle only misdemeanor trials. Where the latter practice is followed, the defense will have to deal with different prosecuting attorneys at different stages of the proceedings.

14. What's the advantage of a grand jury to a prosecutor?

Though judges most often favor the prosecution in preliminary hearings, grand juries—perhaps in part because they are not publicly scrutinized—are usually even more prosecution-friendly. Moreover, the defense doesn't get to cross-examine witnesses who appear before a grand jury, which deprives the defense of a very valuable discovery tool.

Do Not Confuse Indictments and Convictions

When a defendant has been indicted, that means a grand jury has found probable cause to believe the defendant guilty, which justifies holding that defendant for trial. It's a far cry from the judge or jury (regular trial jury, called "petit jury") actually convicting the defendant. A conviction only happens after a trial where charges have been proven beyond a reasonable doubt, or upon a plea of guilty or no contest. (More on grand juries in Chapter 6, and more on plea bargains in Chapter 20.)

15. Does the defense have any choice about whether the prosecutor uses a grand jury or a preliminary hearing?

As mentioned above, either state laws or prosecutorial discretion determine whether a grand jury or preliminary hearing (or both) will be used to further the case against a defendant. In rare instances, the defense may force an open-court preliminary hearing, rather than the secret grand jury proceeding, by making a motion for a preliminary hearing to the court.

Section II: Basic Rights During Preliminary Hearings

This section is about the rights a criminal defendant enjoys with regard to a preliminary hearing.

16. Do I have the right to a lawyer at my preliminary hearing?

Yes. Defendants have a right to be represented by counsel at a preliminary hearing (*Coleman v. Alabama,* U.S. Sup. Ct. 1970). And if a defendant cannot afford to hire his or her own lawyer, the court will appoint one. Defendants who initially may have decided to self-represent can change their minds at the preliminary hearing and ask that a lawyer be appointed to represent them from that point on. (See Chapter 7 for more on court-appointed lawyers.)

17. What will I have to say or do at the preliminary hearing?

The defense usually opts not to put on evidence at the preliminary hearing. Of course, by not putting on evidence, the defense makes it more likely that the judge will rule for the prosecution. However, even when the defense does put on a strong preliminary hearing case, the judge will still usually rule for the prosecution. Thus, by presenting evidence, the defense runs the chance of unnecessarily giving the prosecution a preview of its trial strategy.

18. Can the testimony given at a preliminary hearing be used later in the case?

Yes. Just as in trial, testimony at a preliminary hearing is preserved word for word by either a court reporter or tape recorder. The prosecution, defense, or judge can request that a transcript of the record be prepared, usually for a fee, although a poor defendant is entitled to a transcript at government expense.

Often, the testimony a witness gives at the preliminary hearing is the witness's first statement on the record regarding the facts of the case. And that statement may be useful to the defense at trial if the witness comes up with different testimony.

> **CASE EXAMPLE:** Daniel Marks is charged with driving under the influence (DUI). The arresting officer testifies at the

preliminary hearing that Daniel had an open beer can on the front seat of the car. Later, at trial, the same cop testifies that there was an open beer can on the front seat and five empty beer cans on the floor near the back seat.

Question: Can the officer change his story in this manner?

Answer: Yes, but the defendant's attorney can cross-examine the officer during trial and ask why, if there really were cans on the back floor, did the officer "forget" to mention those cans at the preliminary hearing.

Additionally, a judge may allow the use of testimony given at a preliminary hearing to be entered in evidence at trial if the witness later becomes unavailable (for instance, dies or leaves the country).

CASE EXAMPLE: Same as above. Daniel Marks is charged with DUI. Daniel's friend Julia, a passenger in the car when Daniel was arrested, planned to go on a three-month trek to Nepal. Knowing of Julia's Nepal plans, Daniel's lawyer decides to put Julia on the stand at the preliminary hearing. After the arresting officer testified, Julia testified that she had purchased and brought along with her in Daniel's car a six-pack of canned diet soda. She explained that she was on a diet and often brought her own beverages with her. She further stated that she had held the soda can Daniel had been drinking from when the policemen stopped them because Daniel needed to get his driver's license and couldn't do that while holding the can. Julia said that the remaining five cans of diet soda were on the back seat. The judge found probable cause to hold Daniel for trial and set a trial date (when Julia was scheduled to be in Nepal). Daniel, unwilling to plea bargain, insists he was only drinking soda and feels he was arrested because of his eccentric appearance (blue and green "punk" hair, multiple tattoos, and body piercings). The case goes to trial.

Question: Can Daniel use Julia's testimony from the preliminary hearing at trial to help show that the officer mistook the soda for beer?

Answer: Yes. Daniel can probably have Julia's testimony read to the jury.

Although the defense does not typically present evidence at the preliminary hearing, Daniel Marks's case example above should show why it can be important on occasion to do so. Further, it can be very important for the defense to cross-examine a prosecution witness who presents damaging testimony at the preliminary hearing, because if that person becomes unavailable, the judge will usually allow the prosecution to use that evidence at trial. See Section III, below, for more on defense strategies.

Victims and Prosecution Witnesses May Not Have to Testify at Preliminary Hearings

Many states no longer require witnesses to attend prelims. These states now allow the police to testify to what they've been told by victims and witnesses. Ordinarily this would violate the hearsay rule, but it is allowed because the purpose of the preliminary hearing is to find probable cause rather than determine ultimate guilt. This practice undermines the common defense strategy of using the preliminary hearing as a way of testing the credibility of potential trial witnesses, since the police often cannot answer questions the defense would have put to such witnesses, nor can defense lawyers assess the demeanor of the witnesses who aren't there. See Section III, below, for more on common defense strategies.

19. Does the defense ever win at the preliminary hearing?

The defense might win and the case might be dismissed (or the charges reduced) at the close of a preliminary hearing if:

- The witness identification of the defendant does not hold up under cross-exam, and there is no other credible evidence to show the defendant committed the crime in question. (See Chapter 4.) This may cause the whole case against a particular defendant to unravel, and the judge may readily agree to dismiss the charges (or reduce them to a charge that doesn't require the eyewitness testimony).

- A key prosecution witness fails to show up or becomes reluctant to testify, perhaps because the defendant is a spouse, family member, or friend, and the prelim is being held in a state that requires the witness to attend rather than allowing the police to relate what the witness told them.

- The prosecution fails to put on at least some evidence, as required, to show that each element (part) of the crime charged has some reasonable (albeit minimal) proof. For example, to convict a person for shoplifting, the prosecution usually must show that (1) the defendant, (2) took and carried away, (3) property valued up to $500, (4) of another (person or company), (5) with the intention of depriving that person or company permanently of the property. In the prelim, the prosecution does not have to prove each of these elements beyond a reasonable doubt, but it does have to produce some evidence to substantiate each element. If the prosecution does not put on any evidence as to one or more of the elements, the judge should dismiss the charge.

CASE EXAMPLE: Mary North and a friend were arrested for shoplifting from the cosmetics counter at the Southstrom's department store. At the preliminary hearing, the prosecution puts on evidence to show that Mary and her friend were in the store the day $450 worth of makeup was stolen. They have a videotape of Mary's friend taking lipsticks and putting them in her backpack. There is no tape of Mary. Mary was wearing pants with no pockets and was not carrying a purse, backpack, or anything else at the time. The prosecution presents no evidence whatsoever to show that Mary actually took anything.

Question: Can Mary's lawyer do anything for Mary at this early stage of the case?

Answer: Yes. Mary's lawyer can make a motion (request) for the judge to dismiss the case on the basis that the prosecution failed to put on evidence for one critical element, namely that Mary stole the property in question. In legal jargon, a failure to put on some evidence for each element may be called a failure to establish a *prima facie* (a Latin term pronounced pr-eye-ma fay-sha) case. If the judge denies the motion to dismiss, Mary's lawyer can still try to negotiate a plea bargain with the prosecutor. The prosecutor may be willing to dismiss the charges altogether, or to cut some deal letting Mary go with minimal punishment (probation or some community service).

Section III: Common Defense and Prosecution Strategies at the Preliminary Hearing

This section describes how the defense and the prosecution typically try to use the preliminary hearing to strengthen their own cases without giving away too much to the other side.

20. What can the prosecution and defense gain from a preliminary hearing in terms of their case strategies?

Officially, preliminary hearings protect defendants by weeding out baseless charges. Unofficially, however, each side uses the preliminary hearing to check out the other side's evidence. As a matter of course, both the defense and prosecution tend not to put on so much evidence that they show their whole hand. And, because the defense doesn't have to, it often doesn't put on any evidence at all.

21. What specifically can the defense gain from the preliminary hearing?

Even though the defense doesn't expect to see all the prosecution's cards, the preliminary hearing may give the defense a preview of how strong the prosecution's tangible evidence is, how persuasive the prosecution's witnesses are, and how believable the prosecution witnesses are likely to be should the case go to trial. The defense tries to size up how solid the government's case is as a whole.

Such information can be important to the defense, whether it ultimately settles the case in a plea bargain or proceeds to trial. If the prosecution's case seems weak—if, for example, prosecution witnesses change their earlier stories, forget important details, or are otherwise discredited—the defense may decide it's worthwhile to proceed to trial. The prosecution, on the other hand, may be prompted to offer a generous deal, or at least the defense may gain leverage to push for one. If, however, the government's case seems very strong, this information may help the defense decide to accept a plea bargain, even if it's not what the defense had hoped for, and not waste further energy and money fighting what looks to be a losing battle.

Since over 90% of cases end before trial, it's clear that a primary defense goal at the preliminary hearing is to look for evidence to use to get the best possible result at the plea bargaining table. For example, if an arresting officer's credibility can be undermined during the preliminary hearing, and that officer is the state's main (or only) witness, the prosecutor may then be willing to offer a much better deal following the prelim than the prosecutor would have if the officer had been a better (more believable) witness.

Information gathered at the preliminary hearing will also help the defense if the case is one of the small percentage that do go to trial. Whether or not the defense presents its own witnesses, the defense will usually vigorously cross-examine prosecution witnesses in the preliminary hearing. This cross-examination gives the defense an opportunity to see how the prosecution witnesses will hold up, and to pin them down as to what their testimony will be at trial. (If they change their testimony at trial, the preliminary hearing testimony can be used to impeach their credibility.)

A Case of Destroying the Witness at the Preliminary Hearing

In the 1995 O.J. Simpson double murder criminal trial, the prosecution called the L.A. County coroner, among other witnesses, to testify at the preliminary hearing. The defense's cross-examination of the coroner revealed serious errors—for example, the coroner's office waited too long to examine the bodies and failed to adequately preserve certain evidence taken from the bodies. This cross-examination was so devastating that it forced the prosecution to change its plan to call the coroner to the stand during trial. Because everyone (in and out of court, as the preliminary hearing was nationally televised) saw how poorly the coroner performed during the prelim, the prosecution was forced to find another way to get at least some of the important evidence in without calling the coroner to the stand. They ended up calling another doctor from the coroner's office who, though he didn't actually perform the autopsies, was able to testify about the physical evidence.

Objections During Preliminary Hearings

Sometimes defense lawyers are required by local rules to object to inadmissible evidence during a preliminary hearing in order to preserve their right to object to that evidence later at trial. In the absence of such rules, however, defense lawyers often will choose to remain silent and allow prosecutors to present inadmissible evidence at the preliminary hearing. Why? The defense lawyers are using the preliminary hearing as a discovery device—to learn all they can, good and bad, about the prosecution's case. And since there is no jury at the preliminary hearing to be prejudiced by the damaging evidence, it is often better, from the defense standpoint, to let the prosecution think it has a strong case than it is to educate the prosecution about the problems in the case (which only gives the prosecution a chance to correct the errors and strengthen its case for trial).

As useful as a vigorous cross-examination of prosecution witnesses may be, a sound alternative defense strategy is to cross-examine prosecution witnesses very briefly and politely. This serves two purposes:

- This may relax and lull a witness into admitting damaging evidence either then and there, or later when the defense attorney unexpectedly gets aggressive at trial.

- The defense may save evidence that hurts the witness's credibility (believability) and spring it on the witness at trial. Because the defense did not produce this evidence at the preliminary hearing, the witness may not be expecting it at the trial, and the surprise may fluster the witness and make him look bad in the eyes of the jury.

22. When does it make sense for the defense to waive a preliminary hearing?

The reasons the defense might waive the right to a preliminary hearing include:

- The defendant intends to plead guilty and wants to avoid publicity (and expense if the defendant is represented by private counsel).

- The defendant is guilty of more than the charged offenses and fears further charges from the potentially damning evidence that may come out at the preliminary hearing. Also, if the facts of the case are particularly nasty, and the defendant plans to plead guilty anyway, the less the sentencing judge hears about the facts, the better for the defendant.

- The prosecution's case is strong, and the defense fears that prosecution witnesses may become so entrenched in their positions once they testify under oath at a prelim that they may become angry (or angrier) with the defendant and possibly refuse later interviews with the defense that are sought in the course of preparation for trial.

- The prosecution intends to call witnesses at the prelim who may be unavailable at the time of trial. If the prelim goes forward, this testimony will be available in the form of transcripts from the prelim for the prosecution to use at trial. By waiving the prelim, the defendant may prevent the testimony from coming in when trial time rolls around.

- Defendants who want to stall in the hopes that by the time the case comes to trial the prosecution's witnesses will have either disappeared, forgotten, or become confused about what happened during the alleged crime, may waive the prelim and move for several continuances (delays) of the trial date.

Fundamental Trial Rights of the Defense

You may be familiar with the adage that it's better to let 100 guilty people go free than convict one innocent person. This philosophy is reflected in a number of fundamental trial rights that defendants enjoy. Most of these trial rights trace their pedigree to the U.S. Constitution's Bill of Rights, and they act as an important restraint on governmental power over private citizens. This chapter describes these fundamental trial rights, which, taken together, form a large part of the "due process of law" guaranteed by the Fifth and Fourteenth Amendments to the U.S. Constitution.

Section I: The Defendant's Right to Due Process of Law

The Fifth Amendment to the U.S. Constitution provides in part that a person cannot "be deprived of life, liberty or property without due process of law." This due process clause is the basis for many of the rights afforded criminal defendants and procedures followed in criminal courts.

1. What is meant by the term "due process"?

"Due process" is an abstract term meaning nothing more nor less than what judges and lawmakers say it means. They generally have interpreted it to mean that criminal procedures are supposed to be fair and just. The term has two general dimensions:

- **Procedural due process.** This means that before criminal defendants can be punished, they must be given a legitimate opportunity to contest the charges against them. For example, they are entitled to notice of charges long enough before trial to have a chance to prepare a defense, and are entitled to be tried by fair and impartial judges and juries.
- **Substantive due process.** This means that any actions that the government takes must further a legitimate governmental objective. A common expression that describes substantive due process is that the punishment must fit the crime. For example, a statute that punished drivers who ran stop signs with a year in prison would violate substantive due process.

2. Does the Fifth Amendment's due process clause apply to state governments?

The Fifth Amendment applies directly to the federal government only. However, the Fourteenth Amendment also has a due process clause, which provides, "nor shall any State deprive any person of life, liberty or property without due process of law." The U.S. Supreme Court has interpreted the Fourteenth Amendment so as to make applicable to the states many of the rights set forth in the Bill of Rights. For example:

- The Fourth Amendment's prohibition of unreasonable searches and seizures was made applicable to the states by the case of *Mapp v. Ohio*, U.S. Sup. Ct. 1961.
- The Eighth Amendment's prohibition of cruel and unusual punishment was

made applicable to the states by the case of *Robinson v. California,* U.S. Sup. Ct. 1962.

- The Sixth Amendment's guarantee of the right to counsel was made applicable to the states by the case of *Gideon v. Wainwright,* U.S. Sup. Ct. 1963.
- The Fifth Amendment's establishment of a privilege against self-incrimination was made applicable to the states by the case of *Malloy v. Hogan,* U.S. Sup. Ct. 1964.

The Fifth and Fourteenth Amendments' due process clauses also are the sources of rights not specifically spelled out in the Bill of Rights. For example:

- In *Rochin v. California* (U.S. Sup. Ct. 1952), the Court held that illegal narcotics pumped from a suspect's stomach against his will were inadmissible in court because the police procedures "shocked the conscience" and were "too close to the rack and the screw" to be permitted. However, not every bodily intrusion violates due process. For example, laws requiring blood samples have been upheld against claims that they violate due process.
- In *Stovall v. Denno* (U.S. Sup. Ct. 1967), the Court held that unduly suggestive lineup procedures could violate due process. (See Chapter 4, *Eyewitness Identification: Psychology and Procedures*, for more on lineup procedures.)

3. Does the due process clause prevent the use of involuntary confessions?

Yes. The due process clause has long been interpreted to prohibit the use in court of confessions that are involuntary, even if they may be factually truthful. For example, a confession is likely to be thrown out as involuntary if the police obtain it by using or threatening to use physical force. Likewise, a confession may be unlawfully obtained if the police violate a defendant's *Miranda* rights. (See Chapter 1, Talking to the Police.)

CASE EXAMPLE 1: Jonah, a small man of foreign parentage and limited English skills, is approached on the street and questioned by two police officers. Seeing that the officers are carrying guns and sticks, and having heard reports of police brutality in his neighborhood, Jonah is completely intimidated and answers "Yes" to every police question, including whether Jonah committed a crime.

Question: Did the officers violate Jonah's due process rights?

Answer: No. Though Jonah may have reason to fear the police officers, his confession was voluntary because the officers did nothing to overcome his free will.

CASE EXAMPLE 2: Same case, except that when the officers approach Jonah they tap their gun holsters while telling him that, "It'll be best for you just to confess to doing the robbery last week at the drug store. We know your old Mama's been ill lately, and we don't know how she'll react to the news that her son's been badly hurt." Jonah then admits that he robbed the drug store.

Question: Does the officers' conduct violate Jonah's due process rights?

Answer: Yes. The implied threat of violence to Jonah and its possible impact on his mother would likely amount to sufficient police coercion to overcome Jonah's free will.

CASE EXAMPLE 3: Dad finds illegal drugs under his son's bed, beats his son, and makes him call the police and confess.

Question: Do Dad's actions violate his son's due process rights?

Answer: No. Dad may have committed a crime himself, but unless Dad is working for the police, his conduct isn't a due process violation. Due process limitations apply only to the behavior of government agents like police officers, not private citizens.

4. What other procedures are governed by the due process clause?

Any aspect of the criminal justice system that a defendant thinks violates "fundamental fairness" raises potential due process concerns. Judges' willingness to use the due process clause to invalidate police and prosecution behavior can vary, however, and is probably less in an era when much of the populace wants to get tough on crime. Some of the other important procedures that have

been affected by the due process clause include the following:

- Due process is violated if the government's unreasonable and unexplained delay in charging a defendant with a crime substantially impairs a defendant's ability to mount a defense.

- Due process requires the government to disclose to the defense exculpatory information—that is, information tending to show that the defendant is not guilty. (For further discussion see Chapter 14, *Discovery: Exchanging Information With the Prosecution.*)

- Due process is violated if the government entraps a defendant into committing a crime. (For further discussion, see Chapter 13, *Defense-speak: Common Defenses to Criminal Charges.*)

- Due process requires judges to instruct juries that defendants are presumed innocent of the charges against them.

- Due process may be violated if a prosecutor's arguments are repeatedly factually erroneous, and so angry and intemperate that they prevent the trial from being fair.

- Due process requires that a defendant's guilt be proven beyond a reasonable doubt.

- Due process requires that defendants have a fair opportunity to present evidence. Rules that unduly impinge on that right, for example by preventing a defendant from offering evidence that another person committed the crime with which the defendant is charged, are invalid.

- Due process can affect what happens inside the courtroom during a jury trial. For example, forcing defendants to wear prison clothes rather than street clothes in the courtroom violates due process (*Estelle v. Williams*, U.S. Sup. Ct. 1976). Whether courtroom spectators' conduct can result in a violation of defendants' due process rights varies among jurisdictions. For example, some courts have ruled that due process is violated when spectators watch a trial wearing ribbons or buttons displaying a victim's face. However, other courts have ruled that such spectator conduct does not violate due process (*Carey v. Musladin*, U.S. Sup. Ct. 2006).

Section II: The Prosecution's Burden of Proof

This section explains the burden placed on the prosecution to prove guilt beyond a reasonable doubt.

5. Is it up to the defense to convince a judge or jury of the defendant's innocence?

Absolutely not. The defendant is presumed innocent until the moment a judge or jury finds him or her guilty. It's up to the prosecution to offer enough evidence to convince the judge or jury that the defendant is guilty. Another way of saying this is that the prosecution has the burden of proof.

6. What exactly does the prosecution have to prove to meet its burden of proof?

Most crimes consist of two or more discrete elements. (See Chapter 24.) This means that the prosecution has the burden of proving facts sufficient to satisfy each element of the charged crime. If the prosecution fails to meet its burden with respect to any one element, a defendant should be found not guilty of that crime.

> **CASE EXAMPLE:** Rob Banks is charged with burglary. Assume that the elements of burglary the prosecution has to prove are: (1) Rob, (2) entered, (3) a dwelling, (4) belonging to another, (5) without the owner's permission, (6) with the intent to commit a crime. The jurors are convinced that the prosecution proved (1), (2), (4), (5), and (6), but some don't think that the backyard shed that Rob broke into qualifies as a "dwelling."
>
> **Question:** Should these jurors vote to convict Rob?
>
> **Answer:** No. The prosecution has the burden of proving each and every element of the crime charged. If the prosecution fails to meet the burden of proving any one element, Rob must be found not guilty.

7. How strong a case does the prosecutor have to present to justify a conviction?

The prosecution has to prove the defendant's guilt beyond a reasonable doubt. This is the highest burden of proof the law can impose. (By contrast, a plaintiff in a civil case only has to prove a defendant liable by a preponderance of the evidence.) The term "beyond a reasonable doubt" has no precise meaning. Sometimes, for example, judges tell jurors that "beyond a reasonable doubt" means that jurors must be convinced of guilt to a "moral certainty" before they vote to convict. Though the meaning of "beyond a reasonable doubt" may be imprecise, it reminds judges and jurors that convicting defendants is serious business, and that the prosecution has to overcome all reasonable inferences favoring innocence. At the same time, any doubts should be based on the evidence; that is, the prosecution should not have to disprove all imaginary explanations that might negate guilt.

> **CASE EXAMPLE:** Ida Dunnit is charged with shoplifting. A store security guard and two customers testify that they saw Dunnit put two computer software packages in her purse and leave the store without paying for them. Dunnit offers no evidence at all. During deliberations, one of the jurors says, "I don't think that she's guilty. Who knows—the guard and the two customers may be lying because they're paying her back for something she did to them."
>
> **Question:** Do the juror's misgivings amount to reasonable doubt?
>
> **Answer:** No. Since the juror can't point to any evidence suggesting that the witnesses are taking revenge

on Dunnit by perjuring themselves, the juror's doubts are not reasonable ones. To satisfy its burden of proof, the government does not have to overcome every possible doubt, just rational doubts. However, the legal system cannot prevent a juror from misapplying the concept of reasonable doubt in favor of a defendant. This juror cannot be forced to convict Dunnit.

Beyond a Reasonable Doubt

While each jurisdiction may phrase the prosecution's burden of proof somewhat differently, the following language (taken from a frequently given jury instruction) is typical: "A defendant in a criminal action is presumed to be innocent until the contrary is proved, and in case of a reasonable doubt whether his guilt is satisfactorily shown, he is entitled to a verdict of not guilty. This presumption places upon the State the burden of proving him guilty beyond a reasonable doubt. Reasonable doubt is not a mere possible doubt, because everything relating to human affairs, and depending on moral evidence, is open to some possible or imaginary doubt. It is that state of the case which, after the entire comparison and consideration of all the evidence, leaves the minds of the jurors in that condition that they cannot say that they feel an abiding conviction, to a moral certainty, of the truth of the charge."

Defense lawyers have favorite and sometimes colorful methods of stressing the meaning of beyond a reasonable doubt during closing argument to juries. Some hold their arms away from their sides to resemble a scale, and then tip far to the side to indicate the magnitude of the prosecution's burden. And some use evocative language: "The conscience of this state cannot sanction the conviction of any individual on speculation, on intuition, or on hunches. You are sworn to uphold the law. You are the people who promised during jury selection that you would not convict on speculation. That you would not convict unless the state proved its case beyond a reasonable doubt. You are the people who said that even if you thought that deep down in your hearts that my client was guilty, but that the state had not proven its case beyond a reasonable doubt, you would not convict. That is the conscience of the community, and you are here to uphold it."

Whatever their individual methods, defense lawyers always emphasize to jurors the prosecution's heavy burden of proof.

8. Does the defense ever have the burden to prove anything?

Yes. The defense may have the burden of proving certain affirmative defenses. For example, if the defendant claims to be not guilty by reason of insanity, the defense may have the burden of proving that the insanity claim is accurate. (See Chapter 13 on common defenses to criminal charges.) However, when the defense does have to prove something, its burden of proof is lighter than the government's beyond a reasonable doubt burden. For example, the defense has to convince a judge or jury of insanity only by a preponderance of the evidence or, in some jurisdictions, clear and convincing evidence.

Section III: The Defendant's Right to Remain Silent

This section explains how the defendant's right to remain silent actually plays out in a criminal case.

9. Do I have to testify at my own trial?

No. The Fifth Amendment to the U.S. Constitution provides that a defendant cannot "be compelled in any criminal case to be a witness against himself." In short, the defendant has the right to sit mute. The prosecutor cannot call the defendant as a witness, nor can a judge or defense attorney force the defendant to testify if the defendant chooses to remain silent. This constitutional right to silence is consistent with the prosecution's burden of proof. Even in the absence of a defense case, the defendant must be found not guilty unless the prosecution offers evidence proving guilt beyond a reasonable doubt.

10. Do I have to testify if I'm called as a witness in a criminal trial?

Yes, but a witness may refuse to answer particular questions if the responses would tend to incriminate that witness.

CASE EXAMPLE 1: Greta, a graduate student at Queens University, is subpoenaed as a witness in the criminal trial of Professor Charles for stealing university property. The police have evidence that Greta kept some of the items that Professor Charles is charged with stealing. If the government can prove that Greta knew the items she kept were stolen, she could be found guilty of the crime of receiving stolen property.

Question: May Greta refuse to answer the prosecutor's questions about the theft?

Answer: Yes. Since the prosecution might be able to use Greta's testimony against her in a future criminal proceeding, she has a right not to answer.

CASE EXAMPLE 2: Same case. Greta has told the police that she witnessed Professor Charles's theft of university property, but did not try to prevent the theft or report it to the police. Greta's conduct may violate a portion of the university's code of conduct, and if so she may be placed on academic probation or even dismissed from the university. However, her failure to act is not a crime.

Question: May Greta assert her right to remain silent?

Answer: No. Possible university penalties are not the same as criminal punishment. Since her answers could not be used against her in a criminal proceeding, Greta cannot properly refuse to answer based on the Fifth Amendment.

Question: Might a person in Greta's position nevertheless "take the Fifth"?

Answer: Possibly. Greta can refuse to testify and hope that the judge and prosecutor accept her Fifth Amendment claim at face value. However, the judge can order Greta to testify if she decides that Greta's claim is not well founded. If Greta still refuses to testify, she can then be held in contempt of court and ultimately imprisoned until she agrees to testify.

11. Especially if I'm innocent, why shouldn't I testify in my own case?

Even an innocent defendant runs a variety of risks by testifying, including:

- The judge or a juror may react negatively to the defendant's demeanor.
- Either on direct or cross-examination, the defendant's testimony may accidentally strengthen the prosecution's case.
- The prosecution may be able to attack the defendant's character with the defendant's prior crimes and misdeeds. Such evidence often would be inadmissible if the defendant didn't testify.
- By testifying, the defendant allows the jury to compare the prosecution's story to the defendant's. Subconsciously, the jurors may base their decision on whichever story they find

more convincing rather than hold true to the principle that they must find the defendant guilty beyond a reasonable doubt.

For these and other reasons, defense attorneys often advise their clients not to testify, unless there is no other way to present important evidence to the judge or jury.

12. Won't the judge or jury think I'm guilty precisely because I don't testify?

This question is difficult to answer. Because the defendant has a constitutional right to remain silent and even to refuse to present a defense, the judge or jury may not infer guilt from the defendant's refusal to testify (*Griffin v. California,* U.S. Sup. Ct. 1965). In keeping with this rule, the prosecution may not assert or even imply that a defendant's silence is an indication of guilt. And upon request from the defense, the judge must instruct the jury that it cannot infer guilt from the defendant's silence. Jurors are at least sometimes capable of following such instructions. In the famous murder trial of O.J. Simpson in 1995, Simpson did not testify in his own defense and was nevertheless acquitted of murdering his ex-wife and her friend.

However, no matter what the legal rule, jurors are sometimes suspicious of a defendant who doesn't testify. A juror who is unsure of how to vote once deliberations begin may be subconsciously (and negatively) affected by the defendant's failure to testify. Some jurors may even consciously disregard the judge's instructions by reasoning along these lines: "If I were innocent, I'd sure get on the stand, look the jurors in the eye, and testify to my innocence. Since this defendant was afraid to testify, the defendant must be guilty."

The bottom line is that defendants take risks whether they choose to testify or not. Standard 4-5.2 of the ABA Standards for Criminal Justice instructs attorneys that the decision is for the defendant to make after full consultation. Defendants should carefully consult with their attorneys before deciding whether to testify. Self-represented defendants should consult a legal coach. (See Chapter 7 for more on legal coaches.)

> **CASE EXAMPLE 1:** At the conclusion of a trial in which the defendant neither testified nor called witnesses, Prosecutor Dustin Miojo states during closing argument that, "The state's case is uncontradicted."
>
> **Question:** Does the prosecutor's statement violate the rule against commenting on a defendant's failure to take the stand?
>
> **Answer:** Probably not. A judge would probably rule that the comment is a fair characterization of the state of the evidence rather than an implication that the failure to present a defense indicates guilt. Had the prosecutor repeated the statement several times or made direct references to the defendant's silence, the judge would be more likely to rule that the prosecutor stepped over the line.

CASE EXAMPLE 2: Brigitte Nathan pleads guilty to selling marijuana. During the sentencing hearing, the prosecutor presents a witness, Jill Bobbs, who testifies that she saw Brigitte on numerous occasions selling marijuana to school children. Brigitte says nothing at the hearing, but her lawyer questions Jill and seriously attacks Jill's credibility as a witness.

Question: May the judge impose a harsher sentence on Brigitte because she didn't personally respond to Jill's testimony?

Answer: No. The judge may not draw any negative inferences from a defendant's silence during sentencing hearings (*Mitchell v. U.S.*, U.S. Sup. Ct. 1999).

13. Can I refuse a police request for a blood sample on the grounds that the result might incriminate me?

No. Only evidence that is considered testimonial or communicative—that is, evidence intended to express a person's thoughts—is protected under the Fifth Amendment privilege against self-incrimination. This exception means that the police can require suspects to provide evidence of a purely physical nature without violating the Fifth Amendment (*Schmerber v. California*, U.S. Sup. Ct. 1966). Among the types of physical evidence that a defendant may be required to provide are documents, photographs, fingerprints, and samples of the defendant's voice, hair, saliva, urine, and breath. A suspect may also be required to participate in a lineup and wear certain clothing or repeat certain phrases (for the purpose of voice identification).

14. Can the prosecutor ever overcome a witness's legitimate claim of a Fifth Amendment right not to testify?

Yes. The prosecution can give a witness "immunity" in response to a legitimate refusal to testify based on the Fifth Amendment. The prosecutor can offer one of two forms of immunity, depending on factors such as the seriousness of the immunized witness's own criminal conduct:

- "Transactional immunity," meaning that the person given immunity cannot be prosecuted for any crimes related to the subject matter of the testimony, or
- "Use immunity," meaning that even though the witness given immunity may in the future be prosecuted for a crime related to the topic discussed in this witness's testimony, the immunized testimony itself cannot be used in the future prosecution.

Prosecutors often give immunity to compel small fish to testify against big fish. For example, a prosecutor may give a small-time drug dealer immunity in exchange for the dealer's testimony against the drug lord from whom the dealer purchased the drugs. A witness who refuses to testify after being given immunity can be held in contempt of court by the judge and jailed.

Section IV: The Defendant's Right to Confront Witnesses

This section discusses the right of the defense to face and question witnesses who provide evidence for the prosecution.

15. Is the defense entitled to cross-examine the prosecution's witnesses?

Yes. The "confrontation clause" of the Sixth Amendment gives defendants the right to confront the witnesses against them. Implicit in the right to confront witnesses is the right to cross-examine them (*Douglas v. Alabama*, U.S. Sup. Ct. 1965). Prosecution witnesses have to come to court, look the defendant in the eye, and subject themselves to questioning by the defense. The Sixth Amendment prevents secret trials, and subject to limited exceptions forbids prosecutors from proving a defendant's guilt with written statements from absent witnesses.

> **CASE EXAMPLE 1:** Bea Yussef is on trial for felony hit-and-run. A witness testified for the prosecution, then suddenly became ill and had to go to the hospital before Yussef's attorney could conduct cross-examination.
>
> **Question:** What should the judge do?
>
> **Answer:** The judge should strike the prosecution witness's direct testimony from the record and instruct the jury to disregard it. Even though Yussef's inability to cross-examine the witness is not due to any fault of the prosecution, the prosecution cannot rely on

witnesses whom the defense has not had an opportunity to cross-examine. If the testimony was so important that jurors are unlikely to be able to erase it from their minds, the judge might have to stop the trial (declare a mistrial) and, if the prosecution wishes, start all over again.

> **CASE EXAMPLE 2:** Mary Kontrary is charged with drunk driving. On the day set for her trial, the prosecutor announces that the arresting police officer is on vacation. In lieu of the police officer's testimony, the prosecutor asks the judge for permission to offer into evidence against Mary the officer's police report detailing the reasons for the arrest.
>
> **Question:** Should the judge grant the prosecutor's request?
>
> **Answer:** Under the confrontation clause Mary has a right to confront and cross-examine the police officer. The defense can't cross-examine a police report. Also, the police report does not fit within an exception to the hearsay rule. The judge should dismiss the case or allow the prosecution to delay the trial, time permitting.

16. Is it possible for me to be tried in my absence?

No, with rare exceptions. A defendant's own behavior can cause the defendant to lose the right to personal confrontation. A defendant who voluntarily fails to show up

Hearsay and the Confrontation Clause

The Sixth Amendment's Confrontation Clause guarantees that in criminal cases, defendants have the right to confront the witnesses against them. As a result, prosecutors cannot offer "testimonial" hearsay statements against defendants unless the person whose hearsay is offered testifies as a witness or unless the defendant has previously had a chance to cross-examine the person (say, during a preliminary hearing (*Crawford v. Washington*, U.S. Sup. Ct. 2004)). A hearsay statement is testimonial when government agents such as prosecutors and police officers elicit information in non-emergency situations in order to gather evidence for a later criminal prosecution. For example, information that a witness gives to a grand jury under oath is clearly testimonial. As a result, a prosecutor cannot offer grand jury testimony against a defendant if the person who gave the testimony does not testify at trial and the defendant has not otherwise had a chance to cross-examine

the witness. Likewise, if police officers go to a crime scene and ask witnesses to prepare affidavits, those affidavits are testimonial (*Hammon v. Indiana*, U.S. Sup. Ct. 2006).

On the other hand, statements that people make to 911 operators are generally not testimonial (*Davis v. Washington*, U.S. Sup. Ct. 2006). A 911 operator is not gathering evidence, but rather is trying to figure out what is happening in an ongoing emergency. However, if an emergency has passed, a 911 call may be testimonial. For instance, if a 911 caller reports a kidnapping after the victim has escaped to safety, the report is testimonial. (See *State of Conn. v. Kirby*, Conn. Sup. Ct. 2006.)

Courts are divided as to whether police laboratory reports, such as a report identifying a substance seized from a defendant as cocaine, are testimonial. The U.S. Supreme Court is expected to decide this question sometime early in 2009, in *Melendez-Diaz v. Massachusetts*.

---

for trial can sometimes be tried *in absentia*. And a defendant whose conduct repeatedly disrupts the trial may be removed from the court (*Illinois v. Allen*, U.S. Sup. Ct. 1970). Of course, the defendant's attorney would remain in the courtroom, if the defendant were represented.

CASE EXAMPLE 1: Bea Yussef is still on trial for felony hit-and-run. Bea has a medical problem that causes her to be

highly disruptive unless she has proper medication. Because Bea has been in jail, her doctor has been unable to adjust her medication. As a result, Bea becomes uncontrollable in court and the court orders her removed.

Question: Is the judge's order valid? After Bea's medication is adjusted, should the judge allow her to return to the trial?

Answer: Yes on both counts. The judge is entitled to order Bea's removal if her outbursts constantly disrupt the trial (her attorney would remain, if she has one). At the same time, removing Bea from her trial is a serious step, one that may prejudice the jury against her. The judge must permit Bea to return if medicine enables her to control her behavior. If Bea is representing herself, the judge should temporarily recess the trial if Bea's condition appears to be temporary.

CASE EXAMPLE 2: Stan Desside is charged with assault and battery on Noah Way. Desside claims that he hit Way in self-defense. The prosecutor asks that Desside stay outside the courtroom while Way testifies, because Desside has threatened to attack Way again if Way testifies against him. Desside's attorney can be present during Way's testimony.

Question: Should the judge grant the prosecutor's request?

Answer: No. The confrontation clause gives Desside the right to be personally present when Way testifies. However, based on the threat, the judge can issue a protective order requiring that Desside not annoy Way or come near him. Desside could be punished for violating the order regardless of whether or not he strikes Way.

17. Are there special confrontation rules for child sexual assault cases?

Yes. In recent years, legislators have been concerned about defendants who escape punishment for sexually molesting young children because the children are afraid to testify in the defendant's presence. To address this problem, many states have enacted special rules that authorize judges—in certain situations—to allow children to testify via closed circuit TV. The defendant can see the child on a TV monitor, but the child cannot see the defendant. The defense attorney can be personally present where the child is testifying and can cross-examine the child. The U.S. Supreme Court has upheld the constitutionality of these special procedures (*Maryland v. Craig*, U.S. Sup. Ct. 1990).

Section V: The Defendant's (and the Media's) Right to a Public Trial

This section explains the right of the public, the defendant, and the media to open court proceedings.

18. Has a defendant's right to confront witnesses had an impact on domestic violence cases?

Yes. In an all-too-typical scenario, female victims of domestic violence refuse to cooperate with the police and prosecutors once the initial emergency has passed. At one time, prosecutors were nevertheless able to convict domestic abusers by having police officers testify to victims' hearsay statements describing defendants' abuse. However, many of these statements are "testimonial" and are no longer admissible in evidence. (See *Davis v. Washington*, U.S. Sup. Ct. 2006.) As a result, unless domestic violence victims are willing to testify at trial, charges against their abusers normally have to be dismissed.

19. Can my friends and family attend my trial?

Yes. The Sixth Amendment guarantees public trials in criminal cases. This is an important right, because the attendance of friends, family, ordinary citizens, and the press can all help ensure that court proceedings are conducted fairly and that the defendant's rights are respected.

20. Can I prevent an alleged victim's family and friends from attending court proceedings in my case?

No. The right to a public trial belongs not just to defendants but also to the prosecution, victims, and the public at large.

21. Can the judge limit the number of people who observe my trial?

Yes. As part of maintaining order in the courtroom, judges may restrict the number of people they allow in court, and judges may also order people who disrupt proceedings to leave the courtroom.

Sequestration Rules

Sequestration rules attempt to prevent witnesses from being influenced by the testimony of other witnesses. Sequestered witnesses have to stay outside the courtroom until it is their turn to testify, and they cannot discuss their testimony with other witnesses until those witnesses have been excused from giving further testimony. Thus, if a defendant's friends or relatives are going to testify, sequestration rules may prevent them from being physically present inside the courtroom for much of the trial.

---

22. Does the media have a right to cover criminal proceedings?

Yes. The Supreme Court has recognized that one of the purposes of the First Amendment free speech clause is to protect speech about how the government operates. This includes media access to all open court criminal proceedings, trial and pretrial proceedings alike (*Richmond Newspapers v. Virginia,* U.S. Sup. Ct. 1980; *Globe Newspaper Co. v. Superior Court,* U.S. Sup. Ct. 1982).

The Supreme Court has also indicated that rarely, if ever, will the media be stopped from publishing information about what happens during public court proceedings, even if that information might be harmful to the defendant's ability to get a fair trial (*Nebraska Press Association v. Stuart,* U.S. Sup. Ct. 1976).

23. Are there ever any circumstances that would justify closing criminal proceedings to observers?

Yes, but only as a last resort and as a rare measure to protect an equally important competing right, such as the right to a fair trial or the privacy rights of a child.

CASE EXAMPLE 1: Steven Racci is charged with murdering his criminal law professor. In part because the professor, Kathi Rae, was a beautiful young woman and a frequent guest on law-related talk shows, the case has gotten enormous press coverage. Steven's lawyer has asked the court to close all pretrial proceedings, including the preliminary hearing, and the trial itself to the public. The defense lawyer argues that Steven's right to a fair trial is being denied by the press coverage, in particular that the press is reporting on "evidence" that may not be admitted at trial and so might poison the minds of potential jurors and the public against Steven.

Question: Should the judge close Steven's trial?

Answer: Probably not. In a very few situations, a defendant's right to a fair trial may outweigh the public's right to observe and obtain information about the trial. But a judge may not close a proceeding to the public unless it is necessary to prevent prejudice, and alternative measures that would reasonably protect the defendant are unavail-

able. In Steven's case, alternatives exist, such as screening out jurors whose exposure to the pretrial publicity makes them unfit to serve as fair and impartial jurors. (See Chapter 21, *The Trial Process*, for more on jury selection.)

The judge could also sequester jurors (separate them from the outside world) or order the jurors not to read or watch any news relating to the trial. The judge could also order a change of venue, moving the case to a locale less saturated with pretrial publicity.

CASE EXAMPLE 2: Defense lawyer Bobbie Hulls requests that the court close the trial of his client, Eve Yule, who is on trial for allegedly molesting her young daughter.

Question: Should the judge close Eve's trial to protect the daughter's privacy?

Answer: Again, probably not. Though avoiding further harm to child abuse victims has been found sufficiently important to justify some court closures, the court must first explore other, less drastic, ways of preventing the alleged harm. Here, the court could allow the victim to testify in private and have the testimony transmitted to court via closed circuit TV. Or the judge could close only the portion of the trial when the victim is testifying.

CASE EXAMPLE 3: Same case as above. Eve Yule is on trial for allegedly molesting her young daughter. During jury selection, both prosecution and defense want to ask potential jurors embarrassing questions about their intimate lives.

Question: Should the judge close Eve's trial to protect jurors' privacy?

Answer: No. The judge has an alternative: allowing jurors who wish to do so to answer potentially embarrassing questions in the judge's chambers (with counsel present, of course), rather than in open court.

24. Can judges limit the conduct and number of news media in the courtroom?

Yes. Judges have to protect defendants' rights to a fair trial, and can't allow the media's presence or activities to disrupt courtroom order. For example, in *Sheppard v. Maxwell* (U.S. Sup. Ct. 1966), the Supreme Court found the defendant's right to a fair trial had been denied in part because of "the carnival atmosphere at trial" caused by the media. In that case crowds of news reporters were apparently so loud that it was difficult to hear witnesses and lawyers. Also, reporters were seated so close to the defendant that he could not speak confidentially with his lawyers.

What Not to Wear

Families, friends, and other supporters of victims sometimes come to court wearing buttons, T-shirts, or other items displaying a victim's image, especially in homicide cases. They may be barred from the courtroom, because the emotional impact on the jury may deprive a defendant of a fair trial. (See *Musladin v. Lamarque,* 9th Cir., 2005.)

---

25. Are TV cameras routinely allowed in courtrooms?

No. It is up to the judge. The media may televise a criminal trial at the judge's discretion, unless the defendant shows that the coverage will violate his or her right to fair trial (*Chandler v. Florida,* U.S. Sup. Ct. 1981). Some courts (such as the U.S. Supreme Court) have a policy of not televising proceedings. And following the 1995 televised murder trial of O.J. Simpson, many judges have become more reluctant to permit live televising of trials. The Simpson trial took nine months to complete, and television drew much of the blame for greatly extending the trial. In 1997, when Simpson faced a civil trial based on the same murders for which he had been tried criminally, the judge refused to allow televising and the case was over in a few weeks.

26. Can the judge order my lawyer not to discuss my case with the media?

Yes. A trial judge faced with prejudicial publicity may protect the defendant's right to a fair trial by placing a "gag order" on attorneys, parties, and witnesses, preventing them from discussing a case outside the courtroom. Also, lawyers' ethical rules often limit the type and extent of commentary prosecutors and defense lawyers may make about an ongoing prosecution. For example, gag order or not, a prosecutor is not permitted to interfere with a defendant's right to a fair trial by disclosing negative facts about the defendant if the facts probably are not admissible as evidence.

27. Does the media have the right to investigate crimes?

The media may investigate all they want, as long as they are using lawful means such as interviewing suspects or witnesses who voluntarily wish to talk, or obtaining government documents under the Freedom of Information Act. However, the media does not have the power to force suspects to talk or submit to other procedures. A suspect, of course, does not have to (and usually should not) talk to anyone except his or her own defense lawyer. A suspect may have to submit to police identification procedures, such as appearing in a lineup or giving a blood sample, but has no obligation to give anything to the media.

28. Is it proper for reporters and photographers to come inside my house with police who are searching my home with a search warrant?

No. Under *Wilson v. Layne* (U.S. Sup. Ct. 1999), a homeowner's Fourth Amendment search and seizure rights are violated when police officers allow news people who are on so-called "media ride-alongs" (riding with police officers to crime scenes) to accompany the officers into a home to observe and photograph searches or arrests. Police officers who commit such violations can be personally liable to a homeowner for money damages.

Section VI: A Defendant's Right to a Jury Trial

This section is about a criminal defendant's right to be tried by a jury of his or her peers.

29. As a criminal defendant, am I automatically entitled to a jury trial if I want one?

The Sixth Amendment guarantees jury trials in all criminal prosecutions. However, this right does not extend to petty offenses. The U.S. Supreme Court has defined a petty offense as one that does not carry a sentence of more than six months in jail (*Lewis v. U.S.*, U.S. Sup. Ct. 1996). Since felonies and most misdemeanors carry possible maximum sentences of more than six months in jail, defendants are entitled to a trial by jury in most cases.

30. What if I want a judge trial, but the prosecutor wants a jury trial?

If either the prosecutor or the defendant wants a jury trial, then a jury trial there shall be, assuming the case is serious enough to warrant a jury trial in the first place.

31. If I can't decide whether I want a judge trial or a jury trial, which will I get?

It depends on where the trial takes place. In federal court trials, defendants get jury trials unless they give written notice that they want a judge trial. See Federal Rule of Criminal Procedure 23(a), which provides that a defendant entitled to a jury trial will have one unless the defendant agrees to waive (give up) a jury trial in writing, and the government and the judge accept the defendant's waiver.

Many states have similar provisions. A few states, however, take the opposite approach, and provide that trial will be to a judge unless the defendant expressly requests a jury. Self-represented defendants need to be particularly aware of their state's rule about this matter lest they wind up with a jury when they wanted a judge, or vice versa.

32. Why do juries mostly consist of 12 people?

The United States inherited its jury system from England, and in England juries have consisted of 12 people since the fourteenth century, for reasons nobody is quite sure of. Maybe that's how many spare chairs the first courtroom had. But a jury can consti-tutionally consist of as few as six persons (*Williams v. Florida*, U.S. Sup. Ct. 1970). The size of juries tends to vary depending on the state and the seriousness of the charge. For example, California requires 12-person juries for both felony and misdemeanor tri-als, except that the state and the defendant may agree to less than 12-person juries in misdemeanors (Cal. Constitution, Article I, § 16). Florida law provides for six-person juries in noncapital cases and 12-person juries in capital cases. (Florida Rule of Criminal Pro-cedure 3.270.)

33. Do all jurors have to vote the same way to produce a verdict in a criminal trial?

Not necessarily. Defendants tried by six-person juries can be convicted only if the jury is unanimous in favor of guilt (*Ballew v. Georgia*, U.S. Sup. Ct. 1978). But the U.S. Supreme Court has upheld a state law providing for less than unanimous verdicts by 12-person juries in non-death-penalty cases. Assuming that a state's law provides for less-than-unanimous verdicts in criminal cases, convictions based on nine out of 12 jurors voting for a guilty verdict are constitutionally valid (*Johnson v. Louisiana*, U.S. Sup. Ct. 1972).

Again, however, not all states provide for less-than-unanimous verdicts. In California, for example, unanimous verdicts are required in all criminal cases (California Constitution, Article I, § 16).

For further discussion of how to decide between a judge and a jury trial, and a primer on the jury selection process, see Chapter 21.

Section VII: A Defendant's Right to Counsel

This section is about a criminal defendant's right to be represented by an attorney during all important phases of the criminal justice process.

34. Am I entitled to be represented by an attorney?

Yes. The Sixth Amendment to the U.S. Constitution provides that "in all criminal prosecutions, the accused shall enjoy the right … to have the assistance of counsel for his defense."

35. If I can't afford to hire an attorney, does the government have to appoint one for me?

A judge must appoint an attorney for indigent defendants (defendants who cannot afford to hire attorneys at the going price) at government expense in criminal cases in which the defendant may be imprisoned (*Scott v. Illinois,* U.S. Sup. Ct. 1979). As a practical matter, judges routinely appoint attorneys for indigents in nearly all cases in which a jail sentence is a possibility. Otherwise, the judge would be locked into a nonjail sentence.

For information on arranging for counsel, see Chapter 7. For information on how to achieve an effective attorney-client relationship, see Chapter 8.

36. At what point in a criminal case does the right to counsel go into effect?

An accused person's right to counsel becomes effective at the moment judicial proceedings begin (*Michigan v. Jackson,* U.S. Sup. Ct. 1986). Determining when this moment occurs varies from one case to another. For example, if a criminal case begins with a grand jury indictment, the right to counsel goes into effect with the indictment (even though defendants may not know until they're arrested that they had been indicted). If an arraignment is the first step in a criminal case, then the right to counsel becomes effective when the arraignment takes place. (See Chapter 10 for information about arraignments.)

> **CASE EXAMPLE 1:** Rose Peters is indicted by a grand jury for selling illegal drugs. Rose first finds out about the indictment the next day, when the police come to her apartment to arrest her. While arresting Rose, the police question her and she admits that she's been involved in selling illegal drugs.
>
> **Question:** Did the arresting officers violate Rose's right to counsel?
>
> **Answer:** Yes. The formal criminal proceedings against Rose began with the indictment. At that point she had the right to counsel. Therefore, police questioning in the absence of an attorney was improper, and anything Rose said cannot be introduced into evidence against her in court (*Fellers v. United States,* U.S. Sup. Ct. 2004).

CASE EXAMPLE 2: Same case. After Rose is taken to jail, she waives her *Miranda* rights and agrees to answer the police officer's questions. She then repeats what she told the police officer at the time she was arrested, that she was involved in selling illegal drugs.

Question: Does Rose's waiver of her *Miranda* rights mean that what she told the police at the jail can be offered into evidence against her at trial, or are her jailhouse statements inadmissible as the "fruit of the poisonous tree," the police officer's improper conversation with Rose at the time of her arrest?

Answer: The Supreme Court left this question undecided in its 2004 decision in *Fellers*. Past decisions suggest that a valid waiver of *Miranda* rights sometimes means that defendants' statements can be used against them despite police improprieties earlier in the case. Whether these decisions will apply in a situation like Rose's is uncertain.

37. If I hire a lawyer to defend me for certain offenses, can the police question me about other offenses without my attorney present?

Yes, as long you have been *Mirandized*, the Sixth Amendment right to have your counsel present doesn't extend to uncharged offenses even if the offenses are factually intertwined.

CASE EXAMPLE: Robb was suspected of a burglary in which a man disappeared. Robb was indicted for burglary and an attorney was appointed to represent him. While on bail, Robb confessed to his father that he had killed the man. The father informed the police, who arrested Robb for murder. Robb was given his *Miranda* rights, waived his right to counsel, and confessed to the murder.

Question: Is the confession admissible?

Answer: Yes. The police have the right to question Robb about the murder charge without his attorney being present, because the Sixth Amendment is "offense specific" (*Texas v. Cobb*, U.S. Sup. Ct. 2001). In other words, the Sixth Amendment only precludes the police from questioning a *Mirandized* defendant on the specific offense for which the attorney was retained.

38. What can I do if I'm convicted because of my attorney's incompetence?

It depends. The U.S. Supreme Court has ruled that both indigent defendants who are represented by appointed counsel and defendants who hire their own attorneys are entitled to adequate representation (*Cuyler v. Sullivan*, U.S. Sup. Ct. 1980). But a defendant should not expect a conviction to be overturned just because the defendant's attorney made some mistakes. To result in a guilty verdict being overturned, an attorney's errors have to be so serious that they amount to a denial of a fair trial (*Strickland v. Washington*, U.S. Sup. Ct. 1984).

Here are examples of claims defendants have made against their attorneys that appellate courts have ruled do not justify throwing out a guilty verdict:

- failing to call favorable witnesses at trial
- lawyer using cocaine during the time the representation was taking place
- failing to object to a judge's erroneous instruction to jurors concerning the burden of proof
- eliciting evidence very damaging to the defendant while cross-examining prosecution witnesses
- repeatedly advising a defendant who claimed innocence to plead guilty, and
- representing the defendant while being suspended from the practice of law for failure to pay state bar dues.

On the other hand, circumstances can be sufficiently shocking to justify throwing out a guilty verdict based on an attorney's incompetence. Judges have ruled that the following claims justify a reversal of a guilty verdict:

- putting a law student intern in charge of the defense and leaving the courtroom while the case was going on
- acknowledging during closing argument that the defendant was guilty of a lesser crime without first securing the defendant's approval of this tactic

- during *voir dire* (questioning of the jury), failing to challenge two potential jurors who said they would be bothered by the defendant's failure to testify, and
- failing to investigate a defendant's personal background in a capital punishment case, because the information produced might lead jurors not to sentence the defendant to death (*Wiggins v. Smith*, U.S. Sup. Ct. 2003).

The upshot of all these cases is that defendants should not rely on the appellate courts to ensure that they have the effective assistance of counsel. Understanding the foundations of the attorney-client relationship and insisting on good representation is a defendant's best guarantee of competent counsel. (See Chapter 8.)

39. Can I represent myself in a criminal case?

Defendants have a qualified right to represent themselves. This right depends on whether the judge believes they are competent to do so. Defendants can be mentally competent to stand trial, yet not sufficiently mentally competent to represent themselves (*Indiana v. Edwards*, U.S. Supreme Court 2008). In most cases, criminal defendants are well advised to either hire an attorney or, if they can't afford one, accept an attorney paid for (at least in part) by the government. (See Chapter 7, *Criminal Defense Lawyers*, for further discussion of self-representation, and Chapter 10, *Arraignments*, for a discussion of self-representation at arraignment.)

Section VIII: A Defendant's Right to a Speedy Trial

This section is about how quickly the defendant must be put on trial if the defense fails to "waive time."

40. Does the Constitution specify when my trial will take place?

No. While the Sixth Amendment gives defendants a right to a "speedy trial," it does not specify exact time limits. Thus, judges often have to decide on a case-by-case basis whether a defendant's trial has been so delayed that the case should be thrown out. In making this decision, judges look at the length of the delay, the reason for the delay, and whether the delay has prejudiced the defendant's position. In one case, for example, the U.S. Supreme Court held that a gap of five years between a defendant's arrest and trial did not violate the constitution, because the defendant agreed to most of the delays *(Barker v. Wingo*, U.S. Sup. Ct. 1972).

41. If not in the Constitution, where else can I look for time limits regarding my trial?

Every jurisdiction has enacted statutes that set time limits for moving cases from the filing of the initial charge to trial. For example, federal court cases are governed by the Speedy Trial Act (18 U.S.C. § 3161). This law sets the following time limits:

- The government has to formally charge a defendant with a crime within 30 days of the defendant's arrest.
- The government should bring a case to trial not less than 30 nor more than 70 days after charging a defendant with a crime.

States have their own versions of the Speedy Trial Act. In Florida, for example, a defendant has the right to demand a trial within 60 days of being charged with a crime. In the absence of a demand, the state has 90 days to bring a misdemeanor case to trial, and 175 days to bring a felony case to trial (Rule 3.191, Florida Rules of Criminal Procedure). And in California, the state generally has to bring a felony case to trial within 60 days of filing formal charges in Superior Court. The state has 30 days to bring a misdemeanor case to trial if a defendant is in custody, or 45 days if a defendant is not in custody (Cal. Penal Code § 1382).

42. How set in concrete are these time limits?

Not very. Time limit rules are typically subject to a host of exceptions. For example, when computing the time before trial, delays caused by the absence of the defendant or an important witness may not count. Also, defendants and prosecutors often agree to delay proceedings. As a result, many cases take longer to conclude than a glance at the statutes would suggest.

43. What happens if the prosecutor waits too long to bring my case to trial?

The prosecution's failure to adhere to statutory time requirements generally results in dismissal of the case.

44. Wouldn't it usually be in my interest to delay the trial for as long as possible?

Sure. The longer a case goes on, the more likely it is that the prosecution witnesses will become forgetful, move away, or lose interest in testifying. Prosecutors know this, of course, and often it is prosecutors who oppose defendants' requests for delays. In response to defense delaying tactics, some states (such as California) give the prosecution as well as the defense a right to a speedy trial.

45. Is it ever in a defendant's interest to ask for a trial as soon as possible after charges are filed?

Yes. A very speedy trial can be to a defendant's advantage in cases in which the prosecution has to do a lot of investigation and conduct scientific tests. A quick trial can force the prosecution to go to trial before it is really ready to do so. The defense used this tactic in the 1995 double murder trial of O.J. Simpson. The defense hastened the start of the trial by waiving various hearings it might have insisted on, most notably a hearing on the admissibility of DNA evidence. Many commentators cited the prosecution's possible unpreparedness as a factor that contributed to the jury's not guilty verdict.

Section IX: The Defendant's Right Not to Be Placed in Double Jeopardy

Among the several clauses of the Fifth Amendment to the U.S. Constitution is this well-known provision: "nor shall any person be subject for the same offense to be twice put in jeopardy of life or limb." This section explains the double jeopardy clause, which protects defendants from harassment by preventing them from being put on trial more than once for the same offense. Double jeopardy problems are unusual, because prosecutors usually want to wrap up all their charges in the same case.

46. When is a defendant considered to be "in jeopardy"?

In a jury trial, jeopardy begins when the petit jury (the jury that will decide the case) is given an oath. In a trial before a judge sitting without a jury, jeopardy begins when the first trial witness is sworn in. When a defendant enters into a plea bargain, jeopardy begins when the judge unconditionally accepts the defendant's guilty plea. For example:

- A prosecutor dismisses a case after a jury is selected but before it is given the oath, and then refiles the charges and begins the case all over again. (A prosecutor might do this if an important witness were temporarily unavailable to testify.) The second case can go forward because the defendant was never formally in jeopardy.

- A suspect is subpoenaed to appear before a grand jury, which refuses to issue an indictment. The prosecutor secures additional evidence and again subpoenas the defendant to appear before the grand jury. The second subpoena is valid because the suspect was not formally in jeopardy earlier. (Of course, on both occasions the suspect could refuse to answer questions before the grand jury by invoking the Fifth Amendment.)

- In a trial before a judge, the prosecutor dismisses the case when its principal witness becomes ill while testifying. The case cannot be refiled because jeopardy has already attached.

47. Can I face charges in both state and federal courts for the same conduct?

Generally, yes. Defendants can properly be charged for the same conduct by different jurisdictions. (This happens only infrequently, however, because of limited government resources.) For example, a suspect named Bufford Furrow was arrested in 1999 after shooting at a number of children in a Jewish day care center in California and killing a postal worker in the course of his escape. Furrow was indicted in federal court for murdering a federal employee and committing hate crimes in violation of federal civil rights laws. Furrow could also be charged in a California state court with murder (for killing the postman) and attempted murder (for shooting at the

children). Furrow's prosecution by both the federal and state governments would not violate the double jeopardy clause because they constitute separate jurisdictions.

48. What is the "same offense" for purposes of the double jeopardy clause?

The answer is complex because jurisdictions use two different tests, and the outcome of a double jeopardy claim can depend on which test a jurisdiction uses. Some states use a broad "same conduct" test, meaning that a prosecution is for the same offense if it is for a crime that arose from the same conduct that was the subject of a previous prosecution. Other states (and federal courts) use a narrower "same elements" test, meaning that a prosecution is for the same offense only if all the legal elements (sometimes called material facts) of one crime are the same as for the crime that was the subject of a previous prosecution.

> **CASE EXAMPLE 1:** Jones was charged with the crime of robbery for accosting Hans Supp at gunpoint and taking his wallet. To prove robbery, the prosecution had to show that Jones took Supp's property by means of force or fear. However, Jones was found not guilty. The prosecutor now charges Jones with the crime of theft for taking Supp's wallet. Jones objects that the theft charge violates the double jeopardy clause.

Question: Is the second charge of theft allowable under the double jeopardy clause?

Answer: No, under either test. The second charge is clearly barred under the same conduct test because both the robbery and the theft charges grow out of Jones's attack on Supp. It is also barred under the narrower same elements test, because all of the elements in the crime of theft also are a part of the crime of robbery (that is, a lesser included offense) for which Jones was already put in jeopardy.

CASE EXAMPLE 2: Jones is charged with the crime of robbery for accosting Hans Supp in his office at gunpoint and taking his wallet. The judge dismisses the case after the prosecution's evidence fails to prove that Supp was in his office when Jones stole his wallet. The prosecutor now charges Jones with burglary, claiming that Jones entered Supp's office for the purpose of committing a theft. Jones objects that the burglary charge violates the double jeopardy clause.

Question: Does the burglary charge violate the double jeopardy clause?

Answer: Yes, if the court uses the same conduct test, because both charges arise from the same conduct. But the burglary charge does not violate double jeopardy under the same elements test, because the crimes of robbery and

burglary each contain a legal element that is not part of the other crime. Robbery is theft through force or fear, an element that's not part of the crime of burglary. And burglary involves breaking into and entering a building, an element that's not part of the crime of robbery. Since the elements of the two crimes are different, under the same elements test Jones could be separately charged with both crimes even though both grow out of the same conduct.

49. Can I be retried if I appeal my conviction and the appellate court reverses it?

Yes. In the usual case in which a conviction is overturned because of legal errors during the trial, the defendant can be retried and even given a harsher sentence than after the first trial if convicted a second time.

50. Can I be retried if the judge declares a mistrial during my first trial?

In most cases, yes. A judge may declare a mistrial and call a halt to a case if there is manifest necessity for such an action. For example, a judge may declare a mistrial if:

- the number of jurors falls below the number required by statute because of illness
- the defendant becomes ill and it is not feasible to interrupt the trial for the length of time necessary for the defendant to recover, or

- jurors engage in misconduct (such as by visiting the scene of the crime despite the judge's orders not to do so).

But if the defendant can show that the prosecutor deliberately created the conditions for the mistrial or that there was no manifest necessity for ending the trial, a retrial could be held to violate double jeopardy.

51. Can I be sued civilly for the same conduct for which I faced criminal charges?

Yes. The double jeopardy clause forbids only successive criminal prosecutions growing out of the same conduct. For example, after O.J. Simpson was acquitted of murdering his ex-wife and her friend, their relatives filed a civil suit against him for actual and punitive damages caused by the killings. The civil suits raised no double jeopardy issues, even though punitive damages are a type of punishment, and Simpson was held civilly liable for the deaths.

Basic Evidence Rules in Criminal Trials

This chapter reviews the evidence rules that tend to be most important in criminal trials. Rules of evidence are the trial system's equivalent of the rules of grammar. Just as grammar rules govern how we speak and write, so too do evidence rules control courtroom procedures. Even defendants represented by lawyers need to understand evidence rules, so that they can understand and participate in important strategic decisions in and out of the courtroom.

Section I: Overview

This section is about evidence rules generally: What they are, where they come from and what they accomplish.

1. What is the purpose of evidence rules?

Evidence rules guide how information (evidence) flows from the witnesses to the judge or jury who is hearing the case. The rules control both the **content** of the evidence (that is, what kind of information witnesses can and can't provide), and the **manner** in which witnesses testify (that is, how they relate the information that the law allows them to provide). To take a familiar manner rule, lawyers (and self-represented defendants) are supposed to obtain testimony from witnesses through a series of questions and answers, rather than through a long uninterrupted narrative. An equally familiar yet often misunderstood content rule is the hearsay rule, which bars witnesses from testifying to certain statements made outside the courtroom. (See Section II, below.)

2. Where do evidence rules come from?

Most evidence rules developed through "common law" judicial decisions. Like water droplets in caves that over the years formed stalactites, judges' evidence rulings gradually crystallized into rules that later judges felt compelled to follow.

Today, most court-developed evidence rules have been turned into statutes by Congress and state legislatures. California was among the first states to enact a comprehensive set of evidence laws, known as the California Evidence Code. The California code was a primary model for the Federal Rules of Evidence ("FRE"), a set of laws that governs trials in federal courts. About 40 states have enacted evidence rules based on the Federal Rules of Evidence. Because every jurisdiction's evidence rules are based on the common law and on each other, evidence rules are largely similar throughout the country.

3. Do judges still make evidence rules?

For the most part, no. With some exceptions, legislatures have taken over the development of evidence law. Lawmakers know that evidence rules can affect the outcomes of cases, and they want to have primary influence in shaping the rules. Of course, it's up to judges to interpret the evidence rules that legislators produce, and, in doing so, judges can substantially alter the scope and meaning of the rules. Judges' interpretations can in turn lead to statutory amendments either incorporating the new interpretations or specifically rejecting them. The frequent tug-of-war between judges and legislators to control evidence rules is alternatively fascinating and frustrating to many lawyers.

4. How do trial judges deal with the evidence rules within their courtrooms?

Many evidence rules consist of general guidelines, and judges have the power and responsibility to interpret the guidelines according to the circumstances of individual cases. For example, assume that an evidence rule provides that certain kinds of documents have to be shown to have been prepared in a trustworthy manner before a judge can admit them into evidence. The judge might require greater proof of trustworthiness in a trial involving two multinational corporations than in a trial involving a landlord-tenant dispute. Similarly, one judge may as a matter of personal judicial philosophy generally require greater trustworthiness showings than another judge.

5. Are the evidence rules in criminal cases different from those used in civil cases?

In most jurisdictions, no. The rules known as the Federal Rules of Evidence, for example, apply to both civil and criminal trials. However, certain specific evidence rules apply differently in criminal and civil cases. An example is Federal Rule of Evidence 404-a, which makes certain types of character evidence admissible only in criminal cases.

6. Do the same evidence rules apply to both judge and jury trials?

Yes. Again, most jurisdictions have only one set of evidence rules, applicable generally to all trials in that jurisdiction. In practice, however, judges tend to apply evidence rules much less strictly in cases tried by a judge than in jury cases. One reason for this is that many judges believe that, unlike a jury, they can sort out the legally admissible evidence from that which is not admissible when it comes time to make a decision. A second reason is that information has to be disclosed to judges before they can decide whether or not it's admissible. Since judges hear about information whether or not it's admissible, a ruling excluding evidence is less significant in a judge-tried than in a jury-tried case. Sometimes defendants choose judge trials rather than jury trials because they hope that a judge will be subconsciously influenced by information that is technically inadmissible.

> **CASE EXAMPLE:** Polly Anna is on trial for embezzling funds from the bank where she was formerly employed. Polly wants to attack the credibility of a key prosecution witness by showing that the witness has been previously convicted of a crime. However, because the conviction occurred some years ago and because the judge has discretion as to whether or not to admit evidence

of the conviction, Polly's lawyer is uncertain about its admissibility.

Question: Might this uncertainty affect Polly's decision about whether to ask for a judge or jury trial?

Answer: Yes. The uncertainty about the admissibility of the conviction should incline Polly toward a judge trial. Many judges interpret evidence rules more loosely in judge-tried than in jury-tried cases. Thus, the judge in Polly's case may exclude the conviction if Polly's case is tried to a jury, but admit it if trial is to the judge, figuring that he or she can discount the evidence when deciding the case. And even if the judge were to exclude the conviction from evidence, the judge will at least know of the conviction and might be subtly influenced by it. By contrast, if the judge excludes evidence of the conviction in a jury trial, the jury will never hear about the conviction.

CASE EXAMPLE: Miguel Ito is on trial before a jury for burglary. The prosecution wants to offer into evidence a confession made by Miguel to a police officer shortly after Miguel's arrest. Miguel claims that the confession was taken in violation of the *Miranda* rule (the rule requiring suspects to be informed of their right to remain silent) and therefore is inadmissible.

Question: How will the judge decide whether to admit the confession?

Answer: The judge will conduct a minitrial. After listening to foundational evidence about the confession and whether the police gave a *Miranda* warning, the judge will decide whether to admit the confession into evidence. To prevent the jury from learning about the confession unless the judge rules it admissible, the jury will be excused from the courtroom during the minitrial.

7. What are evidence minitrials?

Judges often have to hear a witness testify before they can determine whether the jury should be allowed to hear that same testimony. Evidence that determines the admissibility of other evidence is called "foundational evidence," and the phase of the trial devoted to foundational evidence is called a "minitrial." In jury trials, to prevent jurors from finding out about evidence that the judge ultimately rules inadmissible, the jury usually is excused from the courtroom during the minitrials.

8. What are "limiting" instructions?

Limiting instructions come into play when, as is often the case, evidence is admissible for one purpose but not for another. A judge will often instruct jurors to consider the evidence only for the legitimate purpose, and ignore it for any other purpose.

Following a limiting instruction can require mental dexterity that few people possess. For example, in an assault case in which the defense is self-defense, the alleged victim may testify, "A day before the fight, my brother told me that the defendant had once killed a man." This testimony may be admissible to show that the victim feared the defendant and therefore did not initiate the fight. At the same time, evidence rules would probably prevent the jury from considering the testimony as evidence that the defendant actually had killed a man (because for this purpose the testimony would be considered hearsay). In this situation, a judge might issue a limiting instruction warning the jurors not to consider the statement as evidence that the defendant actually had killed a man. The judge might say something like, "You may consider the evidence you've just heard only for its possible effect on the alleged victim's state of mind. You may not consider the statement as evidence that the defendant actually killed a man." While limiting instructions are common, their value is dubious because of the mental gymnastics required to follow them.

9. Can the defense assume that the judge will enforce the evidence rules without prompting by the defense?

No. Unlike football and basketball referees, who call fouls without waiting for the fouled team to make a request, most judges do not strike improper evidence on their own volition. Judges usually rule only when the defense or prosecution asks for a ruling by making an objection. To object, all the defense or prosecutor need do is to succinctly point out the reason for the error. For example, if the prosecutor asks a police officer to testify to a statement made by a witness shortly after the commission of a crime, the defense might say, "Objection, hearsay." If the judge finds that the objection is proper, the judge will sustain the objection. Otherwise, the judge will overrule it. If the judge wants clarification of the objection, the judge will ask for it.

10. At my trial my attorney let certain prosecution witnesses give inadmissible testimony without objecting to it. Does this mean my attorney acted incompetently?

Not necessarily. Making objections is as much an art as a science. Even if prosecution evidence is inadmissible, a defense attorney may decide not to object for any number of reasons. For example, the attorney might think the evidence helpful to the defense, or might regard the evidence as so exaggerated that the jury will not believe it. The defense attorney may also decide that objecting will call further attention to damaging evidence, whereas the jury may let the testimony go in one ear and out the next if the attorney simply says nothing. Another concern is that if a defense attorney objects too much (even if the objections are valid), the jury will view him or her as a nuisance or obstructive. Finally, the defense attorney may think that an objection will lead jurors to think that the defense is trying to hide evidence that isn't all that important in the first place. In the heat of trial, defense attorneys typically have to make instantaneous decisions about whether to object; they rarely have time to consult with clients.

Section II: Rules Regulating the Content of Testimony

This section is about what kinds of evidence can and cannot be introduced into a criminal trial for the purpose of influencing the decision of the judge or jury.

11. What's the most basic evidence rule?

Relevance (Federal Rule of Evidence 402) is the basic building block of evidence rules. For evidence to be relevant, some logical connection must exist between the evidence and the factual issue it is offered to prove or disprove. The connection needn't be so strong that any single item of evidence alone proves or disproves a fact. It's good enough if the piece of evidence constitutes a link in a chain of proof along with other pieces of evidence. (As the famous legal authority McCormick put it long ago, "A brick is not a wall.") The main limitation of the relevance rule is that the connection must be based on reason and logic rather than on bias and emotion.

> **CASE EXAMPLE 1:** Ruby Ridge is charged with stealing makeup from a drugstore the night before Halloween. The prosecution wants to offer evidence that Ruby's mom had refused to buy her a Halloween costume.
>
> **Question:** Is this evidence relevant?
>
> **Answer:** Yes. It tends to prove that Ruby had a motive for stealing the makeup.

> **CASE EXAMPLE 2:** Same case. The prosecution also wants to call the drugstore manager to testify that the makeup department suffers more thefts than any other department of the drugstore.
>
> **Question:** Is this evidence relevant?
>
> **Answer:** No. It does nothing to logically connect Ruby to the theft.

> **CASE EXAMPLE 3:** Lance Sellot is charged with drunk driving. The prosecution wants to offer evidence that Lance is a member of a violent street gang.
>
> **Question:** Is this evidence relevant?
>
> **Answer:** No. The crime charged has nothing to do with gang activities, so no logical connection exists between gang membership and whether Lance was drunk at the time he was arrested. The evidence would appeal only to a judge's or jurors' prejudices and emotions.

> **CASE EXAMPLE 4:** Clare Voyant is charged with car theft. Clare was arrested in her home, and the prosecution wants to offer evidence that the arresting officer found marijuana and an unregistered handgun in Clare's home.
>
> **Question:** Is the evidence relevant?
>
> **Answer:** No. No logical connection exists between car theft and possession

of marijuana and a handgun. Again, the evidence would appeal only to a judge's or jurors' prejudices and emotions.

12. Is relevant evidence always admissible?

No. Evidence has to be relevant to have any chance of admissibility, but not all relevant evidence is admissible. Judges often exclude relevant evidence because of some other evidence principle. For example, evidence that is otherwise relevant may have a great potential to unfairly stir a judge's or jurors' emotions and prejudices. In such situations, the judge is supposed to balance the importance of the evidence in the case against the risk of unfair prejudice (Federal Rule of Evidence 403). If the judge determines that the importance outweighs the risk of unfair prejudice, the judge admits the evidence. But if the judge determines that the risk of unfair prejudice substantially outweighs the importance, the judge excludes the evidence. Judges have lots of discretion when it comes to making such rulings. As a general rule, a judge is much more likely to exclude evidence as prejudicial in a jury trial than when the judge is hearing the case without a jury.

CASE EXAMPLE: Kai Ping is charged with assaulting Kevin Pong with a knife; Ping claims self-defense. In a jury trial, the prosecution seeks to offer into evidence the following three items: (a) the knife allegedly used in the assault; (b) a photograph of Pong taken minutes after the fight, showing cuts on Pong's face and arms; and (c) the bloodstained T-shirt that Pong was wearing at the time of the fight.

Question: Are these items admissible in evidence?

Answer: A judge is likely to admit the knife and the photograph into evidence, but exclude the shirt as unduly prejudicial. The size and shape of the knife and the nature of Pong's injuries are rationally related to the issue of whether Ping or Pong was the aggressor in the fight. But the bloody T-shirt has little probative value (that is, it isn't needed to understand what happened and therefore lacks importance to the case), and the sight of the bloody T-shirt may well inflame the jury against Ping.

13. Can I testify that something happened if I didn't personally observe it with one or more of my senses?

No. The "personal knowledge rule" (Federal Rule of Evidence 602) requires all witnesses (except expert witnesses) to testify based on firsthand information. For example, if Monty Vesuvius is going to testify that a defendant charged with drunk driving swilled down four martinis before jumping behind the wheel of a car, Vesuvius must actually have seen the defendant drink the martinis. Suppose Vesuvius says something like:

- "I assumed they were martinis because the defendant was drinking out of glasses that martinis are usually served in,"

- "I figure the defendant drank them because of the four empty glasses on the defendant's table," or
- "I know that the defendant drank the martinis because the bartender told me so."

Each statement shows that Vesuvius lacks personal knowledge and cannot testify to the issue of what the defendant drank. However, very little is required to show that personal knowledge existed. Most often, the judge will tilt toward letting questionable evidence in and leave it to the defense to bring out in cross-examination or closing argument just how shaky the evidence is.

CASE EXAMPLE 1: Babe Bear is charged with trespassing onto property owned by Goldie Locks; Bear's defense is mistaken identity. At trial, the prosecution wants Locks to identify Bear as the individual who ran out of her door when Locks came home after visiting her grandmother. In an evidence minitrial, Bear offers evidence that Locks had been drinking wine and was inebriated when she came home. Bear's evidence also shows that Locks, who normally wears glasses, was not wearing them when she came home.

Question: Should the judge rule that Locks lacks personal knowledge and therefore cannot testify?

Answer: No. Locks is testifying from personal knowledge, because she claims to have personally observed the events to which she is testifying. Whether the problems that Bear pointed out mean that Locks's testimony is not believable is a separate question— dealing with the weight of the evidence—that the judge or jury will have to decide at the end of the case.

CASE EXAMPLE 2: Sue Emmall is charged with possession of heroin. The prosecution plans to call Hy Enlow, Sue's next-door neighbor, to testify that Hy saw Sue holding a baggie of white powder that Hy believed to be cocaine.

Question: Is Hy's testimony proper?

Answer: In part. Hy can testify from personal knowledge that Sue was holding a baggie containing a white powder. However, only an expert drug analyst could testify to whether or not the powder is cocaine. Unless Hy were qualified as an expert, he could not testify to an opinion that the powder was cocaine.

14. As a defendant, can I introduce evidence that I'm really a good person?

Yes. The "mercy rule" allows a criminal defendant to offer evidence of his or her good character as a defense to criminal charges (Federal Rule of Evidence 404-a-1). For example, if the defendant is charged with embezzlement, the defendant could offer evidence that she is honest and law-abiding. (The evidence is relevant on the theory that honest and law-abiding people are less likely to steal money than people without this character trait.) Character evidence offered under the mercy rule is usually in the form of opinions from the defendant's close acquaintances. Like all other evidence, in order to be admissible, character evidence has to be relevant. This means that the trait of the defendant's character to which a witness testifies must have some connection to the charged crime.

> **CASE EXAMPLE 1:** Norman Bates is charged with assaulting Roseanne Fell.
>
> **Question:** Can Bates offer evidence from a close friend that, "In my opinion, Bates is a nonviolent person who wouldn't hurt a fly"?
>
> **Answer:** Yes. The mercy rule allows Bates to offer character evidence suggesting that he has a propensity to be peaceful, making it less likely that he assaulted Fell.
>
> **Question:** Can Bates also offer character evidence that he is honest?
>
> **Answer:** No. The character trait of honesty is irrelevant because the crime charged involves violence, not honesty.

15. Does the defense incur any risks by offering evidence of the defendant's good character?

Most definitely, which is why defendants rarely take advantage of the mercy rule. The primary risks are these:

- The opinion of a defendant's good character usually comes from a close acquaintance and may not, for that reason, carry much weight with a judge or jury.
- The prosecution can cross-examine a defendant's good-character witness, in the process bringing out evidence of a defendant's nasty past misdeeds that otherwise would have been inadmissible.
- Once the defendant introduces evidence of good character, the prosecution can call its own witnesses to testify to the defendant's bad character.

16. If the defense doesn't offer evidence of the defendant's good character, can the prosecutor offer evidence of the defendant's bad character?

In most situations, no. Evidence rules generally forbid prosecutors from presenting "bad" character evidence without the defendant first opening the door by presenting evidence of good character. Character evidence is barred in this situation because it is too prejudicial. A judge or jury might convict a defendant for being a "bad person," even if the evidence that the defendant committed the charged crime is weak.

Noncharacter "Bad Person" Evidence

Despite the rule barring prosecutors from offering evidence of a defendant's bad character, prosecutors routinely avoid the rule by arguing that the bad person evidence is relevant on a noncharacter theory (Federal Rule of Evidence 404-b). For example, a judge would probably permit a prosecutor trying to convict a defendant of assault to offer evidence that the defendant previously assaulted the same victim. A judge would probably rule that it is noncharacter evidence showing that the defendant had a grudge against the victim. A limiting instruction warning jurors against the forbidden character use of the evidence would be appropriate.

Another noncharacter theory that prosecutors often use to admit evidence of a defendant's past misdeeds is *modus operandi*, or "m.o." Under this theory, the prosecutor can offer evidence that the method a defendant used to commit past misdeeds is unique and nearly identical to the method the defendant allegedly used to commit the charged crime. Evidence of the past misdeeds is then admissible, not to paint the defendant as a bad person, but to show that the common m.o. points to the defendant as the perpetrator of the charged crime. Again, for whatever it's worth, a judge might give a limiting instruction.

Character Evidence in Sexual Assault Crimes

Legislatures and judges in many states have become alarmed by a perceived increase in sexual assault crimes such as rape and child molestation. Moreover, they believe that those who commit sexual assaults tend to repeat their crimes and that (especially when the victims are children) the crimes are very difficult to prove in court. As a result, many states have created special exceptions to the character evidence rules for sexual assault cases. The exceptions allow prosecutors to offer evidence that defendants charged with sexual assault or child molestation have committed those crimes in the past (Federal Rules of Evidence 413, 414). The exception for past acts of child molestation was a major factor in the media-saturated trial of Michael Jackson in Santa Maria, California, in 2005. Jackson, an international celebrity, was accused of molesting a teenage boy at Jackson's "Neverland" ranch. The judge allowed the prosecutor to offer evidence that Jackson had previously molested a number of other young boys. The lurid details of the previous crimes consumed many more days of the trial than did the testimony focused on the charged crimes. Jackson was eventually acquitted of all charges.

17. I've been called as a witness in a criminal trial. Can my character be attacked or supported?

Yes. Evidence rules allow the prosecution and the defense to attack the credibility of adverse witnesses by offering evidence of past misdeeds involving dishonesty (Federal Rules of Evidence 608, 609). Usually, such testimony is of one of the following types:

- evidence that a witness has been convicted of a felony, or a misdemeanor involving dishonesty (such as theft)
- evidence in the form of a witness's opinion that another witness is dishonest, or
- evidence that a witness has committed specific acts showing dishonesty, such as lying on a job application.

Evidence concerning a witness's character is limited to the trait of honesty, because only that trait is relevant to the credibility of a witness's testimony.

The Tough Choice Facing Defendants Who Have Previously Been Convicted of Crimes

Defendants who wish to testify in their own defense and who have previously been convicted of crimes are often faced with a difficult choice. If the defendant testifies, the prosecutor may be able to offer the defendant's prior conviction into evidence for the purpose of attacking the defendant's credibility as a witness. Even though the jury will be told that the conviction is relevant only to the defendant's credibility as a witness, the jury may well infer that the defendant is just a bad guy who deserves to be punished. By not testifying, the defendant usually can prevent the jury from finding out about the prior conviction (since the defendant's credibility as a witness is not in issue). But this may deprive the defense of valuable evidence, as well as arouse the suspicions of jurors who wonder why the defendant did not testify. For many defendants, neither option is appealing, and the decision is one that defendants and their attorneys should make only after careful consultation.

---

18. What are rape shield laws?

For many years, evidence rules permitted men on trial for rape to attack their female accusers' credibility by delving into the accusers' sexual histories. Typically the questions were highly embarrassing; the threat of having to answer them scared many women into not reporting the rape in the first place. Moreover, the relevance of previous sexual conduct to the victim's credibility or willingness to engage in sexual intercourse on a particular occasion was highly dubious. As the recognition of these problems grew, almost all jurisdictions enacted "rape shield laws" (see Federal Rule of Evidence 412), which prevent irrelevant inquiries into women's sexual histories. (See Chapter 12, Section V, for more information on rape.)

19. What is hearsay?

Hearsay is an out-of-court statement (or conduct that is the equivalent of a statement or assertion) that is offered for its truth. Out-of-court statements are assertions made in a manner other than by witnesses in court, and their admissibility is governed by what is known everywhere as the "hearsay rule." The purpose of the hearsay rule is to prevent witnesses from testifying to statements made by absentee individuals who can't be seen or cross-examined. In general, the hearsay rule excludes evidence of the "he said, she said" variety.

Nevertheless, as discussed below, out-of-court statements are often admissible in evidence despite the hearsay rule. One reason is that, depending on the purpose for which an out-of-court statement is offered, the hearsay rule may not even apply to it. An out-of-court statement frequently qualifies as "nonhearsay," and is therefore admissible in evidence. The second reason is that the rule is so riddled with exceptions that even when the rule does apply, out-of-court statements are often "hearsay, but admissible."

While the hearsay rule gives defendants the right to confront and cross-examine prosecution witnesses, defendants can forfeit this right if prosecution witnesses fail to testify at trial because the defendant engaged in wrongdoing with the intent of inducing the witnesses not to testify. (See *Giles v. California*, U.S. Sup. Ct. 2008.)

CASE EXAMPLE: Romeo is charged with attempting to kill his former girlfriend Juliet by giving her poison. Juliet survived and immediately told a police officer what happened. A few days before trial, acting on instructions from Romeo, Tybalt visits Juliet and tells her that "if you show up at trial and testify against Romeo, don't expect to survive." Juliet calls the prosecutor, says that she is too scared to testify and disappears.

Question: Has Romeo forfeited his right to cross-examine Juliet?

Answer: Yes. Romeo and Tybalt threatened Juliet with the intent of preventing her from testifying against Romeo. Since the threat succeeded in preventing Juliet from testifying, the judge may allow the police officer to testify to Juliet's hearsay statement describing how Romeo tried to kill her.

The Hearsay Rule Applies to Both Oral and Written Statements

Though the term "hearsay" implies that the rule applies only to oral statements, it applies to written statements as well. Statements in letters, emails, business reports, and other documents may be hearsay or not, depending on the use to which they are put. And just like oral assertions, the contents of documents may be admissible under an exception to the hearsay rule.

20. How do I know whether an out-of-court statement is hearsay?

An assertion whose relevance does not depend on its truth is nonhearsay, and therefore the hearsay rule does not apply. Thus, the first question when analyzing the admissibility of an out-of-court statement under the hearsay rule is, "What is the statement offered to prove?" If the statement is offered to prove something other than its truth, it is nonhearsay.

> **CASE EXAMPLE 1:** Cole Slawson is charged with murdering Barbie Cue on September 6. Cole claims that Barbie was still alive on September 7, and therefore Cole could not have killed her on September 6. Cole calls Sal to testify that Barbie (whose voice she knows well) phoned her on September 7 and said, "I'm still alive."

Question: Is Sal's testimony to Barbie's out-of-court statement barred by the hearsay rule?

Answer: No. It is admissible as nonhearsay to support Cole's defense. Cole is not offering Barbie's statement (through the testimony of Sal) for its truth. That is, it makes no difference whether Barbie's words are true or false. If Barbie utters any words on September 7 (even, "I'm dead"), she clearly could not have died on September 6.

> **CASE EXAMPLE 2:** Barr Nunn is charged with assaulting Slim Pickens with a deadly weapon. To prove that the object with which Nunn struck Pickens was a beer bottle, the prosecutor wants Violet to testify, "The day after the fight, the bartender told me that Nunn hit Pickens with a beer bottle."

Question: Is Violet's testimony hearsay?

Answer: Yes, it is classic inadmissible hearsay. The bartender's statement is relevant to prove that Nunn used a beer bottle only if the words in the statement are true.

> **CASE EXAMPLE 3:** Same case. Nunn's defense is that he is not guilty because Pickens attacked first and Nunn acted in self-defense. To prove that Pickens would not have attacked Nunn, the prosecutor wants Violet to testify, "The night before the fight, Pickens told me that Nunn always carries a gun and is not afraid to use it."

Question: Is Violet's testimony hearsay?

Answer: No. Pickens's statement shows that he feared Nunn. If Pickens feared Nunn, Pickens might not attack him. Thus, even if the statement was inaccurate (that is, even if Nunn did not actually carry a gun), it nevertheless undermines Nunn's self-defense claim, and so it serves the nonhearsay purpose of showing the victim Pickens' state of mind.

CASE EXAMPLE 4: Same case. Hearing the fight, a police officer rushes into the bar to find Slim Pickens lying on the floor, bleeding from a head wound. The police officer looks to the bartender and asks, "Who hit this man?" Without saying a word, the bartender points to Barr Nunn.

Question: Is the officer's question and the bartender's act of pointing at Nunn hearsay that can't be admitted into evidence?

Answer: Yes. The bartender's pointing to Nunn is the equivalent of the statement, "Nunn is the one who hit Pickens." Since the pointing would only be relevant to the case if it were true, it would be considered hearsay and not admissible in evidence—unless one of the exceptions applies.

21. You mean the defense can just avoid the hearsay rule by saying it's offering an out-of-court statement for something other than its truth?

It's not quite that simple. The out-of-court assertion has to be relevant for its nontruth purposes. Otherwise the assertion is inadmissible.

CASE EXAMPLE: As evidence that John committed a crime, the prosecution wants a police officer to testify, "Marcia told me that she saw John commit the crime." When the defense attorney objects on the ground of hearsay, the prosecutor responds, "I'm not offering this to prove that Marcia's statement was true, only that the police officer talked to Marcia."

Question: Should the judge permit the police officer to testify to Marcia's statement?

Answer: No. The fact that a police officer talked to Marcia is irrelevant to John's guilt or innocence. In these circumstances, if the prosecution cannot offer Marcia's out-of-court assertion for its truth, it cannot offer the assertion into evidence at all.

Judges Have Discretion to Exclude Nonhearsay

The fact that an out-of-court statement may be relevant as nonhearsay is not an automatic ticket to admissibility. The judge can exclude nonhearsay if there's a risk the jury will improperly consider the statement for its truth, and such risk substantially outweighs the importance of the nonhearsay use. An example of this arose in a famous 1930s case involving the murder trial of Dr. Shepard. Dr. Shepard was charged with poisoning his wife; he claimed that she committed suicide. The government offered into evidence a statement made by Mrs. Shepard to her nurse shortly before Mrs. Shepard's death. According to the nurse, Mrs. Shepard said, "Dr. Shepard has poisoned me." The government claimed that the statement was admissible as nonhearsay: It wasn't offered for its truth, but as evidence that Mrs. Shepard was not in a suicidal frame of mind. (The government's theory was that people bent on suicide don't accuse others of killing them.) The U.S. Supreme Court said that while the statement might be relevant as nonhearsay, it should have been excluded because its importance to that issue was outweighed by the great danger that the jury would regard it as true. In memorable words, Justice Cardozo wrote for the Court that "Discrimination so subtle is a feat beyond the compass of ordinary minds. The accusatory clang of those words would drown all weaker sounds" (*Shepard v. U.S.*, U.S. Sup. Ct. 1933).

22. Can I testify to my own out-of-court statements?

The hearsay rule applies the same to all statements, whether made by other people or by a testifying witness. Thus, if the relevance of a witness's own statement depends on its truth, the hearsay rule would prevent the witness from testifying to the witness's own out-of-court statement— unless an exception to the hearsay rule applies.

23. If the relevance of an out-of-court statement depends on its truth, does that mean the statement will be automatically barred by the hearsay rule?

No. Expanding on the common law, all jurisdictions recognize various exceptions to the hearsay rule. Most of these exceptions exist because legislators who make the evidence rules think that out-of-court assertions made in specific circumstances are likely to be reliable—simply by force of circumstance. So many exceptions exist that many judges and lawyers think that the rule should be rewritten to say, "Hearsay evidence is admissible, unless an attorney is too dumb to think of an exception." If an exception applies, an out-of-court statement is admissible even though its relevance depends on its truth.

Among the more colorful or popular exceptions are the following.

Excited utterances. This exception admits into evidence statements made under the stress of excitement of perceiving an unusual event. The notion is that people are unlikely to lie when they describe a sudden and exciting event at the time the event occurs. For example, assume that a witness to a bank robbery says right after the robbery, "Oh my God, did you see that? The bank robber had a tattoo on his left ear!" This would qualify as an excited utterance, as it describes an obviously exciting situation and was made immediately afterward. By contrast, in northern California, a motorist's assertion, "By golly, that driver ran the red light," would probably not qualify as an excited utterance. An event has to be unusual to produce the necessary excitement.

Dying declarations. This exception admits into evidence statements made under a sense of immediately impending death. The theory is that such statements are trustworthy because "people don't want to meet their Maker with a lie on their lips."

Admissions by the defendant. This exception makes admissible the defendant's out-of-court statements when offered into evidence by the prosecutor. (Remember, defendants can't offer their own out-of-court statements into evidence.) For example, if a defendant waives her *Miranda* rights and talks to a police officer after she is arrested (see Chapter 1), the prosecutor can call the police officer as a witness and offer the defendant's statement into evidence.

Assertions of state of mind. This exception admits into evidence statements setting forth people's emotions, beliefs, intent, etc. The exception rests in the importance of testimony about mental states in many criminal cases, and people's trustworthiness in describing such matters; for example, why would they lie? In the famous, though grisly, U.S. Supreme Court case that gave rise to this exception (*Hillmon v. Mutual Life Insurance*, U.S. Sup. Ct. 1892), the issue was the identity of a badly-burned corpse found near Crooked Creek, Colorado. Hillmon's widow claimed it was her husband; the insurance company claimed it was a man named Walters. The insurance company wanted to offer into evidence a letter written by Walters to his fiancée a few days before the corpse was found in which Walters said, "I'm going to Crooked Creek to meet up with Hillmon." The Court held that the letter was admissible to show Walters's intent to go to Crooked Creek. Walters's intent to go to Crooked Creek was relevant because it showed that Walters probably did go to Crooked Creek (thus increasing the chance that the corpse was Walters).

Prior inconsistent statements. If a witness's testimony varies in some important way from prior out-of-court statements made by that witness, the prior statements are admissible in evidence. For example, a police officer testifies in court, "I heard what sounded like a smashed window, and went to investigate." But the officer's police report prepared prior to trial states, "After being informed of a smashed window, I went to investigate." The statement in the police report is admissible as a prior inconsistent statement; the defendant may want to offer it into evidence to cast doubt on the accuracy of the officer's testimony.

Business and government records. Written records reflecting regular business and government activities are often admissible under exceptions to the hearsay rule. Presumably, the regularity with which they are prepared, and a business's and government agency's need for accurate records, makes them trustworthy.

Police Report as Government Record

A police report generally consists of an officer's account of events leading up to an arrest, and sometimes of a postarrest investigation. Because a police report often simply recounts statements by witnesses, and no exceptions apply to the witnesses' statements, police reports frequently are barred from evidence by the hearsay rule. However, sometimes, in state courts, a portion of a police report may be admitted into evidence as a government record. For example, if a police officer arrives at the scene of a hit-and-run, measures skidmarks and records the measurements in a police report pursuant to the officer's official duties, that portion of the police report may be admissible in evidence.

Still Confused by the Hearsay Rule?

You're not alone! The ins and outs of the hearsay rule can be very complex; even experienced lawyers and judges sometimes find hearsay issues difficult to resolve. The discussion in this chapter should help a defendant discuss hearsay issues with his or her lawyer. Self-represented defendants should consult with a legal coach if evidence important to the defense or prosecution consists of a witness's written or oral out-of-court statement.

24. What is expert testimony? How does it differ from regular testimony?

Experts have special education, training, or experience that allows them to testify to opinions on matters beyond everyday understanding. Experts are not limited by the personal knowledge rule. (See Question 13, above.) Experts may give opinions based on information provided by other witnesses or contained in written reports. Also, unlike other witnesses, experts can and do demand payment for testifying.

CASE EXAMPLE: Hap Hazard is on trial for robbery; the defense is an alibi. Hap wants the jury to understand the factors that he claims caused the eyewitnesses to mistakenly identify him as the robber.

Question: Can Hap offer expert testimony to support this claim?

Answer: Yes. Most courts have ruled that factors affecting people's ability to observe and recollect are sufficiently beyond everyday understanding to allow experts to testify. In this case, Hap might hire a forensic cognitive psychologist to explain to the jury factors that commonly lead to mis-identifications.

25. Since I'm indigent and represented by a court-appointed lawyer, who will pay the expert witness if one is needed in my case?

Experts are expensive. It's not unusual for an expert to charge defendants a few thousand dollars for a day of testimony, with an additional fee for preparation time. Fees are less of a problem for prosecutors, since fingerprint experts, ballistics experts, and laboratory technicians who testify to such matters as blood alcohol levels in drunk driving cases often are already on the government payroll.

Court-appointed lawyers do not have the funding to hire an expert on every case. However, a court-appointed lawyer can petition a judge for appointment of an expert. If a judge considers an expert's opinion legally necessary or helpful to a fair resolution of the case, the judge can appoint an expert at government expense. For example, an expert who might charge private clients $3,000 might have to accept $750 per day for a court-appointed case (assuming the expert agrees to participate at those rates).

CASE EXAMPLE: Nell Shrap is on trial for making a telephoned bomb threat. The prosecutor's primary evidence is an audiotape of the threat. A government voice identification expert will testify that the voice on the tape is Nell's. Nell is indigent.

Question: How can her court-appointed attorney arrange for expert help?

Answer: Nell's attorney can file a pretrial motion requesting appointment of a voice identification expert at government expense. The defense expert can consult with Nell's attorney, check the procedures of the prosecutor's expert, and testify on Nell's behalf at trial.

Special Interest Organizations as Sources of Expert Witnesses

If a special interest organization believes that a defense has sufficient importance and legal justification, in high-publicity cases the organization may hire an expert to appear in support of the defendant's case. For example, assume that a woman charged with assaulting her husband relies on the defense of battered wife syndrome. Women's rights groups, such as the National Organization for Women, might be willing to provide an expert to testify on the defendant's behalf.

26. What is a "chain of custody"?

A chain of custody is the more complex foundation needed for the admissibility of certain types of exhibits as evidence. Exhibits are tangible objects that are relevant to the facts of a case. A stolen calculator in a shoplifting case; the drugs in an illegal possession of controlled substances case—the photograph of a broken window in a burglary case; the printout of a breathalyzer machine in a drunk driving case; all these are exhibits. Proving that an exhibit being offered into evidence is exactly what it is represented to be—the drugs found on the defendant or the calculator stolen from the store—requires proof of who had possession of the exhibit at all times between the time the evidence was seized and the trial. Proving this chain of custody is especially necessary when exhibits are subject to alteration or are tested prior to trial.

Because criminal prosecutions typically depend on evidence gathered by police officers, it is prosecutors who generally need to establish a chain of custody. In turn, a typical defense strategy is to attack the sufficiency of the prosecutor's chain. If the defense succeeds in preventing the prosecutor from offering an exhibit into evidence, the judge might rule that the prosecutor has insufficient evidence to allow a case to continue.

For example, assume that Hy Immer is on trial for possessing illegal drugs. To prove Immer guilty, the prosecutor must offer the packet of powder that a police officer removed from Immer's pocket into evidence, and prove that the powder is an illegal drug. To establish the chain of custody for the packet, the prosecutor will have to do the following:

- show that the officer who seized the packet marked it in a way that enables the officer to distinguish it from other similar items that may have been taken from other suspects
- prove that the police stored the packet in a way that provides reasonable assurance that nobody tampered with its contents
- call a qualified expert to testify to the chemical composition of the contents of the packet
- establish that the packet given to and tested by the expert is the one that the officer seized from Immer
- prove that the testing procedures were properly carried out, and
- prove that the packet tested by the expert is the same packet as the one the police bring to the trial.

Immer's attorney can challenge each and every step in this foundation. If the prosecutor cannot convince the judge that the foundation is adequate, the judge will rule the packet inadmissible and, in all probability, dismiss the case.

Section III: Rules Regulating the Manner of Testimony

This section is about the rules that govern how information, testimony, and exhibits are actually turned into evidence that can be considered by the judge or jury.

27. Why does the prosecution get to go first in a trial?

The usual explanation is that the prosecution has the burden of proof. It is therefore fair to allow the prosecution to present its evidence first. Actually, this order can be an advantage to a defendant. The prosecution often has to present its case without knowing much about the defense's line of attack. However, the advantage is temporary, since the prosecution has a chance to respond to the defense evidence in a part of the trial called the rebuttal.

28. Can the defense lawyer help me or another defense witness over any rough spots in our testimony?

On direct examination, a lawyer cannot use leading questions to signal the answers that the lawyer wants the witness to give. For example, assume that the defense lawyer wants a defense witness to testify that she arrived home at 9 p.m. The lawyer cannot ask, "Did you arrive home at 9 p.m.?" Instead, the lawyer would have to ask a less leading question such as, "What time did you arrive home?"

However, defense lawyers can use a variety of other methods to help defendants and defense witnesses through their testimony. First, defense lawyers can and should meet with their clients and witnesses before trial to review their testimony. And if the witness forgets something while testifying, the lawyer can show the witness a letter, report, or other document to refresh the witness's memory. Many judges will even permit lawyers to ask leading questions if a witness has had an obvious glitch in recall.

> **CASE EXAMPLE:** Jesse James is charged with armed robbery; his defense is mistaken identity. The prosecutor calls Kit Carson as a witness and asks, "You saw the defendant rob the store, is that correct?"
>
> **Question:** Is this a proper direct examination question?
>
> **Answer:** No. It is a leading question, because it suggests the prosecutor's desired answer. Defense counsel can object and force the prosecutor to ask a nonleading question. For example, the prosecutor might properly ask, "Please look around the courtroom and tell us if you see the person whom you saw with a gun in the store."

29. Will the prosecutor ask me or other defense witnesses questions in the same manner as my lawyer?

No. On cross-examination, lawyers are allowed to ask leading questions. Prosecutors typically ask narrow questions that try to force defendants and their witnesses to provide information helpful to the prosecutors. Of course, defendants and their witnesses must testify truthfully at all times. But they must be careful to avoid going along with misleading information in the prosecutors' leading questions. For example, if a defense witness's story is that an incident occurred "at dusk," the witness should not meekly go along with the prosecutor's leading question, "It was really dark out there, wasn't it?"

To be sure that they testify as truthfully and accurately during a hostile cross-examination as during a friendly direct questioning, defendants and their witnesses must:

- listen carefully to the prosecutor's questions and pause if necessary before answering them
- stay calm and not get into an argument with the prosecutor, and
- tell the judge if they are unable to answer a question. For example, a witness who lacks personal knowledge should say, "I don't know" rather than guess at an answer. And a witness who has to qualify a "yes" or "no" answer to make it accurate should say, "Your Honor, I can answer that question only if I'm allowed to explain my answer."

CASE EXAMPLE: Jesse James is still on trial for armed robbery. After witness Kit Carson testifies and identifies James as the robber, defense counsel cross-examines Carson. Defense counsel asks, "You had drunk three whiskeys within a half hour of entering the store, correct?"

Question: Is this a proper question?

Answer: Yes. The question is leading, but leading questions are permitted on cross-examination. Since Carson is likely to be hostile to the cross-examiner, Carson likely won't agree with the cross-examiner if the information is false.

30. Will I have to deal with the kind of nasty and aggressive questioning that I see on TV and in the movies?

No. How TV and film lawyers ask questions is largely a product of past history and the screenwriter's imagination. Attorneys are officers of the court, and must respect the institution of trial no matter what their views of the opposing witnesses. Lawyers also don't want the jury to think they are bullies, for fear that the jurors will then sympathize with the witness under attack. Defendants and defense witnesses who are confronted by improper prosecutorial questioning must remain cool and allow the defense attorney to object to the prosecutors' tactics. Defendants and their witnesses must also know how to protect themselves if defense counsel fails to object.

Common forms of improper questions include the following:

a. Argumentative questions (popularly known as "badgering the witness")

These questions do not ask for information. Instead, they are derisive comments or legal arguments put by the prosecutor in the form of questions. Typical argumentative questions are:

- "You expect the jury to believe that story?"
- "Shouldn't the jury believe the police officer who testified rather than you?"
- "With all the evidence against you, how can you deny that you stole the watch?"

Self-protection note: Defendants and their witnesses should not argue with the prosecutor. Instead, they can use an argumentative question as an opportunity to reinforce favorable testimony. For example, a witness might respond to the first question above by testifying, "I don't expect the jury to believe anything. I'm just here telling you what happened."

b. Questions that assume facts not in evidence

Prosecutors are supposed to ask questions, not testify. Questions that assume facts not in evidence violate the rule by making factual assertions to which witnesses have no chance to respond. Consider these examples:

- "Most people are terrified at the sight of a weapon, yet you were calm at the time of the robbery?"
- "Even though there were at least ten people in front of the electronics counter, you recognized immediately that Jones was a security guard?"

Self-protection note: Defendants and their witnesses can respond to the prosecutor's assumed fact while reinforcing prior testimony. For example, to the first question a witness might say, "I can't tell you how most people react to a gun. All I can tell you is that on this occasion, I was calm." Similarly, in the second example a witness might testify, "I wasn't counting how many people were at the counter. I can only repeat that for the reasons I already gave, I immediately picked out Jones as a security guard."

c. Questions that misquote witnesses

During cross-examination, prosecutors sometimes refer to testimony that a witness has previously given. But they cannot try to alter the meaning of the testimony by misquoting it. Consider these examples:

- On direct examination, a defendant testifies, "I was at the movies with a friend at 9 p.m." The prosecutor asks, "You say that you were with a friend at some point in the evening?"
- On direct examination, a defense witness testifies, "I had a couple of beers." The prosecutor: "You admit that you were a bit high yourself, right?"

Self-protection note: Witnesses should remind prosecutors of their actual testimony. For example, the witness's response in the second case might be, "I didn't say that I was high, I said that I had a couple of beers."

d. Questions that ask witnesses to speculate or draw improper conclusions

These questions improperly ask witnesses to testify to matters outside their personal knowledge. Consider these examples:

- "If you had seen Stephanie on the corner, would you have tried to make a drug deal?"
- "Dressed as you were, would Katz have been pretty frightened of you when you walked in?"

Self-protection note: Witnesses should not speculate. They often lose credibility in front of a jury by speculating about things they know nothing about. Thus, in the first case the witness might respond, "I can't tell you what might have happened if I'd seen Stephanie on the corner."

31. Can I listen while other witnesses testify?

Sequestered witnesses cannot watch the trial until they have finished testifying. However, unlike witnesses, defendants can't be excluded from a courtroom. Defendants have a constitutional right to be present throughout a trial. Defendants often take advantage of this right by testifying last. By testifying last, defendants can listen to all the other witnesses and direct their testimony to conflicts or ambiguities in the defense case.

RESOURCE

For more on the rules of evidence, see *Represent Yourself in Court: How to Prepare & Try a Winning Case,* by Paul Bergman and Sara J. Berman (Nolo).

Section IV: Scientific Evidence

This section is about what's called forensic evidence—evidence such as fingerprints and DNA analysis that depend on scientific techniques for their reliability.

32. What is scientific evidence?

Scientific evidence is information that has been developed through a process known as the "scientific method." Typically (but not always), scientific evidence has been published in journals, tested by other scientists, and generally accepted as valid within the relevant scientific community. Common examples of scientific evidence include DNA analysis, hair and fiber comparisons, fingerprints, and voice identification evidence. Since scientific evidence is by definition beyond the realm of judges' and jurors' everyday experiences, the prosecution and the defense use qualified expert witnesses to introduce scientific evidence into the courtroom.

33. How does a judge decide whether to admit scientific evidence?

Judges accept many scientific theories as so well established that testimony from a qualified expert witness based on those theories is always admissible. For example, an expert seldom is called on to convince a judge of the validity of fingerprint analysis or radar speed testing devices. However, whenever an expert testifies, the party calling the expert has the burden of convincing the judge that the testimony is reliable and therefore appropriate for consideration by the judge or jury. This is true whether the expert's testimony is based on scientific principles, such as those underlying DNA testing, or nonscientific principles, such as an expert jewelry appraiser's estimate of a gem's value (*Kumbo Tire Co. v. Carmichael,* U.S. Sup. Ct. 1999).

To establish the reliability of scientific evidence, the party seeking to introduce the evidence ordinarily schedules a minitrial (see Question 7, above) in which an expert testifies and explains the scientific methodology. For example, to use DNA evidence for the purpose of identifying a suspect (by comparing samples taken from the suspect with samples found at the crime scene), the prosecutor is still required by some judges to first establish the reliability of that evidence in a minitrial. If the judge is then convinced of its reliability, DNA evidence can be used in that case.

"Junk Science"

Scientific evidence has become a routine part of most trials. In turn, many judges and lawyers have become concerned about so-called junk science. There is no clear definition of junk science. Generally, the term applies when information offered by a prosecution or defense witness is claimed to have a scientific basis whereas, judged by the standards of mainstream scientists, it doesn't. The fear is that juries will be easily bamboozled by pseudo-experts who will testify to anything for a price. The burden falls mainly on judges (very few of whom are trained in the scientific method) to distinguish between valid and invalid scientific testimony.

---

34. How reliable and accurate is expert testimony based on scientific principles and testing?

Since its inception, DNA testing has exonerated about 200 convicts, including some who were on death row. A significant portion of these wrongful convictions were based on scientific failures. (Mistaken eyewitness identification testimony is the number one cause of wrongful convictions.)

Expert scientific testimony may be inaccurate either because the underlying principles are wrong, or because crime lab tests are unreliable or carried out sloppily. Here are some of the documented failures:

- The Chief Serologist of the West Virginia Police Crime Lab was found to have falsified test results in at least 134 cases over a ten-year period.

- A forensic chemist in the Oklahoma City Police Crime Laboratory was repeatedly rebuked by appellate courts for withholding exonerating test results from defense attorneys and for gross delays in providing defendants with test results.

- Experts have frequently connected defendants to crimes based on hair comparison analysis principles that are scientifically unreliable.

- A study of Houston's Police Crime Lab revealed so many problems with its procedures that a Texas state senator concluded that "the validity of almost any case that has relied upon evidence produced by the lab is questionable."

- The FBI Crime Laboratory, generally regarded as the country's premier forensic facility, has admitted to a variety of mistakes. Technicians at the lab misidentified the explosive charge in the Oklahoma City bombing case, falsified DNA testing procedures, relied on a method of bullet lead analysis that lacked scientific validity, and reported fingerprint matches when none existed.

A 2009 report prepared by the prestigious National Academy of Sciences describes the problems in U.S. crime labs and recommends a variety of reforms. These include standardization of testing procedures, increased training for lab technicians, and increased reliance on random proficiency testing. Of course, such reforms are costly and not easy to implement rapidly. The report will no doubt stimulate many criminal defense attorneys to increase their attacks on the accuracy of the results produced by police crime labs.

Compared to other types of testimony on which prosecutors commonly rely (for example, eyewitness identification, confessions, and police informants), scientific evidence has the potential to be far more neutral and reliable. Hopefully, the scientific community will take the lead in enhancing the accuracy and reliability of expert testimony based on scientific testing. (For further information, refer to the excellent article by Paul Giannelli, "Wrongful Convictions and Forensic Science: The Need to Regulate Crime Labs" in Vol. 86 of *The North Carolina Law Review*, pages 163–235 (2007).)

Galileo's Return

Before the U.S. Supreme Court decided the case of *Daubert v. Merrill Dow Pharmaceuticals* in 1993, in most jurisdictions a party seeking to offer scientific evidence had to establish that a particular scientific methodology was "generally accepted" among scientists. Many critics thought this test was unduly conservative. They pointed out that this test would have prevented Galileo from testifying that the world was round, since the earth's roundness was not generally accepted among scientists in Galileo's day. Under *Daubert*, general acceptance is simply one of many factors a judge can consider when deciding whether to admit novel scientific evidence. However, a number of states, most notably California, still follow the general acceptance rule. The result is that new scientific approaches to crime detection often are not used for years after their development—until they win general acceptance in the scientific community. (See Question 36 about lie detector tests for a good example of how this works.)

35. Is DNA evidence routinely admissible at trial?

Yes. Most judges today accept expert evidence based on DNA analysis. The universally-accepted theory underlying DNA analysis is that every person (except an identical twin) has a unique molecular makeup. Different methodologies allow experts to identify the portions of DNA molecules that establish a person's uniqueness. The most common of these methodologies is RFLP, or the Restriction Fragment Length Polymorphism Technique. By comparing an individual's known DNA with a sample of DNA from a crime scene (for example, in a droplet of blood or a strand of hair), an expert can give an opinion concerning the likelihood that both samples came from the same individual.

36. Can DNA evidence ever benefit the defense?

Certainly. The defense may offer DNA evidence to establish that the defendant is not guilty of a charged crime by showing that DNA found on the victim could not have come from him. In some instances, DNA evidence has resulted in the belated release of incarcerated defendants who were wrongly convicted before DNA technology was available for use in court.

A "CSI Effect"?

A currently popular television show called *CSI: Crime Scene Investigation* glamorizes the role of forensic scientists who use sophisticated scientific techniques to link defendants to crimes. Many prosecutors claim that *CSI* has made actual jurors reluctant to vote to convict when, as is typically true, forensic evidence is neither necessary nor available.

37. Are the results of a polygraph (lie detector) test admissible at trial?

Usually, no. The theory underlying polygraph testing is that lying is stressful, and that this stress can be detected and recorded on a polygraph machine if the defendant lies in response to the examiner's questions. Lie detectors are called polygraphs because the test consists of simultaneously monitoring several of the suspect's physiological functions (breathing, pulse, and galvanic skin response) and printing out the results on graph paper—which in turn can demonstrate exactly when in the questioning period the greatest stress occurred. If the period of greatest stress lines up with the key questions on the graph paper, this testing method presumes the subject is lying.

Supporters of lie detector tests claim that the test is reliable because (1) very few people can control all three physiological functions at the same time, and (2) polygraph examiners run preexamination tests on the suspect that enable the examiners to measure that individual's reaction to telling a lie. Critics of polygraph testing argue that (1) many subjects can indeed conceal stress even when they are aware that they are lying, and (2) there is no reliable way to distinguish an individual's stress generated by the test and the stress generated by a particular lie.

Most jurisdictions continue to doubt the reliability of lie detector tests. Some states do admit the results of polygraph tests at trial, at least if the prosecution and defendant stipulate (agree) prior to the test that its results will be admissible.

38. If a prosecution witness was hypnotized sometime before trial, can this affect the admissibility of the witness's testimony?

Yes. The police sometimes use hypnosis as an investigative tool. The police hope that while under hypnosis, victims or witnesses will recall details that they could not recall while fully conscious. At trial, the prosecutor may ask a witness to testify to details that the witness first recalled while under hypnosis.

However, many judges are skeptical of the reliability of details that emerge while a person is under hypnosis. For example, judges fear that some people will make up details in a subconscious effort to please the hypnotist, and that previously hypnotized witnesses will be impervious to cross-examination because they have faith in whatever they recalled while under hypnosis, regardless of its objective accuracy. Thus, some states do not allow previously hypnotized witnesses to testify at all, forcing police and prosecutors to choose between hypnotizing a witness to develop leads for investigation and using the witness at trial. Other states do allow previously hypnotized witnesses to testify, but limit their testimony to information that the witnesses recalled and reported to the police prior to being hypnotized.

39. What is neutron activation analysis?

Neutron activation analysis (NAA) is a method of identifying, analyzing, and comparing numerous types of physical evidence. For example, the NAA technique can:

- detect gunshot residue on the hand of a person who recently fired a gun
- identify the color, brand, and composition of paint, and
- detect the presence of certain narcotics.

The NAA technique measures gamma rays emitted by a sample of material after that material has been bombarded with neutrons in a nuclear reactor. NAA analysis tends to be expensive, and therefore used only when a case warrants it. Judges generally accept expert testimony concerning NAA results, though some judges still require a minitrial to establish the validity of NAA methodology.

40. How may the authenticity of unusual documents be established?

By experts known as "questioned document examiners." These people apply scientific techniques to explain when and how a particular document originated, and whether a particular signature or other handwriting on the document is authentic or a forgery. Judges routinely admit testimony from questioned document examiners into evidence. For example, questioned document examiners may:

- compare two handwriting samples and give an opinion as to whether the same person wrote both. For example, the testimony of questioned document examiners who looked at ransom notes was crucial to the 1932 conviction of Bruno Hauptmann for kidnapping and killing the Lindbergh baby. The experts testified that, among many other things, both Hauptmann and the author of the ransom notes wrote "t" in the word "the" in such a way that it resembled a "u."

- give an opinion as to the make and model typewriter used to prepare a typed document. For example, an expert may trace vertical misalignment in certain characters to a particular typewriter.

- restore burned or water-damaged documents sufficiently to read them.

41. What does fingerprint evidence consist of?

Fingerprint evidence rests on two basic principles: (1) a person's "friction ridge patterns" don't change, and (2) no two people have the same pattern of friction ridges. Because judges normally accept these principles as true, parties seeking to offer fingerprint evidence at trial do not have to convince the judge of the validity of the methodology underlying fingerprint evidence.

> ## More About Fingerprint Evidence
>
> Friction ridges (that are the same on each person's fingers and foot soles) contain rows of sweat pores. Sweat mixed with other body oils and dirt produces fingerprints on smooth surfaces. Fingerprint experts use powders and chemicals to make such prints visible. The age of fingerprints is almost impossible to determine. Therefore, defendants often try to explain away evidence that their fingerprints were found at crime scenes by testifying that they were at the scene and left the prints at a time other than the time of a crime.
>
> Police officers can use fingerprints to identify defendants and crime victims if a print matches one already on file. People's fingerprints can be on file for a variety of reasons. For example, people may be fingerprinted when they are arrested, or when they join certain occupations.

42. What are forensic pathologists?

Forensic pathologists, often coroners, testify to the time and causes of death. For example, based on medical training and pathological expertise, a forensic pathologist may testify that a victim found dead in water actually died from strangulation before entering the water. Or a pathologist may give an opinion as to the type of object used to deliver a blunt force injury.

Section V: Privileged (Confidential) Information

This section summarizes evidence rules that establish "privileges." Privileges are rules that sometimes prevent the disclosure of private communications made in the course of confidential relationships. The rules are complex and can vary greatly from one state to another. Nevertheless, this general summary will give you an idea of what's going on should a privilege issue arise in a case in which you're involved.

43. What are "privileged communications"?

Privileged communications are statements made in private and in the course of a relationship that is privileged under a state's laws. For example, all states grant privileges for private communications between:

- attorneys and clients
- physicians (and other medical personnel) and patients
- spouses, and
- ministers and congregants.

Privilege laws such as these encourage clients to talk freely and openly to attorneys and clients, spouses to talk freely and openly to each other, and congregants to speak freely and openly to priests, ministers, rabbis, and other religious representatives. States create such privileges because lawmakers have decided that society has a greater interest in protecting these relationships than in placing before judges and jurors all the evidence that might be relevant to case outcomes.

In addition to the standard privileges that exist in all states, other states have additional privilege rules that protect private communications between:

- journalists and informants, and
- psychotherapists and patients.

CASE EXAMPLE: When they are alone, Greg Airias admits to his father that he committed a burglary. Greg is later charged with burglary, and at trial the prosecutor calls the father as a witness and asks the father to testify to Greg's statement.

Question: Can Greg's father refuse to answer the question by claiming a privilege, since the communication was a private one between a parent and a child?

Answer: Greg's father probably would have to answer the question. Few states have enacted a privilege for private communications between parents and children.

Question: What could happen if Greg's father refuses to testify despite the judge's order to do so, because he swore to his son that he would never reveal what the son told him?

Answer: The judge would have the power to hold Greg's father in contempt of court and commit him to jail for refusing a valid order to testify. Most judges, however, would be reluctant to send Greg's father to jail in these circumstances.

44. What is the consequence of a judge's ruling that a communication is privileged?

The person protected by a privilege, known as the "holder" of a privilege (for example, a client who communicates with an attorney), can legally refuse to disclose what was said. The other party to the communication (for example, the attorney to whom the client spoke) must also refuse to disclose what was said unless authorized by the holder of the privilege to speak. The privilege bars disclosure at every stage of a criminal case, including pretrial hearings, at trial, and during postconviction proceedings.

> **CASE EXAMPLE:** Sue Cherr receives medical treatment for a knife wound she received during a fight in a tavern. While she is being treated, Sue describes to the doctor the circumstances leading up to her being wounded.
>
> **Question:** Can the prosecution compel either Sue or her doctor to disclose what Sue said to the doctor as to how she came to be wounded?
>
> **Answer:** No. Sue's private statements to her doctor would probably be privileged, meaning that neither Sue nor the doctor can be compelled to disclose what Sue said.
>
> **Question:** Sue wants the doctor to testify to what she said about how she came to be wounded in the knife fight because she thinks the testimony will

help her defense. Can Sue "waive" (give up) the privilege and allow the doctor to testify?

> **Answer:** Yes. Sue is the holder of the privilege so she has the power to authorize the doctor to reveal her (Sue's) statement as to how she came to be wounded.

45. When a privilege exists, does it protect all communications made in the course of that confidential relationship?

No. Nearly every privilege is subject to a variety of exceptions. For example:

- If a client seeks a lawyer's help in planning a future crime, the client's statements to the lawyer will not be privileged.
- No privilege exists for communications made in public places where they can be overheard.
- A privilege will cease to exist if the holder of a privilege discloses a privileged communication to a third party.

> **CASE EXAMPLE 1:** Lucy is charged with knowingly selling adulterated chocolates. In the courthouse elevator, she tells her lawyer Desi, "I should have known that they'd find out about the chemicals I added to that batch of chocolates." Fred, the other passenger in the elevator, overhears the statement. The prosecutor calls Fred as a witness to testify to what Lucy said to Desi.

Question: Is Lucy's statement protected by the attorney-client privilege?

Answer: No. Lucy waived the privilege by speaking to her lawyer in a public area.

CASE EXAMPLE 2: Same case, but this time Lucy made the statement to her lawyer Desi while alone with him in Desi's law office. When she leaves Desi's office and goes back to work, Lucy tells her coworker Ethel, "I told my lawyer about how worried I was that they'd find out that I put the chemicals in the batch of chocolates." The prosecutor calls Ethel as a witness to testify to what Lucy said to her.

Question: Is Lucy's statement protected by the attorney-client privilege?

Answer: No. By revealing to Ethel what she told her lawyer, Lucy waived the attorney-client privilege.

46. What privileges commonly exist for spouses?

Two privileges exist for spouses. The "spousal communications" privilege protects communications between spouses. To be privileged, a communication must be made by one spouse to the other in private, while the spouses are married. A communication made in these circumstances remains privileged even if the spouses are separated or divorced by the time a case goes to trial. Like the attorney-client and doctor-patient privileges, the privilege for spousal communications is subject to exceptions.

For example, in most states no privilege exists in prosecutions for spousal abuse.

The "spousal testimony" privilege is a second spousal privilege that exists in most states. This privilege allows one spouse to refuse to testify against the other spouse without risk of punishment. The privilege allows the spouse to refuse to testify even as to events that occurred before the marriage. On the other hand, this privilege does not exist if the parties are no longer married by the time a case comes to trial. (And in the early days of this privilege, one spouse had the power to forbid the other spouse from testifying. For example, a husband charged with bank robbery could prevent his wife from testifying that she saw him run into the house with the loot from the robbery, even if the wife wanted to testify against him. Almost all states have abolished this aspect of the privilege; each spouse has the right to decide whether to testify against the other spouse or rely on the privilege and refuse to testify.)

CASE EXAMPLE: Hank O'Hare is charged with embezzling sales receipts from his employer. On a number of occasions prior to his arrest, Hank told his wife Hedda in private how he was able to carry out the scheme. Hedda also occasionally went with Hank when he deposited money in an out-of-town bank under a false name.

Question: Can the prosecution call Hedda as a witness in Hank's trial to testify to seeing Hank make bank deposits under a false name and to what Hank told her about how he carried out the embezzlement scheme?

Answer: As to testifying to Hank's statements to her, the answer is "no." Hank's statements to Hedda are protected by the spousal communications privilege. Hedda could not testify to Hank's statements even if she wanted to. As to Hedda's observation of Hank's criminal activities, it's up to Hedda. She can choose to exercise her privilege not to testify against Hank, meaning that she can decide not to testify about seeing Hank make bank deposits under a false name.

Question: What if at the time the prosecution calls Hedda to testify against Hank, Hank and Hedda have gotten divorced?

Answer: Hedda cannot testify to what Hank told her as to how he was able to carry out the embezzlement scheme. Hank's statements were privileged when they were made, and they remain covered by the spousal communications privilege after divorce. However, Hedda no longer has access to the spousal testimony privilege to refuse to testify against Hank. If called by the prosecution to testify, Hedda would have to testify to seeing Hank make bank deposits under a false name.

47. Do privileges exist that might protect statements made by crime victims?

Crime victims often incur both physical and psychic injuries, and thus may receive medical treatment and/or psychological counseling. Statements made by crime victims to medical personnel, psychiatrists, and clinical psychologists are generally protected from disclosure by the same privilege rules that may protect defendants' statements from disclosure. In addition, many states have enacted a privilege for statements made by victims of sexual attacks to crisis counselors.

Defendants charged with crimes often argue that their constitutional rights to a fair trial and to confront the witnesses against them should outweigh these victim privileges. For example, a defendant may ask to see a crisis counselor's notes regarding statements made by an alleged sexual assault victim in order to discover whether the alleged victim told a different story to the counselor than to the police. Few privileges are absolute, and judges sometimes allow defendants access to crisis counselors' records, especially when a defendant has some evidence that an alleged victim has given conflicting accounts of events.

Motions and Their Role in Criminal Cases

This chapter describes motions that parties commonly bring and argue in criminal cases. A motion is a request for a judge to make an order or ruling on a legal issue in the case. A motion may be made orally and involve a simple scheduling matter, such as one party's desire to postpone a preliminary hearing (a Motion for a Continuance). Or, a motion may consist of a written brief that raises complex legal issues that cut to the very heart of a case. For example, a defendant's Motion to Suppress Evidence may ask a judge to rule that crucial prosecution evidence is inadmissible at trial because the police seized it illegally. If a judge rules in the defendant's favor, the prosecution may have to dismiss charges.

> **CAUTION**
>
> **Motions can be confusing.** This chapter highlights a few of the many important rules and procedures involved in handling motions in a criminal case. But it is not a comprehensive guide. Unrepresented defendants who need to make or respond to motions would be wise to consult counsel or, at the very least, to thoroughly research local court rules and procedures governing motions.

Section I: The Basic Procedures

This section provides an overview of how motions are brought and handled in the typical criminal case.

1. When during a criminal case are motions made?

Parties may make motions before, during, or after a trial depending on what they are requesting. For example, a Motion to Set Aside a Jury Verdict obviously can't be made until after a trial is over. Before trial, defendants often file motions to attack the admissibility of certain types of prosecution evidence. A ruling in favor of the defense on such a motion may result in dismissal of charges or at least a plea bargain highly favorable to the defendant.

2. What exactly does the average motion involve?

Typically, motions involve three distinct stages.

a. Giving notice (advising an adversary that you are making a motion)

Notice can be given orally or in writing, depending on the type of motion. To give notice orally, a defense attorney might say during a defendant's arraignment, "Your Honor, the defense intends to move the court for a ruling that the prosecution may not offer the knife in evidence." Written notice is given by preparing a Notice of Motion. The notice is filed with the court and mailed to the adversary.

Most jurisdictions require that the notice and accompanying papers:

- identify the specific order a party wants the judge to make
- explain the facts giving rise to the motion (in writing, in the form of an

affidavit or declaration under penalty of perjury), and

- explain the legal basis for the request in a document that is sometimes called a Memorandum of Points and Authorities. This document resembles an appellate brief, and may consist of many pages of legal arguments and case citations.

b. Hearing the motion

During the hearing, each party has a chance to make oral arguments that may convince a judge to grant ("sustain") or deny the motion.

c. Judge's ruling

The judge hearing the motion may rule immediately after the argument, or the judge may "take the matter under submission" and issue a ruling days, even weeks, later. In complex situations, the judge may invite the parties to submit further written legal arguments before making a ruling.

3. Do all motions involve this three-step process?

No. The defense or prosecution sometimes make motions and argue them immediately, especially if the motions are made in the middle of trial. Even before or after trial, the parties may agree to waive (give up) the right to advance notice of a motion and argue immediately. Also, the parties may forgo oral argument and ask the judge to just rule on a motion "based on the papers."

4. Who can make a motion in a criminal case?

Typically, only the actual parties to the case (the defense and prosecution) can file motions. Sometimes, others who want to assert rights may file motions. For example, in several recent high-profile cases, TV stations have filed motions requesting that judges allow the televising of court proceedings.

Written Arguments Can Help Defendants

Even when not required to do so, many defense lawyers routinely support their motions with written briefs for three reasons: (1) a judge may take written arguments more seriously; (2) judges often make up their minds based on written arguments, before the attorneys argue orally during a hearing; and (3) the defendant will have a record on which to rely during an appeal should the judge deny a particularly important motion. (For more on court records and appeals, see Chapter 23.)

---

5. What happens during a motion hearing?

Hearings on motions are usually relatively short, sometimes just a few minutes. Judges handle motion hearings by themselves, without juries. The judge normally has read the parties' briefs before the hearing, and therefore doesn't want the parties to simply repeat what they wrote. The judge may ask questions and then give the prosecution and defense each a chance to answer and make an argument to persuade her of their position.

6. Can stipulations be used in lieu of motions?

Yes. Before making motions, defense lawyers often ask prosecutors (or vice versa) to stipulate (agree voluntarily) to a request. For example, a defense attorney who wants to continue (delay) a preliminary hearing may simply ask the prosecutor to agree to a new date. If the prosecutor agrees to the delay, the defense need not make a formal motion. Instead, the parties might simply file a written stipulation in court informing the court of the new date. However, some court rules require the judge to approve any stipulations before they are put into effect.

> **CASE EXAMPLE:** The prosecutor, Rose Martinez, and the defense lawyer, Armando Lindan, agree to postpone the preliminary hearing of defendant Julie Daniels from March 8, the originally scheduled date, to April 25, a date that has been cleared with the court clerk.
>
> **Question:** What do the prosecutor and defense lawyer do then, after they agree to the new date?
>
> **Answer:** One of the attorneys prepares a stipulation and files it with the court.

Hallway Hearings

Procedures in criminal courts are often informal. A defense attorney and prosecutor may work out a continuance (or other pretrial issue) informally while standing in a hallway waiting for the judge to call the case. In most cases, judges merely rubber-stamp voluntary agreements. When an agreement results in a defendant waiving (giving up) legal rights, however, the judge often asks the defendant to personally waive the rights on the record. For example, a judge might ask the defendant to personally stipulate to a continuance to show that the defendant is not insisting on a speedy trial.

---

7. Is it risky to file a motion just to delay the case?

Motions filed for the sole purpose of delaying proceedings are considered frivolous (baseless or made for an improper purpose) and can lead to the offending party being fined by the judge.

8. Can my lawyer make motions without consulting me first?

Attorneys often make decisions about what motions to file and when to file them without involving their clients. In some cases, this is because the attorney views the decision to file a particular motion as a tactical one, which the attorney believes he is better qualified to determine than the client. In other cases, the issue comes up suddenly, and the attorney has no time to consult the defendant. Defendants who want more hands-on involvement in their cases should probably ask their lawyers ahead of time to consult them whenever possible. (See Chapter 8 for more on working with defense counsel.)

Section II: Common Pretrial Motions

This section describes the types of pretrial motions most commonly brought in criminal cases.

Motion	Question
Motion to Modify Bail	9
Motion to Dismiss Complaint	10
Motion for Bill of Particulars	11
Motion to Reduce Charges	12
Motion for a Change of Venue	13
Motion to Strike a Prior Conviction	14
Motion for Discovery	15
Motions to Preserve Evidence	16
Motion to Disclose Identity of an Informant	17
Motion to Examine Police Personnel File	18
Motion to Suppress Evidence	19
Motion for Speedy Trial	20

9. Can I file a motion asking the judge to lower my bail or change bail to release O.R.?

Defendants can ask for a change in their bail status with a Motion to Reduce Bail. Motions to reduce bail are common. Bail may have been set originally by some standard measure, perhaps by police at the station house. And defendants often file motions to reduce that bail based on their individual circumstances. Even if a judge has already set bail, the defendant may bring new circumstances to the judge's attention in a Motion to Reduce Bail. (See Chapter 5 for more on the factors that may persuade a judge to lower bail.)

CASE EXAMPLE: Ken Ahura was arrested for driving under the influence. Ken and his family recently moved from another state, and at the time of his arrest Ken was unemployed. Using a bail schedule, the police set Ken's bail at $10,000, far in excess of what he could afford.

Question: How can Ken get a judge to lower bail?

Answer: At Ken's first court appearance, Ken's lawyer should make a motion for a reduction of bail. The lawyer would stress the hardship to Ken and his family of his being in jail, and any factors indicating that Ken will show up as necessary and abide by conditions of bail. Defense motions for reduced bail are often made orally. Even if the judge rejects Ken's first motion to reduce bail, Ken may make additional bail reduction motions if there is a change in circumstances, such as a job offer or a person well known and respected in the community who is willing to vouch for him.

10. What can I do if the prosecutor made mistakes in the document used to charge me with a crime?

A defendant can attack an improper complaint with a Motion to Dismiss for Vagueness or a Motion to Dismiss Based on Improper Jurisdiction. A criminal complaint must specify the crime(s) charged, the defendant(s) accused of such crime(s), and the authority for the prosecution to make such charge(s). The complaint must also allege that the defendant committed each and every element of the crime(s) charged. For example, the crime of larceny (theft) typically includes the following elements: (1) the taking and carrying away, (2) of property of another, (3) with the intent to deprive that person permanently of the property in question. Theoretically, the failure of the complaint to allege each of these elements should result in the case being dismissed upon a motion by the defense. However, those kinds of motions are uncommon. Prosecutors use the same forms over and over, and toss out defective ones. Also, the prosecution is usually free to amend (change) any mistakes, so motions to dismiss based on technical violations are rarely useful. However, this is not always true. For example, a successful dismissal

motion may prevent the prosecution from refiling charges when a statute of limitations (a law that requires a complaint to be filed within a specified time period) will expire before new charges can be filed.

11. How can I find out the details of what the prosecution claims I did wrong?

The defendant can file a Motion for Bill of Particulars to learn the basis of the formal charge that the defendant faces. If the motion is granted, the judge will then order the prosecutor to describe with particularity just what the defendant did wrong. Among other benefits, this may help the defense figure out an appropriate strategy to fight the charges. In most jurisdictions, this type of motion usually is unnecessary, as the defense is routinely given a copy of the police report upon which the criminal complaint was based. However, if the police report does not provide adequate guidance as to facts underlying the prosecution's charge, a motion for a bill of particulars can be very useful. (See Chapter 14 for more on police reports.)

12. Can I get a judge to decide whether the charges against me are too severe given the facts of the case?

Yes, by filing a Motion to Reduce Charges. This is not a common motion, because (1) in most states judges do not normally review the evidence against a defendant prior to trial in misdemeanor cases, and (2) in felony cases, most states have a procedure called a preliminary hearing (see Chapter 16) in which the judge decides whether the prosecution's felony case is adequately supported by the evidence. More typically, defendants seek reduced charges by plea bargaining with prosecutors, offering to plead guilty to lesser crimes. (See Chapter 20 for more on plea bargaining.)

13. What motion can I file if I don't think I can get a fair trial in my town or city?

A defense Motion for Change of Venue asks the judge to relocate the case to a different location. Generally, criminal court proceedings (pretrial and trial) take place in the county where the alleged crime occurred. Defendants sometimes ask for a change of venue (location) when excess pretrial publicity makes it difficult to find unbiased jurors in the locality where a case is pending. If the judge agrees and determines that as a result of the publicity the defendant is unable to get a fair trial, the judge may grant the motion.

Even where the defendant has received extensive negative publicity, the defense may choose not to ask to have the case moved because:

- the case may be sent to an even more undesirable location
- the defendant may end up far away from family and friends
- defense counsel may be at a disadvantage not having an office close by the courtroom, or
- the cost of a trial away from the defense attorney's home base may be more than the defendant can afford.

14. Can I ask the judge to disregard previous convictions on my record when she is imposing sentence on me?

Defendants can sometimes reduce the severity of charges by filing a Motion to Strike a Prior Conviction. Defendants with prior records are often sentenced much more harshly than first offenders, and may even be charged with more serious offenses at the outset. (See Chapter 22 for more on sentencing, and Chapter 6 for more on charging.) For example, a misdemeanor may be filed as a felony if a defendant is a repeat offender. For these reasons, it is especially critical to an effective defense to challenge prior convictions where appropriate.

The most common reason for a judge to strike a prior conviction is a procedural irregularity or constitutional violation associated with the prior conviction. For example, the defendant may have been denied counsel at a critical stage of the case that resulted in the prior conviction, or the defendant may have entered into a plea bargain unknowingly or because of coercive practices by the police. (See Chapter 20 for more on plea bargaining.) Sometimes defense counsel can convince the judge in the current case that fairness requires the prior conviction to be disregarded—struck—where the defendant has since engaged in a long period of good behavior or formal rehabilitation.

Court Records Can Be Wrong

It is not unusual for rap sheets (records of prior convictions) to contain mistakes. For example, a misdemeanor conviction may have been erroneously recorded as a felony. As a routine matter, defense lawyers typically review conviction records for errors, and sometimes have defendants review the records as well.

15. How can I find out what evidence the prosecution plans to use in my trial?

Defendants can file a Motion for Discovery to find out information in prosecutors' files. Technically, such motions are unnecessary. Prosecutors have a legal duty to turn over any information that might help the defendant, even if the defendant fails to ask for it. And many prosecutors voluntarily hand over all the information that the defense is entitled to see, such as police reports and lab tests. But a thorough defense lawyer may be convinced that it's still a good idea to put a formal motion for discovery on the record. (For more information about discovery, see Chapter 14.)

16. Can I require the prosecution to give my own expert an opportunity to examine evidence in the prosecutor's possession?

Defendants can file a Motion to Preserve Evidence to force prosecutors to keep evidence safe long enough for the defense

to run its own tests. For example, if a police lab indicates that the percentage of alcohol in a defendant's blood was 0.12%, the defendant may want a judge to order the prosecutor to preserve the blood sample so that the defense can run its own test. (See Chapter 24 for more on blood alcohol tests.)

17. How can I find out if a witness is actually a government informant?

Defense attorneys can find out whether the prosecution is relying on a government informant by filing a Motion to Disclose Identity of a Confidential Informant. Defense attorneys often try to attack a witness's credibility by showing that the witness is a paid informant who has something to gain (frequently money or reduced charges in the informant's own case) by testifying against the defendant. With this motion, the defense may request that the court order the prosecution to reveal an informant's identity and location. The prosecution can be counted on to vigorously oppose this motion in order to protect the identity of the informant. If the judge grants the motion, the prosecution may even dismiss the case rather than lose a valuable police resource.

18. How can I find out if the officer who arrested or questioned me has behaved improperly in the past?

When a police officer's past history is relevant to the defense, the defendant may gain access to portions of the police officer's personnel file by filing a Motion to Examine Police Officer's Personnel File. If successful, the defense can review the file to determine whether the officer has been implicated previously in any wrong-doing. The record may reveal that the officer has been reprimanded in the past for use of excessive force, planting evidence, or exhibiting racial prejudice. If so, the defense may be able to use this informa-tion to deflate the officer's credibility and, accordingly, weaken the prosecution's case. However, judges do not let defendants go on fishing expeditions into police officer files. Unless a defendant can demonstrate a specific purpose for the request, this motion probably won't be granted. (See Chapter 14 for more on discovery.)

19. How can I show that the police seized evidence illegally and ask the court to keep it out of evidence?

One of the most common pretrial motions is a Motion to Suppress (exclude) improper evidence. This motion can request the exclusion of evidence obtained as a result of:

- an improperly obtained confession (for additional information about confessions, search and seizure, and identification procedures, see Chapters 1, 2, and 4, respectively)
- an improper search or arrest, or
- a tainted identification such as a lineup.

20. My trial date keeps getting postponed by the prosecution. How can I bring my case to trial?

Defendants are entitled to be tried relatively quickly unless they give up (waive) this right somewhere during the case. A defendant can enforce his right to be tried quickly by filing a Motion for a Speedy Trial. The defense can file this motion to force the prosecutor to abide by rules limiting the amount of time that can pass before the defendant is brought to trial. Because delays often benefit the defendant (witnesses' memories fade or they move or die, evidence is lost, and prosecutors lose momentum and are often more willing to deal), defense lawyers typically don't insist on speedy trials. (For additional discussion of speedy trial rights, see Chapter 17.)

Section III: Motions During Trial

This section provides an overview of the motions that the defense commonly brings during a trial.

21. Can I ask the trial judge to rule that certain prosecution evidence is inadmissible before the prosecutor tries to introduce it?

Yes, by making a Motion *in Limine*. This bit of Latin means "at the very beginning." By attacking prosecution evidence through a Motion *in Limine* rather than waiting until the prosecution introduces the evidence at trial, a defendant tries to prevent the jury from ever hearing about evidence that the judge rules inadmissible. Motions *in Limine* are often made orally, though they may be supported with a Memorandum of Points and Authorities. (For more information on this motion, see Chapter 21, Section IV.)

CASE EXAMPLE: Grant Jordan faces trial on drunk driving charges. The prosecutor plans on introducing testimony from several witnesses, including Dr. Joyce, who performed Grant's postarrest blood test. In the doctor's report (reviewed during discovery by the defense), the doctor noted that she'd seen the accused "plastered" in a local bar a week before the accident.

Question: Is there anything the defense lawyer can do to make sure the jury never hears about what the doctor saw the week before?

Answer: Yes, the defense can file a Motion *in Limine* requesting that the doctor's notes about the week before be stricken from the report so the jury never sees them. That the doctor thought the defendant was drunk the week before is irrelevant to the defendant's state at the time of the accident, and the "plastered" comment is highly prejudicial. The doctor will still be able to testify about the results of the blood alcohol test.

Some courts routinely conduct conferences with counsel before jurors are selected, to handle procedural matters related to the trial, including any Motions *in Limine* the lawyers plan to make.

Motions *in Limine* are a critical component of the typical criminal case. Even though there are many ways to discredit witnesses, once a witness refers to damaging evidence, it's difficult for jurors to disregard what they've heard—to, as they say, "unring the bell." So much the better, therefore, to address the question in advance and not let the bell be rung in the first place.

22. It's really important to my defense that the jury actually visit the scene. How can I accomplish this?

The defendant can ask the judge to escort jurors on a visit to scenes of important events by filing a Motion to Allow Jury to View the Crime Scene. Unfortunately, judges incur costs and time delays by granting such motions. Thus, a defendant has to support such a motion with a strong argument as to why the jurors should visit a scene, and the inadequacy of an alternative (such as photographs or videotape).

23. What can the defense do when a prosecution witness blurts out testimony that is both unexpected and damaging?

Ideally, attorneys can object to improper evidence before jurors hear it. If the evidence is anticipated, the objection can be made in a Motion *in Limine*. (See Question 21.) But it's obviously impossible to anticipate everything a witness will say. When jurors do hear improper evidence, the defense can make a Motion to Strike Testimony, followed up by asking the judge to instruct the jurors to disregard the stricken testimony. Even though it is difficult for jurors to disregard something they have heard, it is important for defendants to move to strike improper testimony for at least four reasons:

- Even though the witness should not have made the statement in the first place, jurors can consider evidence unless it is formally stricken by the judge.
- If jurors, during deliberations, ask for testimony to be read back, they will not hear the stricken testimony.
- The instruction may hurt the credibility of a prosecution witness. When jurors are told to disregard portions of a witness's testimony, the jurors may perceive the witness as a partisan who is unwilling to follow the rules of trial.
- Stricken testimony does not become part of the record on appeal. (More on appeals in Chapter 23.)

24. The prosecution's case was weak. Can I try to end the case without putting on evidence?

Yes, by filing a Motion for Dismissal (or acquittal). After the prosecution presents all of its evidence, the defense can ask the judge to acquit the defendant at once on the ground the prosecution hasn't made out a strong enough case to convict. Defense lawyers try to make this motion out of the

presence of the jury so that if the judge denies the motion (and likely the judge will), the jury won't interpret the denial as meaning the judge thinks the defendant is guilty.

CASE EXAMPLE: Vic Trola is a public defender representing Yu Kaleili on kidnapping charges. The prosecution's main evidence was the victim's testimony that Kaleili intentionally forced the victim to enter his car and would not let her leave. During Trola's cross-examination, the victim admitted to entering Kaleili's car willingly. The victim also testified that Kaleili never tried to stop the victim from leaving the car; the victim stated that it was her "impression" that Kaleili would not permit her to leave. After the prosecution rested its case, Trola made a Motion for Dismissal, arguing that the prosecution had failed to prove an essential element of kidnapping: that Kaleili detained the victim against the victim's will.

Question: Will Trola's motion be granted?

Answer: Quite possibly. The victim's testimony casts doubt on whether Kaleili detained the victim by force. If the judge believes that a jury would be unjustified in concluding beyond a reasonable doubt that Kaleili detained the victim, the judge should grant the Motion to Dismiss.

Section IV: Motions After Trial

This section describes the motions that are commonly brought by the defense after the trial has concluded with a guilty verdict.

25. If a judge or jury finds me not guilty, can the prosecutor ask (move) for a new trial?

No. That's the end of the case. If a jury or judge finds a defendant not guilty as to all charges, the prosecution cannot appeal, nor can the prosecution ask the judge to set aside the verdict and order a new trial. A retrial would violate the defendant's constitutional right against double jeopardy. Even if the judge, prosecutor, and half the nation think a jury's decision is wrong, a not guilty verdict is final. The only motion following not guilty is normally the defendant leaving the courtroom as quickly as possible.

26. What can I do if a jury convicts me and I disagree with their decision?

Defendants who think they've been wrongfully convicted have a number of options.

The defendant can make a motion asking the trial judge to overturn the jury's guilty verdict and enter a verdict of not guilty. A judge who believes that a guilty verdict was unreasonable can change it to not guilty. Judges seldom acquit defendants in the face of a jury's guilty verdict, since the jury is supposed to decide factual disputes. Technically, the judge could order an acquittal based on defense evidence,

but this would only happen if the defense presented compelling proof of factual or legal innocence, something that seldom happens outside of the movies and Perry Mason.

A defendant can move for a new trial—that is, ask the judge to set aside the jury's verdict, declare a mistrial, and start over. Defendants may move for new trials based on a variety of grounds. The broadest rules give judges the power to grant a new trial "if required in the interest of justice" (Federal Rule of Criminal Procedure 33). Other rules identify specific grounds on which judges can grant new trials. For example, Florida Rule of Criminal Procedure 3.600 authorizes judges to grant new trials for reasons including the following:

- The defendant has discovered new and important evidence that couldn't have been discovered prior to trial.
- The jurors engaged in misconduct during the trial.
- The judge or prosecutor committed an important legal error.
- The judge gave an improper jury instruction.

Defendants are not entitled to a perfect trial. Typically, even when there are mistakes, judges consider them harmless error—not so serious as to require the setting aside of a verdict—if they probably had little or no effect on the jury when it reached its guilty verdict.

If the trial judge does grant the defense motion for a new trial, the prosecution can appeal and challenge the judge's decision.

But the judges who hear appeals commonly allow trial judges wide discretion in their decisions to grant or deny new trial requests. Appellate judges know that they only review a written record, while the trial judge actually saw and heard the witnesses. Accordingly, appellate judges only reverse trial judges' decisions to grant new trials when the written record clearly shows the trial judge's decision was wrong (or "clearly erroneous," as appellate court judges like to say).

Defendants can appeal (ask a higher court to reverse the conviction) because the trial judge or jurors made a mistake.

Deadline to Move for New Trial

Defendants who want to make a motion for a new trial must typically do so very soon after the jury reaches a verdict. In federal court, new trial motions must be made within seven days, unless they are based on newly-discovered evidence, and even those must be made within three years after the final judgment. (See Federal Rule of Criminal Procedure 33.)

CASE EXAMPLE 1: Motion for New Trial Because of Juror Misconduct. (The following case example illustrates one reason a judge might grant a new trial: juror misconduct.)

Julio Daniels was convicted for burglarizing the Lomida Candy Shoppe. After the verdict, one juror, Rosalie Man-Doe, told a reporter about the deliberations. Rosalie said a juror named Kelsey Oblido had gone to the Shoppe and measured the opening in a broken window. Oblido told them it was "plenty big enough for Daniels," and urged them to ignore defense arguments that no one of Daniels's size could have climbed through. Oblido's "evidence" persuaded Rosalie and another juror, Linda Rogers. Rogers was apparently unsure but said she wanted to do what was right; if the others were sure, then she, too, would convict. Another juror, Clayton Travis, had made racial slurs about the defendant. Among other things, Travis announced that he "knew" Julio Daniels was guilty because "all those people are criminals."

Question: Based on Rosalie's report, does Daniels have grounds to move for a new trial?

Answer: Yes. Juror misconduct is proper grounds for a new trial, and all of the following are prohibited:
- jurors considered evidence not presented in court (Oblido's field trip experiments)
- at least one juror convicted to go along with others and not out of personal conviction (Rogers), and
- one juror (Travis) appeared to have based his verdict on racial prejudice.

CASE EXAMPLE 2: Anna Rose was convicted by a jury of burglary. John Fell testified for the prosecution and identified Anna as the burglar. Anna's attorney moves for a new trial based on Fell's having whispered after the verdict that he believed he'd made a mistake.

Question: Must the judge grant Anna's motion?

Answer: No. Judges often believe that witnesses and even jurors suffer from post-verdict remorse, and too easily want to take back what they did or said. Here the judge might conclude that Fell's recantation is not believable, or that even without Fell's testimony the prosecution had sufficient evidence to convict Anna, in which case any error would be harmless. In either event, the judge would deny Anna's motion.

27. My trial is before a judge alone, no jury. What recourse do I have if the judge convicts me?

For many of the same reasons that a defendant may move for a new jury trial, a convicted defendant may ask the judge to:

- modify the verdict (for instance, change it from conviction on one charge to conviction on a lesser charge); or
- vacate the verdict (withdraw it altogether and order a new trial).

Because these motions ask the judge to—in effect—overrule herself, they are not usually successful. Nonetheless, in certain situations, such a motion might be worth a try—for instance, where new and important evidence is discovered that might persuade the judge to change her mind.

28. What types of new evidence make it possible that I'll get a new trial after being convicted by a judge or jury?

As mentioned earlier, one reason a judge may grant a new trial is that the defense discovers new and helpful evidence that for some very good reason was not available at the time of trial. Defense counsel's being on vacation and not having adequate time to prepare is not considered a good reason. But the recent surfacing of an alibi witness who had fled to Argentina may be. Another possible good reason is that scientific evidence that was not available at trial becomes available. Old cases have been reopened, for instance, to analyze blood samples with new DNA technology.

> **CASE EXAMPLE:** Guy Goode was convicted of rape; his defense was mistaken identity. One year after Goode's conviction, scientists develop a new test that demonstrates that he was not the source of the semen found in the rape victim.
>
> **Question:** Should the trial judge grant a new trial based on this information?
>
> **Answer:** Yes. The information qualifies as newly-discovered evidence, since the scientific test was unknown at the time of Goode's trial. Moreover, the evidence is important; had it been offered at the time of trial, it might well have produced a different verdict.

Writ Proceedings in the Trial Court

Writs, discussed further in Chapter 23, are generally orders from higher courts to lower courts. However, in some states defendants can seek special relief from the trial court itself, in limited situations, through a proceeding called a *writ coram nobis*. For example, using this writ a defendant might ask the trial court itself to reopen a case to review facts that the defendant could not present during trial, either because they were not known or for some other extraordinary reason (for instance, the defendant had been threatened and was afraid to present facts that would have led to an acquittal).

Plea Bargains: How Most Criminal Cases End

A plea bargain is an agreement between the defense and the prosecutor in which the defendant agrees to plead guilty or no contest in exchange for an agreement by the prosecution to drop some charges, reduce a charge to a less serious charge, or recommend to the judge a specific sentence acceptable to the defense.

As criminal courts become ever more crowded, prosecutors and judges alike feel increased pressure to move cases quickly through the system. Trials can take days, weeks, or sometimes months, while guilty pleas can often be arranged in minutes. Also, the outcome of any given trial is usually unpredictable, whereas a plea bargain provides both prosecution and defense with some control over the result—hopefully one that both can live with to some extent.

For these reasons and others, and despite its many critics, plea bargaining is very common. More than 90% of convictions come from negotiated pleas, which means less than 10% of criminal cases end up in trials. And though some still view plea bargains as secret, sneaky arrangements that are antithetical to the people's will, the federal government and many states have written rules that explicitly set out how plea bargains may be arranged and accepted by the court. (See Federal Rule of Criminal Procedure 11(e).)

Section I: Plea Bargaining—The Basics

This section provides a general overview of the plea-bargaining process.

1. Are there other terms for a "plea bargain"?

A plea bargain may also be called a plea agreement or negotiated plea. Lawyers may also casually say they got a great deal or that the prosecution offered a particular sentence.

Different Types of Plea Bargaining

Plea bargaining can be conveniently divided into two types: sentence bargaining and charge bargaining. Sentence bargaining is a method of plea bargaining in which the prosecutor agrees to recommend a lighter sentence for specific charges if the defendant pleads guilty or no contest to them. Charge bargaining is a method where prosecutors agree to drop some of the counts of a charge or reduce the charge to a less serious or less prejudicial offense in exchange for a plea by the defendant.

2. When are plea bargains made?

This depends on the court and the jurisdiction. Some jurisdictions only allow plea bargains during certain phases of the criminal process. In many other places, however, plea bargains can be worked out virtually any time—from shortly after the defendant is arrested (before the prosecutor files criminal charges) up to the time a verdict is reached—even during trial itself. Also, if the trial results in a hung jury (the jurors are split and cannot make the unanimous decision required), the prosecution and defense can (and frequently do) negotiate a plea rather than go through another trial.

Section II: The Pros and Cons of Plea Bargains

This section explains why a defendant may or may not wish to enter into a plea bargain.

3. If I plead guilty or no contest, will I have a criminal record?

A guilty or no contest plea entered as a judge-approved plea bargain results in a criminal conviction; the defendant's guilt is established just as it would be after a trial. The conviction will show up on a criminal record (rap sheet). And the defendant loses any rights or privileges, such as the right to vote, that the defendant would lose if convicted after trial.

4. What does it mean to plead "no contest" (*nolo contendere*) rather than guilty?

A no contest or *nolo contendere* plea in essence says to the court, "I don't choose to contest the charges against me." This type of plea, often part of a plea bargain, results in a criminal conviction the same as a guilty plea. And a no contest plea will show up on a criminal record. However, if the defendant is later sued in civil court by the victim, the no contest plea itself sometimes cannot be used in the civil case as an admission of guilt. A guilty plea, on the other hand, does serve as an admission of guilt and can be introduced in civil cases as evidence against the defendant.

5. What incentives do I have to enter into a plea bargain?

For most defendants, the principal benefit to plea bargaining is receiving a lighter sentence for a less severe charge than might result from taking the case to trial and losing.

> **EXAMPLE:** David Neustadt is charged with 20 counts of burglary—from a spree of burglaries in his neighborhood. Assistant District Attorney Rachel Marks offers to drop the charges to two counts of burglary if David pleads guilty right away. David takes the deal, because his sentence will be shorter and he will be eligible for parole earlier than if he were convicted on every charge at trial.

Another fairly obvious benefit that defendants can reap from plea bargaining is that they can save a bundle on attorneys' fees (assuming they are represented by private counsel). It almost always takes a lot more time and effort to try a case than to negotiate and handle a plea bargain, so defense counsel typically charge a much higher fee if the case goes to trial.

There may also be other benefits for defendants who plead guilty or no contest, such as the following.

a. Getting out of jail

In-custody defendants who either do not have the right to bail or cannot afford bail may get out of jail immediately following the judge's acceptance of a plea. Depending on the offense, the defendant may get out altogether or on probation, with or without some community service obligations. Or, the defendant may have to serve more time, but will still get out much sooner than if he insisted on going to trial.

Benefits of Move From Jail to Prison

Even if the plea results in the defendant being moved from jail to prison, this also, paradoxically, may occasionally be a benefit. A move to prison can be a step up if the jail conditions are worse than prison conditions. And convicts in prison may have privileges that defendants awaiting trial in jail don't have. Furthermore, even when defendants go to prison, there is some intangible benefit to simply having resolution—knowing how long they will be in, rather than what may feel like endless waiting around in jail.

---

b. Getting the matter over quickly

This has the intangible benefit, touched on above, of providing resolution to what is almost always a stressful event (being charged with a crime). People who are charged with a crime, for example, while on vacation might opt for a plea bargain in order to get back home sooner. And defendants with jobs who are charged with minor offenses may prefer to resolve the case in one court appearance rather than missing work repeatedly. Going to trial usually requires many more court dates than a plea bargain takes.

c. Having fewer and/or less serious offenses on one's record

Pleading guilty or no contest in exchange for a reduction in the number of charges or the seriousness of the offenses looks a lot better on a defendant's record than the convictions that might result following trial. This can be particularly important if the defendant is ever convicted in the future. For example, a second DUI conviction may carry mandatory jail time, whereas if the first DUI offense had been bargained down to reckless driving (for example), there may be no jail time for the second DUI arrest. (See Chapter 24 for more on the penalties associated with repeat drunk driving offenses.)

Even for people who are never rearrested, getting a charge reduced from a felony to a misdemeanor, or from a felony that constitutes a strike under a "three strikes" law to one that doesn't, can prove to be a critical benefit. Some professional licenses must be forfeited upon conviction of a felony. Future employers may not want to hire someone previously convicted of a felony. Felony convictions may be used in certain court proceedings (even civil cases) to discredit people who testify as witnesses. Felons can't own or possess firearms. And in many jurisdictions, felons can't vote.

d. Having a less socially stigmatizing offense on one's record

Prosecutors may reduce charges that are perceived as socially offensive to less offensive charges in exchange for a guilty plea. For example, a prosecutor may reduce a molestation or rape case to an assault. This can have a major impact on the defendant's relationship with friends and family. Perhaps even more critical, sometimes defendants convicted of stigmatizing offenses may be at a greater risk of being harmed (or killed) in prison than if they are convicted of an offense that doesn't carry the same stigma.

e. Avoiding hassles

Some people plead guilty, especially to routine, minor first offenses, without hiring a lawyer. (See Chapter 10.) If they waited to go to trial, not only would they have to pay money to a lawyer but they would have to find and hire a lawyer and might well spend time working with the lawyer to prepare for trial.

f. Avoiding publicity

Famous people, ordinary people who depend on their reputation in the community to earn a living, and people who don't want to bring further embarrassment to their families all may chose to plead guilty or no contest to get (and keep) their names out of the paper as quickly as possible.

While news of the plea itself may be public, the news is short-lived compared to news of a trial. And rarely is a defendant's background explored in the course of a plea bargain to the extent it may be done in trial.

g. Keeping others out of the case

Some defendants plead guilty to take the blame (sometimes called the "rap") for someone else, or to end the case quickly so that others who may be jointly responsible are not investigated.

Factors That Affected Detective Fuhrman's Plea Bargain

Retired detective Mark Fuhrman, infamous for having denied using racial slurs during the O.J. Simpson criminal trial, pleaded no contest to perjury charges. Fuhrman apparently "didn't have the money to wage a long court battle and didn't want to put his family through such a trial." Said Fuhrman, "… I don't think the city of Los Angeles either deserves or could handle a trial like this … I cut my losses and everybody else's." (From "Fuhrman Grants Interview, Apologizes for Slurs," *L.A. Times*, October 8, 1996, at B1).

---

6. What's in a plea bargain for the prosecution? Why does the court accept them?

For judges, the primary incentive to accept plea bargains is to move along their crowded calendars. Most judges simply don't have time to try every case that comes through the door.

Additionally, because jails are over-crowded, judges may face the prospect of having to let convicted people (housed in the same facilities as those awaiting trial) out before they complete their sentences. Judges often reason that the quicker those offenders who are not likely to do much jail time anyway are "processed" out of jail (by plea bargains), the fewer problems with overcrowding, and the less frequently serious offenders will be let go before their full sentence has been served.

For a prosecutor, the judge's concerns about clogged calendars are the prosecutor's concerns as well. When the judge is bogged down, the judge yells at prosecutors to move cases along quicker. To keep judges happy (and keep the machine rolling), prosecutors must keep "the bodies" moving (as criminal defendants are most unfor-tunately referred to by some courthouse regulars).

Prosecutors are, of course, also con-cerned for their own calendars. Clogged calendars mean that the prosecutor's staff is overworked. Plea bargains tend to lighten the staff's caseloads. Since plea bargains are much quicker and require less work than trials, they are also easier on the prosecutor's budget. With today's cutbacks on already slim resources, D.A.s feel they will have additional time and resources for more important cases if they conclude a large number of less serious cases with plea bargains.

Another benefit to the prosecution is an assured conviction. No matter how strong the evidence, no case is ever a slam dunk. The prosecution may wage a long, expensive, and valiant battle, and still lose the case (as did prosecutors in the O.J. Simpson criminal trial).

Plea bargains also allow prosecutors to protect government informants. Many informants have criminal records. If a case were to go to trial and the informant were to testify, the defense in many cases could impeach the informant with his or her past criminal history. But in the context of a plea bargain, the prosecution does not have to turn over an informant's criminal history to the defense (*United States v. Ruiz*, U.S. Sup. Ct. 2002).

Plea bargains also give prosecutors flexibility. For instance, they can offer a deal to someone who, though guilty, has given testimony about a codefendant or helped resolve some other unsolved case.

CASE EXAMPLE: Brad Hillary, an experienced criminal with a long rap sheet, planned to rob Danny's Liquor store. He recruited Aliza Michaels to be his lookout. Aliza has no criminal history and is just 18. She merely stood guard; she was not armed and did not know Brad had a gun. As Brad threatened Danny and emptied the cash, his gun accidentally fired. Danny suffered serious but not fatal injuries; Brad and Aliza fled. Aliza later confessed to the police. Brad pleads guilty to armed robbery and gets sentenced 25 years to life in prison—ironically, the same sentence he likely would have gotten after trial, because of his record and the nature of the robbery. Aliza, though technically guilty of armed robbery, is offered a plea to larceny (theft), for which she may serve up to one year in prison, in exchange for her testimony against Brad.

Question: Can the prosecutor do this?

Answer: Yes. The prosecutor likely justified the deal by reasoning that Aliza helped to get the really bad guy and played a minor role in the robbery, and that this was her first offense. These last two factors would ordinarily tend to lighten Aliza's sentence even without her cooperation. (See Chapter 22 for more on factors that tend to mitigate (lessen) or aggravate (increase) a defendant's sentence.)

Finally, prosecutors may use plea bargains to circumvent laws they don't agree with. For instance, a prosecutor may disagree with laws prohibiting possession for personal use of small amounts of marijuana, so the prosecutor's office may have an unwritten policy of giving all such offenders "offers they can't refuse," such as a $25 fine and ten hours of community service.

7. How might a plea bargain benefit victims?

Victims can also benefit from plea bargains, especially when a victim wants to avoid the stress and publicity of trial. A guilty or no contest plea is quicker and tends to receive less press than a trial.

Section III: The Plea Bargaining Process

This section sheds light on how plea bargains come to be made.

8. What happens in a plea bargain?

In a typical plea bargain, the defense lawyer and prosecutor confer (talk), and one or the other proposes a deal. The negotiations can be lengthy and conducted after both parties have had a chance to research and investigate the case. Or, they can be minute-long interchanges in the courthouse hallway.

> **CASE EXAMPLE:** Deputy Public Defender Durlofsky passes Assistant District Attorney Van Lowe in the hallway on their way into the courtroom. The following interchange takes place.
>
> **P.D.** "Mornin', V.L. Got a good offer for me in the Reback case?"
>
> **D.A.** "That's the possession case?"
>
> **P.D.** "Yeah. Honor student, nice guy, caught with some coke in his dorm room. He's been in since last night. How 'bout time served and probation?"
>
> **D.A.** "Fine."
>
> **P.D.** "Okay, what about the Cooper case?"
>
> It is quite likely that a plea bargain in a misdemeanor drug possession case would take place this quickly and this informally, especially when the deal is between a prosecutor and court-appointed attorney who work with each other every day and are friendly. "Time

served" means that the jail time will be just what the defendant has already spent in jail—in this case overnight.

Question: Can the public defender agree to the deal without consulting the defendant (Reback)?

Answer: No. (See Question 9, below.) But this is likely a deal Reback would want to take. If the case went to trial and Reback lost, his sentence might be more severe—more jail time, perhaps a fine, and some community service or mandatory enrollment in a drug treatment program. By accepting the deal, Reback not only gets out of jail but has the certainty of knowing the case is over.

9. Can my lawyer arrange a plea bargain without me?

Yes, but the decision about whether or not to accept the plea bargain ultimately rests with the client. For practical purposes, however, defense counsel often urge defendants to accept deals, convincing them they'll get a much harsher sentence if they go to trial (and they're often right). And defendants tend to take the deals defense counsel recommend.

10. What role does the judge play in plea bargaining?

It is up to the judge to impose sentence in a criminal case; no one else has the authority. On the other hand, it is up to the prosecutor to decide what charges to bring; the judge has no authority in that sphere

except to dismiss a charge that the judge feels is wrong. This means that a prosecutor may agree to change the charges or even drop some charges in exchange for the defendant's plea, and the judge can't stop it. However, if the plea bargain involves the type of sentence to be imposed by the judge, the prosecutor cannot guarantee the result without the judge's agreement.

Much of the time, plea bargaining negotiations take place privately between the defense lawyer and prosecutor, outside of court. The judge has no formal role until the plea is offered in open court. In some courts, however, the judge is actively involved in pushing both sides to negotiate, even facilitating negotiations in the judge's chambers (office). On occasion, the judge will provide guidance to the defense and prosecutor by indicating what sort of a sentence would be acceptable.

11. Does the judge have to go along with the deal the lawyers work out?

In many courts, prosecutors agree to recommend the bargained-for sentence without obtaining any explicit agreement beforehand from the judge. But the prosecutors know from past experience and the judge's reputation whether the judge can be counted on, as many can, to rubber-stamp the prosecutor's recommendation. If the judge rebels or simply doesn't follow the track record, and imposes a harsher sentence than the one the defendant was led to expect, the defendant is usually allowed to withdraw the plea and reassert his or her right to go to trial. But if the prosecutor has made it clear that the judge might not accept the recommendation, and the defendant pleads guilty anyway, the defendant may be stuck with the judge's sentence. In other words, sometimes bargaining for the prosecutor's recommendation will produce a sure result; other times it simply means that the defendant can test what the judge is willing to do; and still other times it guarantees nothing at all and risks a harsh sentence.

Prosecutors Who Back Out of a Deal

Sometimes, prosecutors agree to certain deals out of court and then change their minds in front of the judge. In most places, the defendant caught in such a situation would have the right to simply withdraw a plea of guilty. To deter prosecutors from going back on a deal, defendants should have the agreed-to terms put in writing before going before the judge. Where the prosecutor agrees only to make a recommendation or to not oppose the defense lawyer's request for a certain sentence, however, the court may refuse to allow the defendant to withdraw the plea. See Federal Rule of Criminal Procedure 11(e) (2); *Santabello v. N.Y.,* U.S. Sup. Ct. 1971.

12. Do victims have a role in the plea bargaining process?

Many victims are dissatisfied when defendants are allowed to enter plea bargains, feeling that the harms they suffered were disregarded and the defendants got off too easily. As a result of the efforts of victims' rights groups, laws in many states now allow victims to have a say in the plea bargaining process. Michigan, for example, requires prosecutors to consult with victims before entering into plea bargains. In other states, victims have a legal right to come to court and address a judge personally before the judge decides whether to accept a plea bargain. Still a third possibility for victims in many states is to consult with the probation officers before the probation officers prepare the pre-sentence reports that often influence the terms of plea bargains. (For more information on probation reports and their role in the sentencing process, see Chapter 22.) Increased victim participation in plea bargaining means that for many defendants, good deals may be increasingly hard to come by.

13. What factors enter into a judge's decision to accept or reject a plea bargain?

As a practical matter, many judges will go along with a plea bargain as long as the agreed-upon sentence is within the range of what he considers fair. Usually this means determining if, given the seriousness of the crime and the defendant's criminal record, the sentence seems appropriate in light of other sentences the judge has handed down.

There are some other variables that may come into play, however. Particular judges might (rightly or wrongly) take into their calculation whether they remember the defendant from a previous appearance in their courtroom and how they and members of the community feel (especially if the judge is up for reelection) about the crimes in question. Sometimes such whimsy as whether the judge woke up in a good mood or had a rough morning can also have an impact on his decisions later that day.

14. Assuming the agreement reached in a plea bargain is in the ballpark, what additional role will the judge play?

Even if the deal seems fair to the judge, he is supposed to ask questions to determine whether the defendant is making what is known as a "knowing and intelligent" plea. What this means, essentially, is that the defendant knows and understands:

- the charges against him
- the consequences of the plea (both the sentence as it stands and the possible sentences that could be given were the defendant to have a trial), and
- the rights he is waiving (giving up) by pleading guilty, including: (1) the right to counsel if unrepresented, (2) the right to a jury trial, (3) the right to exercise his privilege against self-incrimination, and (4) his right to confront his accusers.

Defendants should also know that, if they are not U.S. citizens, they risk deportation when they are convicted of a crime. Defendants are competent to waive counsel and plead guilty so long as they are capable of understanding the proceedings (*Godinez v. Moran*, U.S. Sup. Ct. 1993).

In some courts, defendants who are pleading guilty are asked to fill in or sign a form waiving their rights.

Pleas That Aren't Knowing and Intelligent

If a defendant entered into a plea without counsel and did not appear, from a later review of the record, to have made a knowing and intelligent plea, that defendant may have grounds to request that the conviction stemming from the plea be stricken (removed) from the defendant's record, or at least not be considered in any future proceedings. As discussed more fully in Chapter 19, it can be important to try to strike prior convictions, because offenders tend to be sentenced more severely with each repeat offense. However, the United States Supreme Court has decided that even if a defendant did not have counsel or waived counsel before pleading guilty, as long as the defendant was not incarcerated after the plea was entered, the conviction may later be used to make future sentences more severe (*Nichols v. U.S.*, U.S. Sup. Ct. 1994).

Usually the judge asks the defendant a fairly long list of questions to determine whether the plea is knowing and intelligent. And the defendant, following his attorney's advice, quietly answers "yes" to all the judge's questions.

If the judge is satisfied after hearing the defendant's answers, she will typically accept the deal. In some cases, she may want to see a pre-sentence report prepared by the probation department, consult with the crime victim, or hear arguments from both the defense and prosecution supporting their deal. (See Chapter 22 for more on presentence reports and sentencing hearings.)

> **EXAMPLE:** Assuming that Deputy Public Defender Durlofsky and Assistant District Attorney Van Lowe have agreed on the plea bargain in the Reback case from the previous example, the following might take place in the courtroom:
>
> **Clerk:** "Court is now in session, the Honorable Judge Kevin Lu presiding."
>
> **Judge:** "In the matter of the *State vs. Reback,* Mr. Reback, how do you plead?"
>
> **Defendant Reback:** "Guilty, your Honor."
>
> **Judge:** "Counsel, have you reached a settlement?"
>
> **D.A.:** "Yes, your Honor. The people have agreed to time served and probation."

Judge: "Mr. Reback, do you know that by pleading guilty you lose the right to a jury trial?"

Defendant Reback: "Yes, your Honor."

Judge: "Do you give up that right?"

Defendant Reback: "Yes, your Honor."

Judge: "Do you understand what giving up that right means?"

Defendant Reback: "Yes."

Judge: "Do you know that you are waiving the right to cross-examine your accusers?"

Defendant Reback: "Yes."

Judge: "Do you know that you are waiving your privilege against self-incrimination?"

Defendant Reback: "Yes."

Judge: "Did anyone force you into accepting this settlement?"

Defendant Reback: "No."

Judge: "Are you pleading guilty because you in fact possessed cocaine as charged?"

Defendant Reback: "Yes."

Judge: "Mr. Reback, you are hereby sentenced to 12 hours in jail, which you have already served, and to two years' probation."

15. I don't want to plead guilty, but I'm told the judge will treat me worse if I go to trial and lose. Is this true?

In most cases, defendants are made aware in one way or another that the judge will be harsher on them if they go to trial and lose than if they accept a deal. This threat to punish people more severely if they go to trial, often communicated to the defendant directly and indirectly by the judge, prosecutor, and even defense counsel, sometimes causes innocent people to plead guilty. Innocent people also may be offered a "good deal" because the prosecutor may have little evidence against them. On the other hand, people against whom there is a strong case may have nothing to lose by going to trial, as they will likely not be offered very good deals to begin with.

Such punitive practices blatantly violate the Constitution, because they punish a person for exercising the constitutional right to a jury trial. They continue because appellate courts tend not to interfere in the day-to-day aspects of how cases are handled in criminal courts. Nevertheless, a statute is unconstitutional if it allows for harsher punishment of defendants who ask for jury trials than for defendants who plead guilty (*U.S. v. Jackson*, U.S. Sup. Ct. 1968).

Making Sure the Defendant Really Is Guilty

In addition to ensuring that pleas are knowing and intelligent, judges are also supposed to determine if there is an adequate basis in fact for accepting the plea; that is, whether the defendant committed the charged crime. When a defendant formally pleads guilty or no contest but all the while says he is innocent, a judge does not have to accept the plea (*North Carolina v. Alford*, 400 U.S. 25, 91 S.Ct. 160, 1970). In federal courts, defendants who want to plead guilty, or *nolo contendere*, must testify under oath to facts establishing their guilt.

16. What happens after a plea bargain is reached?

Once the deal is worked out, the prosecution and defense will arrange a court hearing and inform the judge about the agreement. Assuming the judge accepts the deal or suggests changes that are satisfactory to both sides, the judge will hear the guilty or no contest plea in open court so that it becomes part of the record. Then, the defendant will be sentenced—either at the same time, which is typical in some less serious cases, or at a later sentencing hearing. (See Chapter 22 on sentencing.)

In-custody defendants may be brought to court soon after the agreement is reached for a special hearing in which the judge takes the plea. Otherwise, the taking of the plea (and sometimes sentencing) will occur at the next scheduled hearing. Depending on when the deal is struck, the next scheduled appearance may be the arraignment, preliminary hearing, or trial.

Section IV: The Strategy of Negotiating Plea Bargains

Just as with other negotiations, such as those of a buyer and seller in a real estate transaction, there are strategies involved with plea bargaining.

17. When prosecutors file charges, do they already have a plea bargain in mind?

Prosecutors often initially charge defendants with more serious or multiple offenses expecting to reduce or drop some as bargaining chips. Because a great many plea bargains occur when the prosecutor agrees to drop one or more of the charges facing a defendant in exchange for a guilty or no contest plea on one or more of the remaining charges, prosecutors tend to charge high in the beginning.

CASE EXAMPLE: Officer Rhett Cutler stopped Charlotte O'Hara for an unsafe lane change. While writing the ticket, Officer Cutler spotted what looked like a small amount of marijuana on the back seat. O'Hara was arrested and charged with the original unsafe lane change offense, possession of marijuana, and DUI (driving under the influence, here of a drug). The charges were filed even though this was a first offense, O'Hara's blood alcohol level (tested just after arrest) was within the legal limit and there was no other evidence of the DUI (other than the marijuana itself and the unsafe lane change).

Question: Why would the prosecutor charge such a serious offense, DUI, for what seems like a routine traffic violation and simple possession?

Answer: It's entirely likely that the prosecutors overcharged O'Hara in order to give themselves room to drop some charges so that O'Hara would feel that she is getting a good deal by pleading guilty. Other factors, such as strict time limits to get charges filed against a defendant, also can contribute to initial overcharging. (For more on charging, see Chapter 6.)

18. Will different defendants charged with the same crime in the same court end up with pretty much the same plea bargain?

Not necessarily. The sentence may differ from case to case depending on a number of factors, such as:

- whether the defendant has any prior convictions ("priors")
- how serious the offense was (whether it was a violent crime), and
- how strong the prosecution's case (evidence) is.

A comprehensive study of plea bargains, conducted in the mid-1980s, found that defense lawyers also look for specific characteristics of the defendant that may be used to argue for leniency in any given case. (See "Plea Bargaining: Critical Issues and Common Practices," U.S. Department of Justice, July 1985.)

One defense lawyer described plea bargaining as follows:

"Everyone in the system knows roughly what a given case is 'worth.' By balancing the seriousness of the crime and the defendant's record (how much time the prosecution wants the defendant to do), against the strength of the evidence and the skill of the defense lawyer (how likely the prosecution is to get a conviction), a specific deal is arrived at." *(How Can You Defend Those People: The Making of a Criminal Lawyer,* James S. Kunen (McGraw-Hill).)

19. What is a "standard deal"?

For many common offenses, prosecutors in a given courthouse will have worked out what is, in effect, a "price list" setting out the typical sentences for different offenses. For example, in one area, it may be the prosecutors' practice to uniformly reduce all first-time DUI (driving under the influence) offenses where blood alcohol tests reveal a marginal or borderline level to a lesser offense such as reckless driving. (See Chapter 24 for more on driving under the influence.)

20. How can I find out what the standard deal is for my case?

Standard deals are typically not written down anywhere. Defense lawyers have to figure out what the "going price" (standard deal) is in a particular jurisdiction for

the crime the defendant is charged with. Lawyers often find out by asking around among their colleagues. Also, some public defender offices keep internal records that they may share with private defense counsel. Because lawyers tend to be clannish, it can often be very difficult for a self-represented defendant to learn about a standard deal. The best place to start, however, even for a layperson, may be a local public defender.

21. What other factors might influence the deal in my case?

A number of other factors may influence particular plea bargains, including:

- where the case is
- what court the case will be heard in and how congested the court calendar is
- which prosecutors are in charge and what their reputation is, and
- which judge will preside over the case and how lenient or tough she is.

Good defense lawyers should know this "lay of the land" information. Defense lawyers who are not personally familiar with these details tend to call and rely on colleagues who are more familiar with the local scoop. Such local factors can be critical. If the judge has a reputation for leniency, for instance, the defense lawyer may be able to get a better deal out of the prosecutor than if the judge has a get-tough reputation. Defendants also tend to find themselves in stronger bargaining positions when their cases are to be heard in busier courts such as in large, metropolitan areas where many judges' (and prosecutors') foremost concern is to get through their backlog.

22. How tricky is it to arrange a plea bargain? Do I have to have a lawyer to negotiate a good deal?

Most of the time, "very tricky" and "yes." To get a good deal, a defense lawyer may have to lobby the district attorney. And just as a child lobbying a parent for a later bedtime must curry favor, so too must defense lawyers; it's critical to make sure at least that they don't irritate the D.A. in charge.

Some suggest, among various other strategies, approaching the D.A. very early on, before any affirmative steps are taken to further the case, and trying to appeal to the D.A.'s sense of compassion. Once prosecutors start working a case, they may become more entrenched in their position. It may then become more difficult to persuade them to drop or reduce certain charges. Further, when lobbying the D.A., wise defense attorneys often start at the bottom of the ladder in the prosecutor's office. If a less experienced D.A. says no, a defense lawyer can always talk to a supervisor. But once the supervising lawyer says no, the defense may be out of luck.

These tactics suggest how cautiously defense lawyers proceed with plea negotiations. And, if defense lawyers have to be careful about how they negotiate a deal, self-represented defendants must be even more careful.

First, there are traps for the unwary pro per. For instance, though technically there are rules of evidence that prevent the use of information discussed in the course of a plea bargain from being used in trial (see Federal Rule of Criminal Procedure 11(e)(6)), the prosecution may find ways around this. The prosecution may, for instance, look for independent evidence that they find from leads given away by the defendant during these negotiations.

Second, defense lawyers may be able to negotiate more effectively because they may have an emotional distance from the case that the defendant lacks.

Third, it is quite likely that the prosecutor will have a bias against defendants representing themselves—or at least a preference for working with fellow lawyers—and will not offer the defendant the same deal he would give a defense lawyer. In one study, prosecutors flatly admitted personal prejudice against unrepresented defendants. (See "Plea Bargaining: Critical Issues and Common Practices," U.S. Department of Justice, July 1985 at 43.) In misdemeanor cases in Texas, the study reported, unrepresented defendants discuss their cases directly with the prosecutors, "who generally advise them to plead guilty to avoid being 'creamed' if they go to trial and in order to get probation or diversion right away." One prosecutor further admitted that in a weak case, "If there is a defense attorney, I'll dismiss it … If there is no attorney, I'll try to get the defendant to plead guilty."

23. How do I know when to take the deal?

One of the reasons why plea bargaining is so common is that both sides often have something to gain when cases are disposed of by guilty pleas. There is no way to know for sure, however, when the best time to take the deal is—when to hold off, when to stall, and when to just accept the sentence and move on. Plea negotiations are somewhat of a poker game.

General wisdom suggests that it is often beneficial for defendants to hold off accepting the first offers. Underlying this theory is the idea that the more time that passes after the alleged offense, the weaker the state's case may become. Witnesses disappear and forget, physical evidence may be lost. And all that time, the defense has a chance to build a better case. So, for some cases, the longer the defendant can hold out, the better the deal will be.

Some prosecutors have a hard and fast policy, however, of escalating their demands if their first offer isn't accepted. Many times, prosecutors who play such hardball have reputations that precede them, and defense lawyers know to accept their first offers if it's reasonably clear that they would lose the case if it went to trial. Also, even if delays are beneficial to the defense, waiting is usually easier for those defendants who are out on bail than it is for in-custody defendants.

Because of these variables, defendants should consult with their lawyers or a legal coach about strategies of waiting versus taking the deal, or going to trial.

In some instances, such as where a prosecutor's deal is no better than the likely sentence and where the defendant has a strong defense, the defendant may want to go to trial.

24. Don't defense lawyers just push people to take deals because it's easier for the lawyers?

Many defendants have the perception that their lawyers just want to get them to plead to make life easier for the lawyers. And that perception seems to be stronger where court-appointed lawyers are involved. Often, before the first meeting with the client, the defense lawyer will have seen the police report, spoken with the D.A., and possibly even agreed upon a tentative plea bargain. In one study from years back, defendants reported most often hearing, as the first words their lawyers spoke, "I can get you ... if you plead guilty." (See *American Criminal Justice: The Defendant's Perspective,* by Jonathan D. Casper (Prentice Hall).) Many defendants today echo this sentiment, and some feel that their lawyers don't even ask for the defendant's version of the crime.

These perceptions are based on some sound evidence. It is clearly true that it is less work for a lawyer to plead a client guilty than to go through a complete trial. Therefore, defendants must make sure their lawyer is working for their best interests, fairly explaining the pros and cons of any deals offered and not rushing or pressuring the defendant into accepting a deal. The final decision on whether or not to plead rests with the clients; defendants have a right to a trial if they want one.

CASE EXAMPLE: Tonya Herding was caught on camera Thursday afternoon stealing clothes, jewelry, and perfume from Mays Department store. She was arrested at the store, taken to jail, and booked. Bail was set at $1,500, but Herding had no money to post bail. She told the police she would need a court-appointed lawyer. She spent the night in jail and was arraigned the next day. In court, just before her case was called, Herding met Nancy Herrigan, the P.D. assigned to the case. Herrigan told Herding she got a good deal and thought Herding should accept it to get out of jail.

Question: Should Herding take the deal?

Answer: It's hard to say. If Herding has people she can contact to lend her the money, she could probably get a bail bond for $150, and for another $150 or so she may be able to get a second opinion from a private defense lawyer. At a minimum, Herding should ask Herrigan to explain what the deal is and why it's a good one. Is it, for example, the standard deal for such offenses? She should also possibly ask what Herrigan thinks of requesting a continuance and lobbying the D.A. further before accepting the present offer.

However, the perceptions can also be incorrect. Some studies show that public defenders do engage in more plea bargaining than private defense lawyers, but the deals they work out tend to be equivalent to or better for defendants on the whole than the results private counsel obtain from going to trial. In other words, some private counsel may push to go to trial when it would be better for the defendant to take the deal.

25. Can I do anything if I feel that I made a bad deal?

Plea bargains are usually binding. Defendants cannot get out of deals just because they changed their minds. In certain (albeit rare) circumstances, however, where it would be unfair to allow a deal to stand, defendants may be allowed to withdraw guilty pleas. Examples of such circumstances may include where a defendant:

- does not have the "effective assistance of counsel" in making the deal (see Chapter 17 for more on effective assistance of counsel)—for instance, the defendant was forced to plead before a public defender could be appointed
- is not informed of the underlying charges before agreeing to the deal or does not voluntarily agree to the deal, or
- is given a sentence that differs from the agreed-upon deal.

The Trial Process

This chapter explains criminal trial procedures and tactics. The discussion is general, since even judges in the same courthouse are apt to conduct trials differently. However, defendants who understand the general procedures and tactics associated with criminal trials are better able to help their attorneys make important trial decisions. Defendants can then also make an educated choice about whether to plead guilty before trial (perhaps as part of a plea bargain) or go to trial.

Section I: Summary of the Trial Process

The many rituals associated with modern trials have developed over centuries. America's common law heritage makes it possible for all states and the federal government to follow a largely uniform set of procedures. In summary form, those procedures are as follows.

Judge or jury: The defense and prosecution decide whether they want the case tried by a judge or a jury.

Select the jury: If a jury trial, the defense and prosecution select the jury through a question and answer process called *voir dire.*

Address evidence issues: The defense and prosecution request the court in advance of trial to admit or exclude certain evidence (these requests are called motions *in limine*).

Opening statements: The prosecution and then the defense make opening statements to the judge or jury.

Prosecution case-in-chief: The prosecution presents its main case through direct examination of prosecution witnesses by the prosecutor.

Cross-examination: The defense cross-examines the prosecution witnesses.

Redirect: The prosecution reexamines its witnesses (called redirect).

Prosecution rests: The prosecution rests its case.

Motion to dismiss: The defense has the option of making a motion to dismiss the charges.

Motion to dismiss denied: Almost always, the judge denies the defense motion to dismiss.

Defense case-in-chief: The defense presents its main case through direct examination of defense witnesses.

Cross-examination: The prosecutor cross-examines the defense witnesses.

Redirect: The defense reexamines the defense witnesses.

Defense rests: The defense rests its case.

Prosecution rebuttal: The prosecutor offers evidence to rebut the defense case (called rebuttal).

Instructions settled: The prosecution and defense get together with the judge and figure out what instructions the judge should give the jury.

Prosecution closing argument: The prosecution makes its closing argument, summarizing the evidence as the prosecution sees it, and explaining why the jury should render a guilty verdict.

Defense closing argument: The defense makes its closing argument, summarizing the evidence as the defense sees it, and explaining why the jury should render a not guilty verdict (or at least a guilty verdict on a lesser charge).

Jury instructed: The judge instructs the jury about what law to apply to the case and how to carry out its duties. (Some judges "preinstruct" juries, reciting instructions before closing argument or even at the outset of trial.)

Jury deliberations: The jury (if it is a jury trial) deliberates and tries to produce a verdict by (usually) unanimous agreement.

Posttrial motions if guilty verdict: If the jury produces a guilty verdict, the defense often makes posttrial motions (requesting the judge to override the jury and either grant a new trial or order the defendant acquitted).

Posttrial motions denied: Almost always, the judge denies the defense posttrial motions.

Sentencing if guilty verdict: Assuming a conviction, the judge either sentences the defendant on the spot, or sets sentencing for another day.

Section II: Choosing a Judge or Jury Trial

This section is about what a defendant should consider when deciding whether to ask for a jury trial.

1. Am I entitled to a jury trial?

The U.S. Constitution guarantees the right to trial by jury in all but "petty" cases (cases in which the defendant cannot be imprisoned for more than six months). Defendants charged with felonies and serious misdemeanors are entitled to jury trials. Defendants charged with minor misdemeanors punishable only by fines—called infractions (for example, speeding)—are not. (See Chapter 17 for more on the right to a jury trial.)

2. Am I likely to be better off with a judge or a jury?

Defendants should normally opt for jury trials unless they have a good reason to waive (give up) a jury and leave the decision to a judge sitting without a jury. The reasons this is often the best choice are that it allows defendants to:

- **Play the percentages.** Most jurisdictions require unanimous jury verdicts. For example, if a case is tried to a 12-person jury, the prosecutor has to convince all 12 of the defendant's guilt. A reasonable doubt in the mind of any single juror will prevent the defendant's conviction—assuming the juror acts conscientiously. By contrast, a judge offers the defense but one mind in which to raise a reasonable doubt.

- **Have a hand in selecting jurors.** Before the start of a jury trial, the defense can question and excuse (dismiss) some potential jurors during jury *voir dire*. In most states, however, unless it can prove actual bias on the part of the judge, the defense has to accept the judge assigned to the case.

Despite these reasons, the defense is sometimes better off with a judge trial. For example, the background of a certain judge might make her sympathetic to the defense. Or, the success of the defense case may rest on a technical legal argument that the judge is more likely than a jury to adopt.

The "One Free Bite" Rule

Some states allow the defense to dismiss a judge without having to prove that the judge is biased. The defense simply files an affidavit stating, in effect, "We want a different judge." (See, for example, Cal. Civ. Proc. Code § 170.6.) But the defense can use this affidavit procedure only once; the defense must accept the next judge assigned to the case—unless, of course, the defense can show actual bias.

3. Who should make the decision about judge or jury?

The judge vs. jury trial decision is an important one, and the defendant should normally make it after consulting with her attorney. (This is specified in Standard 4-5.2, ABA Standards for Criminal Justice.) Usually, defense attorneys have greater access than defendants to information about judges, their backgrounds and their attitudes, and to the technical merits of the case. But a defendant may be as equally equipped as the attorney in gauging the mood of the community toward the police

and the type of crime with which the defendant is charged, and in assessing the emotional appeal of the case.

The Jury Trial "Penalty"

Some judges apply an unwritten and unfair jury trial penalty policy, giving harsher sentences to defendants who opted for a jury rather than a judge trial. For example, in off-the-record conversations, judges often tell defense attorneys something like, "If your client takes a bench (judge) trial and is convicted, he's looking at a couple of years in jail. But if he insists on a jury trial, all bets are off." The implication is that defendants who put the system to the added time and expense of a jury trial will pay for it in their sentences. Before deciding on a judge or jury, defendants should try to find out what the risks are.

4. What happens if I want a judge trial and the prosecutor asks for a jury trial?

If either side requests a jury—prosecutor or defense—trial will be to a jury.

5. If I ask for a jury trial, do I have to pay the jurors?

No. Unlike in civil trials, in which the parties pay the jury fees, the government pays jury fees in criminal cases.

The Jury Waiver in the Leopold and Loeb Case

The trial of Leopold and Loeb took place in Chicago in the 1930s. Thinking themselves too smart to be caught, two wealthy but mentally disturbed young men in search of a thrill killed a young boy. After their arrest, their parents hired the famous Clarence Darrow to defend them. Dramatically, Darrow waived a jury trial and pleaded his clients guilty. Under then-existing Illinois law, a judge and not a jury then had to sentence Leopold and Loeb. Darrow figured that he had a better chance of saving his clients' lives in front of a judge. He was right; they were given life sentences, and Leopold was eventually paroled.

Section III: Jury *Voir Dire*

This section is about the process of selecting a jury in a criminal trial.

6. What is jury *voir dire*?

Usually pronounced "vwar deer," jury *voir dire* is the jury selection process. Potential jurors answer questions about their backgrounds and attitudes, and the prosecutor and defense can challenge potential jurors who demonstrate from their answers that they might not be fair and impartial. If a judge allows a challenge (and sometimes the judge has no choice), the challenged juror is excused and replaced from a larger pool of potential jurors.

7. What kinds of questions can be put to potential jurors?

Some *voir dire* questions are routine; they are put to potential jurors in just about every criminal case. For example, potential jurors are routinely asked whether they know the attorneys, the defendant, or any witnesses, where they work, and whether they have ties to law enforcement. Other questions are case-specific. For example, if the defendant is charged with making a fraudulent insurance claim, potential jurors will undoubtedly be asked about their attitudes toward and experiences with insurance companies.

In some types of cases (for example, rape cases), *voir dire* questions can be very invasive of the potential jurors' privacy. When this occurs, judges often give the potential jurors an option to answer in the judge's chambers, outside the presence of the other potential jurors.

8. Who asks the questions on *voir dire*—the judge or the attorney?

In the past, attorneys did all *voir dire* questioning—except the handful of routine questions that the judge would ask. In many state courts, this is still true. However, it's increasingly common for judges to do most of the questioning in an effort to speed up *voir dire* and prevent attorneys from using *voir dire* to build rapport with the jurors and plant ideas about their side of the case.

Especially in the federal courts, the prosecution and defense may be limited to submitting written questions that they want the judge to ask.

9. What can the defense do to keep potential jurors they don't want off the jury?

The defense and prosecution can each challenge potential jurors. A challenge is a request for the judge to excuse (dismiss) the potential juror in question. The rules allow for two types of challenges: (1) challenges for cause, and (2) peremptory challenges.

A challenge for cause asks the judge to excuse a potential juror on the ground that the juror's answers demonstrate actual bias. Both sides are entitled to jurors who are fair and impartial. Jurors who are predisposed in favor of one side or the other cannot legally serve on a jury. For example, a judge will undoubtedly grant a defendant's challenge for cause if a potential juror says something like, "I think police officers do a marvelous job under almost impossible conditions. I'd find it very difficult to disbelieve any testimony a police officer gives." Such an answer shows that the juror is predisposed to believe a police officer over the defendant, and is not, therefore, fair and impartial. Defendants often seek to exercise challenges for cause privately—perhaps in the judge's chambers. That way, if the judge denies the challenge, the defendant is not faced with an angry juror.

Peremptory challenges allow either side to excuse potential jurors even if their answers do not demonstrate actual bias. If the defense or prosecution has a hunch or an intuition that a potential juror favors the adversary, that side can use a peremptory challenge to excuse that juror. Express bias aside, a defense attorney may think that a juror's background will incline that juror against the defense and will use a peremptory challenge to bump that juror. For instance, if defense counsel believes that older jurors are most likely to accept the defendant's account of events, the attorney will use peremptory challenges to bump younger jurors, hoping that their replacements will be older.

The judge must grant a peremptory challenge, regardless of whether the judge believes the challenged juror is biased. However, each side is given only a limited number of peremptory challenges. (See Question 10 for limits on peremptory challenges.)

> **CASE EXAMPLE:** Marcus Nieman is charged with stealing merchandise from Southstrom's Department Store. One potential juror, Victoria Macy, is employed as a clerk in a different department store. In response to Nieman's questions, Macy states that shoplifters hurt everyone because they force shops to raise prices, and that she supports cameras in dressing rooms and plainclothes floor detectives as good methods of deterring theft. Macy insists that she will be fair to both sides and is not predisposed to believe the department store's security guard.

Nieman challenges Macy for cause, asking the judge to excuse her on grounds of bias.

Question: Will the judge grant the challenge and dismiss Macy?

Answer: Probably not. Macy's feelings are likely to be shared by the public at large. Since Macy insists that she is open-minded and will base her verdict on the evidence, she will remain as a juror unless Neiman uses a peremptory challenge to bump her.

Judges Do Not Often Grant Challenges for Cause

Even though a potential juror's background suggests a probable partiality toward one side or the other, most judges will allow the juror to sit as long as the juror insists that she can give both sides a fair trial. For instance, assume that an alleged victim and a potential juror are both plumbers. The defendant may believe that the juror will subconsciously favor the prosecution. Nevertheless, if the potential juror swears to be open-minded and fair, the judge would probably deny the defendant's challenge for cause. The defense might then use one of its peremptory challenges to strike this juror.

Constitutional Limits on Peremptory Challenges

Until the mid-1980s, attorneys could exercise peremptory challenges for whatever reasons they chose. Since then, courts have ruled that attorneys cannot excuse potential jurors because of the jurors' race or gender. For example, if a defendant claims that a prosecutor has exercised a peremptory challenge against a prospective juror based on the juror's race, the prosecutor has to show that the challenge was based on a valid, race-neutral reason (*Snyder v. Louisiana*, U.S. Sup. Ct. 2008).

Alternate Jurors

In many cases, judges try to seat regular and alternate jurors. The alternates sit in throughout a trial, but will not step in and decide the case unless one of the regular jurors becomes ill or for some other reason has to be excused from the jury. Without an alternate, the judge might have to declare a mistrial and start a trial all over again.

10. How many potential jurors can I challenge?

Each side has an unlimited number of challenges for cause. However, the number of peremptory challenges is very limited. For example, Federal Rule of Criminal

Procedure 24 grants each side only three peremptory challenges in misdemeanor cases. Most states have similar limits. In cases involving murder and other very serious charges, each side may have as many as 20–25 peremptory challenges. Regardless of the number, the defense has to carefully save its peremptory challenges for potential jurors whom they cannot successfully challenge for cause, but who are most likely to harbor biases in favor of the prosecution or otherwise be likely to favor the prosecution or reject the defense story.

> **CASE EXAMPLE:** In the Marcus Nieman example in the previous section, assume that the judge denies Nieman's challenge to Victoria Macy for cause.
>
> **Question:** Should Nieman use a peremptory challenge to kick Macy off the jury?
>
> **Answer:** This is a difficult judgment for Nieman (and his lawyer) to make. Since Nieman has only a few peremptory challenges in this misdemeanor case, he has to think about whether other potential jurors (including those who might replace Macy) are even more unacceptable than Macy. Nieman should at least try to challenge Macy for cause out of the jury's hearing. If Macy knows that Nieman unsuccessfully challenged her fitness to serve on the jury, Nieman may have no choice other than to use one of his precious peremptory challenges after the judge denies the challenge for cause.

11. Who decides which jurors to challenge?

Many defense attorneys think that deciding which jurors to challenge is a matter of professional craft that the defendant should leave to the attorney. Standard 4-5.2 of the ABA Standards for Criminal Justice supports the lawyers' attitude, though it advises attorneys to consult with clients before challenging potential jurors "where feasible and appropriate." Defendants are often at least as sensitive to potential jurors who give off "bad defense vibes" as are attorneys, and ordinarily defendants should ask their attorneys to consult them during jury selection.

Jury Consultants

Defendants who can pay for it often hire jury consultants to assist in the selection of jurors. Typically, jury consultants investigate people's attitudes in the locality where a trial will take place and develop profiles of jurors who are likely to favor either the defense or the prosecution. For example, a jury consultant may report that "college-educated females under the age of 35 are likely to favor the defense." The defense can take such information into account when deciding which jurors to challenge.

12. Can the defense use *voir dire* to preview its case?

Attorneys have often tried to use *voir dire* to begin persuading jurors to vote their way. The ensuing delays in starting trials were a major reason that judges in many areas have taken over *voir dire* questioning. Nevertheless, the defense can use even a limited questioning opportunity to "educate" jurors about the fundamental rules favoring defendants. Consider these questions that the defense might ask:

- "Does each of you understand that the mere fact that Mr. Binder has been arrested and charged with a crime is not evidence of guilt?"
- "Does anyone disagree with the principle that as she sits here now and throughout the entire trial, Ms. Ouspenskaya is presumed innocent unless and until the prosecution convinces you beyond a reasonable doubt of her guilt?"

The defendant would not really expect a potential juror to disagree with such basic principles. The questions emphasize to the jurors that the burden of proof favors defendants and that all defendants are presumed innocent until proven guilty.

Section IV: Motions *in Limine*

This section is about getting the judge to rule on the admissibility of evidence before a party tries to introduce it in front of the jury.

13. Can I find out before trial starts whether a judge will admit damaging prosecution evidence that I think is inadmissible?

Sometimes, by making a *Motion in Limine.* A defendant can file a written Motion *in*

Limine, or make the motion orally. The purpose of the motion is to ask a judge for a pretrial order that evidence a prosecutor intends to offer at trial is inadmissible. For example, a defendant might ask for a ruling that "the prosecution cannot refer to the fact that the defendant has previously been convicted of a crime." If the judge grants the Motion *in Limine,* neither the prosecutor nor prosecution witnesses can refer to the conviction during the trial.

14. If the defense doesn't make a Motion *in Limine,* can the defense make an objection to prosecution evidence during the trial?

Yes. The defense can wait until a prosecutor offers evidence during trial, and then make an objection. But waiting until trial raises the danger that jurors will hear objectionable evidence before the defense has a chance to object. For example, testimony might unfold as follows:

Prosecutor: "Had you ever seen the defendant before?"

Witness: "Yes, the defendant was in a fight in a different bar the week before."

Defendant: "I object to any reference to an earlier fight, it's irrelevant."

Judge: "I agree. The testimony is stricken, and I instruct the jurors to disregard it."

Even though the judge upholds the defense objection and tells the jurors to disregard the improper evidence, some jurors may be influenced by it. As attorneys are wont to say, "It's hard to unring a bell."

By making a Motion *in Limine*, the defense hopes to prevent jurors from hearing improper evidence in the first place.

And in cases where the judge rules that the evidence in question is admissible, it may still benefit the defendant to file a Motion *in Limine*, because even when the judge rules against the defense in a Motion *in Limine*, at least the defense knows ahead of time that the damaging evidence will be allowed in at trial, and can plan its strategy accordingly.

15. Can the judge delay ruling on a Motion *in Limine* until trial?

Yes, and judges often do so. The judge may want to wait until the trial is under-way before ruling on the admissibility of evidence. Nevertheless, a Motion *in Limine* is a useful way for defendants to "red flag" an objection to important but potentially highly prejudicial prosecution evidence. If and when the prosecutor attempts to in-troduce the particular evidence, the judge will have been given notice by the pretrial motion that this is critical evidence and may be more willing to take the time during the trial to carefully consider its admissibility.

Section V: Opening Statements

This section is about the introductory statements to the jury that attorneys are permitted to make at the start of the case.

16. What is an opening statement?

An opening statement is an opportunity for the defense and prosecution to describe what they will try to prove and what evidence they plan on offering. The prosecution and defense cases often emerge piecemeal from a number of witnesses, and are likely to be interrupted by court recesses, cross-examination, and the like. Thus, an opening statement allows each side to make it easier for the judge or jury to follow their case. Good opening statements are like roadmaps and movie previews. Like a roadmap, an opening statement tells a judge or jury where the defense or prosecution case is headed. And like a movie preview, a good opening statement whets a judge's or jury's appetite for the evidence to come.

17. Can evidence be introduced during an opening statement?

No. What is said during opening statement is not evidence. The judge or jury cannot rely on facts referred to during the opening statements when deciding the case. For example, assume that during opening statement a prosecutor says, "You'll hear the defendant's next-door neighbor testify that the defendant drank three beers before leaving for work that morning." If the next-door neighbor does not testify, or testifies but fails to mention three beers, the judge or jurors cannot use the prosecutor's assertion as evidence that the defendant drank three beers. Rather, during closing argument the defense attorney would most likely attack the prosecution's case by pointing out the prosecutor's failure to deliver the evidence promised in the opening statement.

18. When does the defense make its opening statement?

In most jurisdictions, the defense can make an opening statement either immediately after the prosecutor's (before any witnesses testify), or after the prosecution's case-in-chief is over (before defense witnesses testify).

When given the choice, defendants usually choose the first option. Even though judges repeatedly admonish jurors not to evaluate a case until all the evidence is in, jurors weigh information as they hear it. This gives prosecutors a big advantage, because they get to present evidence first. Defense opening statements are one way to keep jurors' minds open until defendants get to present their evidence.

On the other hand, if the defense strategy is to defer certain key decisions—such as whether the defendant will testify—until after the prosecution case is finished, it may be better to defer the defense opening statement until the beginning of the defense case.

19. Can the prosecution or defense argue the merits of their case during opening statement?

No. Since opening statement serves only as a preview, neither the defense nor the prosecution can argue their case. For example, a defendant cannot explain why the defense case is stronger than the prosecution's.

Some judges allow more argument during opening statement than other judges. Whatever leeway a judge allows a prosecutor should also be given to the defense.

> **CASE EXAMPLE:** Rex Kars is on trial for assaulting Herman Shepherd. Kars claims that he acted in self-defense. The prosecutor makes the following remarks during opening statement: "Frank Enstein will testify that he saw the defendant Kars strike the first blow. I submit that Enstein is totally credible. He had the best view of anyone at the scene and is completely unbiased, and his testimony is more credible than any evidence the defendant will offer."
>
> **Question:** Is this a proper opening statement?
>
> **Answer:** No. The prosecutor is making an argument. Opening statement is limited to a preview of evidence; it is not the time to argue which side's evidence is more credible.

Section VI: Prosecution's Case-in-Chief

This section is about the prosecution's case—what the prosecutor has to prove and how strong the proof has to be.

20. Why does the prosecution get to put on its case first?

The prosecution goes first because it has the burden of convincing the judge or jury of the defendant's guilt. Until the prosecution puts on enough evidence to satisfy this burden, there's no reason for the defense to put on a case at all.

21. How can I find out exactly what the prosecutor has to prove in order to convict me?

To figure out what the prosecutor has to prove, defendants have to very carefully read the criminal laws they are charged with violating. Often, the legal definition of a crime differs from its popular understanding. For example, in many jurisdictions drivers may be convicted of drunk driving simply because their blood alcohol level exceeded the legal limit. The prosecution does not have to prove how the alcohol affected their driving.

Most crimes consist of two or more discrete subcomponents called elements. To prove a defendant guilty, a prosecutor has to support each element with proof. If the prosecutor fails to prove any one element beyond a reasonable doubt, the defendant should be found not guilty.

For example, assume that Phil Thee is charged with grand theft. In many states, grand theft consists of the following elements:

1. the defendant
2. took property of another
3. worth more than $200
4. with the intent to permanently deprive the owner of the property that was taken.

If the prosecution fails to offer enough evidence to satisfy each element during its case-in-chief, Phil must be acquitted. For instance, the prosecution may prove that Phil took someone's property, but fail to prove the property's value (Element 3). Or,

the prosecution may prove the value of the taken property, but fail to prove that Phil intended to permanently deprive the owner of possession (Element 4). In either instance, the judge or jury would have to acquit Phil.

22. To obtain a verdict of not guilty, does the defense have to mount an attack on every element of the charged crime?

No. The prosecution has the burden of proving beyond a reasonable doubt each and every element of the crime. This means that if the defense raises a reasonable doubt as to any one element, the defendant must be found not guilty. This is why the defense typically focuses its attack on one or two elements.

For example, return to the case of Phil Thee, the defendant charged with grand theft. In response, Phil might attack just one of the elements that the prosecution has to prove. For example, Phil may concede that someone may have stolen property worth more than $200, but offer evidence that it wasn't he who stole it. Or, Phil may concede that he took property worth more than $200, but claim that he was borrowing it pursuant to an agreement he had made with its owner. Whatever the basis of attack, defendants rarely contest every element of a charge. (For more information about focusing on the elements of a crime as a defense, see Chapter 13. For more information about finding and interpreting criminal statutes, see Chapter 12 and Chapter 27.)

Section VII: Direct Examination of Witnesses

This section explains how a party or the party's attorney must question that party's own witnesses.

23. What is the purpose of the oath that all witnesses take?

The purpose of the oath is to impress on witnesses the seriousness of testifying in court. By swearing to tell the truth, witnesses also subject themselves to perjury charges should they lie about an important matter. (Witnesses who for religious or other reasons do not care to take an oath and swear to tell the truth may instead "affirm" that they will testify truthfully. Whether a witness "swears" or "affirms" to tell the truth, the effect is the same.)

Rarity of Perjury Prosecutions

Witnesses bent on perjury have little to fear from prosecutors. Perjury isn't a high priority crime for most prosecutors, in part because it can be difficult to prove actual knowledge of falsity. An exception to this might be in cases widely reported in the media. When a witness appears to commit perjury in full view of millions, prosecutors may have no choice other than filing perjury charges. An example of this was Detective Mark Fuhrman, who pled guilty to perjury after lying during the 1995 internationally televised murder trial of O.J. Simpson.

24. If I testify in my case, I just want to be able to tell what happened in my own words. Can I do this?

Probably not. Testimony is supposed to emerge in question-and-answer form, not as an unbroken narrative. When witnesses respond to specific questions, adversaries know ahead of time what general information the witness is likely to provide, and have time to object if necessary. This means that defendants represented by attorneys usually have to tell their story in response to the attorney's questions.

Self-represented defendants, on the other hand, can't sensibly pose questions to themselves. (Woody Allen demonstrated this to great comic effect in the famous movie *Bananas*.) Thus, judges usually permit self-represented defendants to testify in narrative form—that is, to tell their story in their own words. But many judges will interrupt the defendant's narrative to ask questions.

25. Can the defense decide the order in which its witnesses testify?

Yes. The defense can call witnesses in whatever order it chooses. However, the defendant often testifies last (if at all). Since the defendant cannot be excluded while other witnesses testify, a defendant who testifies last has the benefit of hearing what the other witnesses have said and listening to the prosecutor's cross-examinations.

Tips for Witnesses

People whose testimony is needed in court are usually served with subpoenas, which are court orders. (See the sample subpoena at the end of this chapter.) Subpoenaed witnesses who fail to appear in court on the subpoena date can be taken into custody. Witnesses should understand the following rules:

- Witnesses can and should discuss their testimony ahead of time with the attorney for the side that called them. Witnesses should know generally what questions will be put to them.

- Witnesses can talk informally to the attorney for the other side if they want to, but they do not have to.

- When testifying, witnesses should limit their answers to the questions asked. They should not volunteer additional information. Even if they are just trying to be helpful, what they say may be legally improper—and it may end up hurting rather than helping.

- Witnesses who don't understand a question should ask the questioner to rephrase it.

- Witnesses often needn't worry if they have a temporary loss of memory. After a witness replies, "I don't remember," evidence rules allow attorneys to show the witness letters, reports, memos, or any other documents to remind the witness of forgotten information. However, after having his or her memory stimulated in this manner (called "refreshing recollection"), the witness must still be able to testify from memory. If the witness says, after viewing a document, "You know, I still can't remember," the witness will not be allowed to simply testify to what's in the document.

- Witnesses who are worried about wasting time in court until they testify should ask the attorney who subpoenaed them about an "on call" procedure. Witnesses who are on call agree to be available to come to court and testify on short notice, but in the meantime can go about their daily tasks.

- Witnesses should keep their cool during cross-examination, and answer an adversary's questions in the same manner that they answered questions asked by the attorney for the side favored by their testimony—that is, make sure they understand the question and limit their answers to what the questions ask.

26. Can the prosecutor call the defendant as a witness?

No. Under the Fifth Amendment to the U.S. Constitution, the defendant has an absolute right not to be called as a witness nor to testify unless he chooses to do so.

Section VIII: Cross-Examination

This section is about whether a party or a party's attorney may question witnesses called by the other party.

27. What is cross-examination?

After a witness has been called by the defense or prosecution and given testimony under direct examination, the other side has an opportunity to question the witness about the testimony. Most trial attorneys agree that cross-examination is one of the most important tools for getting at the truth.

28. What kind of information does a cross-examining prosecutor want to get out of a defense witness?

A prosecutor's usual cross-examination goal is to undermine the credibility (believ-ability) of testimony given by the defendant and other defense witnesses during direct examination. The defense can expect cross-examination to cover these possible areas:

- The witness's prior criminal record, if any, for the purpose of impeaching the witness's credibility. Prior arrests are not generally admissible in evidence, but prior convictions that bear on the ability of the witness to be truthful are, especially if the convictions are for felonies.
- Inconsistencies between the witness's testimony and any statements the witness gave to police officers or others.
- If the witness is the defendant, the defendant's motive to commit the crime. For example, if the defendant is charged with the crime of theft, the prosecutor might ask questions suggesting that the defendant needed a large sum of cash.
- If the witness is the defendant, the defendant's physical ability to do whatever the defendant claims to have done. For example, the prosecutor may try to cast doubt on the defendant's claim to have gotten from one house to another in 15 minutes, or to have been able to observe the color of a car at night.

29. Can the defense attorney help the defendant prepare for cross-examination?

Yes. Defense attorneys often play the part of a prosecutor and rehearse the prosecutor's likely cross-examination with defendants (and defense witnesses) before trial. Such rehearsals are perfectly legal and proper.

30. After the prosecutor cross-examines a defense witness, can the defense attorney ask that witness additional questions?

Yes. This is known as redirect examination, and it gives the defendant or witness a chance to respond to the prosecutor's credibility attacks during cross-examination. For example, if the prosecutor asked the defendant about a prior inconsistent statement, the defendant will have a chance to explain the reason for the inconsistency. Also, redirect gives the defendant or other witness an opportunity to clarify testimony that was cleverly but misleadingly elicited by the prosecutor during cross. For other evidence rules affecting cross-examination, see Chapter 18, Section III.

Section IX: Defense Motion to Dismiss

This section is about when the defense can ask the judge to dismiss the charges in the middle of the trial.

31. After the prosecution rests, can the defense ask the judge to rule on whether the prosecution has provided enough evidence to justify a conviction?

Yes. Even in a jury trial, the judge has the power to decide that the prosecution's case by itself isn't strong enough to support a guilty verdict. The defense can ask the judge to exercise this power by making a Motion to Dismiss at the conclusion of the prosecution's case-in-chief. If this motion is granted, the defense will be saved the necessity of presenting its own case. And the dismissal will operate as the legal equivalent of an acquittal, which means the defendant cannot be retried.

32. Does the defense have anything to lose by making a Motion to Dismiss?

Generally, no. The motion is made out of the jury's presence. Therefore, even if the judge denies the motion, the jury is unaware that the judge thinks that the prosecution's case is strong enough to justify a guilty verdict. However, to preserve their own reputations, defense attorneys usually don't move to dismiss if the prosecution's case is obviously strong enough to justify a guilty verdict.

Section X: Defendant's Case-in-Chief

This section is about how the defense presents its own case.

33. Are the rules for the defense part of the case the same as for the prosecution's?

Yes. Like prosecutors, the defense can call witnesses in whatever order they wish. Also, they must elicit testimony in question-and-answer form, and cannot ask leading questions of defense witnesses.

34. Is it always a good idea to present a defense case?

No. Sometimes the defendant's best argument is that the prosecution evidence is not strong enough to prove guilt beyond a reasonable doubt. In such situations a defendant may choose to rest on the presumption of innocence and neither call witnesses nor present other evidence. This tactic may be riskier in a jury trial. Jurors are probably more prone than judges to thinking, "If the defendant had a good case, why didn't we get to hear it?" Thus, defendants should carefully review with their lawyers any decision to rest on the presumption.

CASE EXAMPLE: June Buggs is on trial for burglary. June's defense is mistaken identity; she claims to have been at home at the time of the burglary. The defense effectively undermined the credibility of the only prosecution witness who claimed to be able to identify June as the burglar. Moreover, June was home alone at the time of the burglary, and has told her lawyer that her memory of the evening is impaired by the fact that she had been smoking marijuana.

Question: Should June consider not presenting a defense case?

Answer: Yes. The prosecution case is weak, and June may do her case more harm than good if she is unable to remember clearly what she was doing on the night of the burglary. Because her strongest argument may be the prosecution's inability to prove her guilty beyond a reasonable doubt, June may reasonably choose to rest on the presumption.

35. Can the prosecutor respond to the evidence presented by the defense?

Yes. After the defense "rests" (finishes presenting evidence), the prosecutor normally has a chance to offer "rebuttal" evidence. The prosecutor can offer rebuttal evidence only to attack evidence offered during the defense case. The prosecutor cannot use rebuttal as an excuse to rehash the prosecutor's case-in-chief or put in new evidence unrelated to what the defense presents.

CASE EXAMPLE: Cara Way is on trial for grand theft. During the defense's case-in-chief, Cara's attorney calls Chia as an alibi witness to testify that Chia and Cara were at the movies at the time of the theft. On rebuttal, the prosecutor wants to call two witnesses: (1) Cain, to testify that Cain recently overheard Chia tell Cara, "If you're ever in trouble, you can count on me for an alibi," and (2) Abel, to testify that Cara was the person he saw commit the burglary. (Abel already testified to this during the prosecution's case-in-chief.)

Question: Can either Cain or Abel testify on rebuttal?

Answer: Cain can testify, because Cain's testimony attacks evidence presented by Cara. Abel cannot testify, because it would be a rehash of testimony already given.

36. At the end of the case, can the judge instruct the jury to find the defendant guilty?

No. As the representative of the community, the jury has the absolute power to find any defendant not guilty. The judge has no power to instruct the jury to return a guilty verdict. And if the jury comes back not guilty, the judge has no power to change its verdict or order a new trial.

Section XI: Closing Argument

This section is about the function of the closing argument and the limits placed on it by the courts.

37. During its closing argument, can the defense mention evidence it forgot to offer when it was putting on its case?

No. Just as the opening statement is limited to evidence that will be offered (see Question 16), so is closing argument limited to evidence that has been offered. Referring to evidence that was not offered during testimony is improper argument outside the record.

38. If the defense realizes during closing argument that it forgot to offer some important evidence, is there anything it can do?

A defense that rests its case having forgotten to offer important evidence can ask the judge for permission to reopen the case-in-chief. Even during closing argument, the judge has the power to allow the defendant to present additional evidence. The more important the evidence, and the better excuse the defendant can offer for not presenting the evidence earlier, the likelier the judge is to allow a defendant to reopen the defense case.

CASE EXAMPLE: Jezza Bell is on trial for child endangerment for leaving her infant son unattended while she went shopping. Jezza's defense was that she left the child in the care of a responsible babysitter who took off without Jezza's knowledge. Jezza testified that a neighbor, Jebediah, saw the babysitter with Jezza's son when Jezza left. However, Jezza could not locate Jebediah and thus could not call him as a witness. Just before Jezza finishes her closing argument, Jebediah rushes into court, apologizes for having been away and offers to testify as above.

Question: What should Jezza do?

Answer: Jezza should immediately ask the judge for permission to reopen her case-in-chief. Jezza should explain what Jebediah will say, and her inability to produce him as a witness earlier. Jebediah's testimony is important, and the judge should grant Jezza's request.

39. What should the defense talk about during its closing argument?

Closing argument is an opportunity for the defense to explain why the evidence requires a not guilty verdict. Most defense closing arguments include these features:

- a reminder that the prosecution has the burden of proving its case beyond a reasonable doubt, and that the defendant is presumed innocent
- a summary of important evidence with a defense spin, especially if the trial has extended over a few days

- an attack on weaknesses in the prosecution's case. Typically, the defense tries to stress that prosecution witnesses were biased or had motives to lie (for instance, a prosecution witness had charges dismissed in return for testifying against the defendant), or gave inconsistent testimony, or did not have a sufficient opportunity to perceive events, or offered implausible testimony; and
- if the defendant presented evidence, support for the strength of that evidence. For example, the defense may stress that defense witnesses were unbiased, and that they testified in a consistent manner.

40. During closing argument, can the prosecutor play to jurors' emotions, as in movies and TV?

Dramas often misleadingly portray what prosecutors can say during closing argument. Prosecutors are supposed to appeal to jurors' reason, not their emotion and prejudice. Prosecution arguments that emphasize name-calling and community biases rather than evidence are improper. The defense should ask the judge to instruct jurors to ignore such comments. If the prosecutor's comments are very prejudicial, the defense can ask the judge to declare a mistrial.

CASE EXAMPLE: Abner Savage is charged with sexually molesting a young girl. During closing argument, the prosecutor calls Savage "a piece of vermin, a filthy beast who must be locked up like the wild animal that he is." The prosecutor also tells the jurors to "send a message to all other would-be child molesters in our community that this kind of behavior won't be tolerated."

Question: Is this proper argument?

Answer: No. The first part of the argument improperly appeals to the jurors' passions and emotions instead of to their reason. The second part is improper because the message that a verdict sends is irrelevant.

Dramas Often Overemphasize the Importance of Closing Argument

Movies and TV dramas often portray closing argument as the most critical phase of trial. Through words as stirring as Marc Antony's over the fallen Caesar, movie attorneys always seem to sway jurors with last-minute dramatic appeals. (An excellent example is defense attorney Jake Brigance's final argument in *A Time to Kill*.) However, judges and jurors rarely decide a case according to which attorney has the better oratorical skills. Studies indicate that most of the time, judges and jurors have made up their minds before closing argument.

41. Who argues first?

Most judges allow the prosecution to argue first, again on the theory that the prosecution carries the burden of proof.

In fact, many judges also allow the prosecution a rebuttal argument following the defendant's argument. Judges who allow a prosecutor only one argument often allow the prosecutor to choose whether to argue first or second.

Section XII: Instructing the Jury

This section discusses how the jury learns the legal principles it will need to render its verdict, and where these principles come from.

42. How do jurors find out about the rules that they are to apply?

Judges instruct jurors as to the legal principles that apply to a defendant's case. Typically, the judge's instructions are the last words the jurors hear before they begin deliberating. However, some judges prefer to instruct jurors before closing arguments.

43. Where do jury instructions come from?

Prosecutors and defense attorneys submit proposed instructions to judges, who decide which instructions to give. In many cases, the instructions are routine and drawn from books of approved jury instructions. For example, *Federal Jury Practice and Instructions,* by Kevin F. O'Malley, et. al., is widely used in federal court trials. The instructions themselves often are the products of committees formed for the purpose of updating a jurisdiction's jury instructions. Other times, instructions originate in appellate court opinions. In their written opinions, appellate court justices often define crimes or other legal principles (such as the meaning of reasonable doubt). These definitions find their way into jury instruction books, and trial judges in turn read the pertinent principles to juries.

Prosecutors and defense attorneys are not limited to proposing the instructions found in jury instruction books. They may formulate their own instructions because of shortcomings of preapproved instructions. For example, an attorney may have to develop a new instruction when a case raises a legal issue for which no preapproved instruction exists. Or, an attorney may propose an alternative to a preapproved instruction. For example, in a particular appellate court jurisdiction, Cases A, B, and C (decided by different justices at different times) may each provide a somewhat different definition of reasonable doubt. A book of preapproved instructions may include only the definition in Case A. However, if a defense attorney considers the definitions in Case B or C to be more favorable to the defendant, the defense attorney may ask the judge to replace the book's preapproved definition with the more favorable one.

> **CASE EXAMPLE:** Bea Leaver is on jury trial for violating a newly enacted consumer protection law. Bea is the first person to be prosecuted under the new law. It is unclear from the text of

the law itself whether the prosecution has to prove that Bea intended to violate the law, and the local book of preapproved instructions does not cover this new law.

Question: How will the jury instructions for this case be created?

Answer: With no preapproved instructions available, the defense and prosecution attorneys will prepare their own proposed instructions for the judge to give. In this case the defense would most likely propose an instruction telling the jurors that the prosecutor has to prove intent, while the prosecution will propose an instruction stating that intent isn't necessary. The judge will instruct the jury with the instruction that he or she believes is a correct interpretation of the new law.

44. Does it really matter whether the defense can convince a judge to give its desired instruction?

It can be hard for jurors to pay attention while a judge recites a lengthy list of complex jury instructions. However, appellate court justices often take the instructions quite seriously if and when they are asked to review a conviction. Defense attorneys trying to convince appellate courts to overturn guilty verdicts often have their greatest success when they can point to errors in jury instructions, including the

wrongful refusal of the judge to give a jury instruction that the defense had proposed.

CASE EXAMPLE: Same case. Believing that the new consumer protection law does not require proof of Bea's intent to violate the law, the judge refuses to give the defense's proposed instruction to the jury. Bea is convicted, and appeals. The appellate court disagrees with the trial judge, and concludes that the law does require proof of intent to violate.

Question: How might the trial judge's decision not to give the defense's proposed instruction affect the outcome of the appeal?

Answer: The appellate court is likely to fasten on the trial judge's failure to give the correct instruction as a reason to reverse the conviction. It doesn't matter that the jury might have convicted Bea even if the trial judge had given the correct instruction.

45. What do jury instructions typically cover?

Jury instructions encompass a variety of legal principles. The principles that judges typically review when instructing a jury include:

- the elements of the crime(s) with which the defendant is charged (for instance, the elements of burglary)
- the definition of reasonable doubt, the requirement of a unanimous verdict (in most jurisdictions), and

other legal principles that apply to all criminal cases

- factors the jurors may consider when evaluating the credibility of witnesses, and
- housekeeping rules, such as how to select a foreperson and how the jurors should conduct their deliberations.

Even in a short trial, the judge may take up to an hour to read all the necessary instructions to the jurors.

46. When instructing the jury, is it common for a judge to tell the jury what verdict the judge favors?

No. That is a frequent feature of English trials, but American judges rarely if ever express personal views as to what result they think juries ought to reach.

47. Can jurors look at the instructions while they deliberate?

Traditionally, judges read instructions aloud to jurors. If a juror wants an instruction repeated, the jurors have to file back into the courtroom and ask the judge to reread it. Many judges now try to simplify the jury's task by handing out written copies of the instructions.

48. What can the defense do to help jurors understand the instructions critical to the defense?

Studies have repeatedly shown that jurors have great difficulty understanding the meaning of jury instructions. Some states have tried to rewrite their instructions in plain English, but abstract legal terms like reasonable doubt cannot be precisely defined. When a defense rests on the jury's understanding of a legal principle, the defense can:

- stress the meaning of the principle in everyday language during closing argument, and
- draft a version of the principle that the defendant thinks the jury can understand, submit the draft to the judge, and ask the judge to include it with the other jury instructions. Obviously, the draft must be legally accurate as well as understandable.

Section XIII: Jury Deliberations and Verdict

This section is about how the jury conducts its deliberations and reaches a verdict.

49. Can jurors discuss the case before the judge sends them off to deliberate?

No. Judges do not want jurors jumping to conclusions based on partial information. Thus, whenever a break occurs in a trial (for a recess, lunch, or the end of the day), judges admonish jurors "not to discuss the case among yourselves or with anyone else." Jurors who fail to obey the admonition may be removed from the jury, and may even cause a mistrial.

CASE EXAMPLE: Sneezy and Doc are jurors in a felony trial. On the second day of trial, they decide to eat lunch together. During the lunch, Sneezy remarks, "I didn't think much of the witness who said she saw the defendant from across the street. She seemed pretty unsure of her testimony." Doc responds, "Well, remember, this was the only time she's ever been in a courtroom. Maybe she was just nervous." They discuss the witness's testimony for a minute or so, but come to no conclusions. Another juror sitting at a nearby table overhears the conversation. After lunch, the third juror reports Sneezy and Doc's conversation to the judge.

Question: What action should the judge take?

Answer: The judge should talk to Sneezy and Doc in chambers to find out firsthand what they said about the case. The judge should then privately meet with the prosecution and defense to discuss what happened. Depending on the seriousness of the violation and the thoughts of the parties, the judge may (1) allow Sneezy and Doc to remain as jurors after giving them and the other jurors a sterner admonition against talking about the case; (2) remove Sneezy and Doc from the jury and replace them with alternates, or (if the attorneys agree) continue with a smaller jury; or (3) declare a mistrial.

Sequestering Jurors

Judges may take the extraordinary step of sequestering jurors when trials are subjected to intense TV and newspaper coverage. A famous example of this occurred in the 1995 internationally covered O.J. Simpson murder trial. Sequestered jurors can remain together throughout an entire trial or, more commonly, only during the time they are deliberating on a verdict. Sequestered jurors eat meals together and stay in the same hotel, and bailiffs closely monitor what they read and watch on TV.

The purpose of sequestration is to protect jurors from the opinions of reporters and to prevent jurors from hearing about information that is never entered into evidence. However, sequestration can seriously interfere with other aspects of a trial. For example, it's hard to imagine that jurors who are together constantly for weeks—or even nine months, as in the O.J. Simpson case—follow the admonition not to discuss the case before official deliberations begin. In addition, sequestration affects jury composition, since only people who can be separated from their daily lives for a long period of time can serve as jurors.

50. Besides premature case discussion, what other activities constitute juror misconduct during trial?

Jurors have committed a variety of no-nos over the years. These include:

- falling asleep during testimony
- coming into court under the influence of drugs or alcohol—particularly after a lunch recess (in one notorious case, jurors were engaging in drug transactions during testimony!)
- lying about their backgrounds during *voir dire* in order to get a spot on the jury
- conducting independent investigations, such as personally visiting the scene of the crime
- discussing the case with the prosecutor or defense attorney, and
- listening to a friend carry on about the need to convict the defendant to protect society.

Judges and attorneys sometimes find out about such misdeeds either by observing them personally in the courtroom, or from reports from other jurors or third parties. Again, depending on the severity of the conduct, the judge may admonish a wayward juror to shape up, replace the juror with an alternate, continue with a smaller jury, or declare a mistrial.

51. Do jurors stay together until they reach a verdict?

No. In extraordinary cases with great publicity, jurors may be sequestered (required to remain together night and day). Otherwise, jurors deliberate during a normal workday and go home in the evening. However, jurors normally do eat lunch together while they deliberate.

52. How long do jurors have to reach a verdict?

Jury deliberations are not subject to fixed time limits. A judge will order jurors to continue deliberating so long as they are making progress towards a verdict. Meanwhile, the judge will continue to hear other cases. When all of the jurors have agreed on a verdict (in those jurisdictions requiring unanimous verdicts), the foreperson tells the bailiff, the lawyers and defendant return to the courtroom, and the verdict is announced.

53. What happens if the jurors cannot agree on a verdict?

When a foreperson reports that jurors are unable to agree on a verdict (that is, unanimous for guilty or not guilty), a judge is likely to encourage jurors to keep trying. Judges try to achieve verdicts whenever possible, so as to avoid the time and expense of a retrial. But if encouragement fails and a jury is hopelessly deadlocked (called a hung jury), the judge has to dismiss the jurors and declare a mistrial. The prosecution can drop the case, or retry the defendant before another jury. Most of the time, however, cases are settled through plea bargains after mistrials caused by deadlocked juries.

Good Citizenship Rules for Jurors

The jury trial system relies on citizens' willingness to serve as jurors and apply legal rules in a rational and responsible manner. Citizens who are called for jury duty should be aware that:

- Ignoring a summons for jury duty is a crime in many jurisdictions. If you ignore a jury summons in California, for example, you may have to pay a large fine and still have to do jury service. In Connecticut, you may be fined and held in contempt of court. And in New York, in addition to possible civil or criminal penalties, dumping that jury duty summons may also negatively affect your applying for loans or car insurance. Even if you know that you are exempt from jury service (say because you have a medical infirmity or have recently completed jury service), respond to the summons.

- You may be allowed to bring magazines and books to court, but newspapers may be off limits. Cell phones may be banned or their use restricted. You may be allowed to bring a laptop computer, and the courthouse may even offer free Wi-Fi. But you and your computer will probably have to pass through a security system similar to those in airports, so leave pocket knives, nail files, and scissors at home. And sorry, knitters—you may have to leave your knitting needles behind.

- The information in Chapter 9 on Courtroom Behavior, including how to dress for court, applies to you. Casual dress is acceptable, but your apparel should show respect for courts. For example, don't wear shorts, a tank top, or a T-shirt with words or logos that may be offensive or inappropriate.

- Most states still pay jurors for service. Washington pays $10 a day, California pays $15 after the first day, and New York pays $40 per day. (If the pay sounds good, New York residents should know that they can volunteer for jury service every two years.)

A prosecutor does not secure justice when a defendant is wrongfully convicted by a jury that overlooks reasonable doubt, nor is justice promoted by jurors who acquit a guilty person because they don't like the victim. Citizens who serve on juries should keep these principles in mind:

- Potential jurors should honestly answer attorneys' *voir dire* questions. Both sides are entitled to an impartial jury, and justice is not served by jurors who try to hide their backgrounds and predispositions.

- Jurors act as minidemocracies when they deliberate. The foreperson should give all jurors a chance to speak, and jurors should consider each others' views before making up their minds.

Good Citizenship Rules for Jurors (continued)

- Jurors may take notes as they listen to testimony.
- Jurors should not conduct independent research. For example, if there's a dispute as to what is visible from a street corner, jurors should not drive to the corner to see for themselves. In one scene in the famous film *Twelve Angry Men*, juror Henry Fonda disproves the prosecutor's claim that a knife found in a defendant's possession is unusual by easily purchasing a duplicate knife. Fonda's act was improper, and in a real case probably would have resulted in a mistrial (if discovered).
- Jurors should not conduct experiments while deliberating, because the results of those experiments are likely to be misleading. In one actual case, a crucial question was how long bite marks on a person's skin would remain visible. To test this out for themselves, one juror bit another on the arm and waited for the marks to fade. The court ruled that the experiment was improper; differences in skin types and bite pressure made any results misleading.
- Jurors may evaluate testimony in the light of their own common sense and experience. For instance, if a store security guard standing 75 feet away claims that the person who picked up an item of merchandise was the defendant, the jurors may consider their own abilities to see at that distance. (But remember, they can't conduct an experiment in the jury room!)

CASE EXAMPLE 1: Rosetta Stone is on trial for drunk driving. After the jury begins to deliberate, the foreperson announces that one of the 12 jurors has been taken ill and cannot continue. The judge orders the remaining 11 jurors to continue deliberating.

Question: Is the judge's action proper?

Answer: No. Stone is entitled to a 12-person jury, and a judge cannot force her to accept an 11-person jury. Thus, Stone could force the judge to declare a mistrial. In the alternative, Stone could agree to waive the 12-person requirement and continue with the remaining jurors. Stone might choose this option if she is in custody or if she thinks her chances of winning are good.

CASE EXAMPLE 2: Assume that Rosetta Stone's drunk driving case is being tried to Judge Schnell sitting without a jury. As soon as the attorneys finish their arguments, Judge Schnell pronounces Stone guilty.

Question: Can the judge legally arrive at a verdict this quickly?

Answer: Yes. Judges sometimes take cases under submission, which means they'll delay making a decision. But as Judge Schnell did, judges often render immediate decisions.

54. Can I do anything if a jury makes a mistake and convicts me?

Yes. The defense can make a number of motions after a guilty verdict, for example, requesting that the judge overturn the jury's (or the judge's own) decision or grant a new trial. (These motions are discussed in Chapter 19.) The defendant can also appeal. (See Chapter 23.)

Sample Subpoena Duces Tecum (Criminal or Juvenile)

CR-125/JV-525

ATTORNEY OR PARTY WITHOUT ATTORNEY *(Name, State Bar number, and address)*:	FOR COURT USE ONLY

TELEPHONE NO.:   FAX NO. *(Optional)*:

E-MAIL ADDRESS *(Optional)*:

ATTORNEY FOR *(Name)*:

SUPERIOR COURT OF CALIFORNIA, COUNTY OF

STREET ADDRESS:

MAILING ADDRESS:

CITY AND ZIP CODE:

BRANCH NAME:

CASE NAME:

ORDER TO ATTEND COURT OR PROVIDE DOCUMENTS: Subpoena/Subpoena Duces Tecum	CASE NUMBER:

You must attend court or provide to the court the documents listed below. Follow the orders checked in item 2 below.   If you do not the judge can fine you, send you to jail, or issue a warrant for your arrest.

1. To: *(name or business)* _____

2. You must follow the court order(s) checked below:

   a. ☐ Attend the hearing.

   b. ☐ Attend the hearing *and* bring all items checked in c. below.

   c. ☐ Provide a copy of these items to the court (Do not use this form to obtain Juvenile Court records):

   (1)_____

   (2) _____

   (3) _____

   ☐ If this box is checked, provide all items listed on the attached sheet labeled *"Provide These Items."*

   d. ☐ If someone else is responsible for maintaining the items checked in c. above, that person (the Custodian of Records) must also attend the hearing.

   e. ☐ If this box is checked and you deliver all items listed above to the court **within 5 days of service of this order,** you do not have to attend court if you follow the instructions in item 5.

3.
   Court Hearing Date: The court hearing will be at *(name and address of court)*:

   Date: _____ Time: _____ _____

   Dept.: _____ Rm.: _____ _____

   Call the person listed in item 4 below to make sure the hearing date has not changed. If you cannot go to court on this date, you must get permission from the person in item 4. You may be entitled to witness fees, mileage, or both, in the discretion of the court. Ask the person in item 4 after your appearance.

4.   The person who has required you to attend court or provide documents is:

   Name: _____ Phone No.: _____

   Address: _____

   Number, Street, Apt. No.

   _____

   City   State   Zip

   Date: _____ Signature ▶ _____

   Name and Title

   FOR COURT USE ONLY

Form Adopted for Mandatory Use
Judicial Council of California
CR-125/JV-525 [Rev. July 1, 2007]

ORDER TO ATTEND COURT OR PROVIDE DOCUMENTS:
Subpoena/Subpoena Duces Tecum
(Criminal and Juvenile)

Page 1 of 2

Sample Subpoena Duces Tecum (Criminal or Juvenile) (cont'd)

CR-125/JV-525

CASE NAME:	CASE NUMBER:

5 a. Put all items checked in item 2c and your completed *Declaration of Custodian of Records* form in an envelope. (You can ask the person in item 4 where to get this form.) Attach a copy of page 1 of this order to the envelope.

  b. Put the envelope inside another envelope. Then, attach a copy of page 1 of this form to the outer envelope or write this information on the outer envelope:

    (1) Case name
    (2) Case number
    (3) Your name
    (4) Hearing date, time, and department

  c. Seal and mail the envelope to the Court Clerk at the address listed in ☐ item 3 or ☐ The court address in the caption on page 1 . You must mail these documents to the court within five days of service of this order.

  d. If you are the Custodian of Records, you must also mail the person in item 4 a copy of your completed *Declaration of Custodian of Records*. Do *not* include a copy of the documents.

— *The server fills out the section below.* —

Proof of Service of CR-125/JV-525

1. I personally served a copy of this subpoena on:

   Date: _____ Time: _____ ☐ a.m. ☐ p.m.

   Name of the person served: _____

   At this address: _____

   After I served this person, I mailed or delivered a copy of this Proof of Service to the person in item 4 on *(date)*: _____

   Mailed from *(city)*: _____

2. I received this order for service on *(date)*: _____ and was not able to serve *(name of person)*

   _____ after *(number of attempts)* _____ attempts because:

   a. ☐ The person is not known at this address.

   b. ☐ The person moved and the forwarding address is not known.

   c. ☐ There is no such address.

   d. ☐ The address is in a different county.

   e. ☐ I was not able to serve by the hearing date.

   f. ☐ Other *(explain)*: _____

3. Server's name: _____ Phone no. _____

4. The server *(check one)*

   a. ☐ is a registered process server.   d. ☐ works for a registered process server.

   b. ☐ is not a registered process server.   e. ☐ is exempt from registration under Business and Professional Code

   c. ☐ is a sheriff, marshal, or constable.   section 22350(b).

5. Server's address: _____

   If server is a registered process server:

   County of registration: _____ Registration no.: _____

I declare under penalty of perjury under the laws of the State of California that I am at least 18 years old and not involved in this case and the information above is true and correct.

Date: _____

▶ _____   ▶ _____

      TYPE OR PRINT NAME OF SERVER   SIGNATURE OF SERVER

CR-125/JV-525 [Rev. July 1, 2007]   **ORDER TO ATTEND COURT OR PROVIDE DOCUMENTS:**   Page 2 of 2
                               Subpoena/Subpoena Duces Tecum
                               (Criminal and Juvenile)

Sentencing: How the Court Punishes Convicted Defendants

Sentences are the punishments that result from guilty or no contest pleas, or from guilty verdicts following trials. A judge's sentencing options used to be quite limited—a defendant could be incarcerated (put in jail or prison) or ordered to pay a fine, or both. But in recent years, courts and legislatures faced with rapidly growing jail populations have gotten as creative with sentences as stockbrokers have with investments. This chapter examines sentencing policies and procedures.

Section I: Overview of Sentencing

This section explains in general terms how the courts determine the punishment a defendant is to receive upon conviction of a crime.

1. If I'm convicted after a jury trial, who decides what punishment I'll receive?

Judges almost always determine punishment, even following jury trials. In fact, a common jury instruction warns jurors not to consider the question of punishment when deciding a defendant's guilt or innocence.

Juries can play a role in sentencing decisions. When statutes identify circumstances that permit judges to hand down harsher-than-maximum sentences, in a jury trial, a sentence exceeding the maximum is valid only if the jury finds that the circumstance is true (*Apprendi v. New Jersey*, U.S. Sup. Ct. 2001). For example, in capital punishment cases in some states, a

judge cannot hand down the death penalty in a jury trial unless the jury recommends death rather than life in prison.

CASE EXAMPLE: Cunningham is convicted of child molestation following a jury trial. After dismissing the jury and conducting a post-trial sentencing hearing, the judge decides to increase Cunningham's sentence because the victim was particularly vulnerable and Cunningham carried out the molestation in a violent manner.

Question: Is Cunningham's sentence proper?

Answer: No. The judge could have increased Cunningham's sentence only if the jury had decided that the victim was particularly vulnerable and Cunningham carried out the molestation in a violent manner (*Cunningham v. California*, U.S. Sup. Ct. 2007).

2. How can I find out the prescribed punishment for the crime with which I'm charged?

Typically, the law a defendant is charged with violating also identifies the punishment. For example, a statute identifying specific behavior as a misdemeanor might go on to state, "For a first-time offense, an offender may be fined not more than $1,000 or imprisoned for not more than six months, or both." Another statute might describe particular behavior as a misdemeanor without specifying the punishment.

In this situation, the punishment can be found in a separate statute that sets forth the punishment either for that particular misdemeanor or, in some states, for all misdemeanors. (See Chapter 27 for how to research criminal statutes.)

3. Are there any limits on the severity of punishment for the commission of a crime?

Yes. The Eighth Amendment to the U.S. Constitution provides that punishment may not be cruel and unusual. For example, a law that said that all convicted robbers would have their left hands cut off would no doubt violate the Eighth Amendment.

Bad Prison Conditions Rarely Qualify as Cruel and Unusual

In a 1994 decision, the Supreme Court made it very tough for prisoners to challenge substandard prison conditions as "cruel and unusual." *Farmer v. Brennan* requires that, to prevail in a lawsuit based on a "cruel and unusual" claim, a prisoner must prove that: (1) prison officials actually knew about the conditions being challenged, and (2) despite the substantial risk to inmates caused by the conditions, the officials did nothing about them. More on prisoners' rights in Chapter 26.

4. My attorney and the prosecutor made a deal in which I would plead guilty in exchange for a certain sentence. After I plead guilty, can the judge disregard the deal and give me a different sentence?

In many cases yes, though judges almost always rubber-stamp plea deals. To make sure that a deal to plead guilty can be canceled if the judge refuses to go along with it, the defendant should make it clear that she will plead guilty only if the sentencing judge agrees to impose the agreed-upon sentence. (More on plea bargaining in Chapter 20.)

CASE EXAMPLE 1: Mickey Finn is charged with drunk driving. Mickey agrees to plead guilty after the prosecutor promises to recommend that the judge not impose any jail time. The prosecutor also says, "I can't promise that Judge Seagram will follow my recommendation; the judge almost always gives first-timers like you 48 hours in jail." After Mickey pleads guilty, Judge Seagram in fact sentences Mickey to 48 hours in jail.

Question: Can Mickey withdraw the guilty plea?

Answer: No. The deal was not contingent on the judge following the prosecutor's sentence recommendation. Mickey will have to serve the sentence.

CASE EXAMPLE 2: Same case. Again, the prosecutor says, "I can't make any promises that Judge Seagram will go along with the deal." Mickey's attorney then says, "We'll plead guilty only if the judge agrees to no jail time. Let's get an indicated sentence from Judge Seagram." Judge Seagram informs the prosecutor and defense attorney that if Mickey pleads guilty, the sentence will be two days in jail.

Question: Does Mickey have to serve two days in jail?

Answer: No. Mickey never entered a guilty plea, and Mickey's attorney had the right to cancel the deal if the judge refuses to go along with it. Of course, Mickey could end up with an even longer jail sentence if he takes the case to trial and is convicted.

5. Do judges have to give "mandatory sentences" so that everyone convicted of the same crime receives the same punishment?

Some criminal statutes do include mandatory sentences, which require judges to impose specific and identical sentences on all defendants who violate those laws. Mandatory sentencing laws usually reflect what the legislature sees as public sentiment that judges have been too lenient, and a desire to treat all people who break the same law alike.

More commonly, criminal statutes do not carry mandatory sentences, and instead carry a range of possible imprisonment and fines within which the judge can fix the punishment. In these cases, judges can take a number of factors into account when deciding on an appropriate sentence. For instance, judges may consider the defendant's past criminal record, age, and sophistication; the circumstances under which the crime was committed; and whether the defendant expresses genuine remorse. In short, mandatory sentence laws fit the punishment to the crime, whereas judges prefer to fit the punishment to the offender.

Understanding Statutory Sentencing Provisions

Criminal statutes must be carefully studied to understand whether or not they specify mandatory sentences. For example, a statute may say that an offense is punishable "by not more than six months in the county jail." This language is nonmandatory. A judge could sentence an offender to three months, three weeks, three days, or no time at all. On the other hand, a statute might say that an offense is punishable "by no less than 15 years in the state penitentiary." A judge would then have to sentence an offender to at least 15 years. Many criminal laws provide for a range of punishment, such as "not less than one year nor more than three years," and leave it to the judge to decide the precise sentence.

6. In addition to a fine and/or incarceration, are there other future consequences to a conviction?

A judge may make a "restitution order." Unlike fines (which offenders pay to the government), a restitution order requires offenders to compensate victims for economic losses. For example, an offender convicted of robbery may be ordered to compensate the victim up to the value of the stolen property, as well as for wages the victim lost while recuperating from injuries incurred during the robbery. Like civil court judgments, restitution orders may be enforced in a variety of ways—for example, by garnishing an offender's wages.

Laws may also authorize judges to order an offender to forfeit personal property used to commit a crime. For example, a judge may order the forfeiture of the car that an offender used to transport illegal drugs.

In many states, a convicted felon may not vote or hold public office, may lose a professional or business license, and may have great difficulty in obtaining future employment. Even someone convicted of a misdemeanor may be screened carefully and questioned extensively when applying for certain jobs.

Perhaps one of the most serious consequences of having a criminal record is that a defendant will likely be punished much more severely if he is convicted of a future crime. Both prosecutors (conducting plea negotiations) and judges (handing down sentences following guilty verdicts) usually consider a defendant's rap sheet (criminal record) to be a key factor influencing the severity of a sentence. Judges almost always give repeat offenders stiffer sentences than they do to first-timers, sometimes because mandatory sentencing laws require them to do so and other times because the judge believes that the defendant didn't learn his lesson the first time around.

Even Acquittals May Have Later Effects

In 1997, the U.S. Supreme Court held that judges can take into account the defendant's prior crimes during sentencing, even if the defendant has been tried and found not guilty of the prior crimes. The acquittal only means the defendant was not guilty beyond a reasonable doubt; the judge may still believe that a preponderance of the evidence shows the defendant committed the crime (*U.S. v. Watts*, U.S. Sup. Ct. 1997).

7. How do three strikes laws work?

Three strikes laws allow judges to impose lengthy sentences on offenders who have at least two prior convictions for "serious" crimes. In the many states that have three strikes laws, a conviction for a third offense would allow (and sometimes require) a judge to impose a lengthy sentence.

The most controversial aspect of three strikes laws is their use to punish offenders whose third conviction is for a nonviolent crime. In one case, an offender with two strikes already on his record was convicted of stealing about $150 worth of videotapes. Ordinarily, punishment for such a crime might be at most a few months in jail. However, under California's three strikes law, the offender was deemed a "career criminal" and sentenced to 25 years to life. The U.S. Supreme Court upheld the validity of the sentence (*Lockyer v. Andrade,* U.S. Sup. Ct. 2003). At the same time, courts can invalidate three strikes sentences if they are unduly harsh. For example, a life sentence constituted cruel and unusual punishment in violation of the Eight Amendment when a defendant's third strike was a conviction for a short delay in reregistering as a sex offender. (See *Gonzalez v. Duncan*, 9th Cir. Ct. of Appeals 2008.) Groups in many states are trying to change three strikes laws so that they can be used only on offenders whose third conviction is for a crime of violence.

8. I have several previous convictions on my record that happened before three strikes was enacted into law in my state. Is there anything I can do to get rid of those prior convictions?

Perhaps. Given the crucial impact of prior convictions on sentences, it's not surprising that pruning clients' past convictions is often the most important impact a defense attorney can have on the severity of a sentence. For example, attorneys might attempt to:

- seal or expunge juvenile convictions
- void prior convictions, perhaps because a guilty plea was taken improperly, or

- demonstrate that a conviction that appears as a felony on a client's record was only a misdemeanor.

Readers who want more information on pruning past convictions might refer to various attorney's criminal practice guides. (See Chapter 27.)

9. What factors might incline a judge to give me a lighter sentence?

The defense may bring to a judge's attention an infinite number of factual circumstances that, if presented persuasively and if the judge has discretion and is favorably disposed, may well move the judge to impose a lighter sentence. The following are examples of such factors (called "mitigating" factors):

- The offender has little or no history of criminal conduct.
- The offender was an accessory (helped the main offender) to the crime but was not the main actor.
- The offender committed the crime when under great personal stress, for example, had lost a job, rent was due, and had just been in a car wreck.
- No one was hurt, and the crime was committed in a manner that was unlikely to have hurt anyone.

10. What factors might incline a judge to give me a harsher sentence?

Just as mitigating circumstances can sway a judge to lessen a sentence, "aggravating" circumstances can persuade a judge to throw the book at an offender. A previous

Sealing Arrest and Conviction Records ("Expungement")

When records of an arrest or conviction are sealed, or expunged, defendants can, for some purposes, treat the arrests or convictions as though they had never happened. For example, assume that a defendant's conviction for misdemeanor possession of an illegal drug is expunged. On applications for school, a job, or a professional license, the defendant may be able to answer that the defendant has no arrests or convictions (assuming no others exist). However, the rules about who is eligible for expungement and the effect of expungement vary from state to state, and people interested in expungement should seek the advice of an experienced attorney. These general guidelines apply to many expungement programs:

- People have to apply (in writing) for expungement. Arrest and conviction records are not automatically expunged or sealed after a period of years.
- Even though a conviction has been expunged, it can still be used to increase the severity of a sentence should a defendant again be convicted. For example, an expunged conviction may subject a defendant to a three strikes sentencing law.
- Convictions cannot be expunged until about a year after they occur, and then only if the defendant is done serving the sentence and is facing no new charges.
- Not all convictions are eligible for expungement. For example, in many states defendants cannot expunge felony convictions or convictions involving sex offenses. Juvenile and misdemeanor convictions are most often subject to expungement.
- A defendant acquitted of a criminal charge may be able to have the records of the arrest and charge sealed immediately. (See, for example, Cal. Penal Code § 851.85; N.Y. Crim. Proc. Law § 160.50.)

record of the same type of offense is the most common aggravating factor. In other cases, aggravating circumstances grow out of the way a crime was committed, as when an offender is particularly cruel to a victim. However, except for prior convictions, in jury trials judges cannot base harsher sentences on aggravating factors unless the jury has decided that those factors are accurate (*Cunningham v. California*, U.S. Sup. Ct. 2007). Sometimes laws themselves specify aggravating factors. Here are some examples:

- Use of a dangerous weapon when assaulting, intimidating, or interfering with a federal employee carrying out official duties increases the punishment from eight years to 20 years (18 U.S.C. § 111).

Throwing the *Booker* at Federal Sentences

The U.S. Congress passed The Sentencing Reform Act of 1984 in response to concerns that federal judges' sentences tended to be too lenient and too variable from one locale to another. The law created a Sentencing Commission that produced a *Guidelines Manual* that specifies sentences for almost all federal crimes. The manual uses a points system that "awards" points according to type of offense, how it was committed, and an offender's background. An offender who grades out at only one point can be sentenced to no more than six months in jail, while an offender who grades out at the maximum 43 points receives a life sentence.

Congress intended the *Guidelines Manual* to be mandatory. However, many judges complained that in practice they were often too harsh and too rigid. In the case of *U.S. v. Booker* (2005), the U.S. Supreme Court imposed two major limits on the *Guidelines Manual*'s reach.

First, the sentences specified in the *Guidelines Manual* are advisory, not mandatory. That is, federal judges may consult the manual but they are not bound to impose the sentences it provides for. The upshot of *Booker* is that federal court trial judges often have considerable sentencing discretion, and appellate court judges can overturn trial judges' sentences only for an abuse of discretion (*Gall v. U.S.*, U.S. Sup. Ct. 2007). For example, if a federal trial judge believes that the recommended punishment for possession of crack cocaine is unduly harsh—as compared to the recommended punishment for powder cocaine—the trial judge has discretion to give a lesser sentence for possession of crack cocaine, and the judge's decision is final even if it is outside the guidelines' range, so long as it is reasonable (*Kimbrough v. U.S.*, U.S. Sup. Ct. 2007). At the same time, sentences that are within the guidelines' range are presumptively reasonable (*Rita v. U.S.*, U.S. Sup. Ct. 2007).

Federal courts are in disagreement about whether a federal law that provides for *lighter* punishment for some minor drug offenses is mandatory. For a decision ruling that this law is mandatory, see *United States v. Cardenas-Juarez* (9th Cir. 2006).

Second, a judge cannot "enhance" a sentence unless an offender has either admitted to the facts giving rise to the enhancement or a jury has concluded that those facts are true. For example, a judge may consider increasing a sentence because an offender injured someone in the course of committing the crime. In order to stiffen the sentence for this reason, the offender either has to admit that the injury occurred, or, in response to evidence at trial, the jury would have to conclude that the offender caused an injury.

In 2006, a report issued by the U.S. Sentencing Commission concluded that despite the *Booker* decision, most judges hand down sentences that conform to the *Guidelines Manual*. Moreover, the average length of sentences has increased slightly since the decision.

- Committing mail fraud against a financial institution as opposed to an individual or some other type of institution can add $1,000,000 and/ or ten years to the punishment (18 U.S.C. § 1341).

CASE EXAMPLE: Tommy Rotten robbed several teachers from the Kind 'R Garden Nursery School by pointing a loaded gun at the children and demanding the teachers hand over their purses. Bob Bracci, brandishing a silver nail file, robbed a convenience store clerk at 4 a.m.; no customers were present.

Question: Assume Rotten and Bracci are in the same jurisdiction; both took the same amount of money and both were convicted of robbery. Will they get the same sentence?

Answer: Probably not. The judge would likely take aggravating and mitigating factors into account, and these differ greatly in the two cases. Rotten used a clearly dangerous weapon, a loaded gun, and by doing so put many people, including children, at risk. Bracci used a makeshift weapon, a nail file, not an inherently dangerous weapon. He robbed the store in the middle of the night when not many customers, certainly not children, would likely be present. Because of these factors, Rotten would almost certainly get a much harsher sentence than Bracci.

11. Apart from the evidence that may come out if my case goes to trial, how else would a judge find out about the mitigating and aggravating factors in my case?

Especially when jail time is a possibility, judges often ask that a probation officer prepare a presentence report. (See Question 15 for more on presentence reports.) Both the prosecution and defense may also present witnesses in open court, the defendant may personally address the judge, and, increasingly, crime victims may also make statements. (See Questions 21 and 22 for more on statements by defendants and victims.)

 WEBSITE
FAMM is a national group that advocates on behalf of prisoners in the sentencing process. For information, consult FAMM's website at www.famm.org.

Section II: Sentencing Procedures

This section is about when and how sentences are imposed, and the procedures judges must follow when doing so.

12. If I'm convicted, will I be sentenced at once?

In minor misdemeanor cases, judges frequently hand down sentences immediately after the defendant pleads guilty or no contest, or is found guilty after a jury or judge trial. Where the possibility of significant incarceration exists, however, the judge may not impose sentence until some days or weeks later, in a separately scheduled sentencing hearing. The sentencing hearing often follows an investigation by a probation officer, who prepares a presentence report for the judge to review. (See Question 15 for more on probation reports.)

13. If I'm sentenced to do jail time, will I have to go right away or will I have some time to make arrangements?

Defendants who are out on bail when they are sentenced to jail are sometimes hauled off immediately. Other times, the judge may agree to "stay" (delay) the time the defendant must start serving the sentence for at least a few days—to allow the defendant to settle her personal affairs. Defense attorneys will usually be well acquainted with the stay policies of local judges.

14. What is likely to happen during my sentencing hearing?

The sentencing portion of a criminal case often takes only moments—especially where the judge is rubber-stamping the sentence agreed to in plea negotiations. For example, the judge may sentence a defendant to "a fine of $250, ten days in jail suspended, one year probation" while the echoes of the defendant's guilty plea still reverberate in the courtroom. Even felony cases can wrap up quickly when sentences are negotiated as part of a plea bargain. For example, in a recent felony drug possession case involving California's three strikes law, a defendant who pleaded guilty was sentenced to seven years in prison in a hearing that lasted six minutes.

As mentioned, sentencing is not always so brief an affair, especially when the judge has legal authority to order a long period of imprisonment. Typically, a presentence report will have been prepared by the probation department, and the defense and prosecution will spend a fair amount of time arguing against or in favor of the probation officer's recommendations and the factual findings on which the recommendations are based. (See Question 15 for more on the presentence report.)

The judge also must allow the defendant an opportunity to make a personal statement (called the defendant's "allocution") before pronouncing sentence. (See Question 21.) And the defendant can call witnesses to testify to the defendant's good character and rehabilitative efforts. Victims also may make personal pre-sentencing statements to the judge. (See Question 22.)

Self-represented defendants should get advice from an attorney to explore what mitigating evidence (evidence that may help reduce their sentence) they should consider offering during the sentencing hearing.

15. What is a presentence report, and what role does it play in the sentencing?

Especially in felony and more serious misdemeanor cases, judges typically rely for their sentencing decisions on presentence reports prepared by probation officers. Probation officers usually prepare these reports during a several-week interval between the conviction and the date set for sentencing.

To prepare the report, a probation officer (or a social worker or psychologist working for the probation department) first interviews the defendant and checks the defendant's rap sheet (criminal record). The probation officer typically talks to the victim, the arresting officer, and the defendant's family and friends.

In addition to the information gleaned from these sources, most probation presentence reports also describe:

- the circumstances of the offense
- the defendant's personal history, including the defendant's criminal record, and
- a statement by the victim as to what the victim lost or how the victim suffered, sometimes called a victim impact statement.

Good defense lawyers make sure that the probation officer preparing the report hears about all the good things the defendant has done and is doing. For example, if the defendant has enrolled in a treatment or counseling program or has an employer willing to say nice things about him, a defense attorney will transmit that information to the probation officer. It's important that the defense make the presentence report appear as favorable to the defendant as possible, since the report is likely to have a large impact on the judge's sentencing decision.

16. How can I improve my presentence report?

Since judges tend not to have time to investigate the circumstances of individual cases, they usually rely heavily on and often rubber-stamp sentencing recommendations in presentence reports. For this reason, it is important for the defendant to make a positive impact on the probation officer preparing the report.

The defendant should be as prepared as possible before meeting with the probation officer, because in some cases the defendant is not allowed to bring a lawyer into that interview. Preparation is also critical because probation officers may rely, when making their recommendations, on information that would not have been permissible in court at trial, such as inadmissible hearsay and illegally obtained evidence. The defendant must be careful about what he or she says in the interview, because probation officers can use the defendant's statements in their reports.

A Judge's View of Presence Reports

The contents of presence reports and probation officers' sentence recommendations are often crucial, as judges may have little time to exercise independent judgment. As one judge put it:

"Most judges are so burdened with simply getting through the day and 'disposing' of the allotted quota of cases that they are usually too weary to undertake the painful examination of the justice, morality, or common sense of the sentences [that] they impose." (*Criminals and Victims: A Trial Judge Reflects on Crime and Punishment*, by Judge Lois G. Forer (W.W. Norton & Co.).)

17. What types of questions will the probation officer ask me when preparing the presentence report?

Probation officers often question defendants very closely. An officer is likely to want to know a defendant's:

- version of the criminal act giving rise to the conviction
- reason or motive for committing the crime
- prior criminal record, including juvenile record
- personal and family history
- education
- employment history
- health
- past and present alcohol and drug use
- financial status, and
- military record (if any).

The defendant should come to the interview prepared to talk about such topics. Whenever possible, the defendant should bring documents that support her position (for example, a letter from an employer, or military discharge papers). The defendant also should be prepared to explain why she believes that probation or some other lenient sentence is appropriate under the circumstances.

18. How can I make a favorable impression on a probation officer?

What the defendant says and how the defendant behaves in front of the probation officer can be critical. The defendant should meet with his lawyer ahead of time to discuss exactly what he should say to the probation officer. In general, it is important for the defendant to:

- Come to the meeting on time, dressed appropriately. Probation officers have busy schedules and deal with lots of defendants who don't care what happens. Simply showing up on time and being respectful may go a long way in positively influencing the probation officer.
- Stress any mitigating factors when relating the facts surrounding the crime in question and when discussing any past criminal involvement.
- Stress any rehabilitative activities the defendant has engaged in between the time the crime occurred and

sentencing, such as attending a 12-step program, getting a job, enrolling in or going back to school, voluntarily performing community service, or obtaining medical or psychological services.

- Discuss family ties and, if applicable, job stability.

- Show remorse. One thing judges claim to look seriously at in sentencing is the risk of recidivism (repeated criminal behavior). Apparently, many judges believe that defendants who try to rationalize (explain away) the offense are more likely to commit repeat crimes than offenders who admit responsibility and show remorse. It could therefore be of great benefit to the defendant if the probation officer's report notes that the defendant exhibits genuine remorse.

Showing Genuine Remorse

Though many of the regular players in the criminal justice system (judge, prosecutors, defense lawyers, probation officers) are hardened to the stories of criminal defendants, they may still be moved and influenced by a defendant who genuinely expresses remorse and feels bad for the victim hurt by the crime. The opposite is also true. Consider these words written by a probation officer in a 1996 murder case: "To have so violently and completely abused another human being is unthinkable by anyone of conscience .... To show or express no sincere remorse, or acknowledge culpability for his actions, as the defendant has done, discloses the full depth of his malevolent character." (Source: *L.A. Times*, December 17, 1996, A28.)

---

19. Will I be able to read the report, and if so, when?

Defendants and their attorneys usually have access to the presentence report before the sentencing hearing. However, the sentence recommendations and information from any confidential sources may be excluded from the copy given to the defense. The defense should review the report thoroughly for factual mistakes. Procedural rules (such as Federal Rule of Criminal Procedure 32 (i)) typically give the defendant and defense counsel the right to comment on the presentence report at the sentencing hearing and to introduce evidence to rebut any factual mistakes.

20. What can the defense do to assure the fairest possible presentence report?

Probation officers are at least as overworked as other players in the criminal justice system. And they are as susceptible to tough-on-crime public opinion as anyone else. Thus, "boilerplate clauses" (prewritten clauses used in case after case) are common. And the probation officer may prepare a report that justifies predetermined decisions rather than weighs the merits of an individual case.

Defense lawyers, well aware of the limitations under which many probation officers work, often take a number of steps including the following to try to ensure that a judge is aware of information favorable to the defendant. Defense lawyers can:

Counsel's Arguments to Reduce Pizza Sentence

Here are some snippets from arguments made by the prosecution and defense attorney during the January 1997 sentencing hearing in which a life sentence for stealing a pizza (under California's three strikes law) was reduced to six years.

- **The prosecution.** The prosecutor told the judge about the defendant's past criminal record and showed the judge the lengthy rap sheet printout, "which extended from [the D.A.'s] outstretched arm to the floor." The assistant D.A. argued, "This case is not about stealing a single slice of pizza. It is about recidivism [the problem of repeat offenders] and how society deals with it." He further argued, "If the foremost purpose of [the justice system] is to protect society, then [the defendant] is a person we need protection from. He is a repeat offender. He has not learned. He has not repented." And the D.A. went on to say that the defendant did not take the pizza because he was hungry, but, "He took the pizza out of meanness … it was literally taking candy from babies."

- **The defense.** The defense, on the other hand, argued essentially that the punishment was way too extreme for the crime. The public defender "described [the defendant] as a reformed criminal whose last crime was a dumb but hardly life-threatening offense." The P.D. told the judge, "No one is going to suggest to the court that [the defendant's] judgment was not faulty … but [the circumstances of the crime] suggest a lesser sentence."

"Judge Slashes Life Sentence in Pizza Theft Case," *L.A. Times*, January 29, 1997 at A1.

- research possible alternative sentences—such as placing the defendant in a treatment center or under home detention rather than a prison, or requiring extensive community service and restitution—and prepare a concrete plan to implement the desired (or least offensive yet realistic) sentence
- improve the defendant's personal profile by enrolling the defendant in a treatment or rehabilitation program and school, and helping the defendant find an appropriate job or perform volunteer community service
- meet with the probation officer before the defendant does to present helpful information
- prepare a written statement in mitigation of the crime that states why the defendant should receive a lighter rather than a harsher sentence, and
- seek a private presentence report. These are written by private individuals—often retired probation officers—engaged in the business of writing presentence reports for an often hefty fee.

21. Will I get a chance to talk directly to the judge at the sentencing hearing?

When deciding what sentence to impose, judges typically consider oral statements made in open court as well as the probation officer's written presentence report. The people who most commonly speak at a sentencing hearing are the prosecutors, the defense attorney, the victims, and the defendant. Rule 32 (i)(4)(A) of the Federal Rules of Criminal Procedure grants both the defendant and defense counsel the right to speak to the court before a sentence is imposed.

As can be expected, the prosecutor's comments will tend to highlight aggravating factors in the crime and past criminal behavior on the part of the defendant. And defense counsel typically responds with reasons justifying a lighter penalty. Also, if defense counsel has not already pointed out factual mistakes in the presentence report, this would be the last appropriate opportunity to do so.

No one, not even defense counsel, may be able to speak in as persuasive a way as the person facing the sentence. Thus, defendants also have a long-held right to speak on their own behalf before the judge imposes the sentence. This is known as the defendant's right of allocution. Defendants will likely want to work with their lawyers to prepare what, if anything, they will say to the judge.

What Not to Say in Allocution

In 1996, Richard Allen Davis was sentenced to death for the kidnapping, molestation, and murder of a young girl named Polly Klaas. The case had shaken the nation for many reasons, not the least of which was that the victim had been taken from her home in a nice neighborhood during a slumber party with girlfriends. Before being sentenced, Davis spoke on his own behalf. Instead of using the allocution to beg for mercy, show remorse, or at least apologize, legal analysts saw his comments as an obvious attempt to lash out and inflict one last painful blow to the victim's family. In front of a packed courtroom, Davis said that just before he killed Polly she said something like, "Just don't do me like my daddy." The suggestion that Polly's father had sexually abused his daughter, wholly unfounded by all accounts, threw flames into the courtroom, prompting angry retorts from the father, tears from other family members, and the wrath, rather than any sympathy, of the judge.

22. What role does the victim play in sentencing?

It used to be that the victim played a minimal role in a criminal prosecution. The victim's only job, if any, was to testify at trial about the circumstances of the offense. Now victims are participating more, from the beginning, where they are involved in prosecutors' pretrial investigations, to later, when they give statements in court to the judge during sentencing hearings. The victim may tell the judge about the impact the crime has had on the victim's life, pain suffered, and any other details to show why the defendant should receive a harsh sentence. The victim typically will also meet with the probation officer, who will include a victim impact statement in the presentence report. This statement may include the victim's version of the offense and may detail any physical, psychological, or monetary damage the victim suffered as a result of the crime.

Rules in some jurisdictions provide victims with a right to address judges at sentencing proceedings. In these jurisdictions, judges cannot forbid victims from making statements before sentence is pronounced (*Kenna v. District Court,* 9th Cir. 2006).

Preparing Victim Impact Statements

With sentences increasingly reflecting the impact of crimes on victims' lives, a crime victim might seek assistance from a friend or counselor when writing an impact statement. Statements may touch on the physical, emotional, and/or financial effects of crimes. For example, how did a crime change one's daily life or general lifestyle? How did it affect relationships with family members and friends? What medical and/ or psychological treatment has a crime necessitated?

Victims might also be eligible for restitution (from the perpetrator) or crime victim assistance funds (from the county or state), and if so might have to fill in a questionnaire. For further information, ask a court clerk or go online to the Office for Victims of Crime, at www.ovc.gov.

Section III: Sentence Options

Subsection A: Incarceration

This subsection is about when and why certain defendants are ordered to serve time in jail or prison.

23. What are some of the reasons judges order convicted defendants locked up?

Competing theories exist as to why some laws require, and why some judges order, convicted criminals to be incarcerated:

- **Retribution.** Some people think that the primary goal of sentencing is retribution, that prison time serves to take out society's vengeance against a defendant.
- **Rehabilitation.** Others argue that the primary purpose of incarceration is rehabilitation—that the sentence will help the defendant mend his criminal ways and encourage him to adopt a lawful lifestyle. Rehabilitation is commendable in theory, but today's jails and prisons tend not to rehabilitate. Many defendants say that they come out better criminals than they went in, that they learn the tricks of the trade from other prisoners.
- **Deterrence.** Some believe that because prison is so bad, the threat of a prison sentence will deter (stop or prevent) people from committing crimes. Like rehabilitation, deterrence doesn't seem to be effective, for several reasons. Often, crimes are committed on impulse or under the influence of a drug or alcohol, without thought of the possible consequences. Also, frequently, people who commit crimes have spent major parts of their lives in institutions and do not fear incarceration the way people who have been free all their lives might. And finally, a sizable number of criminal defendants actually seek punishment because of various psychological pathologies.

- **Punishment and public safety.** Increasingly, people in the know admit that prison doesn't rehabilitate criminals or deter crime. They just lock defendants up for punishment, and to get them off the streets for as long as possible.
- **Politics.** Finally, and unfortunately, an influential group of leaders emphasize incarceration as a way of getting votes. By building more prisons and locking more people up, politicians can cite statistics that make them look tough on crime—whether or not true crime is actually reduced or the underlying problems causing the crime are ever solved.

Height of Silliness?

In May 2006, Nebraska Judge Kristine Cecava created controversy by sentencing convicted sex offender Richard Thompson to ten years probation rather than ten years in prison because she feared that he might not survive in prison because he was only 5'1" tall. The decision angered victims' rights advocates and puzzled Nebraska prison officials, who reported that many prisoners were shorter than Thompson and that they had never been harmed. The appellate court upheld the sentence as a legitimate exercise of judicial discretion, but Nebraska voters removed Judge Cecava from the bench in a 2008 election.

24. What is the difference between jail and prison?

Jails (sometimes called community correctional centers) are short-term lockups normally run by counties and staffed by county sheriffs. Defendants housed in jails include those awaiting trial and unable to make bail, those serving sentences for misdemeanor offenses, and those felons who have to do jail time as a condition of probation. Because jails are devoted to short-term incarceration, they typically lack many of the facilities and programs that are sometimes available in prisons, such as libraries and exercise areas.

Prisons (also called penitentiaries and, in slang, "the joint," "the pen," "the big house," or "up the river") are normally operated by the federal and state governments, and their purpose is long-term incarceration. Most prison inmates serve sentences well in excess of a year.

25. If the judge orders me incarcerated as part of my sentence, will I know exactly how long I'll be locked up?

Some state laws require the judges to impose what are called determinate sentences. A determinate sentence is a fixed-term sentence pronounced by a judge. For example, a defendant sentenced to "30 days in county jail" or "five years in state prison" has received a determinate sentence. Defendants who receive determinate sentences at least know the maximum period of incarceration as soon as they are sentenced, but they may get out earlier because of parole (see

Section III), or because they have not been a problem (good time credits), or because the jail or prison is overcrowded and their bed is needed for a new inmate.

Other state laws require judges to give indeterminate sentences. Indeterminate sentences are those in which a judge sets a minimum and/or maximum time of incarceration, but leaves the decision as to when to release an inmate to prison officials. For example, a defendant sentenced to "serve not less than two nor more than 20 years in the state penitentiary" has received an indeterminate sentence. As a general rule, indeterminate sentences are only imposed on people who are sentenced to state prison after being convicted of a felony.

26. If I am convicted of two or more separate crimes, what is the effect of the sentences running "concurrently" or "consecutively"?

Judges often have discretion to decide whether to give defendants who are convicted of separate crimes concurrent or consecutive sentences. (See *Oregon v. Ice*, U.S. Sup. Ct. 2009.) If a defendant is convicted of a number of crimes that carry lengthy prison terms, the difference between consecutive and concurrent sentences can be tremendous. The reason is that when sentences run concurrently, defendants serve all the sentences at the same time. When sentences run consecutively, defendants have to finish serving the sentence for one offense before starting to serve the sentence for any other offense. The same factors that judges tend

to consider when deciding on the severity of a sentence (for example, a defendant's past record) also affect their decisions on whether to give concurrent or consecutive sentences.

CASE EXAMPLE 1: Haydn Goseek was convicted of 20 counts of forgery for forging and cashing 20 separate checks. Each count carries a maximum possible prison term of five years.

Question: How might the judge's decision as to whether Haydn's sentences should run concurrently or consecutively affect how long Haydn stays in prison?

Answer: If the judge gives Haydn a maximum sentence on each count and runs the sentences consecutively, Haydn's total sentence would be 100 years in prison. If the judge runs the sentences concurrently, Haydn's total sentence would be five years in prison because he would serve each sentence at the same time. (And whether he receives consecutive or concurrent sentences, Haydn might be released early on parole.)

Question: If Haydn previously had a clean record and forged the checks when he had been temporarily laid off from work, how might this affect the judge's sentencing decision?

Answer: Even if the judge decides that a jail term is warranted, the judge might well sentence Haydn to less than the statutory maximum of five years on each count, and run the sentences concurrently.

CASE EXAMPLE 2: Same case. Haydn's forgery conviction was in Michigan. At the time of the Michigan conviction, Haydn was already serving a sentence in Indiana for forgeries committed in Indiana. (Indiana turned Haydn over to Michigan temporarily to stand trial.) The Michigan judge is about to sentence Haydn on the Michigan forgeries.

Question: How can Haydn's attorney minimize the length of Haydn's sentence?

Answer: Haydn's attorney can ask the Michigan court to allow Haydn to serve the Michigan sentence concurrently with the Indiana sentence. That is, every day that Haydn serves in Indiana counts as though it were served in Michigan.

27. Is it true that I may be released before the end of my jail term because the jail is overcrowded?

It's possible. Overcrowding in jails and prisons has led to early release for many prisoners. For example, one study reported that the average time served on a one-year misdemeanor sentence in Los Angeles had decreased from an average of 200 days to an average of 80 days in the mid-1990s. Nevertheless, many defendants can expect to serve lengthier sentences than ever, despite overcrowding, because of the

One Sentence for Separate Crimes?

Sometimes, a sentencing judge can legally give just a single sentence to a defendant who is convicted of separate crimes. The reason is that a defendant may commit what the law regards as a single unlawful act, yet may be convicted of violating several statutes. For example, assume that a defendant sets a house on fire in an attempt to kill the occupants. The defendant may be convicted both of arson and attempted murder, but could probably be given only a single sentence. Typically, the sentence would be for the more serious crime, which in this instance would probably be attempted murder.

> CAUTION
> The issue of whether a defendant's illegal conduct can legally count only as a single unlawful act for sentencing purposes can be quite complex. Judges often have to consider a variety of uncertain factors, such as a defendant's purpose in committing a crime. A defendant facing conviction of multiple offenses should seek legal advice as to the possibility of receiving separate sentences for each offense.

current get-tough attitude prevalent in the public and the law enforcement community.

28. My lawyer said I might get "time served." What is time served?

Time that defendants spend in jail before they are convicted (called pretrial detention) may be credited toward the total time of the sentence. This is called time served. A defendant unable to make bail may spend time in jail before a plea bargain or a trial takes place—sometimes days, sometimes months, and in very rare instances years. It is not unusual in minor first-time offenses for a plea bargain to be struck whereby the defendant's total punishment is the time served plus probation. (More on plea bargains in Chapter 20.)

29. Time served sounds great—get out of jail right away. Why would anyone refuse?

While time served sounds terrific and most offenders jump at the chance to be let out of jail right away, this option is by no means a "get out of jail free" card. There are some serious consequences that a defendant should not take lightly:

- The offender will still have a criminal record; time served doesn't erase the conviction.
- Time served is almost always given in conjunction with probation and sometimes a fine or community service or both. Probation, as discussed in more detail later in this section (Subsection C), may have onerous conditions attached to it.

Defendants who violate even one of the probation conditions may be sent immediately to jail. Because of this, some defendants may wisely choose to avoid the fine or probation conditions and serve the entire jail time outright, especially if the charge is relatively minor and the local jail is routinely releasing defendants early.

30. What is a "suspended" sentence?

A sentence is suspended when a judge imposes a jail sentence but allows a defendant not to serve all or part of it. For example, a judge may impose a sentence of a "$750 fine and ten days in county jail, five days suspended." The catch is that a suspension is conditional on a defendant's complying with the terms and conditions that a judge specifies. For example, a judge may condition suspension on a defendant's compliance with the conditions of probation or completing a drug treatment program. If a defendant violates one of the conditions (for example, fails to complete a drug treatment program), a judge can order the defendant to serve the suspended portion of the sentence.

Mistreatment in Prison

Most defendants facing imprisonment for the first time are scared, and much of the time with good reason. Jails and prisons nationwide are overcrowded. Many inmates are subjected to brutal conditions both from guards and from fellow prisoners. One thing a defendant should do is to work closely with a lawyer, from arrest on, to develop an effective sentencing plan and present the best possible case for an alternative (nonprison) sentence to the probation officer and the judge. For more information about prisons and prisoners' rights, see Chapter 26.

Subsection B: Fines

This subsection is about when fines may be imposed as part of a sentence and what happens if the fines aren't paid.

31. Can I be fined for committing a crime?

Fines are a common punishment for a variety of crimes, especially less serious offenses committed by first-time offenders. Offenses that are typically punished by a fine include minor drug possession (of a small amount of marijuana, for example), fish and game violations, shoplifting, traffic violations, and even some first-time drunk driving cases. In more serious offenses or when the defendant has a criminal record, many judges combine a fine with other punishments, such as incarceration, community service, and probation. In many parts of the country, laws specify the maximum amount an offender may be fined for a particular offense. The judge is then free to impose a fine up to but not exceeding that amount.

32. What is a "day fine"?

Fines have been subject to a great deal of criticism. One frequent complaint is that they impact rich and poor offenders very differently: "The rich pay the fine, the poor do the time." One recent trend to combat that critique has been the implementation of day fines. With day fines, employed defendants do not have to pay a fine all at once. Instead, they pay a percentage of their earnings on a weekly or monthly basis. The payment amounts vary depending on an offender's salary.

33. Is "restitution" a fancy word for fine?

No. Fines go to the state (or federal or local government prosecuting the crime). Restitution is money paid by the defendant to the victim or to a state restitution fund. In some cases, the "victim" is society, such as in welfare and Medicare fraud schemes, in which case defendants may be sentenced to pay the state back the money defrauded. More typically, in both state and federal jurisdictions, offenders may be required to return or replace stolen or damaged property, to compensate victims for physical injuries and medical and psychological treatment costs, or to pay funeral and other costs where a victim dies.

More About Restitution

In most states, restitution orders are limited to victims' out-of-pocket economic losses, such as medical expenses and lost pay for missing work. With few exceptions—such as when a child has been sexually assaulted by the defendant—a judge cannot order a defendant to compensate a victim for noneconomic damages such as pain and suffering and emotional distress. Victims who want compensation for noneconomic losses have to sue the defendant in a separate civil action.

Courts typically enforce their restitution orders in two ways:

1. If probation is granted, the defendant is required to pay the restitution as a condition of remaining on probation. If the supervising probation officer believes that the defendant is willfully avoiding paying the restitution, he can seek to have the probation revoked and the defendant incarcerated.

2. The restitution order is considered to be the equivalent of a civil judgment and can be enforced by the victim—by attaching or garnishing a defendant's assets or wages. However, under this method of enforcing the restitution order, the defendant can't be put in jail for not paying up.

Recognizing that many criminal defendants may never be in a position to pay full restitution, a number of states also have set up restitution funds to help compensate victims who cannot collect from the defendant.

For example, following the 1999 shooting at a Granada Hills, California, Jewish day care center, the city attorney's Victim of Crime Program initiated an outreach effort. *The L.A. Times* reported that victims who were shot may receive up to $46,000 from a state restitution fund to help pay their medical bills, and victims (and their families) who were present during the incident may be eligible for up to $10,000 for psychological counseling.

Typically, the defendant will be ordered to pay restitution as just one part of the sentence, in addition to prison, community service, probation, and/or some other punishment. Sometimes, plea bargains are struck where criminal charges are dropped altogether if the defendant admits guilt and completely compensates the victim for stolen property or a vandalized car. This type of arrangement is called a "civil compromise." (More on plea bargains in Chapter 20.)

34. I heard about a case in which the police confiscated a defendant's car and boat. Is that a type of fine?

Technically, no. The defendant's property was probably taken as part of a civil forfeiture proceeding, a separate proceeding from the criminal case, in which the government takes property used as part of criminal activities. In 1996, the U.S. Supreme Court held that civil forfeiture is not punishment and therefore forfeiture proceedings do not violate the prohibition against double jeopardy (*U.S. v. Ursery*, U.S. Sup. Ct. 1996).

Subsection C: Probation

This subsection is about probation: What it is, when it is imposed, and what happens if it doesn't work out.

35. How does probation work?

Probation is a figurative leash that the criminal justice system puts on defendants in lieu of incarceration in jail or prison. Offenders who are put on probation (either instead of or in addition to any other punishment they might receive) are typically required to adhere to a number of conditions of probation. Common conditions of probation include:

- obeying all laws (breaking even petty laws like jaywalking have been known to land a probationer back in jail)
- abiding by any court orders, such as an order to pay a fine or restitution

- reporting regularly to the probation officer
- reporting any change of employment or address to the probation officer
- abstaining from the excessive use of alcohol or the use of any drugs
- refraining from travel outside of the jurisdiction without prior permission of the probation officer, and
- avoiding certain people and places (for example, an offender convicted of assaulting his ex-wife may have as one condition of probation that he avoid any contact with his ex-wife or her family).

Probation officers also can check in on a probationer—at home or at work, announced or unannounced. Some probationers, such as those convicted on drug charges, are also subject to random searches and drug tests. Most courts have concluded that probationers do not have the same Fourth Amendment rights to be free from unreasonable searches and seizures as other people. (More on search and seizure in Chapter 2.)

36. If I get probation, does that mean I won't go to jail?

Not necessarily. A sentence may be straight probation with no other punishment, or it may be probation following some time in jail. Most commonly, the judge sentences the defendant to a certain period of time in jail, but suspends (puts on hold) the jail time and lets the defendant serve the remaining portion of the sentence on probation. If the defendant violates any of the probation conditions, however, the judge can lift the suspension and put the original sentence back in place.

37. What factors will the judge consider when deciding whether to give me probation?

When deciding whether to give the defendant probation, the judge will look at the defendant's criminal record and the seriousness of the crime. The judge will also consider:

- whether the crime was violent
- whether the defendant is a danger to society
- whether the defendant made or is willing to make restitution to the victim, and
- whether the victim was partially at fault.

38. What type of supervision does the probation officer provide?

Reporting to a probation officer can mean a number of things. The offender may be required to go to the probation office once a week, monthly, or even less frequently. In some busy metropolitan areas it may only mean mailing the probation officer a postcard once per month. As stated above, probation officers may also search probationers, may show up at their homes or workplaces, and may require probationers to submit to drug tests.

39. If my probation conditions are too difficult to live with, is there a way I can get them changed?

If a defendant can show good cause why a judge should change the original probation order, the judge may grant the request and modify the terms of probation.

> **CASE EXAMPLE:** Greta Charles was sentenced to 48 hours in jail, a large fine, community service, and probation on a second drunk driving offense. One condition of probation was that she not drive for one year. Six months later, Greta got a job that required her to drive. With her lawyer, she contacted the probation officer, who agreed that she had complied with all of the probation conditions for the first six months. The P.O. (probation officer) told them he would not oppose their request to the judge to lift the ban on driving for the remainder of the probation term.
>
> **Question:** Will the judge let Greta drive?
>
> **Answer:** Probably. Although the judge has authority to deny such requests, most judges tend to follow the probation officer's recommendations. In this case, the judge is likely to grant the request because Greta:
>
> - served the jail term
> - abided by her probation
> - paid her fine and performed her community service, and
> - made the request so that she could be gainfully employed (Greta had

proof in the form of documentation from the new employer).

40. If I violate a condition of my probation, what's likely to happen to me?

Defendants caught (either by police or probation officers) violating a condition of probation are subject to having their probation revoked (taken away) and all or part of the original suspended jail or prison sentence reimposed. Since one typical condition of probation is to obey all laws, a probationer who is rearrested on even a minor charge may then be subject to penalties for both the current arrest and the probation violation.

41. Do I get a hearing before my probation is revoked?

Yes. If a probation violation is discovered and reported, it is likely that the court will conduct a probation revocation hearing. If the defendant violated probation by breaking a law, the probation revocation hearing will probably take place after the new offense has been disposed of. If the violation was not a new criminal offense but nevertheless broke a condition of probation (for instance, socializing with people the judge prohibited a defendant from contacting), then the revocation hearing may take place as soon as practicable after the violation is reported. Defendants are entitled to written notification of the time, place, and reason for the probation revocation hearing.

42. What happens at a probation revocation hearing?

A probation revocation hearing is like a minitrial without a jury. Both the defense and prosecution may present evidence to show the judge why the defendant should or should not be subjected to whatever penalty the judge originally imposed. The defendant is allowed counsel at this hearing, but the judge does not have to follow strict rules of evidence.

Additionally, the legal standard in a probation revocation hearing is lighter than the beyond a reasonable doubt standard of criminal trials. In the revocation hearing, typically, the prosecution will only have to prove by a preponderance of the evidence that the defendant violated a condition of probation. (These legal standards are difficult to quantify, but essentially this means that it doesn't take as much evidence, or that the evidence doesn't have to be as compelling, to take away someone's probation as it does to find someone guilty of a crime in the first place. In essence, probation is a privilege that can be lost more easily than one's initial freedom.)

43. Is it possible to plea bargain a probation revocation charge?

Yes. When a defendant arrested on new charges is found also to be in violation of an earlier probation order, the defense may negotiate a new plea bargain to cover both offenses in one package deal. This is especially common in busy, big-city courts where calendars are backlogged. (See Chapter 20 for more on plea bargaining.)

Subsection D: Community Service

This subsection is about when the court may order the defendant to do some work in the community as an alternative to spending time in jail.

44. Can the judge make me work as part of my sentence?

Yes. Judges can sentence defendants to perform unpaid community work called "community service" to repay a debt to society for having committed the offense. The defendant may be required to perform community service in addition to receiving some other form of punishment, such as probation, a fine, or paying restitution.

45. What kind of work does community service usually involve?

Typically, offenders are assigned to work for nonprofit or government agencies, such as parks, libraries, schools, cemeteries, religious institutions, and drug and alcohol treatment centers. They may be sentenced to do a wide range of work—from cleaning highways to lecturing students on the dangers of drunk driving. In one very effective community service program, gang member offenders work in a home for mentally and physically challenged children, helping them to dress, eat, and play.

Some offenders do community service work in group settings, with other offenders; other times they work alone.

They may be supervised directly by the nonprofit group or government agency they are sent to work for or by the probation department. And they may have to report to the court or probation officer at regularly scheduled times to prove that they are complying with the community service order.

Subsection E: Miscellaneous Alternative Sentences

This subsection is about some of the more creative sentencing alternatives that have been tried in recent years.

46. Are there any other kinds of sentences I might get?

Yes. There are many different types of "alternative sentences." Alternative sentencing is the buzzword for an increasingly visible movement in the criminal justice system. Largely inspired by overcrowded and nonrehabilitative prisons, some judges are beginning to work with prosecutors and defense lawyers to impose nontraditional sentences, especially in cases that don't involve violence.

To some, alternative sentencing means anything other than incarceration. And it is true that many alternative sentences are simply variations of probation—perhaps with a fine and community service thrown in. But alternative sentencing can also include fairly innovative punishments. People have been required to:

- install breathalyzer ("ignition interlock") devices in their cars so that their cars will not start unless the offender blows into the device and has "clean" breath (after drunk driving convictions)

- drive around with signs on their cars notifying others they'd been convicted of a drunk driving offense. (This may be a modern equivalent of the scarlet letter)
- give lectures or teach classes about the dangers of criminal behavior
- attend lectures given by crime victims (convicted drunk drivers may be required to listen to families of people who were killed or maimed in alcohol-related accidents)
- complete a drug or alcohol treatment program
- do weekend jail time
- stay at home under house arrest; a person under house arrest may be required to wear an electronic monitoring device, such as an ankle bracelet
- live in their own slummy building, and
- serve time in private jails. private contractors provide jail services for a fee, which they charge both governments and inmates.

Another alternative approach to handling offenses, especially minor ones and those for which prosecutors have declined to press charges, is for the prosecutor to send the defendant and the victim to a neighborhood justice center to resolve their dispute through a process known as mediation. In mediation, a neutral third party helps the disputing parties arrive at a mutually satisfactory agreement.

"Megan's Law" (Sex Offender Registration)

A "Megan's Law," in effect in many jurisdictions, applies to offenders who have been convicted of certain types of sexual crimes, especially sexual crimes against children. (The law was named after Megan Kanka, a seven-year-old New Jersey girl who was raped and killed by a previously convicted child molester who lived across the street from Megan's family.)

A Megan's Law typically requires an offender to register with police authorities, usually upon release from prison. Depending on an assessment of the risk that an offender will commit a future sexual crime, a Megan's Law also requires police agencies to notify schools, other agencies, and the public at large as to a registered offender's whereabouts. The names of registered offenders become part of a national database of sex offenders.

Some types of sexual conduct that once were crimes have in recent years been decriminalized. For example, the U.S. Supreme Court invalidated laws prohibiting consensual sex between a same-sex couple (*Lawrence v. Texas*, U.S. Sup. Ct. 2003). People convicted under such laws who had to register may be able to apply to their state's justice department to have their name removed from its sex offender database.

47. I've heard that some states have drug courts to handle certain types of drug cases. What are they, and how do they work?

Drug courts are a variation of the same current push for alternative sentencing. Founded in the late 1980s, drug courts originally dealt with first-time drug offenders but now admit some repeat offenders. In a slightly different setting than the usual courtroom, the judge and lawyers work together to keep the defendants enrolled in a drug treatment program for a certain minimum period of time. Attorneys in drug courts do not speak as advocates on behalf of their clients; the judge actually talks directly to defendants, who must in turn answer directly. The treatment programs include acupuncture, counseling, education, and job training, along with regular, frequent court appearances and drug testing. The results from some of these programs have been so positive that other jurisdictions are now beginning to set up their own drug courts. By the mid-1990s, there were some 80 drug courts nationwide and many more in the works. Among other achievements, studies show significantly less recidivism (rearrests) in drug court graduates than among regularly sentenced defendants.

48. What is parole, and how does it work?

Parole is early jail or prison release granted by prison officials. Parole is similar to probation in that the offender is free from prison, with rights limited by the parole conditions. Conditions of parole tend to be similar but more restrictive than probation conditions. See Chapter 26 for information about parole.

49. How is a pardon different from probation and parole?

A pardon (also sometimes called a "grant of clemency") is an order from a jurisdiction's chief executive (a state's governor or the president of the United States) relieving a convicted person of the penalties for having committed a crime. While a pardon does not necessarily erase a conviction, a pardon normally restores a person's civil rights. See Chapter 26 for more information about pardons.

Section IV: The Death Penalty

This section examines the basic rules and procedures concerning the ultimate criminal sentence, the death penalty.

50. What is the current status of the death penalty in the United States?

As of March 2009, 36 states authorize capital punishment. (New Jersey in 2007 and New Mexico in 2009 are the most recent states to abolish the death penalty.) A few of the states that authorize capital punishment have not carried out any executions since 1976, the year that the U.S. Supreme Court decided in *Gregg v. Georgia* that the death penalty was a valid form of punishment under properly revised statutes. Though some states provide for the possibility of capital punishment in cases involving drug trafficking, aircraft hijacking, and other crimes, all or virtually all of the prisoners now on "death row" have been convicted of murder.

Federal criminal laws authorize capital punishment for those convicted of more than 40 different kinds of crimes, including treason, aggravated murder, and drug trafficking. Among the most notable people executed by the federal government are Ethel and Julius Rosenberg, executed in 1953 after being convicted of espionage for passing atomic secrets to the Soviet Union, and Timothy McVeigh, executed in 2001 for blowing up a federal office building in Oklahoma City and killing 168 people. However, comparatively few cases involving the death penalty arise in federal court.

As of the beginning of 2009, a total of 3309 inmates were on death row. The number of executions carried out in 2008 continued to decrease to the lowest number in 14 years. Thirty seven prisoners (all of them male) were executed in 2008. By comparison, 42 executions were carried out in 2007, 53 executions were carried out in 2006, 60 in 2005, 59 in 2004, 65 in 2003 and 71 in 2007. Only 111 death sentences were handed down in 2008, also continuing the recent years' decline in the number of people sentenced to death.

Since 1976, when the U.S. Supreme Court upheld the legality of revised death penalty statutes in the case of *Gregg v. Georgia*, a total of 1,136 executions have been carried out. Twenty-two of these executed prisoners were under age 18 when they committed the crimes for which they were sentenced to death, a practice that the U.S. Supreme Court later declared unconstitutional (*Roper v. Simmons*, U.S. Sup. Ct. 2005).

Among the 36 states that provide for capital punishment, the rate at which executions are carried out varies greatly by region of the country. Since 1976, Southern states have accounted for the great majority of the executions. In 2008 alone, Southern states accounted for 35 of the 37 executions that were carried out; 18 of the 35 executions took place in Texas. For additional statistical information on the death penalty, visit www.deathpenaltyinfo.org/2008YearEnd.pdf.

Lethal injection (depicted in graphic detail in the film *Dead Man Walking*), is generally considered to be the most humane form of execution and is currently the most common method of carrying out executions. The most common type of lethal injection is a "three-drug cocktail" that sedates, paralyzes, and then kills. Though administration of the "three-drug cocktail" sometimes causes excruciating pain, this method of execution does not constitute cruel and unusual punishment in violation of the Eighth Amendment (*Baze v. Rees,* U.S. Sup. Ct. 2008). A few states still authorize methods such as electrocution and the gas chamber, but they are rarely used. Hanging and firing squads are outmoded forms of execution that may remain "on the books" in a few states but are no longer used. Dissection and dismemberment, two favorites of the eighteenth century, designed to make the idea of capital punishment as frightening as possible, are long gone.

51. What factors determine whether a death penalty law is valid under the U.S. Constitution?

Decisions of the United States Supreme Court have established a variety of standards with which capital punishment laws must comply to satisfy the federal Constitution. The most important standards are:

- Statutes authorizing judges and juries to impose the death penalty must set out specific sentencing guidelines that they must consider when determining whether to sentence a particular defendant to death (*Gregg v. Georgia*, U.S. Sup. Ct. 1976). These statutory guidelines consist of "aggravating factors" (factors suggesting that a defendant might merit a harsher sentence) and "mitigating factors" (factors suggesting leniency). For example, a statute might instruct jurors who have convicted a defendant of a capital crime to take factors such as these into account when deciding on punishment:
  - whether a defendant has previously engaged in violent criminal activity
  - whether a defendant has prior felony convictions
  - whether a defendant was at the time a crime was committed under extreme duress or the domination of another person
  - a defendant's character, background, history, and mental and physical condition, and
  - evidence of innocence that the defendant had offered into evidence

at trial (*Oregon v. Guzek*, U.S. Sup. Ct. 2006).

So important are these factors that a defense attorney's failure to investigate a defendant's personal background thoroughly can constitute "ineffective assistance of counsel" that requires a sentence of death to be reversed (*Wiggins v. Smith,* U.S. Sup. Ct. 2003).

Defendants tried by juries are entitled to have jurors rather than judges consider the sentencing guidelines and decide whether the death penalty is appropriate (*Ring v. Arizona,* U.S. Sup. Ct. 2002).

- The trial must be "bifurcated." That is, a jury has to first decide whether a defendant is guilty of a capital crime. Then, in a separate proceeding, the jury considers evidence relating to aggravating and mitigating factors and decides whether to sentence a defendant to death or impose a lesser sentence. In many states, if a jury recommends death, the judge retains the power to decide on a lesser sentence, such as Life Without Possibility of Parole (LWOP). On the other hand, should a jury in one of these states recommend a life sentence, the judge has no power to impose the death penalty.
- The Eighth Amendment's ban on "cruel and unusual punishment" limits the crimes for which the death penalty can be imposed. For

example, a defendant convicted of rape of an adult cannot constitutionally be sentenced to death (*Coker v. Georgia*, U.S. Sup. Ct. 1977).

- The death penalty cannot be carried out on prisoners who are mentally retarded (*Atkins v. Virginia*, U.S. Sup. Ct. 2002).
- The death penalty cannot be imposed on offenders who were under age 18 at the time they committed a crime potentially punishable by death (*Roper v. Simmons,* U.S. Sup. Ct. 2005). Imposition of death in these circumstances violates both the Eighth ("cruel and unusual punishment") and Fourteenth ("due process of law") Amendments.
- A death sentence cannot be given to defendants who are convicted of raping children (*Kennedy v. Louisiana*, U.S. Sup. Ct. 2008). The Court decided that sentencing child rapists to death constitutes cruel and unusual punishment in violation of the Eighth Amendment.

52. What are "special circumstances"?

Among the 37 states that authorize capital punishment, many limit its possible use to murder cases in which "special circumstances" exist. In these states, a prosecutor has to file a murder charge as a "special circumstances" case and prove beyond a reasonable doubt that one or more of the charged circumstances apply. Here are some "special circumstances" that

might lead a prosecutor to seek the death penalty:

- A murder was committed for the purpose of financial gain.
- The defendant has a prior conviction for murder.
- The murder was committed for the purpose of escaping from custody.
- The victim was a police officer, firefighter, or government official.
- The murder was committed by means of poison or an explosive device.
- The murder was carried out in a particularly heinous and cruel manner.

CASE EXAMPLE: Shemp is charged with first degree murder for killing Moe "with malice aforethought." The jury convicts Shemp of murder and on the verdict form indicates that "we the jury conclude that Shemp carried out the murder in such a vicious and cruel manner that he ought to be put to death."

Question: If the state's laws allow the death penalty for a murder committed in a vicious and cruel manner, is the death sentence proper?

Answer: No, for two reasons. First, a death sentence may be handed down only if the prosecutor seeks the death penalty at the outset of a case and identifies in advance the "special circumstances" that allow the death penalty to be handed down; the jury must also be told that the special circumstances must be proved beyond a reasonable doubt. Second, the death penalty can be imposed only after a separate penalty hearing in which both sides have an opportunity to present evidence of aggravating and mitigating factors.

53. Do prosecutors use special procedures when deciding whether to seek the death penalty?

Yes. In the usual case in which capital punishment is not an option, charging decisions are made by a single prosecutor who reviews police reports and decides what charges to file. (See Chapter 6.) By contrast, a charging decision in a capital case is usually made by a team of a District Attorney's most experienced prosecutors, often including the District Attorney personally. Before deciding to seek the death penalty, the prosecutorial team must of course be convinced that it can be proved that a defendant committed a capital crime. Charging decisions may also be influenced by factors such as the following:

- **Costs.** Compared to cases in which LWOP is the ultimate sentence, capital cases normally add to a case's costs and complexity. For example, capital cases ordinarily take longer to try and may involve automatic appeals. Also, in some states a defendant facing the death penalty is entitled to two government-paid lawyers rather than one.

- **Adverse jury reaction.** A prosecutor may fear that a jury will acquit a defendant for whom it may feel some sympathy rather than see the defendant face the possibility of execution. (This was apparently a major factor in the L.A. District Attorney's decision not to ask for the death penalty in the 1995 famous prosecution of O.J. Simpson. Of course, Simpson was acquitted anyway.)

- **Popular support.** A prosecutor may believe that continued popular support of the death penalty depends on seeking it only in the most egregious cases.

- **Excuse of defense-minded jurors.** A prosecutor who seeks the death penalty is entitled to remove potential jurors who have serious qualms about voting for capital punishment. Because the jurors removed by this process may be defense-oriented, prosecutors may seek capital punishment in order to select a jury that may be prosecution-minded.

- **Improper biases and prejudices.** Some commentators contend that prosecutors are more likely to seek the death penalty when defendants are poor or members of ethnic minorities, especially when their victims are Caucasian. On the other hand, if the jury recommends LWOP, the judge has no power to impose the death penalty.

54. What are the issues in the death penalty debate?

The debate over the morality and wisdom of the death penalty began to heat up in the latter half of the twentieth century. One factor was that many Western European and other countries, including Canada, Mexico, and New Zealand, abolished the death penalty in the period between 1950 and 1970, leaving the United States increasingly isolated as a country with both a modern and complex criminal justice system and capital punishment. Another factor was that the appeal process began to lengthen, making death row prisoners increasingly visible. Among the most famous of these was Caryl Chessman, the so-called "red light bandit," who was sentenced to death in California in 1948 for committing a number of "lovers lane" kidnappings (he killed nobody). A series of appeals kept Chessman alive until his execution in 1960. While in prison he wrote four books that called international attention to the United States' use of the death penalty—some of his books were translated into other languages and became popular in other countries. (One of his books became a 1955 film, "Cell 2455, Death Row.")

Polls indicate that somewhere between 60% and 70% of Americans continue to support capital punishment, a figure that has dropped somewhat since states have created the alternate sentence of life without possibility of parole. However, the debate over the legitimacy of the death penalty is likely to continue for many years. One reason is that at the center of the debate are conflicting beliefs about the morality of the death penalty, and attitudes based on what people view as moral imperatives are not easily changed.

A second issue dividing death penalty proponents and opponents concerns deterrence. Proponents argue that the death penalty deters at least some people who would otherwise commit murders from doing so, and that its deterrent effect would be even greater were unnecessary delays in carrying out death sentences eliminated. However, the answer to the question of whether the death penalty acts as a deterrent is uncertain. Many social science researchers have investigated the deterrence hypothesis; some studies have shown a deterrent effect while others have not. Whatever their conclusions, the weakness in all these studies is that consensus is lacking on how to "model" the murder rate. That is, deterrence can be measured only by comparing murder rates in different jurisdictions that have or don't have the death penalty using variables such as poverty rates, racial makeup, and the like. Since researchers don't agree on which variables to include and how much weight to give them, there exists "a raging methodological disagreement over how best to pick the variables, and a nagging suspicion that researchers' own attitudes toward capital punishment were subconsciously influencing the forms of equations" (*The Death Penalty: An American History*, by Stuart Banner (Harvard Press)). The claim that the death penalty's deterrent effect would be greater were it carried out more quickly or frequently is also untestable because the federal constitution prevents states from eliminating or severely cutting back on prisoners' access to the courts.

A third issue concerns the risk of executing innocent prisoners. The use of DNA testing and other scientific techniques has revealed that a few death row prisoners were factually innocent. In recent years, at least two states, Illinois and Maryland, have placed a moratorium on carrying out the death penalty because of worries that innocent people may be put to death. Death penalty proponents of course have no desire to execute innocent prisoners and generally agree that its use should be confined only to those whose guilt is beyond dispute and who are in fact "the worst of the worst." However, some support for the death penalty has been undermined by the fact that mistakes have been made in the past and the risk that, despite the wide use of scientific technology at trial, others may be made in the future.

A fourth issue concerns what opponents claim is the disparate racial impact of the death penalty. The U.S. Supreme Court has ruled that racial disparities in the use of the death penalty, if any, do not render its use unconstitutional (*McCleskey v. Kemp*, U.S. Sup. Ct. 1987). Nevertheless, in an effort to convince states to abolish capital punishment, opponents argue that the disparity in the use of the death penalty concerns not the defendants but the victims of crimes. The death penalty is unfair, they argue, because research studies tend to show that it is imposed when victims are Caucasian much more often than when they are Black or members of other racial minorities. However, the merits of this argument are unclear. As Banner points out, "Most murders involved criminals and victims of the same race, so equalizing the treatment of victims would cause more black defendants to be sentenced to death. From the point of view of one concerned with race discrimination, was that a desirable outcome?" Banner concludes that the consequences of the racial disparity argument are unclear (*The Death Penalty: An American History*, by Stuart Banner (Harvard Press)).

A final concern involves the costs of administering the death penalty. The costs are much higher than for prisoners given other types of sentences, including life without possibility of parole. The high costs are attributable to the legal system itself. For example, in many states defendants facing the death penalty who cannot afford to hire private attorneys (and that is almost all defendants) will be represented by two lawyers rather than one, both paid for by the government. Also, both the prosecution and the defense are likely to call on a variety of expert witnesses both at the guilt and sentencing phases of capital cases, adding significantly to their cost. Another reason for the high costs of capital punishment is that death penalty verdicts typically generate lengthy appeals and "collateral attacks" via habeas corpus and other procedures. Finally, "death rows" themselves entail higher costs, in part because states take extra precautions with prisoners sentenced to death. If opponents succeed in convincing states to eliminate capital punishment, the reason may be that people come to believe that the financial impact of the death penalty on state budgets outweighs the death penalty's merits.

RESOURCE

More information on the death penalty are provided by the following references:

- *The Death Penalty: An American History*, by Stuart Banner (Harvard Press), is a thorough and largely neutral account of the history of the use of the death penalty.

- *Actual Innocence: Five Days to Execution and Other Dispatches from the Wrongly Convicted*, by Jim Dwyer, et. al. (Doubleday), explains the use of DNA evidence in murder trials and describes a number of fascinating cases of "getting the wrong guy."

- The Cornell Death Penalty Project (http://library2.lawschool.cornell.edu/death) is an anti-capital-punishment website administered by the Cornell Law School.

- The American Civil Liberties Union provides anti-capital-punishment information at its website (www.aclu.org/capital/index.html).

- Pro-Death Penalty.com (www.prodeathpenalty.com) is one of the few sites with information supporting the death penalty and links to other websites, both pro and con.

- The Death Penalty Information Center (www.deathpenaltyinfo.org) sponsors an anti-death-penalty website.

Appeals: Seeking Review by a Higher Court

A not guilty verdict on all charges normally ends a criminal case. The prosecution cannot appeal once a defendant has been acquitted of the originally charged offenses and any additional offenses the judge may allow the jury to consider.

A guilty verdict, however, on some or all the charges, does not necessarily mean the case is over. Defendants who think they've been wrongfully convicted have a number of options:

1. The defendant can make a motion asking the trial judge to overturn the jury's guilty verdict and enter a verdict of not guilty.

2. A defendant can move for a new trial—that is, ask the judge to set aside the jury's verdict, declare a mistrial, and start over.

3. Defendants can appeal (ask a higher court to reverse the conviction because the jurors made a mistake).

Chapter 19 discusses the motions that a defendant can bring after a jury or judge has found the defendant guilty. This chapter discusses common questions about appeals to higher courts.

Section I: Appeals

This section provides an overview of the appeal process in a criminal case.

1. What is an appeal?

An appeal is a request to a higher (appellate) court to review and change the decision of a lower court. Because posttrial motions requesting trial courts to change their own judgments or order new jury trials are seldom successful, the defendant who hopes to overturn a guilty verdict must usually appeal. The defendant may challenge the conviction itself or may appeal the trial court's sentencing decision without actually challenging the underlying conviction.

2. If I had a private lawyer at trial, can that lawyer handle my appeal?

As a general rule, a convicted defendant should try to find a lawyer who is experienced in appeals. While this may be the same lawyer who tried the case, often attorneys who handle criminal appeals possess a special expertise regarding that process—an expertise that many trial lawyers lack. Also, many appeals involve the possibility of challenging the competency of the trial attorney as a basis for appeal.

3. Can I remain free on bail during the time I'm appealing the conviction?

Defendants who have been at liberty during the pretrial and trial phases of a case often are allowed to remain at liberty pending an appeal, although some states impose extra requirements. For instance, in felony cases in California, the defendant must show by clear and convincing evidence that she is not a danger to the community or to other people. (See Cal. Penal Code § 1271.1(3)(b).)

Self-Representation on Appeal

As mentioned throughout this book, in most circumstances self-representation in a criminal case can be risky because:

- the rules are complex
- the stakes can be high—liberty or life—not "just" losing money as in civil cases, and
- court personnel, judges, and even jurors are often hostile toward self-represented defendants.

If these factors are present in pretrial and trial proceedings, they are even more evident in appeals, which tend to be more formal and to involve more written work and pickier rules. Appellate courts have requirements for every aspect of appellate practice; written briefs are no exception. Rules for briefs often specify the number of pages, type and color of paper, binding, size of spacing, and even print type.

For these reasons, and because the law can be complex, drafting an appellate brief can be difficult even for an experienced attorney.

Counsel may have to undertake extensive legal research to effectively understand and make appropriate references to necessary statutes, court cases, and administrative regulations, and sometimes even the state or federal constitution. Appellate courts also have their own sets of rules for oral arguments, which may differ from the rules in trial courts.

Thus, even defendants who represented themselves at trial may want to hire an attorney for an appeal.

That said, it is possible (though undoubtedly rare) for a self-represented defendant to get extra sympathy on appeal. In at least one instance known to the authors, an earnest, enthusiastic law clerk who felt sorry for a self-represented defendant researched the issues and "rewrote" the defendant's brief in order to more effectively present that defendant's arguments to an appellate court judge.

4. When can I file an appeal?

The general rule is that cases may not be appealed until the trial court enters a final judgment. The entry of judgment is the official recording of the judge or jury's guilty verdict or the judge's order denying any posttrial motions. Not surprisingly, this is known as the "final judgment rule." The policies behind the final judgment rule are to prevent piecemeal and repetitive appellate review of trial judges' rulings, and to eliminate appeals altogether in cases that end with not guilty verdicts.

> **CASE EXAMPLE:** Eileen Johnson is on trial for assault with a deadly weapon. During the testimony of a prosecution witness, the judge admits evidence that

Eileen's attorney thinks is improper hearsay.

Question: Can Eileen immediately appeal the trial judge's decision to admit the testimony?

Answer: No. Under the final judgment rule, Eileen cannot appeal until the case is over. If Eileen is convicted, Eileen can ask the appellate court to set aside the judgment based on the erroneous admission of hearsay evidence and on any other grounds that may exist.

5. How long do I have to decide whether I want to appeal?

Appeals are subject to strict time limits. A defendant may have to file a paper called a notice of appeal very soon, often within seven to ten days after the entry of the final judgment.

A notice of appeal tells the prosecution and the court that the defendant intends to bring an appeal. Defendants who later change their minds may withdraw notices of appeal without penalty, but if they don't first file their notices in time, they will likely have lost their right to appeal.

6. How long will the whole appeal process take?

The appeals process usually takes many months. A trial transcript must be prepared, and both the defense and prosecution prepare briefs and respond to each other's briefs. Also, some cases go through two or even three levels of appellate courts. (See the list at the end of this chapter.)

7. During trial my lawyer said we have to "make a good record for appeal." What does this mean?

Appellate court judges do not consider new evidence. Their rulings are based only on the trial court "record." A record includes such materials as a transcript of testimony, documents or other exhibits that the trial judge admitted into evidence, pre- and post-trial motions, and the parties' arguments. A record can also include information that the parties unsuccessfully sought to introduce into evidence.

Thus, to make a good record is to put before the trial court judge all the information that you want an appellate court judge to have when deciding whether to uphold or reverse the outcome of the trial. In addition to offering all the testimony and documents supporting their claims, the actions that attorneys can take to produce a good trial court record include:

- **Make offers of proof.** An offer of proof typically consists of a summary of the testimony that a witness will give if the judge allows the witness to testify. If the trial court judge rules that the testimony is inadmissible, by making an offer of proof you provide an appellate court with a basis for determining the ruling was wrong.
- **Translate gestures into words.** If a court reporter can't transcribe testimony, an appellate court judge may be unable to determine its meaning

or admissibility. For example, assume that a witness testifies, "I was standing this close to her," and holds up his hands to indicate the distance. The distance may be clear to everyone in the courtroom, but not to appellate court judges who are limited to what appears on the record. To make a good record, translate the gesture into words: "For the record, the witness is holding his hands about two feet apart."

- **Make all legitimate objections and arguments.** As a general rule, appellate court judges ignore objections and arguments that you make for the first time on appeal. The idea is that if you fail to give the trial court judge a chance to rule on the admissibility of the adversary's evidence, you've given up the right to argue on appeal that the evidence should not have been allowed. (The "plain error rule" is an exception to this requirement. If the trial court judge makes an obvious mistake that affects a defendant's substantial rights and the integrity of the trial process, an appellate court may reverse a conviction even though the defendant failed to object during the trial. See Federal Rule of Evidence 103(d).)

It is especially important for the defense to make a good record, because most criminal trials end in guilty verdicts. If the defendant wants a shot at a reversal on appeal, the trial court record must be solid.

As mentioned, if something bad happens to the defendant during trial that does not become a part of the record, the appellate court cannot consider it. If the appellate court can't even consider what happened, it is not likely to reverse a guilty verdict. By contrast, the more complete the record, the better the defendant's chances on appeal (assuming, of course, that mistakes were made that likely influenced the outcome).

CASE EXAMPLE 1: A prosecution witness, the alleged victim Suzie Fels, sneers at the defendant Andrew Williams while he is testifying. Suzie mouths in a whisper (so the court reporter can't hear) to the jury, "Evil man … I hope he hangs."

Question: What, if anything, should the defense do?

Answer: Speak up and say something like, "Your Honor, let the record reflect that the witness is making faces at my client and whispering things to the jury. Please instruct the witness to stop that prejudicial behavior and instruct the jury to disregard her actions and statements."

Question: If Andrew's lawyer did not stop the proceedings and put the facts on the record, could he later complain to the appellate court that, "the verdict should be overturned because Suzie made faces at my client and whispered disparaging remarks to the jury"?

Answer: No. If the behavior does not appear in the record, it won't be considered by the appellate court.

CASE EXAMPLE 2: Same case. The trial court judge gives the instruction for the jury to disregard Suzie's remarks, as desired by the defense, but Andrew is convicted anyway. On appeal, Andrew argues, "The trial court judge should have stopped the trial immediately and dismissed the charges because of Suzie's grossly prejudicial behavior."

Question: Will an appellate judge consider this argument?

Answer: Probably not. Andrew neglected to argue for dismissal during the trial. Since Andrew didn't give the trial court judge a chance to consider this argument, an appellate judge needn't rule on it. To make a good record, the defense should have argued for dismissal during the trial.

CASE EXAMPLE 3: Dave Lenoman is on trial for burglary. Dave's defense is an alibi. During the trial, Dave asks the judge to receive into evidence a hotel receipt showing that Dave was out of town on the evening of the burglary. The judge rules that the receipt is inadmissible hearsay, and refuses to admit the receipt into evidence unless Dave offers evidence showing that the receipt is a business record, a type of admissible hearsay. Dave fails to offer such evidence. On appeal, Dave

submits an affidavit from the hotel clerk demonstrating that the receipt was a business record.

Question: Will an appellate judge rule that the trial judge should have admitted the receipt into evidence as a business record?

Answer: No. Dave failed to offer the necessary evidence at trial, and can't offer it for the first time on appeal.

CASE EXAMPLE 4: Same case. During Dave's trial, the prosecutor offers evidence that Dave had been previously convicted of drunk driving. Dave neglects to object to this evidence.

Question: On appeal, can Dave argue that the trial judge should have excluded evidence of the conviction?

Answer: No. Since Dave neglected to object to the evidence during trial, he cannot object on appeal.

8. How do I get a copy of the trial transcript?

As part of preparing an appeal, the defense must order a trial court transcript from the court reporter. Transcripts are usually quite costly. However, indigents (poor defendants) may obtain transcripts at little or no cost.

9. What happens after I've given notice I want to appeal?

Once the defense decides to appeal a case and files a notice of appeal, the appellate court will typically set a schedule. The court will tell the parties when their briefs (written arguments) must be filed and when the parties must appear in court, if at all, to present their case orally to the court (called "oral argument").

10. What is an "appellant" and an "appellee"?

When the appellate process starts, the defendant is usually called the appellant or petitioner. And the prosecution is called the appellee or respondent.

11. What information do appellate courts consider when ruling on an appeal from a trial court conviction or sentence?

An appellate court will not look at new evidence or hear witnesses. Unlike trial courts that decide issues of fact (deciding who is telling the truth or what happened), appellate courts decide issues of law. Appellate judges read the parties' briefs and make decisions such as whether a trial court decision should be overturned or whether a sentence should be modified.

12. What exactly goes into a written appellate brief?

Briefs typically refer to:
- Specific parts of the trial transcript. (Appellate judges generally look only at those portions of the record cited in the briefs submitted by the parties.)
- Statutes and previous court opinions that the lawyers are relying on as

authority for the appellate court to uphold or overturn the trial judge's rulings. Lawyers develop the arguments in briefs by doing legal research into how other courts have decided similar legal problems and then applying the reasoning in these earlier decisions to the present case. (More on legal research in Chapter 27.)

Typically there are three briefs in an appeal from a criminal case:
- the appellant files an opening brief
- the respondent files a responding brief, and
- the appellant files a reply brief.

13. What happens after the briefs are written and filed?

After briefs are filed, the lawyers may have the opportunity to appear before the appellate court to orally argue the appeal. It is an increasingly common practice, however, for courts to decide appeals on the briefs and trial record without hearing argument. If an oral argument does take place, it will likely be limited in time—from two to five minutes in some state appellate courts to 30 minutes in some federal courts. Because both sides will have submitted their arguments in writing ahead of time, the appellate judges will know what the issues are and often limit the discussion to specific questions. An appellate court may take days, weeks, or even months to decide an appellate case.

14. If an appellate court decides that an error occurred during the trial, will a conviction be reversed?

Often, the answer is, "No." As appellate court judges sometimes say, "Defendants are entitled to fair trials, but not perfect ones." Appellate courts reverse guilty verdicts only if a trial court error affected a "substantial right" of a party (see Federal Rule of Evidence 103). An error that affects a party's substantial right is called a "reversible error." Since appellate courts do not usually rule that errors are reversible, only a very small percentage of convictions are reversed on appeal.

Appellate court judges deem most errors to be "harmless." A harmless error is one that does not affect a party's substantial right. For example, assume that despite the defendant's objection, a trial judge allows a prosecutor to offer improper hearsay evidence connecting a defendant to a crime. If the prosecution's properly admitted evidence leaves no doubt of the defendant's guilt, the appellate court will probably rule that the trial judge's error was harmless.

Sentences are a different matter. When a trial judge has discretion over the type or length of sentence, an appellate will rarely reverse the judge's sentencing decision, and then only if the judge committed an abuse of discretion. However, if a sentence is legally improper, the appellate court will either correct the error itself or send the case back to the trial court for re-sentencing. For example, a familiar rule provides that a defendant can only be punished once for engaging in a criminal act, even if that act results in convictions of separate crimes. If a trial court judge were to mistakenly punish a defendant separately for each conviction that was based on a single criminal act, an appellate court would rectify the mistake itself or order the trial court judge to do so.

Section II: Writs

This section is about some of the ways a criminal defendant can get help from a higher court outside of the regular appeals process.

15. What is a writ?

The word "writ" traces its roots to English common law. In Old English, writ means a letter, often written by an attorney. Writ was the name for an action in the courts. There were different kinds of writs for different actions—writs to recover land or personal property, to enforce judgments, to seek damages for broken contracts. Most of the common law writs have been abolished and replaced by the civil actions we know today.

In another sense, the word "writ" meant, and still means, an order. For example, an "original writ" in old England was a letter from the king to the local sheriff ordering someone who committed a wrong to either make repairs to the person wronged or appear in court to face formal accusations. In this context, the original writ is most like our "summons" ordering a party to appear in court.

In most modern American jurisdictions, a writ is an order from a higher court to a lower court or to a government official such as a prison warden. Defendants may seek several types of writs from appellate judges directed at the trial court or at a lower appellate court. (Many states have two levels of appellate courts—an intermediate appellate court and the state Supreme Court.) This section merely provides an overview about common writs. Writs, like appeals, are complex and involve picky details. Defendants facing situations in which they may be entitled to take a writ should consult counsel.

16. What's the difference between a writ and an appeal?

Writs usually are considered to be extraordinary remedies, meaning they are permitted only when the defendant has no other adequate remedy, such as an appeal. In other words, a defendant may take a writ to contest a point that the defendant is not entitled to appeal. Any one of the following reasons, for example, may prohibit an appeal (and justify a writ):

- The defense did not lodge a timely objection at the time of the alleged injustice.
- The matter at issue concerns something that goes beyond the trial record.
- A final judgment has not yet been entered in the trial court, but the party seeking the writ needs relief at once to prevent an injustice or unnecessary expense.

- The matter is urgent. Writs are heard more quickly than appeals, so defendants who feel wronged by actions of the trial judge may need to take a writ to obtain an early review by a higher court.
- The defendant has already lodged an unsuccessful appeal. (In some cases, defendants may file multiple writs, but the right to appeal is limited to one.)

17. What is a writ of habeas corpus?

Defendants who want to challenge the legality of their imprisonment—or the conditions in which they are being imprisoned—may seek help from a court by filing what is known as a "writ of habeas corpus."

A writ of habeas corpus (literally to "produce the body") is a court order to a person (prison warden) or agency (institution) holding someone in custody to deliver the imprisoned individual to the court issuing the order. Many state constitutions provide for writs of habeas corpus, as does the United States Constitution, which specifically forbids the government from suspending writ proceedings except in extraordinary times—such as war (U.S. Constitution, Article 1, § 9(2)).

Known as "the Great Writ," habeas corpus gives citizens the power to get help from courts to keep government and any other institutions that may imprison people in check. In many countries, police and military personnel, for example, may take people and lock them up for months—even years—without charging them, and those imprisoned have no legal channel by which to protest or challenge the imprisonment. The writ of habeas corpus gives jailed suspects the right to ask an appellate judge to set them free or order an end to improper jail conditions, and thereby ensures that people in this country will not be held for long times in prison in violation of their rights. Of course, the right to ask for relief is not the same as the right to get relief; courts are very stingy in granting their writs.

 CAUTION

Rules governing writs are complex and changing. Defendants seeking review through writs, especially writs of habeas corpus, must be aware that the rules governing these proceedings are even more complex than the rules governing appeals, and the law in this area changes frequently. For more information on postconviction proceedings generally, see *Advanced Criminal Procedure in a Nutshell,* by Mark Cammack and Norman Garland (Thomson-West Publishing). For information on federal habeas corpus proceedings ask a law librarian to help you locate the federal habeas corpus laws at 28 U.S.C. § 2254 and the reference volume *Rules Governing § 2254 Cases in the United States District Courts.* For more on habeas proceedings in the U.S. Supreme Court see Chapter 11, "Extraordinary Writs," in *Supreme Court Practice,* by Robert L. Stern et. al. (BNA Books), and on federal habeas proceedings generally see *Federal Habeas Corpus Practice and Procedure,* 3rd ed., by Randy Hertz and James Liebman (LexisNexis).

Suspension of the Great Writ

During the Civil War, President Lincoln suspended the right of habeas corpus, pursuant to Article 1, § 9 of the U.S. Constitution. Generals in the field thus had authority to arrest and keep people in custody whom they considered "threats to public safety"; those arrested no longer had the right they previously enjoyed to challenge the legality of the imprisonment in the court system.

In the aftermath of the September 11, 2001, terrorist attacks, the Bush administration also curtailed the right of habeas corpus. So-called terrorists who were classified as enemy combatants had no right to question in court their detention until a special "combatant status review tribunal" reviewed their status. In the case of *Boumediene v. Bush* (U.S. Sup. Ct. 2008), the Supreme Court declared this policy invalid and that terrorism suspects had the right to file writs of habeas corpus to challenge in federal court the lawfulness of their detention. This ruling potentially affected the rights of some 270 people arrested for suspected terrorist activities, some of whom had been imprisoned as long as six years without a court hearing to review their imprisonment.

CASE EXAMPLE: Defendant Ed Ippus was convicted of murder. He contends that the only reason he was convicted was that his attorney, Johnny Baily, was incompetent. The basis for Ed's contentions is that his attorney came to court drunk every day during the trial, thus depriving Ed of his Sixth Amendment right to effective assistance of counsel.

Question: Can Ed make such an argument if the trial court's official record (transcripts of the proceedings) does not reveal that counsel was intoxicated?

Answer: Yes, Ed may file a request for a writ of habeas corpus, either by itself or in conjunction with an appeal. If the appellate court is persuaded, it may go beyond the record and consider new evidence, for example, testimony of a juror who smelled alcohol on Baily's breath in the elevator during court recesses.

18. Can habeas corpus be used for anything other than getting me out of jail?

In recent decades, defendants have filed increasing numbers of habeas corpus petitions requesting new and unusual forms of relief. For example, defendants have filed writs (successfully or unsuccessfully) to:

- reduce or set bail
- speed an arraignment
- contest being denied a jury trial
- challenge a conviction when not informed of the right to counsel at certain pretrial proceedings, and
- contest prison overcrowding, excessive solitary confinement, or other prison conditions.

Custody Doesn't Only Mean Jail

A person doesn't have to be in jail or prison to use the writ of habeas corpus. A defendant committed to a mental institution, for example, after pleading not guilty by reason of insanity, may also use the writ of habeas corpus to contest an illegal commitment or unlawful conditions.

19. What other writs might be relevant to my case?

The writ of prohibition and the writ of mandamus are also sometimes used in criminal cases. These writs, often used together and sometimes interchangeably, are in essence complements of one another. The writ of prohibition is an order from an appellate court to the trial court to stop some particular action. A writ of mandamus (also known as a writ of mandate) orders a lower court to do something. The purpose of both writs is in essence to keep lower courts (and others affected) from exceeding their lawful jurisdiction.

Because of their similarity to appeals, writs are discussed in this chapter on post-conviction proceedings. But parties may take a writ (apply to an appellate court for relief through a writ proceeding) before, during, or after a trial.

CASE EXAMPLE: Rodney Prince, facing charges of resisting arrest, objected to the trial judge's ruling to exclude evidence of the arresting officer's personnel file. The file noted numerous incidents in which the arresting officer, Noah Kontrol, had been reprimanded for beating suspects. In order to effectively raise his defense that he was forced to resist Kontrol because he threatened to beat him, Prince needs the information in the personnel file.

Question: Is there anything Prince can do to force the judge to admit the evidence?

Answer: Prince may be able to get the relief he needs by requesting a writ of mandamus from a higher court requiring the judge to admit the evidence. However, the higher court would probably refuse to issue the writ, since this is likely a point that Prince could argue on appeal if he were to be convicted.

20. Can I use a writ of habeas corpus to challenge the legality of a conviction based on a law or court decision that came into effect after I was convicted?

Generally, after any appeals have concluded and a conviction is final, the conviction cannot be challenged based on a new rule that goes into effect (*Teague v. Lane,* U.S. Sup. Ct. 1989). For example, assume that Joe was tried and convicted at a time before the U.S. Supreme Court decided the case of *Crawford v. Washington,* which established the rule that "testimonial hearsay" is inadmissible against criminal defendants unless the defendants have had

a chance to cross-examine the speakers. (For more information about *Crawford,* see Chapter 17.) Based on the *Teague* ruling, Joe could not use the writ of habeas corpus to challenge the legality of his conviction based on Crawford—that is, he cannot claim that the prosecution offered hearsay evidence against him that would not have been allowed by the *Crawford* court (*Wharton v. Bockting,* U. S. Sup. Ct. 2007).

Teague's general policy that new rules may not be used retroactively is subject to limited exceptions. For example, if a court decides that the law that a defendant was convicted of breaking was beyond the power of the government to enact, then the defendant can bring a writ of habeas corpus to attack the conviction, even if the conviction is final. As a silly example, assume that Marsha is convicted of violating a law making it a crime to make a funny face at a chicken. Years after Marsha's conviction is final, a court rules that the government had no power to make that law. Marsha could use the writ of habeas corpus to ask a court to set aside her conviction.

Teague defines the scope of the writ of habeas corpus only for purposes of *federal* law. States have their own provisions for writs of habeas corpus. A state may decide to retroactively apply new rules to cases that are final, even though they are not required to do so (*Danforth v. Minnesota,* U.S. Sup. Ct. 2008).

In *Danforth,* the defendant, Danforth, was convicted of sexually assaulting a minor. The minor did not testify at trial;

Potential Postconviction Remedies

As discussed in this chapter, convicted defendants can take a number of steps—motions, appeals, and writs—to challenge guilty verdicts and/or to correct violations of constitutional rights. The following list illustrates these steps. A defendant who loses at one may go on to the next step, all the way down the list (up the legal chain) in a process that can take many years—especially for serious felonies such as death penalty cases.

CAUTION
This list is merely an illustration of possible postconviction proceedings—some of which may only be used in certain cases. Also, defendants usually must have unsuccessfully sought relief through the available state remedies first before they will be allowed to seek relief in federal courts. For these reasons, and because of the complexities of these proceedings and what is at stake (liberty or life), defendants should consult counsel to determine which remedies are available to them.

List of Writ/Appeals Process

- **Motion for Acquittal.** Requests that the judge decide that there is not enough evidence to convict the defendant. Depending on whether the trial is before a judge or a jury and depending on court rules, this motion may be made either after the prosecution presents its evidence or after all the evidence is presented.

- **Motion for a New Trial.** Requests that the trial judge declare a mistrial and grant a new trial.

- **Appeal to State Appellate Court.** Contends that the trial judge made some legal error.

- **Petition for Rehearing to State Appeals Court.** Requests that appeals court judges change their own decision.

- **State Supreme Court Appeal.** Requests that the highest court in the state review and overturn the decision of the midlevel appeals court.

- **U.S. Supreme Court Appeal.** Requests that the highest court in the nation intervene to correct an error on the part of the state courts that violates the U.S. Constitution.

- **State Court Habeas Corpus Petition.** Requests that the state appeals courts order the jail or prison holding the defendant to release the defendant upon a showing that he is being held in violation of some state law or constitutional right.

- **Federal Habeas Corpus Petition to District Court.** Requests the federal trial court to order the jail or prison holding the defendant to release him because he is being held in violation of the U.S. Constitution.

- **Appeal of Federal Habeas Corpus Petition to Circuit Court.** Requests the midlevel federal court to review the federal trial court's decision denying the writ.

- **Appeal of Federal Habeas Corpus Petition to U.S. Supreme Court.** Requests the highest court in the land to review the midlevel federal court's decision denying the writ.

rather, the jury saw a recorded interview in which the minor described the assault. Though this method of offering evidence was lawful as of the time of Danforth's trial, almost a decade later (and long after the conviction had become final), the U.S. Supreme Court decided in *Crawford v. Washington* that the Confrontation Clause of the U.S. Constitution's Sixth Amendment requires that defendants have an opportunity to cross examine the witnesses against them. Had *Crawford* been the law at the time Danforth was tried, the prosecutor would not have been allowed to introduce the minor's interview into evidence. Under *Teague,* because his conviction is final, Danforth could not use the *federal* writ of habeas corpus to challenge his conviction. However, should Minnesota choose to, the *Danforth* decision recognizes that the state has the power to allow Danforth to use its *state* writ of habeas corpus to challenge his conviction.

How the Criminal Justice System Works: A Walk Through Two Drunk Driving Cases

This chapter walks through two fairly routine criminal cases in which the defendants are both charged with "DUI," driving under the influence of alcohol or drugs. The first section gives some background on the law of DUI. The second section shows what happens to the defendants, Shelly Rogers and Julian Daniels, from the time they are arrested until the day they are sentenced by the court. Readers will get a chance to review the police reports, and "listen in" on the interviews the defendants have with their public defender and on the court proceedings they face. Since more than 90% of criminal cases end in plea bargains rather than going to trial, both of these defendants' cases end in plea bargains. (See Chapter 20 for more on plea bargaining.) The sentences each defendant receives, however, are very different, due among other reasons to the fact that Rogers is a repeat offender whereas this offense is Daniels's first. (See Chapter 22 for more on sentencing.)

Section I: Questions and Answers About DUI (Driving Under the Influence)

This section provides general information about how drunk driving cases are handled in the courts.

1. I've never heard the term DUI. Are there other terms for what I think of as drunk driving?

States have different terms for DUI. Some of these are:

- DUIL (driving under the influence of liquor)
- DWI (driving while intoxicated)
- OMVI (operating a motor vehicle intoxicated)
- OWI (operating while intoxicated), or
- OUI (operating under the influence).

2. What type of behavior describes a DUI offense?

In many states, a DUI offense consists of the following facts (elements):

- driving or operating (sometimes even sitting behind the wheel will suffice)
- a motor vehicle (typically a car, but a motor vehicle can also be a truck, a motorcycle, a golf cart, a tractor, a bicycle, a horse, and possibly even a skateboard), and
- while under the influence of an intoxicating beverage or drug, or with a certain blood alcohol level over the legal limit (0.08% in many states or 0.01% or above for persons under 21 years of age).

The Popular Term "Drunk Driving" Misses the Point

Notice the difference between the legal term "driving under the influence" and the more familiar term "drunk driving." The former does not have the word "drunk" in it. This difference can have tremendous legal importance in a criminal case. It means that the prosecution does not have to show the defendant was drunk, but simply that the defendant had enough alcohol in her system to possibly be affected by it when in control of a motor vehicle. It may in some cases be enough, for example, to have the arresting officer testify that the defendant's breath smelled of alcohol or that the defendant's eyes were bloodshot (red). The prosecution may offer evidence that the defendant, when questioned by the officer, said that she felt "happy" or "relaxed," even though that defendant may not have meant at all to imply that she was drunk. Bottom line: What the typical DUI defines as a crime can differ drastically from the image many people have in mind when they hear the word "drunk."

3. What are "illegal per se" laws?

In states that have illegal per se laws, defendants whose blood alcohol levels meet or exceed the legal limit (usually, a blood alcohol content of 0.08) are DUI, regardless of whether the alcohol has in fact affected their behavior or whether they are actually intoxicated. In those states, the only facts (elements) the prosecution has to prove are:

- the defendant was driving or in physical control of a vehicle (in some places on a public road), and
- at the time the defendant was driving or in physical control of the vehicle, the defendant's blood alcohol level was above the legal limit. (In some states, the accused does not even have to be driving. If a driver has pulled over to get some rest, but is still behind the wheel in a position to drive, the police may make a lawful arrest.)

By contrast, in states that do not have illegal per se laws, the prosecution may use the defendant's blood alcohol level as evidence of being under the influence. But typically, the prosecution will also have to provide further evidence that either the defendant suffered from symptoms of the influence of alcohol (for instance, bloodshot eyes or smell of alcohol on the breath) or that the defendant's driving was impaired (for example, weaving in and out of lanes, or following too closely to the car in front).

Even in states that have illegal per se laws, observations of police officers (sometimes called field evidence) are still relevant to proving a DUI case. Also, prosecutors sometimes bring charges under both general driving under the influence laws and per se laws. Then, if the defense pokes holes in one of the approaches (for instance, the testing procedure was faulty or the officer's observations were not trustworthy), the prosecution will have the other approach to use to secure a conviction.

4. I've been charged with DUI. What are my chances of getting the prosecutor to agree to change it to a less serious offense?

Most often, when the evidence of DUI is strong, prosecutors will not agree to reduce this crime to a lesser offense, especially if the DUI is a repeat offense or it involved an accident that resulted in injury or substantial property damage. However, if the evidence is weak or marginal (for instance, the defendant was driving well and tested just above the legal limit), the prosecutor may be willing, in exchange for a plea of guilty, to reduce the charges to an offense such as:

- reckless driving (which in most states is a less serious misdemeanor), or
- speeding (only an infraction).

For more on plea bargaining, see Chapter 20.

Many times, when charges are reduced to a less serious offense, the punishment will be less severe. But even when the sentence for the lesser crime is tough, it still carries less stigma than a DUI conviction. And though, of course, all efforts should be made to avoid driving under the influence, if a defendant were to be charged in the future with a second offense, the sentence in that future case would likely be much more severe if the first offense had remained a DUI than if the first offense had been reduced to a lesser charge. Many states, for example, give mandatory jail sentences to second-time DUI offenders. (See the chart illustrating sentences for DUI offenses accompanying Question 15, below.)

Use of Plea in a Later Civil Trial

Defendants who end up plea bargaining a DUI case in which injuries or property damage occurred usually plead no contest rather than guilty. This is because, in most jurisdictions, a no contest can't be admitted as evidence in a later civil case, whereas a guilty plea can (as an admission of guilt). (For more on this issue, see Chapter 20.)

---

5. Will a DUI conviction have any effect on my driver's license or operator's permit?

In most states, in addition to criminal proceedings, an accused drunk driver also faces administrative proceedings in which the agency in charge of motor vehicles and licenses will try to take the person's driver's license away for a lengthy period of time (often six to 12 months).

The impact of this on a defendant differs from place to place. In large urban areas where public transportation is convenient, it may be less damaging to have a license taken away than in suburban or rural areas. Also, many states restrict rather than completely suspend licenses so people may drive to and from work—though usually nowhere else. But in states that do suspend licenses for first-time DUI offenses, for those who need their cars to work, the administrative penalty may actually end up being more severe than the judge's sentence.

6. What is a field sobriety test?

Field sobriety tests, or FSTs, are tests given by police officers to drivers in order to determine if they are driving under the influence of alcohol or drugs. The word "field" means at the scene of the stop (usually the side of the road or highway), as opposed to the station house. The classic FSTs involve the police asking suspected DUI offenders to:

- touch their nose
- stand on one foot
- walk a straight line, and
- recite the alphabet, forward or backward.

Also, the police may conduct blood alcohol tests (discussed below) in the field using a portable machine that tests blood alcohol content by analyzing a suspect's breath. Other blood alcohol tests, such as blood or urine tests, are typically done at the police station or a local hospital.

7. What are blood alcohol tests?

Three commonly used tests measure the amount of alcohol in a suspect's body: blood, breath, and urine tests. Blood tests directly measure the amount of alcohol in a suspect's bloodstream. Breath and urine tests measure essentially the same thing but do so by using a mathematical formula to convert the percentage of alcohol in the breath or urine to the likely corresponding blood alcohol content. Some states no longer require breath percentages to be converted to blood alcohol content, however. Instead, the laws of those states now define a legal urine alcohol or breath alcohol limit.

There are, of course, a number of variables that can affect the overall accuracy of these tests—human factors, such as the rate at which different people absorb alcohol, and technical factors, such as the competence of the person performing the tests and the accuracy of the testing machines.

 RESOURCE

For more on blood alcohol tests, see *Challenging the Breath Test at Trial: A Practical Guide for Defense Attorneys*, by Michael S. Taheri, et al. (Dimensions). Nolo also publishes *Fight Your Ticket & Win in California* (geared to California law) and *Beat Your Ticket* (a national book), both by David W. Brown. Both include easy-to-understand yet detailed discussion of blood alcohol testing that may assist readers.

Get an Independent Blood Test

Many devices used by police officers to take a breath test out in the field are equipped to capture two samples. One of these is for the police laboratory to analyze, while the other one is preserved for possible testing in an independent laboratory at the behest of the defendant. It is almost always a good idea for a defendant to arrange for an independent test—unless the status of the defendant's sobriety isn't in serious question.

8. What will happen to me if I refuse to take a blood alcohol test?

Some drivers refuse to cooperate with the police when the police attempt to conduct a blood alcohol test. Whether this is wise depends on the situation—see the related case example below on refusal to take a breath test.

In many states, the law assumes that as a condition of obtaining a driver's license, drivers consent to alcohol or drug testing if the police have probable cause to believe they are driving under the influence. Such laws are called "implied consent" laws. Under these laws, drivers do not have the right to refuse to take a blood alcohol test, and failure to cooperate typically results in the loss of driving privileges for a specified period of time, regardless of what happens in the underlying DUI case. Often, a license suspension for failure to take the test is as long as (or longer than) what results from a DUI conviction (to eliminate any incentive not to take the test). In addition, a refusal may increase a defendant's ultimate jail time if that defendant is convicted.

Some DUI defendants have tried to argue a constitutional right to refuse to take the test on the grounds that a mandatory test violates their Fifth Amendment right against self-incrimination. However, as discussed more fully in Chapter 1, the U.S. Supreme Court has decided that the Fifth Amendment only gives people the right to refuse to give evidence that is testimonial in nature, such as answering questions on the witness stand. Activities like giving blood and performing field sobriety tests are considered nontestimonial, and there is thus no constitutional right to refuse them. And evidence that a defendant refused the test can be admitted against the defendant in court as evidence of a guilty state of mind.

Sometimes a Sound Defense Strategy Dictates Against Taking the Test

Almost always, if a driver has never before been convicted of DUI, it makes sense to take the test, even if the defendant is drunk. This is because the penalty for refusal is usually as or more severe than the DUI offense itself. However, for second or subsequent offenses, the decision is not quite so simple. Sometimes, the penalty for a second offense may be so severe that it makes tactical sense to refuse the test— thereby possibly depriving police of the evidence they need to obtain a conviction. As one former public defender confessed, "When arrestees would call me up in the middle of the night to ask whether they should take the BAC test, I had pretty much of a standard routine. I'd first ask if they had in fact been drinking. They'd invariably answer, yeah, but just a couple. I'd then ask if they had ever been busted for DUI before. If not, I told them to take the test. But if they had a prior, I'd tell them to refuse the test. It was the best legal advice I could give under the circumstances."

CASE EXAMPLE: George Kramer is arrested on suspicion of drunk driving. When approached by Officer Elaine Costanza, Kramer shows Officer Costanza his driver's license and politely answers her questions about where he was coming from and where he is heading. When she asks him to submit to a breathalyzer to test his blood alcohol level, however, he flatly refuses.

Question: What consequences will Kramer's refusal have?

Answer: If the state has an implied consent law, Kramer will lose his driver's license for refusing the blood alcohol test. More important, however, if Kramer is ultimately charged with DUI and if the case were to go to trial, a jury might infer guilt from Kramer's refusal.

9. Can I choose which blood alcohol test I want to take?

Under the typical implied consent law, drivers are, in most circumstances, allowed to choose whether to take a blood, breath, or urine test. (In many states, police officers must advise drivers that they have such a choice.) There are differing thoughts on which test a driver should take if given the choice. For example, many in the scientific community have found urine tests to be the most unreliable of the tests, and therefore the most susceptible to challenge in court. The blood test is generally considered the most accurate of the tests and should therefore be preferred by people who are convinced they are under the legal limit.

10. Is there anything I can do to protect myself if I am asked to take a field sobriety test (FST)?

Yes. Just because a driver may not refuse to take a test does not mean that there aren't steps the driver can take to help his situation. A driver asked to stand on one foot or walk a straight line should pay attention to any road conditions such as a soft shoulder or incline that make performing such tests particularly difficult. If any such conditions exist, a driver charged with DUI should report them as soon as possible to his lawyer. They may later be used to invalidate the tests.

People wearing tight shoes or heels may want to ask the police for permission to remove their shoes before trying to stand on one foot or walk a straight line. Drivers suspected of DUI should never, though, reach down to remove their shoes—or make any other movements for that matter, especially with their hands—without first asking permission. Such movements may be interpreted by police as an attempt to grab a weapon.

The Old Backward Alphabet Trick!

Here is a warning for those asked to recite the alphabet backward. Many people cannot say the alphabet backward when they are sober. And police officers have been known to use this as a trick to get people to blurt out, "I can't even do that sober," thereby admitting they are in fact drunk.

11. What type of evidence is used in a typical DUI trial?

Typically, arresting police officers testify in DUI cases. They will answer the prosecutors' questions about symptoms they may have noticed, such as a defendant's driving pattern, bloodshot eyes, and the smell of alcoholic beverages on the breath. Prosecutors may also introduce documents to prove their case, such as photographs of the scene or people involved, and scientific evidence such as doctor's reports, lab analyses, and blood, breath, or urine test results. The police or arrest report and the officer's notes, while they may not be introduced as evidence in the case, may nonetheless be used to "refresh the officer's recollection" if the officer forgets something in the report. (More on admitting evidence and refreshing recollection in Chapter 18.)

12. Are there some particular things I should do or not do if I'm involved in a DUI-related accident?

Other than calling for emergency medical assistance (for anyone who is hurt) or filing a report on the accident as may be required by state law, defendants involved in DUI-related accidents should avoid making any oral or written statements to:

- **Police officers.** As discussed more thoroughly in Chapter 1, suspects do not have to and almost always should not talk to the police.
- **Witnesses or victims.** Even statements like "I'm sorry" can come back to haunt a defendant, because in court

they can sound like admissions of wrongdoing.

It may be helpful to get names, addresses, and phone numbers of potential witnesses, especially for drivers who feel they were not at fault, since that information may not be in the police report. Also, as soon as possible after the accident, defendants should write down their version of what happened and note the date and time of the writing (perhaps also mailing a copy of the statement to themselves in order to retain a postmark with the date on it). At the top of any such statement, defendants should write "Confidential: Attorney-Client Privileged," and they should not show the document to anyone except their attorney (assuming they use one).

13. What are my chances in court if I decide to fight a DUI charge?

Not surprisingly, it depends on a lot of factors. In reality, defendants whose blood alcohol tested clearly above the legal limit seldom win at trial, especially if they also failed the field sobriety tests. Where there is no blood test, or where the test results are at or below the limit, there is a much greater chance of successfully fighting the charges.

Though many prosecutors' offices are tough on DUI cases these days, skilled defense lawyers can sometimes get an acquittal by undermining the prosecutor's case. For instance, some defense lawyers routinely request maintenance and accuracy records for breathalyzer machines, and may mount a successful defense based on a machine's failure to be properly serviced or calibrated.

14. What sentences are typically handed down for violating DUI laws?

DUI sentences vary greatly depending on factors such as whether it's a first-time or repeat offense, and whether or not anyone was injured. But, as with most crimes, the typical sentence includes a fine and perhaps a few days of jail time. Convicted defendants may also suffer other consequences. For instance, they may:

- lose their driver's license, at least temporarily
- have to submit to an alcohol- or drug-related treatment program, and
- see their car insurance rates climb astronomically.

Additionally, there is a growing movement toward what is known as alternative sentencing. Some of the newer punishments that have been given in DUI cases require that convicted drunk drivers:

- have a breath test device (called a certified ignition interlock device) installed in their cars—at their own expense—which prevents the car from being started if alcohol is detected
- display a bumper sticker on their car that states that they've been convicted of a DUI
- carry a restricted driver's license allowing only trips to and from work, for example, and

- perform community service such as lecturing high school or college students, telling them about the arrest experience and urging them not to drive drunk.

(For more on sentencing, see Chapter 22.)

15. What type of sentence am I facing if I have a previous DUI conviction on my record?

Repeat offenders are routinely sentenced more severely than first offenders. The chart below, based on possible sentences for drunk driving in California (Cal. Veh. Code § 23152), shows how states can raise the punishment ante for repeat offenders.

16. What kind of lawyer should I get to fight a DUI charge?

First off, defendants should always try to hire a lawyer who practices criminal law as opposed to civil law (noncriminal, such as divorce and contract cases). (See Chapter 7 on criminal defense lawyers.) Second, DUI cases often involve unique considerations. Even a criminal lawyer who specializes in something other than DUIs may not be as effective in representing a defendant's interests in a DUI charge as one who concentrates on this particular type of case. For example, the top-notch defense lawyer who has gotten five people acquitted of murder charges may be the best in the business, but may not be familiar with the latest research on breathalyzers or blood or urine testing for alcohol.

Possible Sentences for Drunk Driving in California (California Vehicle Code § 23152)			
First offense (or no prior offense within 7 years):	**Second offense (within 7 years):**	**Third offense (within 7 years):**	**Fourth offense (within 7 years; can be filed as a felony):**
3–5 years of probation	3–5 years of probation	3–5 years of probation	3–5 years of probation
$390–$1,000 fine	$390–$1,000 fine	$390–$1,000 fine	$390–$1,000 fine
Mandatory enrollment in alcohol treatment program, and either 48 hours to 6 months in jail or 90-day driver's license restriction allowing offender to drive to work and the treatment program	48 hours to 1 year in jail, 18–30-month treatment program, and license restriction allowing offender to drive to work and the treatment program only for the length of the program; or 10 days to 1 year in jail and an 18-month license suspension	18-month treatment program if offender hasn't completed one, and 4 months to 1 year jail time, and 3-year revocation of driver's license	18-month treatment program, if offender hasn't completed one, and 6 months to 1 year in jail, and 4-year revocation of driver's license

Sometimes an Attorney Can't Help

If a first-time DUI defendant is clearly guilty and the state can prove this by a high blood alcohol test or field sobriety tests, the defendant may be better off representing himself and pleading guilty than paying a lawyer to accomplish pretty much the same result. The fact is, because of political pressures and heightened awareness of the serious harm that DUI can cause, many DAs refuse to plea bargain DUI cases, and many judges impose a "standard" sentence on first-time offenders, whether or not they are represented by an attorney. Before deciding whether to self-represent or get a lawyer, a DUI defendant would be wise to talk to a lawyer (at least for an hour or so) about how DUI cases are handled in that court and locality.

17. I was arrested, and my arraignment is coming up. I still haven't found a lawyer. What should I do?

At the arraignment, a defendant will be called on to plead (typically) guilty or not guilty. Defendants who do not yet have counsel may act as their own counsel and enter a not guilty plea. However, there are risks to doing this. (See Chapter 10 for more on arraignments.)

18. Where can I find out more about DUI laws in my state?

In addition to consulting a lawyer, one may find information about DUI laws from:

- a state driving/automobile agency (for instance the Department of Motor Vehicles or DMV—in some states called the Department of Public Safety)
- a traffic school
- a police department, and
- traffic law books, vehicle and penal codes, and other resources typically found in law libraries. (See Chapter 27 for more on legal research.)

Section II: DUI Case Examples

What follows below are case examples involving DUIs that take the defendants from arrest through conviction, in both cases by way of plea bargaining (since that is how the overwhelming majority of these cases end).

CAUTION
Please understand that any particular DUI case may be handled differently depending on:

- the state
- the court
- the attorneys, and
- the facts.

a. The facts leading up to the arrest of Julian Daniels and Shelly Rogers for DUI

On December 1, Shelly Rogers headed home after a party at Keith's Tavern. Officer Wood had noticed her weaving in and out of her lane and following closely behind the car in front of her. Officer Wood put on the flashing red light, and Rogers pulled over.

That same evening, across town, as Julian Daniels drove home from Mick's Pub, he hit a tree in a residential neighborhood. A neighbor heard the crash and phoned the police. Officer Charles drove up a few minutes later, lights flashing. Daniels was standing in front of his car, surveying the damage, when Officer Charles approached him.

About the same time as Daniels hit the tree, Rogers rolled down her window after pulling over. She put her hands on the steering wheel and waited for the police officer to approach. When the officer approached the car, the officer smelled the characteristic odor of an alcoholic beverage on Rogers's breath. The officer asked for Rogers's driver's license, then asked her to step out of the car. Rogers politely complied with both requests.

Question: Does the officer have probable cause to arrest Rogers?

Answer: Yes. (More on arrests in Chapter 3.)

Question: Can the officer also frisk Rogers?

Answer: Yes. (More on police frisking and searching in Chapter 2.)

After frisking Rogers, the officer asked where she'd come from and if she'd been drinking. Rogers politely replied that she'd like to answer but felt that she should not say anything before consulting a lawyer.

Question: Did Rogers do the right thing by asking to speak with her lawyer?

Answer: Yes. (More on not talking to the police in Chapter 1.)

The officer then told Rogers she would need to take a couple of tests and that she didn't have a right to talk to her lawyer before taking them. The officer asked Rogers to recite the alphabet, to stand on one leg, and to touch her finger to her nose. Rogers was successfully able to recite the alphabet but stumbled somewhat when she tried standing on one foot. The officer then shined a flashlight in Rogers's eyes and asked her to look left and right. The officer then gave Rogers a breath test with a PBA (portable breath analyzer). Rogers's BAC (blood alcohol content) measured 0.11 (beyond the legal limit of 0.08 for that state), so she was arrested for DUI (driving under the influence), handcuffed, and put in the back of the squad car. Nothing

further was said by either Rogers or the police officer.

Question: Did the officer err in not giving Rogers her *Miranda* warnings after arresting her?

Answer: No, the officer didn't ask Rogers any questions, so he wasn't required to warn her. (More on *Miranda* warnings in Chapter 1.)

Meanwhile, across town, Daniels was given the same field sobriety tests. Though Daniels passed all three, the officer still suspected DUI because Daniels had red, watery eyes and had hit a tree. Consequently, the officer arrested Daniels and brought him to the station for a blood test. Daniels's blood alcohol content measured 0.09% (just above the legal limit of 0.08%).

b. The booking of Daniels and Rogers

Both Daniels and Rogers were brought to the Main County Station, and both were booked upon arrival. They were photographed, their possessions except for clothes and wristwatches were taken and inventoried (see below), and they were put into jail cells to wait.

Question: Was it right for the police to take their possessions as part of the booking process?

Answer: Yes. (More on booking in Chapter 5.)

Their respective booking records read in part as follows:

Suspect: Julian Daniels

Inventory: Brown leather wallet, containing identification, photos, and $25; 4-door white Toyota Corolla (license _____) impounded.

Suspect: Shelly Rogers

Inventory: Black leather purse containing wallet (with credit card and driver's license, hair brush, nail file, and $62); red Corvette (license _____) impounded.

c. Preparation of the police reports

Later that night, the arresting officers completed their paperwork documenting the arrests, including arrest and investigation reports, a statement for the Department of Motor Vehicles, and additional pages with notes and comments.

> **Question:** Do police typically make written arrest reports in cases like this?
>
> **Answer:** Yes. (See Chapter 14 for more on arrest reports.)

d. The preparation of the criminal complaint

The officers' reports were delivered to the district attorney's intake desk at the courthouse. Both defendants' reports ended up on the desk of D.A. Ira Davidson. Davidson glanced at the police reports and filled in the appropriate blanks on the criminal complaint forms as he had done with nearly 150 criminal complaints that day.

> **Question:** Is it unusual for a D.A. to be so quick about filing a complaint?

> **Answer:** No, especially in large urban areas. (More on charging in Chapter 6.)

e. Phone calls and bail

A couple of hours later, after handling other matters and running computer checks to see if the suspects had criminal records, a police officer went to their respective cells and told Daniels that his bail had been set at $500 and Rogers that hers had been set at $3,500 (Rogers, it turned out, had been convicted of a DUI the year before).

> **Question:** Do police usually set bail?
>
> **Answer:** Sometimes; other times judges set bail amounts. (See Chapter 5 for more on bail.)

Both were allowed to make phone calls. Daniels reached his mother, who came down and paid the $500. He left on bail and was given a summons to appear in court for an arraignment the following week. Rogers wasn't as successful. She was too embarrassed to call her parents, and none of the friends she phoned were home, so she spent the night in jail. (More on bail in Chapter 5.)

f. Rogers goes to court for her arraignment

The next morning, Rogers was taken to court for an arraignment.

> **Question:** Are people usually arraigned that quickly?
>
> **Answer:** If they are in custody, yes. They usually have to be arraigned within at most 48 hours after arrest,

excluding weekends and holidays. (More on arraignment in Chapter 10.)

Rogers spent two hours in the courthouse lockup waiting for Judge Diana Benjamin.

Question: Where is the lockup?

Answer: Usually in an area of the courthouse that is segregated from the courtrooms and public areas, for example, in the basement or on a separate floor. (See Chapter 9 for a tour of a typical courthouse and courtroom.)

When the case was finally called, a bailiff led Rogers into the courtroom. Still handcuffed, Rogers stood before the judge and waited. Judge Benjamin was looking over some papers and talking with her clerk. Rogers stood waiting. She heard the judge ask her clerk for another cup of coffee, then look down and say, "Rogers?"

"That's me."

Question: Should Rogers have said, "That's me, your Honor"?

Answer: Adding "your Honor" would have made Rogers's reply more respectful and certainly couldn't have hurt. (See Chapter 10 for tips on how to speak to a judge.)

"Do you have counsel?"

Question: Does Rogers have the right to counsel at an arraignment?

Answer: Yes. (See Chapter 10 on arraignments.)

"What?"

"Do you have a lawyer?"

"No, your Honor."

"Do you want a lawyer?"

"Yeah. I guess so."

"Have you been given a chance to call a lawyer?"

"They let me make a phone call last night, but no one was home. Umm. But I don't think I have the money to hire a lawyer."

Question: Will Rogers get a public defender if she can't afford a lawyer?

Answer: Yes, or some other court-appointed attorney. (See Chapter 7 on the right to appointed counsel for those who cannot afford a private lawyer.)

"Let's see. You can talk to the public defender if you want, and we'll see you back here this afternoon. Or you can plead now if you intend to plead guilty."

Question: Should Rogers make a plea bargain?

Answer: It depends on a number of details. Here, Rogers hasn't even yet met with a lawyer, though, so she should certainly do that before even considering a plea bargain. (More on plea bargains in Chapter 20.)

"Yes, I'd like a public defender."

The judge called to her clerk, "Get somebody from the P.D.'s office down here." And to Rogers the judge said, "Okay, we'll get you a lawyer and see you back here later."

g. Rogers gets a public defender

The bailiff returned Rogers to the lockup. A few hours later, a young man approached her cell.

"Shelly Rogers?"

"Yes?"

"I'm Andrew Duncan. I'm from the public defender's office. How are you?"

"Tired, bored. Sick of this place."

"Well, unfortunately, I don't think I can get you out today. I talked to the D.A. The D.A. said for a second offense, you gotta do 48 hours—no way around it. But if you plead guilty this afternoon, then you can get out tomorrow with probation. You'll have to pay a fine and do another alcohol program. I see you did a three-month one last time you were arrested. But that's it."

> **Question:** Would Rogers be sentenced to jail time if she went to trial and lost?
>
> **Answer:** Yes. If that's the mandatory state law for a second DUI, she would get the time either way—and possibly even more if she went to trial and lost. (See Chapter 20 on plea bargaining, and Chapter 22 on sentencing.)

"Yeah. Listen, what if I want to fight it?"

"Well. You could fight it, but it doesn't look good." He read from the reports, "Blood alcohol—0.11, failed field sobriety tests ...."

"I did the alphabet, didn't I?" Shelly interrupted.

"Um. Yeah, but you couldn't stand on one foot, your eyes were bloodshot, they smelled some type of alcoholic beverage on your breath. Look, we can talk more in a little bit. I have to go back into court now to meet another client. Your case will be called after lunch. I'll come talk to you again before then. In the meantime, think it over. I'll tell you this much, if you go to trial and lose, on a second DUI a judge might give you a lot more than 48 hours in jail. You can get up to a year in jail, plus the probation, plus fines and an alcohol program. You might want to cut your losses."

Andrew Duncan left Shelly Rogers and ran back upstairs to court to meet with another client.

h. Rogers considers a plea bargain suggested by her public defender

After lunch, Shelly Rogers was hauled back into court. Standing before the judge, still handcuffed, Shelly wondered what was going on. Duncan hadn't been back to see her.

Duncan ran in, put his briefcase down, pulled out a file folder and leaned in to whisper to Shelly.

"I was in another courtroom on another case and couldn't come talk to you. Sorry. I want you to know, though, I spoke to the D.A. If you do the 18-month alcohol rehab program and plead guilty now, they'll let you out tomorrow—as soon as the 48 hours are done. You'll be on probation for three years. And you'll do some community service instead of the fines; they do that where people can't afford to pay them. Okay?"

"Yeah. I guess that's the best I can do."

"Well, you do risk a lot more if you fight and lose."

"Okay."

i. The court takes Rogers's guilty plea under the plea bargain

"All right, just say yes to all the questions the judge asks you and we'll be out of here in three minutes," Andrew told his client.

"All right people, we're back on the record, let's go," the judge called as she sat down at the bench. "What's next?" she asked her clerk.

"Rogers is back—continued from this morning."

"Okay, Ms. Rogers. Let's see, you now have counsel," said the judge.

"Yes."

"And how do you now plead to the charges of second offense driving under the influence?"

"Say 'guilty,'" Andrew Duncan whispered to Rogers.

"Guilty," Rogers said.

"Counsel, have you reached a settlement?"

D.A.: "Yes, your Honor; 18-month program, three years probation, $500 fine which we'll convert to community service hours (because the defendant is indigent), plus 48 hours—if she pleads guilty now."

"Ms. Rogers, do you know that by pleading guilty you lose the right to a jury trial?"

"Yes."

"Do you give up that right?"

"Yes."

"Do you understand what giving up that right means?"

"Yes."

"Do you know that you are waiving the right to cross-examine your accusers?"

"Yes."

"Do you know that you are waiving your privilege against self-incrimination?"

> **Question:** Is that the Fifth Amendment?
>
> **Answer:** Yes.

"Yes."

"Did anyone force you into accepting this settlement?"

"No."

"Are you pleading guilty because you in fact were driving under the influence?"

"Yes."

> **Question:** If Shelly Rogers wants to take the plea bargain, why does the judge need to ask her so many questions?
>
> **Answer:** Because a judge is required by law to ensure that defendants understand what rights they are giving up by pleading guilty and that they are pleading guilty voluntarily. (See Chapter 20 on plea bargaining.)

j. The judge sentences Rogers as prescribed in the plea bargain

"Ms. Rogers, you are hereby sentenced to be incarcerated for a term of 48 hours.

You shall enroll by no later than 14 days from today in a court-approved 18-month alcohol treatment program. You shall be on probation for a period of three years, and you'll have to do 50 hours of community service. Do you understand?"

> **Question:** Will Rogers have to report to a probation officer?

> **Answer:** Yes. (More on probation, community service, and other punishments in Chapter 22, on sentencing.)

"Yes, your Honor."

"Bailiff, take her back to lockup." To Shelly the judge said, "You may go home tomorrow. Counsel will explain the paperwork you have to complete. I don't want to see you back here, Ms. Rogers. I hope you take the alcohol program more seriously this time around."

When Shelly was released the next day, she was given a packet of information from the public defender's office. It included the name and phone number of her probation officer and a list of the court-approved treatment programs. (More on probation in Chapter 22.)

k. Free on bail, Daniels meets his public defender before the arraignment and discusses a possible plea bargain

Daniels, meanwhile, had been free on bail. A week after Shelly Rogers was sentenced, Andrew Duncan, the same public defender, met with Julian Daniels in the hallway outside the courtroom just before Daniels's arraignment.

"Hi. Daniels, right?"

"Yes."

"My name is Andrew Duncan, I'm your lawyer. I spoke with you on the phone a few days ago?"

"Yes. Yes, thank you."

"You've never been arrested before, right?"

"No, never."

"What happened? Says here you hit a tree?"

"Yeah. I was looking down to get a new tape, and next thing I knew I'd plowed into this tree."

"Okay, you were 0.09 …. I think I can get you a decent deal, probably three years probation, three-month alcohol program, and some community service if you plead today."

"Look. I don't need an alcohol program. I had a couple of beers with my girlfriend. That's it. I'm not an alcoholic. What's community service? Is that picking up trash like those guys in orange vests I see out on the roadway?"

"Well, that's one kind of community service, yes. But, we could arrange for you to work in a library or school, or some volunteer program like that."

"How many hours of community service are we talking?"

"They said 200 hours."

"I can't do that. I'm in school full-time and I have a job. Man, I don't want this on my record; I'm applying to grad schools. You know that cop didn't even read me my rights."

"Did the cop question you?"

"Not really. I mean he asked if could say the alphabet and touch my nose, and told me to stand on one foot. Then he put me in the car."

"Well, technically, they don't have to read you your rights unless they question you."

"Oh?"

"Yup. Listen, your girlfriend was with you the whole time at the bar?"

"Yeah."

"She can testify that you only had, how many beers?"

"Two. Two beers. She was with me the whole time. That's all I had."

"And you're in college where?"

"State University. I'm graduating this spring."

"Okay, let me talk to the D.A. There's pretty much no way to get around doing an alcohol program on a DUI—even a first-timer. Our only chance is if she reduces the charge to reckless driving. Come into the courtroom with me, but you sit in the back and wait. Your case will be called in the next hour or two."

"Do your best, Mr. Duncan," Daniels called.

"Thanks."

"Sure."

I. Daniels's lawyer proposes a plea bargain to the prosecutor

In the courtroom, Duncan found the assistant D.A. handling the case, Colleen O'Larky, sitting toward the front in the audience section of the courtroom waiting for her next case. He slid in to the seat next to her.

"Larky," Duncan whispered.

"Yeah," she replied quietly, putting a folder in front of her mouth so the judge wouldn't see she was talking.

"I gotta talk to you about the Daniels case, set for this afternoon. Your case."

"I'm listening."

"Have you looked at it? 0.09—just over the limit, no priors, good kid—finishing college this spring, wants to go to grad school. What can we do here?"

"You know my boss. No forgiveness on DUIs. He spoke at a MADD (Mothers Against Drunk Driving) conference last week. My hands are tied."

"Look, make an exception here. He's a nice kid. He was just looking down to change a tape and hit a tree. Dumb luck. No one was hurt. Knock it down to reckless. It's bad enough this is going to go on his record—he's clean. He passed all the FSTs, says right here on the police report."

Just then the judge called "State v. Molly Patricks." The D.A. jumped up and whispered,

"That's my case, Duncan. Hang on. I'll think about it and get back to you."

"I'm waiting right here," Duncan replied, and the D.A. went up before the judge to handle a different case. Ten minutes later she was back.

"All right, Duncan. But only for you. Reckless. Two years probation, 150 hours community service—best offer. And he pleads today, or no deal."

"Thanks, Larky. I'll talk to him. Sounds good."

Andrew Duncan quietly slipped out and went to the back of the courtroom to find Daniels. He told Daniels the deal the prosecutor had offered, and Daniels agreed to plead.

m. Daniels pleads no contest

Daniels's case was called some time later. And after asking Daniels the same questions Judge Benjamin asked Shelly Rogers earlier (and getting all the same answers from Daniels), she accepted Daniels's plea of no contest.

Question: What is a no contest plea?

Answer: In most respects the same as a guilty plea, but it likely cannot be used as an admission of guilt against Daniels in a later civil suit should the owner of the tree he hit decides to sue for property damage. (More on no contest pleas in Chapter 20.) Daniels was convicted of reckless driving and sentenced as agreed.

Juvenile Courts and Procedures

This chapter provides an overview of the juvenile justice process. Juvenile justice is an umbrella term for the special procedures set up by every state to deal with young people whose cases qualify for handling in juvenile court. Juvenile courts handle most of the cases in which young people (usually called "juveniles" or "minors") are accused of committing crimes. Of course, the treatment of juveniles differs from state to state, judge to judge, and cop to cop. And if differences of opinion generally exist about getting tough on crime, the conflicting opinions on how to deal with minors accused of crimes are greater still. The goal of this chapter is to help anyone involved with juvenile courts to understand their general policies and procedures, particularly where these differ from those found in adult criminal courts. Hopefully, the chapter will make juvenile court seem a little less foreign, a little less intimidating, a little easier to understand and deal with.

Section I: A Brief History of U.S. Juvenile Courts

This section sketches the background of today's juvenile justice system.

1. When were the first juvenile courts established in the United States?

The first juvenile court was established in 1899. However, it wasn't until 1945 that all states had juvenile courts.

2. How were children dealt with before juvenile courts were established?

In the mostly rural society of the nineteenth century, parents, churches, and communities punished children who committed crimes. Children were typically disciplined by force, sometimes brutally.

The urbanization that followed the industrial revolution in the last half of the nineteenth century posed particular problems for children. Many were subject to harsh conditions, including extensive poverty and child labor. At that time, children who got into trouble (whether by committing a crime or by being the victims of abuse or neglect) were often put to work or sent away to relatives. So-called "reform schools," the precursors of modern juvenile halls, were also set up. The ostensible purpose of these schools was to change or reform children, in part by giving them skills and training. In fact, these facilities were often little more than warehouse-type jails, some with deplorable conditions, where most of the learning that occurred was how to become a better criminal.

Around the turn of the twentieth century, many social leaders came to believe that reform schools were not working. They also began to understand children not simply as mini-adults, but as people with special needs who should be treated differently than adults. Consequently, the movement for a separate juvenile justice system began.

Too Young to Punish?

Based on principles developed by English common law, most states consider children under age seven to be legally incapable of forming the *"mens rea"* (guilty state of mind; see Chapter 12) necessary to be morally to blame and therefore subject to criminal punishment. As a result, minors under age seven are usually excused because of their age if they commit acts that would be crimes if committed by adults. Instead, the parents of these children may have to pay restitution (compensation) to the victims. In addition, a court may determine that a child's parents are unfit, remove the child from the parents' custody, and place the child with a relative, foster family, or treatment facility.

Children between the ages of seven and 14 often occupy a middle ground. Using what legal rules often refer to as a "rebuttable presumption," minors in this age range are often presumed to be incapable of forming a guilty mind. However, if a prosecutor can show that a particular child in this age range is capable of forming and did form a guilty mind, the child can be criminally punished.

Once minors reach age 14, most states regard them as fully capable of forming a guilty mind. Therefore, minors older than 14 are usually held accountable for the crimes they commit, either in juvenile or adult court.

3. What are the goals of juvenile courts?

As with adults, juvenile court goals are a mix of rehabilitation, punishment, and community safety. Juvenile courts have traditionally considered children less dangerous and more amenable to rehabilitation than adults. As a result, minors who commit crimes often receive counseling and stay at home in lieu of going to jail. However, citing statistics suggesting that minors increasingly commit more and worse crimes at younger ages, advocates of punishment and community safety want juvenile courts to get young criminals off the streets.

Juvenile Court Paternalism

The roots of paternalism are deep in the juvenile justice system. In part they stem from an English concept called *parens patriae* (Latin for "parent of the country"). Under this concept, minors really belong to the government; parents are temporary custodians. Juvenile and family courts, as the arm of the government, are therefore ultimately responsible for minors. Programs in the juvenile justice system often reflect a paternalistic attitude towards minors. For example, judges may follow "tough love" or "scared straight" programs out of the belief that juveniles benefit from a strict but caring approach.

Section II: Juvenile Court Jurisdiction

This section briefly looks at juvenile court "jurisdiction," which refers to a juvenile court's power to hear cases.

4. Do juvenile courts only have jurisdiction over cases in which juveniles are accused of committing crimes?

No. In addition to having jurisdiction over cases involving crimes committed by minors (often called "juvenile delinquency" cases), juvenile courts in most states also have jurisdiction over:

- Cases involving minors who are allegedly abused or neglected by their parents or guardians. These are often called "juvenile dependency" cases. Abused or neglected minors may be removed from parental homes and placed with relatives or foster parents. At a minimum, parents are often ordered to undergo counseling as a condition of keeping or regaining custody. A juvenile court may also declare parents permanently unfit and approve a minor's adoption.
- Cases involving minors who commit status offenses. A status offense is a type of violation that only a juvenile can commit. For example, a 14-year-old who skips school (is truant) for no valid reason commits a status offense if the law requires all children under the age of 16 to attend school. An adult could not violate this law.

5. Do the same procedures apply to dependency, status offense, and juvenile delinquency cases?

No. Even though juvenile courts may have jurisdiction over all three types of cases, different procedures typically apply to each. This chapter focuses on juvenile delinquency cases, since they are the juvenile court counterpart of adult criminal proceedings. However, keep in mind the following points about status offenses:

- Juvenile court personnel may use the term juvenile delinquency as an umbrella term that covers both juvenile crimes and status offenses.
- Minors who commit status offenses can sometimes end up in custody in juvenile hall. For example, if a minor violates a judge's order to attend school, the judge may send the minor to juvenile hall for disobeying the court order.
- Minors charged with status offenses do not have a constitutional right to counsel. Some states do, however, provide attorneys to minors charged with status offenses.

CASE EXAMPLE: Officer Steve Roberts sees Jack Aranda, who appears to be a teenage boy, shopping at the local mall on a Wednesday morning. When Officer Roberts stops Jack and asks him how old he is, Jack says, "I'm 15." Jack then tells Officer Roberts, "I wanted to shop before the mall gets crowded." Officer Roberts then takes Jack into custody.

Juvenile Justice Lingo

Juvenile courts tend to have their own jargon, in part to portray a gentler image than adult criminal courts. Some of the unique terms that you may encounter if you become involved in juvenile court proceedings are as follows:

- **Adjudication:** A juvenile court trial, similar to an adult trial.
- **Admission of petition:** The juvenile court counterpart to a guilty plea.
- **Camp:** A locked facility for juvenile offenders. Camps often house minors who will be locked up for many weeks or months, while juvenile halls tend to be temporary holding facilities. States may have various types of camps differing in degrees of security, rigidity, and facilities. Many camps have school facilities.
- **Custody order:** An arrest warrant.
- **Dependency court:** A branch of the juvenile court that hears cases involving minors who have allegedly been neglected or abused by parents or guardians.
- **Detention order:** An order that a minor be placed in custody.
- **Disposition:** A juvenile court sentence or other final order, which juvenile court regulars often shorten to "dispo."
- **Dispositional hearing:** A sentencing hearing.
- **Fact-finding hearing:** Along with adjudication, a juvenile court term for a trial.

- **Infant:** A minor, in most states a person under the age of 18. (Few teenagers appreciate being referred to as infants!)
- **Involved:** The juvenile court equivalent of guilty.
- **Juvenile Hall:** A jail (or temporary holding facility) for minors.
- **Petition:** The juvenile court equivalent of a criminal complaint, which charges a child with a violation.
- **Referee:** A judicial officer, usually a lawyer appointed by a court's presiding judge, who performs many of a judge's functions but who has not been formally elected or appointed as a judge.
- **Respondent:** A juvenile court defendant.
- **Suitable placement:** A court order removing a juvenile from the juvenile's parental home and placing the juvenile into a foster home, a group home, a treatment facility, a camp, or some other type of placement.
- **Sustained (Not Sustained):** The equivalent of a verdict, a juvenile court finding that the charge in a petition is (or is not) true.
- **Ward of the court:** A minor who is under the jurisdiction of the juvenile court.

Question: Did Officer Roberts properly arrest Jack?

Answer: Yes. Laws typically require minors to be in school on weekdays. Because Jack appeared to be of school age, the officer had a right to question him. When Jack's responses indicated that he was truant, the officer had a right to arrest him. See Section III for what the officer might do with Jack.

Section III: Deciding Whether to File Charges

This section summarizes the typical processes by which cases are either weeded out of or formally filed in juvenile courts.

6. How do most minors come to the attention of the police?

Unlike adults, juvenile offenders often come to police attention through reports of parents and school officials. When the police decide to file formal charges against a suspect who is a minor, they normally refer the case to a prosecutor or probation officer attached to a juvenile court.

7. Does every minor who is stopped by the police end up in juvenile court?

No; a variety of scenarios are possible. A police officer may:

- detain and warn the minor against further violations, and then let him go free (in juvenile court and police lingo, the minor was "counselled and released")

- detain and warn the minor against further violations, but hold him until his parent or guardian comes for him, or

- place the minor in custody and refer the case to the juvenile court.

8. What happens once a case has been referred to juvenile court?

The following is an overview of how juvenile cases typically flow through the system:

- A prosecutor or a juvenile court intake officer (often a probation officer) decides whether to:
  - dismiss the case
  - handle the case informally, or
  - petition the case (file formal charges).

- In some localities, the probation officer makes only a preliminary assessment of whether to file formal charges, and leaves the final decision to a prosecutor.

- A decision to proceed informally often results in the minor's having to appear before a probation officer or a judge. The minor may receive a stern lecture, and may also be required to attend counseling sessions or after-school classes, repay the victim for damaged property or pay a fine, perform community service work, or go on probation. If the intake officer suspects that a minor taken into custody has been abused or neglected, proceedings to remove her from the custody of parents or guardians may also be started.

- If the decision is to proceed formally, the intake officer or prosecutor files a petition and the case is placed on the juvenile court's calendar. (In large cities, juvenile courts may handle over 300 cases each day.)
- The minor is arraigned (formally charged) before a juvenile court judge or referee. At this point, the juvenile court either takes jurisdiction of the case or waives (transfers) the case to adult criminal court. (See Section V, below, for more on transfers to adult court.)
- If the case remains in juvenile court, the minor either enters into a plea arrangement or faces trial (often called an adjudication).
- If, after trial, the juvenile court judge sustains the petition (concludes that the charges are true), the judge decides on an appropriate sentence (usually referred to as a disposition). (See Section VI below.)
- Postdisposition hearings may occur. For example, a judge's disposition order may require a minor to appear in court periodically so that the judge can monitor the minor's behavior.

9. What factors do intake officers normally consider when deciding whether to file formal charges?

The official factors that an intake officer is likely to consider include:

- **The severity of the offense.** A serious crime is more likely to result in the filing of a petition than a less serious crime.
- **The minor's age.** Petitions are more likely to be filed in cases involving older than younger children.
- **The minor's past record.** Formal charges are more likely when a minor has had previous juvenile court involvement.
- **The strength of the evidence that a minor committed a crime.**
- **The minor's gender.** Formal charges are more likely to be filed against boys than girls.
- **The minor's social history.** Petitions are more likely to be filed when children have a history of problems at home or at school.
- **The parent's or guardian's apparent ability to control the minor.** The greater the lack of parental control over the minor, the more likely the intake officer is to file a petition.

In addition to these official reasons, the filing decisions of many intake officers cannot help but be swayed—off the record—by a number of subjective factors. These may include:

- **The minor's attitude.** Formal proceedings are less likely when a child shows remorse for a bad deed.
- **The minor's manner of dress.** If the minor dresses well, is groomed neatly, and is polite, intake personnel are more likely to handle the case informally than if the minor dresses sloppily or in a way that shows disrespect for the juvenile justice system or obvious gang involvement.

- **Whether the minor has family or community support.**
- **Whether the minor has an attorney.** Disposing of a case informally may be less likely when a child has a lawyer. (See Section IV for more on lawyer involvement in juvenile cases.)
- **Ethnicity and socioeconomic status.** Statistics suggest (though few, if any, intake officers would admit, on or off the record) that the ethnicity and socioeconomic status of minors sometimes affects how aggressively their cases are handled.

10. Does the filing of a formal petition mean that the case has to go to trial or end by plea bargain?

No. Juvenile court judges often informally divert cases. In other words, working with other community service agencies (schools, social services, and child welfare departments) a judge may retain jurisdiction over a case while the minor undergoes a recommended program. For example, the minor (and/or the minor's parents) may have to participate in counseling. Or, the minor may have to pay restitution, repair damaged property, perform community service work, or attend special classes. If the minor fails to complete the recommended program, formal charges may be reinstated. (For information on diversion in adult cases, see Chapter 6.) Juveniles in some cities may also be able to participate in another form of diversion, called "teen court." (See "A Sampling of Innovative Juvenile Justice Programs" in Section VI.)

A Statistical Look at One Year in State Juvenile Courts

In 2003, approximately 1.6 million juvenile delinquency cases were filed in the United States, and of those, about 57% (928,849) were formally processed. About 36% of the formally charged cases were for property offenses and about 12% involved drug offenses. Of the formally charged juveniles around 64% were adjudicated delinquent, and about 63% of those were placed on probation.

The information comes from a database maintained by the National Center for Juvenile Justice, which is a research division of the National Council of Juvenile and Family Court Judges. The database currently contains juvenile court statistics from 1985–2003 and is available at http://ojjdp. ncjrs.org.

Section IV: The Right to Counsel and Other Constitutional Rights

This section demonstrates how in recent decades juvenile courts' procedures have become less informal and more like adult criminal courts. However, important differences remain.

11. Do minors have the same constitutional rights as adults?

No. Until the 1960s, juvenile courts offered few of the rights guaranteed to adult criminal defendants. Up until then, juvenile court judges dispensed justice pretty much as they saw fit. Outside criticism of their sometimes arbitrary approach was rare. Juvenile court proceedings were closed to the public. Parents could not and did not object. Defense lawyers were not often present, and minors had virtually no rights. Since the 1960s, the U.S. Supreme Court has issued several rulings that have afforded minors at least some of the rights enjoyed by adults.

12. Do the police need probable cause to search and arrest a minor?

Yes. However, public officers in quasi-parental relationships with minors (for example, school officials) do not need probable cause to justify the temporary detention and search of a minor. A reasonable suspicion that a child has committed a crime is all that many public officials need to detain and search the minor or the minor's property, such as a school locker. (See Chapter 2 for more on constitutional protections against unreasonable searches and seizures.)

13. Do minors taken into custody have a right to bail?

No. Minors do not have the bail option that most arrested adults have. (See Chapter 5 for more on bail.) Minors who are taken into custody by the police are usually either released to the custody of a parent or guardian, or detained (locked up) until they can be taken before a juvenile court judge for arraignment. (This period may be called

---

Advantages and Risks of Preadjudication Release

Police officers and other intake officers are often willing to release arrested minors to their parents' custody pending a court date. Preadjudication release is usually good for both minor and family. It gives the minor a chance to get cleaned up and prepare for the hearing, and perhaps consult with an attorney. Also, some studies have shown that detained minors consistently receive harsher dispositions.

In some instances, parents may be justifiably reluctant to accept custody of their arrested children. Some state laws make parents liable in certain circumstances for their children's acts of juvenile delinquency. (For example, parents of a minor who steals may have to make restitution to the victim.) Parents who fear that their child may commit further crimes, especially if they fear that the child is violent and beyond their control, may be hesitant to agree to preadjudication release. Parents in such situations should try to determine the extent of their potential liability and inquire (perhaps of a public defender or a private defense lawyer if resources permit) how they can keep their child safely detained with as little damage as possible to the child's chances for receiving rehabilitative treatment.

"preadjudication detention.") Unfortunately, as is the case with some adults, a juvenile who is arrested on a Friday may have to remain in custody until the following Monday (or Tuesday if the Monday happens to be a holiday), when court is in session.

14. Are minors ever locked up with adult offenders?

Yes, despite the fact that laws in most states require that minors be kept in separate juvenile halls or jail facilities. Studies all across the country routinely show that minors are often jailed with adults. The reasons for this vary. Police officers sometimes mistake older minors for adults, and some minors lie to the police about their age. In other instances, juvenile facilities don't exist, are overcrowded, or are located at an inconvenient distance.

15. Do minors have the right to legal representation in juvenile delinquency cases?

Yes. In *In re Gault,* (U.S. Sup. Ct. 1967), the Supreme Court said, "The juvenile needs the assistance of counsel to cope with problems of law, to make skilled inquiry into the facts, to insist upon regularity of the proceedings, and to ascertain whether he has a defense and to prepare and submit it."

16. Does a minor who cannot afford a lawyer have the right to a court-appointed attorney?

Yes. Minors who can't afford a lawyer (which is almost always the case) are entitled to have one provided by the state. (More on court-appointed lawyers in Chapter 7.)

17. Can minors who are locked up make a phone call for help?

Often, yes. Minors who are not quickly released from custody can exercise their right to counsel by politely requesting permission to make a phone call to secure legal representation. If the family situation allows, the minor should probably call a parent or guardian, who can in turn contact a lawyer. Otherwise, the minor may contact a lawyer directly or, if the minor and the minor's family are without adequate funds, ask to speak with a public defender.

"I Won't Talk Until You Call My Parents"

Police officers generally give *Miranda* warnings to arrestees, both adults and juveniles. These warnings advise arrestees of their right to remain silent and consult with a lawyer. (See Chapter 1.) Minors arrested for serious crimes should never talk to the police before consulting either a lawyer or a parent or guardian. Minors can exercise their *Miranda* rights by asking to speak either with a lawyer or with a parent or guardian before talking to the police. If the police ignore the request and continue questioning the minor, nothing the minor says is admissible as evidence of the minor's guilt if the case goes to trial.

18. How and when are lawyers appointed for minors?

In some jurisdictions, public defenders are automatically appointed for minors. In other jurisdictions, minors have to formally request appointed counsel at arraignment.

19. Will a minor who comes from a wealthy family still be eligible for an appointed attorney?

Yes. The right to counsel attaches to the minor, not to the minor's family. While some counties may try to collect payment for legal services from the minor's family, it is doubtful that the family could be legally compelled to pay.

20. Are parents allowed to participate in meetings between their child and the child's lawyer?

Sometimes. Most defense lawyers will initially want to meet with a minor alone, because the minor is the client even if the parents are paying for the lawyer's services. In fact, in order to preserve lawyer-client confidentiality (discussed in Chapter 8), it's important that minors speak privately with their lawyers. However, when the time comes to make important decisions, it is common for lawyers to include parents in the discussion, assuming the minor consents.

Parents may certainly—and should—tell lawyers to keep the parents informed about what is happening. Parents should also ask if they can be of any assistance. For example, parents may be able to provide relevant family history and contact people familiar with the child (for example, teachers, clergypeople, or employers) who might agree to testify or write letters on the child's behalf.

21. Other than the right to counsel, what other constitutional rights do juveniles have?

The *Gault* case (U.S. Sup. Ct. 1967) also decided that in addition to the right to counsel, juveniles charged with crimes have:

- the right to notice of the charges
- the right to confront and cross-examine witnesses, and
- the privilege against self-incrimination (they cannot be compelled to testify).

(For more on these rights, see Chapter 17.)

22. Is there a right to a jury trial in juvenile courts?

Generally, no. Only about ten states allow jury trials in juvenile delinquency cases. Even in those states, the right to a jury trial may be confined to specific types of cases, such as those involving minors who have prior records and are facing serious charges.

States that do not allow jury trials at all in juvenile court include California (Cal. Welf. & Inst. Code § 702.3), New Jersey (N.J. Stat. Ann. 2a:4a-40), and Pennsylvania (42 Pa. Cons. Stat. Ann. 42, § 6336). Massachusetts (Mass. Gen. Laws Ch. 119, § 55-A) and Michigan (Mich. Comp. Laws § 712A.17) afford juveniles a general right to jury trials. Arkansas (Ark. Code Ann. § 9-27-331), Colorado (Colo. Rev. Stat. § 19-2-804), and Illinois (705 Ill. Comp. Stat. § 405/5-35) provide jury trials to juveniles only in limited types of cases.

Is It Helpful for Minors to Have Lawyers in Juvenile Cases?

Almost always, yes. And the attorney should normally be one who specializes in or is at least familiar with juvenile court procedures. Research indicates that effective assistance of counsel can greatly affect a case's outcome. For example, attorneys often can help by:

- getting cases diverted, or handled informally, so the juvenile is not incarcerated and has no juvenile court record

- arranging for a juvenile's release from pre-adjudication detention

- keeping juveniles from being tried as adults, and

- putting together, and convincing a judge to agree to, a creative and compassionate disposition.

Nevertheless, some juvenile court professionals say that a lawyer's involvement often prolongs cases, turning what a prosecutor might be willing to handle informally into a formal adversarial proceeding. Some probation officers, intake personnel, judges, and other juvenile court staff admit that they are hostile to defense attorneys because they think that the attorneys slow down already overcrowded calendars. Some judges threaten to (and some actually do) give harsher treatment to juveniles represented by lawyers.

Since the variables are so great, there are no meaningful guidelines regarding when a lawyer should be used. However, juvenile court regulars, such as a deputy public defender assigned to the court, may have an informed opinion on whether the minor is likely to benefit from legal representation. Also, the more serious the crime and the worse the minor's record, the more important it is to have legal representation. On the other hand, an "A" student with no prior record who is accused of putting graffiti on a school wall may decide that a quick, informal, and satisfactory disposition is more likely if no lawyer is involved.

23. What is the burden of proof in juvenile cases?

To convict an adult of a crime, the government must prove guilt beyond a reasonable doubt. (See Chapter 17.) *In re Winship* (U.S. Sup. Ct. 1970) extended this rule to juvenile court cases in which a minor could be incarcerated if adjudicated a delinquent. However, to sustain charges that will not result in a minor's incarceration, the government only has to prove by a preponderance of the evidence that the minor engaged in illegal conduct.

Section V: Trying Juveniles as Adults

This section provides an overview of the procedures by which juvenile courts can transfer cases to adult criminal courts, where juveniles are tried as adults.

24. What does it mean to be tried as an adult?

Juveniles who are tried as adults are subject to the harsher punishment options of adult criminal courts. For example, juveniles who are tried as adults and convicted can receive sentences that juvenile court judges lack the power to impose (for example, life sentences) and will normally be locked up in adult jails and prisons rather than juvenile treatment facilities. On the other hand, adult criminal courts afford rights that some juvenile courts do not, such as the right to a jury trial.

25. Why might a case be transferred from juvenile to adult court?

A juvenile court judge may transfer a case to adult court when, in the judge's opinion, the minor is not amenable to rehabilitation as a juvenile. Typically, juveniles are transferred to adult court when they are charged with serious offenses and/or have a lengthy juvenile court record. Juvenile court judges usually also take into account the minor's age (older minors are more likely to be transferred to adult courts than younger minors) and mental and physical abilities.

26. At what age can a minor's case be transferred to adult court and the minor tried as an adult?

The age at which a minor may be tried as an adult varies from state to state. In many states, a minor can be tried as an adult only if the minor has reached a minimum age, often 16. In other states, 13-year-olds may be tried as adults. In still other states, a child of any age may be tried as an adult depending on the nature of the crime. Based on a perception of increased lawlessness at younger ages, the current trend is for states to lower the age at which a minor may be tried as an adult.

27. What procedure does a juvenile court judge follow when deciding whether to transfer a case to adult court?

While juvenile court judges can themselves begin transfer proceedings, transfer proceedings are normally initiated at the request of a government prosecutor.

Following the prosecutor's request, a juvenile court judge hears evidence relating to the minor's amenability—or lack thereof—to juvenile court services.

A juvenile's right to a hearing before a case can be transferred to adult court was established by *Kent v. U.S.* (U.S. Sup. Ct. 1966). Minors are entitled to counsel at transfer hearings.

To convince a juvenile court judge to transfer a case to adult court, the prosecutor normally has to offer evidence showing probable cause to believe that the minor committed the charged offense. (This aspect of the hearing is similar to a preliminary hearing, discussed in Chapter 16.) If the judge concludes that probable cause exists, the judge may then hear additional evidence concerning the minor's general background, prior juvenile court record, and amenability to treatment. Then, taking into account the seriousness of the offense, the judge will decide whether to transfer the case to adult court. After transfer to adult court, a case typically goes back to square one, with an adult court arraignment. (See Chapter 10.)

28. What are automatic transfer laws?

Some states have laws mandating that juveniles be tried as adults in certain types of cases. The typical automatic transfer law is activated when a minor has reached a certain age (often 16) and is charged with a serious and violent offense such as robbery, rape, or murder.

Other Names for Transfer Hearings

The hearing in which a judge considers whether to transfer a case to adult court has a variety of names. The hearing may be called a "waiver" hearing, because the juvenile court waives (gives up) jurisdiction by transferring a case to adult court. It may also be called a "fitness" hearing, since the judge decides whether a minor is fit to be tried as an adult. A final common name is a "certification" hearing, because a judge certifies that a minor is fit to be tried as an adult.

---

29. What are reverse transfer hearings?

Juveniles have the right to request a juvenile court transfer hearing even when a case is subject to an automatic transfer law. However, because the law has already automatically transferred the case, a minor is put in the position of trying to convince a juvenile court judge to take back jurisdiction. Thus, the hearing is commonly called a "reverse waiver" or "reverse transfer" hearing.

30. What arguments can a minor's lawyer use to try to persuade a judge not to transfer a juvenile case to adult court?

A recent child advocacy report identified the following arguments that attorneys can make at transfer or reverse transfer hearings:

- Although an offense is serious, the minor is still a child who would benefit from the services available in the juvenile system. Factors indicating that a minor is likely to benefit from juvenile court services include:
  - the minor has close family attachments
  - older friends, teachers, counselors, employers, etc., have submitted statements indicating their belief that a minor has good potential
  - the minor was not thinking as an adult at the time of the offense
  - the minor has good moral judgment and expressed remorse for the improper behavior
  - other minors in similar situations have benefitted from juvenile court services, and
  - it is realistic to expect that a minor's delinquent behavior will improve from services meeting the minor's needs.
- The minor has not in the past had sufficient opportunity to be rehabilitated.
- The minor is likely to suffer physical or emotional harm in the adult system.
- The juvenile court system provides sufficient safeguards so that the community can be protected while the minor undergoes treatment as a juvenile.

(Source: "A Call for Justice: An Assessment of Access to Counsel and Quality of Counsel in Delinquency Proceedings," by the ABA Juvenile Justice Center, the Juvenile Law Center, and the Youth Law Center (1995), p. 35.)

How Can You Help an Accused Minor?

Family members, friends, employers, teachers, and others who want to help a minor can appear in court or write letters demonstrating their support. Supporters should be prepared to give concrete examples of the minor's behavior indicating that the minor is basically a good person who has potential and who should be given an opportunity to turn things around. Supporters can submit school records showing that the minor has attended school regularly. Parents may want to secure and submit to the court a psychological assessment of the minor. The fact that the minor has learning difficulties, for example, can be very relevant and persuasive evidence supporting treatment rather than punishment. Parents may be able to research and suggest to the court possible alternative treatment programs (such as wilderness programs or military schools) instead of a detention camp or juvenile hall. Finally, parents or other supporters can examine the prosecution's file for inaccuracies, particularly concerning the minor's previous juvenile court records.

31. When is it normally in a minor's best interests to be tried as a juvenile rather than as an adult?

Common advantages of being tried in juvenile rather than adult court include:

- Juvenile court records are easier to seal than adult court records. (More on sealing juvenile records in Section VII, below.)
- Juvenile court proceedings are civil, and a finding that a minor committed an offense usually carries less social stigma than an adult criminal record.
- Juvenile courts dispositions are often less severe than adult criminal sentences, and are more likely to be tailored to the minor's personal situation. For example, rather than simply imposing a fine or a jail term, a juvenile court judge may impose a curfew and require a minor to attend school and attend regular counseling directed towards minors.
- Even when incarceration is ordered, a juvenile court judge is less likely to impose a lengthy sentence than an adult court judge. (Juvenile court judges cannot impose the most severe punishments, such as life imprisonment).
- Minors incarcerated by juvenile courts serve their sentences in juvenile facilities rather than adult prisons.

32. Can it ever be in a minor's best interests to be tried as an adult rather than as a juvenile?

Yes. As mentioned, a frequently cited potential benefit of being tried as an adult is that in an adult court a minor can request a jury trial. Jury trials are not available in most juvenile courts. And, depending on factors such as the minor's age and the seriousness of the offense, a jury may be more sympathetic to the minor than a judge would be.

In busy urban areas with crowded court dockets and overcrowded jails, it is also possible that the minor's case will be disposed of more quickly and a minor will receive a lighter sentence in adult than in juvenile court.

Section VI: Sentencing (Disposition) Options

This section briefly reviews the wide range of disposition options often available to juvenile court judges.

33. Can juvenile court judges incarcerate minors?

Yes. After sustaining a petition (finding that a juvenile committed a crime), juvenile court judges can order juveniles confined in a variety of placements. From the least to the most restrictive alternatives, some common confinement options include:

- **Home confinement** (house arrest), in which a minor has to remain at home at designated times, often after a curfew during the week and on weekends.

- **Suitable placement.** A judge may order a juvenile to live with a relative or in a group or foster home.
- **Juvenile jails** (often called juvenile hall or juvenile detention facilities). Similar to adult jails, juvenile jails are designed for short-term incarceration.
- **"Shock probation"** (also called a "split" or "intermittent" sentence), in which an offender is incarcerated for three to six months before going on probation. The place of incarceration may be a "boot camp," in which minor offenders are subject to strict discipline and physical labor. The taste of jail hopefully shocks minors into improved behavior.
- **Secured facilities ranging from minimum to maximum security.** (A juvenile detention camp is a form of secure facility.) Juveniles may be detained in secured facilities for months or even years. Typically, juveniles have to work and attend school and counseling sessions while in a secured facility.
- **Adult jails.** Juvenile judges may have the authority to sentence certain offenders to serve their sentences in adult facilities.

34. Other than confinement, what other dispositions are common in juvenile court?

Juvenile judges can impose a variety of non-incarceration dispositions, either alone or in combination with each other. The most common nonincarceration options are:

- a verbal warning or reprimand
- payment of a fine to the court or restitution to the victim or both
- counseling, either individual or group therapy
- community service
- electronic monitoring, which uses wrist-anklet transmitters to verify a minor's location, and
- probation, which allows minors to remain free if they fulfill specified conditions. For example, regular attendance at counseling sessions is a typical condition of probation. A minor who violates a condition of probation may be incarcerated. The sample Informal Probation Agreement below suggests the wide variety of probation conditions that a juvenile court judge may impose.

You Owe Me a Day in Jail

One recent juvenile court proceeding is suggestive of how judges can tailor probation conditions to a minor offender's personal situation. Following the sustaining of a petition, a judge placed the offender on probation and told the young offender that he would serve one day in juvenile hall for every unexcused school absence and for every unexcused tardy.

Sample Informal Probation Agreement

JV-622

ATTORNEY OR PARTY WITHOUT ATTORNEY *(Name, State Bar number, and address):*	*FOR COURT USE ONLY*

TELEPHONE NO.: FAX NO. *(Optional):*
E-MAIL ADDRESS *(Optional):*
ATTORNEY FOR *(Name):*

SUPERIOR COURT OF CALIFORNIA, COUNTY OF

STREET ADDRESS:
MAILING ADDRESS:
CITY AND ZIP CODE:
BRANCH NAME:

CHILD'S NAME:

INFORMAL PROBATION AGREEMENT	CASE NUMBER:

This agreement is a **CONTRACT** between the probation officer, the above named child, and his or her parent or parents or legal guardian.

The agreement is for up to six (6) months, and during that period and for up to 90 days after that, the probation officer has the right to request that the district attorney file a petition in juvenile court to have the child declared a ward of the court if the child does not successfully complete the terms of the program described below. If within the first 60 days after this agreement is signed, the child does not become involved in the program, the probation officer MUST take the necessary steps to bring the case before the juvenile court.

TERMS AND CONDITIONS OF THE PROGRAM

The child must *(check all that apply to this child):*

1. ☐ Report to the probation officer _____ times each month until or unless directed differently.
2. ☐ Obey all city, county, state, and federal laws and ordinances.
3. ☐ Obey his or her parent or parents or legal guardian.
4. ☐ Attend school regularly, obey school rules and regulations, and not leave the school campus during school hours without permission of school officials or the probation officer.
5. ☐ Not use, possess, or be under the influence of any alcoholic beverage or illegal or intoxicating substance, or possess any associated paraphernalia.
6. ☐ Not use, possess, or be under the influence of the following *(specify):* _____ .
7. ☐ Not possess, own, or handle any firearm, knife, weapon, fireworks, explosives, or chemicals that can produce explosives.
8. ☐ Not contact or associate with _____
   _____ .
9. ☐ Not be a member or associate with any known members of any criminal street gang.
10. ☐ Participate in individual, group, or family counseling, as directed by the probation officer.
11. ☐ Submit to chemical testing in the form of, but not limited to, blood, breath, urine, or saliva on the direction of the probation officer or a peace officer.
12. ☐ Consent to the search of his or her person, vehicle, or place of residence at any time, day or night, with or without a search warrant and without probable or reasonable cause, on the direction of the probation officer or a peace officer.
13. ☐ Perform _____ hours of community service and provide proof of completion by *(date):*_____ .
   Community service to be arranged
   a. ☐ by the child with the approval of the probation officer.
   b. ☐ through the probation officer.

Page 1 of 2

Form Approved for Optional Use
Judicial Council of California
JV-622 [New January 1, 2006]

INFORMAL PROBATION AGREEMENT

www.courtinfo.ca.gov

Sample Informal Probation Agreement (continued)

CHILD'S NAME:	CASE NUMBER:

14. ☐ Be at his or her place of residence between the hours of _____ p.m. and _____ a.m. unless with a parent or legal guardian or with the prior permission of the probation officer.

15. ☐ _____

16. ☐ _____

17. ☐ _____

18. ☐ _____

19. ☐ _____

20. ☐ _____

I have read and understand the terms and conditions. I consent to them and promise to follow them and to cooperate with the probation officer. I understand that if I do not follow the terms and conditions, I may have to go to juvenile court. I have received a copy of this agreement.

Date:

_____
(TYPE OR PRINT CHILD'S NAME)

▶ _____
(SIGNATURE OF CHILD)

I am the ☐ parent ☐ legal guardian of the child, and he or she has agreed to the terms of this agreement. I agree to cooperate with the probation officer and to assist the child to follow the terms and conditions.

Date:

_____
(TYPE OR PRINT NAME)

▶ _____
(SIGNATURE OF PARENT/LEGAL GUARDIAN)

Date:

_____
(TYPE OR PRINT NAME)

▶ _____
(SIGNATURE OF PARENT/LEGAL GUARDIAN)

Date:

_____
(TYPE OR PRINT NAME)

▶ _____
(SIGNATURE OF PARENT/LEGAL GUARDIAN)

A Sampling of Innovative Juvenile Justice Programs

Teen Courts. Teen courts are the product of collaborative efforts of schools, juvenile courts, and probation departments. In teen courts, first-time teenaged offenders agree to be "tried" by a jury of their peers—other teenagers. Usually, the minor gives up the right to be represented by counsel. The jurors hear evidence, often presented by a probation officer. The juvenile being tried may admit to the charges or present additional evidence. Though teen courts cannot fine or imprison offenders, their sentences can carry serious consequences. With the consent of a minor's parents, teen court sentences can impose community service, counseling, drug or alcohol rehab programs, curfews, and restrictions on who the minor can associate with. Teen courts may also impose more creative sanctions, such as requiring a minor to scrub graffiti off a school wall, attend tutoring, write an essay about the minor's improper behavior, or write a letter apologizing to the victim. After a teen court trial, the offender may have to report to the probation department to verify compliance with the sanctions.

L.A.'s Juvenile Traffic Court. Despite its name, the Juvenile Traffic Court has jurisdiction over a variety of cases, including those in which minors are charged with status offenses (truancy and curfew violations) and minor drug or traffic offenses. The Juvenile Traffic Court follows a "fast track" process designed to dispose of cases within 45 days instead of the usual juvenile court average of nine months. In this informal style of court lawyers are not permitted, and judges have great leeway in tailoring dispositions to individual offenders. For example, a judge dismissed the case of one minor who brought to court a certificate showing that she attended school every day, and waived the fine for the student who completed summer school with at least a "C" average.

Denver's Project New Pride. This is a community-based program aimed at hard-core offenders. Minors get tutoring help for school assignments, job counseling, and training. For example, project staff help minors fill out job applications and even start small businesses (for example, providing lawn and garden services) to help defray program costs.

The Boston Offender Project. Targeting violent offenders, the project features decreasing levels of incarceration and case supervisors with low caseloads who provide intensive psychological and employment counseling.

The Allegheny Academy. Minor offenders in this program live at home but attend the academy after school and on weekends. At the academy, minors receive meals, job training, and individual and group counseling.

"Scared Straight"

Scared Straight was a New Jersey program started in the late 1970s. The idea was to frighten juvenile offenders into reforming their behavior by confronting them with adult prison inmates who would curse at the minors and tell them of the horrors of prison life. The program was discontinued when research indicated that it had little effect on the rate at which minors committed crimes.

35. What are blended sentences?

Judges in some jurisdictions have the power to sentence juveniles to serve time both in adult and juvenile facilities. For example, after a case has been transferred from juvenile to adult court, the adult court judge may sentence a minor to serve time in a juvenile facility until age 18 and then complete the sentence in an adult prison. Similarly, a judge may have the authority to sentence a minor to serve time in an adult prison, but suspend that sentence while the minor serves time in a juvenile facility.

36. How do juvenile court judges decide what disposition to give?

Like their adult court counterparts, juvenile court judges take a number of factors into account when deciding on an appropriate disposition. The seriousness of an offense and an offender's prior record are always of major importance. Juvenile court judges tend to rely heavily on the recommendations of probation officers. A juvenile court judge's particular philosophy concerning the proper role of the juvenile court may also influence the disposition. For example, a judge who views the court's primary function as rehabilitative may resist imposing incarceration despite a locality's get-tough-on-crime attitude.

As this last factor suggests, dispositions are often a product of a host of subjective and unpredictable factors. For example, a minor appearing in court at the end of a day after the judge has processed numerous cases, each more depressing than the last, may be treated more harshly than someone whose case happened to be first on the calendar. A disposition may depend on whether a probation officer or judge views the minor as rebellious, confrontational, or remorseful. Even a minor's demeanor and manner of dress may be critical. A minor whose clothes demonstrate respect for the court and who answers questions politely may be given a less harsh disposition than a minor who shows up in gang-type clothing and who rudely mumbles responses. While some of these factors may be unfair, they are a necessary byproduct of a system in which human beings have to decide what is in a minor's and society's best interests.

37. Can a minor's juvenile court record affect a later sentence in adult criminal court?

Yes. Statutes in many states permit (and sometimes require) judges to impose harsher sentences on violators with prior convictions. Often, even though juvenile court proceedings are civil, these laws provide that juvenile court dispositions, especially for serious violations, count as prior convictions. Some prior juvenile offenses may even count as strikes under a state's "three strikes" law. (For further discussion of three strikes laws, see Chapter 22, Section I.)

CASE EXAMPLE: As an adult, Anne Apolis is convicted of attempted murder. Six years earlier, Anne had been declared a ward of the court after a juvenile court adjudication of carjacking. A statute in Anne's state provides for double the mandatory minimum sentence for convicted felons who have previously been convicted of specified crimes, including carjacking.

Question: Might Anne's juvenile court adjudication affect the length of her sentence on the attempted murder conviction?

Answer: Yes. Because Anne has a juvenile prior for carjacking, she will probably be sentenced to double the mandatory minimum. In most states, juvenile court adjudications have the same effect as adult convictions under sentence enhancement laws.

38. Can a minor challenge or alter a juvenile court judge's disposition order?

Yes. Like adults, juvenile offenders have the right to file appeals and writs. (See Chapter 23 for more on appeals and writs.)

Juveniles can also ask a juvenile court judge to modify a disposition based on changed circumstances. For example, a minor who was placed outside the family home in part because a stepparent was a bad influence may ask the judge to return her home when the stepparent moves away. Or, a relative whose home can serve as a suitable placement may be located after a disposition order has been made. A minor may also ask for a change if a placement is unsafe or the minor is not receiving the treatment the judge anticipated at the time of disposition. Juvenile court judges usually have broad power to change their orders, so postdisposition changes are always possible.

Section VII: Sealing Juvenile Court Records

This section outlines basic procedures for sealing (expunging) juvenile court records. Sealing gives former offenders a chance to avoid being hampered in adulthood by their juvenile misbehavior.

39. What is a juvenile court record?

A juvenile court record consists of the documents relating to a juvenile court case. If a minor is arrested and the case is closed without charges being filed, the record will be short, perhaps no more than a record of an arrest. If a minor is adjudicated a ward of the court for violating the law and given an in-custody disposition, the record may be much longer.

40. What does it mean to seal a juvenile court record?

To seal or expunge a juvenile court record means to treat the juvenile court proceedings as though they never took place. Allowing juveniles to keep their records sealed helps people who've cleaned up their acts from forever being haunted by things they did when they were young.

> **EXAMPLE:** Some years ago, Rick was adjudicated a ward of the juvenile court for committing a residential burglary. Rick later went to court and had the record sealed. Then, when Rick applied for a job, the employer asked, "As a minor or an adult, have you ever been convicted of a criminal offense?" Because his juvenile court record was sealed, Rick legally can and should answer "No."

41. Are juvenile court records sealed automatically when a person becomes an adult?

No. Normally, a person who meets a state's eligibility requirements for record-sealing has to file a petition with the juvenile court clerk, often in the county where the juvenile adjudication occurred, formally asking the court to issue a written order sealing the record. However, some states do have limited automatic sealing provisions. (See Cal. Welf. & Inst. Code § 826-a, providing that unless a judge decides that a former juvenile court offender has continued to violate the law, juvenile court records are destroyed automatically on an offender's 38th birthday.)

42. Is it necessary to hire an attorney to have a record sealed?

No. An experienced attorney may be able to quickly complete the necessary paperwork, but will certainly charge a fee to do so. Many states have preprinted fill-in-the-blanks petition forms, available at a court clerk's office. These forms ordinarily contain instructions for completing and filing the petition. In some states, a county probation officer also has the authority to file paperwork on a petitioner's behalf.

43. When is a juvenile offender eligible to seal a juvenile court record?

Eligibility rules vary from state to state. Typically, eligibility for record-sealing depends on such factors as:

- **Age.** Usually, a petitioner must be an adult (18 years or older) to be eligible for record-sealing.
- **How much time has passed since an offense was committed or since the juvenile court proceedings ended.** Often, even if a juvenile offender has reached adulthood, the offender has to wait a specified period of time (perhaps five years) from the date of an offense or from the termination of juvenile court proceedings.
- **Seriousness of the juvenile court offense.** Misdemeanor records may be more readily sealed than felony records.

- **Conduct following the juvenile court proceedings.** A juvenile offender with later criminal violations may be ineligible to have juvenile court records sealed.

44. Can sealed records ever come back to haunt a juvenile offender?

Yes. Record-sealing rewrites history for many, but not all, purposes. For example:

- A sealed record of a juvenile court adjudication may be used to increase the severity of a sentence following a later conviction. (See Question 37, above.)
- An application for a job in law enforcement may trigger a police agency's access to sealed records.
- An application for auto insurance may allow the insurance company to have access to sealed records pertaining to automobile-related offenses.

Further Reading on Juvenile Courts and Procedures

- *Trial Manual for Defense Attorneys in Juvenile Court*, by Randy Hertz, et al. (ALI/ABA), a treatise written for lawyers providing comprehensive instruction on the lawyer's role in juvenile delinquency proceedings.
- *Representing the Child Client*, by Mark Soler, et al. (Matthew Bender), another lawyer's treatise that provides comprehensive analysis of the laws affecting accused children.
- *The Juvenile Justice System Law and Process*, 2nd ed., by Mary Clement (Butterworth-Heinemann), a textbook that gives a clear and detailed introduction to the civil and criminal aspects of the juvenile justice system.
- *No Matter How Loud I Shout*, by Edward Humes (Simon & Schuster), a compelling and personalized account of a year in the life of one California juvenile court judge.

Prisoners' Rules

Prison inmates lose many of their civil rights, including many of the rights enjoyed by nonconvicted criminal defendants that we described earlier in this book. But the Eighth Amendment to the U.S. Constitution, which prohibits "cruel and unusual punishment," as well as many other federal and state laws, ensures that prisoners do not lose all of their rights just because they are behind bars. This chapter discusses important prisoners' rights, focusing on federal rights that are common to prisoners nationwide. This chapter also includes a section on resources for prisoners and their families. Finally, the chapter explains the basics of parole (early release from prison under supervision) and pardons (grants of executive clemency).

Section I: Prisons and Prisoners' Rights

Prisoners retain rights to basic freedoms such as freedom of speech, religion, and equal protection of the laws (meaning a right not to be treated differently than other prisoners just because of race, sex, or religion). Prisoners also have the right to basic—albeit minimum—living standards. However, these rights may be curtailed to some extent because courts must balance them against a prison's need for safety, order, and security. Courts tend to uphold prison rules that limit prisoners' exercise of constitutional rights so long as the prison rules are reasonably related to legitimate prison needs. This section examines the balance that courts have struck between prisoners' rights and prison regulations in a variety of common situations.

1. Do prisoners have the right to decent living conditions?

The Eighth Amendment requires that state and federal prison systems provide at least "the minimal civilized measure of life's necessities" (*Rhodes v. Chapman*, U.S. Sup. Ct. 1981). Because this rule is so vague, prisons can be deficient in a variety of ways yet still meet minimum constitutional standards. To prove that prison conditions are cruel and unusual, prisoners must show that they were forced to live with seriously hazardous or oppressive conditions (an objective test that looks at the conditions themselves) and that prison officials deliberately or maliciously caused the conditions (a subjective test that considers the intent of the officials responsible for them) (*Wilson v. Seiter*, U.S. Sup. Ct. 1991).

Supermax Prisons

Supermax prisons house a state's most dangerous inmates. Among the notorious Supermax prisoners are Theodore Kaczynski (the Unabomber), John Muhammed (the Beltway sniper), and Eric Rudolph (the Atlanta Olympic games bomber). About 30 states currently operate Supermax prisons.

By isolating the "worst of the worst" in separate, super-secure facilities, Supermax prisons are designed to reduce the risk of harm that prison guards and the general prison population would otherwise face. Typically, Supermax prisoners remain in their cells 23 hours a day and eat all their meals while alone in their cells. States need comply only with relatively informal procedures when deciding which inmates to send to Supermax facilities (*Wilkinson v. Austin*, U.S. Sup. Ct. 2005).

How Many Americans Are Behind Bars?

The Bureau of Justice (http://www.ojp.usdoj.gov/bjs/) provides information on many aspects of the criminal justice process. Its figures reveal that as of the start of 2008, nearly 2,300,000 prisoners were housed in state and federal prisons and jails. The number was a small increase from the year before. There are approximately 500 prisoners per 100,000 U.S. residents, but the figures vary according to gender and ethnicity. For example, male prisoners outnumber females by more than 10 to 1. And there were 3,138 black male prisoners for every 100,000 black males in the population, compared to 1,259 Hispanic male prisoners per 100,000 Hispanic males and 481 white male prisoners per 100,000 white males.

In addition to the number of prisoners, more than 5 million men and women were either on parole or probation as of the beginning of 2008.

2. What factors have judges considered when deciding whether prison conditions are adequate?

When determining the adequacy of prison conditions, judges consider both the conditions themselves and how prison officials have subjected inmates to them. Examples of inadequate prison conditions include:

- overcrowding
- lack of supplies necessary for personal hygiene, such as soap and water
- unsanitary food preparation
- nutritionally inadequate food
- lack of access to medical treatment and poor medical care
- failure to protect prisoners' physical safety
- substandard shelter, such as the lack of adequate heating, cooling, clothing, and blankets
- unsafe building conditions, such as exposed wiring and vermin infestation

- inadequate facilities for prisoners put in solitary confinement
- lack of opportunities for prisoners to get physical exercise, and
- inadequate opportunities for prisoners to access the courts, such as a prison law library that has few books or is unavailable to prisoners in solitary confinement.

A condition may be improper even if it affects only a small group of prisoners. For example, prison officials may violate both the First (free exercise of religion) and the Eighth (freedom from cruel and unusual punishment) Amendments if they do not provide pork-free meals to prisoners whose religions forbid eating pork, even if the non-pork-eaters make up a minority of the population.

3. Does the right to equal protection of the laws mean that all prisoners must be treated alike?

No. Prison officials have wide discretion to manage prison life. For example, many prisons classify inmates as maximum, medium, or minimum security risks, and treat them accordingly. As a result, minimum security risk prisoners are usually housed in a section of a prison with fewer restrictions on their movement and greater work opportunities compared to maximum security risk prisoners. Factors that prison officials consider when assessing a prisoner's security classification include:

- the length and severity of the sentence
- previous behavior in other jails or prisons

- medical needs
- gang affiliations (or the existence of known enemies within the prison population)
- work skills
- proximity to outside family (especially where a relative is ill or aged)
- likelihood of rehabilitation, and
- whether a prisoner poses a threat to other inmates, guards, or himself.

Prisoners who are unhappy with their confinement status may seek a review of this process, especially if the prisoner can show proof of specific factors that warrant a lower risk classification, such as work skills or medical needs. But it's most effective to present such documentation when a prisoner is first confined. Prison officials will be less inclined to change their minds once they make a designation, and courts often refuse to second-guess prison officials on a process they view as a prison management function.

4. Can prisoners observe religious holidays, meet with clergy, and wear ritual clothing?

Yes. The First Amendment guarantees free exercise of religion, and that right cannot be denied to prisoners absent valid, rational prison management concerns.

5. Do prisoners have the right to medical treatment?

Yes. To deliberately or intentionally with-hold necessary medical treatment constitutes cruel and unusual punishment under the Eighth Amendment (*Estelle v. Gamble*, U.S.

Sup. Ct. 1976). State and federal rules such as the federal Correctional Officers Health and Safety Act of 1998 also set forth efforts that prisons must make to prevent and detect diseases.

CASE EXAMPLE: Joseph Dabney, a state prison inmate, complained to prison guards several times about chest pains and shortness of breath during outdoor exercise. Joseph saw several prison doctors, none of whom gave Joseph any treatment other than telling him to take it easy. Joseph subsequently suffered a massive heart attack.

Question: Does Joseph have a claim for the unconstitutional denial of medical care?

Answer: Yes. Prison officials (both guards and doctors) were aware of symptoms commonly associated with serious heart trouble yet failed to provide treatment. Joseph could recover money damages because the prison was deliberately indifferent to his medical needs. A judge might also order "injunctive relief," requiring the prison to upgrade its medical procedures.

6. May prison officials withhold food to punish prisoners?

No. Prisons must give enough food to provide sustenance and nourishment to inmates. However, food restrictions of various types may be a permissible form of punishment, especially if they are temporary. For example, a prison may withhold hot foods or provide a prisoner with only one meal a day. In an extreme case, even a temporary diet of bread and water may be permissible.

CASE EXAMPLE: Gene Bogz, a federal prisoner, found mouse parts in the chicken dinner he was served one night.

Question: Does Gene have a valid claim that his Eighth Amendment rights were violated based on being served unsanitary food?

Answer: Gene's claim will not win if the court finds this was an isolated incident, or that prison officials had taken steps to fix the problem (such as hiring exterminators to rid the facility of mice). Gene might have a valid legal claim if the problem were ongoing, if there were other incidents of unclean food, or the court determined that the prison officials knew about the mice and had done nothing to get rid of them.

7. Can prison guards use physical force against inmates?

Prison staff violate the Eighth Amendment when they use force "maliciously and sadistically for the very purpose of causing harm," but they are permitted to use force in a good faith effort to maintain or restore discipline (*Hudson v. McMillan*, U.S. Sup. Ct. 1992). Generally, this means an inmate must show that the force was not used for a legitimate disciplinary purpose, or that the degree of force the officials used was completely out of proportion to the needs of the situation.

CASE EXAMPLE: Andy and Kopkit, prison guards, fire tear gas and plastic bullets into the prison yard after a disturbance in which three inmates from one gang attacked an inmate from a rival gang. Andy and Kopkit then forcibly herd all the prisoners on the yard into their cells. Arvin Waites, an older inmate who was not involved in the disturbance, slipped and fell while being herded back to his cell, suffering a painful sprained ankle.

Question: Does Arvin have a good chance at winning a personal injury lawsuit against Andy, Kopkit, and the prison?

Answer: No. Under the circumstances, the guards' actions were reasonably necessary to quell a disturbance. Especially in such an emergency situation, Arvin would have to prove that the guards acted maliciously (that is, spitefully or wickedly), an extremely difficult task.

8. Do prisons have to protect inmates from attacks by other prisoners?

Yes. But to have a valid legal claim against a prison for failing to protect him from attack, the victimized prisoner has to prove that prison staff was aware that the prisoner had been threatened by a particular inmate and that the staff was deliberately indifferent to the prisoner's safety.

Prison Assault and Rape

Widely acknowledged to be a serious problem for both men and women serving time in prison, prison rape has been condemned by many, including the U.S. Supreme Court: "The horrors experienced by many young inmates, particularly those who are convicted of nonviolent offenses, border on the unimaginable. Prison rape not only threatens the lives of those who fall prey to their aggressors, but it is potentially devastating to the human spirit. Shame, depression, and a shattering loss of self-esteem accompany the perpetual terror the victim thereafter must endure" (*Farmer v. Brennan*, U.S. Sup. Ct. 1994).

According to statistics published by the nonprofit organization Stop Prison Rape, some 80,000 unwanted sexual acts take place behind bars in the United States every day. These include both inmate-on-inmate assaults and guard-on-inmate assaults. A report in *Salon* magazine's 1998 series "Locked Up in America" found that "the vast majority of the more than 138,000 women in U.S. prisons and jails today [said they] have been exposed to some form of sexually related intimidation or assault by corrections officers while serving time."

9. Do prisoners have the right to outdoor exercise?

Prisoners must be afforded reasonable opportunities for physical movement. A few lower courts have recognized access to outdoor exercise as a right that may not be taken away unless justified by other prison needs (such as when a prisoner is denied access because he assaulted another inmate on the prison yard). Other courts have upheld prison programs of indoor-only physical activities.

10. May prison officials search prisoners' cells?

Yes. Although a cell is a prisoner's "home" during incarceration, prisoners have no judicially recognized expectation of privacy in their cells. Therefore the Fourth Amendment right to be free from unreasonable searches and seizures is extremely limited for prisoners. Prison officials do not need warrants to search prisoners' cells, and searches may be random and unannounced. Typically, though, to be considered reasonable, officials must have legitimate reasons for conducting their searches, such as the prison's need to keep the facility free of drugs and weapons.

> **CASE EXAMPLE:** Victor Sales, a prison inmate, filed a complaint against prison officials for failure to provide him with adequate access to the prison law library. After the complaint was filed, guards began waking Victor up twice nightly and searching his cell.

The guards said they were looking for drugs and weapons, but Victor believes that the guards conducted the searches in retaliation for him complaining about the library. Other prisoners were not subjected to these "shakedown" searches after lights out.

Question: Does Victor have a valid legal claim for a violation of his Fourth Amendment rights?

Answer: Yes. Even though the prison officials do not need a warrant to search Victor's cell, cell searches must still be reasonable. A search made in order to intimidate and harass, rather than for a legitimate prison purpose, is not reasonable.

11. Are prison officials allowed to seize a prisoner's property during a "shakedown" search?

Prison officials can almost always justify seizures of prisoners' personal belongings, because they are permitted to take away property in order to maintain security and order.

12. Can prison officials conduct strip searches and body cavity searches of inmates?

Intrusive body searches can be legitimate if they are necessary to maintain prison safety and keep out contraband. However, invasive searches are not valid if they are performed to humiliate or harass a prisoner, or to retaliate against a prisoner for angering a member of prison staff.

13. Can family members and friends visit prisoners?

Visitation has never been declared to be a fundamental constitutional right. Most prisons do allow visits, but if prison officials have valid reasons for placing limits on visitation, judges almost always uphold those restrictions. It is typical for prisons to:

- limit visiting hours
- minimize physical contact, requiring prisoners to communicate with visitors through a barrier such as a wall (though lawyers can usually arrange full contact visits with their clients)
- restrict the numbers and types of visitors (for example, a prison may limit visits to only certain family members, or ban visits altogether from people who have violated prison rules on previous visits or those suspected of gang-related activity), and
- require both a visitor and a prisoner to be searched before and after the visit to ensure that contraband does not enter the prison.

The U.S. Supreme Court has ruled that prison regulations such as these are valid (*Overton v. Bazzetta,* U.S. Sup. Ct. 2003).

14. Do prisoners have a right to privacy during prison visits?

No. Prison officials may monitor most visits. But visits from lawyers must be private enough to allow for confidential communication.

15. Do prisoners have the right to make phone calls?

As a general rule, inmates have a right to make phone calls. However, prisons can severely restrict the right: A typical prison rule limits inmates to two short social calls per week. Prisoners may also be required to pay for long distance phone charges.

16. May prisoners be transferred from one prison facility to another?

Prisoners do not have a right to liberty, and therefore they have no right to be incarcerated in the prison of their choice. If a prisoner wants to contest a scheduled transfer, prison officials must usually give the prisoner a hearing to object to the move. If the prisoner loses at his hearing and takes the case to court, a judge will typically approve the transfer so long as prison officials have a rational basis for their actions.

CASE EXAMPLE: Mohammed is incarcerated in a federal prison in New York. Mohammed's attorney is in New York and his family lives there. Mohammed is then transferred to a prison in New Mexico, though none of his family members can afford to visit him there.

Question: If Mohammed can show that he was transferred because the New York warden is prejudiced against people of Middle Eastern descent, would the transfer be valid?

Answer: No. A prisoner's ethnicity is not a rational reason for a transfer.

Question: Is the transfer valid if the prison shows that Mohammed was transferred in order to testify before a grand jury in Santa Fe, New Mexico?

Answer: Yes. Prisons are often located in remote rural areas where family visits are difficult, so the distance from his home is not enough to invalidate the transfer. And Mohammed's presence as a witness before the grand jury would certainly be a legitimate government reason to move him (*Olim v. Wakinekona*, U.S. Sup. Ct. 1983). Mohammed might more successfully challenge the transfer if he could show that he was transferred as punishment for having requested a pork-free diet, or if he were too weak to travel and could show that the move would cause him serious pain or injury.

How Successful Are Prisons at Rehabilitating Inmates?

Judges often sentence offenders to prison in the hope that they will emerge as lawful, productive citizens. However, the unfortunate fact is that imprisonment generally fails to produce rehabilitation. For example, studies have found that a year after release, 60% of ex-inmates remain unemployed. And the federal Bureau of Justice Statistics has found that two-thirds of parolees are rearrested within three years of their release.

Prisons' typical failure to achieve rehabilitation is due partly to lack of resources, which translates into a lack of prison programs. For example, estimates are that somewhere between 70% and 85% of inmates have substance abuse problems. However, less than 15% of inmates are treated for those problems while they are incarcerated. Similarly, though many inmates are functionally illiterate, prisons do little to enhance their literacy skills.

Compounding the inability of prisons to provide rehabilitative services are a variety of laws that can make life on the outside very difficult for many ex-felons. For example:

- Federal welfare rules bar those convicted of buying or selling drugs from ever receiving food stamps or cash assistance.
- Federal housing laws allow public housing agencies to exclude ex-felons and their families from public housing.
- Federal education laws bar ex-felons who have violated drug laws from receiving student loans.
- Ex-felons may be unable to vote or pursue a wide variety of professions.

For further information see *Gates of Injustice: The Crisis in America's Prisons*, by Alan Eisner (Prentice Hall).

17. Do prisoners have the right to send and receive mail?

Yes, but prison officials may typically open and read the mail first. However, prison censorship must be related to rational prison concerns. For example, they can justify examining incoming mail more strictly than outgoing mail, because mail entering the facility must be more carefully screened for contraband.

18. May prison officials open and read mail to and from a prisoner's lawyer?

Prison officials have a limited right to open letters and packages from lawyers. Officials can open mail to be sure that it does not contain contraband. However, they typically must open it in front of the inmate. Moreover, officials may not read the contents of lawyer-client communications. Lawyers who send mail to prison inmates mark it as "privileged legal communication" or "confidential legal correspondence," and inmates should do the same when they write letters to their lawyers.

19. May prison officials place limits on inmates' mail privileges?

Yes. A prison may limit the people with whom a prisoner corresponds when necessary for prison order, safety, or security. Prisons may also limit the type of mail a prisoner receives. For example, prisons may forbid mail that contains nudity or sexually explicit material.

CASE EXAMPLE: Bruce, who is in a maximum security prison serving time for selling narcotics, has been corresponding with his girlfriend Rainy. A prison guard recently found photos and maps of the land around the prison as well as references in the girlfriend's letter that officials felt might help Bruce to plan an escape.

Question: Can the prison forbid future correspondence between Bruce and Rainy?

Answer: Yes. The prison has an adequate basis for thinking that mail letters to and from Rainy pose a security threat.

20. Are disabled prisoners protected under the Americans with Disabilities Act?

Yes. Prison officials at state and federal facilities must provide reasonable accommodations for disabled prisoners (*Pennsylvania Dept. of Corrections v. Yeskey*, U.S. Sup. Ct. 1998).

CASE EXAMPLE: An informant reported that he had seen Kathi Andrews, a deaf inmate, with a sharpened kitchen knife in violation of prison rules. Kathi was given an informal prison hearing to review the charges but was not provided a sign language interpreter at the hearing.

Question: Did the prison violate Kathi's rights under the Americans with Disabilities Act (ADA)?

Answer: Perhaps. If the hearing officer spoke slowly and looked directly at Kathi so that she was able to understand everything by lip-reading, the prison may have done enough to reasonably accommodate her disability. If, however, the hearing was before a panel of officers and Kathi (who is only able to lip-read one person at a time) could not understand the proceedings without an interpreter, then the prison may have to provide one. In such a case, the prison may also have to remove any restraints on Kathi's hands so that she could respond through the interpreter.

21. May prisoners get married while in prison?

Yes, but prison officials may limit the type and length of any wedding ceremony.

22. Can prisoners be required to work while in prison, and, if so, are they paid?

Yes to both questions. The Thirteenth Amendment, which forbids slavery and other involuntary servitude, has a specific exception for people who have been convicted of a crime. According to the Federal Bureau of Prisons, "All Federal inmates have to work if they are medically able. Most inmates are assigned to an institution job such as food service worker, orderly, plumber, painter, warehouse worker or groundskeeper. These jobs pay from twelve cents to forty cents per hour." Most states pay prisoners similarly low wages for prison work, and some allow for compensation in the form of "credits" toward a reduced sentence rather than money.

Monies earned from prison work are placed in accounts that prisoners may draw on to buy personal items through the prison commissary (store), to make phone calls, pay for court filing fees, or to satisfy court judgments such as victim restitution or child custody.

> **CASE EXAMPLE:** Lynn Felder is in jail awaiting trial on murder charges.
>
> **Question:** Can Lynn be forced to work in the jail's kitchen facility?
>
> **Answer:** No. Lynn has not yet been *convicted* of a crime. The Thirteenth Amendment only permits forced labor as punishment for those convicted of a crime.

23. Is a prison the same thing as a jail?

A jail is a locked facility that generally houses defendants who are awaiting trial and unable to make bail, or who have been convicted of and are serving sentences for misdemeanors (less serious crimes). A prison, also known as a penitentiary, is a locked facility that houses inmates convicted of felonies (more serious crimes). Jails are normally funded and run by local governments, whereas prisons are administered by state or federal prison bureaus.

24. Can prisoners choose the type of work they are required to do in prison?

No. But prison officials may not discriminate against prisoners in making work assignments. For example, officials cannot base work assignments on an inmate's race or religion.

25. Can prisoners lose professional or business licenses as a result of imprisonment?

Whether conviction and imprisonment will cause a prisoner to lose a business or professional license often depends on the rules of the agency that issued the license. For example, in most states lawyers who are convicted of crimes involving fraud will almost certainly be disbarred. To determine how incarceration might affect a particular license, an inmate should consult both state licensing rules and the rules of the organization that issued the license.

26. Can prisoners vote while in prison or after they are released?

Almost all states bar felons from voting while they are in prison. (Only a few states, such as Vermont, allow prisoners to vote by absentee ballot.) At least seven states permanently bar convicted felons from voting. An estimated four million United States citizens are currently prohibited from voting due to felony convictions. Because a disproportionate number of those convicted of felonies are members of minority groups, these bans have prevented a higher percentage of minorities from voting than nonminorities. If you'd like more information on the states that ban voting rights for ex-felons, you can check out a report prepared by Human Rights Watch, at www.hrw.org/reports98/vote.

Even in the states that do not permanently ban those with felony convictions from voting, the restoration of the right to vote is not necessarily automatic. In many states, the right to vote, along with the right to hold public office and serve on a jury, are part of a "package" of civil rights that may be restored upon the completion of a sentence (which means serving out any parole or probationary term in addition to any imprisonment associated with that conviction). In some states, such as California, Utah, and Oregon, these civil rights are restored automatically once a felon finishes the full sentence. In other states, corrections officials must notify the state's Office of Elections, or the released felon must personally obtain a Certificate of Discharge and submit it to the governor's office, affirmatively requesting the restoration of civil rights. To determine how to restore voting and other civil rights in a particular state, contact that state's Department of Corrections.

27. Do prisoners lose custody of their children when they are imprisoned?

Inmate parents do not automatically lose formal custody of their children just because they are sent to prison (although this may happen to parents convicted of crimes involving child abuse or neglect).

Because an imprisoned parent is not available to care for children, however, either the parent or the state must make other custodial arrangements. In some cases, prisoners may even have their parental rights terminated, but when that's at stake the inmate parent must first be given notice and the opportunity for a hearing. There is no federal constitutional right to be provided with a lawyer during a termination of parental rights proceeding, but many states do provide lawyers for prisoners facing this situation.

28. Must a parent who is paying child support continue to make payments while in prison?

Many states require inmates to pay up to 50% of what they earn in prison toward satisfying court judgments like child support or victim restitution. An inmate parent may also be required to make up for any payments missed during the prison term once released and employed. In other states, however, an inmate parent's child support obligations are suspended and do not have to be paid during the time the inmate is incarcerated.

Section II: Legal Resources for Prisoners and Their Families

The following section explains the basics about how prisoners can enforce their legal rights. The section also includes listings of resources that prisoners and their families can use to get more information about prison life.

29. Do prisoners have any recourse when prison officials seek to revoke their privileges for violating prison rules?

Prison officials must normally afford prisoners limited due process before revoking their privileges. This means that officials must provide prisoners with notice of the actions they intend to take and the reasons for them. Inmates can then have a hearing to contest the officials' punitive actions. These hearings are usually informal. Inmates have no right to a lawyer at these disciplinary hearings, and they may even be restricted from presenting witnesses if doing so would create security or safety problems.

> **CASE EXAMPLE:** Mark Oh was found with a sharpened nail file taped to his foot, in violation of prison regulations. Prison officials notified Mark in writing that because of the violation, he would lose all the "good time credits" he had accumulated as a model prisoner (credits that would have gone toward an early release on parole). Mark was told that he could appear before the prison ombudsman to tell his side of the story, but that he would not be allowed to have a lawyer present or to call any witnesses on his behalf.
>
> **Question:** Are the prison procedures legitimate?

Answer: Probably. Because a nail file could be used as a weapon, prison officials had valid security reasons for revoking Mark's good time credits. Also, the officials gave Mark written notice and an opportunity to appear at a hearing. If Mark wanted to call a witness who could explain why he had a legitimate reason for carrying the nail file, then prison officials should allow the witness to appear at the hearing unless officials could show that the appearance threatened safety or security.

30. How can prisoners use the courts to enforce their legal rights?

Prisoners who believe that the conditions in which they are living are unlawful should normally begin by making a written complaint to the prison administration. The courts often will not consider prisoners' complaints unless the prisoners can prove that they first tried to resolve their problem within prison channels. Many facilities have complaint forms; if not, a letter will do. A prisoner may also want to send the complaint to the state or federal agency that is ultimately responsible for the facility's operation. If the complaint fails to remedy the problem, a prisoner may then seek help from the courts. A prisoner can also seek help from a nonprofit prisoners' rights group.

Prisoners' rights legal claims can take a variety of forms. A prisoner may file suit in state court under a state's Tort Claims Act to try to recover money damages for personal injuries, perhaps as a result of physical abuse by a guard or another prisoner. A prisoner may file a federal civil rights claim (also known as a "Section 1983" action) to recover money damages for physical injuries or to redress the violation of a federal civil right, such as interference with the right to practice one's religion. A prisoner's lawsuit may seek money damages or a court order (called "injunctive relief") requiring prison officials to take action, such as improving substandard conditions or transferring the prisoner to another facility.

A federal Court of Appeals discussed a number of prison condition rules in the case of *Foster v. Runnels* (2009). (The case appears at www.ca9.uscourts.gov/datastore/opinions/2009/02/05/0615719.pdf.) Inmate Ronald Foster, representing himself *pro se*, filed a lawsuit against the warden and a correctional officer named Sandra Cole at California's High Desert State Prison. Foster claimed that they violated his civil rights under 42 United States Code 1983 by refusing to serve him 16 meals over a period of 23 days. Cole refused to serve the meals to Foster because he had refused to comply with the warden's order that prisoners not cover their cell windows with paper. The Court noted that "the denial of food can constitute an unjustified and unnecessarily punitive response to a rules violation… The sustained deprivation of food can be cruel and unusual punishment when it results in pain without any penological purpose." The Court decided that the warden had nothing to do with

Cole's decision to deny meals to Foster and dismissed the claim against him. However, unless Foster's conduct posed a realistic threat to Cole's safety or to the functioning of the prison, Cole had no right to prevent Foster from eating. Although the Court ruled in Foster's favor, its decision did not end the case. Unless the parties settle, to succeed, Foster will have to go to trial and convince a judge or jury that Cole's decision to deny meals to him was unjustified.

31. Does the right of access to the courts include the right to counsel?

The right to counsel (meaning the right to assistance from a lawyer, appointed free of charge for those who cannot pay) is guaranteed only through a defendant's first appeal. So as a general rule a prisoner has no right to counsel for the purpose of filing prisoners' rights claims. However, judges have the power to appoint lawyers to represent prisoners who challenge conditions of confinement. Generally, a judge will do so only when a prisoner's complaint raises serious issues that are likely to affect a sizable group of prisoners. One paradox of this approach is that judges may be least likely to find out about and appoint attorneys for the very prisoners who most need the assistance of counsel, such as those in solitary confinement or those who cannot read or write English.

32. What kind of rules apply to prisoners' lawsuits?

The lawsuits filed by prisoners are subject to an array of rules. While some of these rules seem technical or picky, failing to follow them can mean your lawsuit will be delayed—or worse, thrown out completely. For example, a judge may invalidate a claim because the prisoner waited so long to file it that a "statute of limitations" (a rule that sets time limits on claims) ran out.

CASE EXAMPLE: Joe is convicted and sentenced to prison in Illinois. An appeals court overturns the conviction on the ground that the police illegally arrested Joe. After the state decides not to prosecute Joe again, Joe files a civil lawsuit against Illinois seeking damages for being falsely arrested. Illinois' statute of limitation on civil rights claims is two years, and Joe filed his complaint more than two years after the case started.

Question: Did Joe file his complaint in time?

Answer: No. Joe had two years from the time he was brought into court to sue for false arrest, because at that point the illegal arrest concluded. Because Joe waited more than two years to file his civil lawsuit, the judge was correct to dismiss his complaint (*Wallace v. Kato*, U.S. Sup. Ct. 2007).

Prisoners may also have to show they tried to resolve their problems informally within the prison system before going to court (a requirement called "exhausting administrative remedies"). Other rules specify that the prisoner must file with the court that has jurisdiction (power) to hear a case, or may limit the length of documents and require certain papers to be officially witnessed ("notarized").

Because the rules governing these cases can be complex, prisoners who have funds available are usually best served by hiring lawyers to represent them. Most prisoners cannot afford to hire lawyers, and to make matters worse, most public defender groups are not authorized to represent prisoners whose convictions are final. A limited number of lawyers or prison legal rights organizations provide free ("pro bono") legal representation to prisoners. Because these resources are scarce, many prisoners represent themselves, which is called filing a case "pro per" (also called "pro se"). Self-representing inmates have to follow the same rules as lawyers, so they should plan on spending as much time as they are permitted in the prison law library researching the legal basis of their claim as well as the technical requirements for filing their case.

Resources for Prisoners' Lawsuits

Here are some publications for prisoners who are filing a prisoners' right lawsuit without the help of a lawyer (and for their friends and family if they are helping the prisoner with the lawsuit):

- *Prisoner's Self-Help Litigation Manual*, by John Boston and Daniel E. Manville (Oceana Publication, Inc.)
- *Represent Yourself In Court*, by Paul Bergman and Sara J. Berman (Nolo)
- *Rights of Prisoners*, by Michael B. Mushlin (Clark, Boardman, Callaghan), and
- *A Jailhouse Lawyer's Manual* (Columbia Human Rights Law Review).

A Jailhouse Lawyer's Manual provides names, addresses, and other information about prisoner assistance groups across the country. It is available online (www.columbia.edu/cu/hrlr/index.html). In addition, prisoners may purchase both volumes of *A Jailhouse Lawyer's Manual* for $45 (the price for non-prisoners is $90) or one volume for $25. A Spanish language edition is available for $15. The website contains an order form and mailing address.

The Prison Law Office is a nonprofit office that provides assistance to prisoners in California. The group's website (www.prisonlaw.com) includes self-help materials on habeas corpus, parole, personal injury claims, HIV in prison, prison staff misconduct, and problems with confinement conditions.

33. Are prisoners supposed to have access to legal materials?

Yes. Judges have acknowledged that prisoners' legal rights may be meaningless unless prisoners have some ability to enforce them. Inmates therefore have a "right of access" to the courts. To comply with this, prisons must provide inmates with either an adequately stocked prison law library or help from legal assistants. Prisons must also provide supplies necessary to file court documents, such as paper, pens, postage stamps, and sometimes notaries.

Other Sources of Information on Prison Life

Here are some additional places for prisoners and their families to look for information on adjusting to life in prison:

- The ACLU's National Prison Project publishes *The Prisoners' Assistance Directory*, which refers prisoners and their families to helpful support organizations.
- The Federal Bureau of Prisons' webpage is located at www.bop.gov.
- A publication called the *Directory of Programs Serving Families of Adult Offenders* is available through the website of the National Institute of Corrections. This booklet, which you can download from NIC's website (www.nicic.org), lists public and private organizations throughout the United States that serve inmates' families.

The Restrictions on Prisoners' Litigation Are Increasing

Prisoners' lawsuits challenging the conditions of their confinement constitute about 10% of all civil cases filed in federal court. Judges and lawmakers increasingly view many prisoners' legal claims as "frivolous"—that is, unreasonable claims that waste judges' time. This has led to harsh new limitations on cases brought by prisoners.

For example, the United States Supreme Court has ruled that a state has no obligation to "enable [a] prisoner to discover grievances, and to litigate effectively" (*Lewis v. Casey*, U.S. Sup. Ct. 1996). Moreover, a federal law known as the Prison Litigation Reform Act (PLRA) cut back on prisoners' rights to file legal claims *in forma pauperis* (without paying court filing fees). As a result, prisoners may be required to pay part of the fees when they file and to continue making payments during the remainder of their prison term (drawing on earnings from prison labor).

The PLRA also gives federal judges the power to dismiss prisoners' lawsuits immediately unless the prisoners have "exhausted their prison remedies." However, judges have to consider "exhausted" claims even if prisoners' lawsuits improperly add new ("unexhausted") claims. The judges rule on the merits of the "exhausted" claims but ignore the "unexhausted" ones. (*Jones v. Bock*, U.S. Sup. Ct. 2007.)

For more information on the PLRA, see *The PLRA: A Guide for Prisoners*, published by the ACLU's National Prison Project.

Section III: Parole

Parole is the conditional release from prison before the end of a sentence. People on parole (called parolees) remain under supervision until the end of a fixed term, and they normally have significant and strict conditions with which they must comply to remain at liberty. Parolees are supervised by parole department officers; the parole department is usually an arm of the state's prison agency.

34. What are typical parole conditions?

Here is a list of requirements and rules that parolees typically must follow in order to remain at liberty:

- report regularly to a parole officer
- report their whereabouts (some parolees are required to wear electronic monitoring devices that track their location)
- obtain permission in advance for any travel out of a county
- submit to random searches of their homes, cars, and persons (including blood, urine, and saliva testing, for disease, drugs, or other contraband)
- obey all laws
- refrain from using, buying, or selling alcohol or illegal drugs
- avoid certain people, such as victims, witnesses, gang members, or persons with criminal records
- pay money for court-ordered restitution, and
- attend classes or counseling sessions, such as court-ordered drug or alcohol treatment classes or anger management classes.

If the parole board finds that the parolee violated his parole conditions, the parole can be revoked, in which case the parolee returns to prison to serve all or most of the remainder of the sentence. If the parolee violates his parole by committing another crime, the parolee can be forced to serve the remainder of the original sentence (as a parole violation) and then serve a sentence for the new conviction.

35. What is the difference between probation and parole?

Parole is early release from a partially served prison term, granted by a parole board. The parole board is an administrative agency that is part of the state corrections department. In contrast, probation is imposed by a judge at the time of sentencing, to be served as an alternative to or in addition to a jail or prison term. (See Chapter 22 for more on probation.) There is no parole in the federal prison system; a federal prisoner earns "good time" credits for behaving in prison but still has to serve a minimum of 85% of his sentence.

36. How long can I remain on parole?

The length of parole terms vary widely and are a function of the length of time left to serve on the original sentence. Parole may be as short as a year or as long as a lifetime. Upon evidence of good behavior, a parole board may terminate parole before its scheduled end.

37. Can a parolee relocate?

Parole conditions typically prevent a parolee from moving from one county to another within the same state without permission from a parole officer. Reasons that might incline a parole officer to grant a request for a move include:

- to protect the parolee
- to allow the parolee the opportunity to work or study
- to permit the parolee to live closer to family members who can aid in a parolee's rehabilitation, or
- to permit a parolee to obtain necessary medical or mental health treatment.

38. Do judges decide when to release prisoners on parole?

Not usually. Decisions to grant and revoke parole are made by a group of prison officials called a parole board. But in some cases, parolees have the right to appeal the decisions of the parole board to a court, or to a Board of Appeals within the parole agency.

39. What factors do parole boards consider when deciding whether to parole a prisoner?

Although the decision to grant parole is ultimately a subjective one, parole boards are usually required to consider a prescribed set of factors in making a parole determination. These factors typically include:

- the severity of the original offense and any sentencing recommendations affecting parole

- the prisoner's behavior while incarcerated
- statements submitted by victims, and
- a prisoner's chance for successful reintegration into the community.

40. Can victims affect parole decisions?

In many states, victims or their surviving family members have a right to be notified that the prisoner who harmed them is eligible for parole and has an upcoming parole hearing. The victims can submit their views to the parole board either in writing or by making a personal appearance at the hearing.

41. What happens if a parolee violates a condition of parole?

The parole board may revoke parole and order the parolee returned to prison. Before this happens, however, due process entitles a parolee to:

- written notice of the alleged violation(s) and of the evidence against the parolee
- a hearing, usually conducted by a hearing officer or the parole board and not by a judge. At the hearing, a parolee may present witnesses and other evidence and cross-examine adverse witnesses unless the hearing officer or parole board has good cause not to allow witnesses to appear, and
- at the conclusion of the hearing, a written decision setting out the reasons for the parole revocation.

Parolees facing revocation of their parole often try to cut a deal (sometimes called a "screening deal") where they give up the right to a hearing in exchange for receiving less prison time than would have been imposed following a complete hearing and revocation decision.

42. Do parolees have a right to appointed counsel at parole revocation hearings?

No. Parolees may request the court that sentenced them to appoint counsel for a parole revocation hearing. Judges have the discretion to appoint counsel in those circumstances, and they are more likely to do so when facts are seriously disputed or involve complex documentary evidence, or when a parolee is not capable of self-representation because of language or mental deficiencies.

43. What is "temporary release" and how does it differ from parole?

Temporary release allows prisoners to leave prison for a short time to deal with important personal matters. For example, a prisoner might apply for temporary release in order to attend a parent's funeral. Another reason for temporary leave is so that prisoners can work days outside of prison and look for housing prior to being formally paroled. Typically, prisoners who are granted temporary release are considered nonviolent, have behaved well while in prison, do not have extensive histories of criminal behavior, and are virtually certain to return to prison in accordance with the terms of their leave.

Section IV: Pardons

A pardon, also called a grant of clemency, is an order granted to an offender by the chief executive that releases the convicted person from prison and/or from further penalties that result from that conviction.

44. Who has the power to grant pardons?

Only a jurisdiction's chief executive has pardon power. A state's governor has the power to pardon those who have been convicted of state offenses, and the president of the United States can issue pardons for those convicted of federal crimes.

45. What standards must governors or the president follow in deciding whether or not to grant pardons?

Chief executives are accountable only to the political process when making pardon decisions, and those decisions normally are final. Few established standards exist, though many cynics insist that a record of campaign contributions is often a way to influence a chief executive's decisions.

46. Is "sealing" a criminal record the same as a pardon?

No. Sealing criminal records (often called expunging the records) is similar to a pardon in that convicted persons whose records are sealed may lawfully tell prospective employers that they were never convicted of a crime. Unlike pardons, however, decisions to seal criminal records are made by judges. And typically, someone seeking expungement must wait a period of time after completing a sentence for records to be sealed, whereas prisoners may be pardoned at any time. For information on sealing juvenile court records, see Chapter 25.

47. Can DNA tests show that someone who was convicted many years ago is actually innocent?

Yes, and defendants who are cleared by DNA tests are perfect candidates for pardons. (A defendant who obtains a DNA test showing his innocence can also apply for relief by filing a petition for writ of habeas corpus with the courts. For more on habeas corpus, see Chapter 23, Section II.) Some states have passed laws that allow defendants in certain types of cases to demand DNA tests. For information on legal help for inmates challenging convictions based on DNA testing, contact The Innocence Project (see below).

The Innocence Project

The Innocence Project (www.innocence project.org) was established in 1992 with the goal of exonerating the innocent through post-conviction DNA testing. Since its inception, more than 190 innocent people, including 14 who were at one time sentenced to death, have been exonerated by post-conviction DNA evidence. When DNA testing reaffirms a client's guilt, The Innocence Project closes the case, and the results of all testing may become a matter of public record. Through federal legislation that The Innocence Project helped bring about, defendants wrongfully convicted in the federal system are entitled to compensation of $50,000 per year of imprisonment in noncapital cases and $100,000 per year in capital cases. Having determined that mistaken eyewitness identification played a role in 75% of the convictions overturned through DNA testing, The Innocence Project has made strides in achieving eyewitness identification reform in a number of U.S. jurisdictions, thus improving identification procedures used by law enforcement and reducing the number of wrongful convictions. For more information, contact The Innocence Project at 100 Fifth Avenue, 3rd Floor, New York, New York 10011.

Looking Up the Law

Not all criminal cases require legal research. Many cases do not involve complex legal questions, but rather a dispute over whose version of what happened should be believed. Some people, however, may want to look further into the law, especially if there is a search and seizure issue in the case, or there is reason to doubt that the charged crime is supported by the facts known to the defense. To facilitate such inquiries, this chapter introduces some basic legal research techniques and commonly available resources. For a more comprehensive guide to conducting legal research, consult *Legal Research: How to Find & Understand the Law*, by Stephen Elias and the Editors of Nolo (Nolo), an easy-to-read book that provides step-by-step instruction on how to find legal information. This excellent Nolo resource is relatively inexpensive and can often be found in public and law libraries.

Section I: What to Research

This section offers an orientation to the general categories and terms commonly used by publishers of books dealing with criminal law.

1. What additional information can I find out about my case by doing some legal research?

All of the following are different types of rules that may affect a criminal case and that can be researched in most law libraries (see Section II, below, on how to find a law library):

- **Substantive law:** Rules that define crimes (such as murder or extortion) and defenses (such as self-defense).
- **Rules of criminal procedure:** Rules that govern the criminal justice process (for instance, when an arraignment must be held and when a case must come to trial).
- **Constitutional rights:** Rules that protect person, property, and privacy (like a defendant's right not to testify).
- **Rules of evidence:** Rules that govern the type and amount of proof permissible at trial and other court proceedings (like rules generally barring hearsay and character evidence, discussed in Chapter 18).
- **Local rules of court:** Rules that govern customs and regulations in particular geographical locations, courthouses, or even courtrooms.

2. What laws will tell me more about the crimes with which I am charged and the defenses that might be available?

"Substantive" law is the term for rules that govern the heart of a case: the definitions of the crimes with which the defendant is charged and possible defenses to those charges. The term "substantive law" is used in contrast to "procedural" law, which deals with the rules that govern how cases move through the court system. This book, for example, deals primarily with procedural law, though the first section in Chapter 24 does discuss the substantive law of drunk driving.

Probably the most important research task dealing with substantive law is to learn the legal elements of each of the charges and possible defenses in a particular case. Once the elements of a crime are understood, it is possible to determine whether the facts in the case support a conviction for that offense.

For example, assume that Robert Steven Liefert is charged with burglary. The crime of burglary traditionally has been defined as "the breaking and entering into the dwelling of another in the night with intent to commit a felony inside," a definition made up of six elements:

1. the breaking
2. the entering
3. into the dwelling
4. of another
5. in the night
6. with intent to commit a felony inside.

Under this definition of burglary, if Liefert is guilty of the first five elements but did not intend to commit a felony, he should not be convicted of this offense.

In modern times, most jurisdictions have modified this definition of burglary in many respects. For example, they do not limit burglary to houses but include any type of structure, and the crime may be committed at any time of day or night. Lawyers who routinely handle burglary cases would know the current definition of burglary in their state (and if Liefert were representing himself, he would want to research this information).

One good place to find the standard elements of common criminal offenses and defenses is a book that contains model jury instructions. These instructions, which a judge reads to the jury at the close of trial and which judges use themselves in deciding cases without juries, identify the elements that must be proven in order to convict a defendant for a particular criminal offense. Most law libraries will have state-specific jury instruction books (which a reference librarian can help locate) that set out complete jury instructions for common crimes.

 RESOURCE
Here are two of the more commonly used jury instruction books:
- *Federal Jury Practice and Instructions*, by Kevin F. O'Malley, et. al. (Thomson-West Publishing, 5th ed. 2000);
- *Criminal Defense Jury Instructions*, by Harry Ackley (Knowles Law Book Publishing, Inc.).

In addition to understanding the elements of a particular crime, it may be necessary to do some additional research about the meaning of abstract legal jargon used to define the elements. What, for instance, does "breaking and entering" really mean? What if Liefert walked into the building by opening an unlocked back door; is that "breaking"? What if he broke a window and reached his hand in to grab something without ever actually going inside; is that "entering"?

CASE EXAMPLE: Anita Shelter, a homeless person, broke into an abandoned building to get out of the rain.

Question: Could she be convicted of burglary?

Answer: Not under the traditional definition (breaking and entering into the dwelling house of another in the night with the intent to commit a felony inside). The breaking and entering is the act; the intent to commit a felony inside is the mental component. Because Anita's intent was merely to get out of the rain, she did not intend to commit a felony in the building.

Question: What if Anita, once inside, found and then decided to steal a diamond ring. Would she be guilty of burglary?

Answer: No. That would not have been burglary either under the traditional definition, since the intent to take the ring was not formed until after the breaking and entering.

To answer these types of very specific questions, you would need to know how the courts in your state have interpreted your state's burglary statute. Or, if you are charged with a federal crime, you will need to know how the federal courts have dealt with the federal statute in issue. Usually, the best way to start acquiring this information is to get an overview from a secondary resource (a discussion of the law by an expert rather than the text of the law itself).

Just as a lawyer might, a nonlawyer would probably start by asking the law librarian to suggest an appropriate secondary resource on crimes against property—or burglary in particular. The librarian may suggest consulting a general treatise (reference book) about criminal law, a criminal law treatise for your particular state, a chapter about burglary in a legal encyclopedia, or some other resource. (More on these below.)

3. Does the substantive law cover anything other than specific crimes and defenses?

Substantive criminal law also covers certain legal principles that apply to criminal prosecutions in general. One such principle is that most crimes require that some physical act be taken toward commission of the crime (as opposed to just talking about it) and a frame of mind that is consistent with doing something wrong (called the *mens rea*, or guilty mind, requirement). Some offenses also require that the defendant's actions cause a particular result, such as murder, which requires that the defendant's actions cause the death of a person.

4. I've been charged with two crimes. Will I be able to find information about both crimes in the same set of books?

A person can, quite naturally, be charged with more than one crime. The substantive laws governing those crimes may or may not be located in the same book or set of books.

EXAMPLE: Yetta Speed was stopped for DUI (driving under the influence), and the police found illegal drugs in her car. Yetta was charged with both DUI and possession of illegal substances. Laws relating to the DUI might be in a "Vehicle" code, section, or title together with other laws relating to moving violations, while laws relating to illegal substances might be in a "Health and Safety," "Criminal," or "Penal" code, section, or title.

5. What's the difference between state crimes and federal crimes?

States and the federal government both enact criminal laws. Some offenses, like routine drunk driving, would be state crimes, covered by state laws, whereas assaulting a federal officer, like an FBI agent, would likely be a federal offense no matter where it is committed.

But, as with many aspects of the law, even these divisions are not so clear-cut. To commit the crime of assaulting a federal officer (18 U.S.C. § 111), among other things, the victim must have been engaged in the performance of official duties at the time of the assault. If the victim was an off-duty FBI agent, the case might well be governed by a state assault statute (law).

Also, the same conduct may violate both federal and state laws. A well-known case involving federal and state criminal trials stemming from the same incident involved four California law enforcement officers accused of beating motorist Rodney King. The officers were tried and acquitted in state court on assault charges and were tried and convicted in federal court for having violated Rodney King's civil rights.

6. What are the rules that tell me how my case will move through the courts, and where do I find these rules?

Procedural rules govern the process of criminal justice, before, during, and after trial. Rules of criminal procedure control dozens of details including such things as:

- how soon after arrest a suspect must be arraigned
- whether a prosecutor must conduct a preliminary hearing or may seek an indictment from the grand jury, and
- when a jury trial must be requested.

Procedural rules for criminal cases may be grouped together in a particular chapter, title, or section of general laws under a heading called "Criminal Procedure." Some states have conveniently separated rules into collections of books called "codes." In these codes, there may be a separate code of criminal procedure. In other states, people must look up the rules they need in what's called a general index to statutes. The federal courts use the Federal Rules of Criminal Procedure. Again, reference librarians in law libraries are usually most helpful in pointing folks in the right direction.

7. Will my local court have any rules I should know about?

Local court rules also affect procedure, and they can be critical to effectively defending a case. Local rules can govern many details, even things like how many copies of legal documents must be submitted and the type of paper required. These may sound like picky little details, and they are. But they are details that you must follow. Local rules also vary; even different counties within the same state can have different rules.

People can usually obtain a copy of local rules of court from the courthouse law library, the Clerk's Office, or the court clerk or law clerk to a particular judge.

8. What are rules of evidence, and where do I find them?

Evidence rules govern how the defense and prosecution are to present the testimony of witnesses and exhibits they attempt to introduce into evidence, and what types of information qualify to be admitted as evidence in a trial. Chapter 18 explains the most frequently encountered rules of evidence and refers to particular federal rules of evidence. To get an idea of how typical evidence rules are worded, the federal rules are good starting places for research because they have been adopted or used as a guideline in over half the states. But the defense must be familiar with the rules for its specific state and how courts in its state have interpreted these rules. Again, law librarians, upon request, will direct people to the appropriate rules of evidence.

9. Assuming I want to do some research into some legal aspects of my case, where do I start?

Many people faced with the need to do legal research start by floundering for hours through mostly useless material. Fortunately, there are often better and quicker ways to ferret out the sought-after information. One standard method is to ask a human being who is likely to know the answer. Even lawyers like to start research projects by asking their colleagues or law librarians for ideas. And, just as doctors rarely go to family or social events without being asked to diagnose illnesses off the top of their heads, so too are lawyers routinely solicited by friends and family for "quick" answers to legal inquiries.

If you don't have a human being to ask, or need a more detailed answer than you can get from one, probably the best place to start your research is a specialized reference book (such as those described below in Question 15) that explains and organizes the substantive law or procedural law.

10. How can I ask someone to help me research my case when my lawyer told me not to talk to anyone about it?

Because of the potential consequences in a criminal case (where the defendant's liberty and sometimes life is at stake), defendants, as well as their friends and family, must be very careful about whom they talk to about the case. For instance, it is possible that a prosecutor might attempt to find out even from a law librarian who helped the defendant do some research whether the defendant said anything to indicate guilt.

Defendants who reveal confidential information to a librarian or, for that matter, to anyone other than their lawyer, also risk destroying the confidential nature of whatever they've said in the past to their lawyer. (See Chapter 8 for more on the confidential nature of lawyer-client communications.)

With those warnings in mind, the following people may be helpful in certain respects:

- **Law librarians.** Law librarians, who usually have extensive legal training, can be most helpful in pointing out and helping locate resources such as legal forms, reference books explaining particular areas of law, rules of evidence and procedure, court cases, and statutes. Both for the confidentiality reasons discussed above and because it's not a librarian's job, people should not ask or expect a law librarian to do research for them or provide legal

Seeking Help from a Librarian

Just as when you talk to court clerks, it helps to be polite when speaking with a law librarian (or non-law librarian at a public library). You may be outraged about your case, but set emotions aside and stick to the facts. The librarian will likely want to help you, but the librarian is not your lawyer or counselor. And recall the need for confidentiality; do not discuss factual details about your case with anyone other than your lawyer.

Prepare before asking questions, then approach the librarian calmly and try to be specific. For example, say something along the lines of, "I am looking for the laws or code sections that apply to _____ in order to _____ . The case is a criminal matter in _____ court." Or, if you can't be this specific, ask a question that

is more general, helps you identify what you need, and assures the librarian that you are not asking for legal advice. For instance, "I need to understand _____ . Can you suggest some resources?"

As an example, suppose Steve has agreed to help his cousin, who was charged with a DUI. Steve might approach a librarian and say, "I am looking for the code sections that apply to blood alcohol levels because my cousin is charged with a DUI. He lives here in this county. Can you tell me where I should look?"

If you are unfamiliar with legal concepts, you may find it difficult to identify the information you need. Law librarians and other online research assistants often recognize this, and if you plan ahead and are patient, they will often ask questions that can help them point you in the right direction.

advice. Librarians can, however, help find and sometimes explain how to use many important research tools.

- **Courtroom and courthouse clerks.**
Clerks at the court where a case is pending can sometimes be very helpful, especially when it comes to procedural details. They can provide routine (but nonetheless essential) details such as the time court starts and where bathrooms and cafeterias are. They may also help people obtain copies of documents such as court rules, legal forms, and jury instructions. Clerks are sometimes hostile, however, to people they view as wasting the court's time, such as people representing themselves and those perceived as asking for legal advice. But asking how to get forms and court rules is not seeking legal advice.

- Whether asking where the bathroom is or how to fill in a subpoena form, you should try to be especially polite to clerks. They are used to dealing with so many rude and pushy people that someone who is polite may well stand out and have a much better shot at being treated respectfully in kind.

- **A self-help legal coach.** Consulting a lawyer doesn't always have to mean hiring the lawyer to handle the whole case. It may be possible to find a lawyer to give you research tips as you need them. (See Chapter 7 for more on legal coaches.)

Publications That Explain the Law Are Not the Last Word

Explanations and conclusions in encyclopedias or treatises (resource books covering a whole subject such as drunk driving or search and seizure) are not binding law. Rather, they are the opinions of the authors, and authors—even learned scholars—may be wrong. Also, because law can change very quickly, the information may be out of date. Even if the author is right and the information is up to date, a judge in any given case is not required to follow what the author says (true even for the authors of this book!). Rather, the judge is bound only by the law itself, the statutes, and court opinions that speak to the facts of the particular case. Rather than rely on the experts, you will be wise to look up the original law sources (statutes and cases) yourself or double-check with a lawyer. Still, there's no question about it: Background reference sources are good places to start.

---

11. If it's necessary to hit the books, where do I start?

It might help to start with a good legal dictionary. Legal jargon can seem like a foreign language—called "legalese" by some. Though it is not easy, or for that matter even necessary, to become fluent, it does help to at least be comfortable with certain essential legal terms. Many such terms have been defined throughout this book, and there is a glossary of criminal law terms in Section III of this chapter. But people may still want to consult a legal dictionary both for words not defined here or for more detailed explanations.

It is obviously crucial to understand unfamiliar terms. But it can also be important to review familiar terms, because they may have different connotations in legalese. For example, many people think of being "robbed" as having their possessions stolen. Let's say Lisa and her husband Steve come home from a wedding only to find their front door kicked in, furniture broken, and TV missing. Lisa says "Steve, we've been robbed!" While perfectly appropriate in everyday terms, their house had actually been "burglarized." For them to have been robbed, the perpetrator would have to have taken their property directly from them, while they were present, using actual force or intimidation that caused them to be afraid. The difference may seem like word play, but it can be critical. Since robbery is an offense against person as well as property, robbery typically carries a stiffer sentence than burglary, a crime against property only.

RESOURCE

Readable dictionaries. While many lawyers use *Black's Law Dictionary* (West Publishing Co.), the following dictionaries may be easier to understand:

- *Nolo's Plain-English Law Dictionary* (Nolo)
- *Law Dictionary*, by Stephen Gifis (Barron's)
- *Dictionary of Legal Terms: A Simplified Guide to the Language of Law*, by Stephen Gifis (Barron's)

- *Law Dictionary for Non-Lawyers*, by Daniel Oran (Delmar Publishing Co.)
- *Law Thesaurus-Dictionary*, by William Statsky (West Publishing Co.), and
- *Dictionary of American Legal Usage*, by David Melinkoff (West Publishing Co.).

12. So once I have a dictionary, what do I do next?

There are many legal reference books that summarize and explain court cases, statutes, and other rules of law, and these reference books can be important legal research tools. They may provide particular answers (or cite to other helpful resources) or give the big picture. Either way, they are often a good place to start a research project.

13. What are legal encyclopedias, and how can they help me research an issue in a criminal case?

Legal encyclopedias—organized alphabetically by topic with a detailed index at the end of the last volume, like regular encyclopedias—cover virtually every aspect of the criminal justice system. Each entry not only summarizes the law, but also refers to the statutes and cases that provide the legal basis for the entry. Although any given encyclopedia entry may offer a general discussion of the legal principles involved in that particular subject area, crime, or defense, they seldom are specific enough to actually provide an answer. But they can help someone totally unfamiliar with an area of law gain an understanding of the important issues, perhaps suggesting further research in more specifically focused sources.

RESOURCE

Encyclopedias. The two main national law encyclopedias are *American Jurisprudence* (Am. Jur.) and *Corpus Juris*. They include broadly based discussions on the laws of all 50 states. Both are now in their second series, so cites are to "Am. Jur. 2d" and "C.J.S." (*Corpus Juris Secundum*). Many of the larger states have their own encyclopedias as well, for example:

- Pennsylvania Law Encyclopedia
- New York Jurisprudence 2d
- Encyclopedia of Georgia Law
- Florida Jurisprudence, and
- California Jurisprudence 3d.

14. What are "form books," and how can they help me in my criminal case?

Form books are collections of sample legal documents. They include fill-in-the-blanks documents, which can be copied and filled in with appropriate information. Sometimes, they have to be customized to fit the circumstances of a particular case. Some states provide their own fill-in-the-blanks forms, available for small sums of money at local courts. Court clerks, law librarians, and lawyers can help locate form books and court-approved forms. Form books can help in preparing legal paperwork such as subpoenas, pretrial motions (requests to the judge; see Chapter 19), and stipulations. Form books also usually explain the procedural background for each form.

They can provide helpful explanations of the laws that have to be followed as well as instructions for completing the forms, and they often refer to other resources for further information.

Forms can help the following kinds of defendants:

- **Represented defendants.** Looking at forms can give represented defendants a feel for how other lawyers draft certain documents, to see how they compare to what their own lawyers have drafted and possibly to clarify questions they want to ask their lawyers.

- **Defendants doing much of the work themselves but hiring a legal coach on an as-needed basis.** These defendants can consult forms to do a first draft of a motion, for example, and then have their coach edit the motion rather than draft it from scratch. Some lawyers may find this helpful, while others may find it easier and cheaper to draft such a document from scratch.

- **Self-represented defendants.** By reviewing a form, they avoid having to reinvent the wheel.

RESOURCE

Some form books are:
- *Federal Procedural Forms* (Bancroft Whitney/Lawyers Coop);
- *Florida Criminal Procedure* (Bancroft Whitney/Lawyers Coop);

- *New Jersey Criminal Procedure* (Bancroft Whitney/Lawyers Coop)
- *Criminal Law of New York* (Bancroft Whitney/Lawyers Coop)
- *Texas Criminal Practice Guide* (Matthew Bender), and
- *West's California Criminal Defense Motions Forms Manual* (West Publishing Co.).

15. What are "practice guides," and how can they help me research an issue in my criminal case?

In addition to all the other types of resource books discussed in this chapter, lawyers often consult guide books—sometimes called practice guides or manuals or "continuing legal education" (CLE) materials. These guides, published by and for lawyers, include practical tips, suggestions, and forms in areas of state and federal law practice. They cover a huge variety of subjects, such as drunk driving, grand jury practice, criminal appeals, and many more.

Practice guides are available in many states, and some publishers gear their materials specifically toward lawyers in particular states. For example, the Practicing Law Institute (PLI) gears some materials toward New York lawyers, and the Rutter Group and Continuing Education of the Bar (CEB) toward California lawyers.

RESOURCE

Some practice manuals:

- *Trial Guidelines for the Defense of Criminal Cases* (ALI)

- *Defense of Drunk Driving Cases* (Matthew Bender)
- *Prosecution and Defense of Criminal Conspiracy Cases* (Matthew Bender)
- *Defending a Federal Criminal Case* (Federal Defenders of San Diego, Inc.)
- *Representation of Witnesses Before Federal Grand Juries: A Manual for Attorneys* (National Lawyers Guild)
- *West's California Criminal Procedure*, by Laurie L. Levenson (West Publishing Co.), and
- *West's California Criminal Trial Book* (West Publishing Co.).

16. What's the best way to find the law itself?

The law itself consists of constitutional provisions, statutes, court cases, municipal ordinances, and administrative regulations.

a. State and federal statutes

Statutes are rules enacted by federal and state legislatures. Statutes are sometimes called acts or, simply, laws. State statutes are generally grouped by subject matter for the purpose of publication. Most sets of state statutes take up many volumes, but are divided into "codes," "chapters," or "titles," which are in turn divided into sections and subsections.

Federal statutes are published in the United States Code. As with some state collections of statutes, the U.S. Code is divided into titles and sections. Each statute has a particular number, called a citation or cite. With citation to a statute (for example, from this or another Nolo book or a treatise, encyclopedia, or practice manual), one can easily find the statute. For example, the crime of assaulting a federal officer is mentioned above (in Question 5) followed by the number (citation) 18 U.S.C. § 111. To find this statute, one would look in Title 18 of the United States Code (U.S.C.) and then find the volume of that title containing Section 111.

Books containing collections of statutes include an index in the last volume that has references to the location of particular statutes according to their subject matter. To use a subject matter or topical index, it helps to think of a number of possible headings for the particular subject (for ideas, review headings in a treatise or encyclopedia or ask a librarian). If the statute doesn't appear under the first logical heading, it pays to keep searching or perhaps consult a legal dictionary for related words or phrases. Legal subjects also overlap, so helpful information may be listed under more than one heading. For example, laws that relate to protecting a defendant who has been subjected to a police search may be located under any or all of the following (or other) headings: "Search and Seizure" (or either one separately), "Fourth Amendment," or "Exclusionary Rule."

When looking at collections of statutes, it is helpful to use the annotated versions if these are available. Annotated collections of statutes contain the language of the statute along with short summaries of the significant court cases (including their legal citation for easy reference; see below) that

have interpreted the statute, and references to other resource books and articles that have discussed the law.

In order to read and make sense of a statute once it's been found, it is important to:

- understand all the terms. One can do that by looking them up in a legal dictionary or, especially in longer statutes, looking in the beginning part of the statute for definitions of terms used in other parts of the law.
- check that the statute is current. Statutes are often revised and sometimes repealed. So, after finding a statute in the main section of a hardbound collection of statutes, one should look in the paperbound supplement or update (called a "pocket part"), usually located inside the back cover of the book. Pocket parts contain the changes that have been made to a law or its wording since the publication of the hardbound volume. Some pocket parts are also annotated with references, for example, citations to recent cases discussing a statute.

b. Court cases

Sometimes, higher (appellate) courts review the record and decisions of lower (trial) courts, and interpret the meaning of statutes, constitutional provisions, and other court cases. These interpretations commonly make up what's known as "common law" (judge-made law). These appellate court interpretations are documented in written decisions (called opinions, case law, or cases). The typical court opinion includes a summary of the facts that the trial judge or jury found to be true, the actual decision at which the appellate court has arrived in the appeal (called the "holding"), and the legal reasoning for that decision.

The written decisions of appellate courts (cases) are collected and published in hardbound volumes called "reporters," "reports," or "case reports." There are many separate reporters for different courts and geographical areas. For example, a case from the New York Court of Appeals may be published in a series of state reporters called New York Appeals and also in a regional reporter series called Northeastern Reporter, which includes cases from several states. Federal cases are published according to the court that decided them. For example, decisions by the U.S. Courts of Appeal are collected in the Federal Reporter. At present in its third series, this is called Federal Reporter, Third Series (which readers may see cited as "F.3d").

Recent cases, not yet included in a hardbound reporter, are located in softbound supplements. And cases decided in the last few days or weeks may often only be available from the appellate court itself or a computer reporting service—although, as discussed in Section II, below, courts in most states now publish recent decisions on the World Wide Web or on a publicly accessible bulletin board on the Internet. To look up a new case, one just mentioned in the newspaper, for example,

ask a librarian for assistance; it won't yet be in the hardbound books.

Cases, like statutes, have citations to make them easy to find. Let's say someone wanted to read the famous case that produced a rule requiring police to read suspects their rights before conducting any in-custody questioning, *Miranda v. Arizona* (discussed more thoroughly in Chapter 1). Reading this book or an encyclopedia, treatise, or legal dictionary, readers see mention of *Miranda* followed by the citation, 384 U.S. 436 (1966). The first number means the case is located in volume 384. The letters in the middle (U.S.) are the abbreviation for United States Reports, the case reporter series where the *Miranda* case is published. The last number indicates that the case begins at page 436. The names reflect the parties to the lawsuit (Ernesto Miranda was the defendant who appealed; the people of the state of Arizona were the prosecution who opposed the appeal). The date at the end is when the United States Supreme Court decided the case.

The Numbering System for Reporters

Case reporters are published in numbered volumes. After a series accumulates years of numbered volumes, the publisher starts over with another series. So, you may find a cite to a 2d or 3d series. For example, *People v. Gray*, 254 Cal. App. 2d 256 (1967), is at volume 254 of the California Appellate Reports, second series, beginning on page 256.

In addition to the full text of the court's opinions, reporters include "headnotes," short summaries of the legal issues in a case. Headnotes are numbered in the order in which the issues are discussed in a case. They can be quite useful, both for a quick look at what a case is about and as a table of contents to help locate other issues of interest. Headnote numbers also connect to publishers' "digests." If you go to a "digest," you'll find cases organized by headnote numbers. By turning to a headnote number, you can often find numerous cases that address the same specific legal issue. But headnotes are not written by the judge or judges who wrote the opinion; they are written by the reporter's editors. They can be inaccurate and are not "law," so they should not be quoted when making an argument to a judge without first reading the actual decision of the court.

Once court cases are published, they are usually not removed from the books even if later courts conclude that the decision is no longer correct. Thus, before relying on a case, people should always verify that the case is still "good law," meaning that it has not been overruled by a later case. A series of case histories called *Shepard's Citations for Cases* reports the status of published cases. Law librarians—or one of the reference sources mentioned above— can help explain how to use *Shepard's*. *Shepard's* can also be helpful in locating more recent cases that discuss (but don't overrule) a particular case.

Printed versions of Shepard's used to be common in law libraries. But with online research now the norm, many law libraries have abandoned printed research tools. Find out from a law librarian whether your library has free access to *Shepard's* online. If this service is not available for free, you may be able to purchase *Shepard's* (or a similar service) on a "pay as you go" basis. Or you may be able to purchase a limited subscription—for example, you may be able to purchase access to the citation service only.

What Rules Judges Must Follow

Sometimes it can be confusing to know which rules a judge has to follow. Primary authorities (statutes, cases, administrative regulations, and local rules and ordinances) can be mandatory, which means that a court has to follow them. But they can also be just "persuasive," which means a court can consider them but does not have to follow them. For example, a state court in New York may find it helpful and convincing that a California court recently decided the same legal question that is now before the New York court. But the New York court does not have to follow the California court's decision. Judges must, however, follow the decisions of higher courts in their own state. For example, a Los Angeles trial judge must follow a decision of the California Supreme Court (the highest state court in California), but a trial judge in Alabama doesn't have to.

When researching cases, it is thus best to find an appellate court case from the same state (or circuit in the federal court system) where one's case is to be heard. But if the only case available is an out-of-state case that is nonetheless right on point (on the same legal issue with similar facts) and very helpful, it may be worth trying to convince the judge that the out-of-state court's reasoning should be followed.

c. State constitutions and the U.S. Constitution

The U.S. Constitution is the supreme law of the land, which means that all state and federal laws must comply with it. Each state's laws must also conform to their state constitutions. State constitutions cannot limit rights provided by the U.S. Constitution, though they may sometimes provide greater protections. Judges decide whether or not laws comply with constitutional provisions. Judges also interpret the meaning of constitutional provisions, just as they interpret statutes.

Again, a law librarian may be able to point out a helpful resource on constitutional law. But because constitutional law is often complex, it may be very helpful to first consult a lawyer for assistance.

d. Administrative regulations

Administrative regulations ("regs") are enacted by federal, state, and local agencies. For example, the Equal Employment Opportunity Commission, Veterans' Administration, state board of medical quality assurance, or state department of motor vehicles all make their own rules. Administrative laws govern agencies' policies and procedures, such as how they conduct hearings and why they grant or withhold benefits and privileges (such as licenses).

Some criminal cases involve both court hearings and hearings before an administrative agency. For example, in some places defendants charged with DUI will face court proceedings for the criminal statutes they are charged with violating, and administrative proceedings to suspend or take away their driver's licenses. A doctor who assaulted a patient may have to appear in court on criminal charges and may be called before an administrative agency regarding license suspension or revocation.

Someone charged with such an offense may want to research the rules governing the administrative agency, because although an administrative hearing may resemble a court case, in reality it is quite different. For example, most agencies do not follow the rules of evidence, there is no right to a jury, lawyers may be excluded, a defendant may not be able to subpoena witnesses or documents—or even have witnesses testify—and hearings may not be open to the public.

Section II: Where to Do Research

This section is about where you can find and read the various resources described in Section I.

17. Where can I find a law library?

The best place to do legal research is in a law library. In some states, finding a well-stocked law library that is open to the public is no problem; at least one library will be at a principal courthouse in every metropolitan area. But in other states, courthouse libraries are nonexistent or inadequate, and the only decent law libraries open to the public will be located at a publicly funded law school. Some private law schools also open their law libraries to the public, at least for limited hours.

For simple legal research tasks, a public library may be a fine place to start. The main branch of a nearby public library may have a small but helpful legal section, which includes a compilation of the state's criminal laws. Another possibility is to ask for permission to use an attorney's law office library.

18. Can I use a computer to do research online?

Yes. Increasingly, legal resources are available online. Two major private systems, Lexis and Westlaw, maintain online databases of court cases, statutes, legal articles, and a host of other resources (nationwide and, in some instances, worldwide). These providers usually charge for the amount of time spent online, and a search can get quite expensive, especially for those not familiar with the system. If you are willing to pay to use one of these services, call its toll-free number and speak to a research

assistant before you begin your search. You can often get help planning out all the steps in the search to get the most effective results. This will help you conduct an efficient search, potentially saving you a great deal of money. Print out any cases or statutes you find and want to read so that you can end your search (and stop paying), then read the material as slowly as you need to.

Before paying for Lexis or Westlaw:

- Try to find a library that provides free access to online databases. While the access may be limited, it could be adequate for your needs. Again, plan ahead because the library may limit how much time you can spend at a computer terminal.

- Try to use one of the free internet resources listed at the end of this section, or one of the lower-priced internet providers such as VersusLaw (www.versuslaw.com). A growing number of free Internet sites are available.

- If your library still has traditional print resources, start with these. You can search at your leisure, and even if you later need to do some online research, your quest will likely go much faster once you have a better idea of where you are heading.

 CAUTION
Use standard Internet safety tips when searching for information online. For example, whenever possible, enter website

addresses (known as URLs) directly into your web browser rather than clicking on links. That way you'll be sure you are going to the actual site you intend to search. Also, be aware that when you enter key terms into search engines, you may get a lot of advertising sites, such as law firms and lawyers with marketing sites in the area you are researching. Distinguish government or academic sites from marketing sites, and be cautious when you use information from the latter. There are also many very helpful law-related blogs, including several on the Nolo website (www. nolo.com) with extremely useful information in a number of areas. Blogs are an individual's interpretations of the law and may not necessarily be correct. Also, be careful not to enter personal, identifying information into a website, especially if it concerns your criminal case. Confidentiality may be destroyed by talking, writing, emailing, or blogging about any factual details of your case. Chapters 8 and 18 review some important rules about confidentiality.

RESOURCE

For an extended discussion on how to use all of the research tools discussed in this chapter, in print and online, consult *Legal Research: How to Find & Understand the Law*, by Attorneys Stephen R. Elias and the Editors of Nolo (Nolo).

19. Are there any inexpensive online resources?

Many legal reference sources are now becoming available on the World Wide Web. Statutes from many states are now online, as are federal statutes, regulations, and rules. For example, California puts its codes and statutes online at www.leginfo. ca.gov/calaw.html.

Internet sites also link users to courts, to local district attorney and public defender offices, to prosecuting and defense lawyers' organizations, and to the FBI, the Department of Justice, the ACLU, and more. Some Web pages have crime victims or prisoners as their target audience; others aim at more general audiences. Several websites also link users to many of the interesting criminal justice resources currently available online. These can be located by plugging words such as "criminal law," "criminal justice," "crimes," "prisoner's rights," and "victim's rights" into a search engine (such as www.google.com). Some of the sites that point users toward helpful criminal resources at the time of this printing include (not in any particular order):

- Cecil Greek's Criminal Justice Page at www.criminology.fsu.edu/cjlinks
- Jeff Flax's Legal Resource Page at www.jflax.com
- a law locator on the net called FindLaw also has a detailed criminal law section (www.findlaw.com)
- The Association of Federal Defense Attorneys at www.afda.org
- The Vera Institute at www.vera.org
- The Tennessee Criminal Law Defense Resources at www.tncrimlaw.com
- The National Organization for the Reform of Marijuana Laws at www. norml.org
- Cornell University has a helpful resource called the Legal Information

Institute, which has among other resources a free listing of U.S. Supreme Court cases and criminal codes from a number of states, at www.law.cornell.edu

- materials, including sample motions and briefs, are available on the website maintained by the Massachusetts Association of Criminal Defense Lawyers (www.macdl.com)

- Thomas, the Library of Congress' collection of legislative information, a free site which gives information about federal statutes that have been enacted since the 101st Congress (http://thomas.loc.gov), and

- PublicLegal, a categorized index of more than 4,000 select websites in 238 nations and territories, as well as thousands of locally stored Web pages, legal forms, and downloadable files (http://www.ilrg.com).

Section III: Glossary

This section contains simple plain-English definitions of selected criminal law words and phrases, and provides some examples of the use of the words and phrases ("context of use" examples). You may use this glossary as a mini-dictionary for a quick understanding of terms commonly used in the criminal justice system. You may want to consult the book's index for further information, as well as the legal dictionaries listed in Section I of this chapter.

Abuse excuse: A type of self-defense claim with which defendants seek to justify their actions by proving that they were subjected to years of prolonged child or spousal abuse.

Accessory after the fact: A person who takes an active role in concealing criminal activity that has already taken place. ("Jake was convicted of being an accessory after the fact because he destroyed evidence of Steve's failed kidnap attempt.")

Accessory before the fact: A person who aids criminal activity but is not present when the crime is committed. ("Jake was convicted of being an accessory before the fact for helping his friend Steve to plan a kidnapping.")

Accomplices: Partners in criminal activity.

Acquit: A judge or jury "acquits" a defendant by finding the defendant not guilty.

Acquittal: A finding by a judge or jury that the defendant is not guilty.

Action: Another word for a lawsuit. While the term may be more commonly used in civil lawsuits, a criminal action simply means a criminal lawsuit brought by the prosecution against a defendant.

Administrative agency: A government department charged with enforcing laws and developing regulations. For example, the Department of Homeland Security is a federal agency that enforces laws relating to public safety, and it has the power to develop regulations.

Administrative law judge: A judicial officer who presides over cases brought by an administrative agency.

Admissible evidence: Evidence that a trial judge can consider or can allow a jury to consider when reaching a verdict.

Admission: A defendant's out-of-court statement offered into evidence against the defendant by the prosecution as an exception to the hearsay rule.

Adversary: Party on the opposite side of a legal case; opponent. Typically, in a criminal case, the *prosecution* and the *defense* are the adversaries, each on either side of the case.

Affidavit: A written statement of facts and assertions made under oath.

Affirmative defense: A type of *defense* that a defendant has to assert and support with evidence, such as *self-defense* or *alibi*.

Aggravated offense: A crime that is made more serious because of the way in which it was committed. ("Simple assault" may become "aggravated assault" if the attacker uses a deadly weapon.)

Alibi: A defense that asserts that the defendant could not have committed the crime in question because the defendant was somewhere else at the time the crime was committed. ("Defendant Evelyn has a strong alibi. The entire Martinez family can testify that Evelyn was picking her kids up from Linda's house, and therefore could not have committed the bank robbery.")

Allegation: In a formal written criminal complaint, a prosecutor's claim that a defendant violated the law. The term can be used informally to refer to oral claims as to how events occurred. (Context of use: "The guard alleged that the prisoner had a weapon.")

Anticipatory search warrants: Search warrants that police obtain before contraband arrives at the location to be searched.

Appeal: A request to a higher court to review the rulings or decision of a trial court judge. Decisions by courts of appeal often are made by three judges. Appeals in criminal cases rarely revisit the facts of the case, but rather are mostly concerned with errors of law or procedure.

Appellant: The party who brings an appeal to an appellate court.

Appellate court: A higher court that reviews the decision of a lower court. ("The appellate court reviewed and overturned the decision of the trial court to exclude the evidence of Officer Neustadt's use of racial epithets.")

Appellee: The party who responds to an appeal brought by an appellant.

Appointed counsel: A lawyer who represents *indigent* defendants at government expense.

Argument: A persuasive presentation by the *prosecution* or *defense* to the judge or jury that supports the prosecutor's or defendant's case.

Arraignment: Often a defendant's first court appearance, in which the defendant is formally charged with a *crime* and asked to respond by pleading *guilty, not guilty,* or *no contest.* Other matters often handled at the arraignment are arranging for the appointment of *defense counsel* and the setting of *bail* or other conditions of release pending final disposition of the case.

Arrest: An arrest occurs when the police (or a citizen making a *citizen's arrest)* detain a person in a manner that makes it clear she is not free to leave, and continue to hold her for the purpose of bringing criminal charges against her.

Arrest report: A report prepared by an arresting officer summarizing the circumstances leading to the arrest. ("Julia Daniels went to the police station to obtain a copy of the arrest report so that she could compare her story to the police's account of her arrest.")

Arson: The unlawful burning of a building.

Assault: A crime often defined as either an attempt to batter (unlawfully touch) someone, or intentionally placing a person in fear of an immediate battery.

Attempt: Starting but not completing an intended criminal act. Attempts are crimes, often punished less severely than completed crimes.

Attorney: Another name for a lawyer.

Attorney work product: Legal work, including the lawyer's research and development of theories and strategies, that is considered to be *privileged* or confidential and therefore not available for review by the other side.

Authenticate: To identify an object at trial. A defense lawyer or prosecutor "authenticates" an exhibit by offering *testimony* that tells the judge what the exhibit is, where it came from, and its connection to the case.

Bail: Money paid to the court to ensure that an arrested person makes all required court appearances. If not, the bail is forfeited.

Bail bond: A guarantee given to a court by a bail bond seller to pay a defendant's bail should the defendant fail to appear in court. The bail bond seller charges the defendant (or whomever obtains the bond) a nonrefundable premium of approximately 10% of the amount of bail as a condition for making this guarantee.

Bailiff: A uniformed peace officer who maintains order in the courtroom and performs other courtroom duties, such as escorting defendants in custody to and from a courtroom, attending to the needs of a jury, and handing exhibits to witnesses.

Bar: Initially, a partition in courtrooms dividing the space where judges sit from the area where the public may sit. Typically the term now refers to lawyers as a group. Lawyers are called "members of the bar," and often belong to professional organizations called "bar associations." Another meaning of the word "bar" is to prevent something from happening in court. ("Because the defendant did not give early enough notice of his intention to present evidence of an alibi, the defendant will be barred from presenting such evidence at trial.") Lastly, attorneys may sometimes call a case "the case at bar," meaning this particular present case, to distinguish it from some past or future case.

Battery: The uninvited touching of another person. Battery is usually a *misdemeanor,* although it becomes a *felony* if the touching results in—or is intended to cause—serious injury. ("Lorne Cooper committed a battery by striking career counselor Chip Donalds in the face with a leather briefcase.")

Bench: A judge's courtroom chair and desk. "Bench" is also a substitute term for "judge." For example, a defendant might ask for a "bench trial," meaning a trial by a judge without a jury.

Best evidence rule: An evidence rule that restricts a witness from orally testifying to the contents of a document unless the document is produced in court. This rule is also frequently used to require production of the original document rather than a copy.

Beyond a reasonable doubt: The burden of proof that the prosecution must carry in a criminal trial to obtain a guilty verdict.

Bill of Rights: The first ten amendments to the U.S. Constitution—those primarily dealing with rights of individuals. For example, among those rights guaranteed by the Bill of Rights are the right to remain silent (to not incriminate oneself) and the right to a *jury trial*.

Blue card warnings: The name police use for *Miranda warnings* in some locations.

Booking: The procedure in which a jail records pertinent information, often including a *mug shot* and fingerprints, about a person who has been arrested and placed in the jail's custody.

Bounty hunter: Person who chases down defendants who have skipped *bail*, and turns them in.

Brief: A legal document, written to the judge by the prosecution or defense, consisting of a persuasive statement of fact and law that supports that side's position on one or more issues in the case. Can also be used as a verb, "to brief," meaning to write this type of persuasive statement. ("Judge Shupe asked counsel to brief the issue of whether the police officer's personnel record should be admitted into evidence, and ordered that their briefs be submitted by 10:00 a.m. the following morning.")

Burden of proof: The requirement that the *prosecution* convince the judge or jury that the defendant is guilty beyond a *reasonable doubt* of each and every *element* of the crime(s) charged. In a criminal case the burden of proof always rests with the prosecution, except that, in many states and in federal courts, the defendant has the burden to prove an *insanity* or *alibi* defense.

Burglary: The crime of breaking into and entering a building with the intention to commit a felony. The breaking and entering need not be by force, and the felony need not be theft. For instance, someone would be guilty of burglary if he entered a house through an unlocked door in order to commit a murder. For more on burglary, see Chapter 12.

Business records exception: An exception to the *hearsay rule* that allows a business document to be admitted into evidence despite its being hearsay if a proper foundation is laid to show that it is inherently reliable.

Calendar or **court calendar:** Cases a particular judge will hear on a given day. (Context of use: "Dorit's arraignment was on calendar for July 12 at 9:00 a.m.")

Capital crime or **offense:** A crime that can be punished by death or by life in prison.

Caption: A heading on all pleadings (legal documents such as the criminal *complaint* or *information* and *briefs* in support of *motions*) submitted to the court that indicates basic information such as the defendant's name, the court, and the case number.

Case: One meaning for the word case is a criminal action or lawsuit. "Case" also refers to a written decision by a judge, found in books called Case Reporters or Reporters. A party's case, or case-in-chief, also refers to the evidence that party (either the prosecution or the defense) has submitted in support of their position.

Certiorari: An order (known as a "writ") that a higher court (such as the U.S. Supreme Court) will exercise its discretion and review a lower court's ruling.

Challenge: A *prosecution* or *defense* request for the judge to excuse (dismiss) a potential juror—or to remove him or herself as judge (called a *recusal*) because of a conflict of interest.

Challenge for cause: A claim made during jury *voir dire* that a potential juror is legally disqualified from jury service— usually because of factors that would prevent the juror from being fair to one side or the other.

Chambers (also called **judge's chambers**): A judge's private business office, often located adjacent to the courtroom. ("Judge Elias asked counsel to meet in chambers to discuss the possibility of a plea bargain before trial.")

Charge(s): Formal *allegation* or accusation of criminal activity. ("The defendant, Ira Benjamin Rogers, is hereby charged with murder in the first degree.")

Circuit Courts (or **Circuit Courts of Appeals**): The name used for the principal trial court in many states. In the federal system, appellate courts are organized into 13 circuits. Eleven of these cover different geographical areas of the country—for example, the United States Court of Appeal for the Ninth Circuit covers Alaska, Arizona, California, Hawaii, Idaho, Montana, Nevada, Oregon, and Washington. The remaining circuits are the District of Columbia Circuit and the Federal Circuit (that hears patent, customs, and other specialized cases based on subject matter). The term derives from an age before mechanized transit, when judges and lawyers rode "the circuit" of their territory to hold court in various places. For more information, see Chapter 23.

Circumstantial evidence: Evidence that proves a fact by means of an inference. ("From the evidence that Victor Michaels was observed running away from the scene of a crime, a judge or jury may infer that Victor was the person who committed the crime.")

Citizen's arrest: An arrest made by a private citizen, in contrast to the typical arrest made by a police officer. Citizen's arrests are lawful in certain limited situations, such as when a private citizen personally witnesses a violent crime and then detains the perpetrator.

City attorney: A lawyer who works for and represents a city, and who in certain circumstances has the authority to bring criminal prosecutions.

Civil: Noncriminal. Civil lawsuits are generally between two private parties, whereas criminal actions involve government enforcement of the criminal laws. ("After a car accident in which Bob's car hit Steve's car, the state brought criminal charges against Bob for driving under the influence. Later, in a separate civil suit, Steve sued Bob for personal injuries and damages to Steve's car stemming from the same accident.")

Clear and convincing evidence: The *burden of proof* placed on a party in certain types of *civil cases*, such as cases involving fraud. Also, in some jurisdictions, a defendant relying on an insanity defense must prove that defense by clear and convincing evidence (even though the ultimate burden of proof as to guilt remains with the *prosecution*). Clear and convincing is a higher standard than *preponderance of the evidence*, the standard typical in most civil cases, but not as high as *beyond a reasonable doubt*, the burden placed on the prosecution in criminal cases.

Clerk's office: The administrative office in a courthouse where legal documents are filed, stored, and made available to the public. ("The defendant's attorney, Lisa Stevens, stopped by the clerk's office on her way to court to get a copy of the prosecution's *motion* to request a witness list.")

Closing argument (also called **final argument**): A persuasive presentation made by the *prosecution* and the *defense* to the judge or jury at the conclusion of a trial, arguing how, given the law and the evidence presented, that particular side should win. ("In closing argument, the public defender convinced the jury that the prosecutor had not proven all the *elements* of the *charges* against the defendant *beyond a reasonable doubt*.")

Common law: Law that judges create in the course of issuing appellate court decisions. Common law is often contrasted with statutory law, which is enacted by legislatures. As a general rule, *crimes* are defined by statutory law while many aspects of *criminal procedure* are shaped by the common law—often consisting of U.S. Supreme Court decisions that interpret the U.S. Constitution's *Bill of Rights*.

Community service: Unpaid work that benefits the community and that may be required of a convicted defendant as an alternative to a jail *sentence*.

Complaint: A pleading or legal document prepared by the prosecutor's office that formally *charges* the defendant with a crime or crimes. This initial charging document is also sometimes called an *information*.

Concurrent sentences: Sentences for more than one crime that defendants serve at the same time.

Confession: A voluntary statement by an accused, orally or in writing, in which the accused admits guilt of a particular *crime* or crimes. ("After being promised leniency by the police (who did not actually have authority to ensure a light sentence), Colleen O'Larky confessed to having embezzled funds from her employer, Duncan Enterprises.")

Consecutive sentences: Sentences for more than one crime that defendants serve in sequence (that is, one after another).

Conspirators: Two or more people who join together to commit a crime.

Contempt of court: Behavior, punishable by fine or imprisonment, in court or outside of court, that obstructs court administration, violates or resists a court order, or otherwise disrupts or shows disregard for the administration of justice.

Contingency fees: A method of compensating a lawyer for legal services in which the lawyer receives a percentage of the money the client is awarded at the close of a civil trial or by a settlement in a civil case. Contingency fee arrangements are not permitted in criminal cases.

Continuance: A delay in a scheduled court proceeding. The *prosecution* and *defense* can request a continuance when they want the court to postpone a deadline.

Contraband: Property that is illegal to possess or transport.

Conviction: A finding of guilty following a trial or plea bargain.

Corpus delicti: Literally, the "body" of the crime. This Latin phrase refers, for example, to the corpse in a murder case or the burned building in an arson case.

Costs (also, **court costs**): Expenses of trial other than attorneys' fees, such as fees and costs for filing legal documents, witness travel, court reporters, and expert witnesses.

Counsel: Attorneys or lawyers (also called **counselors**). To counsel means to advise.

County attorney: Prosecuting lawyer for county government.

Court: A government building where *criminal* and/or *civil cases* are heard. Can also mean the judge; for example, if the prosecutor says she does not wish to waste the court's time, the prosecutor actually means the particular judge to whom the prosecutor is speaking.

Court clerk: A court employee who assists a judge with the many administrative tasks of moving cases through the court system. For example, the court clerk may prepare and maintain the judge's calendar, retrieve case files from the main clerk's office, administer oaths to witnesses during trial, and prepare orders and verdict forms. Sometimes the court clerk is referred to as the "courtroom clerk" to distinguish her function from that performed by the "courthouse clerk."

Court-martial: A military criminal trial.

Court reporter: The person who records every word that is said during official court proceedings (hearings and trials) and *depositions*, and who prepares a written transcript of those proceedings upon the request of the judge or a party. ("Judge Ellis ordered counsel to speak slower so that the court reporter, Victoria Shirley, could effectively transcribe what counsel said.")

Credibility: Believability. ("The credibility of witness Joe Pepsi was put in grave doubt when he testified that he only drank Coca-Cola.")

Crime: A type of behavior that has been defined as warranting some type of punishment by the state, usually including imprisonment. Crimes, and the punishments for committing the crimes, are defined by Congress and state legislatures.

Criminal: Colloquial for people who commit crimes; also an adjective applied to courts, attorneys, and procedures that are involved in the process of charging and trying a person for a crime.

Cross-examination: The *prosecution's* or *defense's* opportunity to ask questions of the other side's *witnesses*, including the defendant if she chooses to take the stand and *testify*. ("The prosecutor Kris Dawden cross-examined the maid who said she'd seen the defendant's car parked in his driveway at the same time the defendant's ex-wife was murdered.")

Culpability: Guilt.

Culpable: Guilty or blameworthy. ("Many people felt there was no doubt that Johnny Miller was culpable in the murder case brought against him.")

Culprit: Can mean either the person accused or the person found guilty of committing a crime.

Curfew: A law requiring *minors* to get off the streets after a certain hour at night.

Custodial interrogation: Police questioning of an arrestee. See Chapter 1.

Damages: Money that civil courts award to compensate those who have been injured or lost property through another's wrongdoing. (Many crimes can result both in criminal penalties and money damages.)

Defendant: A person who has been formally *charged* by the *prosecutor* or *grand jury* with committing a *crime*. In *civil cases*, the defendant is the party who is sued by the person initiating the lawsuit (the plaintiff).

Defense: (1) A defense(s) is the accused's answer stating why he should not be found guilty of a *crime*. For example, an *alibi* defense is a defense that states that the defendant could not have committed the crime in question because she was physically in a different location from where the crime occurred. (2) The defendant's team, including the defendant, defense lawyer(s) and her assistants, investigators, etc.

Defense lawyer: Person who speaks and acts on behalf of the defendant.

Deposition: More common in *civil cases* and severely limited (in some states prohibited) in criminal cases, a deposition is a pretrial *discovery* (formal investigation) tool in which a party (or the party's lawyer) asks a series of oral questions of another party or *witness*. The questions are answered under oath and transcribed by a court reporter.

Determinate sentences: Sentences for fixed terms, such as for "36 months." Offenders may be released on parole before they have finished serving their sentences.

Dicta: Language in appellate court decisions that indicates judges' attitudes but is unnecessary to case outcomes. ("The statement in the judge's written appellate court opinion that drug use is the country's biggest threat was dicta.")

Direct examination: The initial questioning of a *witness* by the party (*prosecution* or *defense*) who has called that witness.

Discovery (in criminal cases): The procedures used by the *defense* and *prosecution* to find out before *trial* what information the other side has and intends to use if the trial takes place. As a general rule, the defense is entitled to discover more information than is the prosecution (because of the Fifth Amendment rule against mandatory self-incrimination), and in all cases discovery is much more limited in criminal cases than in civil cases.

Dissenting opinion: An appellate court judge's written reasons for disagreeing with the outcome of a case. Judges may prepare dissenting opinions in the hope of influencing judges in higher courts or in future cases, or to encourage legislators to change laws.

District attorney (also called **D.A.** or **prosecutor**): The prosecuting lawyer who works for and represents the local county government in criminal cases. Although district attorneys sometimes also represent state governments, more often such prosecutors are called "state's attorneys."

Diversion: An alternative procedure in which the case is handled outside of the court instead of under the regular criminal justice procedure. Typically, a person who agrees to be diverted will escape *criminal charges* altogether if he stays out of trouble for a specific period of time and cooperates in whatever rehabilitation activities are made available. Diversion is usually only available for very minor crimes and drug offenses when rehabilitation appears to be possible.

Docket: (1) A formal record of all the legal documents that have been filed—and court proceedings and orders that have taken place—in a particular case. (2) A calendar or list of all the proceedings on a court's agenda.

Double jeopardy: A rule from the Fifth Amendment to the U.S. Constitution that prohibits a defendant from being twice put in jeopardy (typically, made to stand trial) for the same offense. There are some exceptions to this rule, and it usually only takes hold when the first juror has been called in a trial.

Due process: A constitutional requirement (from the Fifth and Fourteenth Amendments) guaranteeing procedural fairness when the government seeks to deprive people of property, liberty, or life.

Elements of a crime (also called **legal elements**): Component parts of *crimes*. For example, "Robbery is defined as (1) the taking and carrying away (2) of property of another (3) by force or fear (4) with the intent to permanently deprive the owner of the property." Each of those four parts is an element that the *prosecution* must prove to satisfy its *burden of proof.*

Entrapment: The act by police or their agents to induce a person to commit a crime for the purposes of prosecuting that person for that induced crime. For more information, see Chapters 13 and 17.

Evidence: Information presented to a judge or jury, including the testimony of *witnesses*, documents, and *exhibits* that bear on the question of guilt or innocence.

Ex parte: One-sided. A contact with the judge by one party outside the presence of the other party is considered an *"ex parte* contact" and is generally forbidden unless it concerns a routine scheduling matter that doesn't relate to the substance of the case.

Ex post facto law: A law that attempts to punish behavior that was not illegal when the behavior took place; such laws are generally unconstitutional.

Excited utterance: An exception to the *hearsay rule* that finds an out-of-court statement to be inherently reliable if it is made about a startling event while the person making the statement is experiencing that event.

Exclusionary rule: A judge-created rule that evidence that police seize illegally is generally inadmissible at trial.

Exculpatory evidence: Evidence that points toward a defendant's innocence. *Prosecutors* are required to automatically hand over such evidence to the *defense*, even if the defense doesn't request it, and a showing that this rule was violated can sometimes result in a conviction being reversed.

Exhibit: A tangible object presented to the judge or jury during trial to help the *prosecution* or *defense* establish its case.

Expert witness: A person who, because of special knowledge or training, is permitted to offer an opinion about a set of facts when testifying before the judge or jury. Nonexpert witnesses, by contrast, usually may only testify as to their firsthand observations.

Expunge: Destroy, erase, blot out. Some states will expunge or destroy arrest records, for example, once a certain number of years have passed following the arrest.

False arrest: A tort (a *civil* as opposed to *criminal* wrongdoing) that alleges that a person was unlawfully detained. ("Michael Gleiberman sued Officer Torchin for *false arrest* some weeks after all charges against Gleiberman were dropped. Gleiberman had obtained evidence that Torchin had no *probable cause* to arrest him. Torchin had only arrested Gleiberman because Gleiberman had been having an affair with the wife of Torchin's best friend, Marcus Lesser.")

Felony: Serious *crime* (contrasted with *misdemeanors* and *infractions*, less serious crimes), usually punishable by a prison term of more than one year or in some cases by death. People convicted of felonies also frequently suffer other punishments, such as not being able to vote and not being allowed to own or possess a firearm.

Fifth Amendment right against self-incrimination: The constitutional right of every person to remain silent when being questioned by the police and—as a criminal defendant—to not take the witness stand at trial or other court proceedings.

Forfeiture: Forfeiture laws authorize the government to seize property that was used in connection with certain kinds of criminal activity. For instance, the government may take away the boat a drug dealer used to transport heroin.

Forgery: The act of altering or falsifying a document with the intent to defraud someone. ("Chipeco committed forgery by altering her birth certificate in order to secure a fake ID.")

Foundation: A set of facts explaining the origin of *evidence* such as documents and photographs, thereby establishing their *authenticity*. Before admitting these and similar items into evidence, the judge will require that the party trying to admit them establish an adequate foundation.

Frivolous motion: A *motion* that is made without legally valid grounds, such as a motion that is designed solely to delay proceedings.

Grand jury: A group of 15–23 citizens selected for court service to decide, based on the prosecutor's evidence, whether or not there is *probable cause* to charge a *defendant* with a *crime* or crimes.

Guilty: (1) One of the *pleas* a *defendant* may enter in response to being *charged* with a *crime*. A guilty plea admits the charges and subjects the defendant to punishment for them. (2) The state of being found guilty (*culpable*, the opposite of innocent) by a judge or jury.

Habeas corpus: Literally means "you have the body." A habeas corpus writ (court order) is an order by a court ordering the governmental authority (for example, a prison warden) holding a person in custody to bring that person into court so that the person may challenge the legality of the custody.

Harmless error: A trial judge's mistake that an appellate court decides did not have an impact on a case's outcome.

Hearing: A court proceeding before a judge, typically much shorter than a trial. ("Judge Doherty told her clerk that she had four hearings scheduled before 10 a.m., an *arraignment, a preliminary hearing*, a hearing on a *motion* to exclude illegally seized evidence, and an *ex parte* hearing for the police requesting a *warrant* for the *arrest* of one Gil Davids.")

Hearsay: An out-of-court statement offered in court to prove the truth of what that statement asserts. As a general rule, hearsay cannot be used as evidence. However, there are so many exceptions to the hearsay rule that many knowledgeable observers comment that "hearsay is admissible unless there is no exception to the general rule."

Holding: The rule for which an appellate court opinion stands.

Holding pens or **holding cells:** Courthouse jail cells (also called **lockups** and sometimes **bullpens**) where defendants who are in custody and who are to appear in court are forced to wait. After their court appearance, such defendants are taken back to the regular jail where they are being held.

Hostile witness (sometimes called an **adverse witness**): A witness so hostile to the party who called him or her that *cross-examination* is permitted.

ID: Identification. Can be used as a verb (for example, to ID the perpetrator) or as a noun (for example, the victim made a positive ID).

Immunity: Freedom from prosecution. Prosecutors often grant (give) one defendant immunity as an incentive to testify against another defendant. Prosecutors can also force immunized defendants to testify because if they don't, they can be held in *contempt of court*.

Impanel (sometimes spelled **empanel**): The act of assembling a panel (group) of prospective jurors for jury selection.

Impeach: To discredit. To "impeach a witness's credibility," for instance, is to discredit that person's believability.

In camera: Court session that is closed to the public, not in open court; often conducted in the judge's *chambers*.

Inadmissible: When evidence offered by a party is ruled inadmissible by the judge, that means it is not allowed to become a part of the court record and may therefore not be considered as evidence against the defendant.

Incompetence to stand trial: Lacking the mental ability to understand or participate in legal proceedings. A defendant may be sane at the time a crime was committed yet incompetent to stand trial, or vice versa.

Indeterminate sentences: Sentences for an unfixed period of time, such as "five years to life." A parole board often decides how long an offender given an indeterminate sentence actually serves in prison.

Indigent (**indigency**): Poor. In *criminal* cases, the court will appoint a *public defender* or private lawyer to represent defendants who are so poor that they do not have the money to hire their own private lawyers. In some courts, defendants who have too much money to qualify for a public defender or court-appointed counsel but not enough money to hire a private lawyer may be considered "partially indigent" and allowed appointed counsel for a reduced fee.

Information: The term commonly used for the initial document filed in court by the prosecutor that charges a defendant with one or more crimes.

Inquest: Investigation. Coroners, fire marshals, and legislative agencies, for example, all may have authority to investigate *criminal* cases, conducting what are known as "inquests." ("When *arson* was suspected at the Grand Theater, the fire marshal was called in to conduct an inquest to determine the cause of the fire.")

Insanity: A mental disease or defect that sufficiently interferes with a defendant's ability to control his actions or appreciate the nature of his act so that the defendant is not considered to be legally responsible for his criminal acts.

Interrogatory: Question. The term "interrogatories" usually refers to a set of questions a party to a lawsuit asks of the other party, witnesses, or other people who might have helpful information during the period of time before trial called "discovery." Interrogatories are more commonly used in *civil cases.*

Irrelevant: Not related to. Information that is not logically related to the main issues in the case may not be considered by the judge or jury—whichever is hearing and deciding the case—and may not therefore be introduced into evidence.

Jail: The place where people convicted of minor crimes and defendants awaiting trial are held in custody. Those convicted of more serious crimes usually end up in prison.

Jeopardy: Subject to being convicted of a crime. The Constitution prohibits being twice placed in jeopardy for the same crime. See *double jeopardy.*

Judge: A public officer who presides over court hearings and trials. Sometimes the words "bench" and "court" are used to mean "judge."

Jurisdiction: A court's geographic power and legal authority to hear a particular type of case. ("In California, the superior courts for each county are authorized to grant divorces if at least one of the divorcing parties is a legal resident of the county.") Often the term is used interchangeably with state. ("In some jurisdictions all *felonies* are initiated by *grand jury* proceedings, while in other jurisdictions they are initiated by a prosecutor's *information* or *complaint.*")

Juror: A person selected to serve on a *jury.*

Jury: A group of people who decide the facts of the case and render a verdict, typically guilty or not guilty, on specific

criminal charges defined by the judge in *jury instructions.* (See also *grand jury.*)

Jury instructions: Legal rules given by the judge to the jury. The judge typically gets some of these rules from jury instruction books—which contain the standard rules given by other *criminal* courts in that state—and rules that are custom-drafted by the *prosecution* and *defense* for the particular facts of the case.

Jury selection: See *voir dire.*

Juvenile: A minor, typically a person under 18, although for *criminal* law purposes, some states consider juveniles to be 16 and under and decide on a case-by-case basis whether people between ages 16–18 are juveniles entitled to special treatment as such.

Juvenile court: Special court where actions involving *juveniles* are handled. (See Chapter 25 for more on this subject.)

Larceny: Another word for theft. Although the definition of this term differs from state to state, it typically means the taking of property belonging to another with an intent to permanently deprive the owner of the property of its possession. ("Joe was originally charged with larceny, but he escaped conviction when he convinced the jury that he had just borrowed the car and was intending to return it. He was, however, convicted of joyriding, which doesn't require an intent to permanently deprive the car's owner of the car's possession.")

Law clerk: An assistant to a judge, typically a recent law school graduate, who helps the judge with tasks like researching the issues and drafting court opinions or decisions. Some lawyers also hire law students or recent law graduates whom they call "law clerks" to assist with research, witness interviewing, and other tasks.

Lawyer (also called **attorney**): Person who speaks and acts on behalf of a party. In every state, lawyers are either licensed or certified by a state organization typically consisting of and run by lawyers. With some exceptions, only lawyers may appear in *criminal* courts to represent defendants. The exceptions consist of programs that allow law students—under supervision of a lawyer—to represent people accused of minor crimes. Lawyers are sometimes called "counsel." ("Judge Fels announced that she would continue the arraignment so that the accused may consult counsel before entering a plea.")

Leading question: A question that suggests the answer, often a statement asked as a question. ("Wanting to make sure the *witness* provided the right answer, the lawyer asked the witness, 'That was your coat tangled in the bush when the murder was committed, wasn't it?'")

Legal aid lawyers: See *public defenders.*

Lesser included offense: A *crime* that is made up of some but not all of the *elements* of a more serious crime. For example, residential burglary (a *felony*) typically is defined as breaking and entering into the home of another with the intent to commit a crime inside. Trespass (a *misdemeanor*) is the unauthorized entry onto the property of another. Since every burglary necessarily involves a trespass,

trespass is a lesser included offense of burglary.

Liable: A legal conclusion that an offender is civilly responsible for a victim's losses—the civil equivalent of "guilty" in the criminal justice system. ("Bob not only was convicted of aggravated assault, but he also was found liable civilly and ordered to pay the plaintiff $10,000 in damages.")

Lineup: A procedure in which the police place a suspect in a line with a group of other persons and ask an eyewitness to the crime to pick the person he saw at the crime scene out of the group. If the suspect is selected and later *charged* with the *crime*, the fact of the lineup identification may be introduced as evidence.

Local rules: Rules adopted by specific courts or specific regions regulating aspects of case administration. Local rules sometimes modify state and federal rules. They can affect how *plea bargaining* happens, how hearings are conducted, and the procedures used at trial. Understanding them may be critical to presenting an effective defense.

Loitering: A crime best understood as just hanging out. ("The police instituted a policy of arresting all those people hanging around the boardwalk after 9:00 p.m., for either *curfew* or loitering violations.")

L.W.O.P.: A life prison sentence, literally "life without parole."

Magistrate: A court official who acts as a judge in certain (often lower level) court proceedings. ("Officer Edwin Barry went before Magistrate Talia Nin to request a warrant for Mimi's arrest.")

Malice: Typically, a willful or intentional state of mind to bring about some injury or wrongdoing. Malice can sometimes be found in other ways, such as where someone's actions show recklessness (extreme lack of care). To be found *guilty* of certain crimes, such as murder, the state must prove malice or (for first degree murder) malice aforethought.

Manslaughter: The crime of killing a person but without the malice (evil intent) required to classify the killing as murder.

Marshal (sometimes spelled **marshall**): A law officer who is empowered to enforce certain court rulings and orders. The federal government has U.S. marshals, and some states have marshals (similar to sheriffs).

Memorandum of Points and Authorities: See *brief.* A document that cites (refers to) legal authorities such as statutes and court cases, and explains how those authorities support the position advocated by the party who wrote the memorandum. Often written to support a *motion.*

Mens rea: Mental component of criminal liability. Typically, to be guilty of a *crime,* a defendant must be found to have committed the act (called *"actus reus"*), and to have the requisite (required) criminal intent or *mens rea* (mental component such as recklessness or malice).

Miranda warning: A warning that the police must give to a suspect in custody before interrogating (questioning) the suspect if the police want to use the suspect's answers as evidence in a trial. The *Miranda* warning requires that the suspect be told that she has the right to remain silent, the right to have an attorney present when being questioned, the right to a court-appointed attorney if a private attorney is unaffordable, and the fact that any statements made by the suspect can be used against her in court.

Misdemeanors: Crimes, less serious than *felonies,* punishable by no more than one year in jail. ("The defense lawyer told the defendant, 'You were, as you know, originally charged with possession and sale of marijuana, a felony, but I got the D.A. to agree to simple possession, a misdemeanor—*time served,* a fine, and a couple hundred hours of *community service*—if you plead today. What do you think?'")

Mistrial: A trial that ends before the full proceeding has been completed because of some prejudicial error or wrong that has occurred. ("When the judge heard evidence that the D.A. had spoken with several jurors during court recesses, the judge declared a mistrial, and the defendant's case was reset for trial.")

Motion: A request to the court for an order or ruling. Some motions are made orally, others in writing. Depending on the ruling sought, a motion can be made before, during, or after trial. ("The defense made a motion to suppress the lineup based on the grounds that police conduct made the identification impermissibly suggestive.")

Motion for a continuance: See *continuance*. ("The D.A. and defense lawyer, still engaged in plea negotiations, jointly made a motion to the court for a continuance, which the court immediately granted. The trial was consequently recalendared approximately 45 days later.")

Motion *in limine*: A request for a court order excluding *irrelevant* or prejudicial evidence in advance of it being offered in open court, typically made in jury trials.

Movant: Party making or bringing a *motion*.

Moving party: See *movant*.

Mug shot: Photo taken of the defendant, typically by police, during the *booking* proceeding after arrest.

Mugging: To be mugged has two meanings: (1) to be robbed, or (2) to have your "mug shot" or photo taken during *booking*.

Murder: The unlawful killing of another person when the killing (1) was deliberate and lacked legal justification, or (2) the result of wilful behavior that disregarded the inherent risk to human life (such as shooting a firearm into an inhabited building), or (3) occurred while the defendant was committing an inherently dangerous *felony* (called the "felony-murder rule"). Most states divide murder into three degrees, with first degree murder being the most serious offense and third degree murder (often called manslaughter) being the least serious of the three.

No contest: A *plea* entered by the defendant in response to being charged with a *crime*, whereby the defendant neither admits nor denies guilt of the crime, but agrees to submit to punishment (usually a fine or jail time) as if guilty. The reason why this sort of plea is typically entered is that it often can't later be used as an admission of guilt if a *civil trial* is held after the criminal trial.

Nolo contendere: See *no contest*. Comes from the Latin meaning, "I will not contest it."

Not guilty: A verdict that the defendant has not been proven guilty of the offense charged—issued by a judge or jury after trial. Although a not guilty verdict is often taken to mean that the judge or jury finds the person innocent, it really only means that the judge or jury were unable to find the defendant guilty.

Notice: Notification. To give someone notice of a court *hearing* is to let them know when and where it will take place and other basic information they need to adequately prepare for it.

Notice of Motion: A document that notifies an adversary about when and where a *motion* will be made, what the reason for the motion is, and what supporting documentation will be relied on in making the motion.

Objection: Taking exception to or not agreeing with some statement made by or document filed by an *adversary*. Typically refers to the response the *prosecution* or *defense* makes in court when they don't want some testimony or exhibit admitted into evidence during trial: they then "make an objection."

Offer of proof: A summary of the testimony that a witness will give if the judge allows the witness to testify.

Off-the-record remarks: Comments by judges or lawyers made in court or in other formal settings such as depositions that are intended to be private and therefore do not become part of a case's official record.

Opening statement: A statement made by an attorney or self-represented defendant before the *evidence* is actually introduced to preview the evidence and set the stage for the trial. Many people think of the opening statement as a kind of roadmap to the rest of the proceedings.

Opinions: Appellate court judges' written explanations for and justifications of their decisions.

O.R. (own recognizance): A way the defendant can get out of jail, without paying *bail* money, on the defendant's promise to appear in court when next required to be there. Sometimes called "personal recognizance."

Order: A ruling or decision by a court. A court order can be made orally or in writing. In a judge trial, a *verdict* of guilty may be written up as a court order.

Overrule: Deny. When the judge overrules an objection, the judge denies the objection and the evidence objected to is allowed in.

Own recognizance: See *O.R.*

Party (parties): The *prosecution* and the *defendant* or defendants are the parties to a *criminal* case.

Percipient witness: A *witness* who perceived the facts she testifies about. A percipient witness is an ordinary witness, as contrasted with an expert witness who may testify—because of the wittness's

special knowledge or training—about things she did not actually observe.

Peremptory challenge: An opportunity to challenge (dismiss or excuse) a potential *juror* during *jury selection* without having to give a reason. Parties each get a limited number of peremptory challenges. ("The defense lawyer, Loretta Nay, used one of her three peremptory challenges to excuse (dismiss) Juror number 1, Janet Alan, because of a hunch that Janet would be sympathetic to the police.")

Perjury: A crime committed by lying while under oath (while *testifying* during trial, on a sworn *affidavit,* or in a *deposition* or *interrogatories*).

Petitioner: A party who makes a formal written request to a higher court asking it to review the ruling of a lower court.

Petty theft: Taking property valued less than a certain amount specified by *statute* (in some states $500). Where the property is worth more than that amount, the *crime* would be considered "grand theft."

Phishing: A form of Internet fraud in which a fake website or email is made to resemble a legitimate one, in order to steal valuable information such as credit cards, social security numbers, user IDs, and passwords.

Plain error: An obvious mistake that affects a defendant's substantial rights and the integrity of the trial process.

Plea: The defendant's formal answer to criminal charges. Typically, defendants enter one of the following pleas: *guilty, not guilty,* or *no contest.* Although a plea may be entered at any time during the case, or not at all, it usually comes shortly before the case is scheduled to come to *trial*.

Plea bargaining: The negotiation between *defense* and *prosecution* (and sometimes the judge) of the settlement of a *criminal* case. ("Defendant Charlie Keith got a lighter sentence when prosecutor Ronnie Mick agreed to plea bargain the assault charges to disturbing the peace (a less serious offense) in exchange for Keith's *guilty* plea.")

Pleading: Written document setting out the criminal *charges*.

Points and Authorities: See *Memorandum of Points and Authorities*.

Prejudice: Bias or discrimination.

Prejudicial error: A wrong decision by the judge that in retrospect deprived a convicted defendant of a fair trial and therefore justifies a reversal of the case by an appellate court. ("Judge Pickholtz made a prejudicial error by allowing Officer Janus to describe the cocaine that he had seized from the defendant's apartment. The seizure had previously been found to be an unconstitutional violation of the defendant's Fourth Amendment rights, and therefore no mention of the illegally seized evidence at trial should have been permitted. Because the jury's verdict may have been influenced by the mention of the cocaine, the error was prejudicial and the verdict should be reversed and a new trial ordered.")

Preliminary hearing: A court proceeding in which the *prosecution* must present enough *evidence* for the judge to justify holding the defendant to answer for the *crime(s)*, or the case is dismissed. If the case is dismissed, *charges* may be refiled.

Preponderance of the evidence: The *burden of proof* in most *civil actions* (amounting to something more than 50%). Contrasted with the much higher *prosecution* burden in *criminal* cases, *beyond a reasonable doubt*.

Present sense impression: An exception to the *hearsay rule* that finds out-of-court statements presumptively reliable and therefore admissible if they are made about an event while or just after the event occurs (since the party making the statements wouldn't have time to fabricate them).

Presentence report: A written summary of an investigation conducted by a probation officer, social worker, or psychologist working to help the judge determine a defendant's *sentence*. ("At the direction of Judge Shelly, the probation officer Nettie Solomon prepared a presentence report that included the circumstances of the *crime*, the defendant's personal history, including past *criminal* record, and statements from the victims and one *witness*.")

Presumption of innocence: One of the most sacred principles in American criminal justice, which holds that a defendant is innocent until the *prosecution* proves each *element* of the crime charged *beyond a reasonable doubt*.

Pretrial conference: A meeting between the prosecutor, the defense, and (usually) the judge before *trial* to identify undisputed facts, share *witness* lists or any other required *reciprocal discovery,* and sometimes try to settle (*plea bargain*) the case. Pretrial conferences may be conducted by the judge in or out of court.

Pretrial motion: A request to the court made before *trial* for an order or ruling. Typical pretrial *motions* include a motion for *continuance*, motion to strike a prior conviction, and motions to exclude *evidence* that was illegally seized or evidence of *lineup* that was unfairly conducted.

Prior inconsistent statement: A *procedural* rule that allows certain out-of-court statements to be admitted into *evidence* for the purpose of discrediting a witness by showing that the witness gave a contradictory account of something on a prior occasion. ("The defense lawyer impeached (discredited) the *witness* at trial with a *prior inconsistent statement* the witness made under oath at the *preliminary hearing*.")

Priors: Past convictions, no matter how old.

Privileged: Confidential. ("Counsel objected to the prosecutor's asking the witness, Dr. Davids, to reveal a discussion he had with his patient, the defendant Madhu Rose, on the grounds that the conversation was 'privileged.'")

Privileges: Legal rules and principles that keep certain information confidential and thus out of court or discovery proceedings. Some common privileges include confidential communications made to a spouse, doctor, lawyer, psychotherapist, or clergyperson.

Pro bono: Legal services performed pro bono or on a pro bono basis are done for free or a reduced fee. (Comes from the Latin *pro bono publico*, meaning "for the good of the public.") Because most criminal defendants are entitled to be represented by lawyers paid by the state, few lawyers offer pro bono criminal defense services. However, if the media takes an interest in a case, private lawyers will sometimes step forward and offer pro bono representation because of the media exposure they'll receive.

Pro per (also **pro se**): Self-represented. A Latin term used by lawyers and court personnel for someone who represents him or herself in court without a lawyer.

Pro se (pronounced "pro say"): Same as *pro per.*

Probable cause: Reasonable basis or justification for certain actions by the police that occur early on in the *criminal* process. Probable cause is more than a mere hunch but not so much as to be convinced *beyond a reasonable doubt* (the greater standard for conviction at trial). ("Even though Officer Charles was not convinced that Sally Victors murdered Greta Gaspar, the fact that she had the opportunity to do so and owned a handgun of the same type as that used in the murder provided probable cause to arrest Sally on murder charges.")

Probative: Probative evidence is evidence that tends to prove or disprove some contested issue. The terms "probative" and "relevant" are very close in meaning, but as a general rule evidence that arguably is relevant may still be considered not probative because it doesn't really help the judge or jury decide contested facts.

Procedural law (also called **procedure**): Laws or rules that govern the method of how a *criminal* case is administered and tried in court. Procedural rules are contrasted with rules of *"substantive law"* that define the rights and duties of parties, and the elements of particular *crimes* and *defenses.*

Prosecution: (1) To prosecute, or the prosecution of a case, means to bring a *criminal* case against a defendant. ("Upon the capture of the serial killer A. Tilla, D.A. Shelly Shulam announced that her office would prosecute Tilla swiftly and to the limits of the law.") (2) The prosecution can also refer to the government's team (the defense team's adversary). ("Judge Diana Rogers said that after hearing the defense argument on the *motion in limine,* she wanted to hear the prosecution's response.")

Prosecutors (often called **D.A.s**): Lawyers who work for the government to bring and litigate criminal cases.

Public defenders (in some jurisdictions called **legal aid lawyers**): Lawyers paid by the state or county to work full time representing indigent or poor clients who are assigned to them by the local courts.

Quash: Nullify. ("The prosecutor moved to quash (requested that the judge render null and void) the defendant's subpoena of breathalyzer calibration records from the lab.")

Rap sheet: A defendant's *arrest* and *conviction* record as maintained by one or more criminal justice agencies. ("At the defendant's sentencing hearing, the prosecutor argued that the punishment should be severe in part because the defendant's rap sheet stretches from his arm (held high above the prosecutor's head) to the floor.")

Reasonable doubt: Lingering doubt following serious consideration of a matter; not just any possible doubt. ("The jury refused to convict defendant Sims, contending that despite significant *prosecution* evidence, they still had reasonable doubt that he committed the murders.") Reasonable doubt is the same thing as not being convinced of a defendant's guilt *beyond a reasonable doubt.*

Rebuttal evidence: Evidence offered to contradict evidence presented by the adversary.

Recess: A break in a hearing or trial.

Reciprocal discovery: Laws in some states that require the *prosecution* and *defense* to exchange certain information before *trial,* such as lists of all *witnesses* to be called at trial and reports of any *expert witnesses.* As a general rule, the prosecution has to give the defense more than the defense has to give the prosecution, because the defense's right to not turn over evidence is to some extent protected by the *Fifth Amendment right against self-incrimination.*

Reckless (or child) endangerment: A crime consisting of putting another person at risk of serious injury or death.

Record: The official written *transcript* of court proceedings and evidence in a case. When something goes on the record, it appears in the official transcript. If some aspect of the case is off the record, such as a brief procedural question at sidebar (the judge's *bench*), it will not appear in the official transcript.

Recross-examination: Additional *cross-examination* of *witnesses* called by an adversary on *redirect examination.*

Recuse or **recusal:** When a judge takes herself off a case because of a conflict of interest, the judge is said to recuse herself and the act is considered a recusal.

Redact: To delete or cover up part of a document because it refers to inadmissible evidence.

Redirect examination: Additional direct examination of a *witness* by the party who called that witness just after that witness has been *cross-examined* by the adversary.

Regulations: Rules made by administrative agencies.

Relevancy: A connection or applicability to the issues in the case. Relevant evidence is evidence that helps to prove or disprove some fact in connection with the case.

Relief: A party's desired legal remedy. ("The prisoner sought relief in the form of an order requiring the prison cafeteria to provide vegetarian meals.")

Respondent: The name for the defendant (responding party) in cases where the plaintiff is called a *"petitioner."*

Response (or **Responsive pleading**): A general term for a legal document in which a party responds to an adversary's *pleading, motion,* or *brief.*

Restitution: Money that a judge orders a convicted offender to pay to a victim as compensation for losses directly related to the crime.

Retainer agreement: Contract between a lawyer and client.

Reversible error: A trial court error that affects a substantial right and results in the reversal of a conviction.

Sanctions (**to sanction**): Penalties (often fines) imposed by the court on one or both of the parties for improper conduct during the case.

Seal: To conceal from public record. In some instances, for example, a person's *arrest* or *criminal* records may be sealed, meaning without a court order to inspect them they may not be viewed. ("The criminal record of crimes defendant Cyndi Summer committed as a *juvenile* was sealed.")

Sentence: The full panoply of punishments that a judge metes out in a criminal case. ("Judge Deyda sentenced Defendant Laney Su to five years in state prison after the jury convicted Su on drug charges.")

Sentencing guidelines: Laws that either suggest (are permissive) or dictate (are mandatory) the *sentence* a judge is required to give for specific crimes.

Standing: To have legal standing is to have a sufficient stake in a legal dispute to have a right to go to court and ask for legal relief. ("The passengers in Rich's car did not have standing to complain about the way the police officer searched Rich's pockets.")

Statute: Law enacted by a legislature, often contrasted with *common law* (judge-made law).

Statute of limitations: The legal time limit in which *criminal* charges can be filed against a defendant for a particular *crime*. A few crimes, such as murder, do not have a statute of limitations, and the statute of limitations for criminal acts against children typically is much longer than for crimes against adults.

Stipulation: An agreement between parties. For example, the *prosecution* and *defense* may stipulate to the admissibility of certain testimony or an exhibit. ("Defense and prosecution lawyers met to negotiate a *plea bargain* and stipulated to *continue* the next scheduled court hearing to permit further discussions.")

Stop and frisk: A police officer's brief and limited pat down of a person's outer clothing; an intrusion that is less invasive than a full-scale search.

Strike: To delete testimony from the official court record. ("In the rape trial of the defendant, when the *witness* began recounting the victim's past sexual history, the *prosecutor* immediately moved to strike the witness's testimony, and the motion was granted.")

S.U.: Straight up. When a *prosecutor* writes "s.u." on a defendant's file, it may mean the prosecutor will not *plea bargain* the case.

Subpoena (subpena): A court order compelling someone to appear in court.

Subpoena *duces tecum*: A court order compelling someone to appear in court and bring along with them certain tangible objects or documents.

Substantive law: Rules defining *crimes* and rights and duties of parties (as opposed to *procedural* laws, which govern case administration).

Suspended sentence: A sentence (punishment) that the judge hands down but does not require the defendant to serve right away or at all if certain conditions—such as successfully completing probation—are met.

Sustain: Uphold. When a judge sustains an *objection*, it is upheld, and the evidence objected to is not allowed in.

Testify: To give testimony.

Testimony: Evidence given under oath, in court or in a deposition.

Time served: The time a defendant spends in jail awaiting resolution of his or her case. If convicted, the time served may be credited toward the ultimate *sentence*.

Tort: A legal claim of *civil* (noncriminal) wrong (other than a breach of contract), often referred to as a personal injury. Some actions, such as assault and battery, can be both crimes and torts.

Transcript: A written record of a court proceeding or *deposition*.

Treatise: A legal reference book, usually covering an entire legal subject. ("As part of preparing the defense case, the defense lawyer consulted a respected treatise on drunk driving defense.")

Trial: The in-court examination and resolution of a *criminal* case. ("My lawyer, Kate Johnson, told me that my case probably won't go to trial because more than

90% of criminal cases are settled by *plea bargains* before they go to trial.")

Trial notebook: A notebook or binder lawyers set up to help them organize their case.

U.S. attorneys: *Prosecutors* for the federal government.

Vacate: To overturn a lower court's decision. ("The state Supreme Court vacated the guilty verdict after deciding that the trial judge had not allowed the defendant a sufficient opportunity to cross-examine the police officer.")

Venue: The geographic area in which a court has authority to hear a case.

Verdict: The jury's (or judge's in a judge trial) final decision in a *criminal* case: *guilty* or *not guilty*.

Voir dire: The process of questioning and selecting a jury. The judge, the prosecution, and the defense all question potential jurors for the purpose of deciding whether the jurors will render a fair verdict.

Waive: Give up. ("Marguerite Lorenzo waived her right to a jury trial after deciding a judge would likely be more sympathetic than a jury would be to her defense that the breathalyzer machine malfunctioned.")

Waive time: Give up one's rights to have a *criminal* case against him be prosecuted according to speedy trial rules. ("My lawyer said I should waive time, that it's routine to do so, and that I will not suffer any ill consequences by doing so.")

Warrant: Order from a judge or magistrate authorizing the police to *arrest* someone (arrest warrant) or to search a particular location for evidence (search warrant).

White collar crime: A type of *crime* that typically involves money or property gotten through deception, including fraud, forgery, embezzlement, counterfeiting, and computer tampering.

Witness: A person who *testifies* in court.

Wobbler: A crime that can be charged as either a *misdemeanor* or a *felony*.

Writ: A court order directed by a higher court to a lower court or governmental official ordering some type of action to be taken.

Index

R

NOLO *Law for All*

Find a Quality Attorney

- *Qualified lawyers*
- *In-depth profiles*
- *Respectful service*

When you want help with a serious legal problem, you don't want just any lawyer—you want an expert in the field who can provide up-to-the-minute advice to help you protect your loved ones. You need a lawyer who has the experience and knowledge to answer your questions about personal injury, wills, family law, child custody, drafting a patent application or any other specialized legal area you are concerned with.

Nolo's Lawyer Directory is unique because it provides an extensive profile of every lawyer. You'll learn about not only each lawyer's education, professional history, legal specialties, credentials and fees, but also about their philosophy of practicing law and how they like to work with clients. It's all crucial information when you're looking for someone to trust with an important personal or business matter.

All lawyers listed in Nolo's directory are in good standing with their state bar association. They all pledge to work diligently and respectfully with clients—communicating regularly, providing a written agreement about how legal matters will be handled, sending clear and detailed bills and more. And many directory lawyers will review Nolo documents, such as a will or living trust, for a fixed fee, to help you get the advice you need.

www.lawyers.nolo.com

NOLO | *Online Legal Forms*

Nolo offers a large library of legal solutions and forms, created by Nolo's in-house legal staff. These reliable documents can be prepared in minutes.

Online Legal Solutions

- **Incorporation.** Incorporate your business in any state.
- **LLC Formations.** Gain asset protection and pass-through tax status in any state.
- **Wills.** Nolo has helped people make over 2 million wills. Is it time to make or revise yours?
- **Living Trust (avoid probate).** Plan now to save your family the cost, delays, and hassle of probate.
- **Trademark.** Protect the name of your business or product.
- **Provisional Patent.** Preserve your rights under patent law and claim "patent pending" status.

Online Legal Forms

Nolo.com has hundreds of top quality legal forms available for download—bills of sale, promissory notes, nondisclosure agreements, LLC operating agreements, corporate minutes, commercial lease and sublease, motor vehicle bill of sale, consignment agreements and many, many more.

Review Your Documents

Many lawyers in Nolo's consumer-friendly lawyer directory will review Nolo documents for a very reasonable fee. Check their detailed profiles at **lawyers.nolo.com**.

NOLO *and* USA TODAY

Cutting-Edge Content, Unparalleled Expertise

The Busy Family's Guide to Money

by Sandra Block, Kathy Chu & John Waggoner • $19.99

The Busy Family's Guide to Money will help you make the most of your income, handle major one-time expenses, figure children into the budget—and much more.

The Work From Home Handbook

Flex Your Time, Improve Your Life

by Diana Fitzpatrick & Stephen Fishman • $19.99

If you're one of those people who need to (or simply want to) work from home, let this book help you come up with a plan that both you and your boss can embrace!

Retire Happy

What You Can Do NOW to Guarantee a Great Retirement

by Richard Stim & Ralph Warner • $19.99

You don't need a million dollars to retire well, but you do need friends, hobbies and an active lifestyle. This book shows how to make retirement the best time of your life.

The Essential Guide for First-Time Homeowners

Maximize Your Investment & Enjoy Your New Home

by Ilona Bray & Alayna Schroeder • $19.99

This reassuring resource is filled with crucial financial advice, real solutions and easy-to-implement ideas that can save you thousands of dollars.

Easy Ways to Lower Your Taxes

Simple Strategies Every Taxpayer Should Know

by Sandra Block & Stephen Fishman • $19.99

Provides useful insights and tactics to help lower your taxes. Learn how to boost tax-free income, get a lower tax rate, defer paying taxes, make the most of deductions—and more!

First-Time Landlord

Your Guide to Renting Out a Single-Family Home

by Attorney Janet Portman, Marcia Stewart & Michael Molinski • $19.99

From choosing tenants to handling repairs to avoiding legal trouble, this book provides the information new landlords need to make a profit and follow the law.

Stopping Identity Theft

10 Easy Steps to Security

by Scott Mitic, CEO, TrustedID, Inc. • $19.99

Don't let an emptied bank account be your first warning sign. This book offers ten strategies to help prevent the theft of personal information.

NOLO *Keep Up to Date*

 Go to **Nolo.com/newsletter** to sign up for free newsletters and discounts on Nolo products.

- **Nolo Briefs.** Our monthly email newsletter with great deals and free information.

- **Nolo's Special Offer.** A monthly newsletter with the biggest Nolo discounts around.

- **BizBriefs.** Tips and discounts on Nolo products for business owners and managers.

- **Landlord's Quarterly.** Deals and free tips just for landlords and property managers, too.

 And don't forget to check **Nolo.com/updates** to find free legal updates to this book.

Let Us Hear From You

 Comments on this book? We want to hear 'em. Email us at feedback@nolo.com.

KYR11